The
PHOTOGRAPHIC
HISTORY
of the
CIVIL WAR

THREE VOLUMES IN ONE

The
PHOTOGRAPHIC
HISTORY
of the
CIVIL WAR

THREE VOLUMES IN ONE

Armies & Leaders
The Cavalry
The Decisive Battles

PORTLAND HOUSE

Originally published in separate volumes under the titles:
The Photographic History of the Civil War: Armies and Leaders, foreword
copyright © 1983 by Random House Value Publishing, Inc.
The Photographic History of the Civil War: The Cavalry, foreword copyright © 1983
by Random House Value Publishing, Inc.
The Photographic History of the Civil War: the Decisive Battles, foreword
copyright © 1983 by Random House Value Publishing, Inc., preface copyright © 1983 by
Random House Value Publishing, Inc.

This 1997 edition is published by Portland House,
a division of Random House Value Publishing, Inc.,
201 East 50th Street, New York, New York 10022

Printed and bound in the United States of America

ISBN 0-517-20155-0

8 7 6 5 4 3 2 1

The Photographic History
of The Civil War

—————

Armies & Leaders

GENERAL JAMES CONNOR   GENERAL JOHN W. GEARY   GENERAL JOHN B. MAGRUDER   GENERAL ROBERT D. LILLEY   GENERAL P. G. T. BEAUREGARD   GENERAL LEWIS WALLACE   GENERAL HENRY A. WISE   GENERAL JOSEPH L. BRENT

BLACQUE BEY   GENERAL R. E. LEE   GEORGE PEABODY   W. W. CORCORAN   JAMES LYONS

"SOLDIERS AND CITIZENS"

ROBERT E. LEE WITH FORMER UNION AND CONFEDERATE LEADERS
AFTER THE ARMIES' WORK WAS DONE

By great good fortune this unique photograph, taken at White Sulphur Springs, Virginia, in August, 1869, was preserved more than forty years by a Confederate veteran of Richmond, Mr. James Blair, through whose courtesy it appears here—to sound the key-note of this volume as no preface could. Such a fraternal gathering could have been paralleled after no other great war in history. For in this neighborly group, side by side, are bitter foemen of not five years past. Near the unmistakable figure of Lee stands Lew Wallace, the commander who in 1864 had opposed Lee's lieutenant—Early—at the Monocacy; the division leader who at Shiloh, first grand battle of the war, had fired on the lines in gray commanded by the dashing Confederate general who now touches him on the right—Beauregard. To the left stand Connor and Geary, formerly generals of opposing forces in the Carolinas. There is the tall "Prince John" Magruder, the venerable Henry A. Wise, and other one-time leaders of the Gray. And for a further touch of good citizenship, there is added the distinguished presence of George Peabody of Massachusetts, and W. W. Corcoran of Washington—philanthropists of the noblest type, but not alone in this group "as having helped their fellow men."

The Photographic History of The Civil War

Armies & Leaders

Contributors

Robert S. Lanier
Managing Editor

William Conant Church
Brevet Lieutenant-Colonel, U. S. V.; Editor of "The Army and Navy Journal"; Author of "Life of Ulysses S. Grant," "Life of John Ericsson," etc.

William Peterfield Trent, LL.D.
Professor of English Literature in Columbia University; Author of "Robert E. Lee," "Southern Statesmen of the Old Regime," etc.

Walter Lynwood Fleming, Ph.D.
Professor of History, Louisiana State University; Author of "Secession and Reconstruction of Alabama," etc.

John E. Gilman
Commander-in-Chief, Grand Army of the Republic, 1910–1911

Allen C. Redwood
Artist and Author; Late Army of Northern Virginia; Author of "Johnny Reb Papers," etc.

Hilary A. Herbert
Late Colonel, Eighth Alabama Infantry; Late Secretary of Navy of the United States

Marcus J. Wright
Late Brigadier-General, Confederate States Army; Agent for the Collection of War Records, United States War Department

Samuel A. Cunningham
Late Sergeant-Major, Confederate States Army; Founder and Editor of "The Confederate Veteran"

CONTENTS

PAGE

FRONTISPIECE—*"Soldiers and Citizens"* 4

FOREWORD— 9

INTRODUCTION 11
  Robert S. Lanier

ULYSSES SIMPSON GRANT— 29
  William Conant Church

ROBERT E. LEE 51
  William Peterfield Trent

WILLIAM TECUMSEH SHERMAN— 75
  Walter L. Fleming

"STONEWALL" JACKSON— 97
  Allen C. Redwood

LOSSES IN THE BATTLES OF THE CIVIL WAR—THEIR MEANING 117
  Hilary A. Herbert

  Casualties of Great European Battles 140
  Battles and Casualties of the Civil War—Gen. Marcus J. Wright . . . 142
  Troops Furnished to the Union Army by the States 146
  Casualties in the Union and Confederate Armies 148
  Summaries of Organizations in the Two Armies 150
  Regimental Casualties in the Union Army 152
  Some Striking Confederate Losses 156

THE FEDERAL ARMIES; THE CORPS AND THEIR LEADERS 159

THE CONFEDERATE ARMIES AND GENERALS 239

THE ORGANIZATIONS OF THE VETERANS 287

  THE GRAND ARMY OF THE REPUBLIC 290
    John E. Gilman

  THE UNITED CONFEDERATE VETERANS 296
    Samuel A. Cunningham

GENERAL OFFICERS, UNION AND CONFEDERATE—A COMPLETE ROSTER . . . 301

SELECTED PORTRAITS OF CIVIL WAR LEADERS AND TROOPS 323

PHOTOGRAPHIC DESCRIPTIONS THROUGHOUT THIS BOOK
  Roy Mason
  George L. Kilmer, Late U. S. V.

FOREWORD

ON April 14, 1861, Fort Sumter underwent a thirty-four-hour bombardment by the Confederate Army. As the fighting drew to a close, Union officer Major Robert Anderson lowered the flag and turned the fort over to the Confederacy. The American Civil War had begun. It would be four long, hard-fought years before the guns would finally be silenced.

The Photographic History of the Civil War: Armies and Leaders captures the images of both intense drama and horror created by this internal national conflict. This unique collection of black-and-white photographs takes the reader into the campsites and onto the battlefields where victories were won and lives were lost. The superb text and photograph descriptions present an authoritative yet sensitive portrayal of the War Between the States.

This volume profiles the leaders from both sides of the Civil War and analyzes the makeup of the armies which comprised the fighting ranks. The military leaders discussed here include Ulysses S. Grant, Robert E. Lee, William T. Sherman and "Stonewall" Jackson. While each of these men came from different backgrounds, they all shared an unwavering determination and strong belief in the causes they fought for. The individual armies are descibed here in great detail also. How each troop was formed, its involvement in the war, and the officers who led the soldiers into battle are all carefully described.

An analytical look is taken at the losses suffered by many of these armies throughout the war. Every successful battle was at the expense of many lives. For instance, it appears that almost all of the heavy losses of the Confederate regiments were suffered when they were either winning victories or stubbornly holding on to the field of battle. Several tables included here break down the number of men killed, wounded, or missing during the major battles, and list the number of deaths resulting from all causes in the Union armies, deaths in Confederate armies and the casualties from individual regiments from both armies.

By the 1860s the camera was on its way to becoming an important medium for communication. The method used during this period was known as daguereotype, named after its inventor Frenchman Louis Jacques Mandé Daguerre. By using this wet-plate process, however, the Civil War photographer was unable to capture action shots. Yet this disadvantage did not prevent him from capturing on film the human and material wreckage created by the war—the wistful face of the dying young soldier or the sabotaged railroad. The Battle of Bull Run marked the beginning of American military photography.

The Civil War photographers risked constant danger of battle and worked under the most difficult conditions—the bitter cold during the winters of 1862 and 1863 and the blistering heat in the summer. Important Civil War photographers—including Mathew B. Brady, Timothy O'Sullivan and Alexander Gardner as well as other combat photographers—provided the American people with an inside look at this war through their work.

The photographs gathered here are truly remarkable. The camera lens not only has captured the soldier in uniform, but also the soulful expressions worn by each face weathered by the war. These poignant photographs stirred the hearts of Americans on both sides of the Mason-Dixon line then and will continue to do so today.

K.M.B.

INTRODUCTION

SOLDIERS
AND
CITIZENS

VETERANS AFTER ONE YEAR

SELF-RELIANCE, COURAGE AND DIGNITY ARE IMPRINTED ON THE FACES OF THESE "VETERANS"—MEN OF McCLERNAND'S CORPS IN THEIR QUARTERS AT MEMPHIS, TENNESSEE, AFTER THE COSTLY ATTEMPT ON VICKSBURG BY WAY OF CHICKASAW BLUFFS. YET THEY HAVE BEEN SOLDIERS HARDLY A YEAR—THE BOY ON THE RIGHT, SO SLIGHT AND YOUNG, MIGHT ALMOST BE MASQUERADING IN AN OFFICER'S UNIFORM. OF SUCH WERE THE SOLDIERS WHO EARLY IN THE WAR FOUGHT THE SOUTH IN THE FLUSH OF HER STRENGTH AND ENTHUSIASM

EDWIN M. STANTON
Secretary of War.

MONTGOMERY BLAIR
Postmaster-General.

GIDEON WELLES
Secretary of the Navy.

SALMON P. CHASE
Secretary of the Treasury.

HANNIBAL HAMLIN
Vice-President.

WILLIAM H. SEWARD
Secretary of State.

CALEB B. SMITH
Secretary of the Interior.

MEMBERS OF
PRESIDENT LINCOLN'S
OFFICIAL FAMILY

Other members were: War, Simon Cameron (1861); Treasury, W. P. Fessenden, July 1, 1864, and Hugh McCulloch, March 4, 1865; Interior, John P. Usher, January 8, 1863; Attorney-General, James Speed, December 2, 1864; Postmaster-General, William Dennison, September 24, 1864.

EDWARD BATES
Attorney-General.

JAMES A. SEDDON
Secretary of War.

CHRISTOPHER G. MEMMINGER
Secretary of the Treasury.

STEPHEN R. MALLORY
Secretary of the Navy.

JOHN H. REAGAN
Postmaster-General.

ALEXANDER H. STEPHENS
Vice-President.

JUDAH P. BENJAMIN
Secretary of State.

MEN WHO HELPED PRESI-
DENT DAVIS GUIDE THE
SHIP OF STATE

The members of the Cabinet were
chosen not from intimate friends of
the President, but from the men preferred by the States they represented.
There was no Secretary of the Interior in the Confederate Cabinet.

GEORGE DAVIS
Attorney-General.

VICE-PRESIDENT STEPHENS
AND MEMBERS OF THE
CONFEDERATE CABINET

Judah P. Benjamin, Secretary of
State, has been called the brain of
the Confederacy. President Davis
wished to appoint the Honorable
Robert Barnwell, Secretary of State,
but Mr. Barnwell declined the honor.

AFTER THE GREAT MASS MEETING IN UNION SQUARE, NEW YORK, APRIL 20, 1861

Knots of citizens still linger around the stands where Anderson, who had abandoned Sumter only six days before, had just roused the multitude to wild enthusiasm. Of this gathering in support of the Government the *New York Herald* said at the time: "Such a mighty uprising of the people has never before been witnessed in New York, nor throughout the whole length and breadth of the Union. Five stands were erected, from which some of the most able speakers of the city and state addressed the multitude on the necessity of rallying around the flag of the Republic in this hour of its danger. A series of resolutions was proposed and unanimously adopted, pledging the meeting to use every means to preserve the Union intact and inviolate. Great unanimity prevailed throughout the whole proceedings; party politics were ignored, and the entire meeting—speakers and listeners—were a unit in maintaining the national honor unsullied. Major Anderson, the hero of Fort Sumter, was present, and showed himself at the various stands, at each of which he was most enthusiastically received. An impressive feature of the occasion was the flag of Sumter, hoisted on the stump of the staff that had been shot away, placed in the hand of the equestrian statue of Washington."

[14]

RECRUITING ON BROADWAY, 1861

Looking north on Broadway from "The Park" (later City Hall Park) in war time, one sees the Stars and Stripes waving above the recruiting station, p a s t which the soldiers stroll. There is a convenient booth with liquid refreshments. To the right of the picture the rear end of a street car is visible, but passenger travel on Broadway itself is by stage. On the left is the Astor House, then one of the foremost hostelries of the city. In the lower photograph the view is from the balcony of the Metropolitan looking north on Broadway. The twin towers on the left are those of St. Thomas's Church. The lumbering stages, with the deafening noise of their rattling windows as they drive over the cobblestones, are here in force. More hoop-skirts are retreating in the distance, and a gentleman in the tall hat of the period is on his way down town. Few of the buildings seen here remained half a century later. The time is summer, as the awnings attest.

THE WAR'S GREAT "CITIZEN" AT HIS MOMENT OF TRIUMPH

Just behind the round table to the right, rising head and shoulders above the distinguished bystanders, grasping his manuscript in both hands, stands Abraham Lincoln.   Of all the occasions on which he talked to his countrymen, this was most significant.   The time and place marked the final and lasting approval of his political and military policies.   Despite the bitter opposition of a majority of the Northern political and social leaders, the people of the Northern States had renominated Lincoln in June, 1864.   In November, encouraged by the victories of Farragut at Mobile, Sherman in Georgia, and Sheridan in the Shenandoah Valley, they had reëlected him President of the United States by an electoral vote of 212 to 21.   Since the election, continued Northern victories had made certain the

LINCOLN READING HIS SECOND INAUGURAL ADDRESS ON MARCH 4, 1865

speedy termination of the war. Not long since, his opponents had been so numerous and so powerful that they fully expected to prevent his renomination. Lincoln himself, shortly after his renomination, had come to believe that reelection was improbable, and had expressed himself as ready "to cooperate with the President-elect to save the Union." Yet neither in Lincoln's demeanor nor in his inaugural address is there the slightest note of personal exultation. For political and military enemies alike he has "malice toward none; charity for all." Indeed the dominant feeling in his speech is one of sorrow and sympathy for the cruel sufferings of both North and South. Not only in the United States, but throughout the civilized world, the address made a profound and immediate impression.

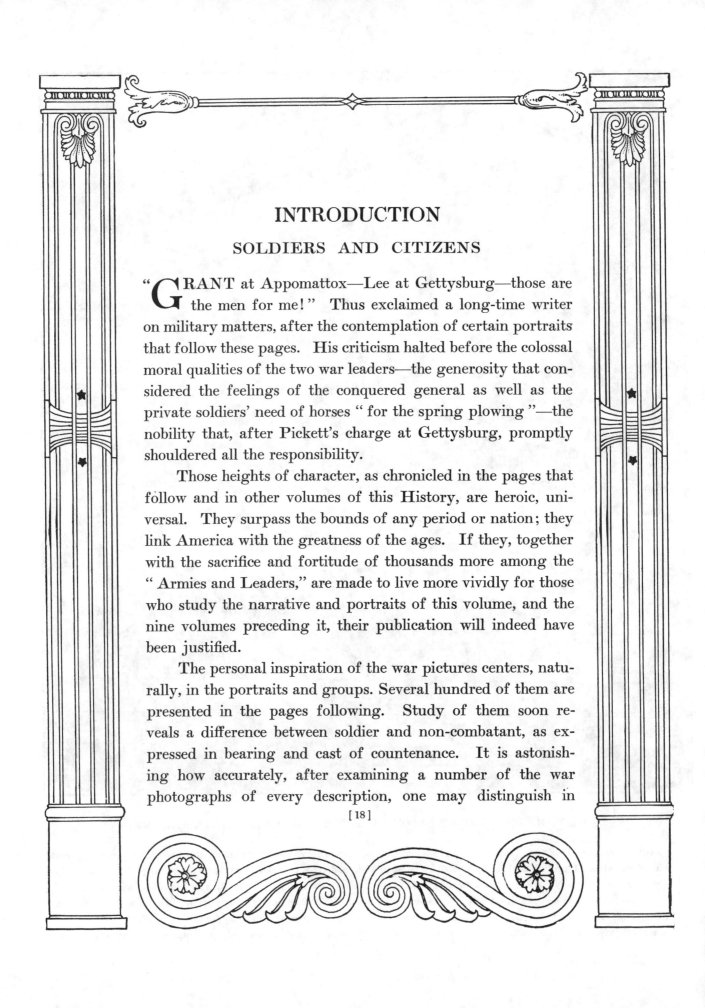

INTRODUCTION

SOLDIERS AND CITIZENS

"GRANT at Appomattox—Lee at Gettysburg—those are the men for me!" Thus exclaimed a long-time writer on military matters, after the contemplation of certain portraits that follow these pages. His criticism halted before the colossal moral qualities of the two war leaders—the generosity that considered the feelings of the conquered general as well as the private soldiers' need of horses "for the spring plowing"—the nobility that, after Pickett's charge at Gettysburg, promptly shouldered all the responsibility.

Those heights of character, as chronicled in the pages that follow and in other volumes of this History, are heroic, universal. They surpass the bounds of any period or nation; they link America with the greatness of the ages. If they, together with the sacrifice and fortitude of thousands more among the "Armies and Leaders," are made to live more vividly for those who study the narrative and portraits of this volume, and the nine volumes preceding it, their publication will indeed have been justified.

The personal inspiration of the war pictures centers, naturally, in the portraits and groups. Several hundred of them are presented in the pages following. Study of them soon reveals a difference between soldier and non-combatant, as expressed in bearing and cast of countenance. It is astonishing how accurately, after examining a number of the war photographs of every description, one may distinguish in

FROM
THE ARMY
TO THE
WHITE HOUSE

War-time portraits of
six soldiers whose
military records
assisted them
to the Pres-
idential
Chair.

Garfield in '63—(left to right) Thomas, Wiles, Tyler, Simmons, Drillard, Ducat, Barnett, Goddard, Rosecrans, Garfield, Porter, Bond, Thompson, Sheridan.

Brig.-Gen. Andrew Johnson
President, 1865–69.

General Ulysses S. Grant
President, 1869–77.

Bvt. Maj.-Gen. Rutherford B. Hayes
President, 1877–81.

Maj.-Gen. James A. Garfield
President, March to September, 1881.

Bvt. Brig.-Gen. Benjamin Harrison
President, 1889–93.

Brevet Major William McKinley
President, 1897–1901.

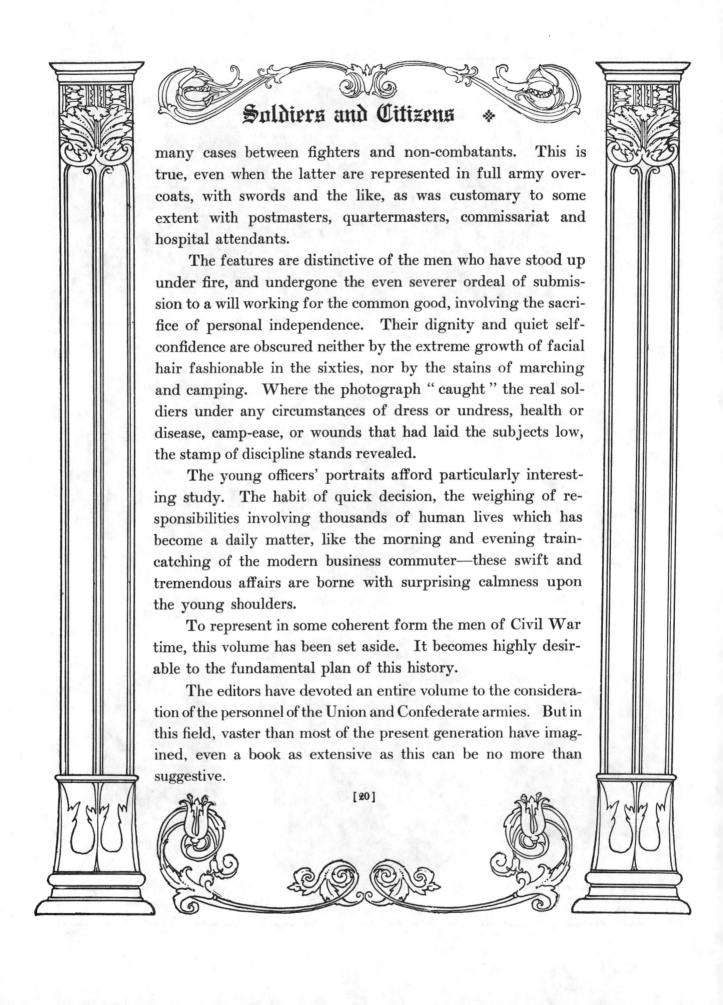

many cases between fighters and non-combatants. This is true, even when the latter are represented in full army overcoats, with swords and the like, as was customary to some extent with postmasters, quartermasters, commissariat and hospital attendants.

The features are distinctive of the men who have stood up under fire, and undergone the even severer ordeal of submission to a will working for the common good, involving the sacrifice of personal independence. Their dignity and quiet self-confidence are obscured neither by the extreme growth of facial hair fashionable in the sixties, nor by the stains of marching and camping. Where the photograph " caught " the real soldiers under any circumstances of dress or undress, health or disease, camp-ease, or wounds that had laid the subjects low, the stamp of discipline stands revealed.

The young officers' portraits afford particularly interesting study. The habit of quick decision, the weighing of responsibilities involving thousands of human lives which has become a daily matter, like the morning and evening train-catching of the modern business commuter—these swift and tremendous affairs are borne with surprising calmness upon the young shoulders.

To represent in some coherent form the men of Civil War time, this volume has been set aside. It becomes highly desirable to the fundamental plan of this history.

The editors have devoted an entire volume to the consideration of the personnel of the Union and Confederate armies. But in this field, vaster than most of the present generation have imagined, even a book as extensive as this can be no more than suggestive.

Brevet Major George Haven Putnam, 176th New York, Prisoner at Libby and Danville in the Winter of 1864-65.

Brevet Lieut.-Colonel Harrison Gray Otis: Twice Wounded; Brig.-Gen. in Spanish War, Maj.-Gen. in Philippines.

Chief of Scouts Henry Watterson, C. S. A., Aide-de-Camp to General Forrest, Chief of Scouts under General Jos. E. Johnston.

REPRESENTATIVE CIVIL WAR OFFICERS—SUCCESSFUL ALSO IN LATER LIFE

George Haven Putnam, publisher and author, led in the move for international copyright. Harrison Gray Otis served as an editor in California more than 30 years, and fought again in the Spanish War. Henry Watterson, as editor of the Louisville *Courier-Journal*, did much to reconcile North and South. Andrew Carnegie's millions, made from iron and steel, went largely to philanthropy and the advancement of peace. Nathan B. Forrest, the daring Confederate cavalryman, later developed two vast plantations. Thomas T. Eckert became President of the Western Union Telegraph Company. Grenville M. Dodge, Chief Engineer of the Union Pacific, built thousands of miles of railroads, opening up the Western empire.

Andrew Carnegie Superintended Military Railways and Government Telegraph Lines in 1861.

Lieut.-General Nathan B. Forrest, C. S. A., Entered as Private; Lieut.-Col., 1861, Maj.-Gen., 1864.

Brevet Brig.-General Thomas T. Eckert, Superintendent of Military Telegraph; Asst. Sec. of War, 1864-66.

Maj.-General Grenville M. Dodge, Wounded Before Atlanta; Succeeded Rosecrans in the Department of Missouri.

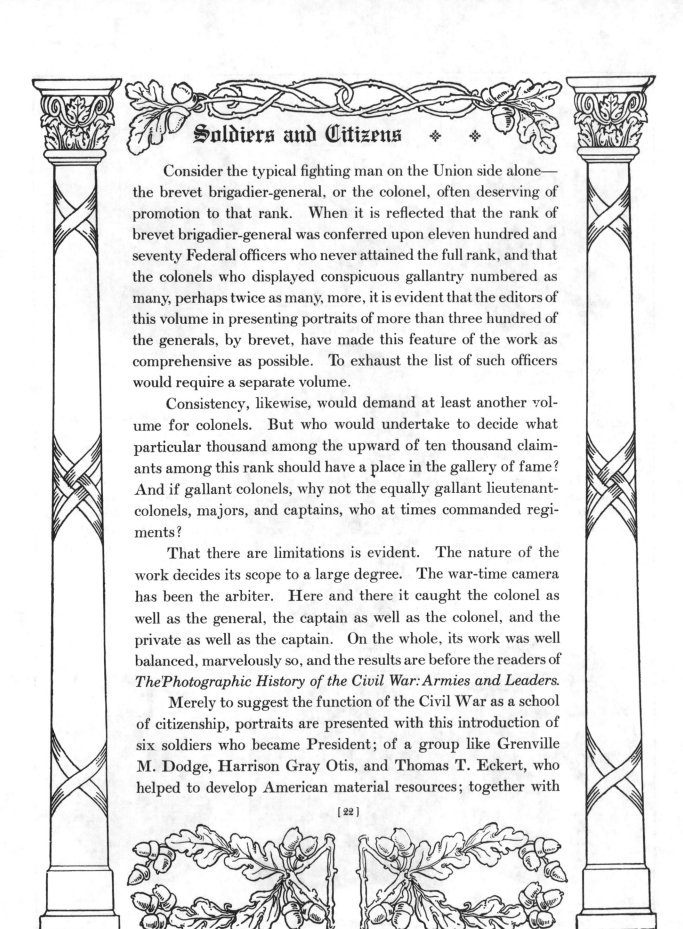

Soldiers and Citizens ✦ ✦

Consider the typical fighting man on the Union side alone—
the brevet brigadier-general, or the colonel, often deserving of
promotion to that rank. When it is reflected that the rank of
brevet brigadier-general was conferred upon eleven hundred and
seventy Federal officers who never attained the full rank, and that
the colonels who displayed conspicuous gallantry numbered as
many, perhaps twice as many, more, it is evident that the editors of
this volume in presenting portraits of more than three hundred of
the generals, by brevet, have made this feature of the work as
comprehensive as possible. To exhaust the list of such officers
would require a separate volume.

Consistency, likewise, would demand at least another volume for colonels. But who would undertake to decide what
particular thousand among the upward of ten thousand claim-
ants among this rank should have a place in the gallery of fame?
And if gallant colonels, why not the equally gallant lieutenant-
colonels, majors, and captains, who at times commanded regiments?

That there are limitations is evident. The nature of the
work decides its scope to a large degree. The war-time camera
has been the arbiter. Here and there it caught the colonel as
well as the general, the captain as well as the colonel, and the
private as well as the captain. On the whole, its work was well
balanced, marvelously so, and the results are before the readers of
The Photographic History of the Civil War: Armies and Leaders.

Merely to suggest the function of the Civil War as a school
of citizenship, portraits are presented with this introduction of
six soldiers who became President; of a group like Grenville
M. Dodge, Harrison Gray Otis, and Thomas T. Eckert, who
helped to develop American material resources; together with

Brevet Brigadier-General Stewart L. Woodford, Lieut.-Gov. of New York, 1866–68; President Electoral College, 1872; M. C., 1873–75; U. S. Dist. Atty., 1877–83; U. S. Minister to Spain, 1879–98.

Brevet Brigadier-General James Grant Wilson, Author of Addresses on Lincoln, Grant, Hull, Farragut, etc.; President New York Gen. and Biog. Soc. and of Am. Ethnological Society.

Brevet Major-General William B. Hazen, Chief Signal Officer, Raised 41st Ohio Volunteers; Marched with Sherman to the Sea; Commanded 15th Army Corps; U. S Military Attaché to France.

WAR–TIME PORTRAITS OF TYPICAL SOLDIERS WHO TURNED TO PUBLIC LIFE AND EDUCATION

Notable as lawyers, writers and statesmen are General Carl Schurz (on the left), who became Minister to Spain, Secretary of the Interior, and editor of the New York *Evening Post;* and General Lewis Wallace (to the right), Governor of New Mexico, Minister to Turkey, and author of "Ben Hur" and other historical novels.

Major-General Carl Schurz.

Major-General Lewis Wallace.

Colonel George E. Waring, Jr., Led a Brigade of Cavalry; Reorganized Street Cleaning System of New York City; Died in Havana, Cuba, Fighting Yellow Fever.

Brevet Brigadier-General Francis W. Palfrey, Register in Bankruptcy in 1872; Author of "Antietam and Fredericksburg" in 1882; Author of Many Scholarly and Important Papers.

Lieutenant E. Benjamin Andrews: Wounded at Petersburg, 1864; Professor of History and Political Economy, Brown University, 1882–88; President thereof, 1889–98.

Brevet Brigadier-General Francis A. Walker, Superintendent Ninth and Tenth Censuses; Commissioner of Indian Affairs in 1872; President Mass. Inst. of Technology, 1881.

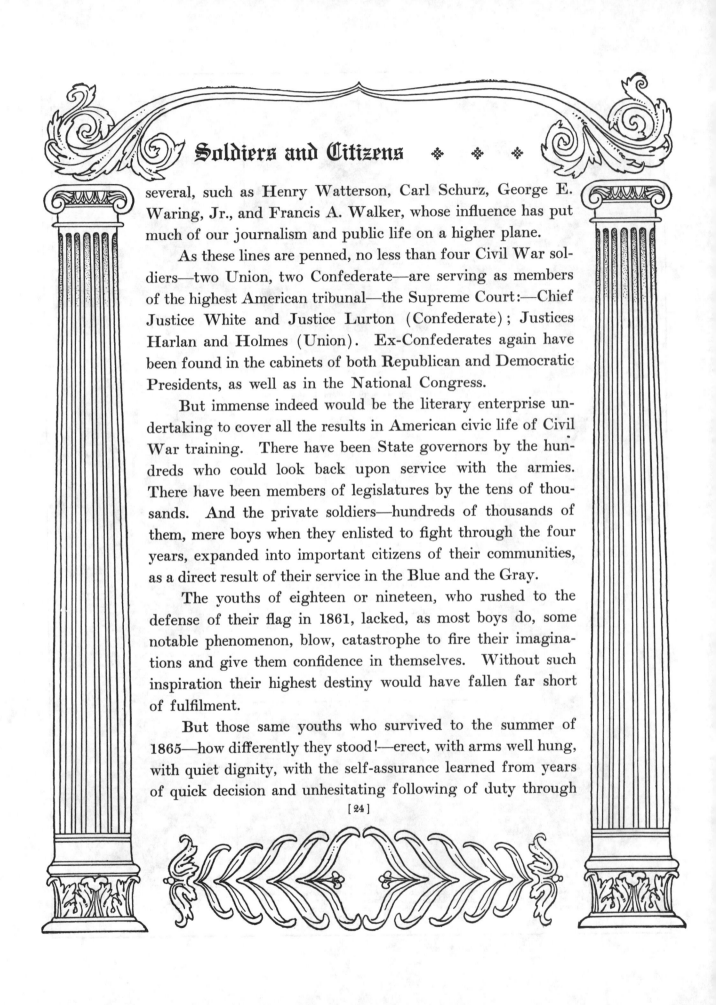

several, such as Henry Watterson, Carl Schurz, George E. Waring, Jr., and Francis A. Walker, whose influence has put much of our journalism and public life on a higher plane.

As these lines are penned, no less than four Civil War soldiers—two Union, two Confederate—are serving as members of the highest American tribunal—the Supreme Court:—Chief Justice White and Justice Lurton (Confederate); Justices Harlan and Holmes (Union). Ex-Confederates again have been found in the cabinets of both Republican and Democratic Presidents, as well as in the National Congress.

But immense indeed would be the literary enterprise undertaking to cover all the results in American civic life of Civil War training. There have been State governors by the hundreds who could look back upon service with the armies. There have been members of legislatures by the tens of thousands. And the private soldiers—hundreds of thousands of them, mere boys when they enlisted to fight through the four years, expanded into important citizens of their communities, as a direct result of their service in the Blue and the Gray.

The youths of eighteen or nineteen, who rushed to the defense of their flag in 1861, lacked, as most boys do, some notable phenomenon, blow, catastrophe to fire their imaginations and give them confidence in themselves. Without such inspiration their highest destiny would have fallen far short of fulfilment.

But those same youths who survived to the summer of 1865—how differently they stood!—erect, with arms well hung, with quiet dignity, with the self-assurance learned from years of quick decision and unhesitating following of duty through

WAR–TIME POR–
TRAITS OF FEDERAL
SOLDIERS WHO CON–
TRIBUTED TO THE
PHOTOGRAPHIC
HISTORY HALF A
CENTURY LATER

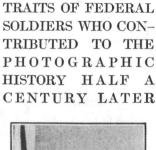

Captain A. W. Greely, 1863; Later Maj.-
Gen., U. S. A.; Chief Signal Service
("Signals"; "Telegraph").

Private Geo. L. Kilmer in '64, Wearing
the "Veteran Stripe" at 18
(Military Editor).

Private J. E. Gilman, Lost an Arm at Gettysburg; Commander-in-Chief G. A. R. 1910–11
("Grand Army of the Republic").

Bvt. Brig.-Gen. T. F. Roden-
bough, U. S. A., in 1865;
Wounded at Trevilian and
Winchester; Later Sec-
retary U. S. Military
Service Institution
("Cavalry" Editor).

Capt. F. Y. Hedley in '64, Age 20; Later Editor
and Author of "Marching Through Georgia"
("School of the Soldier," "Marching
and Foraging").

Col. W. C. Church; Later Edi-
tor of the *Army and Navy
Journal* and Author of Life of
Ulysses S. Grant ("Grant").

T. S. C. Lowe, Military Bal-
loonist in the Peninsula Campaign, 1862—the First War
Aeronaut ("Balloons").

Capt. T. S. Peck; Medal of Hon-
or in 1864; Later Adj.-Gen.
of Vermont (Contributor of
many rare photographs).

Col. L. R. Stegman, Wounded
at Cedar Creek, Gettysburg,
Ringgold and Pine Moun-
tain (Consulting Editor).

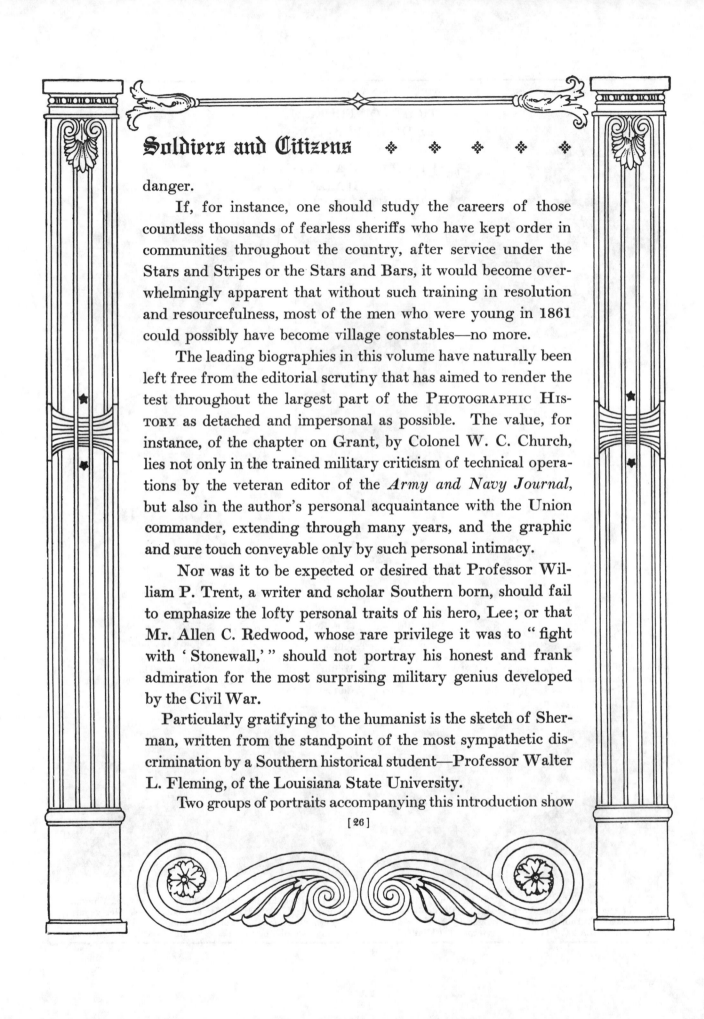

danger.

If, for instance, one should study the careers of those countless thousands of fearless sheriffs who have kept order in communities throughout the country, after service under the Stars and Stripes or the Stars and Bars, it would become overwhelmingly apparent that without such training in resolution and resourcefulness, most of the men who were young in 1861 could possibly have become village constables—no more.

The leading biographies in this volume have naturally been left free from the editorial scrutiny that has aimed to render the test throughout the largest part of the PHOTOGRAPHIC HISTORY as detached and impersonal as possible. The value, for instance, of the chapter on Grant, by Colonel W. C. Church, lies not only in the trained military criticism of technical operations by the veteran editor of the *Army and Navy Journal*, but also in the author's personal acquaintance with the Union commander, extending through many years, and the graphic and sure touch conveyable only by such personal intimacy.

Nor was it to be expected or desired that Professor William P. Trent, a writer and scholar Southern born, should fail to emphasize the lofty personal traits of his hero, Lee; or that Mr. Allen C. Redwood, whose rare privilege it was to " fight with ' Stonewall,' " should not portray his honest and frank admiration for the most surprising military genius developed by the Civil War.

Particularly gratifying to the humanist is the sketch of Sherman, written from the standpoint of the most sympathetic discrimination by a Southern historical student—Professor Walter L. Fleming, of the Louisiana State University.

Two groups of portraits accompanying this introduction show

WAR–TIME PHOTOGRAPHS OF CONFEDERATE SOLDIERS

CONTRIBUTORS TO THE PHOTOGRAPHIC HISTORY

Col. Hilary A. Herbert; Later Member of Congress and Secretary of the Navy ("The Meaning of Losses in Battle").

Lieut.-Col. J. W. Mallet; Later Professor of Chemistry, University of Virginia ("Confederate Ordnance").

Private John A. Wyeth in '61, at 16; Later Organizer of the New York "Polyclinic" ("Confederate Raids").

Lieut. R. H. McKim in '62; Later Rector Church of the Epiphany, Washington, and Military and Religious Writer ("The Confederate Army").

Captain F. M. Colston, Artillery Officer with Alexander ("Memoirs of Gettysburg" and Many Rare Photographs).

Allen C. Redwood, of the 55th Virginia, with "Stonewall" Jackson; Later Artist and Author (Confederate Reminiscences; "Jackson").

Brig.-Gen. M.J. Wright; Later U. S. War Dept. Agent ("Records of the War" and Statistics).

Col. D. G. McIntosh; Later Attorney-at-Law ("Artillery of the Confederacy").

Col. T. M. R. Talcott; Later Civil Engineer ("Reminiscences of the Confederate Engineers").

S. A. Cunningham; Later Editor *Confederate Veteran* ("United Confederate Veterans").

Deering J. Roberts, Surgeon; Later Editor *Southern Practitioner* ("Confederate Medical Service").

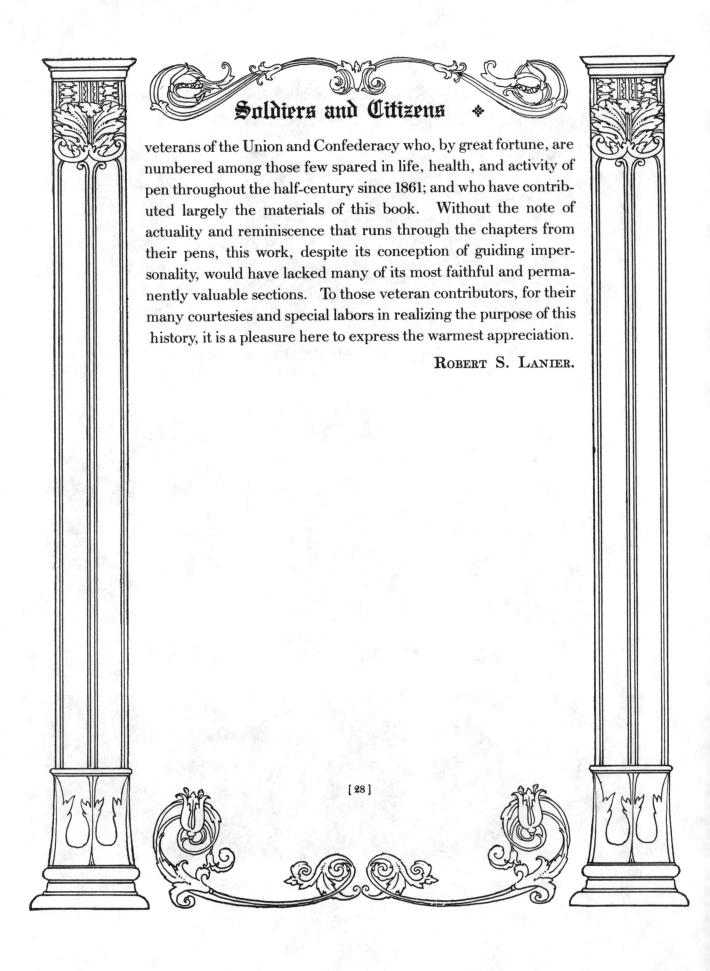

veterans of the Union and Confederacy who, by great fortune, are numbered among those few spared in life, health, and activity of pen throughout the half-century since 1861; and who have contributed largely the materials of this book. Without the note of actuality and reminiscence that runs through the chapters from their pens, this work, despite its conception of guiding impersonality, would have lacked many of its most faithful and permanently valuable sections. To those veteran contributors, for their many courtesies and special labors in realizing the purpose of this history, it is a pleasure here to express the warmest appreciation.

ROBERT S. LANIER.

I

GRANT

DURING THE WILDERNESS CAMPAIGN, 1864

WHEN GRANT LOST AN ARMY BUT SAVED A NATION

GRANT ON LOOKOUT MOUNTAIN—1863

Wearing epaulets and a sword—quite unusual for him—but calm and imperturbable as of old, with his crumpled army hat, plain blouse, his trousers tucked into his boot-tops, and the inevitable cigar, Ulysses S. Grant stands at a historic spot. Less than a week before, when the Union soldiers under Thomas, still smarting from their experience at Chickamauga, stood gazing at the Confederate works behind which rose the crest of Missionary Ridge, the Stars and Stripes were thrown to the breeze on the crest of Lookout Mountain. Eager hands pointed, and a great cheer went up from the Army of the Cumberland. They knew that the Union troops with Hooker had carried the day in their "battle above the clouds." That was the 25th of November, 1863; and that same afternoon the soldiers

AT THE SPOT WHERE HOOKER SIGNALED VICTORY THE WEEK BEFORE

of Thomas swarmed over the crest of Missionary Ridge while Grant himself looked on and wondered. When a few days later Grant visited the spot whence the flag was waved, an enterprising photographer, already on the spot, preserved the striking scene. Seated with his back against a tree, General J. A. Rawlins gazes at his leader. Behind him stands General Webster, and leaning against the tree in Colonel Clark B. Lagow. The figure in the right foreground is Colonel William S. Hillyer. Seated by the path is an orderly. They have evidently come to survey the site of Hooker's battle from above. Colonel Lagow is carrying a pair of field glasses. Less than four months later Grant was commissioned lieutenant-general and placed in general command of the Union armies.

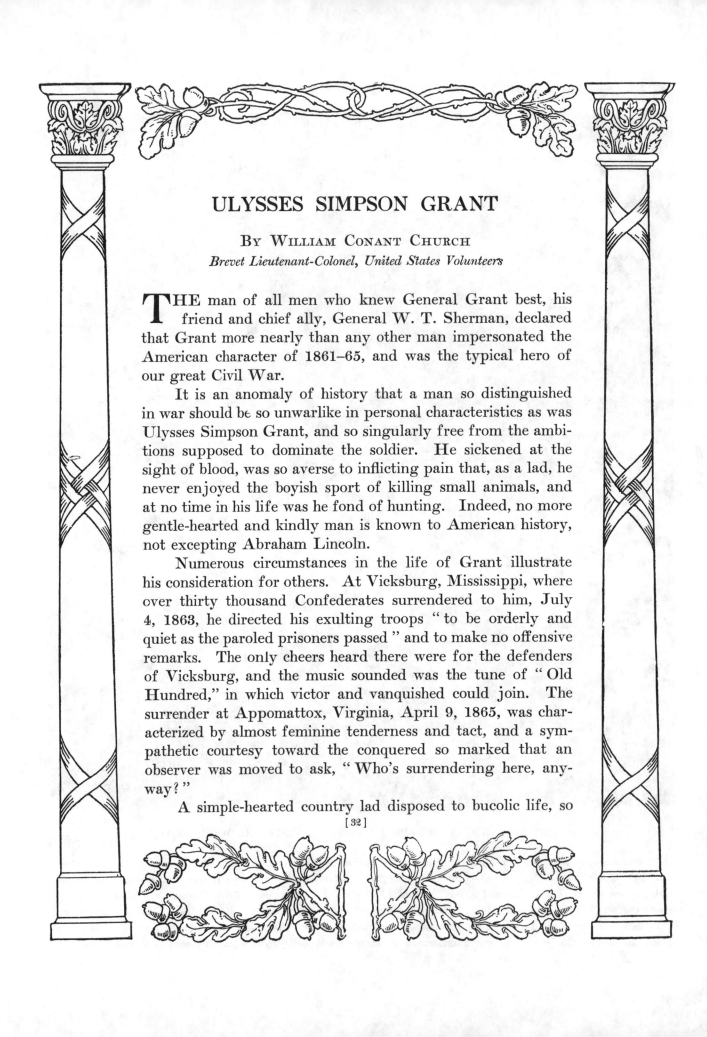

ULYSSES SIMPSON GRANT

By William Conant Church
Brevet Lieutenant-Colonel, United States Volunteers

THE man of all men who knew General Grant best, his friend and chief ally, General W. T. Sherman, declared that Grant more nearly than any other man impersonated the American character of 1861–65, and was the typical hero of our great Civil War.

It is an anomaly of history that a man so distinguished in war should be so unwarlike in personal characteristics as was Ulysses Simpson Grant, and so singularly free from the ambitions supposed to dominate the soldier. He sickened at the sight of blood, was so averse to inflicting pain that, as a lad, he never enjoyed the boyish sport of killing small animals, and at no time in his life was he fond of hunting. Indeed, no more gentle-hearted and kindly man is known to American history, not excepting Abraham Lincoln.

Numerous circumstances in the life of Grant illustrate his consideration for others. At Vicksburg, Mississippi, where over thirty thousand Confederates surrendered to him, July 4, 1863, he directed his exulting troops " to be orderly and quiet as the paroled prisoners passed " and to make no offensive remarks. The only cheers heard there were for the defenders of Vicksburg, and the music sounded was the tune of " Old Hundred," in which victor and vanquished could join. The surrender at Appomattox, Virginia, April 9, 1865, was characterized by almost feminine tenderness and tact, and a sympathetic courtesy toward the conquered so marked that an observer was moved to ask, " Who's surrendering here, anyway? "

A simple-hearted country lad disposed to bucolic life, so

GRANT IN 1863—BEFORE THE FIRST OF HIS GREAT VICTORIES

Grant was described in 1861 as a man "who knows how to do things." In February, 1862, he captured Forts Henry and Donelson, thus opening the way for a Federal advance up the Tennessee River, and was promptly commissioned major-general. His experience at Shiloh in April, coupled with failures in official routine during the Donelson campaign which were not approved by his superiors, left him under a cloud which was not removed until the capture of Vicksburg, July 4, 1863, revealed capacity of a high order. The government's plan of conducting the war was then entrusted to him to work out with practically unlimited power.

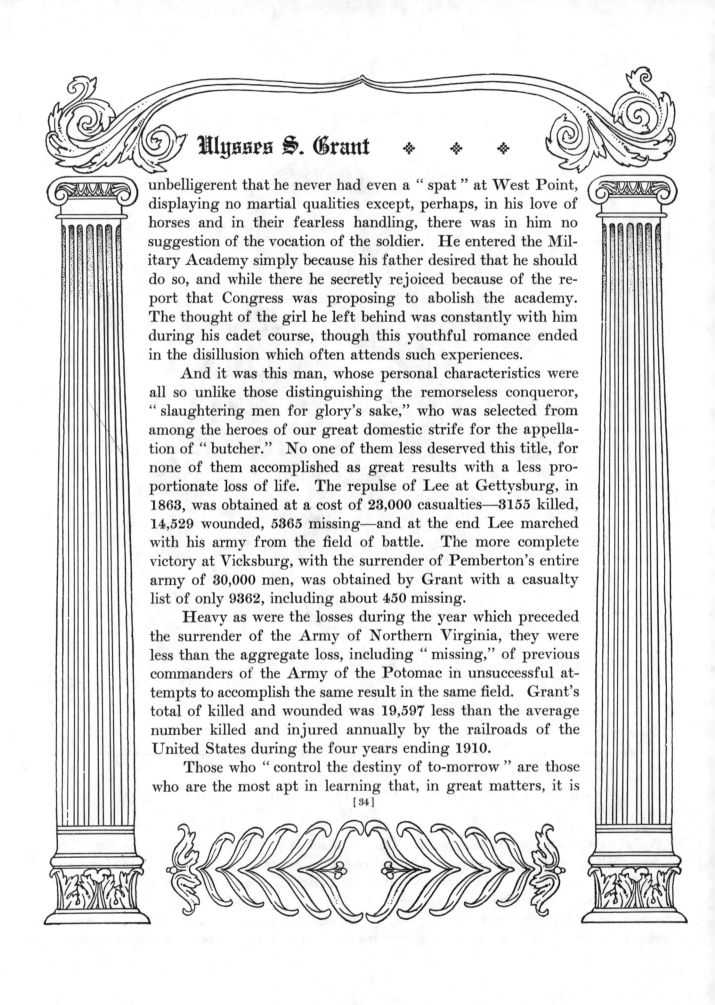

unbelligerent that he never had even a " spat " at West Point, displaying no martial qualities except, perhaps, in his love of horses and in their fearless handling, there was in him no suggestion of the vocation of the soldier. He entered the Military Academy simply because his father desired that he should do so, and while there he secretly rejoiced because of the report that Congress was proposing to abolish the academy. The thought of the girl he left behind was constantly with him during his cadet course, though this youthful romance ended in the disillusion which often attends such experiences.

And it was this man, whose personal characteristics were all so unlike those distinguishing the remorseless conqueror, " slaughtering men for glory's sake," who was selected from among the heroes of our great domestic strife for the appellation of " butcher." No one of them less deserved this title, for none of them accomplished as great results with a less proportionate loss of life. The repulse of Lee at Gettysburg, in 1863, was obtained at a cost of 23,000 casualties—3155 killed, 14,529 wounded, 5365 missing—and at the end Lee marched with his army from the field of battle. The more complete victory at Vicksburg, with the surrender of Pemberton's entire army of 30,000 men, was obtained by Grant with a casualty list of only 9362, including about 450 missing.

Heavy as were the losses during the year which preceded the surrender of the Army of Northern Virginia, they were less than the aggregate loss, including " missing," of previous commanders of the Army of the Potomac in unsuccessful attempts to accomplish the same result in the same field. Grant's total of killed and wounded was 19,597 less than the average number killed and injured annually by the railroads of the United States during the four years ending 1910.

Those who " control the destiny of to-morrow " are those who are the most apt in learning that, in great matters, it is

BEFORE VICKSBURG

AFTER VICKSBURG

The close-set mouth, squared shoulders and lowering brow in this photograph of Grant, taken in December, 1862, tell the story of the intensity of his purpose while he was advancing upon Vicksburg—only to be foiled by Van Dorn's raid on his line of communications at Holly Springs. His grim expression and determined jaw betokened no respite for the Confederates, however. Six months later he marched into the coveted stronghold. This photograph was taken by James Mullen at Oxford, Mississippi, in December, 1862, just before Van Dorn's raid balked the general's plans.

This photograph was taken in the fall of 1863, after the capture of the Confederacy's Gibraltar had raised Grant to secure and everlasting fame. His attitude is relaxed and his eyebrows no longer mark a straight line across the grim visage. The right brow is slightly arched with an almost jovial expression. But the jaw is no less vigorous and determined, and the steadfast eyes seem to be peering into that future which holds more victories. He still has Chattanooga and his great campaigns in the East to fight and the final magnificent struggle in the trenches at Petersburg.

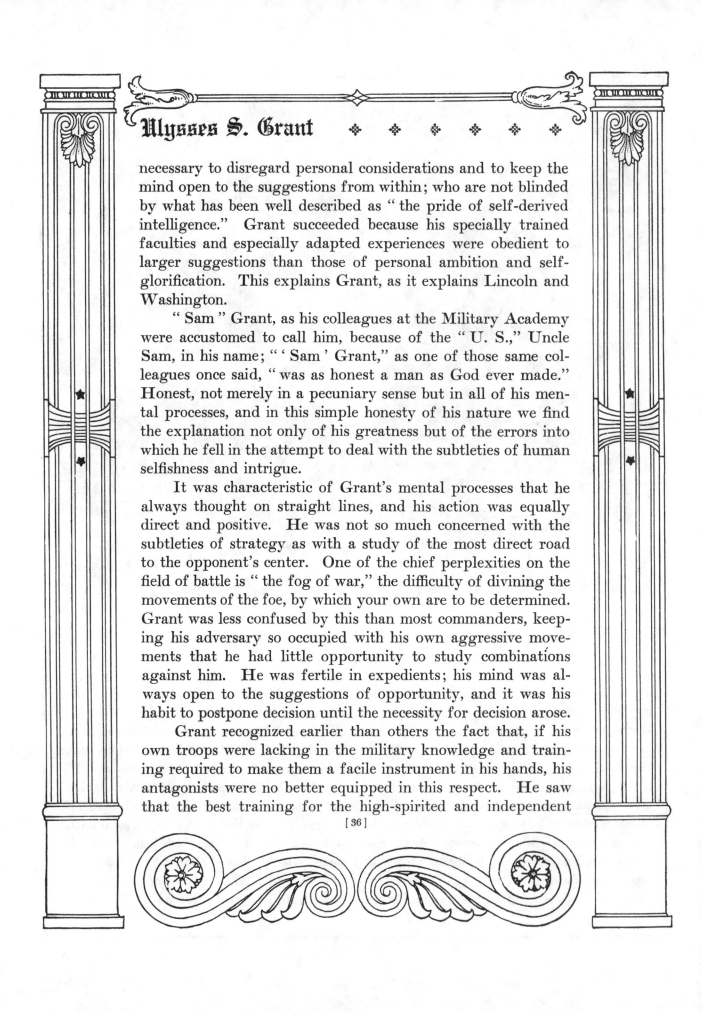

necessary to disregard personal considerations and to keep the mind open to the suggestions from within; who are not blinded by what has been well described as " the pride of self-derived intelligence." Grant succeeded because his specially trained faculties and especially adapted experiences were obedient to larger suggestions than those of personal ambition and self-glorification. This explains Grant, as it explains Lincoln and Washington.

" Sam " Grant, as his colleagues at the Military Academy were accustomed to call him, because of the " U. S.," Uncle Sam, in his name; " ' Sam ' Grant," as one of those same colleagues once said, " was as honest a man as God ever made." Honest, not merely in a pecuniary sense but in all of his mental processes, and in this simple honesty of his nature we find the explanation not only of his greatness but of the errors into which he fell in the attempt to deal with the subtleties of human selfishness and intrigue.

It was characteristic of Grant's mental processes that he always thought on straight lines, and his action was equally direct and positive. He was not so much concerned with the subtleties of strategy as with a study of the most direct road to the opponent's center. One of the chief perplexities on the field of battle is " the fog of war," the difficulty of divining the movements of the foe, by which your own are to be determined. Grant was less confused by this than most commanders, keeping his adversary so occupied with his own aggressive movements that he had little opportunity to study combinations against him. He was fertile in expedients; his mind was always open to the suggestions of opportunity, and it was his habit to postpone decision until the necessity for decision arose.

Grant recognized earlier than others the fact that, if his own troops were lacking in the military knowledge and training required to make them a facile instrument in his hands, his antagonists were no better equipped in this respect. He saw that the best training for the high-spirited and independent

On this page are three photographs of General Grant, taken in the most critical year of his career, the year when he took Vicksburg in July, then in November gazed in wonder at his own soldiers as they swarmed up the heights of Missionary Ridge. The following March he was made general-in-chief of the armies of the United States. Congress passed a vote of thanks to General Grant and his army, and ordered a gold medal to be struck in his honor. But as we see him here, none of these honors had come to him; and the deeds themselves

GRANT IN 1863

were only in process of accomplishment. Even Sherman, the staunch friend and supporter of Grant, had doubts which were only dispelled by the master stroke at Vicksburg, as to the outcome of Grant's extraordinary methods and plans. He was himself conscious of the heavy responsibility resting upon him and of the fact that he stood on trial before the country. Other faithful generals had been condemned at the bar of public opinion before their projects matured. The eyes in these portraits are stern, and the expressions intense.

PORTRAITS OF 1863—SHOWING GRANT IN REPOSE

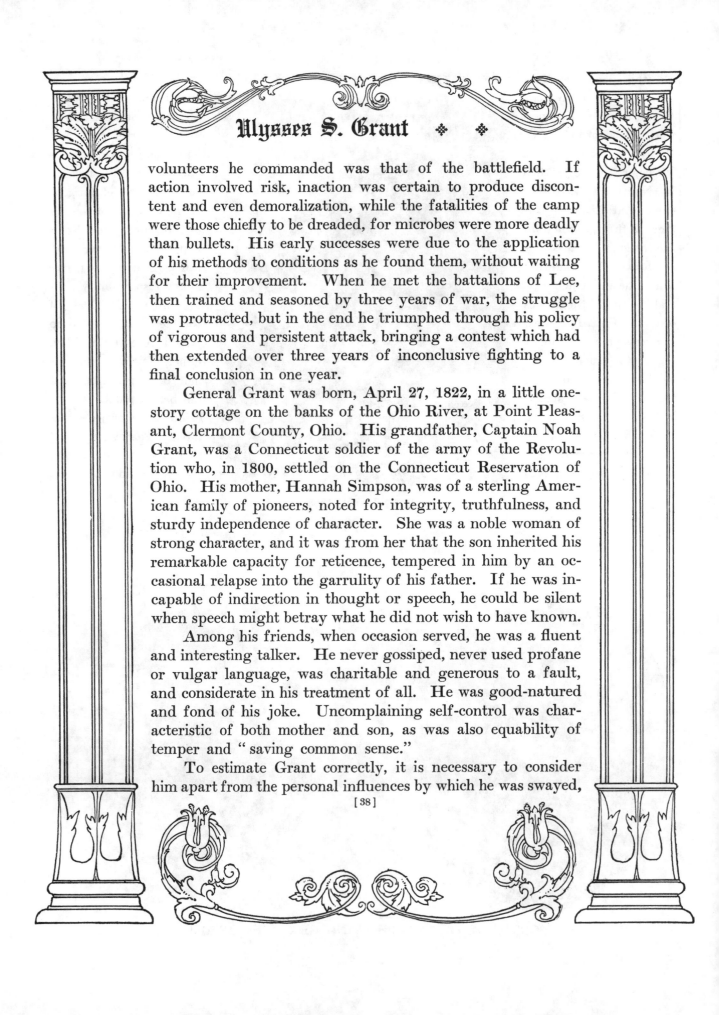

volunteers he commanded was that of the battlefield. If action involved risk, inaction was certain to produce discontent and even demoralization, while the fatalities of the camp were those chiefly to be dreaded, for microbes were more deadly than bullets. His early successes were due to the application of his methods to conditions as he found them, without waiting for their improvement. When he met the battalions of Lee, then trained and seasoned by three years of war, the struggle was protracted, but in the end he triumphed through his policy of vigorous and persistent attack, bringing a contest which had then extended over three years of inconclusive fighting to a final conclusion in one year.

General Grant was born, April 27, 1822, in a little one-story cottage on the banks of the Ohio River, at Point Pleasant, Clermont County, Ohio. His grandfather, Captain Noah Grant, was a Connecticut soldier of the army of the Revolution who, in 1800, settled on the Connecticut Reservation of Ohio. His mother, Hannah Simpson, was of a sterling American family of pioneers, noted for integrity, truthfulness, and sturdy independence of character. She was a noble woman of strong character, and it was from her that the son inherited his remarkable capacity for reticence, tempered in him by an occasional relapse into the garrulity of his father. If he was incapable of indirection in thought or speech, he could be silent when speech might betray what he did not wish to have known.

Among his friends, when occasion served, he was a fluent and interesting talker. He never gossiped, never used profane or vulgar language, was charitable and generous to a fault, and considerate in his treatment of all. He was good-natured and fond of his joke. Uncomplaining self-control was characteristic of both mother and son, as was also equability of temper and "saving common sense."

To estimate Grant correctly, it is necessary to consider him apart from the personal influences by which he was swayed,

IN THE AUTUMN OF 1863—GRANT'S CHANGING EXPRESSIONS

Although secure in his fame as the conqueror of Vicksburg, Grant still has the greater part of his destiny to fulfil as he faces the camera. Before him lie the Wilderness, Spotsylvania, Cold Harbor, and the slow investment of Petersburg. This series forms a particularly interesting study in expression. At the left hand, the face looks almost amused. In the next the expression is graver, the mouth close set. The third picture looks plainly obstinate, and in the last the stern fighter might have been declaring, as in the following spring: "I propose to fight it out on this line if it takes all summer." The eyes, first unveiled fully in this fourth view, are the unmistakable index to Grant's stern inflexibility, once his decision was made.

IN THE AUTUMN OF 1864—AFTER THE STRAIN OF THE WILDERNESS CAMPAIGN

Here is a furrowed brow above eyes worn by pain. In the pictures of the previous year the forehead is more smooth, the expression grave yet confident. Here the expression is that of a man who has won, but won at a bitter cost. It is the memory of the 50,000 men whom he left in the Wilderness campaign and at Cold Harbor that has lined this brow, and closed still tighter this inflexible mouth. Again, as in the series above, the eyes are not revealed until the last picture. Then again flashes the determination of a hero. The great general's biographers say that Grant was a man of sympathy and infinite pity. It was the more difficult for him, spurred on to the duty by grim necessity, to order forward the lines in blue that withered, again and again, before the Confederate fire, but each time weakened the attenuated line which confronted them.

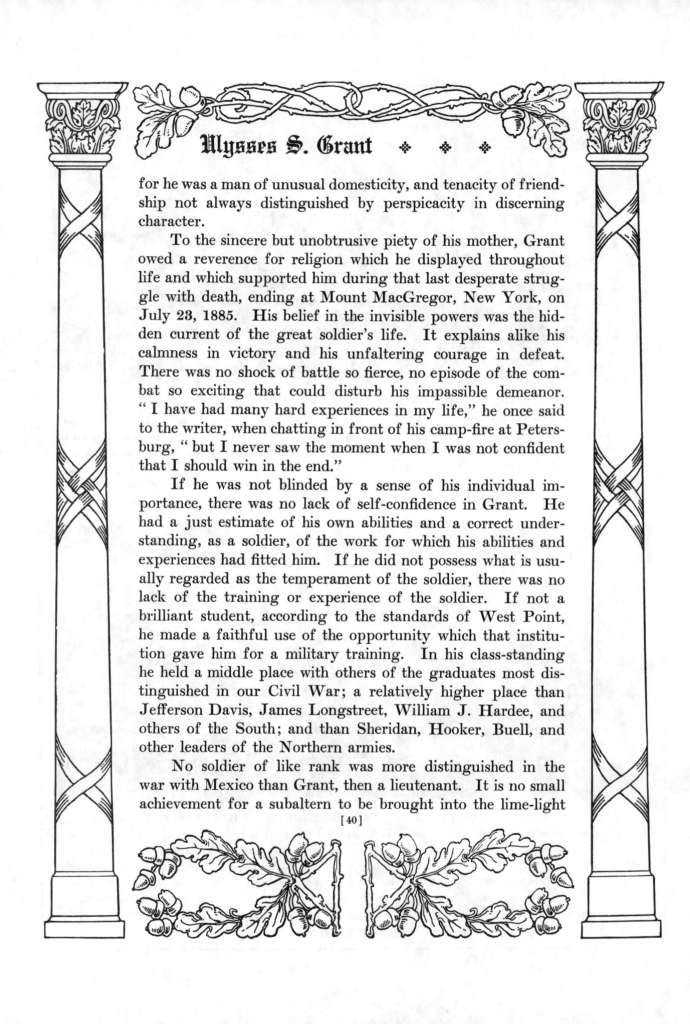

for he was a man of unusual domesticity, and tenacity of friendship not always distinguished by perspicacity in discerning character.

To the sincere but unobtrusive piety of his mother, Grant owed a reverence for religion which he displayed throughout life and which supported him during that last desperate struggle with death, ending at Mount MacGregor, New York, on July 23, 1885. His belief in the invisible powers was the hidden current of the great soldier's life. It explains alike his calmness in victory and his unfaltering courage in defeat. There was no shock of battle so fierce, no episode of the combat so exciting that could disturb his impassible demeanor. " I have had many hard experiences in my life," he once said to the writer, when chatting in front of his camp-fire at Petersburg, " but I never saw the moment when I was not confident that I should win in the end."

If he was not blinded by a sense of his individual importance, there was no lack of self-confidence in Grant. He had a just estimate of his own abilities and a correct understanding, as a soldier, of the work for which his abilities and experiences had fitted him. If he did not possess what is usually regarded as the temperament of the soldier, there was no lack of the training or experience of the soldier. If not a brilliant student, according to the standards of West Point, he made a faithful use of the opportunity which that institution gave him for a military training. In his class-standing he held a middle place with others of the graduates most distinguished in our Civil War; a relatively higher place than Jefferson Davis, James Longstreet, William J. Hardee, and others of the South; and than Sheridan, Hooker, Buell, and other leaders of the Northern armies.

No soldier of like rank was more distinguished in the war with Mexico than Grant, then a lieutenant. It is no small achievement for a subaltern to be brought into the lime-light

GRANT

IN JUNE, 1864—

A SUMMER DAY AT CITY POINT

WHILE

GREAT EVENTS

WERE HANGING IN THE BALANCE

Third from the left sits General Grant at his headquarters at City Point, on a high bluff at the junction of the James and the Appomattox rivers. At this moment his reputation hangs in the balance. In the three successive battles of the Wilderness, Spotsylvania, and Cold Harbor, he has lost 49,000 men, but the still-trusting North hurries fresh men and vast supplies to the front. Always unassuming in appearance, General Grant had changed in this photograph to his summer garb. The general's blouse, like the others, was of plain material, single-breasted, and had four regulation brass buttons in front. It was substantially the coat of a private soldier, with nothing to indicate the rank of an officer except the three gold stars of a lieutenant-general on the shoulder-straps. Judging from the experience of the past few weeks, the outlook for the future was far from bright. Yet here Grant sits serene, undaunted, confident that no army with ever lessening resources can stand the weight of metal and men which he has been hurling for many weeks against Lee.

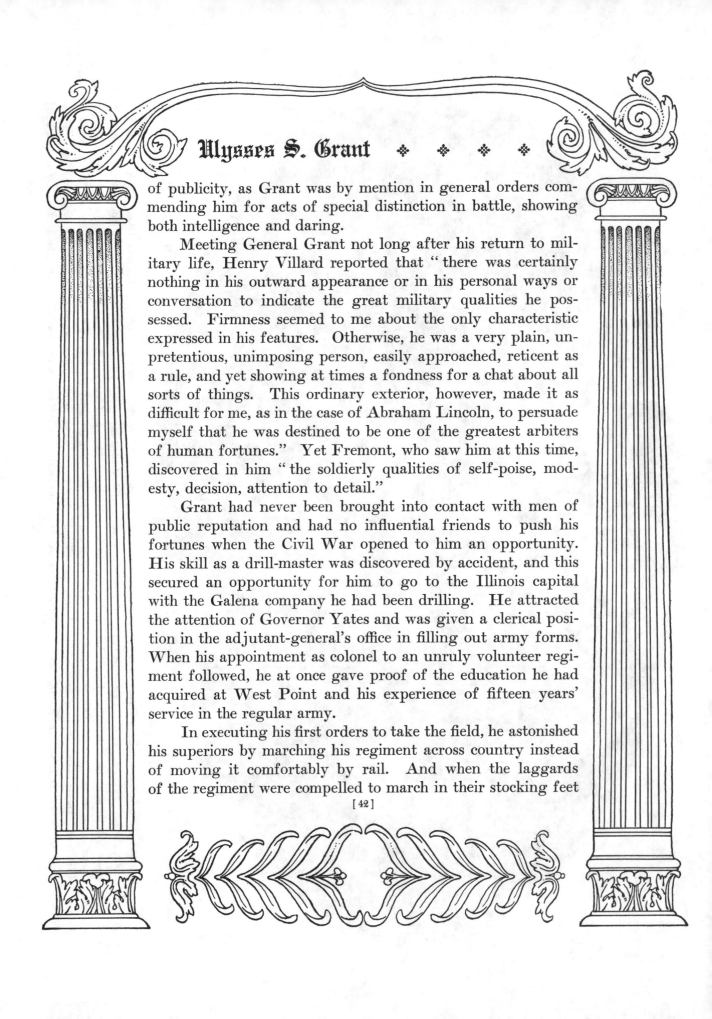

of publicity, as Grant was by mention in general orders commending him for acts of special distinction in battle, showing both intelligence and daring.

Meeting General Grant not long after his return to military life, Henry Villard reported that "there was certainly nothing in his outward appearance or in his personal ways or conversation to indicate the great military qualities he possessed. Firmness seemed to me about the only characteristic expressed in his features. Otherwise, he was a very plain, unpretentious, unimposing person, easily approached, reticent as a rule, and yet showing at times a fondness for a chat about all sorts of things. This ordinary exterior, however, made it as difficult for me, as in the case of Abraham Lincoln, to persuade myself that he was destined to be one of the greatest arbiters of human fortunes." Yet Fremont, who saw him at this time, discovered in him "the soldierly qualities of self-poise, modesty, decision, attention to detail."

Grant had never been brought into contact with men of public reputation and had no influential friends to push his fortunes when the Civil War opened to him an opportunity. His skill as a drill-master was discovered by accident, and this secured an opportunity for him to go to the Illinois capital with the Galena company he had been drilling. He attracted the attention of Governor Yates and was given a clerical position in the adjutant-general's office in filling out army forms. When his appointment as colonel to an unruly volunteer regiment followed, he at once gave proof of the education he had acquired at West Point and his experience of fifteen years' service in the regular army.

In executing his first orders to take the field, he astonished his superiors by marching his regiment across country instead of moving it comfortably by rail. And when the laggards of the regiment were compelled to march in their stocking feet

GRANT—ON HIS FIRST TRIP NORTH

The war is over. Grant has received in a magnanimous spirit, rarely paralleled in history, the surrender of Lee. Here he appears in Philadelphia on his first trip North after the war. His bearing is that of a man relieved of a vast responsibility, but with the marks of it still upon him. He is thinner than the full-chested soldier in the photograph taken in 1863, after the fall of Vicksburg. His dress is careless, as always, but shows more attention than when he was in the field. He looks out of the picture with the unflinching eyes that had been able to penetrate the future and see the wisdom of the plan that proved the final undoing of the Confederacy.

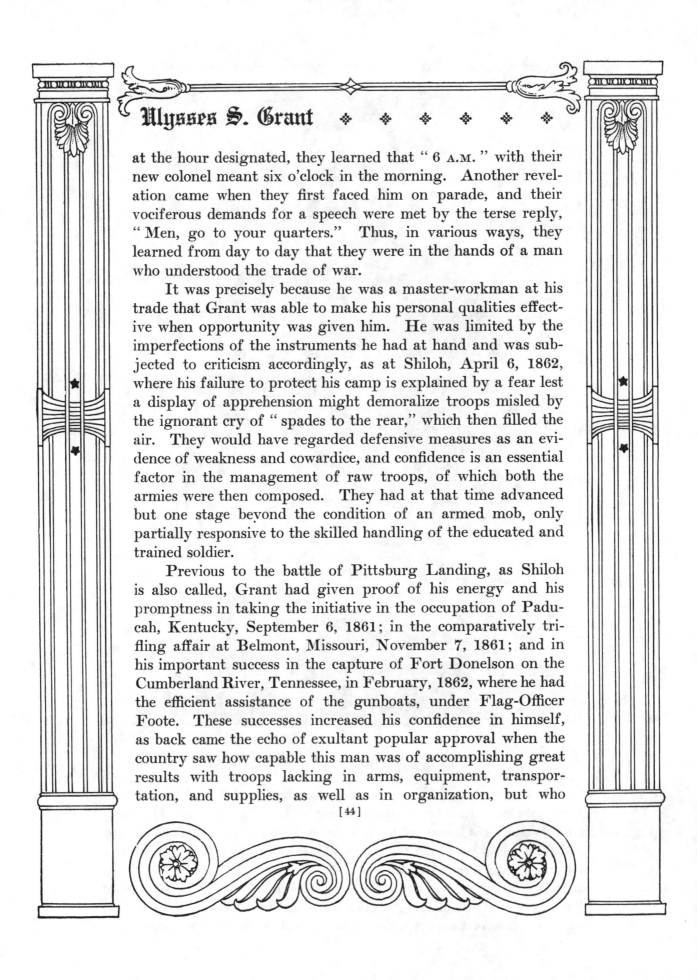

at the hour designated, they learned that "6 A.M." with their new colonel meant six o'clock in the morning. Another revelation came when they first faced him on parade, and their vociferous demands for a speech were met by the terse reply, "Men, go to your quarters." Thus, in various ways, they learned from day to day that they were in the hands of a man who understood the trade of war.

It was precisely because he was a master-workman at his trade that Grant was able to make his personal qualities effective when opportunity was given him. He was limited by the imperfections of the instruments he had at hand and was subjected to criticism accordingly, as at Shiloh, April 6, 1862, where his failure to protect his camp is explained by a fear lest a display of apprehension might demoralize troops misled by the ignorant cry of "spades to the rear," which then filled the air. They would have regarded defensive measures as an evidence of weakness and cowardice, and confidence is an essential factor in the management of raw troops, of which both the armies were then composed. They had at that time advanced but one stage beyond the condition of an armed mob, only partially responsive to the skilled handling of the educated and trained soldier.

Previous to the battle of Pittsburg Landing, as Shiloh is also called, Grant had given proof of his energy and his promptness in taking the initiative in the occupation of Paducah, Kentucky, September 6, 1861; in the comparatively trifling affair at Belmont, Missouri, November 7, 1861; and in his important success in the capture of Fort Donelson on the Cumberland River, Tennessee, in February, 1862, where he had the efficient assistance of the gunboats, under Flag-Officer Foote. These successes increased his confidence in himself, as back came the echo of exultant popular approval when the country saw how capable this man was of accomplishing great results with troops lacking in arms, equipment, transportation, and supplies, as well as in organization, but who

GRANT IN 1865—THE ZENITH OF HIS CAREER

Behind Grant in 1865 lay all his victories on the field of battle; before him the highest gift within the power of the American people—the presidency. He says in his memoirs that after Vicksburg he had a presentment that he was to bring the war to a successful end and become the head of the nation. Grant's sturdy, persistent Scottish ancestry stood him in good stead. He was a descendant of Matthew Grant, one of the settlers of Windsor, Connecticut, in 1635, and a man of much importance in the infant colony. His American ancestors were fighting stock. His great-grandfather, Noah Grant, held a military commission in the French and Indian War, and his grandfather, also named Noah, fought in the Revolution. Henry Ward Beecher summed up the causes of Grant's meteoric rise from store clerk in 1861, to president in 1869, as follows: "Grant was available and lucky." His dominant trait was determination.

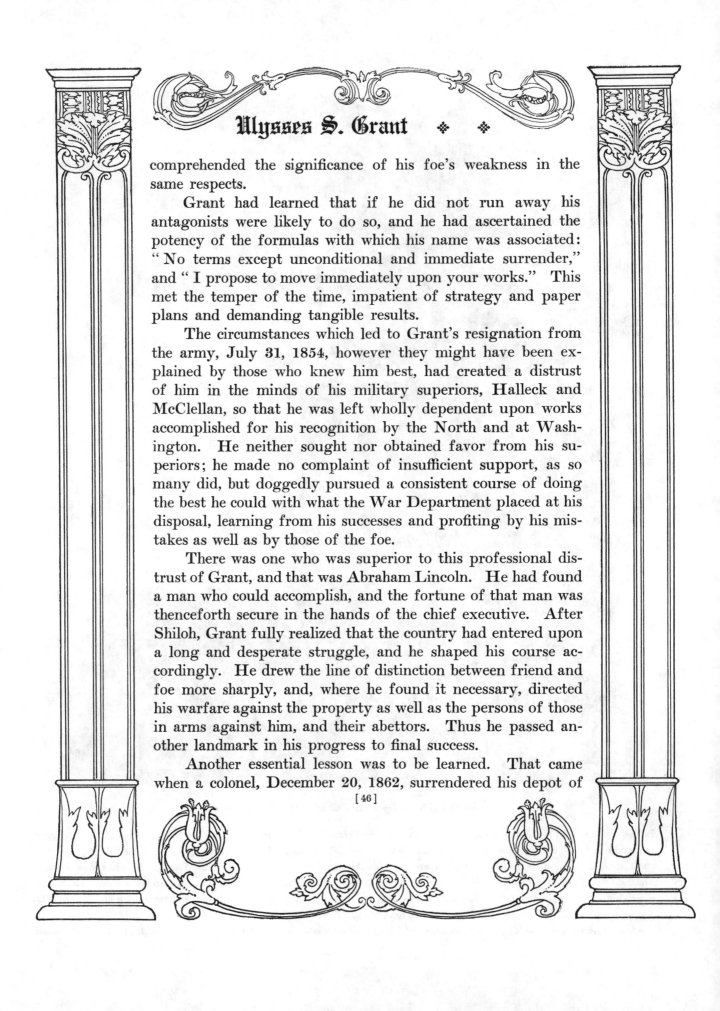

comprehended the significance of his foe's weakness in the same respects.

Grant had learned that if he did not run away his antagonists were likely to do so, and he had ascertained the potency of the formulas with which his name was associated: "No terms except unconditional and immediate surrender," and "I propose to move immediately upon your works." This met the temper of the time, impatient of strategy and paper plans and demanding tangible results.

The circumstances which led to Grant's resignation from the army, July 31, 1854, however they might have been explained by those who knew him best, had created a distrust of him in the minds of his military superiors, Halleck and McClellan, so that he was left wholly dependent upon works accomplished for his recognition by the North and at Washington. He neither sought nor obtained favor from his superiors; he made no complaint of insufficient support, as so many did, but doggedly pursued a consistent course of doing the best he could with what the War Department placed at his disposal, learning from his successes and profiting by his mistakes as well as by those of the foe.

There was one who was superior to this professional distrust of Grant, and that was Abraham Lincoln. He had found a man who could accomplish, and the fortune of that man was thenceforth secure in the hands of the chief executive. After Shiloh, Grant fully realized that the country had entered upon a long and desperate struggle, and he shaped his course accordingly. He drew the line of distinction between friend and foe more sharply, and, where he found it necessary, directed his warfare against the property as well as the persons of those in arms against him, and their abettors. Thus he passed another landmark in his progress to final success.

Another essential lesson was to be learned. That came when a colonel, December 20, 1862, surrendered his depot of

GRANT IN CHARACTERISTIC POSE, WITH HIS STAFF IN 1864

The indifferent attitude of the general-in-chief is most characteristic. Grant had begun the investment of Petersburg when this photograph was taken. Around him are the men who had followed him faithfully through the faith-shaking campaigns of the Wilderness. He never made known his plans for an advance to anyone, but his calm confidence communicated itself to all who listened to him. In the most critical moments he manifested no perceptible anxiety, but gave his orders with coolness and deliberation. At the left of the photograph sits General John A. Rawlins, who has foresworn his customary mustache and beard which the next picture shows him as wearing. He was first aide-de-camp to Grant, then assistant adjutant-general and chief of staff. Behind Grant, who stands in the center with one hand thrust carelessly into his pocket, sits Lieutenant Frederick Grant, later major-general in the United States Army. In front of Grant stands Colonel M. B. Ryan, and on the extreme right sits Colonel Ely S. Parker, military secretary, who was a full-blooded Indian, a grandnephew of the famous Red Jacket, and chief of the tribes known as the Six Nations.

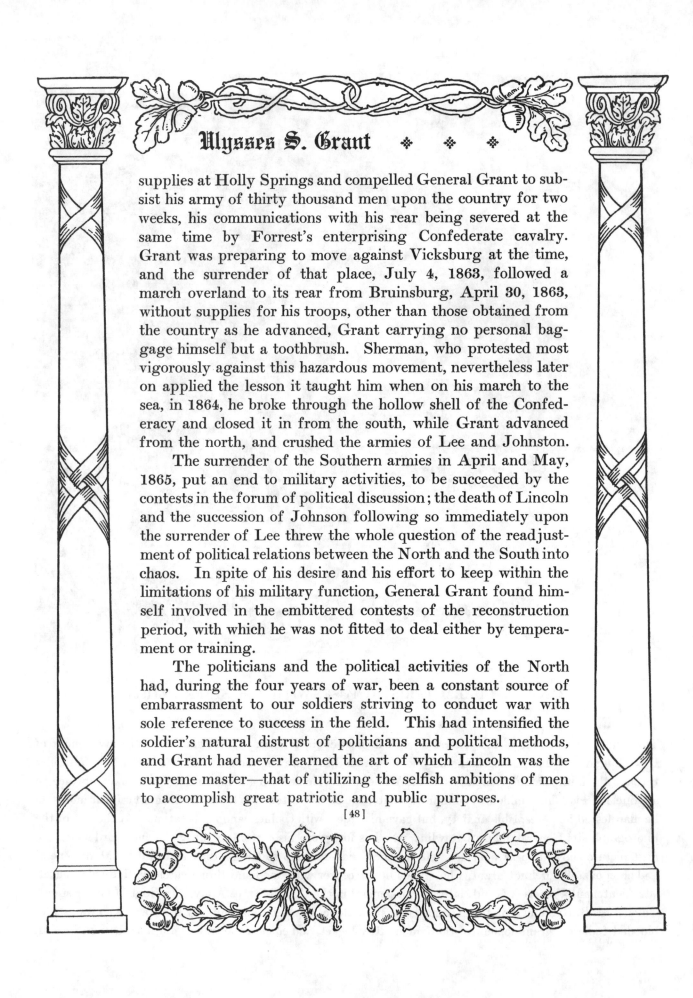

supplies at Holly Springs and compelled General Grant to subsist his army of thirty thousand men upon the country for two weeks, his communications with his rear being severed at the same time by Forrest's enterprising Confederate cavalry. Grant was preparing to move against Vicksburg at the time, and the surrender of that place, July 4, 1863, followed a march overland to its rear from Bruinsburg, April 30, 1863, without supplies for his troops, other than those obtained from the country as he advanced, Grant carrying no personal baggage himself but a toothbrush. Sherman, who protested most vigorously against this hazardous movement, nevertheless later on applied the lesson it taught him when on his march to the sea, in 1864, he broke through the hollow shell of the Confederacy and closed it in from the south, while Grant advanced from the north, and crushed the armies of Lee and Johnston.

The surrender of the Southern armies in April and May, 1865, put an end to military activities, to be succeeded by the contests in the forum of political discussion; the death of Lincoln and the succession of Johnson following so immediately upon the surrender of Lee threw the whole question of the readjustment of political relations between the North and the South into chaos. In spite of his desire and his effort to keep within the limitations of his military function, General Grant found himself involved in the embittered contests of the reconstruction period, with which he was not fitted to deal either by temperament or training.

The politicians and the political activities of the North had, during the four years of war, been a constant source of embarrassment to our soldiers striving to conduct war with sole reference to success in the field. This had intensified the soldier's natural distrust of politicians and political methods, and Grant had never learned the art of which Lincoln was the supreme master—that of utilizing the selfish ambitions of men to accomplish great patriotic and public purposes.

MEN ABOUT TO WITNESS APPOMATTOX

No photographer was present at Appomattox, that supreme moment in our national history, when Americans met for the last time as foes on the field. Nothing but fanciful sketches exist of the scene inside the McLean home. But here is a photograph that shows most of the Union officers present at the conference. Nine of the twelve men standing above stood also at the signing of Lee's surrender, a few days later. The scene is City Point, in March, 1865. Grant is surrounded by a group of the officers who had served him so faithfully. At the surrender, it was Colonel T. S. Bowers (third from left) upon whom Grant called to make a copy of the terms of surrender in ink. Colonel E. S. Parker, the full-blooded Indian on Grant's staff, an excellent penman, wrote

GRANT BETWEEN RAWLINS AND BOWERS

out the final copy. Nineteen years later, General Horace Porter recorded with pride that he loaned General Lee a pencil to make a correction in the terms. Colonels William Duff and J. D. Webster, and General M. R. Patrick, are the three men who were not present at the interview. All of the remaining officers were formally presented to Lee. General Seth Williams had been Lee's adjutant when the latter was superintendent at West Point some years before the war. In the lower photograph General Grant stands between General Rawlins and Colonel Bowers. The veins standing out on the back of his hand are plainly visible. No one but he could have told how calmly the blood coursed through them during the four tremendous years.

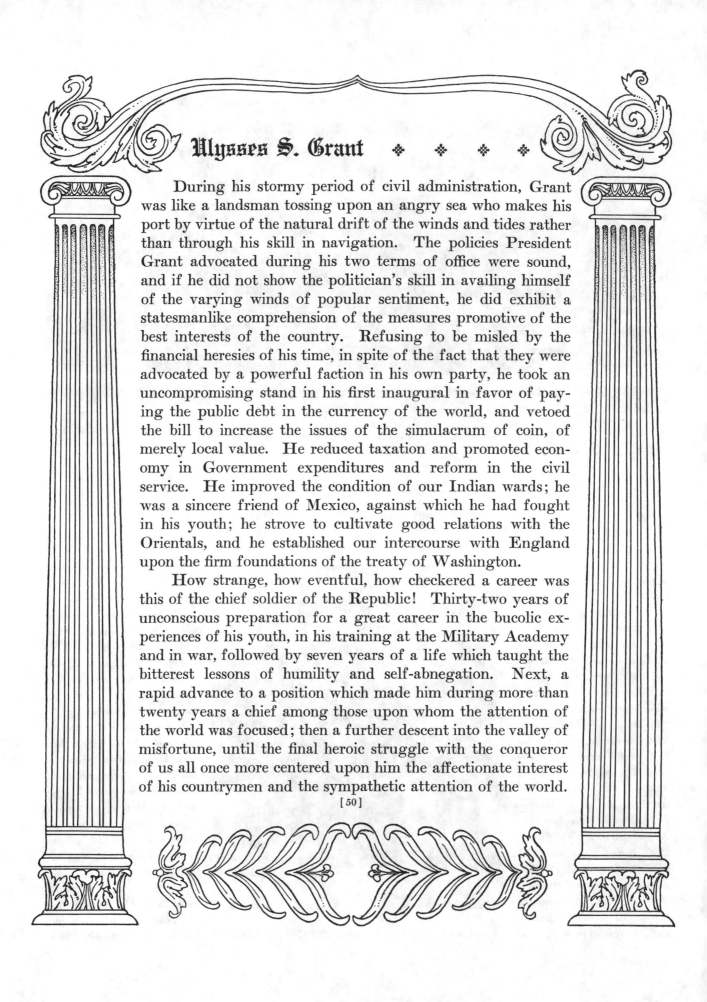

Ulysses S. Grant ✦ ✦ ✦ ✦

During his stormy period of civil administration, Grant was like a landsman tossing upon an angry sea who makes his port by virtue of the natural drift of the winds and tides rather than through his skill in navigation. The policies President Grant advocated during his two terms of office were sound, and if he did not show the politician's skill in availing himself of the varying winds of popular sentiment, he did exhibit a statesmanlike comprehension of the measures promotive of the best interests of the country. Refusing to be misled by the financial heresies of his time, in spite of the fact that they were advocated by a powerful faction in his own party, he took an uncompromising stand in his first inaugural in favor of paying the public debt in the currency of the world, and vetoed the bill to increase the issues of the simulacrum of coin, of merely local value. He reduced taxation and promoted economy in Government expenditures and reform in the civil service. He improved the condition of our Indian wards; he was a sincere friend of Mexico, against which he had fought in his youth; he strove to cultivate good relations with the Orientals, and he established our intercourse with England upon the firm foundations of the treaty of Washington.

How strange, how eventful, how checkered a career was this of the chief soldier of the Republic! Thirty-two years of unconscious preparation for a great career in the bucolic experiences of his youth, in his training at the Military Academy and in war, followed by seven years of a life which taught the bitterest lessons of humility and self-abnegation. Next, a rapid advance to a position which made him during more than twenty years a chief among those upon whom the attention of the world was focused; then a further descent into the valley of misfortune, until the final heroic struggle with the conqueror of us all once more centered upon him the affectionate interest of his countrymen and the sympathetic attention of the world.

II

LEE

RESIDENCE OF ROBERT E. LEE, ON FRANKLIN STREET, RICHMOND, OCCUPIED BY HIS FAMILY DURING THE WAR— THREE OF THE PORTRAITS OF GENERAL LEE THAT FOLLOW WERE TAKEN IN THE BASEMENT OF THIS HOUSE—IT LATER BECAME THE HOME OF THE VIRGINIA HISTORICAL SOCIETY

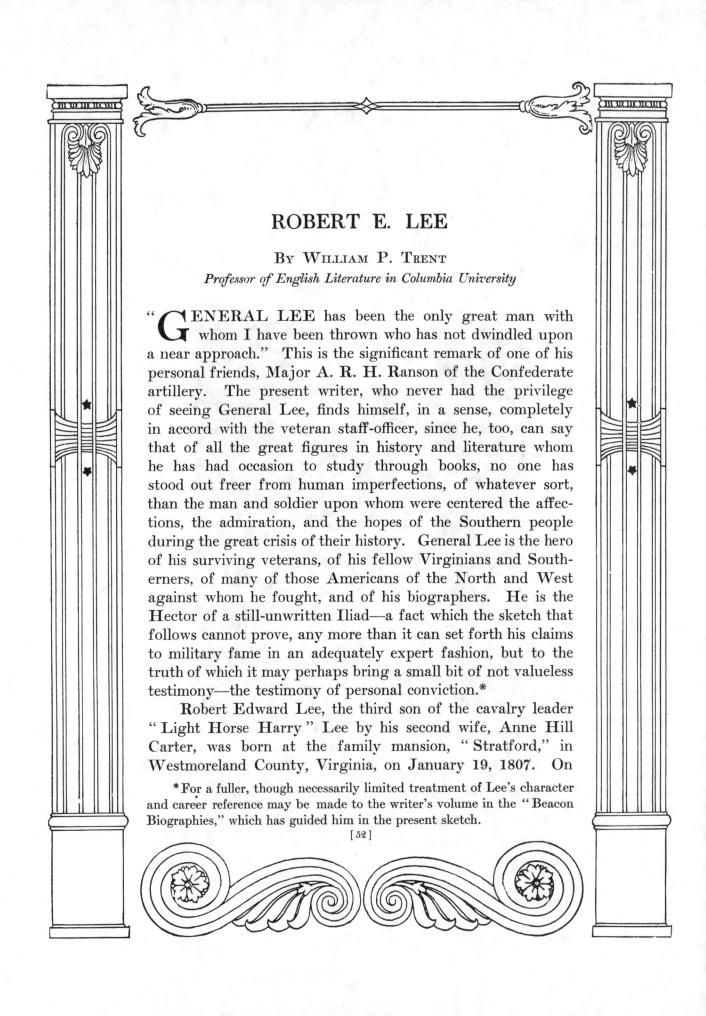

ROBERT E. LEE

By William P. Trent
Professor of English Literature in Columbia University

"GENERAL LEE has been the only great man with whom I have been thrown who has not dwindled upon a near approach." This is the significant remark of one of his personal friends, Major A. R. H. Ranson of the Confederate artillery. The present writer, who never had the privilege of seeing General Lee, finds himself, in a sense, completely in accord with the veteran staff-officer, since he, too, can say that of all the great figures in history and literature whom he has had occasion to study through books, no one has stood out freer from human imperfections, of whatever sort, than the man and soldier upon whom were centered the affections, the admiration, and the hopes of the Southern people during the great crisis of their history. General Lee is the hero of his surviving veterans, of his fellow Virginians and Southerners, of many of those Americans of the North and West against whom he fought, and of his biographers. He is the Hector of a still-unwritten Iliad—a fact which the sketch that follows cannot prove, any more than it can set forth his claims to military fame in an adequately expert fashion, but to the truth of which it may perhaps bring a small bit of not valueless testimony—the testimony of personal conviction.*

Robert Edward Lee, the third son of the cavalry leader "Light Horse Harry" Lee by his second wife, Anne Hill Carter, was born at the family mansion, "Stratford," in Westmoreland County, Virginia, on January 19, 1807. On

*For a fuller, though necessarily limited treatment of Lee's character and career reference may be made to the writer's volume in the "Beacon Biographies," which has guided him in the present sketch.

"LEE WAS ESSENTIALLY A VIRGINIAN"

Old Christ Church at Alexandria, Virginia. The church attended by both Washington and Lee calls up associations that explain the reference of General Adams. In 1811, at the age of four, Robert E. Lee removed from Westmoreland County to Alexandria, which remained his home until he entered West Point, in 1825. During these years he was gaining his education from private tutors and devoting himself to the care of his invalid mother. Many a Sunday he passed through the trees around this church, of which Washington had been one of the first vestrymen, to occupy the pew that is still pointed out to visitors. The town serves to intensify love of Virginia; here Braddock made his headquarters before marching against the French, in 1755, with young George Washington as an aide on his staff; and here on April 13th of that year the Governors of New York, Massachusetts, Pennsylvania, Maryland, and Virginia had met, in order to determine upon plans for the expedition. In the vicinity were Mount Vernon, the estate of Washington, and Arlington, which remained in the family of Washington's wife. The whole region was therefore full of inspiration for the youthful Lee.

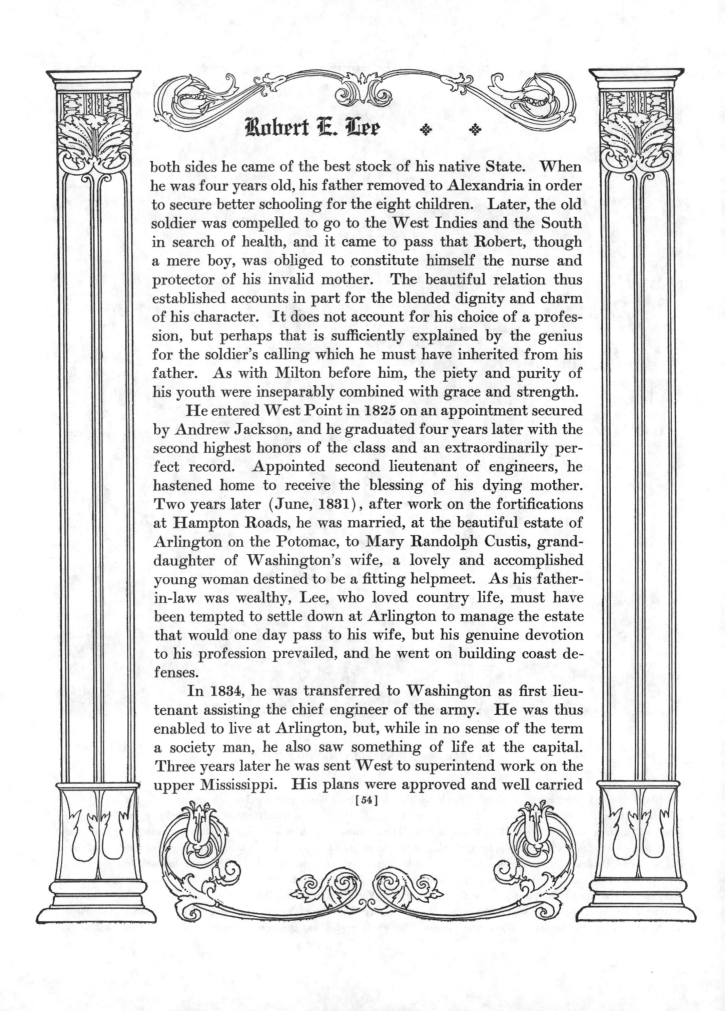

both sides he came of the best stock of his native State. When he was four years old, his father removed to Alexandria in order to secure better schooling for the eight children. Later, the old soldier was compelled to go to the West Indies and the South in search of health, and it came to pass that Robert, though a mere boy, was obliged to constitute himself the nurse and protector of his invalid mother. The beautiful relation thus established accounts in part for the blended dignity and charm of his character. It does not account for his choice of a profession, but perhaps that is sufficiently explained by the genius for the soldier's calling which he must have inherited from his father. As with Milton before him, the piety and purity of his youth were inseparably combined with grace and strength.

He entered West Point in 1825 on an appointment secured by Andrew Jackson, and he graduated four years later with the second highest honors of the class and an extraordinarily perfect record. Appointed second lieutenant of engineers, he hastened home to receive the blessing of his dying mother. Two years later (June, 1831), after work on the fortifications at Hampton Roads, he was married, at the beautiful estate of Arlington on the Potomac, to Mary Randolph Custis, granddaughter of Washington's wife, a lovely and accomplished young woman destined to be a fitting helpmeet. As his father-in-law was wealthy, Lee, who loved country life, must have been tempted to settle down at Arlington to manage the estate that would one day pass to his wife, but his genuine devotion to his profession prevailed, and he went on building coast defenses.

In 1834, he was transferred to Washington as first lieutenant assisting the chief engineer of the army. He was thus enabled to live at Arlington, but, while in no sense of the term a society man, he also saw something of life at the capital. Three years later he was sent West to superintend work on the upper Mississippi. His plans were approved and well carried

LEE IN 1850
FROM THE ORIGINAL DAGUERREOTYPE—WITHOUT THE UNIFORM
PAINTED ON LATER

Through the courtesy of General G. W. C. Lee—who furnished information of much value concerning several portraits in this chapter—there is reproduced above the actual appearance of his distinguished father in 1850. This portrait was copied, embellished with a uniform painted on by hand, and widely circulated. To study the unretouched original is particularly interesting. Lee at this period was in Baltimore, in charge of defenses then being constructed. Three years before, in the Mexican War, he had posted batteries before Vera Cruz so that the town was reduced in a week. After each of the battles of Cerro Gordo, Churubusco, and Chapultepec, he received promotion, and for his services in the last he was breveted colonel. A born soldier, the son of a soldier, this handsome young man is not as handsome by far as the superb general who later lent grace and dignity to the Confederate gray. He little realized the startling future when this photograph was taken.

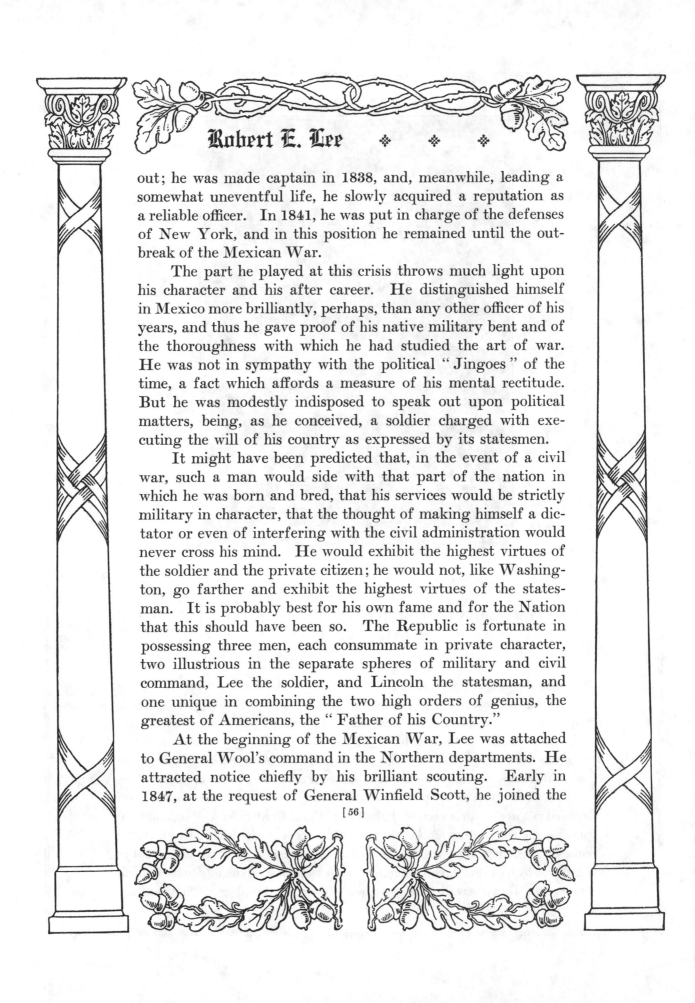

out; he was made captain in 1838, and, meanwhile, leading a somewhat uneventful life, he slowly acquired a reputation as a reliable officer. In 1841, he was put in charge of the defenses of New York, and in this position he remained until the outbreak of the Mexican War.

The part he played at this crisis throws much light upon his character and his after career. He distinguished himself in Mexico more brilliantly, perhaps, than any other officer of his years, and thus he gave proof of his native military bent and of the thoroughness with which he had studied the art of war. He was not in sympathy with the political "Jingoes" of the time, a fact which affords a measure of his mental rectitude. But he was modestly indisposed to speak out upon political matters, being, as he conceived, a soldier charged with executing the will of his country as expressed by its statesmen.

It might have been predicted that, in the event of a civil war, such a man would side with that part of the nation in which he was born and bred, that his services would be strictly military in character, that the thought of making himself a dictator or even of interfering with the civil administration would never cross his mind. He would exhibit the highest virtues of the soldier and the private citizen; he would not, like Washington, go farther and exhibit the highest virtues of the statesman. It is probably best for his own fame and for the Nation that this should have been so. The Republic is fortunate in possessing three men, each consummate in private character, two illustrious in the separate spheres of military and civil command, Lee the soldier, and Lincoln the statesman, and one unique in combining the two high orders of genius, the greatest of Americans, the "Father of his Country."

At the beginning of the Mexican War, Lee was attached to General Wool's command in the Northern departments. He attracted notice chiefly by his brilliant scouting. Early in 1847, at the request of General Winfield Scott, he joined the

ARLINGTON, THE HOME OF LEE, FROM THE GREAT OAK

The beautiful estate by the Potomac came to General Lee from the family of George Washington. While Lee, as a boy and youth, lived in Alexandria he was a frequent caller at the Arlington estate, where Mary Lee Custis, the only daughter of George Washington Parke Custis, was his companion and playfellow. Before he had completed his course at West Point the friendship had ripened into love and the two became engaged. Her father is said to have considered her entitled to a more wealthy match than young Lee, who looked forward to a career in the army. But in 1831, two years after his graduation, the ceremony was performed and on the death of Custis in 1857, the estate passed into the possession of Robert E. Lee as trustee for his children. The management had already been in his hands for many years, and though constantly absent on duty, he had ordered it so skilfully that its value steadily increased. On the outbreak of the Civil War and his decision to cast in his lot with Virginia, he was obliged to leave the mansion that overlooked the national capital. It at once fell into the hands of Federal troops. Nevermore was he to dwell in the majestic home that had sheltered his family for thirty years. When the war was over, he gave the Pamunkey estate to his son Robert and himself retired to the quiet, simple life of Lexington, Virginia, as president of the institution that is now known, in his honor, as Washington and Lee University.

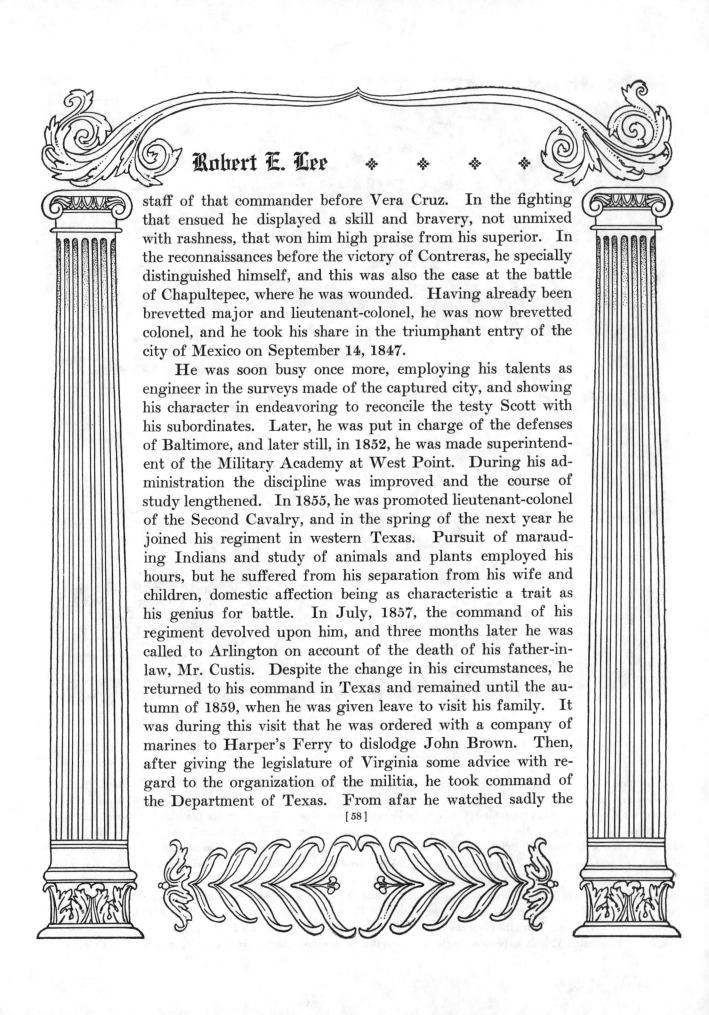

staff of that commander before Vera Cruz. In the fighting that ensued he displayed a skill and bravery, not unmixed with rashness, that won him high praise from his superior. In the reconnaissances before the victory of Contreras, he specially distinguished himself, and this was also the case at the battle of Chapultepec, where he was wounded. Having already been brevetted major and lieutenant-colonel, he was now brevetted colonel, and he took his share in the triumphant entry of the city of Mexico on September 14, 1847.

He was soon busy once more, employing his talents as engineer in the surveys made of the captured city, and showing his character in endeavoring to reconcile the testy Scott with his subordinates. Later, he was put in charge of the defenses of Baltimore, and later still, in 1852, he was made superintendent of the Military Academy at West Point. During his administration the discipline was improved and the course of study lengthened. In 1855, he was promoted lieutenant-colonel of the Second Cavalry, and in the spring of the next year he joined his regiment in western Texas. Pursuit of marauding Indians and study of animals and plants employed his hours, but he suffered from his separation from his wife and children, domestic affection being as characteristic a trait as his genius for battle. In July, 1857, the command of his regiment devolved upon him, and three months later he was called to Arlington on account of the death of his father-in-law, Mr. Custis. Despite the change in his circumstances, he returned to his command in Texas and remained until the autumn of 1859, when he was given leave to visit his family. It was during this visit that he was ordered with a company of marines to Harper's Ferry to dislodge John Brown. Then, after giving the legislature of Virginia some advice with regard to the organization of the militia, he took command of the Department of Texas. From afar he watched sadly the

LEE'S BOYHOOD PLAYGROUND

When Robert E. Lee came over from Alexandria as a boy, to play soldier in the gardens and grounds around this beautiful mansion overlooking the Potomac, he could hardly have thought of its occupation during his life-time by a hostile force determined to bend his native State to its will.   When he was graduated from West Point in 1829 and proudly donned the army blue, he little imagined that thirty-two years later, after he had paced his room all night in terrible perplexity, he would doff the blue for another color sworn to oppose it.   The estate about Arlington house was a fair and spacious domain.   Every part of it had rung in his early youth and young manhood with the voice of her who later became his wife.   He had whispered his love in its shaded alleys, and here his children had come into the world.   Yet here stand men with swords and muskets ready to take his life if they should meet him on the field of battle.   Arlington, once famous for its hospitality, has since extended a silent welcome to 20,000 dead.   Lee's body is not here, but reposes in a splendid marble tomb at Washington and Lee University, where he ruled with simple dignity after the finish of the war.

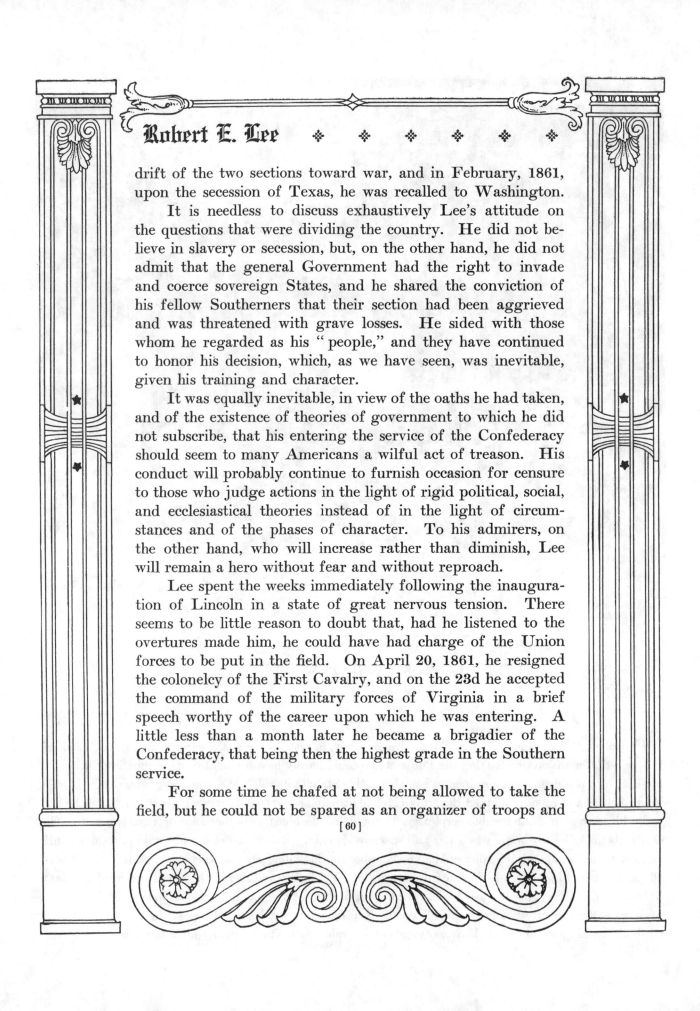

drift of the two sections toward war, and in February, 1861, upon the secession of Texas, he was recalled to Washington.

It is needless to discuss exhaustively Lee's attitude on the questions that were dividing the country. He did not believe in slavery or secession, but, on the other hand, he did not admit that the general Government had the right to invade and coerce sovereign States, and he shared the conviction of his fellow Southerners that their section had been aggrieved and was threatened with grave losses. He sided with those whom he regarded as his "people," and they have continued to honor his decision, which, as we have seen, was inevitable, given his training and character.

It was equally inevitable, in view of the oaths he had taken, and of the existence of theories of government to which he did not subscribe, that his entering the service of the Confederacy should seem to many Americans a wilful act of treason. His conduct will probably continue to furnish occasion for censure to those who judge actions in the light of rigid political, social, and ecclesiastical theories instead of in the light of circumstances and of the phases of character. To his admirers, on the other hand, who will increase rather than diminish, Lee will remain a hero without fear and without reproach.

Lee spent the weeks immediately following the inauguration of Lincoln in a state of great nervous tension. There seems to be little reason to doubt that, had he listened to the overtures made him, he could have had charge of the Union forces to be put in the field. On April 20, 1861, he resigned the colonelcy of the First Cavalry, and on the 23d he accepted the command of the military forces of Virginia in a brief speech worthy of the career upon which he was entering. A little less than a month later he became a brigadier of the Confederacy, that being then the highest grade in the Southern service.

For some time he chafed at not being allowed to take the field, but he could not be spared as an organizer of troops and

WHERE LEE STOOD SUPREME—THE WILDERNESS IN 1864

From the point of view of the military student Lee's consummate feats of generalship were performed in the gloom of the Wilderness. On this ground he presented an always unbroken front against which Grant dashed his battalions in vain. Never were Lee's lines here broken; the assailants must always shift their ground to seek a fresh opportunity for assault. At this spot on the battlefield of the Wilderness the opposing forces lay within twenty-four feet of each other all night. The soldiers, too, had learned by this 1864 campaign to carry out orders with judgment of their own. The rank and file grew to be excellent connoisseurs of the merits of a position. "If they only save a finger it will do some good," was General Longstreet's reply, when his engineer officers complained that their work on Marye's Hill was being spoiled by being built higher by the gunners of the Washington artillery—who had to fight

LEE IN THE FIELD
THE BEST KNOWN PORTRAIT

behind them. For this reason the significance of the lines as shown in many war maps is often very puzzling to the students of to-day, who have never seen the actual field of operations and have no other guide. Much of the ground disputed by the contending forces in our Civil War was quite unlike the popular conception of a battlefield, derived from descriptions of European campaigns, or from portrayals of the same, usually fanciful. For at this variety of warfare, Lee was a master, as well as on the rolling open plains of the Virginia farm. The portrait of Lee opposite was taken during the campaign preceding this test of the Wilderness. The reproduction here is directly from the photograph—taken at Lee's first sitting in war-time, and his only one "in the field." Reproductions of this picture painted, engraved, and lithographed were widely circulated after the war. The likeness was much impaired.

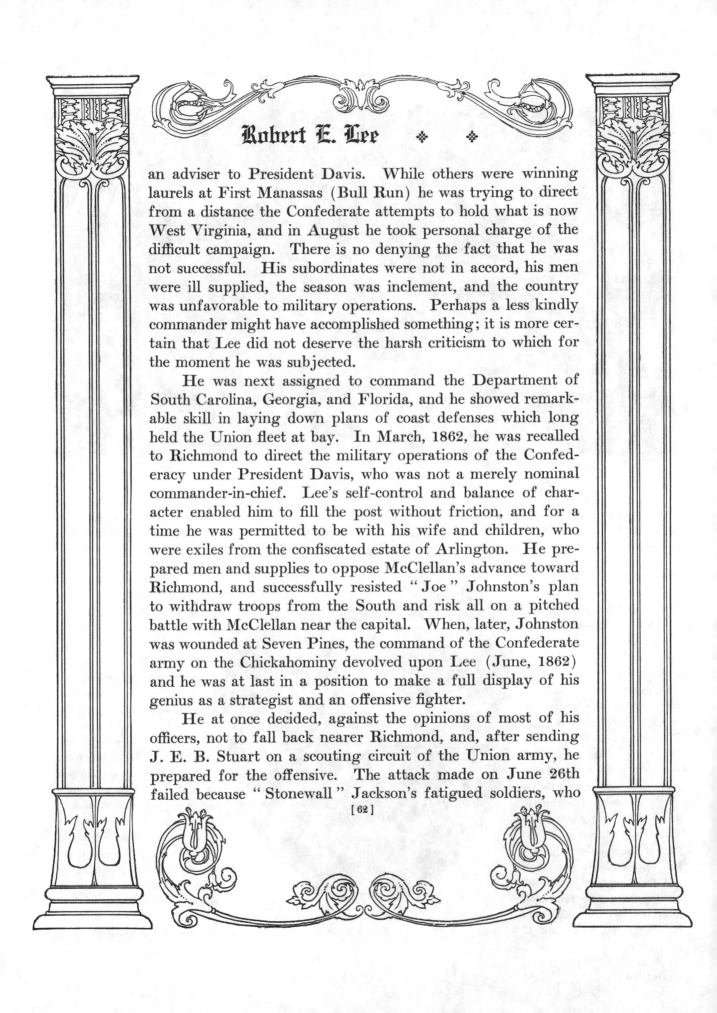

an adviser to President Davis. While others were winning laurels at First Manassas (Bull Run) he was trying to direct from a distance the Confederate attempts to hold what is now West Virginia, and in August he took personal charge of the difficult campaign. There is no denying the fact that he was not successful. His subordinates were not in accord, his men were ill supplied, the season was inclement, and the country was unfavorable to military operations. Perhaps a less kindly commander might have accomplished something; it is more certain that Lee did not deserve the harsh criticism to which for the moment he was subjected.

He was next assigned to command the Department of South Carolina, Georgia, and Florida, and he showed remarkable skill in laying down plans of coast defenses which long held the Union fleet at bay. In March, 1862, he was recalled to Richmond to direct the military operations of the Confederacy under President Davis, who was not a merely nominal commander-in-chief. Lee's self-control and balance of character enabled him to fill the post without friction, and for a time he was permitted to be with his wife and children, who were exiles from the confiscated estate of Arlington. He prepared men and supplies to oppose McClellan's advance toward Richmond, and successfully resisted " Joe " Johnston's plan to withdraw troops from the South and risk all on a pitched battle with McClellan near the capital. When, later, Johnston was wounded at Seven Pines, the command of the Confederate army on the Chickahominy devolved upon Lee (June, 1862) and he was at last in a position to make a full display of his genius as a strategist and an offensive fighter.

He at once decided, against the opinions of most of his officers, not to fall back nearer Richmond, and, after sending J. E. B. Stuart on a scouting circuit of the Union army, he prepared for the offensive. The attack made on June 26th failed because " Stonewall " Jackson's fatigued soldiers, who

ALL

THE ORIGINAL

WAR–TIME PHOTOGRAPHS

OF

ROBERT E. LEE

AS

PRESENTED

IN THIS CHAPTER

AND IN

OTHER VOLUMES

LEE
AT THE HEIGHT OF
HIS FAME
1863

"I believe there were none of the little things of life so irksome to him as having his picture taken in any way," writes Captain Robert E. Lee of his illustrious father. Lee was photographed in war-time on three occasions only: one was in the field, about '62–'63; the second in Richmond in 1863; and the third immediately after the surrender, at his Richmond home. Several of the portraits resulting have appeared in other volumes of this history; all the rest are presented with this chapter. Lee's first sitting produced the full-length on page 235, Volume II, and the full-face on the page preceding this—the popular portrait, much lithographed and engraved, but rarely shown, as here, from an original photograph, with the expression not distorted into a false amiability, but calm and dignified as in nature. Lee's second sitting was before Vannerson's camera in Richmond, 1863. Richmond ladies had made for their hero a set of shirts, and had begged him to sit for a portrait. Lee, yielding, courteously wore one of the gifts. The amateur shirtmaking is revealed in the set of the collar, very high in the neck, as seen in the photographs on this page. Another negative of this second oc-

casion, a full-length, is reproduced in Volume IX, page 123. The third photographing of Lee was done by Brady. It was the first opportunity of the camera wizard since the war began to preserve for posterity the fine features of the Southern hero. The position selected by Brady was under the back porch of Lee's home in Richmond, near the basement door, on account of the better light. The results were excellent. Three appear with this chapter: a magnificent three-quarter view, enlarged on page 63; a full-length, on page 69; and a group with Custis Lee and Colonel Taylor, on page 67. Another view of this group will be found on page 83 of Volume I; and the fifth of these Brady pictures, a seated profile of Lee alone, on page 23 of Volume III. An early daguerreotypist had portrayed Lee in 1850 as a young engineer-colonel —see page 55. The general's later life is covered by his celebrated photograph on "Traveler" in September, 1866, on page 121 of Volume IX; by the two portraits of '67 and '69 on page 73; by the photograph with Johnston, taken in 1869, on page 341 of Volume I, and by the striking group photograph that forms the frontispiece to this volume.

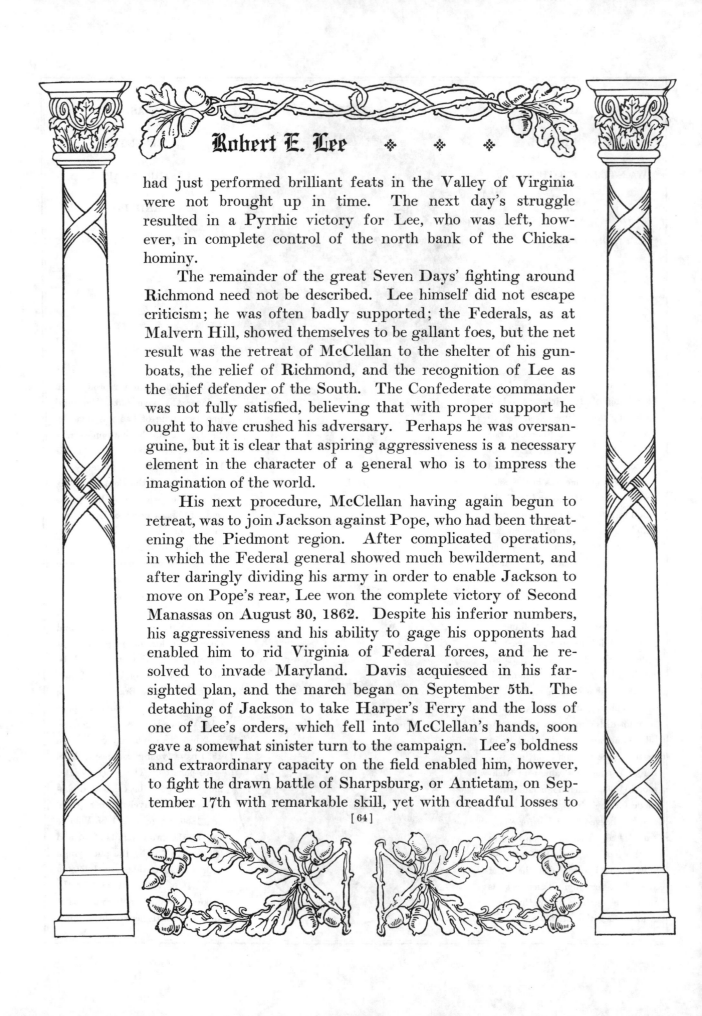

had just performed brilliant feats in the Valley of Virginia were not brought up in time. The next day's struggle resulted in a Pyrrhic victory for Lee, who was left, however, in complete control of the north bank of the Chickahominy.

The remainder of the great Seven Days' fighting around Richmond need not be described. Lee himself did not escape criticism; he was often badly supported; the Federals, as at Malvern Hill, showed themselves to be gallant foes, but the net result was the retreat of McClellan to the shelter of his gunboats, the relief of Richmond, and the recognition of Lee as the chief defender of the South. The Confederate commander was not fully satisfied, believing that with proper support he ought to have crushed his adversary. Perhaps he was oversanguine, but it is clear that aspiring aggressiveness is a necessary element in the character of a general who is to impress the imagination of the world.

His next procedure, McClellan having again begun to retreat, was to join Jackson against Pope, who had been threatening the Piedmont region. After complicated operations, in which the Federal general showed much bewilderment, and after daringly dividing his army in order to enable Jackson to move on Pope's rear, Lee won the complete victory of Second Manassas on August 30, 1862. Despite his inferior numbers, his aggressiveness and his ability to gage his opponents had enabled him to rid Virginia of Federal forces, and he resolved to invade Maryland. Davis acquiesced in his farsighted plan, and the march began on September 5th. The detaching of Jackson to take Harper's Ferry and the loss of one of Lee's orders, which fell into McClellan's hands, soon gave a somewhat sinister turn to the campaign. Lee's boldness and extraordinary capacity on the field enabled him, however, to fight the drawn battle of Sharpsburg, or Antietam, on September 17th with remarkable skill, yet with dreadful losses to

LEE—THE GENERAL WHO SHOULDERED "ALL THE RESPONSIBILITY"

The nobility revealed by the steadfast lips, the flashing eyes in this magnificent portrait is reflected by a happening a few days before its taking. It was 1865. The forlorn hope of the Confederacy had failed. Gordon and Fitzhugh Lee had attacked the Federal lines on April 9th, but found them impregnable. Lee heard the news, and said: "Then there is nothing left me but to go and see General Grant."—"Oh, General, what will history say to the surrender of the army in the field?"—Lee's reply is among the finest of his utterances: "Yes, I know they will say hard things of us; they will not understand how we were overwhelmed by numbers; but that is not the question, Colonel; the question is, is it right to surrender this army? If it is right, then I will take all the responsibility."

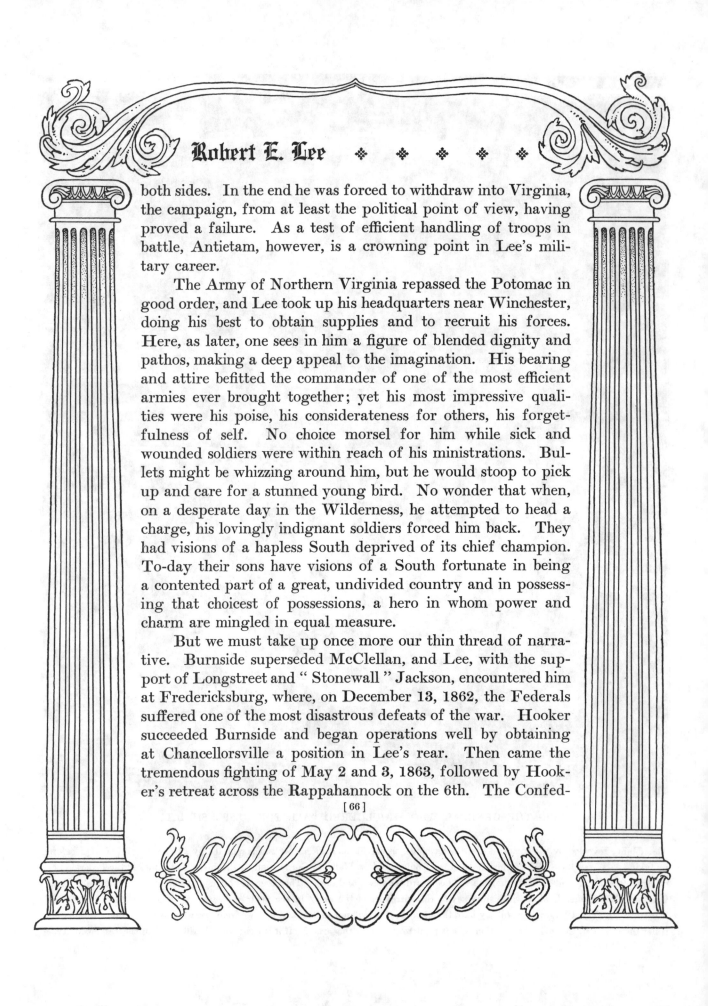

both sides. In the end he was forced to withdraw into Virginia, the campaign, from at least the political point of view, having proved a failure. As a test of efficient handling of troops in battle, Antietam, however, is a crowning point in Lee's military career.

The Army of Northern Virginia repassed the Potomac in good order, and Lee took up his headquarters near Winchester, doing his best to obtain supplies and to recruit his forces. Here, as later, one sees in him a figure of blended dignity and pathos, making a deep appeal to the imagination. His bearing and attire befitted the commander of one of the most efficient armies ever brought together; yet his most impressive qualities were his poise, his considerateness for others, his forgetfulness of self. No choice morsel for him while sick and wounded soldiers were within reach of his ministrations. Bullets might be whizzing around him, but he would stoop to pick up and care for a stunned young bird. No wonder that when, on a desperate day in the Wilderness, he attempted to head a charge, his lovingly indignant soldiers forced him back. They had visions of a hapless South deprived of its chief champion. To-day their sons have visions of a South fortunate in being a contented part of a great, undivided country and in possessing that choicest of possessions, a hero in whom power and charm are mingled in equal measure.

But we must take up once more our thin thread of narrative. Burnside superseded McClellan, and Lee, with the support of Longstreet and " Stonewall " Jackson, encountered him at Fredericksburg, where, on December 13, 1862, the Federals suffered one of the most disastrous defeats of the war. Hooker succeeded Burnside and began operations well by obtaining at Chancellorsville a position in Lee's rear. Then came the tremendous fighting of May 2 and 3, 1863, followed by Hooker's retreat across the Rappahannock on the 6th. The Confed-

LEE IN RICHMOND AFTER THE WAR

The quiet distinction and dignity of the Confederate leader appears particularly in this group portrait—always a trying ordeal for the central figure. Superbly calm he sits, the general who laid down arms totally unembittered, and set a magnificent example to his followers in peace as he had in war. Lee strove after the fall of the Confederacy, with all his far-reaching influence, to allay the feeling aroused by four years of the fiercest fighting in history. This photograph was taken by Brady in 1865, in the basement below the back porch of Lee's Franklin Street house in Richmond. On his right stands General G. W. C. Lee, on his left, Colonel Walter Taylor. This is one of five photographs taken by Brady at this time. A second and third are shown on pages 65 and 69, a fourth on page 83 of Volume I, and a fifth on page 23 of Volume III.

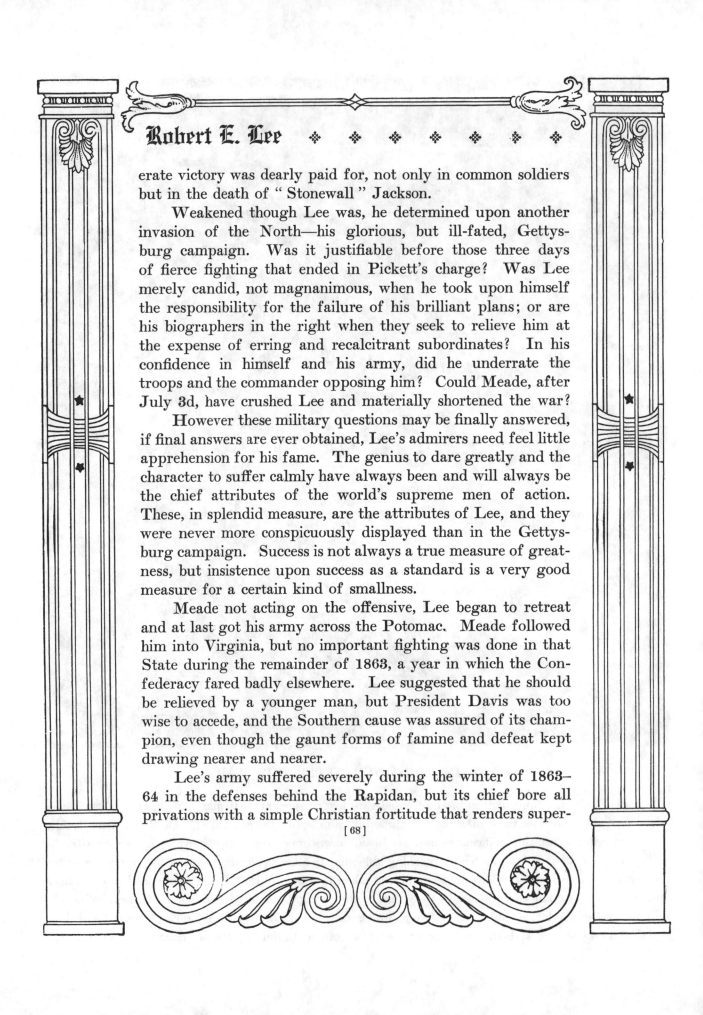

erate victory was dearly paid for, not only in common soldiers but in the death of " Stonewall " Jackson.

Weakened though Lee was, he determined upon another invasion of the North—his glorious, but ill-fated, Gettysburg campaign. Was it justifiable before those three days of fierce fighting that ended in Pickett's charge? Was Lee merely candid, not magnanimous, when he took upon himself the responsibility for the failure of his brilliant plans; or are his biographers in the right when they seek to relieve him at the expense of erring and recalcitrant subordinates? In his confidence in himself and his army, did he underrate the troops and the commander opposing him? Could Meade, after July 3d, have crushed Lee and materially shortened the war?

However these military questions may be finally answered, if final answers are ever obtained, Lee's admirers need feel little apprehension for his fame. The genius to dare greatly and the character to suffer calmly have always been and will always be the chief attributes of the world's supreme men of action. These, in splendid measure, are the attributes of Lee, and they were never more conspicuously displayed than in the Gettysburg campaign. Success is not always a true measure of greatness, but insistence upon success as a standard is a very good measure for a certain kind of smallness.

Meade not acting on the offensive, Lee began to retreat and at last got his army across the Potomac. Meade followed him into Virginia, but no important fighting was done in that State during the remainder of 1863, a year in which the Confederacy fared badly elsewhere. Lee suggested that he should be relieved by a younger man, but President Davis was too wise to accede, and the Southern cause was assured of its champion, even though the gaunt forms of famine and defeat kept drawing nearer and nearer.

Lee's army suffered severely during the winter of 1863–64 in the defenses behind the Rapidan, but its chief bore all privations with a simple Christian fortitude that renders super-

LEE IN 1865

The gray-haired man who wears his uniform with such high distinction is the
general who had shown every kind of bravery known to the soldier, including the
supreme courage to surrender his army in the field when he saw that further fighting
would be a useless sacrifice of lives. This was a photograph taken by Brady,
shortly before Lee left his home to become president of Washington University.

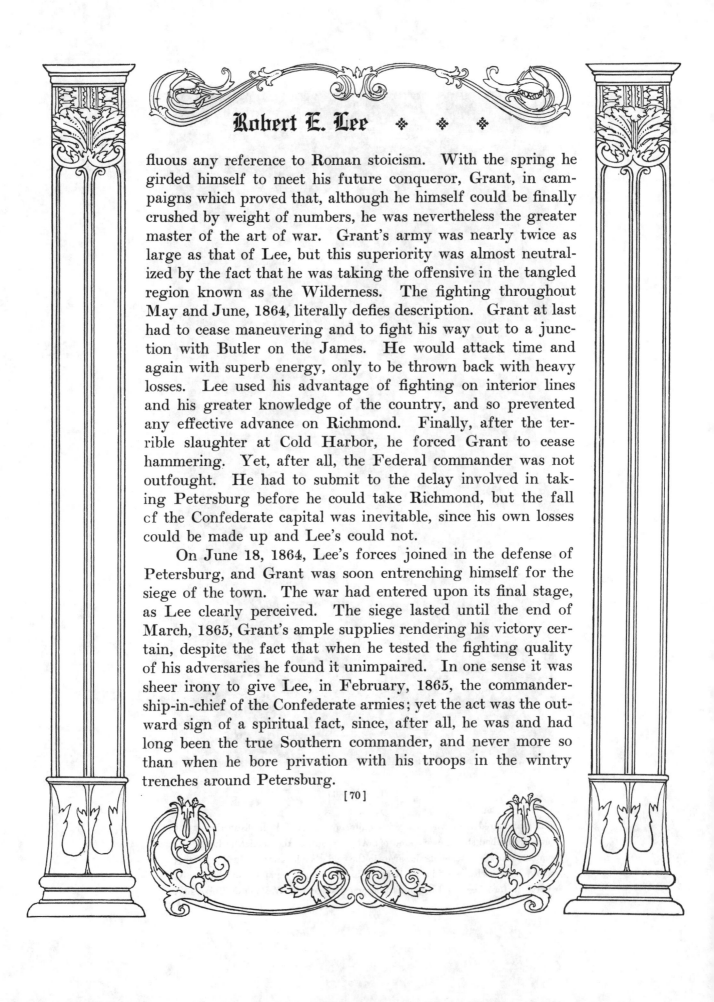

fluous any reference to Roman stoicism. With the spring he girded himself to meet his future conqueror, Grant, in campaigns which proved that, although he himself could be finally crushed by weight of numbers, he was nevertheless the greater master of the art of war. Grant's army was nearly twice as large as that of Lee, but this superiority was almost neutralized by the fact that he was taking the offensive in the tangled region known as the Wilderness. The fighting throughout May and June, 1864, literally defies description. Grant at last had to cease maneuvering and to fight his way out to a junction with Butler on the James. He would attack time and again with superb energy, only to be thrown back with heavy losses. Lee used his advantage of fighting on interior lines and his greater knowledge of the country, and so prevented any effective advance on Richmond. Finally, after the terrible slaughter at Cold Harbor, he forced Grant to cease hammering. Yet, after all, the Federal commander was not outfought. He had to submit to the delay involved in taking Petersburg before he could take Richmond, but the fall cf the Confederate capital was inevitable, since his own losses could be made up and Lee's could not.

On June 18, 1864, Lee's forces joined in the defense of Petersburg, and Grant was soon entrenching himself for the siege of the town. The war had entered upon its final stage, as Lee clearly perceived. The siege lasted until the end of March, 1865, Grant's ample supplies rendering his victory certain, despite the fact that when he tested the fighting quality of his adversaries he found it unimpaired. In one sense it was sheer irony to give Lee, in February, 1865, the commandership-in-chief of the Confederate armies; yet the act was the outward sign of a spiritual fact, since, after all, he was and had long been the true Southern commander, and never more so than when he bore privation with his troops in the wintry trenches around Petersburg.

LEE

AND HIS STAFF

AS THE WAR ENDED

MEN

WHO STAYED

THROUGH APPOMATTOX

These twelve members of General Robert E. Lee's staff surrendered with him at Appomattox Court House, and with him signed a parole drawn up by Grant, to the effect that they would not take up arms against the United States until or unless they were exchanged. This military medallion was devised by the photographer Rockwell during General Lee's stay in Richmond in April, 1865. These facts are furnished by Major Giles B. Cooke (No. 12, above), who had verified them by writing General Lee himself after the surrender.

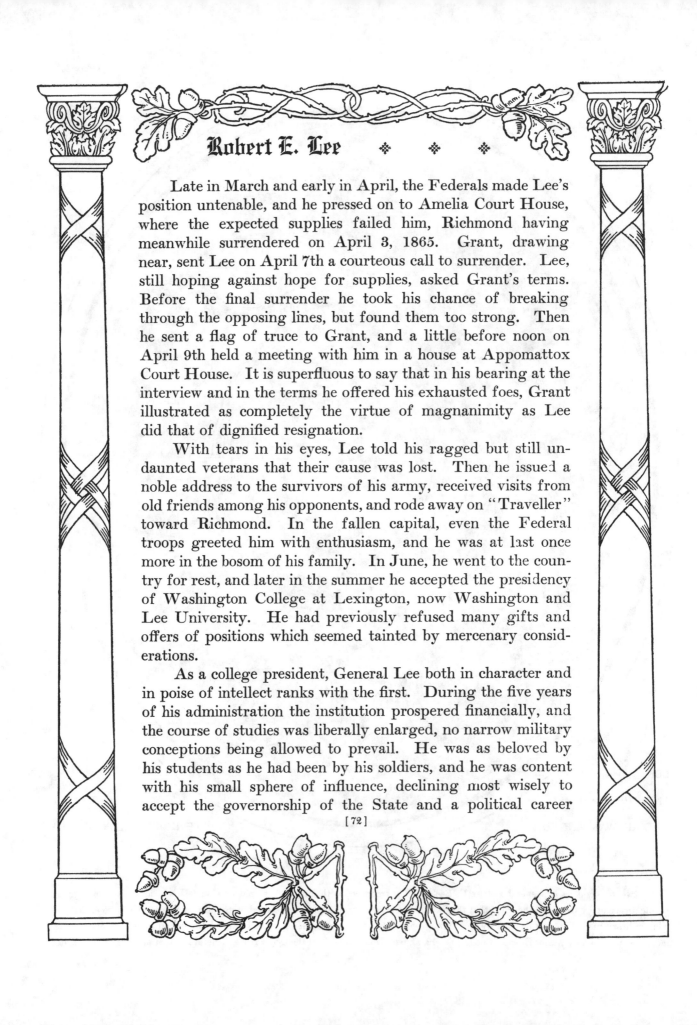

Robert E. Lee ✦ ✦ ✦

Late in March and early in April, the Federals made Lee's position untenable, and he pressed on to Amelia Court House, where the expected supplies failed him, Richmond having meanwhile surrendered on April 3, 1865. Grant, drawing near, sent Lee on April 7th a courteous call to surrender. Lee, still hoping against hope for supplies, asked Grant's terms. Before the final surrender he took his chance of breaking through the opposing lines, but found them too strong. Then he sent a flag of truce to Grant, and a little before noon on April 9th held a meeting with him in a house at Appomattox Court House. It is superfluous to say that in his bearing at the interview and in the terms he offered his exhausted foes, Grant illustrated as completely the virtue of magnanimity as Lee did that of dignified resignation.

With tears in his eyes, Lee told his ragged but still undaunted veterans that their cause was lost. Then he issued a noble address to the survivors of his army, received visits from old friends among his opponents, and rode away on "Traveller" toward Richmond. In the fallen capital, even the Federal troops greeted him with enthusiasm, and he was at last once more in the bosom of his family. In June, he went to the country for rest, and later in the summer he accepted the presidency of Washington College at Lexington, now Washington and Lee University. He had previously refused many gifts and offers of positions which seemed tainted by mercenary considerations.

As a college president, General Lee both in character and in poise of intellect ranks with the first. During the five years of his administration the institution prospered financially, and the course of studies was liberally enlarged, no narrow military conceptions being allowed to prevail. He was as beloved by his students as he had been by his soldiers, and he was content with his small sphere of influence, declining most wisely to accept the governorship of the State and a political career

LEE IN 1867

PRESIDENT OF WASHINGTON COLLEGE, LATER
WASHINGTON AND LEE UNIVERSITY

LEE IN 1869

THE YEAR BEFORE HIS DEATH AT THE AGE
OF SIXTY-THREE

THE DECLINING YEARS

In these portraits the bright eyes of the daring leader have lost none of their fire; the handsome head still remains erect. In October, 1865, Lee had been installed as president of Washington College at Lexington, Virginia, later named in his honor Washington and Lee University. Under his management new chairs were founded, the scheme of study enlarged, and from the moral side it would have been impossible to secure finer results. Lee's greatness of soul was shown in the way in which he urged the Southern people loyally to accept the result of the war. On the morning of October 12, 1870, at the age of sixty-three, he died—mourned throughout the Union which he had helped to reunite, and throughout the civilized world, which had watched with admiration his gallant fight and nobility of soul. "To those who saw his composure under the greater and lesser trials of life," wrote Colonel William Preston Johnson, his intimate friend, "and his justice and forbearance with the most unjust and uncharitable, it seemed scarcely credible that his serene soul was shaken by the evil that raged around him." On his dying bed he fought over the great battles of the war. How strongly he felt his responsibility is shown by nearly his last words: "Tell Hill he must come up."

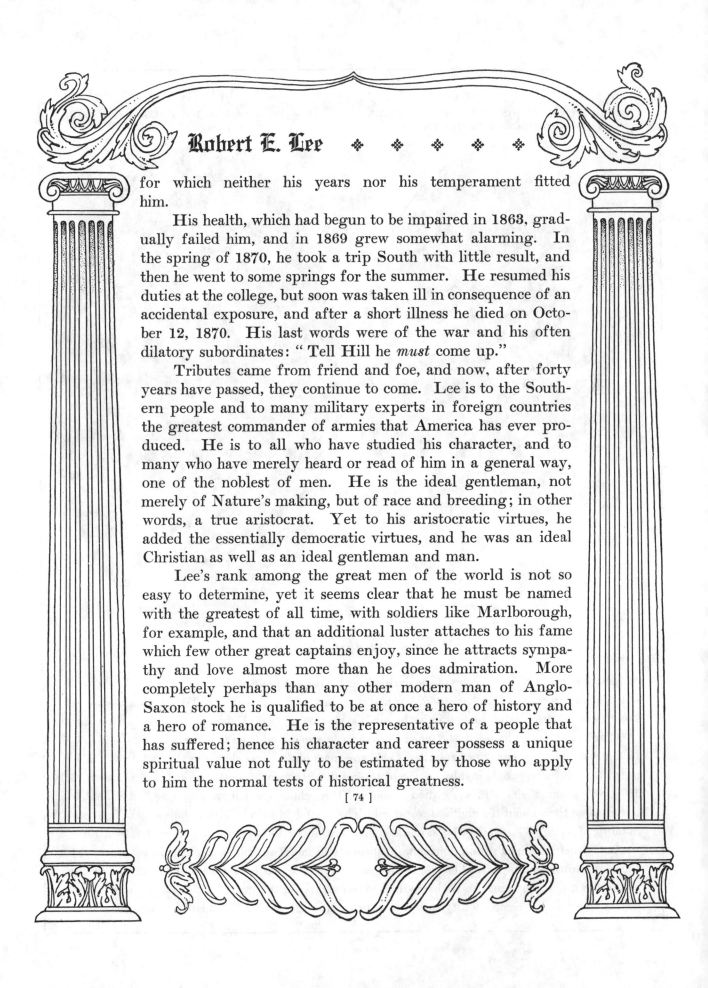

for which neither his years nor his temperament fitted him.

His health, which had begun to be impaired in 1863, gradually failed him, and in 1869 grew somewhat alarming. In the spring of 1870, he took a trip South with little result, and then he went to some springs for the summer. He resumed his duties at the college, but soon was taken ill in consequence of an accidental exposure, and after a short illness he died on October 12, 1870. His last words were of the war and his often dilatory subordinates: "Tell Hill he *must* come up."

Tributes came from friend and foe, and now, after forty years have passed, they continue to come. Lee is to the Southern people and to many military experts in foreign countries the greatest commander of armies that America has ever produced. He is to all who have studied his character, and to many who have merely heard or read of him in a general way, one of the noblest of men. He is the ideal gentleman, not merely of Nature's making, but of race and breeding; in other words, a true aristocrat. Yet to his aristocratic virtues, he added the essentially democratic virtues, and he was an ideal Christian as well as an ideal gentleman and man.

Lee's rank among the great men of the world is not so easy to determine, yet it seems clear that he must be named with the greatest of all time, with soldiers like Marlborough, for example, and that an additional luster attaches to his fame which few other great captains enjoy, since he attracts sympathy and love almost more than he does admiration. More completely perhaps than any other modern man of Anglo-Saxon stock he is qualified to be at once a hero of history and a hero of romance. He is the representative of a people that has suffered; hence his character and career possess a unique spiritual value not fully to be estimated by those who apply to him the normal tests of historical greatness.

III

SHERMAN

A LEADER WHO FOUGHT, BUT WHO WON MORE
BY MARCHES THAN OTHERS WON BY FIGHTING

MAJOR–GENERAL WILLIAM T. SHERMAN AND HIS GENERALS

This photograph shows Sherman with seven major-generals who "went through" with him —fighting their way to Atlanta, and marching on the famous expedition from Atlanta to the sea and north through the Carolinas to the battle of Bentonville and Johnston's surrender.

From left to right they are:

MAJOR-GENERAL
O. O. HOWARD
Commanding the Army of the Tennessee

MAJOR-GENERAL
J. A. LOGAN
Formerly Commanding the Army of the Tennessee

MAJOR-GENERAL
W. B. HAZEN
Commanding a Division in the Fifteenth Army Corps

MAJOR-GENERAL
W. T. SHERMAN
Commanding the Military Division of the Mississippi

MAJOR-GENERAL
JEFF C. DAVIS
Commanding the Fourteenth Army Corps

MAJOR-GENERAL
H. W. SLOCUM
Commanding the Army of Georgia

MAJOR-GENERAL
J. A. MOWER
Commanding the Twentieth Army Corps

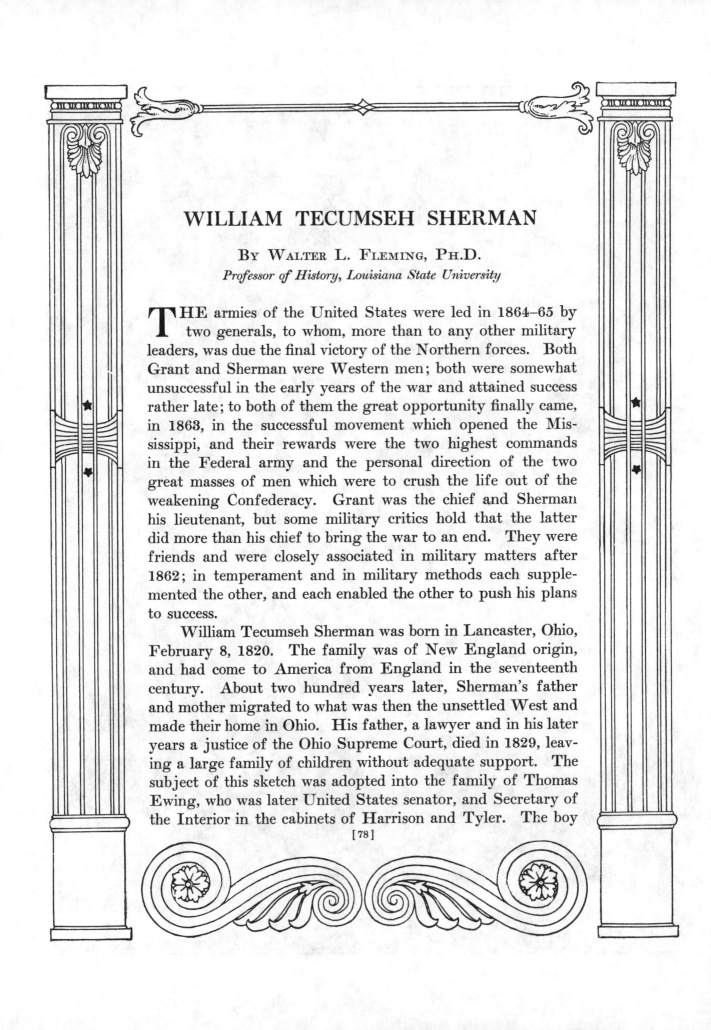

WILLIAM TECUMSEH SHERMAN

By Walter L. Fleming, Ph.D.
Professor of History, Louisiana State University

THE armies of the United States were led in 1864–65 by two generals, to whom, more than to any other military leaders, was due the final victory of the Northern forces. Both Grant and Sherman were Western men; both were somewhat unsuccessful in the early years of the war and attained success rather late; to both of them the great opportunity finally came, in 1863, in the successful movement which opened the Mississippi, and their rewards were the two highest commands in the Federal army and the personal direction of the two great masses of men which were to crush the life out of the weakening Confederacy. Grant was the chief and Sherman his lieutenant, but some military critics hold that the latter did more than his chief to bring the war to an end. They were friends and were closely associated in military matters after 1862; in temperament and in military methods each supplemented the other, and each enabled the other to push his plans to success.

William Tecumseh Sherman was born in Lancaster, Ohio, February 8, 1820. The family was of New England origin, and had come to America from England in the seventeenth century. About two hundred years later, Sherman's father and mother migrated to what was then the unsettled West and made their home in Ohio. His father, a lawyer and in his later years a justice of the Ohio Supreme Court, died in 1829, leaving a large family of children without adequate support. The subject of this sketch was adopted into the family of Thomas Ewing, who was later United States senator, and Secretary of the Interior in the cabinets of Harrison and Tyler. The boy

[78]

BEFORE THE MARCH TO THE SEA

These two photographs of General Sherman were taken in 1864—the year that made him an international figure, before his march to the sea which electrified the civilized world, and exposed once for all the crippled condition of the Confederacy. After that autumn expedition, the problem of the Union generals was merely to contend with detached armies, no longer with the combined States of the Confederacy. The latter had no means of extending further support to the dwindling troops in the field. Sherman was the chief Union exponent of the tactical gift that makes marches count as much as fighting. In the early part of 1864 he made his famous raid across Mississippi from Jackson to Meridian and back again, destroying the railroads, Confederate stores, and other property, and desolating the country along the line of march. In May he set out from Chattanooga for the invasion of Georgia. For his success in this campaign he was appointed, on August 12th, a major-general in the regular army. On November 12th, he started with the pick of his men on his march to the sea. After the capture of Savannah, December 21st, Sherman's fame was secure; yet he was one of the most heartily execrated leaders of the war. There is a hint of a smile in the right-hand picture. The left-hand portrait reveals all the sternness and determination of a leader surrounded by dangers, about to penetrate an enemy's country against the advice of accepted military authorities.

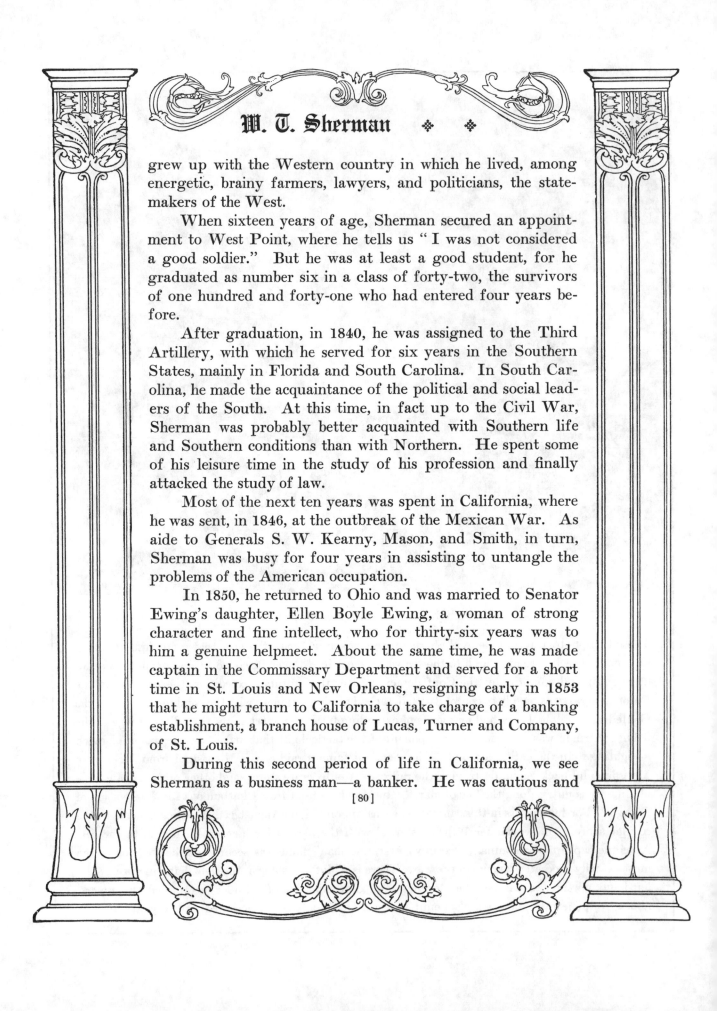

grew up with the Western country in which he lived, among energetic, brainy farmers, lawyers, and politicians, the state-makers of the West.

When sixteen years of age, Sherman secured an appointment to West Point, where he tells us " I was not considered a good soldier." But he was at least a good student, for he graduated as number six in a class of forty-two, the survivors of one hundred and forty-one who had entered four years before.

After graduation, in 1840, he was assigned to the Third Artillery, with which he served for six years in the Southern States, mainly in Florida and South Carolina. In South Carolina, he made the acquaintance of the political and social leaders of the South. At this time, in fact up to the Civil War, Sherman was probably better acquainted with Southern life and Southern conditions than with Northern. He spent some of his leisure time in the study of his profession and finally attacked the study of law.

Most of the next ten years was spent in California, where he was sent, in 1846, at the outbreak of the Mexican War. As aide to Generals S. W. Kearny, Mason, and Smith, in turn, Sherman was busy for four years in assisting to untangle the problems of the American occupation.

In 1850, he returned to Ohio and was married to Senator Ewing's daughter, Ellen Boyle Ewing, a woman of strong character and fine intellect, who for thirty-six years was to him a genuine helpmeet. About the same time, he was made captain in the Commissary Department and served for a short time in St. Louis and New Orleans, resigning early in 1853 that he might return to California to take charge of a banking establishment, a branch house of Lucas, Turner and Company, of St. Louis.

During this second period of life in California, we see Sherman as a business man—a banker. He was cautious and

SHERMAN IN 1865

If Sherman was deemed merciless in war, he was superbly generous when the fighting
was over. To Joseph E. Johnston he offered most liberal terms of surrender for the
Southern armies. Their acceptance would have gone far to prevent the worst of the
reconstruction enormities. Unfortunately his first convention with Johnston was
disapproved. The death of Lincoln had removed the guiding hand that would have
meant so much to the nation. To those who have read his published correspondence
and his memoirs Sherman appears in a very human light. He was fluent and frequently reckless in speech and writing, but his kindly humanity is seen in both.

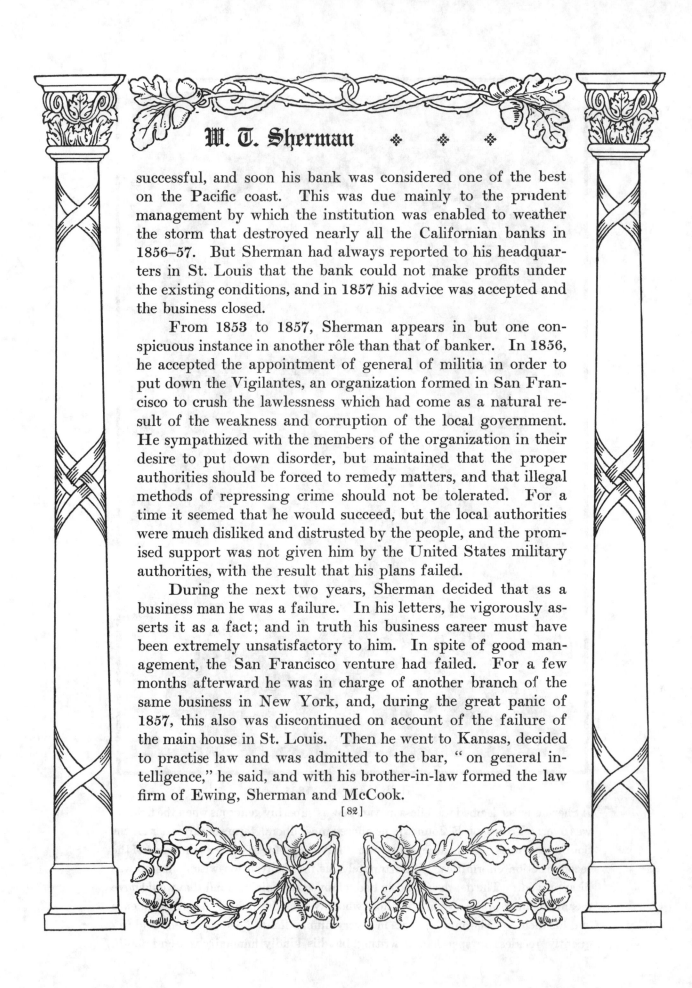

successful, and soon his bank was considered one of the best on the Pacific coast. This was due mainly to the prudent management by which the institution was enabled to weather the storm that destroyed nearly all the Californian banks in 1856–57. But Sherman had always reported to his headquarters in St. Louis that the bank could not make profits under the existing conditions, and in 1857 his advice was accepted and the business closed.

From 1853 to 1857, Sherman appears in but one conspicuous instance in another rôle than that of banker. In 1856, he accepted the appointment of general of militia in order to put down the Vigilantes, an organization formed in San Francisco to crush the lawlessness which had come as a natural result of the weakness and corruption of the local government. He sympathized with the members of the organization in their desire to put down disorder, but maintained that the proper authorities should be forced to remedy matters, and that illegal methods of repressing crime should not be tolerated. For a time it seemed that he would succeed, but the local authorities were much disliked and distrusted by the people, and the promised support was not given him by the United States military authorities, with the result that his plans failed.

During the next two years, Sherman decided that as a business man he was a failure. In his letters, he vigorously asserts it as a fact; and in truth his business career must have been extremely unsatisfactory to him. In spite of good management, the San Francisco venture had failed. For a few months afterward he was in charge of another branch of the same business in New York, and, during the great panic of 1857, this also was discontinued on account of the failure of the main house in St. Louis. Then he went to Kansas, decided to practise law and was admitted to the bar, " on general intelligence," he said, and with his brother-in-law formed the law firm of Ewing, Sherman and McCook.

SHERMAN IN 1876

A SOLDIER TO THE END

The tall figure of "Old Tecumseh" in 1876, though crowned with gray, still stood erect and commanding. Upon the appointment of Grant as full general, in July, 1866, Sherman had been promoted to the lieutenant-generalship. When Grant became President of the United States, March 4, 1869, Sherman succeeded him as general. An attempt was made to run him against Grant in 1872, but he emphatically refused to allow his name to be used. He retired from the army on full pay in February, 1884. Although he was practically assured of the Republican nomination for President that year, he telegraphed that he would not accept the nomination if given, and would not serve if elected. He spent his later years among his old army associates, attending reunions, making speeches at soldiers' celebrations, and putting his papers in order for future historians. He resolutely refused all inducements to enter the political arena, and to the end he remained a soldier.

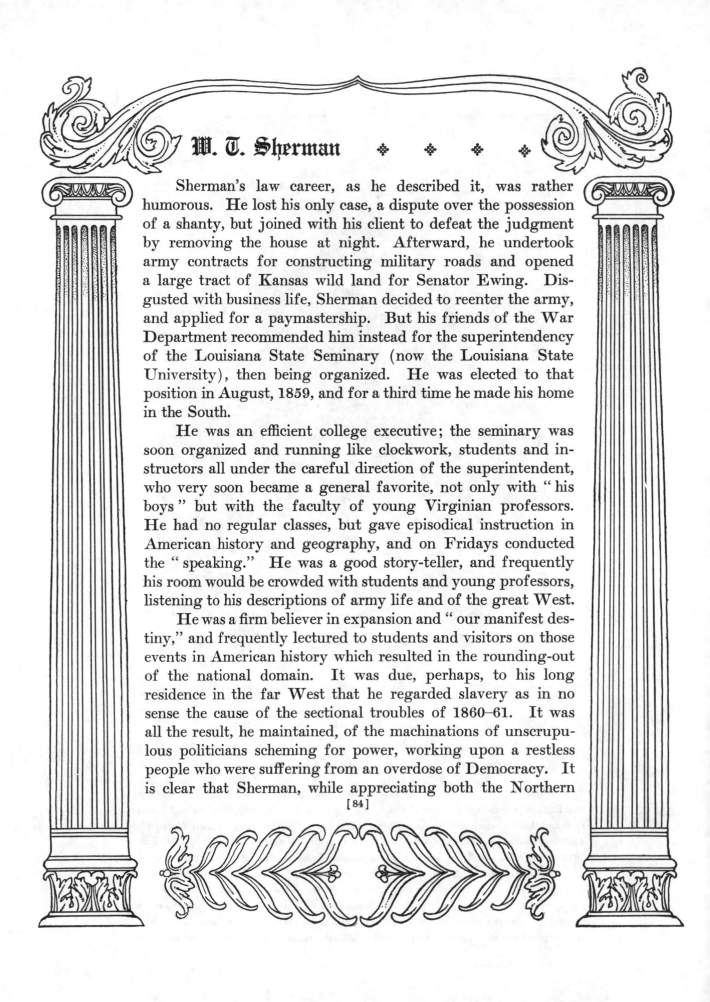

Sherman's law career, as he described it, was rather humorous. He lost his only case, a dispute over the possession of a shanty, but joined with his client to defeat the judgment by removing the house at night. Afterward, he undertook army contracts for constructing military roads and opened a large tract of Kansas wild land for Senator Ewing. Disgusted with business life, Sherman decided to reenter the army, and applied for a paymastership. But his friends of the War Department recommended him instead for the superintendency of the Louisiana State Seminary (now the Louisiana State University), then being organized. He was elected to that position in August, 1859, and for a third time he made his home in the South.

He was an efficient college executive; the seminary was soon organized and running like clockwork, students and instructors all under the careful direction of the superintendent, who very soon became a general favorite, not only with " his boys " but with the faculty of young Virginian professors. He had no regular classes, but gave episodical instruction in American history and geography, and on Fridays conducted the " speaking." He was a good story-teller, and frequently his room would be crowded with students and young professors, listening to his descriptions of army life and of the great West.

He was a firm believer in expansion and " our manifest destiny," and frequently lectured to students and visitors on those events in American history which resulted in the rounding-out of the national domain. It was due, perhaps, to his long residence in the far West that he regarded slavery as in no sense the cause of the sectional troubles of 1860–61. It was all the result, he maintained, of the machinations of unscrupulous politicians scheming for power, working upon a restless people who were suffering from an overdose of Democracy. It is clear that Sherman, while appreciating both the Northern

SHERMAN'S LEADERS IN THE ATLANTA CAMPAIGN

THE FIRST OF FIVE GROUPS OF LEADERS WHO MADE POSSIBLE SHERMAN'S LACONIC MESSAGE
OF SEPTEMBER, 1864: "ATLANTA IS OURS AND FAIRLY WON"

James D. Morgan, Leader of a Division
in Palmer's Corps.

R. M. Johnson, Leader of a Division
in the Fourteenth Corps.

John Newton Led the Second Division
of the Fourth Corps.

Alpheus S. Williams, Leader of a Division
under General Joseph Hooker.

Edward M. McCook, Dashing Leader of a
Cavalry Division in Front of Atlanta.

Wager Swayne, Originally Colonel of the
43d Ohio, Brevetted Major-General.

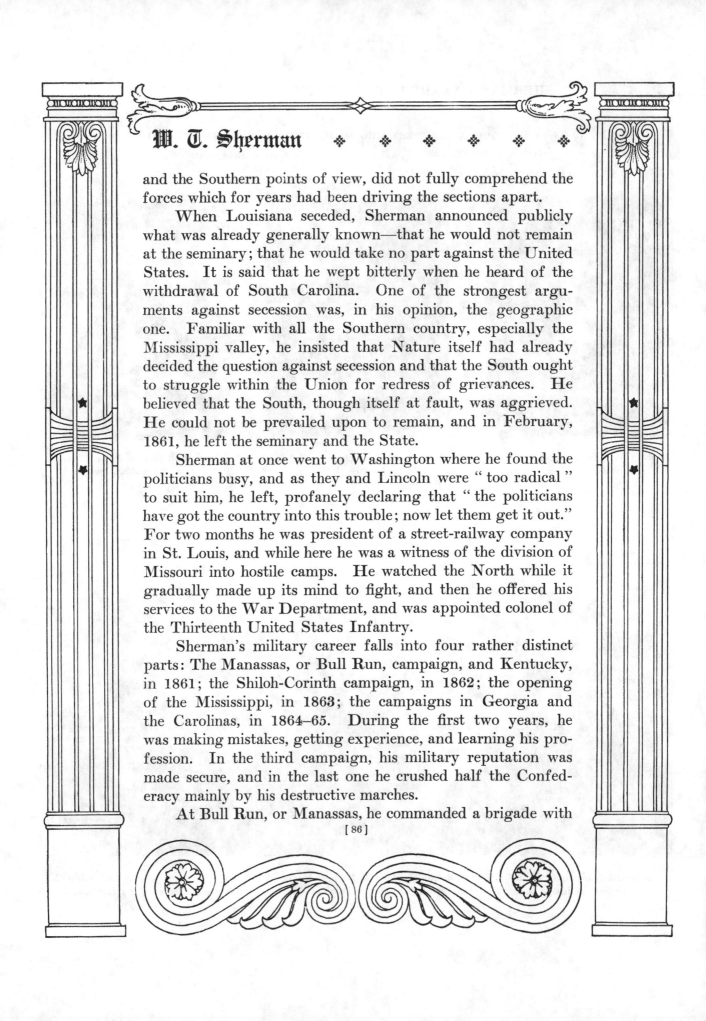

and the Southern points of view, did not fully comprehend the forces which for years had been driving the sections apart.

When Louisiana seceded, Sherman announced publicly what was already generally known—that he would not remain at the seminary; that he would take no part against the United States. It is said that he wept bitterly when he heard of the withdrawal of South Carolina. One of the strongest arguments against secession was, in his opinion, the geographic one. Familiar with all the Southern country, especially the Mississippi valley, he insisted that Nature itself had already decided the question against secession and that the South ought to struggle within the Union for redress of grievances. He believed that the South, though itself at fault, was aggrieved. He could not be prevailed upon to remain, and in February, 1861, he left the seminary and the State.

Sherman at once went to Washington where he found the politicians busy, and as they and Lincoln were " too radical " to suit him, he left, profanely declaring that " the politicians have got the country into this trouble; now let them get it out." For two months he was president of a street-railway company in St. Louis, and while here he was a witness of the division of Missouri into hostile camps. He watched the North while it gradually made up its mind to fight, and then he offered his services to the War Department, and was appointed colonel of the Thirteenth United States Infantry.

Sherman's military career falls into four rather distinct parts: The Manassas, or Bull Run, campaign, and Kentucky, in 1861; the Shiloh-Corinth campaign, in 1862; the opening of the Mississippi, in 1863; the campaigns in Georgia and the Carolinas, in 1864–65. During the first two years, he was making mistakes, getting experience, and learning his profession. In the third campaign, his military reputation was made secure, and in the last one he crushed half the Confederacy mainly by his destructive marches.

At Bull Run, or Manassas, he commanded a brigade with

Thos. H. Ruger Commanded a Brigade under General Hooker.

J. C. Veatch, Division Leader in the Sixteenth Army Corps.

Morgan L. Smith, Leader of the Second Division, Fourteenth Corps.

LEADERS IN THE ATLANTA CAMPAIGN— GROUP No. 2

COMMANDERS OF BRIGADES AND DIVISIONS WHICH FOUGHT UNDER McPHERSON, THOMAS AND HOOKER IN THE CAMPAIGN FOR ATLANTA, SUMMER OF '64

J. D. Cox Commanded a Division under General Schofield.

M. D. Manson, Brigade Leader in the Twenty-third Corps.

Charles Cruft Commanded a Brigade under General Stanley.

J. A. J. Lightburn Led a Division in the Army of the Tennessee.

W. L. Elliott, Chief of Cavalry under General Thomas

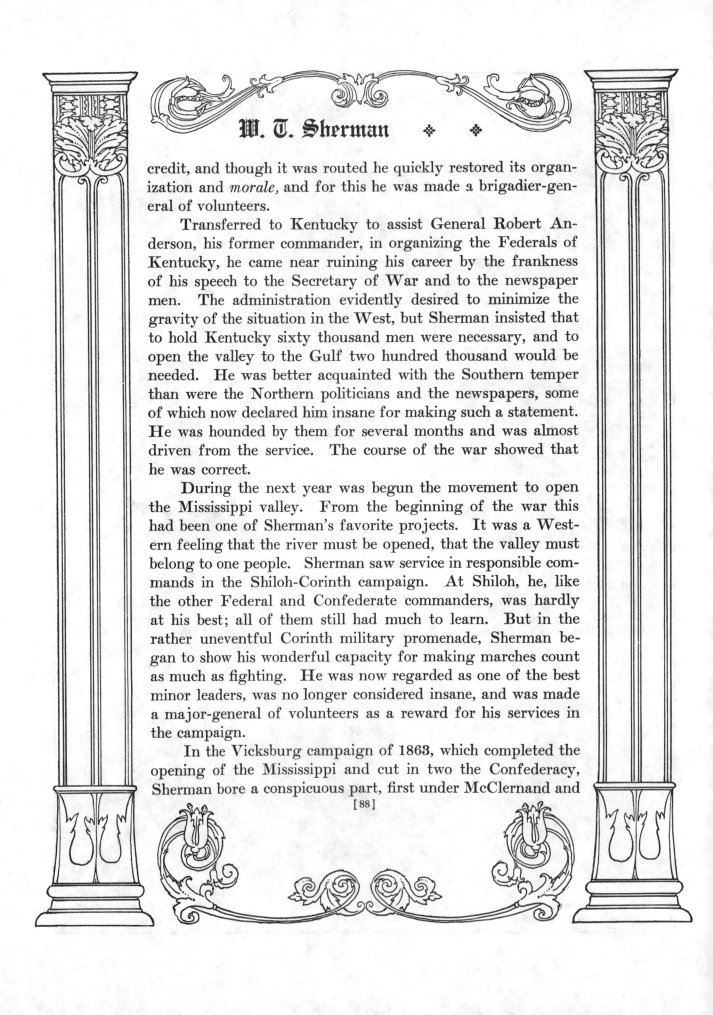

credit, and though it was routed he quickly restored its organization and *morale,* and for this he was made a brigadier-general of volunteers.

Transferred to Kentucky to assist General Robert Anderson, his former commander, in organizing the Federals of Kentucky, he came near ruining his career by the frankness of his speech to the Secretary of War and to the newspaper men. The administration evidently desired to minimize the gravity of the situation in the West, but Sherman insisted that to hold Kentucky sixty thousand men were necessary, and to open the valley to the Gulf two hundred thousand would be needed. He was better acquainted with the Southern temper than were the Northern politicians and the newspapers, some of which now declared him insane for making such a statement. He was hounded by them for several months and was almost driven from the service. The course of the war showed that he was correct.

During the next year was begun the movement to open the Mississippi valley. From the beginning of the war this had been one of Sherman's favorite projects. It was a Western feeling that the river must be opened, that the valley must belong to one people. Sherman saw service in responsible commands in the Shiloh-Corinth campaign. At Shiloh, he, like the other Federal and Confederate commanders, was hardly at his best; all of them still had much to learn. But in the rather uneventful Corinth military promenade, Sherman began to show his wonderful capacity for making marches count as much as fighting. He was now regarded as one of the best minor leaders, was no longer considered insane, and was made a major-general of volunteers as a reward for his services in the campaign.

In the Vicksburg campaign of 1863, which completed the opening of the Mississippi and cut in two the Confederacy, Sherman bore a conspicuous part, first under McClernand and

Nathan Kimball Led a Division in the Fourth Corps.

Samuel Beatty, Leader of a Brigade in the Fourth Corps.

William B. Hazen Commanded a Division under McPherson.

J. M. Corse "Held the Fort" at Alatoona Pass.

Joseph F. Knipe, Leader of a Brigade in the Twentieth Corps.

LEADERS IN THE ATLANTA CAMPAIGN GROUP No. 3

Charles Candy Led a Brigade in Geary's Division of the Twentieth Corps.

GENERAL OFFICERS WHO LED BRIGADES OR DIVISIONS IN THE HUNDRED DAYS' MARCHING AND FIGHTING FROM RESACA TO ATLANTA

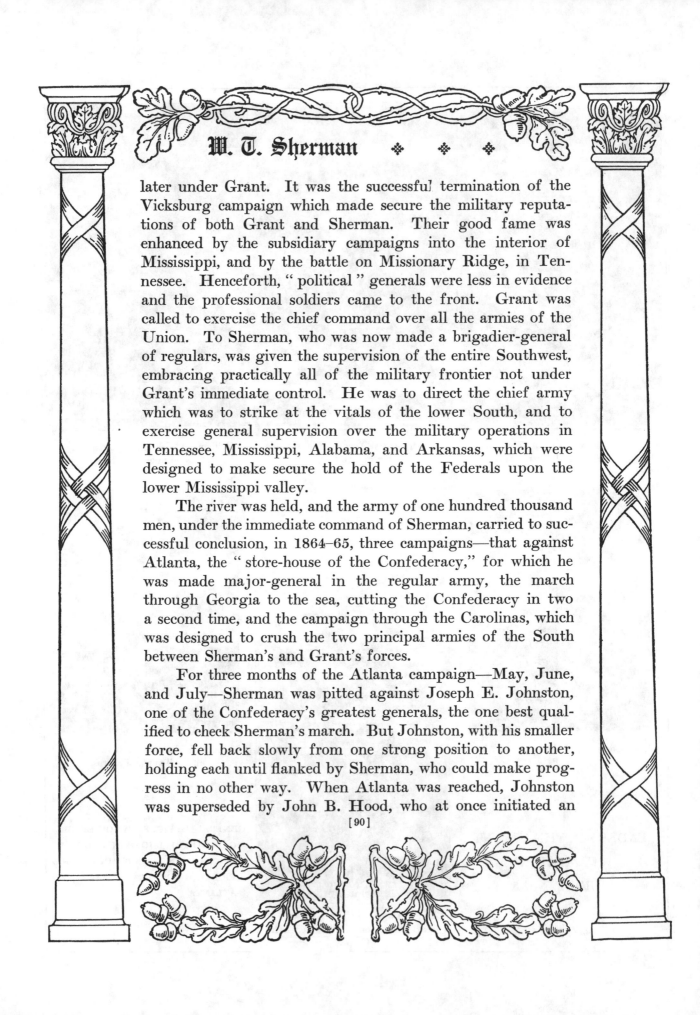

later under Grant. It was the successful termination of the Vicksburg campaign which made secure the military reputations of both Grant and Sherman. Their good fame was enhanced by the subsidiary campaigns into the interior of Mississippi, and by the battle on Missionary Ridge, in Tennessee. Henceforth, "political" generals were less in evidence and the professional soldiers came to the front. Grant was called to exercise the chief command over all the armies of the Union. To Sherman, who was now made a brigadier-general of regulars, was given the supervision of the entire Southwest, embracing practically all of the military frontier not under Grant's immediate control. He was to direct the chief army which was to strike at the vitals of the lower South, and to exercise general supervision over the military operations in Tennessee, Mississippi, Alabama, and Arkansas, which were designed to make secure the hold of the Federals upon the lower Mississippi valley.

The river was held, and the army of one hundred thousand men, under the immediate command of Sherman, carried to successful conclusion, in 1864–65, three campaigns—that against Atlanta, the "store-house of the Confederacy," for which he was made major-general in the regular army, the march through Georgia to the sea, cutting the Confederacy in two a second time, and the campaign through the Carolinas, which was designed to crush the two principal armies of the South between Sherman's and Grant's forces.

For three months of the Atlanta campaign—May, June, and July—Sherman was pitted against Joseph E. Johnston, one of the Confederacy's greatest generals, the one best qualified to check Sherman's march. But Johnston, with his smaller force, fell back slowly from one strong position to another, holding each until flanked by Sherman, who could make progress in no other way. When Atlanta was reached, Johnston was superseded by John B. Hood, who at once initiated an

M. D. Leggett, Division Leader in Blair's Corps.

William Harrow Commanded Division in Logan's Corps.

John W. Fuller, Leader of a Division in Dodge's Corps.

Thomas W. Sweeny Led a Division in Dodge's Corps.

LEADERS IN THE ATLANTA CAMPAIGN—No. 4

PROMINENT LEADERS IN THE ARMY OF THE CUMBERLAND AND THE TENNESSEE IN SHERMAN'S MASTERLY MOVEMENT TO THE HEART OF GEORGIA

George D. Wagner Commanded a Division under Howard.

William F. Barry, Chief of Artillery on Sherman's Staff.

W. W. Belknap, Promoted in Front of Atlanta.

John B. Turchin, Leader in the Fourteenth Corps.

William T. Ward Led a Division under Hooker.

John W. Sprague, Leader in the Sixteenth Corps.

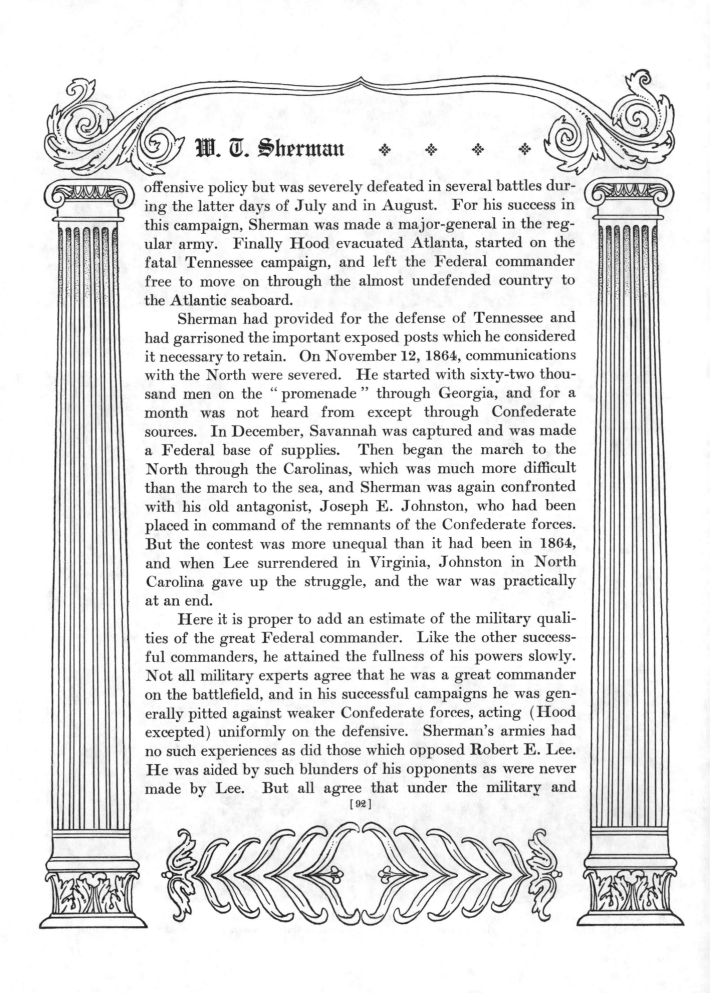

offensive policy but was severely defeated in several battles during the latter days of July and in August. For his success in this campaign, Sherman was made a major-general in the regular army. Finally Hood evacuated Atlanta, started on the fatal Tennessee campaign, and left the Federal commander free to move on through the almost undefended country to the Atlantic seaboard.

Sherman had provided for the defense of Tennessee and had garrisoned the important exposed posts which he considered it necessary to retain. On November 12, 1864, communications with the North were severed. He started with sixty-two thousand men on the "promenade" through Georgia, and for a month was not heard from except through Confederate sources. In December, Savannah was captured and was made a Federal base of supplies. Then began the march to the North through the Carolinas, which was much more difficult than the march to the sea, and Sherman was again confronted with his old antagonist, Joseph E. Johnston, who had been placed in command of the remnants of the Confederate forces. But the contest was more unequal than it had been in 1864, and when Lee surrendered in Virginia, Johnston in North Carolina gave up the struggle, and the war was practically at an end.

Here it is proper to add an estimate of the military qualities of the great Federal commander. Like the other successful commanders, he attained the fullness of his powers slowly. Not all military experts agree that he was a great commander on the battlefield, and in his successful campaigns he was generally pitted against weaker Confederate forces, acting (Hood excepted) uniformly on the defensive. Sherman's armies had no such experiences as did those which opposed Robert E. Lee. He was aided by such blunders of his opponents as were never made by Lee. But all agree that under the military and

Jos. A. Cooper Commanded a Brigade
in the Twenty-third Corps.

M. F. Force Commanded a Brigade
under Blair.

John H. King Commanded a Division
in the Fourteenth Corps.

LEADERS IN THE
ATLANTA AND
NASHVILLE CAMPAIGNS

Milo S. Hascall, Leader of a Division
in the Twenty-third Corps.

GENERAL OFFICERS
CONSPICUOUS IN SHERMAN'S
ADVANCE AND SOME
WHO PROTECTED THE FLANK
AND REAR OF HIS ARMY

David S. Stanley, Leader of the
Fourth Corps; an All-around Soldier.

H. M. Judah Commanded a Division
of the Twenty-third Corps.

Charles C. Walcutt, Leader of a
Brigade in the Fifteenth Corps.

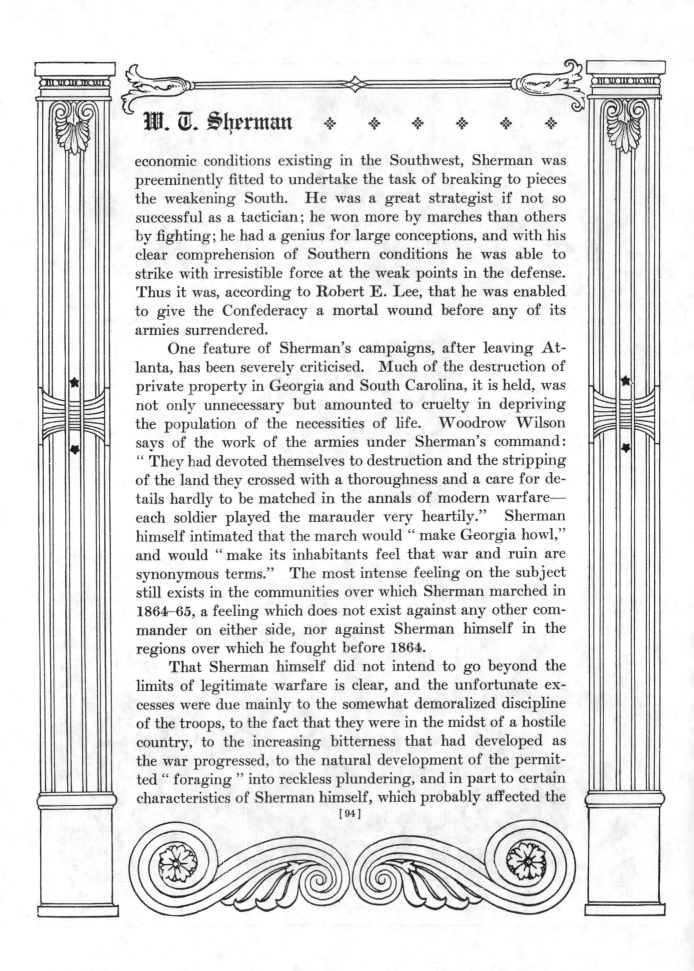

economic conditions existing in the Southwest, Sherman was preeminently fitted to undertake the task of breaking to pieces the weakening South. He was a great strategist if not so successful as a tactician; he won more by marches than others by fighting; he had a genius for large conceptions, and with his clear comprehension of Southern conditions he was able to strike with irresistible force at the weak points in the defense. Thus it was, according to Robert E. Lee, that he was enabled to give the Confederacy a mortal wound before any of its armies surrendered.

One feature of Sherman's campaigns, after leaving Atlanta, has been severely criticised. Much of the destruction of private property in Georgia and South Carolina, it is held, was not only unnecessary but amounted to cruelty in depriving the population of the necessities of life. Woodrow Wilson says of the work of the armies under Sherman's command: "They had devoted themselves to destruction and the stripping of the land they crossed with a thoroughness and a care for details hardly to be matched in the annals of modern warfare—each soldier played the marauder very heartily." Sherman himself intimated that the march would "make Georgia howl," and would "make its inhabitants feel that war and ruin are synonymous terms." The most intense feeling on the subject still exists in the communities over which Sherman marched in 1864–65, a feeling which does not exist against any other commander on either side, nor against Sherman himself in the regions over which he fought before 1864.

That Sherman himself did not intend to go beyond the limits of legitimate warfare is clear, and the unfortunate excesses were due mainly to the somewhat demoralized discipline of the troops, to the fact that they were in the midst of a hostile country, to the increasing bitterness that had developed as the war progressed, to the natural development of the permitted "foraging" into reckless plundering, and in part to certain characteristics of Sherman himself, which probably affected the

ARMY AND CORPS LEADERS WHO ENDED THE WAR IN THE NORTHWEST AND SOUTHWEST

GENERAL EDWARD R. S. CANBY

As Sherman cut the southeastern Confederacy in two by his march to the sea, so Sheridan (center of group above) and Canby (shown below) wiped off the map the theaters of war in the northwest and southwest respectively. With Merritt and Torbert, and the dashing Custer, Sheridan swept the Shenandoah Valley. Canby, as commander of the military division of West Mississippi, directed the Mobile campaign of March-April, 1865, which resulted in the occupation by the Federals of Mobile and Montgomery. A raid by James H. Wilson (second from right) had prepared the way for this result. In May, 1865, Canby received the surrender of the Confederate forces under Generals R. Taylor and E. Kirby Smith, the largest Confederate forces which sur-

rendered at the end of the war. The cavalry leaders in the upper picture are, from left to right: Generals Wesley Merritt, David McM. Gregg, Philip Henry Sheridan, Henry E. Davies, James Harrison Wilson, and Alfred T. A. Torbert. Wilson was given the cavalry corps of the military district of the Mississippi in 1865, and Torbert commanded the cavalry corps of the Army of the Shenandoah under Sheridan. These six great leaders are among the men who handled the Federal cavalry in its last days, welding it into the splendid, efficient, aggressive, fighting force that finally overwhelmed the depleted ranks of their Confederate opponents, Forrest and Wheeler in the West and Rosser, Lomax, Stuart, the two Lees and Hampton in the East.

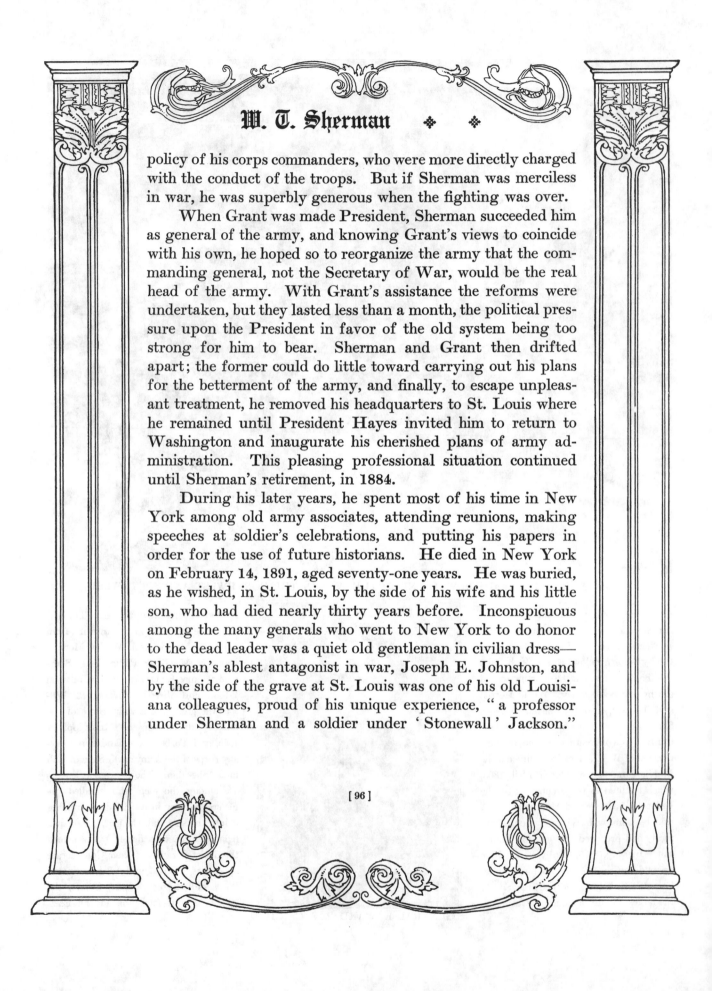

policy of his corps commanders, who were more directly charged with the conduct of the troops. But if Sherman was merciless in war, he was superbly generous when the fighting was over.

When Grant was made President, Sherman succeeded him as general of the army, and knowing Grant's views to coincide with his own, he hoped so to reorganize the army that the commanding general, not the Secretary of War, would be the real head of the army. With Grant's assistance the reforms were undertaken, but they lasted less than a month, the political pressure upon the President in favor of the old system being too strong for him to bear. Sherman and Grant then drifted apart; the former could do little toward carrying out his plans for the betterment of the army, and finally, to escape unpleasant treatment, he removed his headquarters to St. Louis where he remained until President Hayes invited him to return to Washington and inaugurate his cherished plans of army administration. This pleasing professional situation continued until Sherman's retirement, in 1884.

During his later years, he spent most of his time in New York among old army associates, attending reunions, making speeches at soldier's celebrations, and putting his papers in order for the use of future historians. He died in New York on February 14, 1891, aged seventy-one years. He was buried, as he wished, in St. Louis, by the side of his wife and his little son, who had died nearly thirty years before. Inconspicuous among the many generals who went to New York to do honor to the dead leader was a quiet old gentleman in civilian dress— Sherman's ablest antagonist in war, Joseph E. Johnston, and by the side of the grave at St. Louis was one of his old Louisiana colleagues, proud of his unique experience, " a professor under Sherman and a soldier under ' Stonewall ' Jackson."

IV

JACKSON

THOMAS J. JACKSON IN THE FORTIES

A PORTRAIT TAKEN DURING THE MEXICAN WAR,
WHERE JACKSON SERVED AS A SECOND
LIEUTENANT, THE YEAR AFTER HIS
GRADUATION FROM WEST POINT

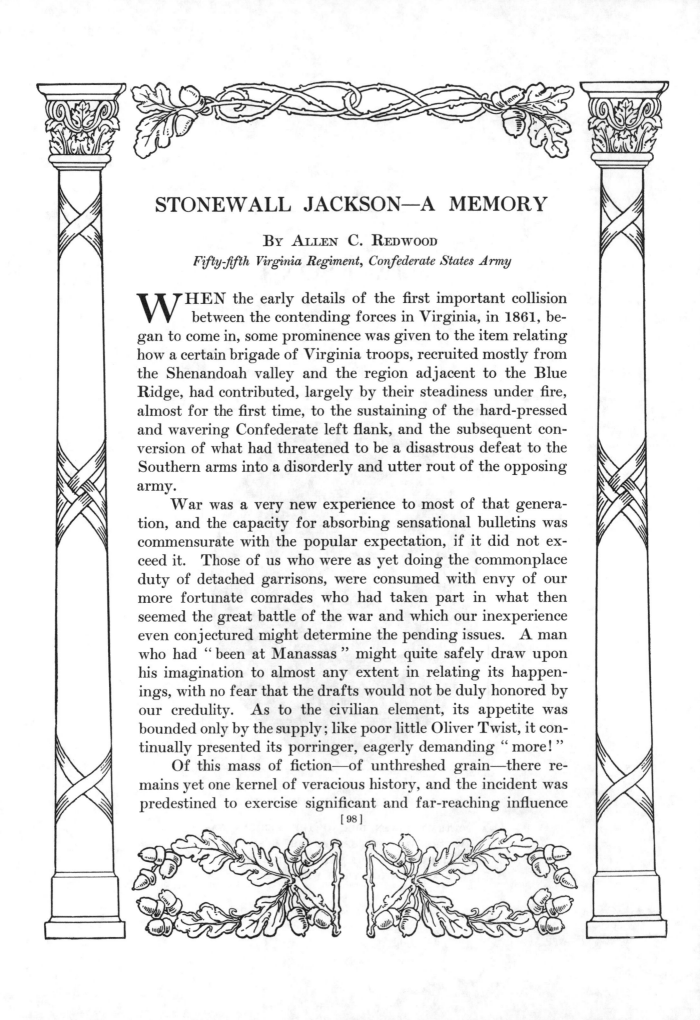

STONEWALL JACKSON—A MEMORY

By Allen C. Redwood

Fifty-fifth Virginia Regiment, Confederate States Army

WHEN the early details of the first important collision between the contending forces in Virginia, in 1861, began to come in, some prominence was given to the item relating how a certain brigade of Virginia troops, recruited mostly from the Shenandoah valley and the region adjacent to the Blue Ridge, had contributed, largely by their steadiness under fire, almost for the first time, to the sustaining of the hard-pressed and wavering Confederate left flank, and the subsequent conversion of what had threatened to be a disastrous defeat to the Southern arms into a disorderly and utter rout of the opposing army.

War was a very new experience to most of that generation, and the capacity for absorbing sensational bulletins was commensurate with the popular expectation, if it did not exceed it. Those of us who were as yet doing the commonplace duty of detached garrisons, were consumed with envy of our more fortunate comrades who had taken part in what then seemed the great battle of the war and which our inexperience even conjectured might determine the pending issues. A man who had "been at Manassas" might quite safely draw upon his imagination to almost any extent in relating its happenings, with no fear that the drafts would not be duly honored by our credulity. As to the civilian element, its appetite was bounded only by the supply; like poor little Oliver Twist, it continually presented its porringer, eagerly demanding "more!"

Of this mass of fiction—of unthreshed grain—there remains yet one kernel of veracious history, and the incident was predestined to exercise significant and far-reaching influence

THOMAS JONATHAN JACKSON

AS FIRST LIEUTENANT, U. S. A.

Jackson's very soul impressed itself on the glass of this early negative through his striking features—more clearly read than later, when a heavy beard had covered the resolute lips, and the habit of command had veiled the deep-seeing, somber eyes. When the quiet Virginia boy with the strong religious bent graduated eighteenth in his class of seventy from West Point in 1846, his comrades little thought that he was destined to become the most suddenly famous of American generals. The year after his graduation he attracted attention by his performances as lieutenant of artillery under General Scott in Mexico, and was brevetted captain and major for bravery at Contreras, Churubusco, and Chapultepec. Fourteen years later he earned his sobriquet of "Stonewall" in the first great battle of the Civil War. Within two years more he had risen to international fame—and received his mortal wound on the field of battle. He was reserved, almost somber with his men, yet he earned the love and enthusiastic devotion of the soldiers who came to be known as "Jackson's foot cavalry," so unparalleled were the marches they made under his leadership. They came to trust his judgment as infallible, and in spite of overwhelming odds they followed no matter where he led.

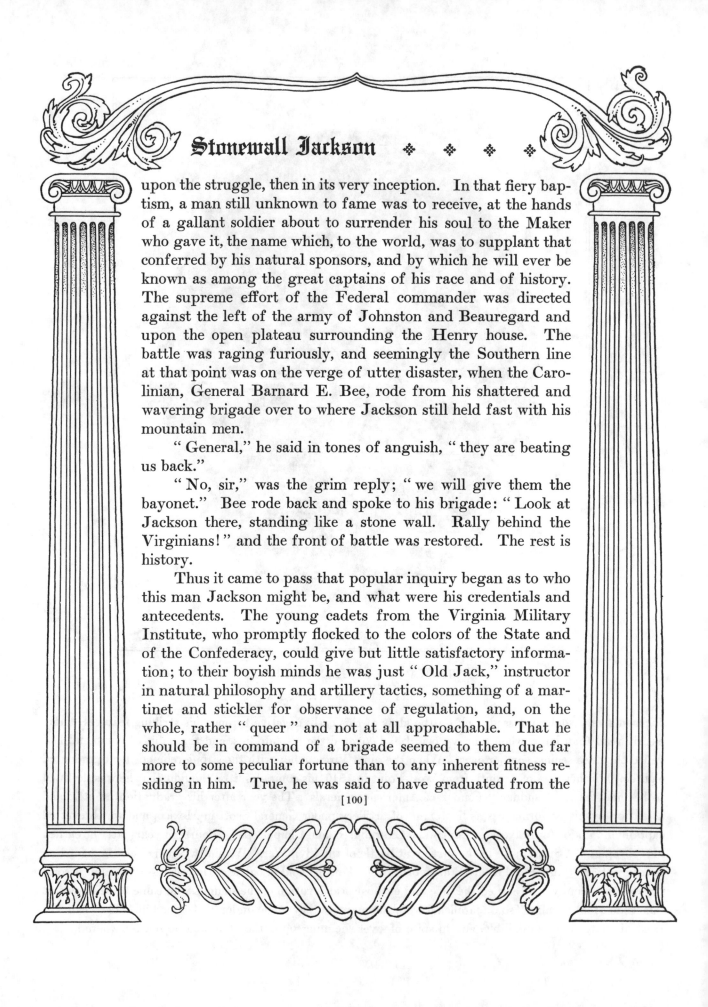

upon the struggle, then in its very inception. In that fiery baptism, a man still unknown to fame was to receive, at the hands of a gallant soldier about to surrender his soul to the Maker who gave it, the name which, to the world, was to supplant that conferred by his natural sponsors, and by which he will ever be known as among the great captains of his race and of history. The supreme effort of the Federal commander was directed against the left of the army of Johnston and Beauregard and upon the open plateau surrounding the Henry house. The battle was raging furiously, and seemingly the Southern line at that point was on the verge of utter disaster, when the Carolinian, General Barnard E. Bee, rode from his shattered and wavering brigade over to where Jackson still held fast with his mountain men.

"General," he said in tones of anguish, "they are beating us back."

"No, sir," was the grim reply; "we will give them the bayonet." Bee rode back and spoke to his brigade: "Look at Jackson there, standing like a stone wall. Rally behind the Virginians!" and the front of battle was restored. The rest is history.

Thus it came to pass that popular inquiry began as to who this man Jackson might be, and what were his credentials and antecedents. The young cadets from the Virginia Military Institute, who promptly flocked to the colors of the State and of the Confederacy, could give but little satisfactory information; to their boyish minds he was just "Old Jack," instructor in natural philosophy and artillery tactics, something of a martinet and stickler for observance of regulation, and, on the whole, rather "queer" and not at all approachable. That he should be in command of a brigade seemed to them due far more to some peculiar fortune than to any inherent fitness residing in him. True, he was said to have graduated from the

JACKSON—HIS MOST REVEALING PHOTOGRAPH

A PICTURE SECURED ONLY BY THE URGING
OF GENERAL BRADLEY T. JOHNSON

Jackson, a modest hero, nearly always shrank from being photographed. At the height of his fame he answered a publisher's letter with a refusal to write the desired magazine article or to send any picture of himself, though the offer was a very flattering one. The photograph above was made in Winchester, in February, 1862, at the Rontzohn gallery, where Jackson had been persuaded to spend a few minutes by the earnest entreaties of General Bradley T. Johnson. Some five months later Jackson was to send Banks whirling down the Shenandoah Valley, to the friendly shelter of the Potomac and Harper's Ferry, keep three armies busy in pursuit of him, and finally turn upon them and defeat two of them. This, with the profile portrait taken near Fredericksburg, shown on page 115 of Volume II, represents the only two sittings of Jackson during the war. Captain Frank P. Clark, who served three years in close association with the general, considered this the best likeness.

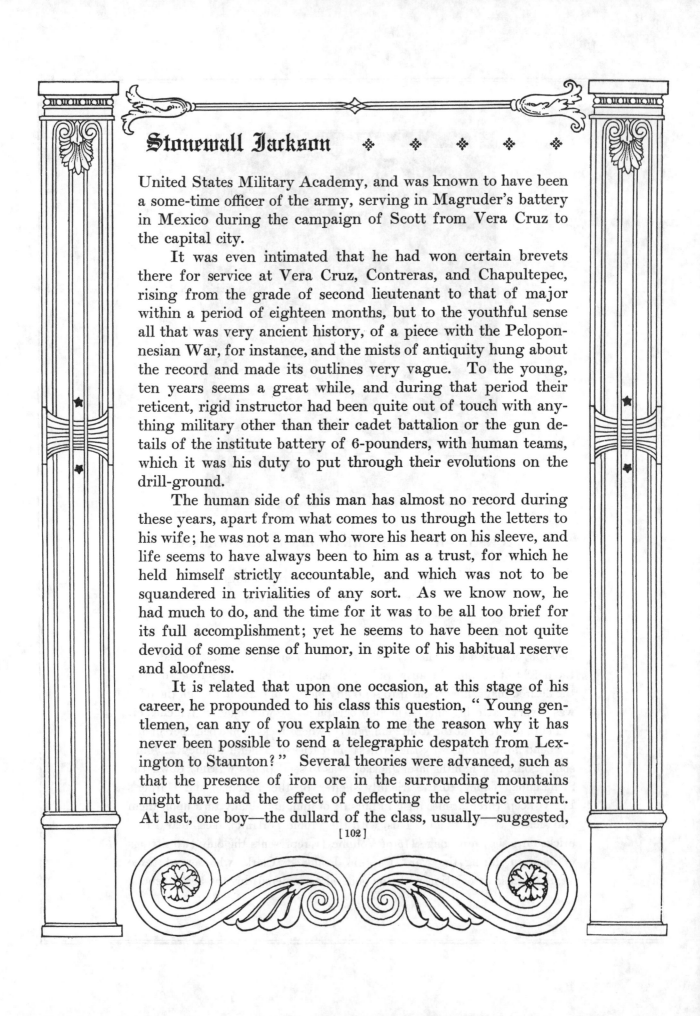

United States Military Academy, and was known to have been a some-time officer of the army, serving in Magruder's battery in Mexico during the campaign of Scott from Vera Cruz to the capital city.

It was even intimated that he had won certain brevets there for service at Vera Cruz, Contreras, and Chapultepec, rising from the grade of second lieutenant to that of major within a period of eighteen months, but to the youthful sense all that was very ancient history, of a piece with the Peloponnesian War, for instance, and the mists of antiquity hung about the record and made its outlines very vague. To the young, ten years seems a great while, and during that period their reticent, rigid instructor had been quite out of touch with anything military other than their cadet battalion or the gun details of the institute battery of 6-pounders, with human teams, which it was his duty to put through their evolutions on the drill-ground.

The human side of this man has almost no record during these years, apart from what comes to us through the letters to his wife; he was not a man who wore his heart on his sleeve, and life seems to have always been to him as a trust, for which he held himself strictly accountable, and which was not to be squandered in trivialities of any sort. As we know now, he had much to do, and the time for it was to be all too brief for its full accomplishment; yet he seems to have been not quite devoid of some sense of humor, in spite of his habitual reserve and aloofness.

It is related that upon one occasion, at this stage of his career, he propounded to his class this question, " Young gentlemen, can any of you explain to me the reason why it has never been possible to send a telegraphic despatch from Lexington to Staunton? " Several theories were advanced, such as that the presence of iron ore in the surrounding mountains might have had the effect of deflecting the electric current. At last, one boy—the dullard of the class, usually—suggested,

"STONEWALL" AND THE MEN WHO BORE HIS ORDERS

Their honors came not easily to Jackson's staff officers.   Tireless himself, regardless of all personal comforts, he seemed to consider others endowed with like qualities.   After a day of marching and fighting it was no unusual thing for him to send a staff member on a thirty or forty mile ride.   He was on terms of easy friendship and confidence with his aides off duty, but his orders were explicit and irrevocable.   He had no confidants as to his military designs—quite the opposite: Before starting on his march to Harper's Ferry he called for a map of the Pennsylvania frontier, and made many inquiries as to roads and localities to the north of Frederick, whereas his route lay in the opposite direction.   His staff, like his soldiers, first feared his apparent rashness, and then adored him for his success.

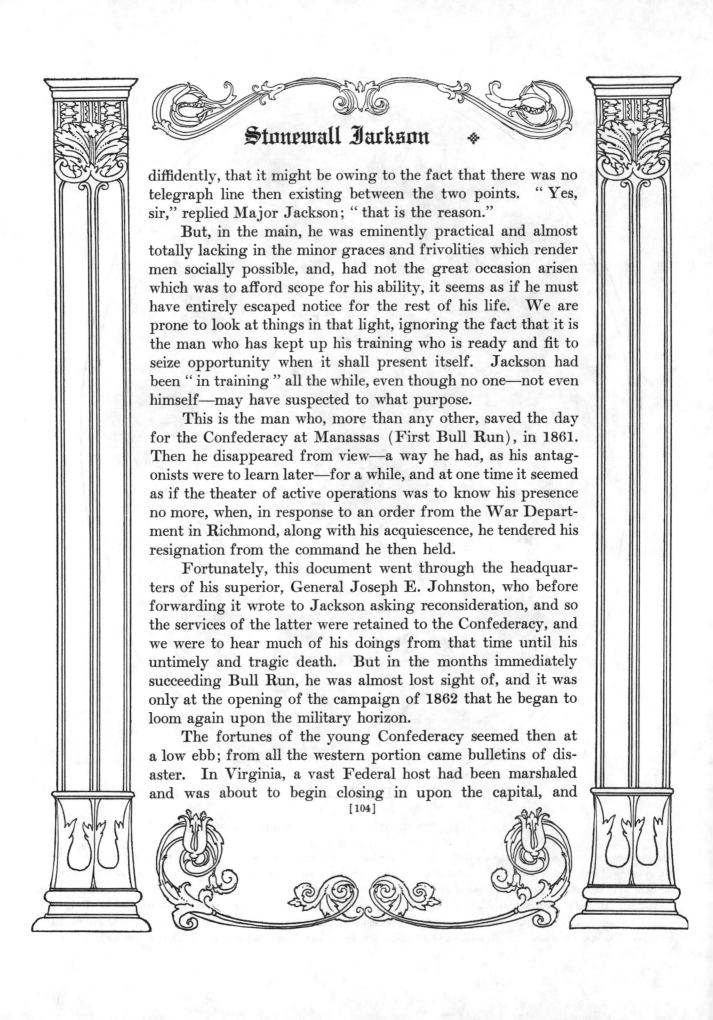

diffidently, that it might be owing to the fact that there was no telegraph line then existing between the two points. " Yes, sir," replied Major Jackson; " that is the reason."

But, in the main, he was eminently practical and almost totally lacking in the minor graces and frivolities which render men socially possible, and, had not the great occasion arisen which was to afford scope for his ability, it seems as if he must have entirely escaped notice for the rest of his life. We are prone to look at things in that light, ignoring the fact that it is the man who has kept up his training who is ready and fit to seize opportunity when it shall present itself. Jackson had been " in training " all the while, even though no one—not even himself—may have suspected to what purpose.

This is the man who, more than any other, saved the day for the Confederacy at Manassas (First Bull Run), in 1861. Then he disappeared from view—a way he had, as his antagonists were to learn later—for a while, and at one time it seemed as if the theater of active operations was to know his presence no more, when, in response to an order from the War Department in Richmond, along with his acquiescence, he tendered his resignation from the command he then held.

Fortunately, this document went through the headquarters of his superior, General Joseph E. Johnston, who before forwarding it wrote to Jackson asking reconsideration, and so the services of the latter were retained to the Confederacy, and we were to hear much of his doings from that time until his untimely and tragic death. But in the months immediately succeeding Bull Run, he was almost lost sight of, and it was only at the opening of the campaign of 1862 that he began to loom again upon the military horizon.

The fortunes of the young Confederacy seemed then at a low ebb; from all the western portion came bulletins of disaster. In Virginia, a vast Federal host had been marshaled and was about to begin closing in upon the capital, and

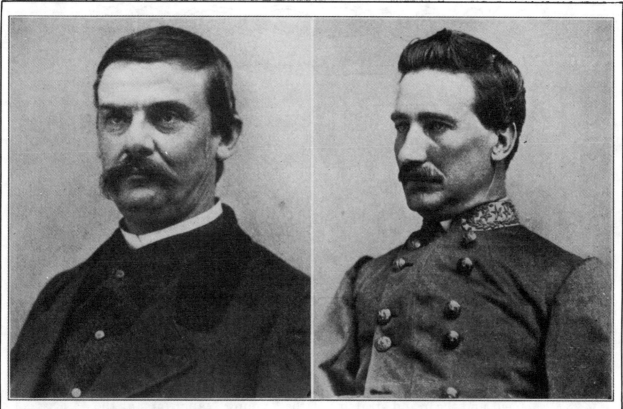

John Echols, Colonel of a "Stonewall" Regiment at Bull
Run; Later Led a Brigade in Lee's Army.

J. D. Imboden, at Bull Run and always with Jackson;
Later Commanded a Cavalry Brigade.

W. B. Taliaferro, with Jackson
throughout 1862; Last, at
Fredericksburg.

Arnold Elzey, a Brigade and
Division Commander under
Jackson and later.

**CONFEDERATE
GENERALS
WITH JACKSON**

**AT THE DAWN
OF HIS
BRILLIANT CAREER**

Isaac R. Trimble.   Where "Stonewall" was,
There was Trimble also.

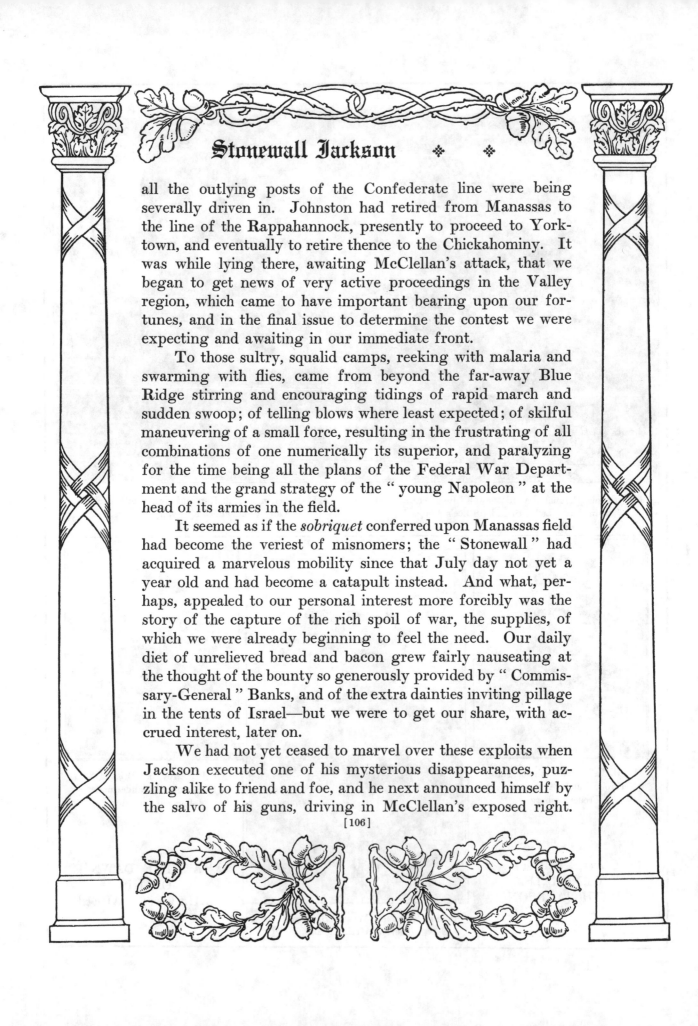

all the outlying posts of the Confederate line were being severally driven in. Johnston had retired from Manassas to the line of the Rappahannock, presently to proceed to York-town, and eventually to retire thence to the Chickahominy. It was while lying there, awaiting McClellan's attack, that we began to get news of very active proceedings in the Valley region, which came to have important bearing upon our for-tunes, and in the final issue to determine the contest we were expecting and awaiting in our immediate front.

To those sultry, squalid camps, reeking with malaria and swarming with flies, came from beyond the far-away Blue Ridge stirring and encouraging tidings of rapid march and sudden swoop; of telling blows where least expected; of skilful maneuvering of a small force, resulting in the frustrating of all combinations of one numerically its superior, and paralyzing for the time being all the plans of the Federal War Depart-ment and the grand strategy of the " young Napoleon " at the head of its armies in the field.

It seemed as if the *sobriquet* conferred upon Manassas field had become the veriest of misnomers; the " Stonewall " had acquired a marvelous mobility since that July day not yet a year old and had become a catapult instead. And what, per-haps, appealed to our personal interest more forcibly was the story of the capture of the rich spoil of war, the supplies, of which we were already beginning to feel the need. Our daily diet of unrelieved bread and bacon grew fairly nauseating at the thought of the bounty so generously provided by " Commis-sary-General " Banks, and of the extra dainties inviting pillage in the tents of Israel—but we were to get our share, with ac-crued interest, later on.

We had not yet ceased to marvel over these exploits when Jackson executed one of his mysterious disappearances, puz-zling alike to friend and foe, and he next announced himself by the salvo of his guns, driving in McClellan's exposed right.

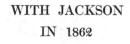

Edward Johnson Led an Independent Command under
Jackson in 1862.

George H. Steuart, Later
a Brigade Commander
in Lee's Army.

James A. Walker Led a
Brigade under Jack-
son at Antietam.

E. M. Law, Conspicuous at South Mountain
and Maryland Heights.

Charles W. Field, Later in Command of
one of Longstreet's Divisions.

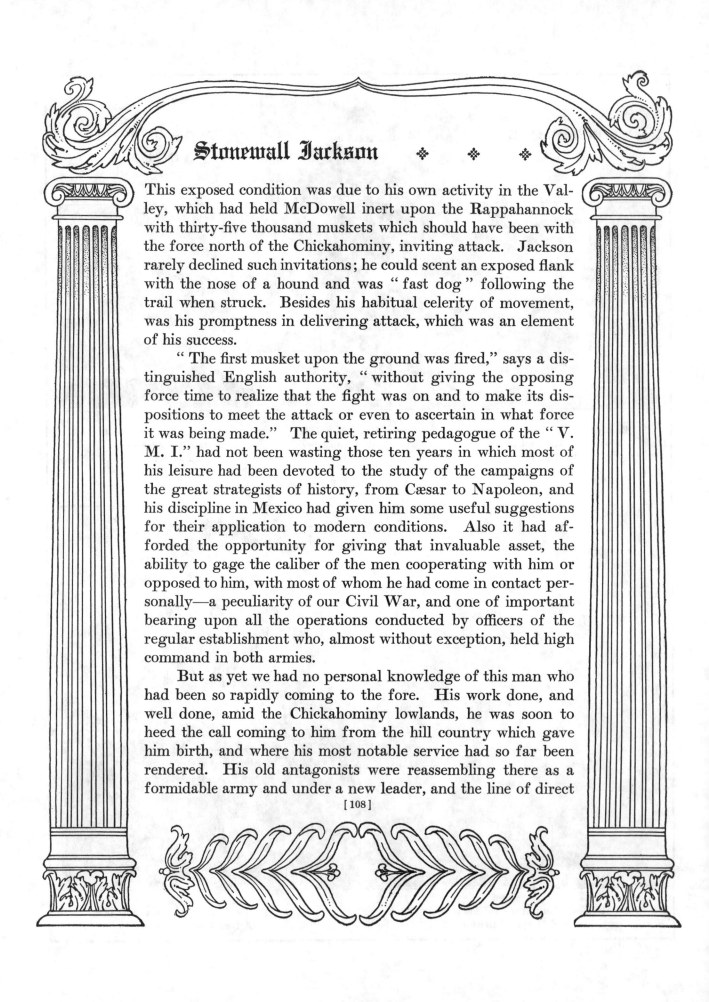

This exposed condition was due to his own activity in the Valley, which had held McDowell inert upon the Rappahannock with thirty-five thousand muskets which should have been with the force north of the Chickahominy, inviting attack. Jackson rarely declined such invitations; he could scent an exposed flank with the nose of a hound and was "fast dog" following the trail when struck. Besides his habitual celerity of movement, was his promptness in delivering attack, which was an element of his success.

"The first musket upon the ground was fired," says a distinguished English authority, "without giving the opposing force time to realize that the fight was on and to make its dispositions to meet the attack or even to ascertain in what force it was being made." The quiet, retiring pedagogue of the "V. M. I." had not been wasting those ten years in which most of his leisure had been devoted to the study of the campaigns of the great strategists of history, from Cæsar to Napoleon, and his discipline in Mexico had given him some useful suggestions for their application to modern conditions. Also it had afforded the opportunity for giving that invaluable asset, the ability to gage the caliber of the men cooperating with him or opposed to him, with most of whom he had come in contact personally—a peculiarity of our Civil War, and one of important bearing upon all the operations conducted by officers of the regular establishment who, almost without exception, held high command in both armies.

But as yet we had no personal knowledge of this man who had been so rapidly coming to the fore. His work done, and well done, amid the Chickahominy lowlands, he was soon to heed the call coming to him from the hill country which gave him birth, and where his most notable service had so far been rendered. His old antagonists were reassembling there as a formidable army and under a new leader, and the line of direct

A. R. Lawton Led
Ewell's Old Di-
vision at the
Battle of
Antie-
tam.

Roswell S. Ripley,
Wounded at
Antietam in
Defense of
Lee's Left
Flank.

R. E. Colston Commanded Trimble's
Division at Chancellorsville.

Henry Heth Commanded the Light
Division at Chancellorsville.

CONFEDERATE

GENERALS

WITH

JACKSON

Jas. J. Archer Commanded a Brigade
at Chancellorsville.

AT ANTIETAM

AND

CHANCELLORS–

VILLE

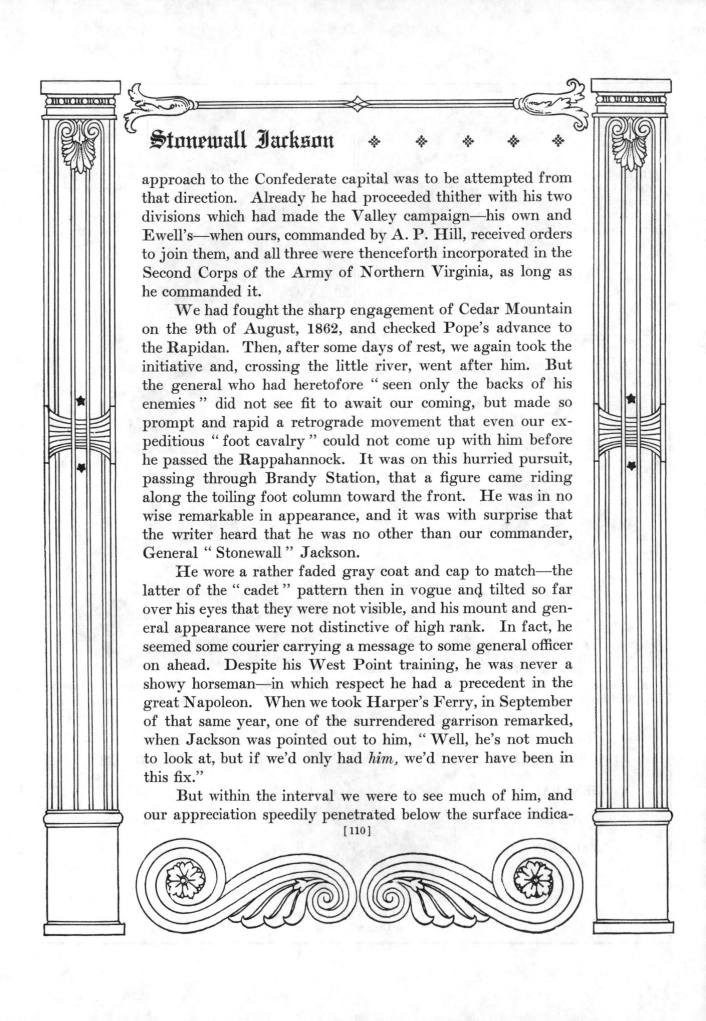

approach to the Confederate capital was to be attempted from that direction. Already he had proceeded thither with his two divisions which had made the Valley campaign—his own and Ewell's—when ours, commanded by A. P. Hill, received orders to join them, and all three were thenceforth incorporated in the Second Corps of the Army of Northern Virginia, as long as he commanded it.

We had fought the sharp engagement of Cedar Mountain on the 9th of August, 1862, and checked Pope's advance to the Rapidan. Then, after some days of rest, we again took the initiative and, crossing the little river, went after him. But the general who had heretofore " seen only the backs of his enemies " did not see fit to await our coming, but made so prompt and rapid a retrograde movement that even our expeditious " foot cavalry " could not come up with him before he passed the Rappahannock. It was on this hurried pursuit, passing through Brandy Station, that a figure came riding along the toiling foot column toward the front. He was in no wise remarkable in appearance, and it was with surprise that the writer heard that he was no other than our commander, General " Stonewall " Jackson.

He wore a rather faded gray coat and cap to match—the latter of the " cadet " pattern then in vogue and tilted so far over his eyes that they were not visible, and his mount and general appearance were not distinctive of high rank. In fact, he seemed some courier carrying a message to some general officer on ahead. Despite his West Point training, he was never a showy horseman—in which respect he had a precedent in the great Napoleon. When we took Harper's Ferry, in September of that same year, one of the surrendered garrison remarked, when Jackson was pointed out to him, " Well, he's not much to look at, but if we'd only had *him,* we'd never have been in this fix."

But within the interval we were to see much of him, and our appreciation speedily penetrated below the surface indica-

B. D. Fry, Colonel of the 13th Alabama ; Later led a Brigade in Pickett's Charge.

F. T. Nichols, Wounded in the Flank Attack on Howard's Corps, May 2, 1863.

Harry T. Hays, Later Charged the Batteries at Gettysburg.

Robert F. Hoke, Later Defender of Petersburg, Richmond and Wilmington.

William Smith, Colonel of the 49th Virginia; Later at Gettysburg.

CONFEDERATE

GENERALS

WITH

JACKSON

J. R. Jones Commanded a Brigade of Virginians in Trimble's Division.

F. L. Thomas Commanded a Brigade in A. P. Hill's Division.

AT THE

LAST—

CHANCEL-

LORSVILLE

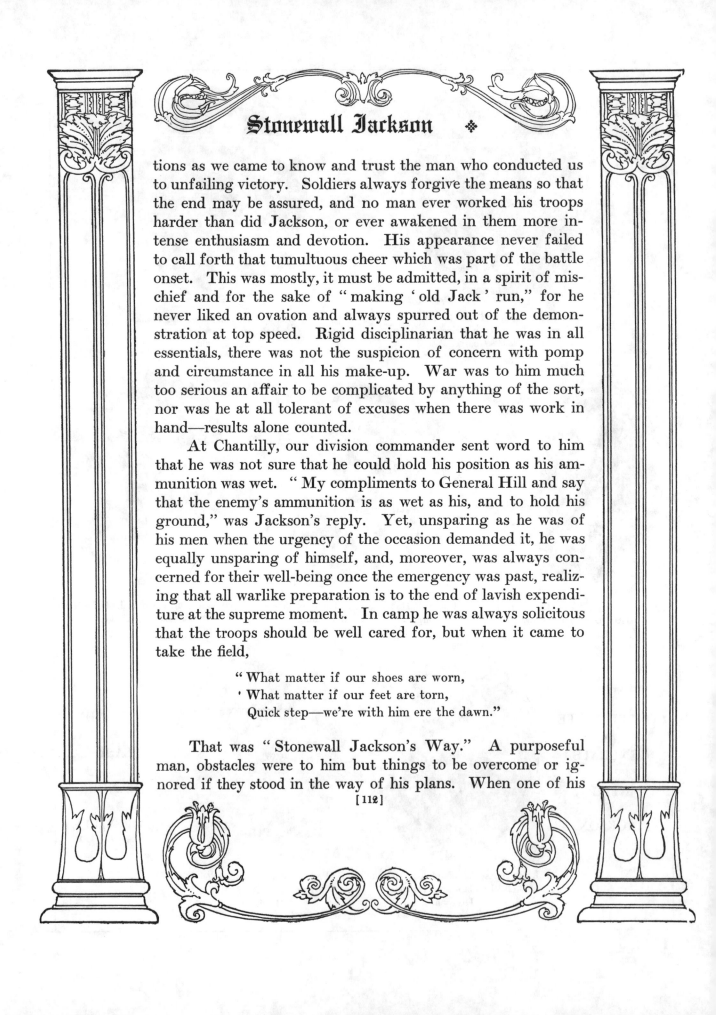

tions as we came to know and trust the man who conducted us to unfailing victory. Soldiers always forgive the means so that the end may be assured, and no man ever worked his troops harder than did Jackson, or ever awakened in them more intense enthusiasm and devotion. His appearance never failed to call forth that tumultuous cheer which was part of the battle onset. This was mostly, it must be admitted, in a spirit of mischief and for the sake of "making 'old Jack' run," for he never liked an ovation and always spurred out of the demonstration at top speed. Rigid disciplinarian that he was in all essentials, there was not the suspicion of concern with pomp and circumstance in all his make-up. War was to him much too serious an affair to be complicated by anything of the sort, nor was he at all tolerant of excuses when there was work in hand—results alone counted.

At Chantilly, our division commander sent word to him that he was not sure that he could hold his position as his ammunition was wet. "My compliments to General Hill and say that the enemy's ammunition is as wet as his, and to hold his ground," was Jackson's reply. Yet, unsparing as he was of his men when the urgency of the occasion demanded it, he was equally unsparing of himself, and, moreover, was always concerned for their well-being once the emergency was past, realizing that all warlike preparation is to the end of lavish expenditure at the supreme moment. In camp he was always solicitous that the troops should be well cared for, but when it came to take the field,

> "What matter if our shoes are worn,
> ' What matter if our feet are torn,
>   Quick step—we're with him ere the dawn."

That was "Stonewall Jackson's Way." A purposeful man, obstacles were to him but things to be overcome or ignored if they stood in the way of his plans. When one of his

A. H. Colquitt, Later Conspicuous in the Defense of Petersburg.

R. L. Walker, Commander of a Light Artillery Brigade.

CONFEDERATE
GENERALS
WITH
JACKSON

IN HIS
MASTERLY
1863
CAMPAIGN

S. McGowan, Later Commanded the South Carolina Brigade which Immortalized His Name.

Alfred Iverson, Later at Gettysburg and with Hood at Atlanta.

E. A. O'Neal Charged with His Brigade in Rodes' First Line at Chancellorsville.

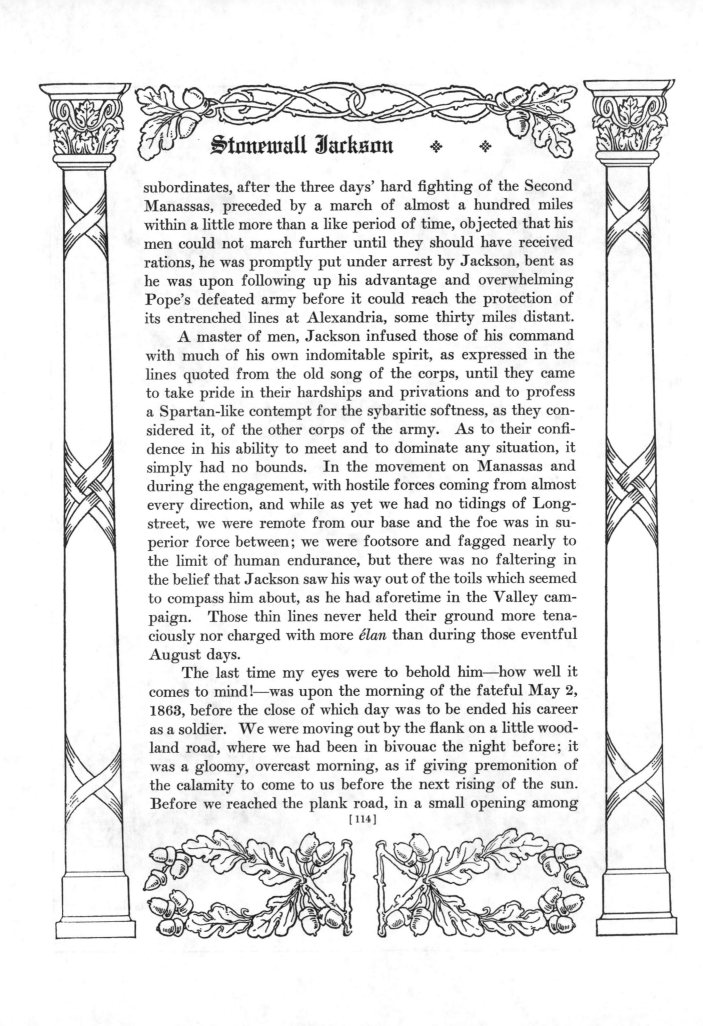

subordinates, after the three days' hard fighting of the Second Manassas, preceded by a march of almost a hundred miles within a little more than a like period of time, objected that his men could not march further until they should have received rations, he was promptly put under arrest by Jackson, bent as he was upon following up his advantage and overwhelming Pope's defeated army before it could reach the protection of its entrenched lines at Alexandria, some thirty miles distant.

A master of men, Jackson infused those of his command with much of his own indomitable spirit, as expressed in the lines quoted from the old song of the corps, until they came to take pride in their hardships and privations and to profess a Spartan-like contempt for the sybaritic softness, as they considered it, of the other corps of the army. As to their confidence in his ability to meet and to dominate any situation, it simply had no bounds. In the movement on Manassas and during the engagement, with hostile forces coming from almost every direction, and while as yet we had no tidings of Longstreet, we were remote from our base and the foe was in superior force between; we were footsore and fagged nearly to the limit of human endurance, but there was no faltering in the belief that Jackson saw his way out of the toils which seemed to compass him about, as he had aforetime in the Valley campaign. Those thin lines never held their ground more tenaciously nor charged with more *élan* than during those eventful August days.

The last time my eyes were to behold him—how well it comes to mind!—was upon the morning of the fateful May 2, 1863, before the close of which day was to be ended his career as a soldier. We were moving out by the flank on a little woodland road, where we had been in bivouac the night before; it was a gloomy, overcast morning, as if giving premonition of the calamity to come to us before the next rising of the sun. Before we reached the plank road, in a small opening among

CONFEDERATE
GENERALS OF
LONGSTREET'S
CORPS

WHO COÖPERAT-
ED WITH JACK-
SON IN
'62 AND '63

Lafayette McLaws With His Division Supported Jackson's
Attacks at Harper's Ferry and Chancellorsville;
Later Conspicuous at Gettysburg and
Chickamauga.

Joseph Brevard Kershaw Captured Maryland Heights, Opposite Jackson's Position at Harper's Ferry.

James L. Kemper Commanded a Brigade
on Jackson's Right at the Second
Battle of Manassas.

Ambrose R. Wright With His Brigade
Closed the Pass Along the Canal
at Harper's Ferry.

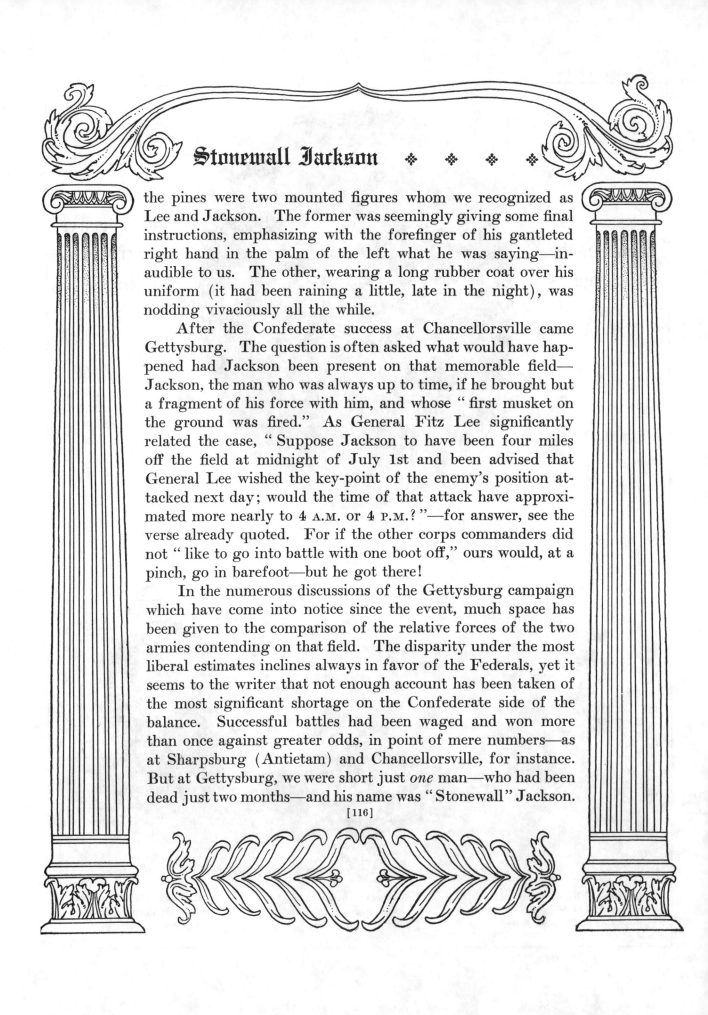

the pines were two mounted figures whom we recognized as Lee and Jackson. The former was seemingly giving some final instructions, emphasizing with the forefinger of his gantleted right hand in the palm of the left what he was saying—inaudible to us. The other, wearing a long rubber coat over his uniform (it had been raining a little, late in the night), was nodding vivaciously all the while.

After the Confederate success at Chancellorsville came Gettysburg. The question is often asked what would have happened had Jackson been present on that memorable field—Jackson, the man who was always up to time, if he brought but a fragment of his force with him, and whose " first musket on the ground was fired." As General Fitz Lee significantly related the case, " Suppose Jackson to have been four miles off the field at midnight of July 1st and been advised that General Lee wished the key-point of the enemy's position attacked next day; would the time of that attack have approximated more nearly to 4 A.M. or 4 P.M.? "—for answer, see the verse already quoted. For if the other corps commanders did not " like to go into battle with one boot off," ours would, at a pinch, go in barefoot—but he got there!

In the numerous discussions of the Gettysburg campaign which have come into notice since the event, much space has been given to the comparison of the relative forces of the two armies contending on that field. The disparity under the most liberal estimates inclines always in favor of the Federals, yet it seems to the writer that not enough account has been taken of the most significant shortage on the Confederate side of the balance. Successful battles had been waged and won more than once against greater odds, in point of mere numbers—as at Sharpsburg (Antietam) and Chancellorsville, for instance. But at Gettysburg, we were short just *one* man—who had been dead just two months—and his name was "Stonewall" Jackson.

V

THE MEANING OF
LOSSES
IN WARFARE

MEN OF THE FAMOUS "VERMONT BRIGADE," ALL FROM THE ONE
STATE, WHICH SUFFERED MORE HEAVILY THAN ANY OTHER FEDERAL
BRIGADE DURING THE WAR—WITHIN A WEEK AT THE WILDERNESS
AND SPOTSYLVANIA, IT LOST 1,645 OUT OF 2,100 EFFECTIVE MEN

THE REGIMENT THAT SUSTAINED THE GREATEST LOSS OF ANY IN THE
UNION ARMY

In the assault on Petersburg, June 18, 1864, these boys from Maine, serving as infantry, sustained the greatest loss of any one regiment in any one action of the war. Before the site where Fort Stedman was subsequently built 635 men were killed and wounded out of nine hundred engaged, a loss of over seventy per cent. in seven minutes. Such slaughter has never been paralleled in any warfare, ancient or modern. Of all the regiments in the Union armies this regiment lost most during the four years. Twenty-three officers and 400 enlisted men were killed and mortally wounded, and two hundred and sixty died of disease. The First Maine Heavy Artillery was organized at Bangor, and mustered in August 21, 1862. It left the State for Washington on August 24th. This section of the tremendous regimental quota—eighteen hundred men—is drilling at Fort Sumner in the winter of 1863. The men little imagine, as they go skilfully through their evo-

THE FIRST MAINE HEAVY ARTILLERY DRILLING IN FORT SUMNER,
ON A WINTER'S DAY OF '63

lutions in the snow, that the hand of death is to fall so ruthlessly on their ranks.   From the defenses of Washington they went to Belle Plain, Virginia, on May 15, 1864, as a part of Tyler's Heavy Artillery Division. Four days later, at Harris's Farm on the Fredericksburg Road, the first of their great disasters fell upon them. In this engagement their killed numbered eighty-two, their wounded 394, and their missing five.   Less than a month later came the awful slaughter at Petersburg.   The remnant of the regiment served until its fall, April 2, 1865.   After taking part in the Grand Review at Washington and remaining in its defenses till September 11th, the organization was mustered out, and ordered to Bangor, Maine.   On September 20, 1865, the survivors of this "fighting regiment" were mustered out.   The Second Wisconsin Infantry lost a greater percentage in killed during its whole term—19.7 per cent. as against 19.2 per cent. in the First Maine.

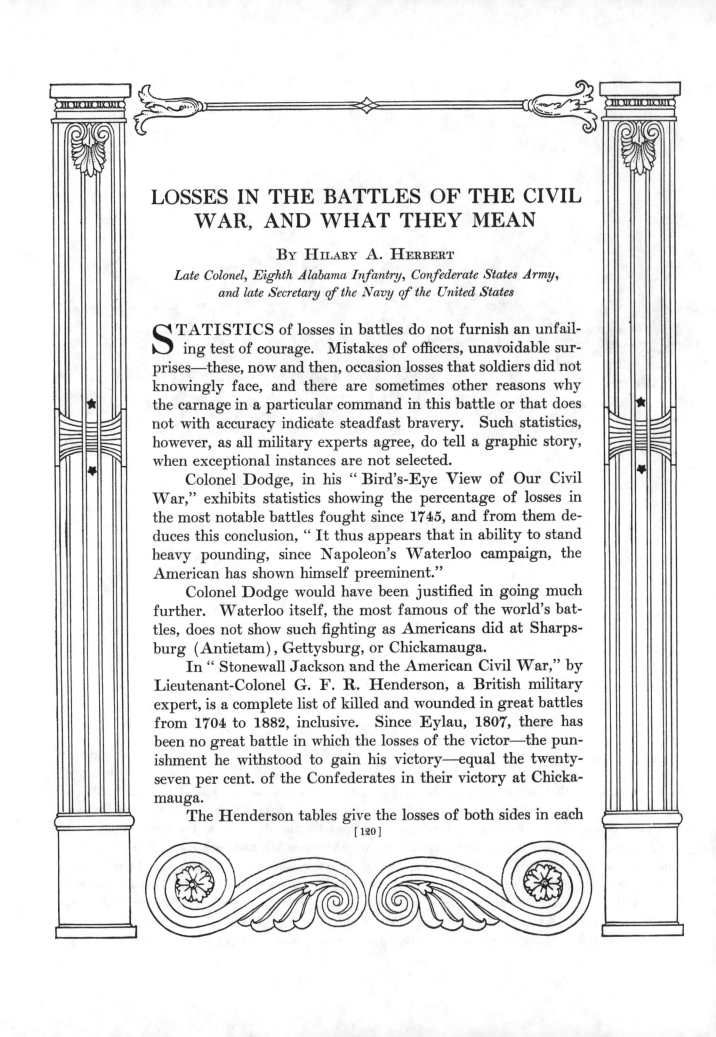

LOSSES IN THE BATTLES OF THE CIVIL WAR, AND WHAT THEY MEAN

By Hilary A. Herbert
*Late Colonel, Eighth Alabama Infantry, Confederate States Army,
and late Secretary of the Navy of the United States*

STATISTICS of losses in battles do not furnish an unfailing test of courage. Mistakes of officers, unavoidable surprises—these, now and then, occasion losses that soldiers did not knowingly face, and there are sometimes other reasons why the carnage in a particular command in this battle or that does not with accuracy indicate steadfast bravery. Such statistics, however, as all military experts agree, do tell a graphic story, when exceptional instances are not selected.

Colonel Dodge, in his " Bird's-Eye View of Our Civil War," exhibits statistics showing the percentage of losses in the most notable battles fought since 1745, and from them deduces this conclusion, " It thus appears that in ability to stand heavy pounding, since Napoleon's Waterloo campaign, the American has shown himself preeminent."

Colonel Dodge would have been justified in going much further. Waterloo itself, the most famous of the world's battles, does not show such fighting as Americans did at Sharpsburg (Antietam), Gettysburg, or Chickamauga.

In " Stonewall Jackson and the American Civil War," by Lieutenant-Colonel G. F. R. Henderson, a British military expert, is a complete list of killed and wounded in great battles from 1704 to 1882, inclusive. Since Eylau, 1807, there has been no great battle in which the losses of the victor—the punishment he withstood to gain his victory—equal the twenty-seven per cent. of the Confederates in their victory at Chickamauga.

The Henderson tables give the losses of both sides in each

MEN OF THE FIFTH GEORGIA

MORE THAN HALF THIS REGIMENT WAS KILLED AND WOUNDED AT THE BATTLE OF CHICKAMAUGA

Lounging beneath the Stars and Bars are eight members of an Augusta, Georgia, company—The "Clinch Rifles." Their new paraphernalia is beautifully marked "C. R." They have a negro servant. In a word, they are inexperienced Confederate volunteers of May, 1861, on the day before their company became a part of the Fifth Georgia Regiment. Pass to November, 1863; imagine six of the soldiers in the group lying dead or groaning with wounds, and but three unhurt,—and you have figured the state of the regiment after it was torn to shreds at the battle of Chickamauga. It was mustered in for twelve months at Macon, Georgia, May 11, 1861, being the last regiment taken for this short term. The Sixth Georgia and those following were mustered in for three years or the war. The Clinch Rifles were sent to garrison Pensacola, Florida, where General Braxton Bragg would occasionally come from his headquarters, eight miles away, to drill them. The ten companies were all from towns, or cities, and nicely uniformed, though each in a different style. This led Bragg to name them his "Pound Cake Regiment." In July and August, 1862, the Fifth marched from Chattanooga, Tennessee, to Bardstown, Kentucky, thence to the eastern part of the State, and down through Cumberland Gap to Knoxville, 800 miles in all. It lost heavily in the battle of Murfreesboro. At bloody Chickamauga, September 19 and 20, 1863, its killed and wounded were more than 54 per cent. of the regiment—surpassed by few organizations in history. It suffered again at Missionary Ridge, and in the spring of 1864, when it stood against Sherman through the Atlanta campaign. The regiment fought on through the campaigns from Savannah, Georgia, up to North Carolina, and in the last combat at Bentonville, North Carolina. It surrendered at Greensboro, April, 26, 1865.

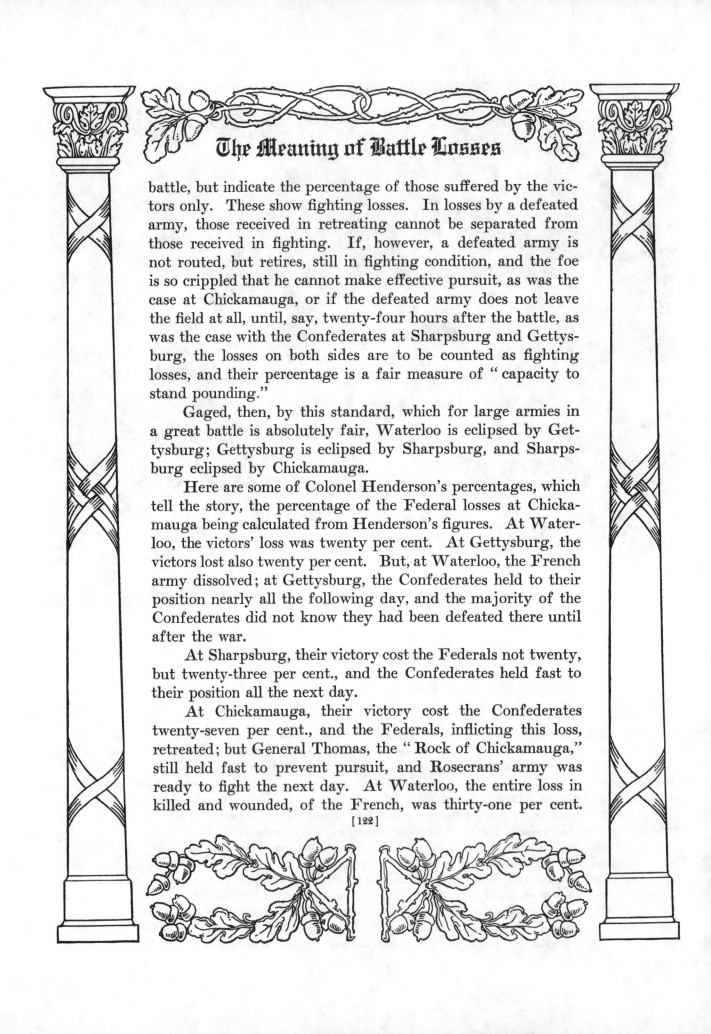

battle, but indicate the percentage of those suffered by the victors only. These show fighting losses. In losses by a defeated army, those received in retreating cannot be separated from those received in fighting. If, however, a defeated army is not routed, but retires, still in fighting condition, and the foe is so crippled that he cannot make effective pursuit, as was the case at Chickamauga, or if the defeated army does not leave the field at all, until, say, twenty-four hours after the battle, as was the case with the Confederates at Sharpsburg and Gettysburg, the losses on both sides are to be counted as fighting losses, and their percentage is a fair measure of " capacity to stand pounding."

Gaged, then, by this standard, which for large armies in a great battle is absolutely fair, Waterloo is eclipsed by Gettysburg; Gettysburg is eclipsed by Sharpsburg, and Sharpsburg eclipsed by Chickamauga.

Here are some of Colonel Henderson's percentages, which tell the story, the percentage of the Federal losses at Chickamauga being calculated from Henderson's figures. At Waterloo, the victors' loss was twenty per cent. At Gettysburg, the victors lost also twenty per cent. But, at Waterloo, the French army dissolved; at Gettysburg, the Confederates held to their position nearly all the following day, and the majority of the Confederates did not know they had been defeated there until after the war.

At Sharpsburg, their victory cost the Federals not twenty, but twenty-three per cent., and the Confederates held fast to their position all the next day.

At Chickamauga, their victory cost the Confederates twenty-seven per cent., and the Federals, inflicting this loss, retreated; but General Thomas, the " Rock of Chickamauga," still held fast to prevent pursuit, and Rosecrans' army was ready to fight the next day. At Waterloo, the entire loss in killed and wounded, of the French, was thirty-one per cent.

OFFICERS OF A WESTERN FIGHTING REGIMENT—THE 36TH ILLINOIS

Of the Illinois regiments the Thirty-sixth fought in every important battle of the entire war in Western territory, and suffered in killed alone a loss of no less than 14.8 per cent., a figure exceeded among Illinois organizations only by the 14.9 per cent. of the Ninety-third. No Federal regiment lost as much as 20 per cent. killed and only 200 out of the 3,559 organizations as much as ten per cent. The Thirty-sixth Illinois lost 204 men out of a total enrollment of 1,376. These figures refer to deaths alone, excluding wounded and missing. At the battle of Stone's River, Tennessee, the regiment lost forty-six killed, 151 wounded, and fifteen missing, a total of 212. This was its heaviest blow in any one battle. It fought at Pea Ridge, an early engagement in the West, at Chaplin Hills, at the bloody battle of Chickamauga, and on the corpse-strewn slopes of Missionary Ridge. It fought under Sherman from Resaca to Atlanta, and when that general marched away on his expedition to the coast, the Thirty-sixth turned back to suffer its fourth largest loss in killed at the battle of Franklin, and to help Thomas crush Hood at the battle of Nashville. Such were the Western fighting regiments.

A REGIMENT
THAT LOST
14.8% IN
KILLED ALONE

ILLINOIS
INFANTRY
IN THE
WEST

OFFICERS OF THE 36TH ILLINOIS

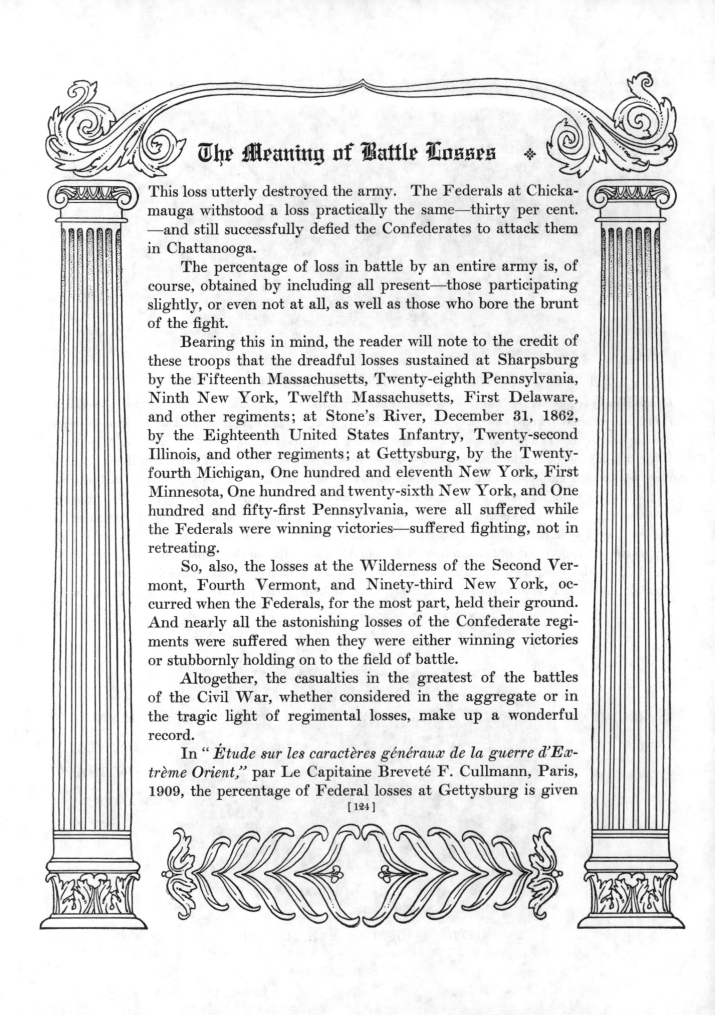

This loss utterly destroyed the army. The Federals at Chicka-mauga withstood a loss practically the same—thirty per cent.—and still successfully defied the Confederates to attack them in Chattanooga.

The percentage of loss in battle by an entire army is, of course, obtained by including all present—those participating slightly, or even not at all, as well as those who bore the brunt of the fight.

Bearing this in mind, the reader will note to the credit of these troops that the dreadful losses sustained at Sharpsburg by the Fifteenth Massachusetts, Twenty-eighth Pennsylvania, Ninth New York, Twelfth Massachusetts, First Delaware, and other regiments; at Stone's River, December 31, 1862, by the Eighteenth United States Infantry, Twenty-second Illinois, and other regiments; at Gettysburg, by the Twenty-fourth Michigan, One hundred and eleventh New York, First Minnesota, One hundred and twenty-sixth New York, and One hundred and fifty-first Pennsylvania, were all suffered while the Federals were winning victories—suffered fighting, not in retreating.

So, also, the losses at the Wilderness of the Second Vermont, Fourth Vermont, and Ninety-third New York, oc-curred when the Federals, for the most part, held their ground. And nearly all the astonishing losses of the Confederate regiments were suffered when they were either winning victories or stubbornly holding on to the field of battle.

Altogether, the casualties in the greatest of the battles of the Civil War, whether considered in the aggregate or in the tragic light of regimental losses, make up a wonderful record.

In "*Étude sur les caractères généraux de la guerre d'Extrème Orient,*" par Le Capitaine Breveté F. Cullmann, Paris, 1909, the percentage of Federal losses at Gettysburg is given

COMMANDERS OF UNION BRIGADES CONSPICUOUS FOR LOSSES

These brigades from the Armies of the Potomac, the Cumberland, and the Tennessee, are mentioned specifically by Colonel William F. Fox, on account of their notable losses in action.

Iron Brigade
SOLOMON MEREDITH
Originally Colonel of the 19th Indiana.

Michigan Cavalry Brigade
PETER STAGG
Originally Colonel of the 1st Michigan Cavalry.

Harker's Brigade
LUTHER P. BRADLEY
Originally Colonel of the 51st Illinois.

Vermont Brigade
LEWIS A. GRANT
Originally Colonel of the 5th Vermont.

First New Jersey Brigade
WILLIAM H. PENROSE
Originally Colonel of the 15th New Jersey.

Iowa Brigade
WILLIAM W. BELKNAP
Originally Colonel of the 15th Iowa.

Willich's Brigade
AUGUST WILLICH
Originally Colonel of the 32d Indiana.

Opdycke's Brigade
EMERSON OPDYCKE
Originally Colonel of the 125th Ohio.

Excelsior Brigade
JOSEPH B. CARR
Originally Colonel of the 2d New York.

Philadelphia Brigade
DE WITT CLINTON BAXTER
Originally Colonel of the 72d Pennsylvania.

Irish Brigade
THOMAS FRANCIS MEAGHER
Commanded the Brigade in 1862.

Steedman's Brigade
JAMES B. STEEDMAN
Originally Colonel of the 14th Ohio.

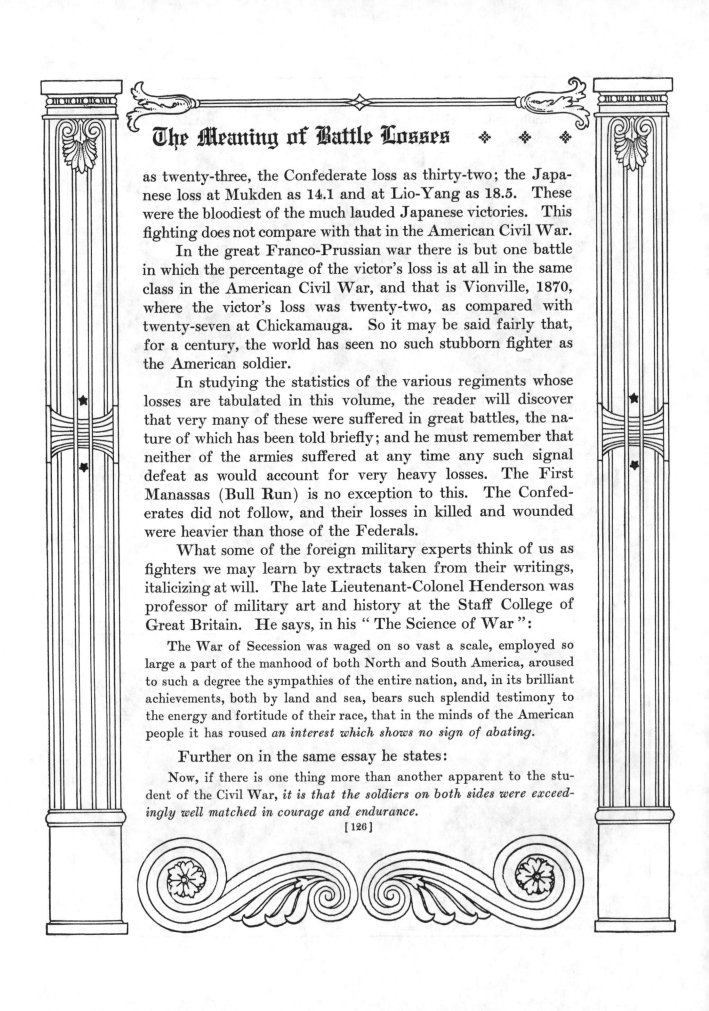

as twenty-three, the Confederate loss as thirty-two; the Japanese loss at Mukden as 14.1 and at Lio-Yang as 18.5. These were the bloodiest of the much lauded Japanese victories. This fighting does not compare with that in the American Civil War.

In the great Franco-Prussian war there is but one battle in which the percentage of the victor's loss is at all in the same class in the American Civil War, and that is Vionville, 1870, where the victor's loss was twenty-two, as compared with twenty-seven at Chickamauga. So it may be said fairly that, for a century, the world has seen no such stubborn fighter as the American soldier.

In studying the statistics of the various regiments whose losses are tabulated in this volume, the reader will discover that very many of these were suffered in great battles, the nature of which has been told briefly; and he must remember that neither of the armies suffered at any time any such signal defeat as would account for very heavy losses. The First Manassas (Bull Run) is no exception to this. The Confederates did not follow, and their losses in killed and wounded were heavier than those of the Federals.

What some of the foreign military experts think of us as fighters we may learn by extracts taken from their writings, italicizing at will. The late Lieutenant-Colonel Henderson was professor of military art and history at the Staff College of Great Britain. He says, in his " The Science of War ":

The War of Secession was waged on so vast a scale, employed so large a part of the manhood of both North and South America, aroused to such a degree the sympathies of the entire nation, and, in its brilliant achievements, both by land and sea, bears such splendid testimony to the energy and fortitude of their race, that in the minds of the American people it has roused *an interest which shows no sign of abating.*

Further on in the same essay he states:

Now, if there is one thing more than another apparent to the student of the Civil War, *it is that the soldiers on both sides were exceedingly well matched in courage and endurance.*

WILLIAM T. WOFFORD
Led his Brigade in the Maryland, Gettysburg, Wilderness and Shenandoah Campaigns.

DANIEL S. DONELSON
Led his Brigade in the Tennessee Campaign, notably at Murfreesboro.

ROBERT H. ANDERSON
Colonel of the 5th Georgia Cavalry; Promoted Brigadier-General July 26, 1864.

JAMES H. LANE
Led his Brigade at Fredericksburg, Gettysburg and in the Wilderness Campaign.

WILLIAM B. BATE
Led his Brigade in Bragg's Tennessee Campaigns, notably at Chickamauga.

ROGER ATKINSON PRYOR
Fought his Brigade on the Peninsula, where it bore a conspicuous part at Seven Pines.

CADMUS M. WILCOX
Led his Brigade at Manassas, Fredericksburg, Chancellorsville and Gettysburg.

WINFIELD SCOTT FEATHERSTON
Originally Colonel of the 17th Mississippi; Promoted for Gallantry at Ball's Bluff; Led his Brigade on the Peninsula.

HENRY L. BENNING
Led his Brigade in the Principal Battles of Longstreet's Corps, including Gettysburg, Chickamauga and the Wilderness.

EDWARD AYLESWORTH PERRY
Commanded a Regiment on the Peninsula; was wounded at Frayser's Farm; Led his Brigade at Gettysburg and the Wilderness.

COMMANDERS OF
CONFEDERATE BRIGADES WHICH SUFFERED HEAVILY IN BATTLE

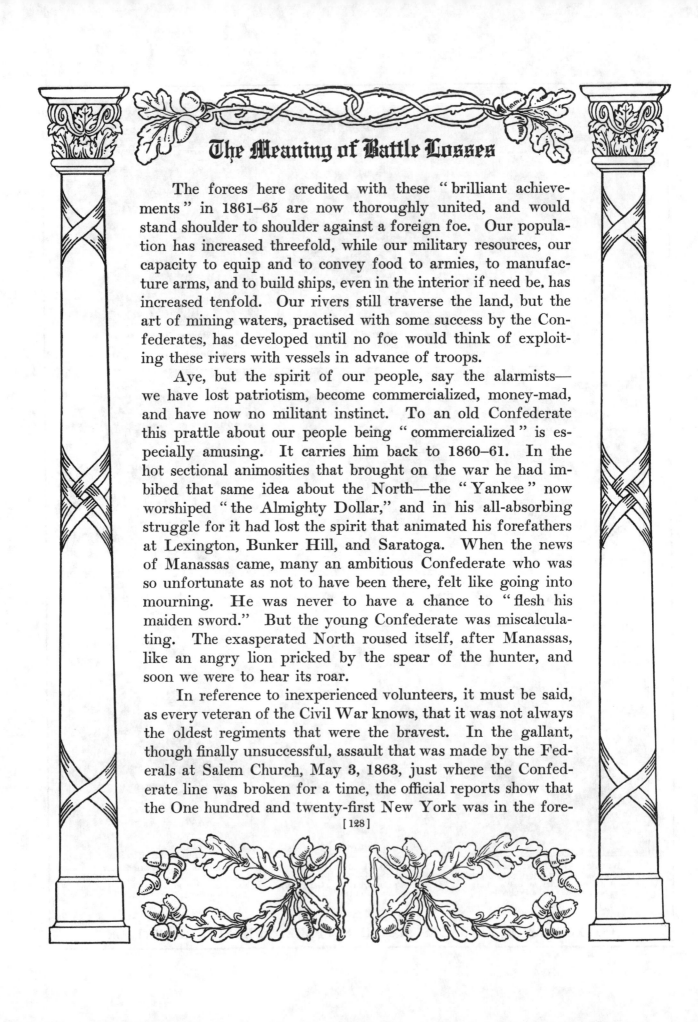

The Meaning of Battle Losses

The forces here credited with these "brilliant achievements" in 1861–65 are now thoroughly united, and would stand shoulder to shoulder against a foreign foe. Our population has increased threefold, while our military resources, our capacity to equip and to convey food to armies, to manufacture arms, and to build ships, even in the interior if need be, has increased tenfold. Our rivers still traverse the land, but the art of mining waters, practised with some success by the Confederates, has developed until no foe would think of exploiting these rivers with vessels in advance of troops.

Aye, but the spirit of our people, say the alarmists—we have lost patriotism, become commercialized, money-mad, and have now no militant instinct. To an old Confederate this prattle about our people being "commercialized" is especially amusing. It carries him back to 1860–61. In the hot sectional animosities that brought on the war he had imbibed that same idea about the North—the "Yankee" now worshiped "the Almighty Dollar," and in his all-absorbing struggle for it had lost the spirit that animated his forefathers at Lexington, Bunker Hill, and Saratoga. When the news of Manassas came, many an ambitious Confederate who was so unfortunate as not to have been there, felt like going into mourning. He was never to have a chance to "flesh his maiden sword." But the young Confederate was miscalculating. The exasperated North roused itself, after Manassas, like an angry lion pricked by the spear of the hunter, and soon we were to hear its roar.

In reference to inexperienced volunteers, it must be said, as every veteran of the Civil War knows, that it was not always the oldest regiments that were the bravest. In the gallant, though finally unsuccessful, assault that was made by the Federals at Salem Church, May 3, 1863, just where the Confederate line was broken for a time, the official reports show that the One hundred and twenty-first New York was in the fore-

MAJ.-GEN. JAMES B. McPHERSON
Atlanta, July 22, 1864.

MAJ.-GEN. JOS. K. MANSFIELD
Antietam, September 18, 1864.

MAJ.-GEN. JOHN SEDGWICK
Spotsylvania, May 9, 1864.

MAJ.-GEN. JOHN F. REYNOLDS
Gettysburg, July 1, 1863.

FEDERAL GENERALS KILLED IN BATTLE—GROUP No. 1—ARMY AND CORPS COMMANDERS

On this and the following six pages are portraits of the fifty-one Union generals killed in battle. Beneath each portrait is the date and place of death, or mortal wounding. Since no such pictorial necrology existed to aid the editors of this History, many questions arose—such as the determination of the actual rank of an officer at a given date, or the precise circumstances of death in certain instances. The list of Colonel W. F. Fox, presented in his work on "Regimental Losses in the Civil War," has been followed.

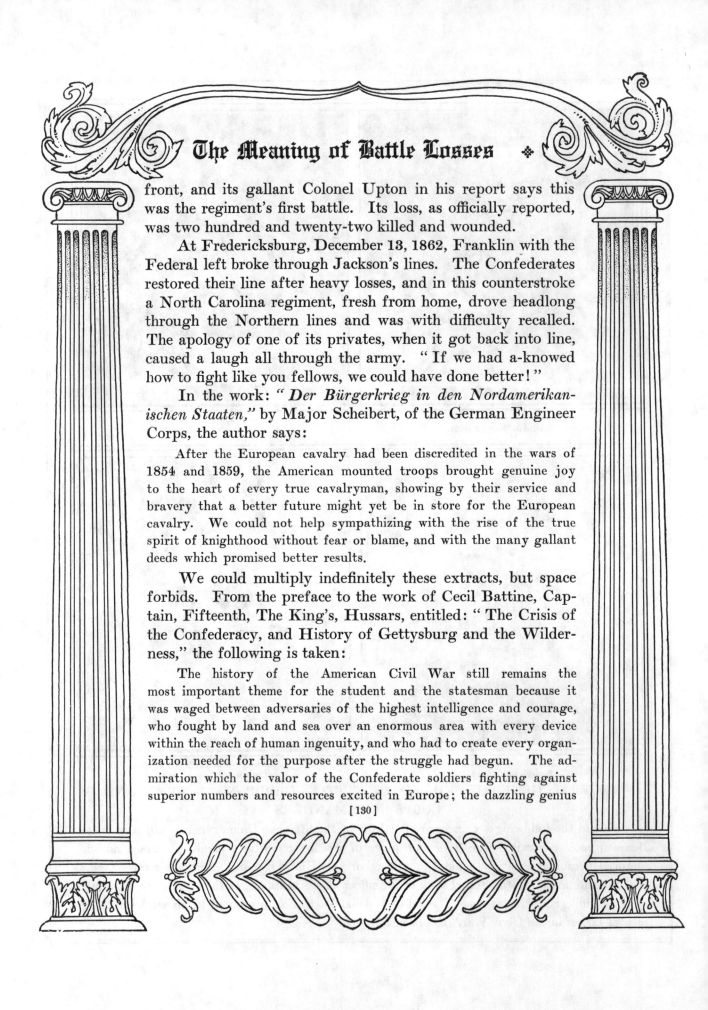

front, and its gallant Colonel Upton in his report says this was the regiment's first battle. Its loss, as officially reported, was two hundred and twenty-two killed and wounded.

At Fredericksburg, December 13, 1862, Franklin with the Federal left broke through Jackson's lines. The Confederates restored their line after heavy losses, and in this counterstroke a North Carolina regiment, fresh from home, drove headlong through the Northern lines and was with difficulty recalled. The apology of one of its privates, when it got back into line, caused a laugh all through the army. "If we had a-knowed how to fight like you fellows, we could have done better!"

In the work: "*Der Bürgerkrieg in den Nordamerikanischen Staaten,*" by Major Scheibert, of the German Engineer Corps, the author says:

After the European cavalry had been discredited in the wars of 1854 and 1859, the American mounted troops brought genuine joy to the heart of every true cavalryman, showing by their service and bravery that a better future might yet be in store for the European cavalry. We could not help sympathizing with the rise of the true spirit of knighthood without fear or blame, and with the many gallant deeds which promised better results.

We could multiply indefinitely these extracts, but space forbids. From the preface to the work of Cecil Battine, Captain, Fifteenth, The King's, Hussars, entitled: "The Crisis of the Confederacy, and History of Gettysburg and the Wilderness," the following is taken:

The history of the American Civil War still remains the most important theme for the student and the statesman because it was waged between adversaries of the highest intelligence and courage, who fought by land and sea over an enormous area with every device within the reach of human ingenuity, and who had to create every organization needed for the purpose after the struggle had begun. The admiration which the valor of the Confederate soldiers fighting against superior numbers and resources excited in Europe; the dazzling genius

PHILIP KEARNY
Chantilly
September 1, 1862.

ISRAEL B. RICHARDSON
Antietam
November 3, 1862.

FEDERAL
GENERALS KILLED
IN BATTLE

GROUP No. 2

MAJOR-GENERALS
COMMANDING
DIVISIONS
AND CORPS

ISAAC I. STEVENS
Chantilly
September 1, 1862.

AMIEL W. WHIPPLE
Chancellorsville
May, 7, 1863.

HIRAM G. BERRY
Chancellorsville
May 3, 1863.

JESSE L. RENO
South Mountain
September 14, 1862.

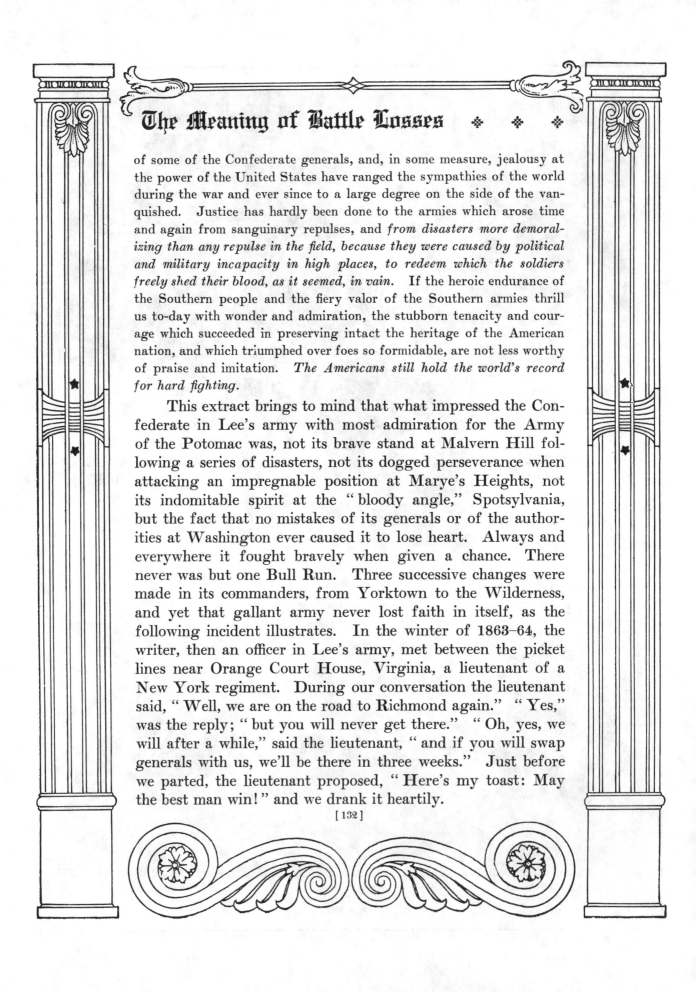

of some of the Confederate generals, and, in some measure, jealousy at the power of the United States have ranged the sympathies of the world during the war and ever since to a large degree on the side of the vanquished. Justice has hardly been done to the armies which arose time and again from sanguinary repulses, and *from disasters more demoralizing than any repulse in the field, because they were caused by political and military incapacity in high places, to redeem which the soldiers freely shed their blood, as it seemed, in vain.* If the heroic endurance of the Southern people and the fiery valor of the Southern armies thrill us to-day with wonder and admiration, the stubborn tenacity and courage which succeeded in preserving intact the heritage of the American nation, and which triumphed over foes so formidable, are not less worthy of praise and imitation. *The Americans still hold the world's record for hard fighting.*

This extract brings to mind that what impressed the Confederate in Lee's army with most admiration for the Army of the Potomac was, not its brave stand at Malvern Hill following a series of disasters, not its dogged perseverance when attacking an impregnable position at Marye's Heights, not its indomitable spirit at the "bloody angle," Spotsylvania, but the fact that no mistakes of its generals or of the authorities at Washington ever caused it to lose heart. Always and everywhere it fought bravely when given a chance. There never was but one Bull Run. Three successive changes were made in its commanders, from Yorktown to the Wilderness, and yet that gallant army never lost faith in itself, as the following incident illustrates. In the winter of 1863–64, the writer, then an officer in Lee's army, met between the picket lines near Orange Court House, Virginia, a lieutenant of a New York regiment. During our conversation the lieutenant said, " Well, we are on the road to Richmond again." " Yes," was the reply; " but you will never get there." " Oh, yes, we will after a while," said the lieutenant, " and if you will swap generals with us, we'll be there in three weeks." Just before we parted, the lieutenant proposed, " Here's my toast: May the best man win! " and we drank it heartily.

BRIG.-GEN.
THOMAS WILLIAMS
Baton Rouge, August 5, 1862.

BRIG.-GEN. ISAAC P. RODMAN
Antietam, September 30, 1862.

BRIG.-GEN.
WILLIAM H. L. WALLACE
Shiloh, April 10, 1862.

FEDERAL GENERALS KILLED IN BATTLE, GROUP No. 3

BRIG.-GEN.
JAMES E. JACKSON
Chaplin Hills, October 8, 1862.

BREVET MAJ.-GEN. JAMES S. WADSWORTH
Wilderness, May 8, 1864.

BREVET MAJ.-GEN.
DAVID A. RUSSELL
Opequon, September 19, 1864.

The Meaning of Battle Losses

Major G. W. Redway, referring to the volunteers of the Army of the Potomac, 1864, writes as follows:

The American volunteer who had survived such battles as Bull Run, Shiloh, Antietam, and the Seven Days' fighting around Richmond, was probably *such a soldier as the world had never seen before.* He needed no instruction as to his duty in the field, and, in fact, often exercised the functions of instructor both to officers and men less experienced than himself.

The impressions Federal and Confederate soldiers made on foreign critics were not lost on themselves. They were testing each other's courage, endurance, and patriotism, and coming to understand the situation as well. Four-fifths of the Confederates had never owned a slave. It was not slavery —both armies were fighting for the preservation of the same free institutions, for what each believed to be his Constitutional rights.

The first step toward reunion was being taken when picket shooting was stopped; and the armies of Northern Virginia and of the Potomac went far beyond that, when encamped on opposite banks of the Rappahannock, near Fredericksburg, during the winter and spring of 1862–63. They chatted, traded tobacco for sugar and coffee, and frequently visited each other across the narrow stream. A Confederate officer riding along the bank visiting his outposts was often saluted by a picket across the river, within easy gunshot. Similar compliments passed between pickets in gray and officers in blue. These soldiers were testifying their respect for each other, with little idea, on the part of the Confederates, that they would ever again be fellow countrymen.

Eventually both generals, Hooker and Lee, issued orders strictly forbidding all intercommunication. Just after these orders, an incident occurred which the writer long ago gave to the newspapers in the hope, which proved vain, that he might hear from the Union soldier. A Confederate officer

BREVET BRIG.-GEN.
JAMES A. MULLIGAN
Winchester, July 26, 1864.

BRIG.-GEN.
THOS. G. STEVENSON
Spotsylvania, May 10, 1864.

BREVET MAJ.-GEN.
THOMAS A. SMYTH
Farmville, April 9, 1865

BRIG.-GEN.
ROBT. L. MCCOOK
Decherd, Tenn., August 6, 1862.

FEDERAL

GENERALS

KILLED

IN BATTLE

GROUP No. 4

BRIG.-GEN.
NATHANIEL LYON
Wilson's Creek, August 10, 1861.

BRIG.-GEN.
HENRY BOHLEN
Freeman's Ford, August 22, 1865.

MAJ.-GEN.
GEO. C. STRONG
Fort Wagner, July 30, 1863.

BREVET MAJ.-GEN.
S. K. ZOOK
Gettysburg, July 3, 1863.

BREVET MAJ.-GEN.
FREDERICK WINTHROP
Five Forks, April 1, 1865.

BREVET MAJ.-GEN.
ALEXANDER HAYS
Wilderness, May 5, 1864.

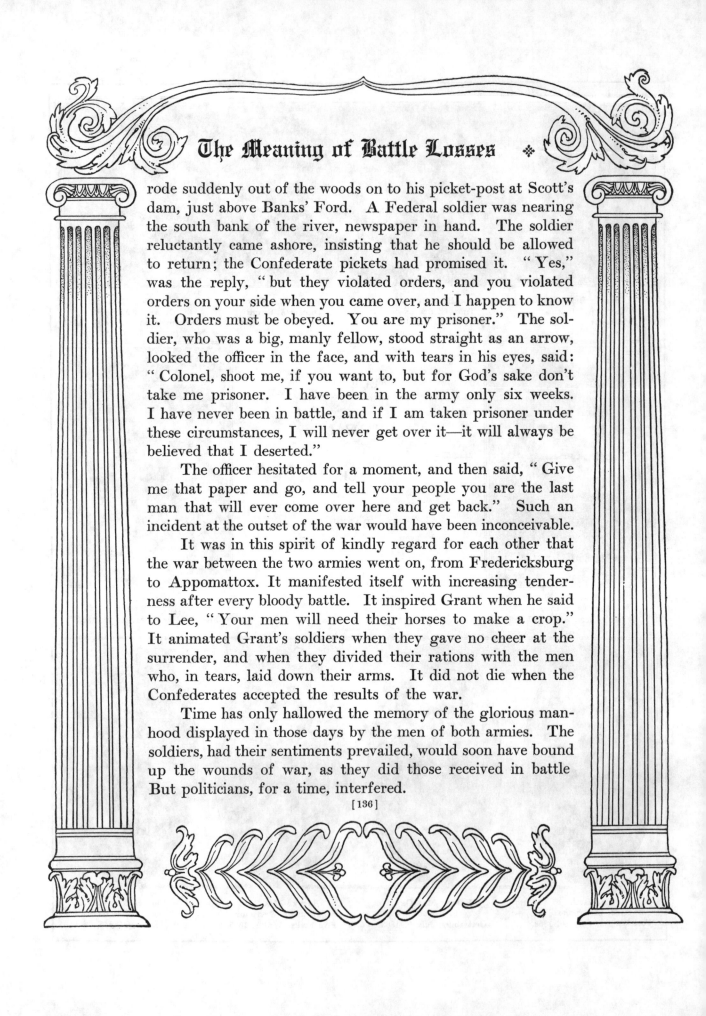

rode suddenly out of the woods on to his picket-post at Scott's dam, just above Banks' Ford. A Federal soldier was nearing the south bank of the river, newspaper in hand. The soldier reluctantly came ashore, insisting that he should be allowed to return; the Confederate pickets had promised it. "Yes," was the reply, "but they violated orders, and you violated orders on your side when you came over, and I happen to know it. Orders must be obeyed. You are my prisoner." The soldier, who was a big, manly fellow, stood straight as an arrow, looked the officer in the face, and with tears in his eyes, said: "Colonel, shoot me, if you want to, but for God's sake don't take me prisoner. I have been in the army only six weeks. I have never been in battle, and if I am taken prisoner under these circumstances, I will never get over it—it will always be believed that I deserted."

The officer hesitated for a moment, and then said, "Give me that paper and go, and tell your people you are the last man that will ever come over here and get back." Such an incident at the outset of the war would have been inconceivable.

It was in this spirit of kindly regard for each other that the war between the two armies went on, from Fredericksburg to Appomattox. It manifested itself with increasing tenderness after every bloody battle. It inspired Grant when he said to Lee, "Your men will need their horses to make a crop." It animated Grant's soldiers when they gave no cheer at the surrender, and when they divided their rations with the men who, in tears, laid down their arms. It did not die when the Confederates accepted the results of the war.

Time has only hallowed the memory of the glorious manhood displayed in those days by the men of both armies. The soldiers, had their sentiments prevailed, would soon have bound up the wounds of war, as they did those received in battle But politicians, for a time, interfered.

ELON J. FARNSWORTH
Gettysburg
July 3, 1863.

STEPHEN H. WEED
Gettysburg
July 2, 1863.

EDW. P. CHAPIN
Port Hudson
May 27, 1863.

VINCENT STRONG
Gettysburg
July 7, 1863.

CONRAD F. JACKSON
Fredericksburg
December 13, 1862.

PLEASANT A. HACKLEMAN
Corinth
October 3, 1862.

FEDERAL

GENERALS

KILLED IN

BATTLE

GROUP No. 5

BRIGADIER–

GENERALS

JOSHUA W. SILL
Stone's River
December 31, 1862.

GEO. D. BAYARD
Fredericksburg
December 14, 1862.

WM. R. TERRILL
Perryville
October 8, 1862.

GEO. W. TAYLOR
Manassas (Second Bull Run)
August 31, 1862.

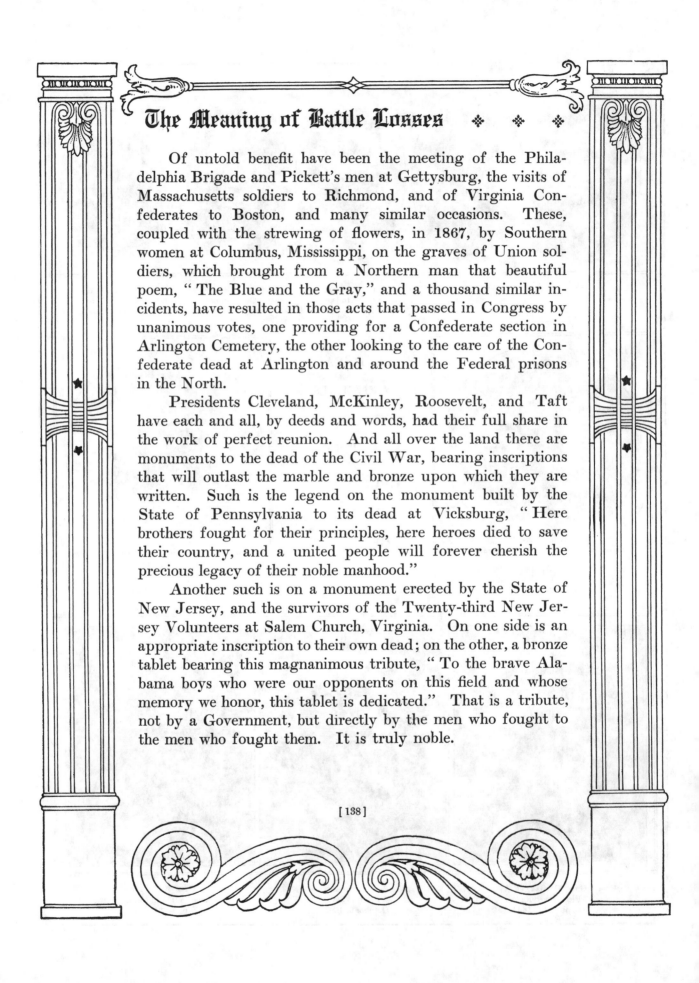

The Meaning of Battle Losses ❖ ❖ ❖

Of untold benefit have been the meeting of the Philadelphia Brigade and Pickett's men at Gettysburg, the visits of Massachusetts soldiers to Richmond, and of Virginia Confederates to Boston, and many similar occasions. These, coupled with the strewing of flowers, in 1867, by Southern women at Columbus, Mississippi, on the graves of Union soldiers, which brought from a Northern man that beautiful poem, "The Blue and the Gray," and a thousand similar incidents, have resulted in those acts that passed in Congress by unanimous votes, one providing for a Confederate section in Arlington Cemetery, the other looking to the care of the Confederate dead at Arlington and around the Federal prisons in the North.

Presidents Cleveland, McKinley, Roosevelt, and Taft have each and all, by deeds and words, had their full share in the work of perfect reunion. And all over the land there are monuments to the dead of the Civil War, bearing inscriptions that will outlast the marble and bronze upon which they are written. Such is the legend on the monument built by the State of Pennsylvania to its dead at Vicksburg, "Here brothers fought for their principles, here heroes died to save their country, and a united people will forever cherish the precious legacy of their noble manhood."

Another such is on a monument erected by the State of New Jersey, and the survivors of the Twenty-third New Jersey Volunteers at Salem Church, Virginia. On one side is an appropriate inscription to their own dead; on the other, a bronze tablet bearing this magnanimous tribute, "To the brave Alabama boys who were our opponents on this field and whose memory we honor, this tablet is dedicated." That is a tribute, not by a Government, but directly by the men who fought to the men who fought them. It is truly noble.

WILLIAM P. SANDERS
Knoxville
November 19, 1863.

WILLIAM H. LYTLE
Chickamauga
September 20, 1863.

JAMES C. RICE
Spotsylvania
May 10, 1864.

CHARLES G. HARKER
Kenesaw Mountain
June 27, 1864.

FEDERAL GENERALS

KILLED IN BATTLE

GROUP No. 6

BRIGADIER-GENERALS

HIRAM BURNHAM
Fort Harrison
September 30, 1864.

SAMUEL A. RICE
Jenkins' Ferry
July 6, 1864.

DANIEL McCOOK
Kenesaw Mountain
July 17, 1864.

J. H. KITCHING
Cedar Creek
Died January 10, 1865.

DANIEL D. BIDWELL
Cedar Creek
October 19, 1864.

Casualties in Great European Battles

COMPILED FROM HENDERSON'S "STONEWALL JACKSON AND THE AMERICAN CIVIL WAR"

LIST OF KILLED AND WOUNDED (EXCLUDING PRISONERS)

THE VICTORIOUS SIDE IS GIVEN FIRST IN EACH CASE

BATTLE	NUMBER OF TROOPS		KILLED AND WOUNDED	TOTAL	TOTAL PERCENTAGE	PERCENTAGE OF VICTOR
Blenheim, 1704	Allies,	56,000	11,000 ⎞ 20,000 ⎠	31,000	26	19
	French,	60,000				
Oudenarde, 1708	Allies,	85,000	10,000 ⎞ 10,000 ⎠	20,000	11	11
	French,	85,000				
Malplaquet, 1709	Allies,	100,000	14,000 ⎞ 20,000 ⎠	34,000	17	14
	French,	100,000				
Prague, 1757	Prussians,	64,000	12,000 ⎞ 10,000 ⎠	22,000	17	18
	Austrians,	60,000				
Zorndorf, 1758	Prussians,	32,760	12,000 ⎞ 20,000 ⎠	32,000	38	37
	Russians,	52,000				
Kunnersdorf, 1759	Allies,	70,000	14,000 ⎞ 17,000 ⎠	31,000	27	20
	Prussians,	43,000				
Torgau, 1760	Prussians,	46,000	12,000 ⎞ 12,000 ⎠	24,000	22	26
	Austrians,	60,000				
Austerlitz, 1805	French,	65,000	9,000 ⎞ 16,000 ⎠	25,000	16	13
	Allies,	83,000				
Eylau, 1807	French,	70,000	20,000 ⎞ 22,000 ⎠	42,000	33	28
	Russians,	63,500				
Heilsberg, 1807	Russians,	84,000	10,000 ⎞ 12,000 ⎠	22,000	13	11
	French,	85,000				
Friedland, 1807	French,	75,000	10,000 ⎞ 24,000 ⎠	34,000	23	13
	Russians,	67,000				
Aspern, 1809	Austrians,	75,000	20,000 ⎞ 25,000 ⎠	45,000	26	26
	French,	95,000				
Wagram, 1809	French,	220,000	22,000 ⎞ 22,000 ⎠	44,000	11	10
	Austrians,	150,000				
Borodino, 1812	French,	125,000	30,000 ⎞ 45,000 ⎠	75,000	28	24
	Russians,	138,000				
Bautzen, 1813	French,	190,000	12,000 ⎞ 12,000 ⎠	24,000	8	6
	Allies,	110,000				
Leipsic, 1813	Allies,	290,000	42,000 ⎞ 50,000 ⎠	92,000	20	14
	French,	150,000				
Ligny, 1815	French,	73,000	12,000 ⎞ 12,000 ⎠	24,000	15	16
	Prussians,	86,000				
Waterloo, 1815	Allies,	100,000	20,000 ⎞ 22,000 ⎠	42,000	24	20
	French,	70,000				
Solferino, 1859	Allies,	135,000	16,500 ⎞ 15,000 ⎠	31,500	10	11
	Austrians,	160,000				
Königgrätz, 1866	Prussians,	211,000	8,894 ⎞ 18,000 ⎠	26,894	6	4
	Austrians,	206,000				
Vionville, 1870	Germans,	70,000	15,800 ⎞ 17,000 ⎠	32,800	19	22
	French,	98,000				
Gravelotte, 1870	Germans,	200,000	20,000 ⎞ 10,000 ⎠	30,000	9	10
	French,	120,000				
Plevna, September 11, 1877	Turks,	35,000	16,000 ⎞ 3,000 ⎠	19,000	16	8
	Russians,	80,000				

GRIFFIN A. STEDMAN, JR.
Petersburg
Died August 6, 1864.

GEO. D. WELLS
Cedar Creek
October 13, 1864.

SYLVESTER G. HILL
Nashville
December 15, 1864.

FEDERAL GENERALS KILLED IN BATTLE—GROUP No. 7

ARTHUR H. DUTTON
Bermuda Hundred
Died June 4, 1864.

CHARLES R. LOWELL
Cedar Creek
October 20, 1864.

THEODORE READ
High Bridge
April 6, 1865.

TABULAR STATEMENT OF LOSSES IN BOTH THE UNION AND CONFEDERATE ARMIES IN THE PRINCIPAL BATTLES OF THE CIVIL WAR, 1861-1865, COMPILED FROM OFFICIAL REPORTS BY MARCUS J. WRIGHT, CHIEF OF THE DIVISION OF CONFEDERATE RECORDS, U. S. WAR DEPARTMENT

	Union Army				Confederate Army			
	Killed	Wounded	Missing	Total	Killed	Wounded	Missing	Total
Bull Run, Va., July 21, 1861	481	1,011	1,216	2,708	387	1,582	12	1,981
Wilson's Creek, Mo., Aug. 10, 1861	223	721	291	1,235	257	900	27	1,184
Fort Donelson, Tenn., Feb. 12–16, 1862	500	2,108	224	2,832	2,000	.....	14,623	16,623
Pea Ridge, Ark., Mar. 7, 1862	203	980	201	1,384	600	.....	200	800
Shiloh, Tenn., Apr. 6–7, 1862	1,754	8,408	2,885	13,047	1,723	8,012	959	10,694
Williamsburg, Va., May 4–5, 1862	456	1,410	373	2,249	1,570	.....	133	1,703
Fair Oaks, Va., May 31–June 1, 1862	790	3,594	647	5,031	980	4,749	405	6,134
Mechanicsville, Va., June 26, 1862	49	207	105	361	1,484	.....	.....	.....
Gaines' Mill, Va., June 27, 1862	894	3,107	2,836	6,837	8,751	.....	.....	.....
Peach Orchard, Savage Station, Va., June 29, 1862								
White Oak Swamp, Glendale, Va., June 30, 1862	724	4,245	3,067	8,036	8,602	.....	875	9,477
Malvern Hill, Va., July 1, 1862								
Seven Days, Va., June 25–July 1, 1862	1,734	8,062	6,075	15,849	3,478	16,261	875	20,614
Cedar Mountain, Va., Aug. 9, 1862	314	1,445	594	2,353	231	1,107	.....	1,338
Manassas and Chantilly, Va., Aug. 27–Sept. 2, 1862	1,724	8,372	5,958	16,054	1,481	7,627	89	9,197
Richmond, Ky., Aug. 29–30, 1862	206	844	4,303	5,353	78	372	1	451
South Mountain, Md., Sept. 14, 1862	325	1,403	85	1,813	325	1,560	800	2,685
Antietam, or Sharpsburg, Md., Sept. 16–17, 1862	2,108	9,549	753	12,390	2,700	9,024	1,800	13,524
Corinth, Miss., Oct. 3–4, 1862	355	1,841	324	2,520	473	1,997	1,763	4,233
Perryville, Ky., Oct. 8, 1862	845	2,851	515	4,211	510	2,635	251	3,396
Prairie Grove, Ark., Dec. 7, 1862	175	813	263	1,251	164	817	336	1,317
Fredericksburg, Va., Dec. 13, 1862	1,284	9,600	1,769	12,653	595	4,061	653	5,309
Stone's River, or Murfreesboro, Tenn., Dec. 31, 1862, and Jan. 2, 1863	1,677	7,543	3,686	12,906	1,294	7,945	2,476	11,715
Arkansas Post, Ark., Jan. 11, 1863	134	898	29	1,061	28	81	4,791	4,900
Chancellorsville and Fredericksburg, Va., May 1–4, 1863	1,575	9,594	5,676	16,792	1,665	9,081	2,018	12,764

**CONFEDERATE
GENERALS
KILLED
IN
BATTLE**

GROUP NO. 1
ARMY
AND CORPS
COMMANDERS

On this page and following are portraits of all the 73 general officers of the Confederacy killed in battle, with the exception of "Stonewall" Jackson, portraits of whom appear in a preceding chapter of this volume (See Index also).

GENERAL ALBERT SIDNEY JOHNSTON
Shiloh
April 6, 1862.

LIEUT.-GENERAL LEONIDAS POLK
Pine Mountain
June 14, 1864.

LIEUT.-GENERAL AMBROSE POWELL HILL
Petersburg
April 2, 1865.

Continued from page 142

Battle								
Champion's Hill, Miss., May 16, 1863	410	1,844	187	2,441	381	1,769	1,670	3,851
Assault on Vicksburg, Miss., May 22, 1863	502	2,550	147	3,199	Full reports not available			
Port Hudson, La., May 27, 1863	293	1,545	157	1,995	....	235	....	....
Port Hudson, La., June 14, 1863	203	1,401	188	1,792	22	25	....	47
Gettysburg, Pa., July 1–3, 1863	3,155	14,529	5,365	23,049	3,903	18,735	5,425	28,063
Fort Wagner, S. C., July 18, 1863	246	880	389	1,515	36	133	5	174
Chickamauga, Ga., Sept. 19–20, 1863	1,657	9,756	4,757	16,170	2,312	14,674	1,468	18,484
Chattanooga, Tenn., Nov. 23–25, 1863	753	4,722	349	5,824	361	2,160	4,146	6,667
Mine Run, Va., Nov. 27–Dec. 1, 1863	173	1,099	381	1,653	110	570	65	745
Pleasant Hill, La., Apr. 9, 1864	150	844	375	1,369	....	987	4,720	5,707
Wilderness, Va., May 5–7, 1864	2,246	12,137	3,383	17,666	Reports of losses not complete			
Spotsylvania, Va., May 10, 1864	753	3,347	....	4,100	Reports incomplete			
Spotsylvania, Va., May 12, 1864	....	6,020	800	6,820	Records of losses not shown			
Drewry's Bluff, Va., May 12–16, 1864	390	2,380	1,390	4,160	Reports incomplete			
Cold Harbor, Va., June 1–3, 1864	12,000			....	Reports incomplete			
Petersburg, Va., June 15–30, 1864	2,013	9,935	4,621	16,569	Estimated loss in Hill's Corps and Field and Kershaw's divisions, 2,970			
Atlanta Campaign, Ga., May, 1864 (including Buzzard's Roost, Snake Creek Gap and New Hope Church)	1,058		1,240	2,298	Killed and wounded, 9,187			
Assault on Kenesaw Mt., Ga., June 27, 1864	1,999		52	2,051	270		172	342
Tupelo, Miss., July 13–15, 1864	77	559	38	674	210	1,116		1,326
Atlanta, Ga., July 22, 1864 (Hood's attack)	430	1,599	1,733	3,722	2,890		851	3,741
Jonesboro, Ga., Aug. 31, 1864	....	179	....	....	1,640			
Jonesboro, Ga., Sept. 1, 1864	233	946	105	1,274	No full return of losses			
Winchester, Va., Sept. 19, 1864	697	3,983	338	5,018	276	1,827	1,818	3,921
Chaffin's Farm and Forts Harrison and Gilmer, Va., Sept. 29–30, 1864	383	2,299	645	3,327	No full report of losses			
Cedar Creek, Va., Oct. 19, 1864	644	3,430	1,591	5,665	320	1,540	1,050	2,910
Franklin, Tenn., Nov. 30, 1864	189	1,033	1,104	2,336	1,750	3,800	702	6,252
Nashville, Tenn., Dec. 15–16, 1864	387	2,562	112	3,061	No report of killed and wounded			
Bentonville, N. C., Mar. 19, 1865	139	794	170	1,103	195	1,313	610	2,118
Appomattox, Va., Mar. 29–Apr. 9, 1865	1,316	7,750	1,714	10,780	No report of losses			
Petersburg, Va., Apr. 2, 1865	625	3,189	326	4,140	No report of losses			

WILLIAM D. PENDER
Gettysburg
July 18, 1863.

STEPHEN D. RAMSEUR
Cedar Creek
October 19, 1864.

CONFEDERATE

GENERALS

KILLED

IN BATTLE

J. E. B. STUART
Yellow Tavern
May 12, 1864.

GROUP

No. 2

MAJOR–

GENERALS

W. H. T. WALKER
Atlanta
July 22, 1864.

PATRICK R. CLEBURNE
Franklin
November 30, 1864.

ROBERT E. RODES
Opequon
September 19, 1864.

Summary of Union Troops Furnished by the Several States and Territories

STATES AND TERRITORIES	White Troops	Sailors and Marines	Colored Troops	Indian Nations	Aggregate	Total Deaths, All Causes
Alabama	2,578	....	....	....	2,578	345
Arkansas	8,289	....	....	....	8,289	1,713
California	15,725	....	....	....	15,725	573
Colorado	4,903	....	....	....	4,903	323
Connecticut	51,937	2,163	1,784	....	55,864	5,354
Dakota	206	....	....	....	206	6
Delaware	11,236	94	954	....	12,284	882
District of Columbia	11,912	1,353	3,269	....	16,534	290
Florida	1,290	....	....	....	1,990	215
Georgia	....	....	....	....	....	15
Illinois	255,057	2,224	1,811	....	259,092	34,834
Indiana	193,748	1,078	1,537	....	196,363	26,672
Iowa	75,797	5	440	....	76,242	13,001
Kansas	18,069	....	2,080	....	20,149	2,630
Kentucky	51,743	314	23,703	....	75,760	10,774
Louisiana	5,224	....	....	....	5,224	945
Maine	64,973	5,030	104	....	70,107	9,398
Maryland	33,995	3,925	8,718	....	46,638	2,982
Massachusetts	122,781	19,983	2,966	....	146,730	13,942
Michigan	85,479	498	1,387	....	87,364	14,753
Minnesota	23,913	3	104	....	24,020	2,584
Mississippi	545	....	....	....	545	78
Missouri	100,616	151	8,344	....	109,111	13,885
Nebraska	3,157	....	....	....	3,157	239
Nevada	1,080	....	....	....	1,080	33
New Hampshire	32,930	882	125	....	33,937	4,882
New Jersey	67,500	8,129	1,185	....	76,814	5,754
New Mexico	6,561	....	....	....	6,561	277
New York	409,561	35,164	4,125	....	448,850	46,534
North Carolina	3,156	....	....	....	3,156	360
Ohio	304,814	3,274	5,092	....	313,180	35,475
Oregon	1,810	....	....	....	1,810	45
Pennsylvania	315,017	14,307	8,612	....	337,936	33,183
Rhode Island	19,521	1,878	1,837	....	23,236	1,321
Tennessee	31,092	....	....	....	31,092	8,777
Texas	1,965	....	....	....	1,965	151
Vermont	32,549	619	120	....	33,288	5,224
Virginia	....	....	....	....	....	42
Washington Territory	964	....	....	....	964	22
West Virginia	31,872	133	196	....	32,068	4,017
Wisconsin	91,029	....	165	....	91,327	12,301
Indian Nations	....	....	....	3,530	3,530	1,018
Regular Army	....	....	....	....	....	5,798
Colored Troops	....	....	*99,337	....	99,337	**36,847
Veteran Volunteers	....	....	....	....	....	106
U. S. Volunteers***	....	....	....	....	....	243
U. S. Sharpshooters and Engineers	....	....	....	....	....	552
Veteran Reserves	....	....	....	....	....	1,672
Generals and Staffs	....	....	....	....	....	239
Miscellaneous—Bands, etc.	....	....	....	....	....	232
	2,494,592	101,207	178,975	3,530	2,778,304	359,528

* Colored troops recruited in the Southern States.
** Includes all the deaths in the 178,975 Colored Troops.
*** Ex-Confederate Soldiers.
Eighty-six thousand seven hundred and twenty-four drafted men paid commutation and were exempted from service.

BRIG.-GEN.
BENJAMIN MCCULLOCH
Pea Ridge, March 7, 1862.

BRIG.-GEN.
BARNARD E. BEE
First Bull Run, July 21, 1861.

MAJ.-GEN.
JOHN PEGRAM
Hatcher's Run, February 6, 1865.

CONFEDERATE GENERALS
KILLED IN BATTLE

GROUP No. 3

BRIG.-GEN.
FELIX K. ZOLLICOFFER
Mill Springs, January 19, 1862.

BRIG.-GEN.
FRANCIS S. BARTOW
First Bull Run, July 21, 1861.

BRIG.-GEN.
ROBERT SELDEN GARNETT
Rich Mountain, July 13, 1861.

DEATHS FROM ALL CAUSES IN UNION ARMIES

Cause	Officers	Enlisted Men	Total
Killed and died of wounds....................	6,365	103,705	110,070
Died of disease...............................	2,712	197,008	199,720
In prison.....................................	83	24,873	24,866
Accidents....................................	142	3,972	4,114
Drowning....................................	106	4,838	4,944
Sunstroke....................................	5	308	313
Murdered....................................	37	483	520
Killed after capture..........................	14	90	104
Suicide......................................	26	365	391
Military execution...........................	....	267	267
Executed by enemy...........................	4	60	64
Causes unclassified..........................	62	1,972	2,034
Cause not stated.............................	28	12,093	12,121
Totals....................	9,584	349,944	359,528

DEATHS IN CONFEDERATE ARMIES

A tabulation of Confederate losses as compiled from the muster-rolls on file in the Bureau of Confederate Archives. (In the report for 1865–66, made by General James B. Fry, United States Provost Marshal-General.) These returns are incomplete, and nearly all the Alabama rolls are missing. Still the figures show that at least 74,524 Confederate soldiers were killed or died of wounds, and that 59,297 died of disease.

STATE	KILLED			DIED OF WOUNDS			DIED OF DISEASE		
	Officers	Enlisted Men	Total	Officers	Enlisted Men	Total	Officers	Enlisted Men	Total
Virginia...........	266	5,062	5,328	200	2,319	2,519	168	6,779	6,947
North Carolina.....	677	13,845	14,522	330	4,821	5,151	541	20,061	20,602
South Carolina.....	360	8,827	9,187	257	3,478	3,735	79	4,681	4,760
Georgia...........	172	5,381	5,553	140	1,579	1,719	107	3,595	3,702
Florida...........	47	746	793	16	490	506	17	1,030	1,047
Alabama..........	14	538	552	9	181	190	8	716	724
Mississippi........	122	5,685	5,807	75	2,576	2,651	103	6,704	6,807
Louisiana.........	70	2,548	2,618	42	826	868	32	3,027	3,059
Texas.............	28	1,320	1,348	13	1,228	1,241	10	1,250	1,260
Arkansas.........	104	2,061	2,165	27	888	915	74	3,708	3,782
Tennessee........	99	2,016	2,115	49	825	874	72	3,353	3,425
Regular C. S. Army.	35	972	1,007	27	441	468	25	1,015	1,040
Border States......	92	1,867	1,959	61	672	733	58	2,084	2,142
Totals........	2,086	50,868	52,954	1,246	20,324	21,570	1,294	58,003	59,297

Colonel W. F. Fox, the authority on Civil War Statistics, states: "If the Confederate rolls could have been completed, and then revised—as has been done with the rolls of the Union regiments—the number of killed, as shown above (74,524), would be largely increased. As it is, the extent of such increase must remain a matter of conjecture. The Union rolls were examined at the same time, and a similar tabulation of the number killed appears, also, in General Fry's report. But this latter number was increased 15,000 by a subsequent revision based upon the papers known as "final statements" and upon newly-acquired information received through affidavits filed at the Pension Bureau."

WM. Y. SLACK
Pea Ridge
March 8, 1862.

ADLEY H. GLADDEN
Shiloh
April 11, 1862.

ROBERT HATTON
Fair Oaks
June 1, 1862.

RICHARD GRIFFITH
Savage Station
June 30, 1862.

GEORGE B. ANDERSON
Antietam
Sept. 17, 1862.

CONFEDERATE

GENERALS KILLED

IN BATTLE

GROUP No. 4

TWELVE BRIGADIER–

GENERALS

HENRY LITTLE
Iuka
September 19, 1862.

L. O'B. BRANCH
Antietam
September 17, 1862.

TURNER ASHBY
Harrisonburg
June 6, 1862.

WILLIAM E. STARKE
Antietam
September 17, 1862.

JAMES MCINTOSH
Pea Ridge
March 7, 1862.

CHARLES S. WINDER
Cedar Mountain
August 9, 1862.

SAMUEL GARLAND, JR.
South Mountain
September 14, 1862.

TABULAR STATEMENT OF ORGANIZATIONS IN THE UNION SERVICE

	REGIMENTS	BATTALIONS	COMPANIES	BATTERIES
Cavalry............................	272	45	78	...
Heavy artillery....................	61	8	36	...
Light artillery....................	...	9	...	432
Engineers.........................	13	1	7	...
Sharpshooters.....................	4	3	35	...
Infantry..........................	2,144	60	351	...
Totals........................	2,494	126	507	432

SUMMARY OF ORGANIZATIONS IN THE CONFEDERATE ARMY

Any attempt to present in statistical form the strength of the Confederate armies is manifestly impossible, as was explained by General Marcus J. Wright in his introductory chapter in Volume I of the PHOTOGRAPHIC HISTORY. The same conditions also render futile any accurate comparison of the troops furnished to the Confederate armies by the various states of the South. Nevertheless, by tabulating the various organizations and bearing in mind the limitations of the method as well as the original data, a slight basis is afforded to gain some idea of the relative numbers contributed by the different States. Furthermore, the numbers of the organizations when summarized are of interest in comparison with those given above.

No complete official roll of regiments and other organizations in the Confederate army is to be found either in the archives of the United States War Department or published in the War Records, and it is difficult, if not impossible, to give either an accurate list or the total number. Various lists have been compiled by private individuals, but none of these show absolute accuracy, and all differ among themselves. A list prepared by Colonel Henry Stone, a member of the Military Historical Society of Massachusetts, was made the basis of the following table by Colonel Thomas L. Livermore, which is published in his volume "Numbers and Losses in the Civil War." This list General Wright states is as accurate as can be found.

TABLE MADE BY COLONEL LIVERMORE FROM COLONEL STONE'S LIST

	INFANTRY				CAVALRY				ARTILLERY		
	Regiments	Legions	Battalions	Companies	Regiments	Legions	Battalions	Companies	Regiments	Battalions	Companies
Alabama..............	55	..	18	4	6	..	18	10	..	2	17
Arkansas.............	42	..	14	2	4	..	5	4	..	2	16
Florida..............	9	..	1	16	2	..	3	6	..	1	15
Georgia..............	67	3	14	9	7	..	21	...	..	..	...
Kentucky.............	9	..	...	..	11	..	1	...	..	..	...
Louisiana............	33	..	22	..	3	..	13	8	5	3	19
Mississippi..........	53	..	21	..	25	1	4	...	..	1	9
Missouri.............	30	..	...	..	7	..	...	...	..	..	...
North Carolina.......	74	1	12	4	6	..	12	2	2	..	9
South Carolina.......	53	3	14	8	7	..	7	13	3	3	25
Tennessee............	78	..	24	..	10	..	11	17	..	1	35
Texas...............	35	1	4	14	33	..	8	15	2	..	24
Virginia.............	99	1	19	5	16	..	40	26	4	12	58
Confederate or Prov. Army...........	5	..	...	..	...	..	...	...	..	..	...
Total...........	642	9	163	62	137	1	143	101	16	25	227

MAXCY GREGG
Fredericksburg,
December 13. 1862.

E. D. TRACY
Port Gibson
May 1, 1863.

THOMAS R. R. COBB
Fredericksburg
December 13. 1862.

GROUP No. 5

CONFEDERATE GENERALS

KILLED IN BATTLE

LLOYD TILGHMAN
Champion's Hill
May 16, 1863.

ROGER W. HANSON
Stone's River
December 30, 1862.

E. F. PAXTON
Chancellorsville
May 3, 1863.

JAMES E. RAINS
Stone's River,
Dec. 31, 1862.

LEWIS A. ARMISTEAD
Gettysburg
July 3, 1863.

WILLIAM BARKSDALE
Gettysburg
July 2, 1863.

MARTIN E. GREEN
Vicksburg
June 27, 1863.

Regimental Casualties in the Union Army

IN any discussion of the total or relative casualties suffered by a military organization in a war, or in any particular engagement, it must be borne in mind that the entire subject is one around which many questions center. The general consideration has been discussed by Colonel Hilary A. Herbert in the preceding chapter. It now remains to give the readers of the PHOTOGRAPHIC HISTORY some few exact statistics of the losses suffered in both great armies.

In the official records there are summarized with considerable completeness the enlistments and casualties for the various regiments and other organizations of the Union army. The reports for the most part are complete and comprehensive, admitting of full discussion, yet often there is great difficulty in reducing the vast amount of material to a common denominator for purposes of comparison. The problem is to consider the various elements in their relations one to another. Thus, it is possible to take those regiments where the number killed or died of wounds during the entire period of service stood at a maximum in comparison with other organizations. Furthermore, it is possible to consider such casualties relatively, depending upon the strength of the organization, and this latter method gives a clear indication of the efficiency of the regiment during its entire period of service. Large total losses mean that the regiment was at the fore-front of the fighting in many battles and not necessarily unduly exposed at one particular action.

Such is the list to be found on page 154, compiled from the authoritative work of Lieutenant-Colonel William F. Fox, U. S. V.—" Regimental Losses in the Civil War." It is, indeed, a record of valor; the fifty regiments here listed are entitled to places of high honor on the scroll of history. It is, all things considered, the most useful basis of making a comparison of the services of the different regiments, and it is one which unfortunately cannot be made for the regiments comprising the Confederate army, on account of the absence of suitable rosters and reports.

Now, if we should consider the maximum percentage of casualties based on the total of killed, wounded, and missing, a similar roll could be constructed. It would be headed by the First Minnesota Infantry, which, at the battle of Gettysburg, with 262 men engaged on the second day, lost 168 wounded and 47 killed, or a percentage of 82. In fact, other regiments standing at the top of such a list are worthy of note, and a few such, as listed by Colonel Fox, are given in the table at the bottom of this page.

The tabular statement on page 154 must be considered, therefore, as suggestive rather than complete. The selection of fifty regiments is an arbitrary one; for, of over two thousand regiments in the Union army, 45 infantry regiments lost over 200 men killed or mortally wounded in action during the war. In fact, Colonel Fox has compiled a list of 300 fighting regiments, which lost over 130 who were killed and died of wounds during the war, or which, with a smaller enrollment, suffered an equivalent percentage of casualties.

REGIMENT	BATTLE	Killed	Wounded	Missing	Total	Engaged	Per Cent.
1st Minnesota	Gettysburg	47	168	—	215*	262	82.0
141st Pennsylvania	Gettysburg	25	103	21	149	198	75.7
101st New York	Bull Run	6	101	17	124	168	73.8
25th Massachusetts	Cold Harbor	53	139	28	220	310	70.0
36th Wisconsin (4 Cos.)	Bethesda Church	20	108	38	166	240	69.0
20th Massachusetts	Fredericksburg	25	138	—	163	238	68.4
8th Vermont	Cedar Creek	17	66	23	106	156	67.9
81st Pennsylvania	Fredericksburg	15	141	20	176	261	67.4
12th Massachusetts	Antietam	49	165	10	224	334	67.0
1st Maine H. A.	Petersburg	115	489	28	632	950	66.5
9th Louisiana Colored	Milliken's Bend	62	130	—	192	300	64.0
5th New Hampshire	Fredericksburg	20	154	19	193	303	63.6

* Action of July 2d,—8 companies engaged; total casualties at Gettysburg were 224.

RICHARD B. GARNETT
Gettysburg
July 3, 1863.

W. R. SCURRY
Jenkins Ferry
April 30, 1864.

PAUL J. SEMMES
Gettysburg
July 10, 1863.

CARNOT POSEY
Bristoe Station
November 13, 1863.

KILLED

IN

BATTLE

JAMES DESHLER
Chickamauga
September 20, 1863.

BENJAMIN H. HELM
Chickamauga
September 20, 1863.

JOHN M. JONES
Wilderness
May 2, 1864.

L. A. STAFFORD
Wilderness
May 11, 1864.

GROUP

No.

6

J. J. PETTIGREW
Falling Waters
July 17, 1863.

THOMAS GREEN
Blair's Landing
April 12, 1864.

ALFRED MOUTON
Sabine Cross Roads
April 8, 1864.

PRESTON SMITH
Chickamauga
September 20, 1863.

Casualties of Fifty Union Regiments During Entire Term of Service

KILLED AND DIED OF WOUNDS—MAXIMUM PERCENTAGES OF ENROLLMENT

COMPILED FROM FOX'S "REGIMENTAL LOSSES IN THE CIVIL WAR"

REGIMENT	DIVISION	CORPS	Enrolled	Killed	Per Cent.
2d Wisconsin	Wadsworth's	First	1,203	238	19.7
1st Maine H. A.	Birney's	Second	2,202	423	19.2
57th Massachusetts	Stevenson's	Ninth	1,052	201	19.1
140th Pennsylvania	Barlow's	Second	1,132	198	17.4
26th Wisconsin	Schurz's	Eleventh	1,089	188	17.2
7th Wisconsin	Wadsworth's	First	1,630	281	17.2
69th New York	Hancock's	Second	1,513	259	17.1
11th Penn. Reserves	Crawford's	Fifth	1,179	196	16.6
142d Pennsylvania	Doubleday's	First	935	155	16.5
141st Pennsylvania	Birney's	Third	1,037	167	16.1
19th Indiana	Wadsworth's	First	1,246	199	15.9
121st New York	Wright's	Sixth	1,426	226	15.8
7th Michigan	Gibbon's	Second	1,315	208	15.8
148th Pennsylvania	Barlow's	Second	1,339	210	15.6
83d Pennsylvania	Griffin's	Fifth	1,808	282	15.5
22d Massachusetts	Griffin's	Fifth	1,393	216	15.5
36th Wisconsin	Gibbon's	Second	1,014	157	15.4
27th Indiana	Williams'	Twelfth	1,101	169	15.3
5th Kentucky	T. J. Wood's	Fourth	1,020	157	15.3
27th Michigan	Willcox's	Ninth	1,485	225	15.1
79th U. S. Colored	Thayer's	Seventh	1,249	188	15.0
17th Maine	Birney's	Third	1,371	207	15.0
1st Minnesota	Gibbon's	Second	1,242	187	15.0
93d Illinois	Quinby's	Seventeenth	1,011	151	14.9
36th Illinois	Sheridan's	Fourth	1,376	204	14.8
8th Penn. Reserves	Crawford's	Fifth	1,062	158	14.8
126th New York	Barlow's	Second	1,036	153	14.7
49th Pennsylvania	Wright's	Sixth	1,313	193	14.6
9th Illinois	Dodge's	Sixteenth	1,493	216	14.4
20th Indiana	Birney's	Third	1,403	201	14.3
15th Kentucky	Johnson's	Fourteenth	956	137	14.3
2d Massachusetts	Williams'	Twelfth	1,305	187	14.3
55th Illinois	Blair's	Fifteenth	1,099	157	14.2
4th Michigan	Griffin's	Fifth	1,325	189	14.2
15th Massachusetts	Gibbon's	Second	1,701	241	14.1
15th New Jersey	Wright's	Sixth	1,702	240	14.1
145th Pennsylvania	Barlow's	Second	1,456	205	14.1
28th Massachusetts	Barlow's	Second	1,778	250	14.0
1st Michigan	Morell's	Fifth	1,329	187	14.0
8th New York H. A.	Gibbon's	Second	2,575	361	14.0
7th West Virginia	Gibbon's	Second	1,008	142	14.0
37th Wisconsin	Willcox's	Ninth	1,110	156	14.0
5th Michigan	Birney's	Third	1,883	263	13.9
10th Penn. Reserves	Crawford's	Fifth	1,150	160	13.9
13th Penn. Reserves	Crawford's	Fifth	1,165	162	13.9
63d Pennsylvania	Birney's	Third	1,341	186	13.8
5th Vermont	Getty's	Sixth	1,533	213	13.8
6th Iowa	Corse's	Sixteenth	1,102	152	13.7
155th New York	Gibbon's	Second	830	114	13.7
49th Ohio	T. J. Wood's	Fourth	1,468	202	13.7

ABNER PERRIN
Spotsylvania
May 12, 1864.

W. E. JONES
Piedmont
June 5, 1864.

GEORGE DOLES
Bethesda Church
May 30, 1864.

ROBERT H. ANDERSON
Antietam
October 6, 1862.

CONFEDERATE

GENERALS

KILLED

IN BATTLE

GROUP No. 7

BRIGADIER–

GENERALS

JOHN H. MORGAN
Greenville
September 4, 1864.

JOHN R. CHAMBLISS, JR.
Deep Bottom
August 16, 1864.

JUNIUS DANIEL
Spotsylvania
Died May 13, 1864.

JAMES B. GORDON
Yellow Tavern
May 11, 1864.

J. C. SAUNDERS
Weldon Railroad
August 21, 1864.

MICAH JENKINS
Wilderness
May 6, 1864.

C. H. STEVENS
Peach Tree Creek
July 20, 1864.

SAMUEL BENTON
Ezra Church
July 29, 1864.

Some Casualties of Confederate Regiments

By General Marcus J. Wright, Confederate States Army

At the time when Lieutenant-Colonel William F. Fox, U. S. V., published his valuable and exceedingly accurate work, entitled "Regimental Losses of the American Civil War, 1861–1865," many regimental reports were missing or inaccessible, so that this work, in many respects a standard as far as Confederate material was concerned, necessarily is incomplete.

No compilation of statistics exists corresponding to that given for the Union armies on a preceding page, and but little exact statistical information of a broad character is available. Therefore, it seems desirable here to give on a following page a table from Colonel Fox's book, which shows remarkable percentages of losses in Confederate regiments at particular engagements. This list contains only a few of the many instances of regiments suffering a heavy percentage of loss. The list is compiled from the few cases in which the official Confederate reports on file in the United States War Department mention the number of effectives taken into action as well as the actual losses.

Because of these statistical deficiencies, no complete catalogue of distinguished Confederate regiments based on the records of battlefield casualties is possible. This is especially regrettable to those who recall the conspicuous services of many organizations from the very outset.

In addition to Colonel Fox's table we give a few other notable instances. At the first battle of Bull Run, the 33d Virginia lost 45 killed and 101 wounded, and the 27th Virginia lost 19 killed and 122 wounded. Hampton's Legion lost 19 killed and 100 wounded.

The 2d Georgia had the longest service of any infantry regiment from that State. In the Seven Days' around Richmond, with 271 men in the field, it lost 120. At Malvern Hill, it lost 81 men and about the same number at Gettysburg.

At Mills Springs, Ky., the 15th Mississippi Regiment lost 46 killed and 153 wounded. The 8th Kentucky regiment at Fort Donelson, Tenn., lost 27 killed and 72 wounded. The 4th Tennessee, at Shiloh, lost 36 killed and 183 wounded, while the 4th Kentucky lost 30 killed and 183 wounded. The 12th Mississippi, at Fair Oaks,

Va., lost 41 killed and 152 wounded. Hampton's Legion, a South Carolina organization, at Fair Oaks lost 21 killed and 122 wounded. The 20th North Carolina lost, at Gaines' Mill, 70 killed and 202 wounded. At Gaines' Mill and Glendale the 14th Alabama lost 71 killed and 253 wounded, the 19th Mississippi 58 killed and 264 wounded, the 14th Louisiana 51 killed and 192 wounded, and the 12th Mississippi 34 killed and 186 wounded. At Malvern Hill, the 2d Louisiana lost 30 killed and 152 wounded. The 21st Virginia lost, at Cedar Mountain, Va., 37 killed and 85 wounded.

At Manassas (Second Bull Run), Va., the 5th Texas lost 15 killed and 224 wounded; the 2d Louisiana lost 25 killed and 86 wounded. At Richmond, Ky., the 2d Tennessee lost 17 killed and 95 wounded. At Antietam, or Sharpsburg, the 13th Georgia lost 48 killed and 169 wounded; the 48th North Carolina lost 31 killed and 186 wounded. At Iuka, Miss., the 3d Texas, dismounted cavalry, lost 22 killed and 74 wounded. At Corinth, Miss., the casualties of the 35th Mississippi were 32 killed and 110 wounded, and of the 6th Missouri, 31 were killed and 130 wounded. At Chaplin Hills, Ky., from the 1st Tennessee regiment, 49 were killed and 129 wounded.

At Fredericksburg, Va., the 57th North Carolina lost 32 killed, 192 wounded, and the 48th North Carolina 17 killed and 161 wounded. At Stone's River, the 29th Mississippi lost 34 killed and 202 wounded.

At Chancellorsville, Va., the losses of the 37th North Carolina were 34 killed and 193 wounded; the 2d North Carolina, 47 killed and 167 wounded. At Vicksburg, Miss., the 3d Louisiana lost 49 killed, 119 wounded, and the 6th Missouri lost 33 killed and 134 wounded. At Helena, Ark., the 7th Missouri lost 16 killed and 125 wounded. At Gettysburg, the 42d Mississippi lost 60 killed and 205 wounded, and the 1st Maryland, with 400 present for duty, had 52 killed and 140 wounded.

At Charleston Harbor, the 21st South Carolina lost 14 killed and 112 wounded, and the 25th South Carolina 16 killed and 124 wounded. At the bloody battle of Chickamauga, Alabama regiments suffered great losses.

ARCHIBALD GRACIE, JR.
Petersburg Trenches
December 2, 1864.

JOHN ADAMS
Franklin
November 30, 1864.

H. B. GRANBERRY
Franklin
November 30, 1864.

JAMES DEARING
High Bridge
April 6, 1865.

CONFEDERATE

GENERALS

KILLED

IN

BATTLE—

GROUP No. 8—

BRIGADIER-

GENERALS

JOHN DUNOVANT
Vaughn Road,
October 1, 1864.

JOHN GREGG
Darbytown Road,
October 7, 1864.

STEPHEN ELLIOTT, JR.
Petersburg
Died in 1864.

OSCAR F. STRAHL
Franklin
November 30, 1864.

ARCHIBALD C. GODWIN
Opequon
September 19, 1864.

S. R. GIST
Franklin
November 30, 1864.

VICTOR J. GIRARDEY
Petersburg
August 16, 1864.

Casualties of Fifty Confederate Regiments

From Fox's "Regimental Losses in the Civil War"

Showing Remarkable Percentages of Losses at Particular Engagements Based on Official Reports

Note—This list does not aim to include all the notable instances of remarkable casualties of regiments in the Confederate Army. It was based by Colonel Fox on available records where the numbers taken into action as well as the casualties were specified in official reports. The list is suggestive rather than complete, as many regiments omitted might with propriety claim to be included in any roll of "Fifty Fighting Regiments."

REGIMENT	BATTLE	DIVISION	Present	Killed	Wounded	Missing	Per Cent.
1st Texas	Antietam	Hood's	226	45	141	..	82.3
21st Georgia	Manassas	Ewell's	242	38	146	..	76.0
26th North Carolina	Gettysburg	Heth's	820	86	502	..	71.7
6th Mississippi	Shiloh	Hardee's	425	61	239	..	70.5
8th Tennessee	Stone's River	Cheatham's	444	41	265	..	68.2
10th Tennessee	Chickamauga	Johnson's	328	44	180	..	68.0
Palmetto Sharpshooters	Glendale	Longstreet's	375	39	215	..	67.7
17th South Carolina	Manassas	Evans'	284	25	164	1	66.9
23d South Carolina	Manassas	Evans'	225	27	122	..	66.2
44th Georgia	Mechanicsville	D. H. Hill's	514	71	264	..	65.1
2d N. C. Battalion	Gettysburg	Rodes'	240	29	124	..	63.7
16th Mississippi	Antietam	Anderson's	228	27	117	..	63.1
27th North Carolina	Antietam	Walker's	325	31	168	..	61.2
6th Alabama	Seven Pines	D. H. Hill's	632	91	277	5	59.0
15th Virginia	Antietam	McLaws'	128	11	64	..	58.5
8th Georgia	Antietam	Hood's	176	13	72	16	57.3
1st S. C. Rifles	Gaines' Mill	A. P. Hill's	537	81	225	..	56.9
10th Georgia	Antietam	McLaws'	148	15	69	..	56.7
18th North Carolina	Seven Days	A. P. Hill's	396	45	179	..	56.5
3d Alabama	Malvern Hill	D. H. Hill's	354	37	163	..	56.4
17th Virginia	Antietam	Pickett's	55	7	24	..	56.3
7th North Carolina	Seven Days	A. P. Hill's	450	35	218	..	56.2
12th Tennessee	Stone's River	Cheatham's	292	18	137	9	56.1
9th Georgia	Gettysburg	Hood's	340	27	162	..	55.0
5th Georgia	Chickamauga	Cheatham's	353	27	167	..	54.9
16th Tennessee	Stone's River	Cheatham's	377	36	155	16	54.9
4th North Carolina	Seven Pines	D. H. Hill's	678	77	286	6	54.4
27th Tennessee	Shiloh	Hardee's	350	27	115	48	54.2
12th South Carolina	Manassas	A. P. Hill's	270	23	121	2	54.0
4th Virginia	Manassas	Jackson's	180	18	79	..	53.8
4th Texas	Antietam	Hood's	200	10	97	..	53.5
27th Tennessee	Perryville	Cleburne's	210	16	84	12	53.3
1st South Carolina	Manassas	A. P. Hill's	283	25	126	..	53.3
49th Virginia	Fair Oaks	D. H. Hill's	424	32	170	22	52.8
12th Alabama	Fair Oaks	D. H. Hill's	408	59	156	..	52.6
7th South Carolina	Antietam	McLaws'	268	23	117	..	52.2
7th Texas	Raymond	John Gregg's	306	22	136	..	51.6
6th South Carolina	Fair Oaks	D. H. Hill's	521	88	181	..	51.6
15th Georgia	Gettysburg	Hood's	335	19	152	..	51.0
11th Alabama	Glendale	Longstreet's	357	49	121	11	50.7
17th Georgia	Manassas	Hood's	200	10	91	..	50.5
3d North Carolina	Gettysburg	Johnson's	312	29	127	..	50.0
4th Virginia	Chancellorsville	Trimble's	355	14	155	3	48.4
1st Maryland	Gettysburg	Johnson's	400	52	140	..	48.0
8th Mississippi	Stone's River	Jackson's	282	20	113	..	47.1
32d Virginia	Antietam	McLaws'	158	15	57	..	45.5
18th Mississippi	Antietam	McLaws'	186	10	73	..	44.6
14th South Carolina	Gaines' Mill	A. P. Hill's	500	18	197	..	43.0
33d North Carolina	Chancellorsville	A. P. Hill's	480	32	167	..	41.4
5th Alabama	Malvern Hill	D. H. Hill's	225	26	66	..	40.8

FEDERAL ARMIES, CORPS AND LEADERS

THE SECOND CORPS, ARMY OF THE POTOMAC

MARCHING DOWN PENNSYLVANIA AVENUE IN 1865—THE SECOND CORPS HAD A RECORD OF LONGER CONTINUOUS SERVICE, A LARGER ORGANIZATION, HARDEST FIGHTING, AND GREATEST NUMBER OF CASUALTIES, THAN ANY OTHER IN THE EASTERN ARMIES—IT CONTAINED THE REGIMENT WHICH SUSTAINED THE LARGEST PERCENTAGE OF LOSS IN ANY ONE ACTION; THE REGIMENT WHICH SUSTAINED THE GREATEST NUMERICAL LOSS IN ANY ONE ACTION; AND THE REGIMENT WHICH SUSTAINED THE GREATEST NUMERICAL LOSS DURING ITS TERM OF SERVICE—OF THE HUNDRED UNION REGIMENTS WHICH LOST THE MOST MEN IN BATTLE, THIRTY-FIVE BELONGED TO THE SECOND CORPS

ORDERLY   ORDERLY   COLONEL JOSEPH J. REYNOLDS   COLONEL WILLIAM G. LE DUC   CAPTAIN H. W. PERKINS

"FIGHTING JOE HOOKER" WITH HIS STAFF

"Fighting Joe Hooker" was a man of handsome physique and intense personal magnetism. He graduated at West Point in 1837 in the same class with Jubal A. Early and Braxton Bragg. Having fought through the Mexican War, he resigned from the army in 1853. On May 17, 1861, he was appointed brigadier-general of volunteers, and on May 5, 1862, major-general of volunteers. He was active throughout the Peninsular campaign, and at Bristoe Station, Second Bull Run, Chantilly, South Mountain and Antietam. He commanded the center grand division of the Army of the Potomac at Fredericksburg. At last, on January 26, 1863, he was assigned by President Lincoln to the command of the Army of the Potomac. On the 4th of May, 1863, his right flank was surprised by Jackson at Chancellorsville, and his 90,000 soldiers were forced to recross the Rappahannock. While fighting in the East he was wounded at

WALKER, THE ARTIST	CAPTAIN R. H. HALL	GENERAL	GENERAL	COLONEL
LIEUTENANT	MAJOR WILLIAM	JOSEPH	DANIEL	JAMES D.
SAMUEL W. TAYLOR	H. LAWRENCE	HOOKER	BUTTERFIELD	FESSENDEN

ON THE SPOT WHENCE HE DIRECTED HIS "BATTLE ABOVE THE CLOUDS"

Antietam, and stunned at Chancellorsville by a cannon-ball which struck a pillar against which he was leaning.   In September, 1863, he was sent with the Eleventh and Twelfth Corps to reënforce Rosecrans at Chattanooga.   On November 24th, in the "battle among the clouds" at the head of his new command, he led a charge against the Confederate artillery and infantry posted on Lookout Mountain.   For his conduct on this occasion he was brevetted major-general in the regular army.   He further distinguished himself under Sherman at Dalton and Resaca, and in the attack on Atlanta.   At his own request (July 30, 1864) he was placed on waiting orders September 28th, when he was put in command of the Northern Department.   He retired from active service October 15, 1868, with the full rank of major-general in the regular army.   General Hooker died at Garden City, Long Island, New York, October 31, 1879.

THE ARMY OF GEORGIA—ON PARADE, GENERAL SLOCUM AT THE HEAD

Very different from the march through Georgia and the Carolinas was this magnificent parade of the Army of Georgia down Pennsylvania Avenue. In front ride General Slocum and his staff. Behind come the long straight lines of men who proved the Confederacy a hollow shell with all of its fighting men at the front. Eagerly crowding close to the line of march are the citizens of Washington who had alternately clamored for action, and shaken in their boots when the daring Confederate leaders pressed close to the Northern capital. Many a heartfelt prayer of thanks and relief was offered when mothers saw their boys march past, unscathed by the war and about to reënter civil life. Many a tear fell for those who could not be there to share the glory.

At Gaines' Mill, Slocum's Division of the Sixth Corps was sent to the support of General Porter, and lost 2,021 out of less than 8,000 present in the hot engagement. It was in front of Fredericksburg May 3, 1863, under General Sedgwick, that the Corps made its most brilliant display of dash and daring. It carried at the point of the bayonet Marye's Heights, the strong position before which there had fallen, gloriously but in vain, nearly 13,000 men the previous December. Most of the Corps was held in reserve at Gettysburg, and its casualties there were slight, but it added again to its laurels at Rappahannock Sta-

THE NINETEENTH ARMY CORPS

THE SIXTH ARMY CORPS IN THE GRAND
REVIEW—THE CORPS THAT SAVED
WASHINGTON FROM CAPTURE

tion. In the battles of the Wilderness and Spotsylvania it encountered its hardest fighting, the percentage of killed of the Fifteenth New Jersey in the latter battle being equaled in only one instance during the whole war. At Cold Harbor it suffered heavily again, and the appearance of two of its divisions at Fort Stevens checked Early's advance on Washington. It pursued Early up the Shenandoah, and fought at Opequon and Cedar Creek. In the final assault on Petersburg it played an important part. It was no less prominent in its final appearance at the Grand Review in Washington.

THE TWENTIETH ARMY CORPS

The Armies of the United States in the Civil War

BY THE PROVISIONS of the Constitution, the President of the United States is commander-in-chief of the army and navy. During the Civil War, this function was exercised in no small degree by President Lincoln. As Secretaries of War, he had in his cabinet Simon Cameron, from March 4, 1861, to January 14, 1862; and Edward M. Stanton, who served from January 15, 1862, throughout Lincoln's administration, and also under Johnson until May 28, 1868, except for a short interval during which he was suspended. There were four generals-in-chief of the armies: Brevet Lieutenant-General Scott, Major-Generals McClellan and Halleck, and Lieutenant-General Grant. The last named has been considered in previous pages of this volume, but the lives and services of the other three are summarized below, in addition to the treatment received in other volumes. (CONSULT INDEX.) This is true of all the army leaders not separately described in the pages that follow. The Index will refer to treatment in other volumes.

LIEUTENANT-GENERAL WINFIELD SCOTT was born near Petersburg, Virginia, June 13, 1786. After being graduated from William and Mary College, he studied law, was admitted to the bar, and then entered the army at the age of twenty-two. His career was one of bravery and incident. He was captured by the British, but exchanged in 1813, fought in the battle of Lundy's Lane, and was severely wounded. After the close of the war he was raised to the rank of major-general, and in 1841 succeeded General Macomb as commander of the United States army. In the war with Mexico, he won great fame and was nominated by the Whigs for President in 1852; but he carried only four States. In 1855, Congress revived the rank of lieutenant-general and conferred it by brevet upon Scott, the appointment being dated March 29, 1847, the day of his brilliant capture of Vera Cruz. It was evident that his age and infirmities would prevent his taking any active part in the Civil War, and on November 1, 1861, he was retired from the chief command of the army of the United States. He wrote an autobiography, and made a European trip in 1864, dying May 29, 1866, at West Point, New York.

MAJOR-GENERAL HENRY WAGER HALLECK (U.S.M.A. 1839) was born in Westernville, New York, January 16, 1815. He served in California and on the Pacific coast during the Mexican War. He retired from the army with the rank of captain in 1854 to practise law, but after the outbreak of the Civil War reentered the regular service, with the grade of major-general. He was in command of the Department of Missouri (afterward Department of Mississippi) from November 19, 1861, to July 11, 1862, when he became general-in-chief of all the armies. Grant succeeded him, March 9, 1864, and Halleck was his chief-of-staff until the close of the war. He continued in the army as head, successively, of the Military Division of the James, the Department of the Pacific, and Department of the South until his death at Louisville, Kentucky, January 9, 1872.

MAJOR-GENERAL GEORGE BRINTON McCLELLAN (U.S.M.A. 1846) was born in Philadelphia, December 3, 1826. He served in the Engineer Corps during the Mexican War, distinguished himself by gallant service, and reached the rank of captain in 1855, having been so brevetted in 1847. He became assistant instructor in practical engineering at West Point, later accompanied the Red River exploring expedition, and was sent on a secret mission to Santo Domingo. During the Crimean War, he was one of a commission of three appointed by Congress to study and report upon the whole art of European warfare. He remained some time with the British forces. McClellan's report was a model of comprehensive accuracy and conciseness, and showed him to be a master of siege-tactics. In 1857, McClellan resigned his army commission to devote himself to the practice of engineering. He became vice-president of the Illinois Central Railroad Company, and later president of the Eastern Division of the Ohio and Missouri Railroad. He made his home in Cincinnati until the outbreak of the Civil War, when he tendered his services to his country and was made major-general of volunteers, April 21, 1861. The Department of the Ohio was constituted, and McClellan took command, May 13th, his appointment as major-general dating from the following day. He drove the Confederates from northwestern Virginia and saved that section to the Union, an accomplishment of the most vital importance, since, in the event of the establishment of the Confederacy, the Union territory would have been contracted at

The upper photograph, as beautifully "composed" as a classic painting, shows General and Mrs. Scott at their home, Elizabeth, New Jersey, in 1862. A closer portrait study of the general appears below. Winfield Scott became the first general-in-chief of the United States Army during the Civil War, being already in that position when the war broke out. He was then nearly seventy-five years old. The aged hero owed his exalted rank and his military fame to his dashing and vigorous achievements as commander in the Mexican War. He directed until retired by his own request in November, 1861. Scott possessed an imposing figure and courage equal to every danger. He was exacting in discipline—that power which the French call "the glory of the soldier and the strength of armies.

Major-General Henry Wager Halleck assumed command of the Army and Department of Missouri in 1861, and from his headquarters at St. Louis directed the operations of the forces which early in 1862 compelled the Confederates to evacuate Kentucky and Central and West Tennessee. After he assumed control of all the armies as successor to McClellan in July, 1862, he made his headquarters in Washington, performing duties similar to those of a chief-of-staff in a modern army. His military decisions in particular crises as Fredericksburg, Chancellorsville and Gettysburg were not always approved by critics; nevertheless, he bore a reputation for genius as a commander. He was succeeded in the duties of general-in-chief in February, 1864, by Lieutenant-General Ulysses S. Grant.

SCOTT AND HALLECK—TWO GENERALS–IN–CHIEF OF THE UNITED STATES ARMY

this point into a neck but little more than one hundred miles in width. After this success, Mc-Clellan was placed, July 25, 1861, at the head of the newly created District (afterward Department) of the Potomac, and began the organization and training of the army of that name. From November 5, 1861 to March 11th of the following year, he was general-in-chief of the armies of the United States, and after the latter date continued in command of the Army of the Potomac until November 9, 1862, when he was replaced by Major-General A. E. Burnside. He took no further part in the war. His removal was due to dissatisfaction with his methods that gradually developed among President Lincoln and his advisers. The

failure of the army to capture Richmond in the Peninsula campaign, and the non-pursuit of Lee immediately after Antietam were the chief reasons. As the nominee of the Democratic party, he was defeated for the presidency in 1864, and his resignation from the army was accepted on November 8th. He now spent several years abroad, returning to live in New Jersey, of which State he became governor in 1877. Aside from his military abilities, McClellan was a man of fine tastes in literature and art, and also took an active interest in promoting the manufacturing industries of the State. He wrote his autobiography, and several works of a military nature. His death occurred October 29, 1885, at Orange.

Army of the Potomac

By THE CONSOLIDATION of the Department of Washington and the Department of Northeastern Virginia, July 25, 1861, the Military District of the Potomac was constituted and placed under command of Major-General George B. McClellan. On August 15, 1861, the Department, or Army of the Potomac was created from it, and as such it was known thereafter. Major-General McClellan assumed command of this army August 20, 1861. As then constituted, it was organized in fourteen brigades composed largely of the troops (regular army and volunteer) of the Department of Northeastern Virginia, under Brigadier-General Irvin McDowell, and new organizations. Most of these brigades had artillery and some of them cavalry. McClellan immediately applied his military knowledge to remodeling the army, and in October a new organization was announced. The division was now the unit, and there were fourteen, including one stationed at Baltimore. There were also one provisional brigade, a provost-guard, a cavalry command, and a cavalry reserve. During the winter of 1861–62, the Army of the Potomac was thoroughly drilled. A new organization was announced in March, 1862, and this the army retained, except while Burnside created the grand division, until it was discontinued, June 28, 1865. The corps were the units, and their number varied from time to time. There were also the provost-guard, the guard for general headquarters, a full artillery, and cavalry reserve. A cavalry division was formed in July, 1862, and reorganized as a cavalry corps in February, 1863. The successive commanders of the Army of the Potomac were:

Major-General George B. McClellan to November 9, 1862; Major-General A. E. Burnside to January 26, 1863; Major-General Joseph Hooker to June 28, 1863, being succeeded by Major-General George G. Meade, who remained at its head until it was discontinued, June 28, 1865, except for a short interval in January, 1865, when Major-General John G. Parke was in temporary command.

MAJOR-GENERAL AMBROSE EVERETT BURNSIDE (U.S.M.A. 1847) was born in Liberty, Indiana, May 23, 1824. He served in the artillery with the rank of first lieutenant, resigned his commission, in 1853, to take up the manufacture of a breech-loading rifle which he had invented. At the outbreak of the Civil War he was an officer of the Illinois Central Railroad Company. For gallant service at Bull Run he was made brigadier-general of volunteers, and in March, 1862, major-general of volunteers. He organized an expeditionary corps in December, 1861, and this was merged in the Department of North Carolina, of which Burnside was the head from January to July, 1862. He captured Roanoke Island and occupied New Berne. From these troops and others was organized, July 22, 1862, the Ninth Corps, with Burnside at its head. He served under McClellan at South Mountain, and at Antietam, where he commanded the left wing, and succeeded him in the command of the Army of the Potomac. Later, Major-General Burnside was assigned to command of the Department of the Ohio. Burnside and the Ninth Corps were with Grant in the

ANOTHER GENERAL–IN–CHIEF
McCLELLAN, WITH HIS WIFE

Major-General George Brinton McClellan began his war career as commander of the Department of Ohio. After he had defeated and scattered the Confederate forces commanded by General Robert E. Lee, securing West Virginia to the Union, he was appointed general-in-chief of the United States Armies as successor to General Scott, in November, 1861. He planned and directed the expeditions which, under General A. E. Burnside captured the coast of North Carolina, under Butler and Farragut opened up the lower Mississippi, and in Kentucky and Tennessee resulted in the capture of Fort Donelson. He led the Army of the Potomac in the Peninsula and Antietam campaigns. Meade, its last commander, said: "Had there been no McClellan there could have been no Grant."

Virginia campaign of 1864. Major-General Burnside resigned his commission at the close of the war and resumed his career as a railroad projector and manager. He was governor of Rhode Island from 1866 to 1869, and senator from 1875 until his death, which occurred September 3, 1881, at Bristol, Rhode Island.

MAJOR-GENERAL JOSEPH HOOKER (U.S.M.A. 1837) was born in Hadley, Massachusetts, November 13, 1814. He entered the artillery and was brevetted lieutenant-colonel for distinguished services in the Mexican War. He resigned his commission in 1853. At the outbreak of the Civil War he was living in California as a farmer and civil engineer. He tendered his services to the Government and was appointed brigadier-general of volunteers. In March, 1862, he was made a division commander in the Army of the Potomac, with a promotion to major-general of volunteers in May. An appointment as brigadier-general of the regular army followed the battle of Antietam, in which he was wounded. In September, 1862, he rose to corps commander, and was at the head of the Center Grand Division in Burnside's organization. He was commander of the Army of the Potomac from January 26, 1863, to June 28th. Later, he exhibited great gallantry as corps commander at Lookout Mountain, and

in the Atlanta campaign. On October 1, 1864, he was placed at the head of the Northern Department, and served at the head of other departments until he was retired, as the result of a paralytic stroke, with full rank of major-general, in October, 1868. His death occurred at Garden City, New York, October 31, 1879.

MAJOR-GENERAL GEORGE GORDON MEADE (U. S.M.A. 1835) was born in Cadiz, Spain, December 31, 1815, while his father was American naval agent at that city. He saw service in the Seminole War, and then resigned in 1836 to take up the practice of civil engineering. He reentered the army and served with the Topographical Engineer Corps during the Mexican War. He was afterward employed on river and harbor improvements, lighthouse construction, and the survey of the Great Lakes, until the Civil War broke out, when he was commissioned brigadier-general of volunteers and put in command of a brigade in the Pennsylvania Reserve in the Army of the Potomac. Later, he commanded the First and Fifth corps and was made general commanding of the army, June 28, 1863. He was in chief command at Gettysburg. On August 18, 1864, he received a commission as major-general in the regular army, and served therein until his death, in Philadelphia, November 6, 1872.

Army of the Tennessee

THE TROOPS in the Military District of Cairo were under the command of Brigadier-General U. S. Grant from August 1, 1861, until February, 1862. The District of West Tennessee was organized February 17, 1862, and Grant was at its head until October 16th. His forces were known as the Army of West Tennessee, and were included in those of the Department of Mississippi, under Major-General Halleck. With this force, consisting of six divisions and some unassigned troops, Grant fought the battle of Shiloh. On October 16, 1862, the Department of Tennessee was created to include Cairo, western Kentucky and Tennessee, and northern Mississippi. Grant was commander until October 24, 1863, when the Military Division of the Mississippi was organized to include the Departments of the Ohio, Tennessee, Cumberland, and of Arkansas. The troops in the Department of Tennessee were designated the Thirteenth Army Corps until December 18, 1862,

when they were reorganized into the Thirteenth, Fifteenth, Sixteenth, and Seventeenth corps. Succeeding Grant, this force, usually called the Army of the Tennessee, was successively commanded by Major-Generals W. T. Sherman, James B. McPherson, John A. Logan, and O. O. Howard. This army took part in the capture of Vicksburg, battle of Chattanooga, Atlanta campaign, and Sherman's campaigns in Georgia and the Carolinas. A detachment of it was with the Red River expedition, in 1864.

MAJOR-GENERAL JAMES BIRDSEYE McPHERSON (U.S.M.A. 1853) was born in Sandusky, Ohio, November 14, 1828. He practised engineering in the Government employ and also taught it at West Point. When the war broke out, he raised a force of engineers, and later he was aide to Major-General Halleck. In December, 1862, he was given command of the Seventeenth Corps. His services

AMBROSE EVERETT BURNSIDE
Commander of the Army of the Potomac During
the Fredericksburg Campaign, November, 1862, to January, 1863.

GEORGE GORDON MEADE
Commander of the Army of the Potomac in the
Gettysburg Campaign, also in the Wilderness
Campaign and Siege of Petersburg.

MAJOR–GENERALS

BURNSIDE,

HOOKER,

MEADE

COMMANDERS

OF

THE ARMY OF

THE POTOMAC

JOSEPH HOOKER
Commander of the Army of the Potomac During the Chan-
cellorsville Campaign and the Opening of the
Gettysburg Campaign.

in reenforcing Rosecrans after Corinth, October, 1862, won him the rank of major-general of volunteers, and after the fall of Vicksburg he received the commission of brigadier-general of the regular army. He succeeded Major-General William T. Sherman in the command of the Army of the Tennessee, March 12, 1864, and was killed at the battle of Atlanta, July 22, 1864.

MAJOR-GENERAL JOHN A. LOGAN was born in Jackson County, Illinois, February 9, 1826. He served in the Mexican War, rising from a private to the rank of second lieutenant. He was afterward admitted to the bar and finally reached Congress. During his term here the Civil War broke out and he enlisted and fought at Bull Run. Returning to the West, he raised the Thirty-first Illinois Infantry, afterward becoming its colonel. He was wounded at Fort Donelson and shortly afterward was made major-general of volunteers. In the Vicksburg campaigns he commanded a division of the Seventeenth Corps. In 1863, he took command of the Fifteenth Corps and served in the Atlanta campaign and led his troops through the Carolinas. He was made head of the Department of the Tennessee May 19, 1865. He was elected to the United States Senate in 1871, and was defeated for the vice-presidency of the United States on the Republican ticket of 1884. He died in Washington, December 26, 1886.

MAJOR-GENERAL OLIVER OTIS HOWARD (U.S. M.A. 1854) was born in Leeds, Maine, November 8, 1830. He served as chief of ordnance, and as first lieutenant taught mathematics at West Point until the Civil War broke out, when he left the regular army to command the Third Maine Volunteers. He headed a brigade in the first battle of Bull Run and was promoted to brigadier-general of volunteers in September, 1861. At Fair Oaks, where he lost his right arm, he achieved distinction as an able fighter. After Antietam, he commanded a division of the Second Corps, and later, as major-general of volunteers, the corps itself for a short time. On April 2, 1863, the Eleventh Corps was given him, and it was these troops that were so badly routed by "Stonewall" Jackson at Chancellorsville. In September, 1863, Howard and his corps were transferred to the Army of the Cumberland, in which he became leader of the Fourth Corps, April, 1864. Howard's services at Gettysburg, Lookout Mountain, and Missionary Ridge were conspicuous. He accompanied Sherman to the relief of Knoxville, and fought in all the battles of the Atlanta campaign, succeeding Major-General McPherson to the command of the Army of the Tennessee, and marching with Sherman through Georgia and the Carolinas. After the close of the war he commanded the Nez Percé Indian expedition of 1877, the Bannock, and Piute campaigns, and from 1880 to 1882, was superintendent of the Military Academy, West Point. He was (1865–74) commissioner of the Bureau of Refugees, Freedmen, and Abandoned Lands, and in 1895 founded the Lincoln Memorial University and the industrial school at Cumberland Gap, Tennessee. Major-General Howard was a noted total-abstinence advocate and was much interested in Sunday-school work. He was retired with full rank in 1894, and he died at Burlington, Vermont, October, 26, 1909.

Army of the Ohio and Army of the Cumberland

THE DEPARTMENT OF KENTUCKY, which constituted the whole of that State within a hundred miles of the Ohio River, was merged in the Department of the Cumberland, comprising the States of Kentucky and Tennessee, August 15, 1861. On November 9th, it was renamed the Department of the Ohio, the States of Ohio, Michigan, and Indiana being added. The troops in this region (over whom McClellan, Rosecrans, O. M. Mitchel, Robert Anderson, and W. T. Sherman had, at different times and places, control) were now organized into the Army of the Ohio, with Major-General Don Carlos Buell in command. Although the department was merged into that of Mississippi in March, 1862, the Army of the Ohio retained its name. This was the body that brought such timely assistance to Grant at Shiloh and drove Bragg out of Kentucky. The army was organized into three corps in September, 1862, but the following month (October 24th) the Department of the Cumberland was recreated to consist of eastern Tennessee, Alabama, and Georgia, and the Army of the Ohio, which had operated chiefly in that region, now became officially the Fourteenth Army Corps, but better known as the Army of the Cumberland. On October 30th, Buell was

GEORGE HENRY THOMAS

Commander of the Army of the Cumberland in the Tennessee and Georgia Campaigns, including Stone's
River, Chickamauga, Chattanooga and Atlanta.

JOHN ALEXANDER LOGAN

Commander of the Army of the Tennessee in Front of
Atlanta. He subsequently resumed Command of a
Corps and Led it Through the Carolinas.

MAJOR–GENERALS

THOMAS

LOGAN

HOWARD

ARMY OF THE

CUMBERLAND

AND ARMY OF

THE TENNESSEE

OLIVER OTIS HOWARD

Commander of the Army of the Tennessee in Part
of the Atlanta Campaign and in the March
Through Georgia and the Carolinas.

replaced by Major-General W. S. Rosecrans, and the Fourteenth Corps was reorganized into the Right Wing, Center, and Left Wing, later the Fourteenth, Twentieth, and Twenty-first Army corps. The last two were afterward consolidated as the Fourth Corps. With this army, Rosecrans fought the battle of Stone's River, drove Bragg across the Tennessee, and was defeated at Chickamauga. Major-General George H. Thomas succeeded to the command October 20, 1863. The army distinguished itself on Missionary Ridge and through the Atlanta campaign (as a part of the Military Division of the Mississippi), and in the campaign against Hood in Tennessee. The army had four divisions of cavalry. It had a reserve corps for a short time, and received two corps from the Army of the Potomac, which were finally consolidated into the reorganized Twentieth Corps.

MAJOR-GENERAL DON CARLOS BUELL (U.S. M.A. 1841) was born March 23, 1818, near Marietta, Ohio, and served in the Mexican War. When the Civil War broke out he assisted in the organization of volunteers, and in November, 1861, took charge of the Department and Army of the Ohio. He was soon raised to the rank of major-general of volunteers. His last service in this army was the driving of Bragg out of Kentucky, for this, with the preceding Tennessee campaign during the summer of 1862, aroused such criticism that he was replaced, October 30th, by Major-General Rosecrans and tried before a military commission. An adverse report was handed in, and Buell resigned from the army June 1, 1864. He then became president of the Green River Iron Company, and, 1885–89, was pension-agent at Louisville. He died near Rockport, Kentucky, November 19, 1898.

MAJOR-GENERAL WILLIAM STARKE ROSECRANS (U.S.M.A. 1842) was born at Kingston, Ohio, September 6, 1818. He served in the Engineer Corps and as assistant professor at West Point. In 1854, he resigned from the army to practise architecture and civil engineering, but at the outbreak of the Civil War he tendered his services to the Government and was made brigadier-general of the regular army, and major-general of volunteers in March, 1862. He succeeded McClellan at the head of the army of occupation in western Virginia after his victory at Rich Mountain, and held it until Major-General Fremont took charge of the Mountain Department, March 29, 1862. From June 26th until the end of October, Rose-

crans was Pope's successor in the Army of the Mississippi and, taking command of the District of Corinth, he defeated the Confederate forces at Iuka and Corinth. He now replaced Buell in the Army of the Cumberland. As general commanding he won the battle of Stone's River, but was defeated at Chickamauga, and was succeeded by Major-General George H. Thomas. He then spent a year in command of the Department of Missouri, during which he drove Price out of the State, and on December 9, 1864, was relieved of active command. After resigning his commission, in 1866, he was United States minister to Mexico, and was in Congress from 1881 to 1885. In 1889, Congress restored him to the rank and pay of brigadier-general. He died at Redondo, California, March 11, 1898.

MAJOR-GENERAL GEORGE HENRY THOMAS (U. S.M.A. 1840) was born in Southampton County, Virginia, July 31, 1816. He served in the Seminole and Mexican wars, and had risen to the grade of lieutenant-colonel when the Civil War broke out. In August, 1861, he was made brigadier-general of volunteers. His first services in the war were rendered in the Departments of Pennsylvania and of the Shenandoah. His division of the Army of the Ohio defeated the Confederate forces at Mill Springs, Kentucky, January 19, 1862. This victory first brought him into notice, and shortly afterward he was made major-general of volunteers. He was put at the head of the Center (Fourteenth Corps) of the reorganized Army of the Cumberland, and in October, 1863, he assumed the chief command, distinguishing himself at Missionary Ridge, in the Atlanta campaign, and in the crushing defeat of Bragg at Nashville. He was promoted to major-general in the regular army for his services at Nashville, December 15, 1864. He narrowly escaped this honor, for, impatient at his delay in attacking Hood—a delay occasioned by the very inclement weather—Grant had sent Major-General Logan to relieve him, and the latter was on the way. He had also shown himself a gallant fighter in the earlier battles of Stone's River, and Chickamauga, where he held the left wing of the army against tremendous odds. This feat is considered one of the most glorious of the whole war. With the right wing of the army routed and in utter confusion, Thomas kept his position against the whole of Bragg's army until ordered to withdraw. He declined the brevet of lieutenant-general, which President Johnson offered him in 1868. Two years later he died in San Francisco, March 28, 1870.

JOHN McALLISTER SCHOFIELD

Commander of the Army of the Frontier and of the
Department and Army of the Ohio.

DON CARLOS BUELL

Commander of the Army of the Ohio in the Shiloh
Campaign and Afterward of a Department.

JOHN POPE

Commander of the Army of Virginia, June to September, 1862, Including Second Bull Run.

WILLIAM STARKE ROSECRANS

Commander of the Army of the Ohio (Cumberland) in
the Campaign of Stone's River and Chickamauga.

COMMANDERS OF THE ARMIES OF THE OHIO AND VIRGINIA

Army of the Ohio

THE DEPARTMENT OF THE OHIO having been merged in that of Mississippi, March, 1862, it was recreated on August 19th, to consist of the States of Ohio, Michigan, Indiana, Illinois, Wisconsin, and Kentucky, east of the Tennessee River, and Major-General H. G. Wright was placed at the head. The troops of the department were scattered through many districts. Some of the brigades constituted the Army of Kentucky, of which Major-General Gordon Granger was in command. Wright was replaced March 25, 1863, by Major-General A. E. Burnside, and shortly afterward the troops in the department were reorganized into the Twenty-third Army Corps, and this force is the Army of the Ohio associated with the Knoxville, Atlanta, and Nashville campaigns. The Ninth Corps was attached to the department from March, 1863, to March, 1864. Burnside was succeeded in turn by Major-Generals J. G. Foster, J. M. Schofield, and George Stoneman. A cavalry division organized in April, 1864, was headed by Major-General Stoneman, and afterward by Colonels Capron and Garrard. On January 17, 1865, the troops still in the department (the Twenty-third Corps having gone to North Carolina) were annexed to the Department of the Cumberland.

MAJOR-GENERAL JOHN MCALLISTER SCHOFIELD (U.S.M.A. 1853) was born in Chautauqua County, New York, September 29, 1831. After garrison duty in Florida and South Carolina, he held the chair of natural philosophy at West Point and later at Washington University, St. Louis, where the outbreak of the Civil War found him. He had command of the District of St. Louis, Department of Missouri; Army of the Frontier; of a division in the Fourteenth Corps; the Department and Army of the Ohio, and of the Twenty-third Corps, which was transferred to North Carolina late in the war. He was made major-general of volunteers in November, 1862. His most noteworthy active services were rendered during the Atlanta campaign and at the battle of Franklin. After the Civil War he was Secretary of War *ad interim*, after the resignation of General Grant. He was commander of the United States army from 1888 to 1895, rising to the rank of lieutenant-general, at which he was retired in September, 1895. He died at St. Augustine, Florida, March 4, 1906.

Army of the Mississippi

THE ARMY OF THE MISSISSIPPI had a short existence, being organized February 23d, and discontinued October 26, 1862. Its first commander was Major-General John Pope, who was succeeded, June 26th, by Major-General W. S. Rosecrans. This army consisted of five divisions, a flotilla brigade, and several brigades of cavalry, and operated on the Mississippi in the spring of 1862, capturing Island No. 10; before Corinth in May, 1862, and at Iuka and Corinth in September and October, 1862. Most of the troops went into the Thirteenth Army Corps.

Army of Virginia

TO OBTAIN CLOSER ORGANIZATION in the various commands operating in Virginia, President Lincoln, on June 26, 1862, constituted the Army of Virginia out of Major-General Fremont's forces (Mountain Department), those of Major-General McDowell (Department of the Rappahannock), those of Major-General Banks (Department of the Shenandoah), and Brigadier-General Sturgis' brigade from the Military District of Washington. This last, an unorganized body of troops, did not join the army at once. Major-General John Pope was placed at the head of the new organization, which was divided into three corps. Exclusive of Sturgis' troops it numbered between forty and fifty thousand men, and was augmented later by troops from three corps of the Army of the Potomac. A corps of the Army of Virginia checked " Stonewall " Jackson's advance

Eugene A. Carr, Commander of the Army
of the Southwest; Led Troops at
Wilson's Creek and Pea Ridge.

FEDERAL

MAJOR–GENERALS

COMMANDING

ARMIES

Quincy Adams Gillmore, Commander of the
Department and Army of the South
at the Siege of Charleston.

Frederick Steele, Commander of the Army
of Arkansas; Engaged at Little
Rock.

Benjamin Franklin Butler, Commander of the Department and
Army of the Gulf in 1862, and
of the Army of the James
in 1864. With this Army
he Operated Against Rich-
mond in May and June.

Gordon Granger, Commander of the Army
of Kentucky in 1862; Noted at
Chickamauga.

James G. Blunt, Commander in Kansas
and of the Army of the Frontier; at
Prairie Grove.

OPERATING

ON THE GULF

AND ALONG THE

WESTERN FRONTIER

David Hunter, Head of a Division at Bull
Run and later of the Department
of the South.

at Cedar Mountain, on August 9th, but the entire organization was defeated at Manassas by Jackson and Longstreet, August 29th and 30th, and withdrew to the lines of Washington. On September 12th, the Army of Virginia was merged in the Army of the Potomac.

MAJOR-GENERAL JOHN POPE (U.S.M.A. 1842) was born in Louisville, Kentucky, March 16, 1822. He served in the Mexican War, rising to the rank of captain. After this he did much work on engineering service in connection with the development of the West. When the Civil War broke out, Pope was sent to Cairo, Illinois, and later to command the troops in northern Missouri. From February to June, 1862, he headed the newly created Army of the Mississippi, during which time he was made major-general of volunteers and brigadier-general of the regular army. His most notable achievement was the capture of Island No. 10, as a result of which he was put in command of the Army of Virginia, June 26, 1862. The reverse of Second Bull Run caused him to ask to be relieved of this command, and he was sent to the Department of the Northwest, to carry on the war against the Sioux Indians. He headed other departments in the West until he was retired, in 1886. His last command was the Department of the Pacific. He was brevetted major-general in March, 1865, for his services at Island No. 10, and received the full rank in 1882. Major-General Pope died at Sandusky, Ohio, September 23, 1892.

Army of the Southwest

CREATED December 25, 1861, from troops in portions of the Department of Missouri. It was merged in the District of Eastern Arkansas, Department of Tennessee, December 13, 1862, and was commanded during its existence by Brigadier-Generals S. R. Curtis, Frederick Steele, E. A. Carr, and W. A. Gorman. This army fought many minor but important engagements in Missouri and Arkansas, including Bentonville, Sugar Creek, and Pea Ridge.

MAJOR-GENERAL SAMUEL RYAN CURTIS (U.S. M.A. 1831) was born near Champlain, New York, February, 1807, and resigned from the army to become a civil engineer and, later, a lawyer. He served as colonel of volunteers in the Mexican War, and afterward went to Congress. He was made brigadier-general of volunteers in May, 1861, and was commander of the Army of the Southwest from December, 1861, to August, 1862. He conducted an active campaign against Van Dorn and Price, during which he won the battle of Pea Ridge, March 7-8, 1862, and was made major-general of volunteers that same month. Later, he was unable to hold Arkansas and was compelled to march to the Mississippi River. He was in command of the Department of Missouri, September, 1862, to May, 1863, and of Kansas, January, 1864, to January, 1865, after which he was at the head of that of the Northwest. He negotiated treaties with several Indian tribes, and was mustered out of the volunteer service April 30, 1866. He died at Council Bluffs, Iowa, December 26, 1866.

MAJOR-GENERAL FREDERICK STEELE (U.S.M. A. 1843) was born in Delhi, New York, January 14, 1819, and served in the Mexican War. He was a major when the Civil War broke out and rose to be major-general of volunteers in November, 1862. Steele served with distinction in Missouri, and was given a division in the Army of the Southwest in May, 1862. For a short time, he had command of the army itself. When it was broken up, he was finally transferred into the Department of the Tennessee, having a division on Sherman's Yazoo Expedition, McClernand's Army of the Mississippi, and the new Fifteenth Army Corps, with which he took part in the Vicksburg campaign. In August, 1863, he was given charge of the Arkansas Expedition, which developed into the Seventh Army Corps, at the head of which he remained until December, 1864. He was given a separate command in the district of West Florida, and assisted Major-General Gordon Granger at the final operations around Mobile. After muster-out from the volunteer service, he returned to the regular army as colonel, having already received the brevet of major-general for the capture of Little Rock. He died at San Mateo, California, January 12, 1868.

MAJOR-GENERAL EUGENE ASA CARR (U.S.M. A. 1850) was born in Erie County, New York, in

GEORGE CROOK

Commander of the Army of West Virginia in 1864. Later Crook led a Cavalry Division under Sheridan in the Appomattox Campaign at Five Forks and during the pursuit of Lee.

JOHN C. FREMONT

Commander of the Mountain Department and Army in West Virginia in 1862. Fremont was in Command in Missouri in 1861 and at one time gave orders to Brigadier-General Grant.

NATHANIEL PRENTISS BANKS

Commander of the Department and Army of the Shenandoah in 1862 and of the Army of the Gulf in 1863–4. With this Army Banks captured Port Hudson in 1863.

PHILIP HENRY SHERIDAN

Commander of the Army of Shenandoah in 1864. Sheridan Led a Division at Chickamauga and Chattanooga and Commanded the Cavalry Corps of the Army of the Potomac in the Wilderness Campaign.

HENRY WARNER SLOCUM

Commander of the Army of Georgia in the Carolinas. Slocum Commanded the Twelfth Corps, Army of the Potomac, at Chancellorsville and Gettysburg and the Twentieth Corps in Front of Atlanta.

JOHN A. McCLERNAND

Commander of the Army of the Mississippi in 1862–3. McClernand Led Troops at Shiloh and later Commanded the Army of the Mississippi operating against Vicksburg; Head of a Corps in Grant's Siege.

COMMANDERS OF THE ARMIES OF WEST VIRGINIA, SHENANDOAH, GEORGIA AND MISSISSIPPI

1830, and served in the mounted rifles in Indian warfare until the opening of the Civil War, when he became colonel in the Illinois cavalry. His appointment of brigadier-general of volunteers was dated March 7, 1862. His service was chiefly in the Southwest, in the Army of the Southwest, the Thirteenth, Sixteenth, and Seventeenth corps, the Districts of Arkansas, and of Little Rock. For short periods he was at the head of the Army of the Southwest and of the left wing of the Sixteenth Corps. His gallant and meritorious serv-ice in the field won him a medal of honor and successive brevets in the regular army, and he showed especial bravery and military ability at Wilson's Creek, Pea Ridge, Black River Bridge, and the capture of Little Rock. He was mustered out of the volunteer service in January, 1866, with the brevet of major-general in the regular army. He returned to the army, and consinued in service on the frontier. In 1892, he was made brigadier-general and was retired February 15, 1893. He died in Washington, D. C., December 2, 1910.

Army of West Virginia

THE TROOPS in the Department of West Virginia were taken from the Eighth Army Corps when the department was reorganized, June 28, 1863. The department commanders were Brigadier-General B. F. Kelley, Major-Generals Franz Sigel, David Hunter, George Crook, Brigadier-General J. D. Stevenson, Brevet Major-General S. S. Carroll, and Major-Generals W. S. Hancock and W. H. Emory. In the campaign against Lieutenant-General Early (June-October, 1864), the two divisions (about seventy-five hundred men) under Crook were called the Army of West Virginia. This force was prominent at the Opequon, Fisher's Hill, Cedar Creek, and other engagements. After the campaign, the troops returned to the various districts in the department.

MAJOR-GENERAL DAVID HUNTER (U.S.M.A. 1822) was born in Washington, July 21, 1802, and rose to rank of major in the Mexican War. As brigadier-general of volunteers, he commanded the Second Division at Bull Run, where he was severely wounded. Shortly afterward, he was made major-general of volunteers. He succeeded Fremont in the Western Department, and was at the head of the Department of Kansas, November, 1861, to March, 1862, then of the South, until September, and of the Tenth Corps from January to June, 1863, and in May, 1864, he succeeded Major-General Sigel in the command of the Department of West Virginia. Hunter was the first general to enlist colored troops, and presided at the court which tried the Lincoln conspirators. He was retired in 1866, having been brevetted major-general, and died in Washington, February 2, 1886.

MAJOR-GENERAL GEORGE CROOK (U.S.M.A. 1852) was born near Dayton, Ohio, September 8, 1828. He spent the nine years before the opening of the Civil War in California. As brigadier-general of volunteers in the Army of the Cumberland, he commanded a division of cavalry. He succeeded Major-General David Hunter in the command of the Department of West Virginia in August, 1864, and shortly afterward was made major-general of volunteers. He was active in the Shenandoah campaign under Sheridan; also at Five Forks and Appomattox. In 1866, as lieutenant-colonel of the regular army, he was sent to the West, where he remained in constant warfare with the Indians for many years. He obtained charge of all the tribes and did much for their advancement. In 1888, he attained the rank of major-general, and died in Chicago, March 21, 1890.

Department of Virginia and North Carolina, Army of the James

THE DEPARTMENT OF VIRGINIA was created in May, 1861, and the troops therein were organized into the Seventh Army Corps on July 22, 1862. This corps was divided between Fort Monroe, Norfolk, Portsmouth, Yorktown, and other places. The Eighteenth Army Corps, created December 24, 1862, from troops in the Department of North Carolina was transferred to the Department of Virginia and North Carolina July 15, 1863, when the two departments were united, and the troops

Irvin McDowell Commanded the 1st
Corps in Front of Washington.

A. A. Humphreys Commanded the
2d Corps at Petersburg.

John Newton Commanded the 1st
Corps at Gettysburg and After.

Darius N. Couch Commanded the
2d Corps at Fredericksburg and
Chancellorsville.

Edwin Vose Sumner Commanded the
2d Corps on the Peninsula
and in Maryland.

Winfield Scott Hancock; Under Him
the Second Corps Earned the
Name "Old Guard."

FEDERAL MAJOR–GENERALS COMMANDING THE FIRST AND SECOND ARMY CORPS

Army and Department of the Gulf

therein were all merged in the Eighteenth Corps. This was reorganized in April, 1864, and the Tenth Corps being transferred from the Department of the South, the whole force was called the Army of the James. Its principal commander was Major-General Benjamin F. Butler, although Major-Generals E. O. C. Ord and D. B. Birney held command for short periods. On December 3, 1864, the two corps were discontinued, the white troops being formed into the Twenty-fourth Army Corps and the colored into the Twenty-fifth. On January 31, 1865, the two departments were again separated.

MAJOR-GENERAL BENJAMIN FRANKLIN BUTLER was born in Deerfield, New Hampshire, November 5, 1818, and was graduated from Waterville College in 1838. He practised law and entered political life. As a brigadier-general of the Massachusetts State Militia, he answered President Lincoln's call and was placed in command of the Department of Annapolis. In May, 1861, he was made major-general of volunteers and given the Department of Virginia, and in August led the troops that assisted in the capture of Forts Hatteras and Clark. On March 20, 1862, he was put in command of the Department of the Gulf and his troops occupied New Orleans on May 1st. His army gained possession of most of the lower Mississippi, and in December he was relieved by Major-General Banks. On November 1st, he assumed command of the Department of Virginia and North Carolina and personally led the Eighteenth Corps (Army of the James) until May 2, 1864. He was sent to New York city in October to cope with the anticipated disturbance during the presidential election. Following an unsuccessful expedition (December 1864) against Fort Fisher, he was removed by Lieutenant-General Grant. He was elected to Congress as a Republican, in 1866. In 1883, he was Democratic governor of Massachusetts, and in the following year was the unsuccessful presidential candidate of the Greenback-Labor and Anti-Monopolist parties. He died in Washington, January 11, 1893.

Army and Department of the Gulf

CONSTITUTED February 23, 1862, comprising, in a general way, the territory of the Gulf States occupied by the Federal troops. Major-General Benjamin F. Butler was the first commander. He was followed by Major-Generals N. P. Banks, S. A. Hurlbut, and E. R. S. Canby, who commanded after the close of the war. There were, at first, many separate bodies of troops scattered over the department. One of these, the Nineteenth Army Corps, was organized in January, 1863, and was discontinued as a corps in this department November 7, 1864. The Thirteenth Army Corps joined this army from that of the Tennessee in August, 1863, and remained until June, 1864. A detachment of the Sixteenth Corps, also from the Army of the Tennessee, joined for the Red River expedition, in March, 1864. On May 7, 1864, the Department of the Gulf was merged in the Military Division of West Mississippi, but retained a separate existence.

MAJOR-GENERAL NATHANIEL PRENTISS BANKS was born in Waltham, Massachusetts, January 30, 1816. He received a common-school education, practised law, and was a prominent member of Congress from 1853 to 1857. He was governor of Massachusetts from 1858 until 1861, and when the Civil War broke out he was president of the Illinois Central Railroad Company, but immediately offered his services to the Government. He was made major-general of volunteers, and was appointed to the command of the Department of Annapolis, and then to the Department of the Shenandoah. In the organization of the Army of the Potomac in March, 1862, he was assigned to the Fifth Corps, but his force was detached April 4, 1862, and remained in the Shenandoah Valley, where Banks had command until that corps was merged in the Army of Virginia, June 26, 1862. After the Army of Virginia was discontinued, Banks was at the head of the Military District of Washington until October 27, 1862. He succeeded Major-General B. F. Butler in command of the Department of the Gulf, and was actively engaged along the lower Mississippi and Red rivers. He resigned his commission after the disastrous Red River expedition of 1864, and was reelected to Congress. In 1890, owing to an increasing mental disorder, he was obliged to retire from public life. He died at his home in Waltham, September 1, 1894.

[180]

TWO COMMANDERS
OF THE
THIRD ARMY CORPS,
SICKLES
AND
HEINTZLEMAN

Daniel E. Sickles
Commanded the
Third Corps at
Chancellorsville
and Gettysburg.

S. P. Heintzelman
Led the Third Corps
at Fair Oaks and
Second Bull Run.

FEDERAL

MAJOR–

GENERALS

COMMANDERS OF THE

THIRD AND FOURTH

ARMY CORPS

W. H. French Commanded the
Third Corps in the Mine
Run Campaign.

T. J. Wood Commanded the Fourth Corps
(West) at Nashville, 1864.

Erasmus D. Keyes Commanded the Fourth
Corps (East) on the Peninsula.

Army of Georgia

MAJOR-GENERAL EDWARD RICHARD SPRIGG CANBY (U.S.M.A. 1839) was born in Kentucky in 1819. Entering the army, he served in the Seminole and Mexican wars. When the Civil War broke out, he served first as colonel in New Mexico, held that territory for the Union, and prevented a Confederate invasion of California. Then, for some time, he was on special duty in the North and East. In May, 1864, with the rank of major-general of volunteers, he assumed command of the Military Division of West Mississippi. He captured Mobile, April 12, 1865, and the following month arranged for the surrender of the Confederate forces in the Trans-Mississippi Department. June 3, 1865, he succeeded to the command of the Army and Department of the Gulf. After the close of the war he was made brigadier-general in the regular army, and was put in command of the Department of the Columbia. While engaged in attempting to settle difficulties between the Government and the Modoc Indians, he was treacherously murdered by their chief, April 11, 1873.

MAJOR-GENERAL GORDON GRANGER (U.S.M.A. 1845) was born in New York city in 1821, and served in the Mexican War and on the Southwestern frontier. When the Civil War broke out, he was made captain and rose through successive grades until his appointment of major-general of volunteers was dated September 17, 1862. He fought at Wilson's Creek, and later commanded the cavalry and had a brigade in the Army of the Mississippi. Then he had charge of the so-called Army of Kentucky, from August to October, 1862, and served in the Department of the Ohio until put in charge of the newly organized Reserve Corps of the Army of the Cumberland. At Chickamauga, he rendered most timely assistance to Thomas and won a brevet of lieutenant-colonel in the regular army. He was the first commander of the new Fourth Corps until April, 1864, when he was sent to command the district of South Alabama, the troops of which were merged in the Reserve Corps, Department of the Gulf (afterward called New Thirteenth Army Corps) of which Granger took command in January, 1865. He commanded the land forces at the fall of Forts Morgan and Gaines (August, 1864), and in the operations around Mobile that resulted in its capture, April, 1865. After the war, Major-General Granger was mustered out of the volunteer service and received the commission of colonel in the regular army. He was brevetted major-general in March, 1865. He died in Santa Fé, New Mexico, January 10, 1876.

Army of Georgia

THE FOURTEENTH AND TWENTIETH ARMY CORPS on the march to the sea and through the Carolinas (November 1864–April 1865) were so known. This force was commanded by Major-General Henry W. Slocum, and constituted the left wing of Sherman's army.

MAJOR-GENERAL HENRY WARNER SLOCUM (U.S.M.A. 1852) was born in Delphi, New York, September 24, 1827, and, beginning the practice of law at Syracuse, New York, he resigned his commission as first lieutenant in 1855. At the outbreak of the Civil War, he joined McDowell's troops as colonel of the Twenty-seventh New York Volunteers, and at Bull Run was severely wounded. In August, 1861, as brigadier-general of volunteers, he commanded a brigade of Franklin's Division of the Army of the Potomac, and later had a division in the Sixth Corps. At Gaines' Mill and Glendale, General Slocum took a prominent part, and after the battle of Malvern Hill he was pro-moted. As major-general of volunteers, he was given the Twelfth Corps in October, 1862. He fought with the armies of the Potomac and of Virginia, and was sent by Major-General Meade to command the army on the first day of Gettysburg. He went West with his corps, and was commanding at Tullahoma during the battle of Chattanooga. For short periods, in 1864 and 1865, he had charge of the District of Vicksburg. In the Atlanta campaign, he was in command of the Twentieth Corps and during the march to the sea and the Georgia and Carolina campaigns, he was at the head of the Army of Georgia, which formed the left wing of General Sherman's army. At the battle of Bentonville, North Carolina, General Slocum repulsed Johnston's attack, and later was present at the surrender of the Confederate Army. He resigned his commission in 1865, and devoted himself to the law. He died in Brooklyn, New York, April 14, 1894.

Fitz John Porter Commanded the
Fifth Corps on the Peninsula.

George Sykes Commanded the Fifth
Corps at Gettysburg.

William Farrar Smith Led the
Sixth Corps at Fredericksburg.

FEDERAL MAJOR–GENERALS
COMMANDERS OF THE FIFTH AND SIXTH ARMY CORPS

Horatio G. Wright Commanded the
Sixth Corps in the Shenandoah
and Petersburg Campaigns.

William Buel Franklin Commanded
the Sixth Corps on the Peninsula
and at Antietam under McClellan.

Gouverneur Kemble Warren, Long
Associated with the Fifth Corps,
finally as Corps Commander.

Army of the Shenandoah

A FORCE belonging to the Middle Military Division, organized for Major-General P. H. Sheridan, in August, 1864, in order to drive Lieutenant-General Early from the Shenandoah valley. It consisted of the Sixth Corps from the Army of the Potomac, and a detachment of the Nineteenth Corps, Army of the Gulf. There was also a cavalry corps made up of two divisions of the cavalry of the Army of the Potomac. With it acted the troops of the Department of West Virginia, a force created from the Eighth Corps (Middle Department), and sometimes called the Army of West Virginia, under the command of Major-General George Crook. Major-General Wright of the Sixth Corps had charge of the Army of the Shenandoah for a few days in October, 1864, and Major-General A. T. A. Torbert assumed the command in February, 1865, when Sheridan rejoined the Army of the Potomac with the cavalry.

Army of the Frontier

THE FIELD FORCES in Missouri and Kansas were organized into the Army of the Frontier on October 12, 1862. It was commanded by Major-Generals J. M. Schofield and F. J. Herron, and by Major-General James G. Blunt temporarily. It was very active during its existence, and fought many minor engagements in the Southwest, including Clark's Mill, Missouri, and Prairie Grove, Arkansas, and the capture of Van Buren, Arkansas. The army went out of existence June 5, 1863, and its troops were scattered among the districts in Tennessee and Missouri.

MAJOR-GENERAL FRANCIS JAY HERRON was born in Pittsburgh, Pennsylvania, in 1837, and gave up his business career in Iowa to go to the front as lieutenant-colonel of an Iowa regiment. He served in the Army of the Southwest, and was captured at Pea Ridge after conduct that brought him great praise and a medal of honor. He was given a division of the Army of the Frontier, which he commanded at Prairie Grove. From March to June, 1863, he was, as major-general of volunteers, at the head of the army itself. Later, as division commander of the Thirteenth Corps, he was present at the fall of Vicksburg, and also held command in Texas and at Port Hudson. He received the surrender of the Confederate forces west of the Mississippi in May, 1865. He resigned from the service in June, 1865, and practised law in New Orleans and New York. He died January 8, 1902.

MAJOR-GENERAL JAMES G. BLUNT was born in Trenton, Maine, in 1826, and became a physician. He settled in Kansas, where he became prominent for his work in the anti-slavery movement. He went to the Civil War as lieutenant-colonel and was made brigadier-general of volunteers in April, 1862. He was placed at the head of the Department of Kansas on May 5, 1862, and when that department was merged in that of Missouri, on September 19th, he was given a division in the Army of the Frontier. On December 7th, his division and that of Brigadier-General F. J. Herron checked, at Prairie Grove, Arkansas, the advance of Major-General Hindman into Missouri. Blunt was senior officer in command of both divisions in the battle. From June, 1863 to January, 1864, he was at the head of the District of the Frontier, that army having been broken up. From October, 1864, to the end of the war he commanded the District of South Kansas. He died in Washington, D. C., July 25, 1881.

Army of the Mountain Department

CREATED March 11, 1862, from the Department of Western Virginia. On March 29th, Brigadier-General Rosecrans turned over the troops therein to Major-General John C. Fremont. This force co-operated with Banks and McDowell against "Stonewall" Jackson in the Shenandoah valley, and its principal engagements were those at McDowell and Cross Keys. On June 26, 1862, the Mountain Department became the First Corps, Army of Virginia.

John A. Dix Commanded the Seventh Corps
(East) in 1862.

J. J. Reynolds Commanded the Seventh
Corps (West) in 1864.

FEDERAL
MAJOR–
GENERALS
COMMANDERS
OF THE
SEVENTH,
EIGHTH
AND NINTH
ARMY
CORPS

Robert C. Schenck Commanded the Eighth
Corps in 1863.

John E. Wool Commanded the Eighth Corps
in 1862.

John G. Parke Commanded the Ninth Corps
at Petersburg.

Orlando B. Willcox Commanded the Ninth
Army Corps in 1863–4.

First Army Corps

MAJOR-GENERAL JOHN CHARLES FREMONT was born in Savannah, Georgia, January 21, 1813. He became professor of mathematics in the United States navy, and was commissioned second lieutenant in the Corps of Topographical Engineers, in 1838. He conducted several exploring expeditions to the Far West, during one of which he fomented a revolt against Mexican rule in California and raised the Bear Flag in that region. Later, he assisted in the Mexican War and was made civil governor of California by Commodore Stockton. Trouble arose between him and General Kearny, who had been charged with the establishment of the Government, which resulted in a court martial and Fremont's resignation from the army. He settled in California, represented that State in the Senate, and was the unsuccessful Republican candidate for President, in 1856. At the outbreak of the Civil War, he was appointed major-general, and on July 25, 1861, put at the head of the Western Department, with headquarters at St. Louis, where he made an attempt to free the slaves of Southern sympathizers. This act led to his removal in November, and the following March he was given command of the newly created Mountain Department. He refused to serve as corps commander under Major-General Pope when his troops were merged in the Army of Virginia. He resigned from the army in June, 1864. He became interested in railroad building and was governor of Arizona (1878–1882). In 1890, he was reappointed major-general and was retired with that rank on April 28th. He died July 13, 1890.

First Army Corps

THE FIRST ARMY CORPS was originally planned to consist of the troops of the Mountain Department, earlier known as the Department of Western Virginia, under command of Brigadier-General W. S. Rosecrans, but by order of the President, the First Corps, from troops of the Army of the Potomac, was placed under command of Major-General Irvin McDowell, March 13, 1862. On April 4th, the First Corps was discontinued and the troops sent to the Department of the Rappahannock, and then in turn merged in the Army of Virginia, as the Third Corps, on June 26, 1862. The First Corps, Army of the Potomac, was recreated September 12, 1862, from the troops of the Third Corps, Army of Virginia, coming successively under command of Major-General Joseph Hooker, Brigadier-General George G. Meade, Brigadier-General J. S. Wadsworth, Major-Generals J. F. Reynolds, Abner Doubleday, and John Newton. This corps rendered gallant service at South Mountain, Antietam, Fredericksburg, Chancellorsville, and Gettysburg, among the more important engagements. It was discontinued March 24, 1864, when it became merged in the Fifth Corps, Army of the Potomac.

MAJOR-GENERAL IRVIN McDOWELL (U.S.M.A. 1838) was born in Columbus, Ohio, October 15, 1818. He rendered distinguished service in the Mexican War. As brigadier-general at the head of the Department of Northeastern Virginia, he had command of the Union army at First Bull Run. Afterward, with a commission of major-general of volunteers, he had a division in the Army of the Potomac. In further reorganizations and changes he headed his troops as commander of the First Corps, Army of the Potomac; Department of the Rappahannock, and Third Corps, Army of Virginia. His conspicuous services at Cedar Mountain won him the brevet of major-general, which full rank he attained in 1872. Immediately after Second Bull Run he was relieved from field service, and was president of several army boards. In July, 1864, he was placed at the head of the Department of the Pacific, and after the war held various commands. He was retired in 1882, and died in San Francisco, May 4, 1885.

MAJOR-GENERAL ABNER DOUBLEDAY (U.S. M.A. 1842) was born at Ballston Spa, New York, June 26, 1819, and served in the Mexican and Seminole wars. As captain of the artillery he was at Fort Sumter under Major Anderson, and fired upon the Confederates the first Federal gun of the Civil War. He served under Major-General Patterson in the Valley, and on February 3, 1862, was made brigadier-general of volunteers and placed in charge of the defenses of Washington. He had a brigade in the Third Corps, Army of Virginia, and afterward a division, which he retained when the corps again became the First

J. M. Brannan Commanded the
Tenth Corps in 1862–63.

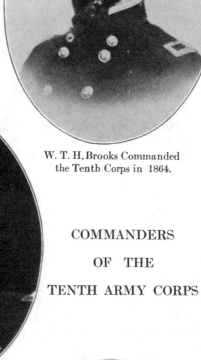

W. T. H. Brooks Commanded
the Tenth Corps in 1864.

FEDERAL

MAJOR–

GENERALS

David B. Birney Commanded
the Tenth Corps in 1864.

COMMANDERS

OF THE

TENTH ARMY CORPS

Ormsby M. Mitchel Commanded the
Tenth Corps in 1862.

Alfred H. Terry Commanded the Tenth
Corps in 1864–65.

Corps, Army of the Potomac. In November, 1862, he became major-general of volunteers. He fought at Fredericksburg and Chancellorsville. When Reynolds was killed on the field of Gettysburg, the command of the First Corps fell upon him for the day, July 1, 1863, until he was succeeded by Major-General John Newton. After being mustered out of the volunteer service, he served as colonel in the regular army until he was retired in 1873. He had been brevetted brigadier and major-general in 1865. Major-General Doubleday was the author of several important military works. He died January 27, 1893, at Mendham, New Jersey.

MAJOR-GENERAL JOHN NEWTON (U.S.M.A. 1842) was born in Norfolk, Virginia, August 24, 1823. After graduation he taught engineering at West Point for three years, and then devoted himself to the construction of fortifications. The outbreak of the Civil War found him chief engineer of the Department of Pennsylvania, and he assisted in preparing the defenses of the national capital. The rank of brigadier-general of volunteers was given him in September, 1861, and he remained with the organization which was eventually the First Corps, Army of the Potomac, as brigade and division commander, being made major-general of volunteers in March, 1863. He succeeded to the command of the corps after Reynolds' death at Gettysburg, July 1, 1863, and led it until it was discontinued, March 24, 1864. His appointment as major-general of volunteers expired in April, 1864, and with his former title he succeeded Sheridan in a division of the Fourth Corps,

Army of the Cumberland. After the war, he continued in the regular army and reached the grade of brigadier-general in 1884, being retired in 1886. His most renowned achievement was the removal of the reefs at Hell Gate in the harbor of New York. General Newton was commissioner of public works, New York city, from 1887 to 1888, and then president of the Panama Railroad Company. He died, May 1, 1895.

MAJOR-GENERAL JOHN FULTON REYNOLDS (U. S.M.A. 1841) was born in Lancaster, Pennsylvania, September 20, 1820, and served in the Mexican War, and in the Rogue River Indian and Utah expeditions. At the outbreak of the Civil War, he was commandant at West Point, but with the rank of brigadier-general of volunteers took active part in the operations of the Army of the Potomac from August, 1861. He commanded a brigade of the Pennsylvania Reserves which was merged in the First Corps, Army of the Potomac. He went with McDowell to the Department of the Rappahannock but returned to the Army of the Potomac at the head of a brigade in the Fifth Corps, for the move to the James. He was taken prisoner at Glendale but was exchanged. The brigade joined the Third Corps, Army of Virginia, in which Reynolds commanded a division. Again with the Army of the Potomac, Reynolds was given the First Corps on September 29, 1862, and later was made major-general of volunteers. On the first day of Gettysburg, July 1, 1863, he was killed by a Confederate sharpshooter. Reynolds' loss was most keenly felt in the Federal army.

Second Army Corps

CREATED by the general order of March 3, 1862, chiefly from Sumner's and Blenker's divisions of the Army of the Potomac as constituted in October, 1861. Major-General Sumner was its first commander, and his successors were Major-Generals D. N. Couch, John Sedgwick, O. O. Howard, W. S. Hancock, G. K. Warren, D. B. Birney, A. A. Humphreys, Brevet Major-Generals Gershom Mott, N. A. Miles, and F. C. Barlow, and Brigadier-Generals John Gibbon, William Hays, and J. C. Caldwell. The Second Corps was with the Army of the Potomac all through the war and took part in all its great engagements. It suffered most severely at Antietam. It was discon-

tinued June 28, 1865. The Second Corps made a notable record for itself. One interesting fact is that until the battle of Spotsylvania, on May 10, 1864, it never lost a gun or a color.

MAJOR-GENERAL EDWIN VOSE SUMNER was born in Boston, January 30, 1797, enlisting in the army in 1819. He rendered distinguished service in the Black Hawk and Mexican wars, and was military governor of New Mexico from 1851 to 1853. As brigadier-general, he superseded Brevet Brigadier-General Albert Sidney Johnston in the command of the Department of the Pacific in April, 1861. He came East to participate in

Franz Sigel Commanded the 11th Corps.

FEDERAL

MAJOR–GENERALS

Innis M. Palmer Commanded the 14th Corps.

Jeff C. Davis Commanded the 14th Corps.

COMMANDERS

OF THE

ELEVENTH

TWELFTH

THIRTEENTH

AND

FOURTEENTH

ARMY CORPS

C. C. Washburn Commanded the 13th Corps.

George W. Morgan Commanded the 13th Corps.

Alpheus S. Williams Commanded the 12th Corps.

the Civil War, and became the first commander of the Second Army Corps. He was made major-general of volunteers, July 4, 1862. He was wounded in the Peninsula campaign and also at Antietam. Upon Burnside's reorganization of the army, he commanded the Right Grand Division. When Hooker was put at the head, Major-General Sumner was relieved at his own request, and sent to the Department of Missouri. But he died on the way there, at Syracuse, New York, March 21, 1863.

MAJOR-GENERAL DARIUS NASH COUCH (U.S. M.A. 1846) was born in Putnam County, New York, July 23, 1822, and served in the Mexican and the Seminole wars, being brevetted first lieutenant in the former. In 1855, he resigned from the army and entered mercantile life in New York city, but returned to his profession at the opening of the Civil War as colonel of volunteers. He was identified with the Department and Army of the Potomac, first as brigade commander (August, 1861–March, 1862), then as division commander in the Fourth Army Corps to September, 1862, when he was made major-general of volunteers and his division was transferred to the Sixth Corps. In October, 1862, Couch was placed at the head of the Second Corps, which he led at Fredericksburg and at Chancellorsville. From June, 1863, to December, 1864, he was at the head of the Department of the Susquehanna, when he was given a division of the Twenty-third Army Corps, and fought at the battle of Nashville. He resigned from the army in 1865, and was defeated for governor of Massachusetts on the Democratic ticket in the same year. Subsequently, he was collector of the port of Boston, and quartermaster-general and adjutant-general of Connecticut. He died in Norwalk, Connecticut, February 12, 1897.

BRIGADIER-GENERAL WILLIAM HAYS (U.S.M.A. 1840) was born in Richmond, Virginia, in 1819, and served in the Mexican War. As lieutenant-colonel he had a brigade of horse artillery in the Army of the Potomac through the Peninsula campaign, the artillery reserve at Antietam, and the artillery of the Right Grand Division at Fredericksburg. In November, 1862, he was made brigadier-general of volunteers, and at Chancellorsville, in command of a brigade in the Second Army Corps he was wounded and captured. He was exchanged, and after the wounding of Hancock at Gettysburg, he had command

of the corps for a short time. Then he spent some time in the Department of the East and later had a brigade in the Second Corps. He died in Fort Independence, Boston Harbor, February 7, 1875.

MAJOR-GENERAL GERSHOM MOTT was born in Trenton, New Jersey, April 7, 1822, and served in the Mexican War. He went to the front in the Civil War as lieutenant-colonel of the Fifth New Jersey Infantry, and later became colonel of the Sixth New Jersey. In September, 1862, he was promoted to brigadier-general of volunteers, and had a brigade in the Third Corps from December, 1862, to March, 1864, and then had consecutively two divisions of the Second Corps. Several times he took command of the corps during the absence of Major-General Humphreys. Mott was brevetted major-general of volunteers in August, 1864, and received the title May 28, 1865, shortly before being mustered out. After the war, he was at one time treasurer of the State of New Jersey, and died in New York city, November 29, 1884.

MAJOR-GENERAL NELSON APPLETON MILES was born in Westminster, Massachusetts, August 8, 1839. He entered mercantile life, but went to the front in the Civil War as first lieutenant in the Twenty-second Massachusetts Infantry, and in May, 1862, he was made lieutenant-colonel of the Sixty-first New York Infantry. By September he had risen to a colonelcy of volunteers. He fought with the Army of the Potomac in all its battles and was wounded at Chancellorsville. From March to July, 1864, he had a brigade in the Second Corps and was made brigadier-general in May. The rank of major-general of volunteers was given him in October, 1865. After the war he entered the regular army as colonel, and his chief service was against the Indians in the West. In the Spanish-American War he commanded the United States army, and personally led the Porto Rico expedition, and upon the reorganization of the Army of the United States he was appointed lieutenant-general (1900), being retired with that rank three years later.

MAJOR-GENERAL WINFIELD SCOTT HANCOCK (U.S.M.A. 1844) was born in Montgomery Square, Pennsylvania, February 14, 1824. He served in the Mexican War and in the border troubles in Kansas, and had risen to the rank of captain when the Civil War broke out. He was

FEDERAL

MAJOR–

GENERALS

P. J. Osterhaus Commanded the Fifteenth
Corps in 1864.

S. A. Hurlbut Commanded the Sixteenth
Corps in 1863.

J. A. Mower Commanded the Seventeenth
Corps in the Carolinas.

J. G. Foster Commanded the Eighteenth
Army Corps in 1864.

COMMANDERS

OF THE

FIFTEENTH

SIXTEENTH

SEVENTEENTH

EIGHTEENTH

AND

NINETEENTH

ARMY CORPS

John H. Martindale Commanded the Eighteenth Corps in Front of Richmond.

William H. Emory Commanded the Nineteenth Corps in the Shenandoah Valley.

made brigadier-general of volunteers in September, 1861, and had a brigade in the Fourth Army Corps at Williamsburg, where McClellan called him "Hancock the Superb." At Antietam, he distinguished himself, and succeeded Richardson at the head of a division of the Second Corps. In November, 1862, he was made major-general of volunteers. His troops did noteworthy work at Fredericksburg and Chancellorsville, and Hancock received the Second Corps, in May, 1863. At Gettysburg, Meade sent him to take charge on the first day, after Reynolds' death, and on the third day he himself was severely wounded. In March, 1864, he resumed command of the Second Corps. He took charge of the Department of West Virginia and Middle Military Division in March, 1865. After the war, he became major-general in 1866, and commanded various departments. He was an unsuccessful candidate for the presidency against Garfield. Of Hancock, General Grant once said: "Hancock stands the most conspicuous figure of all the general officers who did not exercise a separate command. He commanded a corps longer than any other one, and his name was never mentioned as having committed in battle a blunder for which he was responsible." He died on Governor's Island, New York, February 9, 1886.

MAJOR-GENERAL ANDREW ATKINSON HUMPHREYS (U.S.M.A. 1831) was born in Philadelphia, November 2, 1810. He was closely associated with engineering and coast-survey work until the outbreak of the Civil War, when, as major, he became a member of Major-General McClellan's staff. In April, 1862, he was made brigadier-general of volunteers and was chief topographical engineer of the Army of the Potomac during the Peninsula campaign. He had a division of the Fifth Corps from September, 1862, to May, 1863, and fought at Fredericksburg and Chancellorsville. He was then given a division of the Third Corps, and after Gettysburg was promoted to major-general of volunteers and made General Meade's chief of staff. In the final campaign against Lee, he had the Second Corps (November, 1864, to June, 1865). After being mustered out of the volunteer service, September 1, 1866, he was made brigadier-general and placed at the head of the Engineer Corps of the United States army. He was retired in July, 1879, and died in Washington, December 27, 1883. He received brevets for gallant and meritorious services at the battles of Fredericksburg, Va., Gettysburg, Pa., and Sailors Creek, Va.

MAJOR-GENERAL JOHN GIBBON (U.S.M.A. 1847) was born in Holmesburg, Pennsylvania, April 27, 1827, and served in the Mexican War. Later, he was instructor in artillery practice and quartermaster at West Point. He had reached the grade of captain when the Civil War broke out, and became McDowell's chief of artillery. He was promoted to brigadier-general of volunteers in May, 1862. He had a brigade in the Third Corps, Army of Virginia, and a brigade and division in the First Corps, Army of the Potomac. He was given a division in the Second Army Corps, which he held for the most part until August, 1864. When Hancock was sent by Meade to take charge at Gettysburg on the first day, Gibbon was given temporary command of the corps and was seriously wounded. As major-general of volunteers, he had command of the Eighteenth and Twenty-fourth army corps for short periods. When mustered out of the volunteer service, he continued in the regular army as colonel, and rose to be brigadier-general in 1885. He did much Indian fighting, and in 1891 was retired from active service. He died in Baltimore, February 6, 1896.

MAJOR-GENERAL FRANCIS CHANNING BARLOW was born in Brooklyn, New York, October 19, 1834, and was a Harvard graduate of 1855. He enlisted as a private in the Twelfth New York Militia, and after the three months' service had expired, he returned to the field as lieutenant-colonel of the Sixty-first New York. His rise was rapid, due to ability displayed in the Army of the Potomac, and he was made brigadier-general of volunteers after the battle of Antietam (September, 1862), where he was badly wounded. He had a brigade in the Eleventh Corps at Chancellorsville, and a division at Gettysburg, when he was again badly wounded. On recovery, he was assigned to duty in the Department of the South and afterward given a division in the Second Army Corps, March 1864, and served until the Army of the Potomac was discontinued. He was made major-general of volunteers in May, 1865, for his conspicuous gallantry at the battle of Spotsylvania. In April and May, 1865, he had command of the Second Corps. General Barlow resigned from the army November 16, 1865, and returned to New York, where he entered political life and resumed the practice of law. He was secretary of state of New York 1865–1868, and attorney-general for New York from 1871 to 1873, in which capacity he conducted the prosecution of "Boss" Tweed and other municipal officials. He died in New York city, January 11, 1896.

FEDERAL
MAJOR–GENERALS
COMMANDERS
OF
ARMY
CORPS

TWENTIETH

TWENTY-FIRST

TWENTY-SECOND

TWENTY-THIRD

TWENTY-FOURTH

AND

TWENTY-FIFTH

CORPS

A. McD. McCook Commanded the
Twentieth Corps at Chickamauga.

Thos. L. Crittenden Commanded the
Twenty-first Corps in 1863.

C. C. Augur Commanded the Twenty-
second Corps at Port Hudson.

G. L. Hartsuff Commanded the Twenty-
third Corps in 1863.

E. O. C. Ord Commanded the Twenty-
fourth Corps in 1865.

Godfrey Weitzel Commanded the
Twenty-fifth Corps in 1864-5.

Third Army Corps

On the reorganization of the Army of the Potomac in March, 1862, a body of troops, chiefly from Heintzelman's, Porter's and Hooker's divisions of the earlier organization, was constituted the Third Army Corps. In May, Porter's men were transferred to the new provisional Fifth Army Corps. The future additions to the corps were chiefly from the Eighth and Twenty-second corps. The corps fought in the battles of the Army of the Potomac, and two divisions were sent to the assistance of the Army of Virginia at Second Bull Run and Chantilly. On March 24, 1864, it was merged in the Second Corps. Its commanders were Brigadier-Generals S. P. Heintzelman and George Stoneman, and Major-Generals D. E. Sickles, D. B. Birney, and W. H. French.

Major-General Samuel Peter Heintzelman (U.S.M.A. 1826) was born in Manheim, Pennsylvania, September 30, 1805, and served on the frontier, in Florida, in the Mexican War, and in California and Texas. At the opening of the Civil War he was promoted to a colonelcy, and became inspector-general of the defenses of Washington. In May, 1861, he was placed in command at Alexandria, Virginia. He headed the Third Division at Bull Run, and in subsequent organizations of the Army of the Potomac he had a brigade, a division, and afterward the Third Corps, which he commanded until November, 1862. His conduct at Fair Oaks won him a brevet of brigadier-general, for he was now major-general of volunteers. He fought through the Peninsula campaign, and was sent to assist Pope at Second Bull Run and Chantilly. He was in command of the defenses and later of the Department of Washington (Twenty-second Army Corps) from September, 1862, to October, 1863. After this, he took no active part in the war, but was commander of the Northern Department from January to October, 1864, and then served on court martials. He was mustered out of the volunteer service August, 1865, and was retired from the army with the rank of major-general, February 22, 1869. He died in Washington, May 3, 1880.

Major-General George Stoneman (U.S.M.A. 1846) was born in Busti, New York, August 8, 1822, and was captain in command at Fort Brown, Texas, when the Civil War broke out. He refused to obey the order of General Twiggs to surrender the property of the United States Government to the State of Texas, and escaped by steamer to New York. His first active service in the Civil War was as major in the West Virginia campaign, and as brigadier-general of volunteers he had the cavalry command in the Army of the Potomac. It was his troops that brought on the action at Williamsburg in May, 1862. After the death of Major-General Kearny, at Chantilly, he succeeded eventually to the command of his division, and later succeeded Major-General Heintzelman in the command of the Third Army Corps, which he led at Fredericksburg. He was promoted to major-general of volunteers in command of the Cavalry Corps, Army of the Potomac, and led a famous raid toward Richmond during the Chancellorsville campaign. From January to April, 1864, he was in command of the Twenty-third Army Corps, and then received the cavalry division of the same organization. After a raid in the Atlanta campaign, in which he was captured and held prisoner for three months, he assumed command of the Department of the Ohio, and later the District of East Tennessee, where his operations were very successful, especially his raid into North Carolina, in April, 1865. He was retired from the regular army with the rank of colonel, in 1871, and went to California, of which State he was governor from 1883 to 1887. He died in Buffalo, New York, September 5, 1894.

Major-General Daniel Edgar Sickles was born in New York city, October 20, 1825. Admitted to the bar in 1846, he afterward served in the State legislature, the diplomatic service, and in Congress, where he was when the Civil War broke out. He raised the Excelsior Brigade of five New York regiments, which served in the Army of the Potomac with Sickles as brigadier-general of volunters at its head. In March, 1862, it was incorporated in the Third Army Corps. He led his brigade through the Peninsula campaign, commanded a division at Fredericksburg and, as major-general of volunteers, the Third Corps at Chancellorsville and Gettysburg. In the latter battle he lost a leg on the second day. He continued in the army after the close of the war, and was retired with rank of major-general in 1869. He went on a secret diplomatic mission to South America in 1867, and was minister to Spain, 1869–1873. He was sheriff of New York County, in 1890, and Democratic member of Congress, 1892–94, as well as president of the New

John E. Phelps, of Arkansas—
Colonel of the 2d Cavalry.

Marcus La Rue, of Arkansas—
Promoted for Gallantry.

John B. Slough, of Colorado—
Engaged in New Mexico.

Patrick E. Connor, of California—Colonel of the 3d Infantry.

FEDERAL GENERALS—No. 1—ARKANSAS (first two above). COLORADO (third above).
CALIFORNIA (fourth above and six below).

James Shields, Brave Irish Soldier,
A Friend of Lincoln.

George S. Evans, Originally Colonel
of the 2d Cavalry.

George W. Bowie, Originally Colonel
of the 5th Infantry.

Edward McGarry, Brevetted for
Conspicuous Gallantry.

James W. Denver; Denver, Colo.,
Named After Him.

J. H. Carleton Commanded a Column
in March Across Arizona.

This is the first of 29 groups embracing representative general officers of 34 states and territories. On preceding pages portraits appear of many leaders, including all the commanders of armies and army corps, and all generals killed in battle. Many others appear in preceding volumes, as identified with particular events or special branches, such as cavalry and artillery and the signal and medical corps. Information of every general officer can be found through the index and the roster concluding this volume.

Fourth Army Corps (Potomac)

York State Board of Civil Service Commissioners for several years.

MAJOR-GENERAL WILLIAM HENRY FRENCH (U.S.M.A. 1837) was born in Baltimore, January 13, 1815, and served in the Seminole and Mexican wars. In September, 1861, he was appointed brigadier-general of volunteers and major-general of volunteers the following year. He had a brigade in Sumner's Division, a division in the Second Corps, Army of the Potomac, and for a short time a command in the Eighth Corps, that joined the Third Corps after the battle of Gettysburg. He was in command of the Third Corps, from July 7, 1863, to January 28, 1864, and again from February 17th to March 24, 1864. In May, 1864, he was mustered out of the volunteer service, and was brevetted major-general the following year. In the regular army he rose to the rank of colonel in 1877, and, in 1880, was retired from active service. He died in Baltimore, May 20, 1881.

Fourth Army Corps (Potomac)

CREATED March 3, 1862, chiefly from troops in Couch's, W. F. Smith's, and Casey's divisions of the earlier Army of the Potomac, together with some new organizations. It was commanded by Major-General E. D. Keyes. The corps fought through the Peninsula campaign and remained in that region when the rest of the Army of the Potomac withdrew. The troops were gradually sent to other corps of the army—to North Carolina, Washington, and other places, and the corps was discontinued on August 1, 1863.

MAJOR-GENERAL ERASMUS DARWIN KEYES (U. S.M.A. 1832) was born in Brimfield, Massachusetts, May 29, 1810. He did duty on the Western frontier until the Civil War began, when he was raised to a colonelcy and made brigadier-general of volunteers in May, 1861. He commanded a brigade at Bull Run, and eventually was put in command of the Fourth Army Corps when it was created. His appointment as major-general of volunteers was dated from the battle of Williamsburg, and he received a brevet of brigadier-general in the regular army for his gallant and meritorious service at Fair Oaks. He resigned from the army in May, 1864, and went to California. He died in Nice, France, October 11, 1895.

Fourth Army Corps (Cumberland)

THE TWENTIETH AND TWENTY-FIRST army corps were consolidated on September 28, 1863, and the new organization was designated the Fourth Army Corps—the first one of that name, in the Army of the Potomac, having passed out of existence. It was commanded by Major-Generals Gordon Granger, O. O. Howard, D. S. Stanley, and Brigadier-General T. J. Wood. The corps fought in the battle of Chattanooga, was sent to the relief of Knoxville, and took part in the Atlanta campaign. When Sherman turned back toward Atlanta from Gaylesville, Alabama, the Fourth Corps went into Tennessee for the campaign against Hood. It fought at Franklin and Nashville, and was discontinued April 1, 1865.

MAJOR-GENERAL DAVID SLOAN STANLEY (U.S. M.A. 1852) was born in Cedar Valley, Ohio, June 1, 1828. He distinguished himself by his services, at the beginning of the Civil War, in the Southwest, at Dug Springs and Wilson's Creek. As brigadier-general of volunteers he had a division in the Army of the Mississippi and fought at Island No. 10, Iuka, and Corinth. In November, 1862, he became chief of cavalry in the Army of the Cumberland, and soon afterward was made major-general of volunteers. In November, 1863, he received a division of the Fourth Corps and became its head in July, 1864, when Major-General Howard took command of the Army of the Tennessee. Major-General Stanley was wounded at Franklin, November 30, 1864, and this ended his active service in the war, although he again headed the corps from February to August, 1865. Later on, he was given a colonelcy in the regular army and fought against the Indians in the

Orris S. Ferry, of Connecticut, Colonel of the 5th Regiment, Later U. S. Senator.

Joseph R. Hawley, of Connecticut, Distinguished at the Battle of Olustee.

Henry W. Birge, of Connecticut, Commander of a Division in the 19th Corps.

Henry W. Wessells, of Connecticut, Led Troops on the Peninsula in 1862.

H. H. Lockwood, of Delaware, Commander of a Brigade at Gettysburg.

Robert O. Tyler, of Connecticut, Commanded Artillery at Fredericksburg.

Lorenzo Thomas, of Delaware, Adjutant-General of the United States Army.

Daniel Tyler, of Connecticut, Led the Advance at Bull Run, 1861.

FEDERAL

GENERALS

No. 2

CONNECTICUT

DAKOTA

DELAWARE

John B. S. Todd, of Dakota Territory, Appointed Brigadier-General to Date from September 19, 1861.

Northwest. He was made brigadier-general in 1884, and was retired in 1892. He died in Washington, D. C., March 13, 1902.

MAJOR-GENERAL THOMAS JOHN WOOD (U.S. M.A. 1845) was born in Mumfordville, Kentucky, September 25, 1823, and served in the Mexican War. As brigadier-general of volunteers he had a brigade and then a division in the Army of the Ohio, a division of the Left Wing (Fourteenth Corps), Army of the Cumberland, which was continued in the Twenty-first Corps when the Left Wing was reorganized, and likewise in the Fourth Corps until it was discontinued. He had command of the Twenty-first and Fourth corps for short periods, succeeding Stanley in the latter at Franklin and leading it at Nashville. He was wounded at Stone's River and in the Atlanta campaign. He was made major-general of volunteers in January, 1865, and was mustered out of the volunteer service in 1866, having been brevetted major-general in 1865. He was retired in 1868, and died in Dayton, Ohio, February 25, 1906.

Fifth Army Corps

ON THE ORGANIZATION of the Army of the Potomac into corps, March 3, 1862, the Fifth Army Corps was created and given to Major-General N. P. Banks. But this corps was detached, April 4th, from the Army of the Potomac and assigned, with its commander, to the Department of the Shenandoah, and was made the Second Corps of the Army of Virginia, in June. On May 18th, a new Fifth Corps was created and existed provisionally until confirmed by the War Department. It was composed, at first, of Brigadier-General Porter's division of the Third Corps, and Brigadier-General Sykes' troops of the regular army. Other bodies of troops were added from time to time, and the First Corps was merged in it, when the Army of the Potomac was reorganized in March, 1864. It was commanded from time to time by Brigadier-General F. J. Porter, Major-General Joseph Hooker, Brigadier-General Daniel Butterfield, Major-Generals George G. Meade, Charles Griffin, George Sykes, and A. A. Humphreys, Brevet Major-General S. K. Crawford, and Major-General G. K. Warren. The corps fought in whole or in part through all the battles of the Army of the Potomac.

MAJOR-GENERAL FITZ JOHN PORTER (U.S.M.A. 1845) was born in Portsmouth, New Hampshire, June 13, 1822, served in the Mexican War, and afterward taught at West Point. He was assistant adjutant-general in Albert Sidney Johnston's Utah expedition, in 1857. When the Civil War broke out, he was appointed brigadier-general of volunteers and served as chief of staff to Patterson and Banks. He was given a division in the Army of the Potomac, and after it had been assigned to the Third Corps it was made the basis of the Fifth Corps, of which Porter was given command on May 18, 1862, just before McClellan's advance to the Chickahominy. After fighting through the Peninsula campaign, Porter was made major-general of volunteers, and went with his corps to the assistance of Pope and the Army of Virginia. At Second Bull Run, his action on an order from Major-General Pope led to his dismissal from the army. After long years of struggle, in 1886 he succeeded in being restored to the army with the rank of colonel, and shortly afterward was retired. He was engaged in business in New York and held several municipal offices. He died in Morristown, New Jersey, May 21, 1901.

MAJOR-GENERAL DANIEL BUTTERFIELD was born in Utica, New York, October 31, 1831, and was graduated from Union College. Early in the Civil War he became colonel of the Twelfth New York Volunteers, and brigadier-general of volunteers, taking part in the campaigns of McClellan, Burnside, Hooker, and Pope. At Fredericksburg, he had command of the Fifth Army Corps, and afterward became chief-of-staff to the commanding general. He went with Hooker to Chattanooga in October, 1863, and was his chief-of-staff until given a division in the Twentieth Army Corps, which he commanded until July, 1864. At the close of the war he was mustered out of the volunteer service and was brevetted major-general in the United States Army. He resigned from the army in 1869, and was United States treasurer in New York city, 1869–1870. He died at Cold Spring, New York, July 17, 1901.

FEDERAL
GENERALS
No. 3

DISTRICT OF
COLUMBIA
(UPPER TWO)

ILLINOIS
(NINE BELOW)

George W. Getty Led a Division
in the Army of the Potomac.

Samuel Sprigg Carroll, Brevetted
for Gallantry at Spotsylvania.

Isham Nichols
Haynie, Orig-
inally Colonel
of the 48th Reg-
iment.

Joseph Adal-
mon Maltby,
Originally Col-
onel of the 45th
Regiment.

Thomas E. G. Ranson Commanded
the 16th Army Corps.

John F. Farnsworth, Originally
Colonel of the 8th Cavalry.

E. N. Kirk, Severely Wounded in Resisting the Attack on Johnson's
Division at Stone's River.

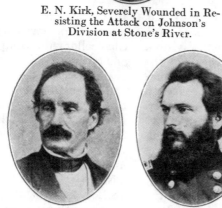

Alexander C. McClurg, Chief of
Staff, 14th Army Corps.

Abner Clark Harding,
Promoted for Gallan-
try at Donelson.

Charles E. Hovey, a
Gallant Division
Commander.

John McArthur, Conspicuous
as a Division Commander.

Sixth Army Corps

MAJOR-GENERAL GOUVERNEUR KEMBLE WARREN (U.S.M.A. 1850) was born at Cold Spring, New York, January 8, 1830. He made a specialty of topographical engineering, and was assistant professor of mathematics at West Point until the beginning of the Civil War, when he came into active service as lieutenant-colonel of the Fifth New York Volunteers. His promotion was rapid, and he reached the rank of major-general of volunteers in May, 1863. He served as brigade and division commander in the Fifth Army Corps, and in January, 1863, became chief topographical engineer, and, later, chief engineer of the Army of the Potomac. His service to the Union cause in defending Little Round Top at Gettysburg won him a brevet of colonel in the regular army. For a short time after Gettysburg he was in command of the Second Corps, and from March, 1864, to April, 1865, of the Fifth Corps, Army of the Potomac; after which he served for a short time in the Department of Mississippi. He left the volunteer service in May, 1865, having received the brevet of major-general in the regular army, in which he remained until February 13, 1866, when he resigned. His last years were spent on surveys and harbor improvements, and he died at Newport, Rhode Island, August 8, 1882.

MAJOR-GENERAL GEORGE SYKES (U.S.M.A. 1842) was born in Dover, Delaware, October 9, 1822, and served in the Mexican and Seminole wars. As major, he entered the Civil War, and was commissioned brigadier-general of volunteers in September, 1861. He led a division of the Fifth Army Corps and was commander for several short periods, notably at the battle of Gettysburg. His commission of major-general of volunteers was dated November 29, 1862. In September–October, 1864, he was in command of the District of South Kansas. After leaving the volunteer service he was made colonel in the regular army, where he remained until he died in Brownsville, Texas, February 9, 1880.

MAJOR-GENERAL CHARLES GRIFFIN (U.S.M.A. 1847) was born in Licking County, Ohio, in 1826, and served in the Mexican War and on the frontier. He was captain when the Civil War broke out, at the head of the Fifth Artillery. His battery fought with great bravery at Bull Run. As brigadier-general of volunteers, he had a brigade and then a division in the Fifth Army Corps, and took part in most of its important battles. He was given command of the corps on April 1, 1865, from which dated his appointment as major-general of volunteers. He led his corps in the final operations against Petersburg, and at Lee's surrender he received the arms and colors of the Army of Northern Virginia. He was one of the commission to carry out the terms of the surrender. After the close of the war, as colonel in the regular army, he was in command of the Department of Texas, where, during an outbreak of yellow fever, he refused to leave his post. Contracting the disease, he died in Galveston, September 15, 1867.

Sixth Army Corps

THE CREATION of this corps was similar to that of the Fifth, on May 18, 1862. Its basis was Brigadier-General W. B. Franklin's division, which was transferred from the Department of the Rappahannock (McDowell's command) and Brigadier-General W. F. Smith's division of the Fourth Army Corps. Franklin was the first commander, and he was followed by Major-Generals W. F. Smith, John Sedgwick, Brigadier-General J. B. Ricketts, Major-General H. G. Wright, and Brevet Major-General G. W. Getty. One division of the corps was prominent at Gaines' Mill, where there were about twenty thousand men present for duty, and it was partially engaged at Second Bull Run, South Mountain, Antietam, and Fredericksburg.

In the last battle it was in the Left Grand Division. The corps carried Marye's Heights in the Chancellorsville campaign, but, excepting one brigade, it was held in reserve at Gettysburg. Several changes were made in the reorganization of March, 1864, and with about twenty-five thousand men at the opening of the Wilderness campaign, it fought with the Army of the Potomac as far as Petersburg, when it was sent to the defense of Washington. Afterward it joined the Army of the Shenandoah and was prominent at the Opequon, Fisher's Hill, and Cedar Creek. In December, 1864, the corps returned to Petersburg and continued with the Army of the Potomac until it was discontinued, June 28, 1865.

P. S. POST. Originally Colonel of the 59th Regiment, Led a Brigade at Stone's River and Nashville.

JOHN W. TURNER, Commander of a Division at Drewry's Bluff and in the Siege of Petersburg.

JULIUS WHITE, Originally Colonel of the 37th Regiment.

JAMES GRANT WILSON, Originally Colonel of the 4th U. S. Cavalry.

AUGUST MERSY, Originally Colonel of the 9th Infantry.

BENJAMIN M. PRENTISS, Noted for His Heroic Defense at Shiloh.

JOHN EUGENE SMITH, Originally Colonel of the 45th Regiment.

LEONARD F. ROSS, Originally Colonel of the 17th Regiment.

RICHARD J. OGLESBY, Conspicuous at Corinth, where He was Wounded.

JOHN C. BLACK, Originally Colonel of the 37th Regiment.

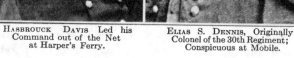

HASBROUCK DAVIS Led his Command out of the Net at Harper's Ferry.

ELIAS S. DENNIS, Originally Colonel of the 30th Regiment; Conspicuous at Mobile.

MICHAEL K. LAWLER Promoted for Gallant Service Throughout the War.

FEDERAL GENERALS—No. 4—ILLINOIS

GILES A. SMITH Commander of a Division in Georgia and the Carolinas.

Seventh Army Corps

MAJOR-GENERAL WILLIAM BUEL FRANKLIN (U.S.M.A. 1843) was born in York, Pennsylvania, February 27, 1823, and served in the Mexican War. He was also an engineer, and taught at West Point. At the opening of the Civil War, as colonel, he had a brigade at Bull Run, and subsequently a division in the First Corps, Army of the Potomac, which formed the nucleus of the Sixth when it was ordered to McClellan on the Peninsula, after having gone with McDowell to the Department of the Rappahannock. Franklin rose to be major-general of volunteers, his commission being dated July 4, 1862. In Burnside's reorganization of the Army of the Potomac, he commanded the Left Grand Division at Fredericksburg. His conduct in this battle was unsatisfactory to Burnside, and Franklin was relieved from duty in the service. In August, 1863, he was put in command of the Nineteenth Army Corps, serving until May, 1864, and was wounded at Sabine Cross Roads on the Red River expedition. From December, 1864, to November, 1865, he was at the head of a board for retiring disabled officers. On the latter date he resigned from the volunteer service, and gave up the regular army, in which he had been brevetted major-general on March 15, 1866. He then became vice-president of the Colt Firearms Company, and was American commissioner-general to the Paris Exposition of 1889. He died in Hartford, Connecticut, March 8, 1903.

MAJOR-GENERAL JOHN SEDGWICK (U.S.M.A. 1837) was born in Cornwall, Connecticut, September 13, 1813. He served with great distinction in the Mexican and Seminole wars. At the outbreak of the Civil War, he was lieutenant-colonel in the cavalry, and he rose to major-general of volunteers by July, 1862. After having a brigade in the Army of the Potomac, he was given a division of the Second Corps, and it met with frightful loss at Antietam, where Sedgwick was twice wounded. After recovery he took command of the Second and Ninth corps for short periods, and in February, 1863, he became head of the Sixth Army Corps, with which his name is so nobly associated. His brave attack upon the heights of Fredericksburg in May, 1863, won him renown. At Gettysburg, which he reached by a forced march on the second day, the left wing of the army was under his command. He was killed by a Confederate sharpshooter near Spotsylvania Court House, May 9, 1864.

MAJOR-GENERAL HORATIO GOUVERNEUR WRIGHT (U.S.M.A. 1841) was born in Clinton, Connecticut, March 6, 1820. At the beginning of the Civil War he had the rank of captain, having been in the Engineers Corps since his graduation. He was chief engineer of the expedition that destroyed the Norfolk Navy-Yard and occupied the same position in the Port Royal expedition. He was division commander in the Department of the South, and was then placed at the head of the re-created Department of the Ohio in August, 1862. Later, he was division and corps commander of the Sixth Army Corps. Being sent by Grant to defend Washington, he took part in the Shenandoah campaign and rejoined the Army of the Potomac before Petersburg. He led the assault on April 2, 1865, which ended the siege. He was promoted to major-general of volunteers in May, 1864. He served on several important commissions after the war, being made brigadier-general in 1879, and was retired from the army in 1884. He died in Washington, July 2, 1899.

Seventh Army Corps

THE TROOPS in the Department of Virginia at Fort Monroe, Norfolk, Portsmouth, and elsewhere, were organized into the Seventh Army Corps, on July 22, 1862, which existed until discontinued on August 1, 1863, when the troops were merged in the Eighteenth Army Corps. It was commanded in turn by Major-General John A. Dix and Brigadier-Generals H. M. Naglee and G. W. Getty. Its principal engagements were the affair at Deserted House, Virginia, and the defense of Suffolk, when besieged by Longstreet in 1863. Its greatest strength, present for duty, was about thirty-three thousand.

MAJOR-GENERAL JOHN ADAMS DIX was born in Boscawen, New Hampshire, July 24, 1798. In 1812, he entered the United States army as a cadet, and continued in military service until 1828, when he settled in Cooperstown, New York, to practise law. He served one term in the United States Senate, and became Secretary of the Treasury under President Buchanan. On the outbreak of the Civil

Robert Francis Catterson, Originally Colonel of the 97th Regiment.

Silas Colgrove Forwarded Lee's "Lost Order" Before Antietam to McClellan.

Thomas T. Crittenden, Originally Colonel of the 6th Infantry.

Robert Sanford Foster, Brevetted for Gallantry.

Alvin P. Hovey, Gallant Division Commander.

Thomas John Lucas, Originally Colonel of the 16th Infantry.

George F. McGinnis, Originally Colonel of the 11th Infantry.

James W. McMillan, Originally Colonel 1st Artillery.

John F. Miller, Colonel of the 29th Regiment; wounded at Stone's River.

Charles Cruft, Conspicuous at Stone's River and Chattanooga.

Jeremiah C. Sullivan Fought in the Shenandoah and Vicksburg Campaigns.

Robert A. Cameron, Originally Colonel of the 34th Regiment.

W. P. Benton Commanded a Brigade at Pea Ridge.

F. Knefler, Originally Colonel of the 79th Regiment.

Walter Q. Gresham, Engaged in the Nashville Campaign.

William Grose Led a Brigade under Thomas.

FEDERAL GENERALS—No. 5—INDIANA

War, Dix was appointed major-general of volunteers, and was given command of the Department of Annapolis (afterward Maryland, and finally merged in the Department of Pennsylvania, July, 1861). Then he was given a division at Baltimore, which became part of the Army of the Potomac, when it was organized. On March 22, 1862, Dix's Division was organized with other troops into the Middle Department, which he headed until June, when he was transferred to the Department of Virginia, the troops of which were organized into the Seventh Army Corps, in July. In July, 1863, Dix was transferred to the Department of the East with headquarters at New York, and remained there until the end of the war. He was twice minister to France (1866-69) and was governor of New York, 1873-75. He died in New York city, April 21, 1879.

Seventh Army Corps (Department of Arkansas)

ANOTHER CORPS designated the Seventh was created on January 6, 1864, to consist of the troops in the Department of Arkansas. The command was given to Major-General Frederick Steele, who was succeeded by Major-General J. J. Reynolds in December, 1864. For a year from May, 1864, the corps was a unit of the Military Division of West Mississippi and was discontinued August 1, 1865. The principal fighting done by the Seventh Corps was in Steele's Arkansas Expedition, especially at Jenkins' Ferry.

MAJOR-GENERAL JOSEPH JONES REYNOLDS (U. S.M.A. 1843) was born in Flemingsburg, Kentucky, January 4, 1822. He taught at West Point and, after resigning, at Washington University, St. Louis, and finally engaged in business in Lafayette. Indiana. He entered the Civil War as colonel of the Tenth Indiana Volunteers, and reached the rank of major-general of volunteers in November, 1862. After active service in Western Virginia, he had a division in the Army of the Cumberland, and was chief-of-staff to Rosecrans in October, 1863. In December, he was put in command of the defenses of New Orleans, and on July 7, 1864, he took command of that portion of the Nineteenth Army Corps which remained in Louisiana, going from there to the head of the Gulf Reserve Corps. On December 22, 1864, he took command of the Seventh Army Corps (Arkansas) until it was discontinued, August 1, 1865. Mustered out of the volunteer service, he returned to the regular army as colonel in the cavalry and received the brevet of major-general. He was retired June 25, 1877, and died in Washington, February 25, 1899.

Eighth Army Corps

THE TROOPS in the Middle Department were organized into the Eighth Army Corps on July 22, 1862. The forces were stationed at various points in Maryland. Its first commander was Major-General John E. Wool, and he was succeeded by Major-Generals R. C. Schenck, Brevet Brigadier-General W. W. Morris, Brigadier-Generals E. B. Tyler, H. H. Lockwood, and Major-General Lewis Wallace. The Eighth Corps saw little active fighting except in West Virginia. Wallace was in command at the Monocacy (July 9, 1864), and the First Separate Brigade under Brigadier-General E. B. Tyler took part, but that battle was fought chiefly by a division of the Sixth Corps. The Eighth Corps was discontinued, August 1, 1865.

MAJOR-GENERAL JOHN ELLIS WOOL was born in Newburg, New York, February 20, 1787. He became a lawyer, but raised an infantry company at Troy and entered the War of 1812. He remained in the army, and in 1841 was raised to the rank of brigadier-general. He selected the American position at Buena Vista in the Mexican War, and for his skill and courage received a vote of thanks and a sword from Congress. He was in command of the Department of the East when the Civil War broke out, and was transferred, in August, 1861, to the Department of Virginia, where he succeeded in saving Fort Monroe to the Federal Government. In May, 1862, his troops occupied Norfolk and Portsmouth

JOHN EDWARDS
Colonel of the 18th Infantry.

ALEXANDER CHAMBERS
Promoted for Gallantry.

WILLIAM T. CLARK
Promoted at Atlanta.

FITZ-HENRY WARREN
Colonel of the 1st Cavalry.

CYRUS BUSSEY
Daring Leader of Cavalry.

JAMES B. WEAVER
Brevetted for Gallantry.

JAMES MADISON TUTTLE
Colonel of the 2d Infantry.

JAMES A. WILLIAMSON
Colonel of the 4th Infantry.

EDWARD HATCH
Brilliant Cavalry Commander.

JACOB G. LAUMAN
Conspicuous at Belmont.

MARCELLUS M. CROCKER
At Corinth and Vicksburg.

FEDERAL GENERALS

No. 6

IOWA

E. W. RICE
Colonel of the 19th Regiment.

JAMES G. GILBERT
Colonel of the 27th Infantry.

after the Confederate evacuation, and at this time he was made major-general. He was given command of the Middle Department in June, and headed the Eighth Army Corps when it was organized in July. In January, 1863, he went back to the Department of the East, which had been recreated, and remained there until July 18th. He was retired from the army on August 1, 1865, and died in Troy, New York, November 10, 1869.

MAJOR-GENERAL ROBERT CUMMING SCHENCK was born in Franklin, Ohio, October 4, 1809. He became a lawyer, and was minister to Brazil, 1851–53. When the Civil War broke out he was made brigadier-general of volunteers, and commanded a brigade at the battle of Bull Run. His force was transferred to the Department of Western Virginia, and he aided in saving that valuable region to the Union. In the new Mountain Department, Schenck had an independent brigade, and he commanded the Federal right at the battle of Cross Keys. He was given a division of the First Corps, Army of Virginia, when the Mountain troops were merged in that army. He was severely wounded at Second Bull Run, where his gallantry won him promotion to major-general of volunteers. After recovery, he was given the Eighth Army Corps (troops of the Middle Department), December 22, 1862. He resigned from

the army December 3, 1863, having been elected member of Congress, where he served until 1870. In 1871, he was a member of the commission which drew up the treaty of Washington, and from 1871 to 1876 was United States minister to Great Britain. He died in Washington, March 23, 1890.

MAJOR-GENERAL LEWIS WALLACE was born in Brookville, Indiana, April 10, 1827. He became a lawyer and served in the Mexican War. At the commencement of the Civil War he headed the Eleventh Indiana Infantry, and was made brigadier-general of volunteers in September, 1861. At Fort Donelson and Shiloh he was in command of a division, and after the former battle he was promoted to major-general of volunteers. In 1863, he superintended the construction of the defenses of Cincinnati. In March, 1864, he took command of the Eighth Army Corps and was defeated by Lieutenant-General Early at the Monocacy. He resigned from the army in November, 1865. After the war he was appointed Governor of New Mexico, and from 1881 to 1885 was United States minister to Turkey. Major-General Wallace was the author of " Ben-Hur," the " Prince of India," and other well-known books, in addition to enjoying great popularity as a lecturer. He died at Crawfordsville Indiana, February 15, 1905.

Ninth Army Corps

THE TROOPS that Major-General Burnside took with him to North Carolina in December, 1861, which were then known as Burnside's Expeditionary Corps and which made a record for themselves at Roanoke Island, New Berne, and elsewhere, were merged in the Department of North Carolina in April, 1862. They and some others from the Department of the South were transferred to the Army of the Potomac in July, and on the 22d, the Ninth Army Corps came into existence. At first, it contained less than five thousand men. Its commanders were Major-Generals Burnside, J. L. Reno, Brigadier-General J. D. Cox, Major-Generals John Sedgwick, W. F. Smith, J. G. Parke, Brigadier-General R. B. Potter, and Brevet Major-General O. B. Willcox. Two divisions went to the assistance of Pope, and fought at Second Bull Run and Chantilly. Afterward,

the corps distinguished itself at South Mountain, Antietam, and Fredericksburg. After the latter battle, Burnside was transferred to the Department of the Ohio (March, 1863) and two divisions of the corps (one having gone to the Seventh) went West with him. The corps took part in the siege of Vicksburg, and was itself besieged in Knoxville, where it suffered great hardships. Early in 1864, the corps was ordered East for reorganization, with Burnside at the head. At the end of May, it became part of the Army of the Potomac, having acted as a separate command through the earlier battles of Grant's campaign. It was very prominent in the siege of Petersburg, and the famous mine was constructed and exploded in front of its lines. The flags of the Ninth Corps were the first that were shown on the public buildings of Petersburg. In June, 1865, the corps was

FEDERAL
GENERALS
No. 7

KANSAS
(THREE TO LEFT AND
EXTREME RIGHT
SECOND ROW)

LOUISIANA
(EXTREME RIGHT
THIRD ROW)

KENTUCKY
(TEN REMAINING)

GEORGE W. DEITZLER
Originally Colonel of the 1st Infantry.

THOMAS EWING, JR.
Originally Colonel of the 11th Cavalry.

THOMAS MOONLIGHT
Originally Colonel of the 11th Cavalry.

SPEED S. FRY
Noted for his Encounter at
Mill Springs.

STEPHEN G. BURBRIDGE
Cavalry Leader in the Morgan
Campaigns.

JOHN T. CROXTON
Led a Brigade in Tennessee and
Georgia.

POWELL CLAYTON
Of Kansas—Later Governor of
Arkansas.

EDWARD H. HOBSON
Noted for the Pursuit of Morgan's
Raiders.

WALTER C. WHITTAKER
Commander of a Brigade at
Chickamauga.

THEOPHILUS T. GARRARD
Defender of Kentucky and East
Tennessee.

D. J. KEILY
Of Louisiana—Colonel of the
Second Cavalry.

JAMES M. SHACKELFORD
Prominent in the Pursuit of Morgan's Raiders.

WILLIAM NELSON
Commanded a Division in Buell's
Army at Shiloh.

JEREMIAH T. BOYLE
Defender of Kentucky and
Tennessee.

N. B. BUFORD
Leader of Cavalry in Kentucky
and Tennessee.

transferred to the Department of Washington and was discontinued on August 1st. This organization is often referred to as the "wandering corps," for it fought in seven States.

MAJOR-GENERAL JESSE LEE RENO (U.S.M.A. 1846) was born in Wheeling, West Virginia, June 20, 1823, and served in the Mexican War, where he was severely wounded at Chapultepec. He was a captain when the Civil War broke out, but was commissioned brigadier-general of volunteers and commanded a brigade in Burnside's Expeditionary Corps, a division in the Department of North Carolina, and the same in the Ninth Army Corps, when it was created. He fought at Roanoke Island, New Berne, Camden, Manassas, and Chantilly and was placed in command of the Ninth Corps, September 3, 1862. He was killed at South Mountain on the 14th. His commission of major-general of volunteers was dated July 18, 1862.

MAJOR-GENERAL JOHN GRUBB PARKE (U.S. M.A. 1849) was born in Chester County, Pennsylvania, September 22, 1827, and entered the Corps of Topographical Engineers. He was first lieutenant when the Civil War broke out, and his commission of brigadier-general of volunteers was dated November 23, 1861. He commanded a brigade in Burnside's expedition to North Carolina, and later had a division in the Ninth Corps. As major-general of volunteers he was Burnside's chief-of-staff at Antietam and Fredericksburg. He went with the corps to the West as its commander, fought through the Vicksburg campaign, and was at the siege of Knoxville. He also commanded the corps after August, 1864, in the operations around Petersburg. He was in command of the Twenty-second Army Corps and at Alexandria, in 1865. After the war he rose to the rank of colonel in the regular army, with the brevet of major-general. He was engaged in engineering, and as superintendent of West Point until he was retired in July, 1889. He died in Washington, December 16, 1900.

BREVET MAJOR-GENERAL ORLANDO BOLIVAR WILLCOX (U.S.M.A. 1847) was born in Detroit, Michigan, April 16, 1823. He served in Texas, in Florida, and in the Mexican War, resigning his commission of first lieutenant in 1857 and taking up the practice of law. He hastened to the front at the outbreak of the war, as colonel of the First Michigan Infantry, and was present at the occupation of Alexandria (May 24, 1861). He commanded a brigade at the battle of Bull Run, where he was severely wounded and captured. For his services here he was made brigadier-general of volunteers. He was exchanged (February, 1862), and later had a division of the Ninth Army Corps, and headed the corps itself at the battle of Fredericksburg. For a short time he was stationed in Indiana and Michigan, and had charge of the district of East Tennessee. He served again with the Ninth Corps in the Knoxville campaign and was at its head for a short period. As division commander he fought through the Wilderness campaign and in the last operations of the Army of the Potomac until July, 1865, except for short periods when he was at the head of the corps. He received the surrender of Petersburg. In August, 1864, he was brevetted major-general of volunteers. After being mustered out of the volunteer service, he became a colonel in the regular army and brigadier-general in 1886. The following year he was retired, and he died at Coburg, Ontario, May 10, 1907.

MAJOR-GENERAL JACOB DOLSON COX was born in Montreal, Canada, October 27, 1828. He became a lawyer and a member of the Ohio State Senate. He entered the Civil War as brigadier-general in the Ohio militia, and was made brigadier-general of volunteers in May, 1861. After distinguished service in western Virginia and under Pope, he succeeded to the command of the Ninth Army Corps upon the death of Major-General Reno, at South Mountain. He was in command of forces in West Virginia and of the Military District of Ohio in 1862-63. On March 4, 1863, his appointment of major-general of volunteers, which dated from October 6, 1862, expired, and it was renewed December 7, 1864. He received a division of the Twenty-third Army Corps in April, 1864, and during the Atlanta and Tennessee campaigns was several times in command of the corps itself. After the battle of Nashville, the corps was moved to North Carolina, where Major-General Cox served in various capacities, and finally as head of the corps from April to June, 1865. In 1866, he resigned from the volunteer service. From 1866 to 1868, he was governor of Ohio, and President Grant's Secretary of the Interior in 1869. He was prominent in politics, finance, and the law until his death, which occurred at Magnolia, Massachusetts, August 4, 1900.

Jonathan P. Cilley, Gallant
Cavalry Leader.

Selden Connor, Colonel
of the 19th Regiment.

Joshua L. Chamberlain, Active at Round Top.

L. G. Estes, Promoted at
the Close of the War.

Cyrus Hamlin, Colonel of the
80th U. S. Colored Infantry.

James D. Fessenden, Brevetted for Meritorious Service.

Francis Fessenden, Active in
the Red River Campaign.

George L. Beal, Brevetted for
Conspicuous Gallantry.

Albion P. Howe, Leader of the Light
Division at the Storming of
Marye's Heights, May 3, 1863.

Neal Dow, Captured and Exchanged for a
Son of Gen. R. E. Lee.

Joseph Dickinson, Brevetted for
Gallantry on Staff Duty
at Gettysburg.

FEDERAL GENERALS

No. 8—MAINE

Tenth Army Corps

CREATED September 3, 1863, to consist of the troops in the Department of the South. Its commanders were Brigadier-General John M. Brannan, and Major-Generals O. M. Mitchel, David Hunter, and Q. A. Gillmore. It took part in the various operations around Charleston Harbor, and in February, 1864, one division went to Florida, where it suffered severely in the battle of Olustee. In April, 1864, the corps entered the Army of the James, in which its commanders were Brigadier-General A. H. Terry, Major-General Q. A. Gillmore, Brigadier-General W. H. T. Brooks, Major-General D. B. Birney, and Brigadier-General Adelbert Ames. It fought around Drewry's Bluff, and two divisions went to Cold Harbor, forming a third division of the Eighteenth Corps. After this, the corps fought at Deep Bottom, Darbytown Road, and Fair Oaks. It was discontinued December 3, 1864 and merged in the new Twenty-fourth Corps. One division and a brigade of the Twenty-fourth, under Major-General Terry, went to Fort Fisher, and, after its capture, the Tenth Corps was reorganized March 27, 1865, in the Department of North Carolina, from Terry's troops. Besides Major-General Terry, Brevet Major-General Adelbert Ames had command from May 13 to August 1, 1865, when the corps was discontinued.

MAJOR-GENERAL ORMSBY MCKNIGHT MITCHEL (U.S.M.A. 1829) was born in Union County, Kentucky, August 28, 1810, and served as assistant professor of mathematics at West Point until 1831, later becoming professor of mathematics, philosophy, and astronomy at Cincinnati College. For a time he practised law. He was director of the Dudley Observatory at Albany, New York, when the Civil War broke out, and entered the army, receiving a commission of brigadier-general of volunteers. From September to November, 1861, he was at the head of the Department of the Ohio, and had a division in the Army of the Ohio, December, 1861, to July, 1862, during which he made a brilliant expedition into Alabama, and won promotion to major-general of volunteers. In September, he was placed at the head of the Tenth Army Corps and died at Hilton Head, South Carolina, of yellow fever, October 27, 1862. He made several important astronomical discoveries.

BREVET MAJOR-GENERAL JOHN MILTON BRANNAN (U.S.M.A. 1841) was born in the District of Columbia in 1819, and served in the Mexican War. He had reached the rank of captain when the Civil War broke out, and was promoted to brigadier-general of volunteers in September, 1861. He was commander of the Department of Key West from February, 1862, until it was merged, the following month, in the Department of the South, of which he was twice in command, as well as temporarily at the head of the Tenth Army Corps between September, 1862, and January, 1863. During this period he led the St. John's River expedition and took part in the battle of Pocotaligo. After this, he commanded divisions in the Twenty-first and Fourteenth corps. He reorganized the artillery in the Army of the Cumberland, and placed the artillery for the defense of Atlanta. He was mustered out of the volunteer service, having been brevetted major-general of volunteers, in May, 1866, and continued in the regular army as lieutenant-colonel and colonel, but with the brevet of major-general, serving at various posts until he was retired in April, 1882. He died in New York city, December 16, 1892.

MAJOR-GENERAL QUINCY ADAMS GILLMORE (U.S.M.A. 1849) was born at Black River, Ohio, February 28, 1825. He entered the Engineer Corps, and served as assistant instructor in engineering at West Point. Before the Civil War broke out he had done much work on fortifications and other engineering projects connected with the army. As captain and chief engineer, he accompanied Burnside to North Carolina, and later planned the details of the successful attack on Fort Pulaski, which feat won him the rank of brigadier-general of volunteers. After this, he held a command in West Virginia and also served in the Department of the Ohio. In June, 1863, he took command of the Tenth Army Corps and held it for a year, participating in the operations around Charleston Harbor, Bermuda Hundred, and the battle of Drewry's Bluff. His commission of major-general of volunteers was dated July 10, 1863. He went to the defense of Washington against Early with the Nineteenth Corps in July, 1864. Resigning from the volunteer service after the war, he rose to rank of colonel in the regular army and was connected with many great engineering projects until his death, which occurred at Brooklyn, New York, April 7, 1888.

MAJOR-GENERAL ALFRED HOWE TERRY was born in Hartford, Connecticut, November 10, 1827. He was colonel of the Second Connecticut

Charles H. Smith, Conspicuous as a
Cavalry Leader.

George F. Shepley, Originally Colonel
of the 20th Regiment.

Elias Spear, Colonel of the 20th
Regiment.

FEDERAL GENERALS—No. 9—MAINE (ABOVE) MARYLAND (BELOW)

Frank Nickerson, Originally
Colonel of the 4th
Regiment.

Daniel White, Brevetted for
Gallantry at the
Wilderness.

Nathaniel J. Jackson, Originally Colonel of the 1st
and 5th Infantry.

Cuvier Grover, Division
Leader in the East and
in the West.

James M. Deems, Brevetted for
Gallantry.

John R. Kenly, Originally Colonel of
the 1st Regiment.

James Cooper, In Command of Maryland Volunteers in 1861.

Volunteers at Bull Run. He returned home to raise the Seventh Connecticut Volunteers, and with this regiment served under Brigadier-General T. W. Sherman at the capture of Port Royal and under Major-General Hunter at Fort Pulaski, which he then commanded. Being raised to brigadier-general of volunteers in April, 1862, he commanded several districts in the Department of the South (Tenth Army Corps), and took command of this corps when it was transferred to the Army of the James, in April, 1864. As brevet major-general of volunteers he headed the Twenty-fourth Army Corps which was organized out of the Tenth, December, 1864, to January, 1865. On the latter date, he was put in command of the provisional corps organized for the capture of Fort Fisher and Wilmington. After these events had taken place, his corps became the reorganized Tenth Corps, and Major-General Terry was in command until May 13, 1865, when he took charge of Richmond. After leaving the volunteer service, he rose to the rank of major-general in the regular army (1886) and was retired in April, 1888. He died in New Haven, Connecticut, December 16, 1890. For the capture of Fort Fisher he was tendered the thanks of Congress.

Major-General William Thomas Harbaugh Brooks (U.S.M.A. 1841) was born in New Lisbon, Ohio, January 28, 1821, and served in the Seminole and Mexican wars, and in Texas and New Mexico. He had reached the rank of captain when the Civil War broke out, and was made brigadier-general of volunteers in September, 1861. He commanded a brigade in the Sixth Army Corps until October, 1862, and a division until after the Chancellorsville campaign, when, as major-general of volunteers, he was at the head of the Department of the Monongahela until Grant's operations against Lee and Richmond began. His commission of major-general of volunteers having expired, Brigadier-General Brooks was then in command of a division of the Eighteenth Army Corps, and on June 21, 1864, was put at the head of the Tenth Corps. He resigned from the volunteer service the following month, and died in Huntsville, Alabama, July 19, 1870.

Major-General David Bell Birney was born in Huntsville, Alabama, May 29, 1825. He practised law in Philadelphia until 1861, when he entered the Federal army as lieutenant-colonel of a Pennsylvania regiment and reached the rank of brigadier-general of volunteers, in February, 1862. He had a brigade in the Third Army Corps through the Peninsula campaign and was with Pope at Second Bull Run and Chantilly, taking the division temporarily after Brigadier-General Kearny was killed. As major-general of volunteers, he had a division at Fredericksburg and Chancellorsville and commanded the Third Corps at Gettysburg after Major-General Sickles was wounded, holding it from time to time until February, 1864. In the new organization of the Army of the Potomac (March, 1864), he had a division in the Second Corps until July, when he was given command of the Tenth Corps, Army of the James. While in this position he contracted a fever, and died in Philadelphia, October 18, 1864.

Eleventh Army Corps

When the Army of Virginia was discontinued, September 12, 1862, its First Corps, which had been the troops of the Mountain Department under Rosecrans and Fremont, and had been led by Sigel in the Pope campaign, was merged in the Army of the Potomac as the Eleventh Corps. It remained on the line of Manassas during the Antietam campaign, did not reach Fredericksburg in time for the battle, and at Chancellorsville was badly routed by "Stonewall" Jackson, because its commander allowed himself to be surprised. In this battle about twelve thousand troops were present. It was one of the two corps heavily engaged on the first day at Gettysburg. After that battle, one division was sent to Charleston Harbor, and the other two went with Hooker to Tennessee to assist Grant in the Chattanooga campaign. These two divisions then went with Sherman to the relief of Knoxville, and shared all the great hardships of the march. In April, 1864, these troops were merged in the new Twentieth Army Corps, for the Atlanta campaign. The leaders of the Eleventh Corps were Major-General Franz Sigel, Brigadier-General J. H. Stahel, Major-General Carl Schurz, Brigadier-General A. von Steinwehr, and Major-General O. O. Howard.

Stephen M. Weld, Jr., Leader of Colored Troops at the Crater Battle.

William F. Bartlett Led His Brigade at the Crater and Was Captured.

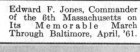

Oliver Edwards Led a Brigade at the "Bloody Angle," Spotsylvania; Brevetted for Gallantry at Sailor's Creek.

Edward F. Jones, Commander of the 6th Massachusetts on Its Memorable March Through Baltimore, April, '61.

Frederick W. Lander, One of the Early Heroes of the War.

Charles J. Paine, Noted Leader of Colored Troops.

George H. Gordon Led a Charge at Cedar Mountain.

Charles P. Stone, Later Distinguished in the Service of Egypt.

Albert Ordway, Promoted at the Close of the War.

Henry L. Eustis, Originally Colonel of the 10th Regiment.

N. A. Miles Commanded a Brigade at Chancellorsville and Later Led a Division in the Army of the Potomac.

FEDERAL GENERALS—No. 10—MASSACHUSETTS

Twelfth Army Corps

MAJOR-GENERAL FRANZ SIGEL was born in Sinsheim, Baden, November 18, 1824, and was graduated from the Military School at Carlsruhe, becoming a champion of German unity and minister of war to the revolutionary Government of 1848, which was overthrown by Prussia. Later, having withdrawn to Switzerland, the Government expelled him, and he emigrated to America in 1852. He taught in a military institute in St. Louis and edited a military periodical. When the Civil War broke out, he organized the Third Missouri Infantry and an artillery battery, and after assisting Captain Lyon in the capture of Camp Jackson, he served in Missouri, at Carthage and at Springfield. As brigadier-general of volunteers, he was conspicuous for his bravery at Pea Ridge, and as major-general of volunteers was placed in command of Harper's Ferry in June, 1862. Then he served in the Army of Virginia, in command of its First Corps, out of which the Eleventh Corps, Army of the Potomac, was created. He relinquished the latter in January, 1863. On March 10, 1864, he succeeded Brigadier-General B. F. Kelley in the command of the Department of West Virginia, but after the defeat at New Market, May 15th, he was relieved by Major-General Hunter and given the division at Harper's Ferry, where he successfully held out against Lieutenant-General Early. In July, 1864, he was relieved from his command, and he resigned from the army in May, 1865. After the war, he edited a German paper in Baltimore, and later was register and United States pension-agent in New York city. He was well known as a lecturer and editor of the "New York Monthly," a German periodical. He died in New York city, August 21, 1902.

MAJOR-GENERAL CARL SCHURZ was born in Cologne, Prussia, March 2, 1829, studying there in the gymnasium and later at the University of Bonn. He was engaged in the revolutionary movement in 1848, and was compelled to seek refuge in Switzerland. In 1852, he came to the United States and settled in Philadelphia, later going to Milwaukee, Wisconsin, where he began the practice of law. Lincoln appointed him United States minister to Spain, but he resigned to take part in the Civil War. As brigadier-general of volunteers, he commanded a division of the First Corps, Army of Virginia, at Second Bull Run, and at Chancellorsville a division of the Eleventh Corps. At Gettysburg he had command, as major-general of volunteers, of the Eleventh Corps, temporarily, and again in January and February, 1864. At Chattanooga, he took an active part. In March, 1864, he was put in charge of a corps of instruction near Nashville, and at the close of the war was chief-of-staff to Major-General Slocum in the Army of Georgia. He resigned from the volunteer service in May, 1865, and became a newspaper correspondent in Washington, and, in 1866, founded the *Detroit Post*. He was senator from Missouri (1869-1875), and Secretary of the Interior from 1877 to 1881, and editor of the New York *Evening Post* from 1881 to 1884. He was an enthusiastic advocate of civil-service reform and other political movements. He was a writer and speaker of note, and died in New York city, May 14, 1906.

Twelfth Army Corps

CREATED September 12, 1862, from the Second Corps, Army of Virginia, the troops of which, under Major-General N. P. Banks, had been in the Department of the Shenandoah, and in earlier organizations of the Army of the Potomac. It was the smallest corps in the army, and in the early days contained about twelve thousand men. The command was given to Major-General J. F. K. Mansfield, who was killed at Antietam, the first battle of the new corps. Its next battle was that of Chancellorsville where, with the Third, it bore the real brunt of the fight. After Gettysburg, in which we remember the Twelfth by its gallant defense of Culps' Hill, it went with Hooker to Tennessee where one division opened the line of supplies to the starving Army of the Cumberland and fought "the battle in the clouds" on Lookout Mountain. In April, 1864, the Twelfth Corps was merged in the newly formed Twentieth, for the Atlanta campaign. After Mansfield's death, the command of the Twelfth Corps was held by Major-General H. W. Slocum except for very brief periods, when it was headed by Brigadier-General A. S. Williams, the senior division commander. In its short career, the corps is said to have never lost a gun or a color.

JOHN C. PALFREY
Chief Engineer of the 13th
Army Corps.

EDWARD W. HINKS
Originally Colonel of the 8th
Infantry.

MASSACHUSETTS

(ABOVE)

CHARLES DEVENS
Colonel of the 15th Regiment.
Later Commanded Division.

GEORGE L. ANDREWS
Engaged in the Siege and Capture
of Port Hudson.

MICHIGAN

(BELOW)

J. M. OLIVER
Originally Colonel of the
15th Regiment.

HENRY BAXTER
Promoted for Gallantry at
the Wilderness.

JOSEPH T. COPELAND
Originally Colonel of the
5th Cavalry.

FEDERAL

GENERALS

No. 11

WM. R. SHAFTER
Later Commander at Santiago, Cuba.

CHARLES C. DOOLITTLE
Originally Colonel of the 18th Infantry;
Promoted for Merit.

BYRON R. PIERCE
Originally Colonel of the
3d Infantry.

HENRY A. MORROW
"Here to fight, not to surrender"—Gettysburg, July 1.

RALPH ELY
Leader of the Brigade which
was first in Petersburg.

Thirteenth Army Corps

Major-General Joseph King Fenno Mansfield (U.S.M.A. 1822) was born in New Haven, Connecticut, December 22, 1803, and served in the Mexican War and in the Engineer Corps. From May, 1861, to March, 1862, he had charge of the Department of Washington, and as brigadier-general of volunteers commanded the District of Suffolk of the Seventh Army Corps, and captured the town of Norfolk in May. As major-general of volunteers, he was put at the head of the newly formed Twelfth Army Corps on September 12, 1862, and was mortally wounded at Antietam, on the 17th.

Brevet Major-General Alpheus Starkey Williams was born in Saybrook, Connecticut, September 10, 1810, was graduated from Yale College, and held various political positions in Detroit where he also practised law. As colonel of a Michigan regiment, when the Civil War broke out, he was made brigadier-general of volunteers and headed a brigade in the Department of Pennsylvania. Passing through the various organizations of the Army of the Potomac, he was given a division in the Fifth Corps, which became the Second Corps, Army of Virginia, and the Twelfth Corps, Army of the Potomac, and finally was merged in the Twentieth Corps, Army of the Cumberland. Williams was the only general to lead the same division through the whole of the war, although at various times he temporarily headed the corps in which he was placed. He was corps commander at Antietam, after Mansfield fell; at Gettysburg, and also on the march to the sea and in the campaign through the Carolinas. His brevet of major-general of volunteers for marked ability and energy, was dated January 12, 1865, and a year later he was mustered out of the service. After the war, he was United States minister to San Salvador (1866–69), and member of Congress from 1874 until his death, which occurred in Washington, December 21, 1878.

Thirteenth Army Corps

On October 24, 1862, the troops in the newly created Department of the Tennessee, under Major-General Grant, were designated the Thirteenth Army Corps, and Major-General W. T. Sherman was put in command. The troops were scattered in many districts. Sherman organized four of the divisions into the Yazoo Expedition, and started on the campaign that ended in failure at Chickasaw Bluffs, December 29, 1862. On December 18th, the corps was subdivided, and the Army of the Tennessee now consisted of the Thirteenth, Fifteenth, Sixteenth, and Seventeenth corps. Brigadier-General Morgan succeeded Sherman, who commanded the whole department, at the head of the new Thirteenth Army Corps. The corps went with Major-General McClernand (January 4-12, 1863) on the expedition to Arkansas Post, the expedition being known as McClernard's Army of the Mississippi, in which the Thirteenth Corps became the First Corps for that period. Following Morgan, the commanders of the Thirteenth Corps were Major-Generals J. A. McClernand, E. O. C. Ord (who succeeded when McClernand was relieved at Vicksburg), and C. C. Washburn. One division fought the battle of Helena (July 4, 1863), and the battle of Port Gibson (May 1, 1863) was fought almost entirely by it.

After Vicksburg, the corps invested Jackson, and on August 7th it was transferred to the Army of the Gulf, where its chief active service (two divisions) took place in the Red River campaign of 1864. New commanders of the corps while in the Army of the Gulf were Major-General N. J. T. Dana, and Brigadier-Generals T. E. G. Ransom, R. A. Cameron, M. K. Lawler, and W. P. Benton. On June 11, 1864, the troops of the corps were transferred to other commands, but they were largely brought together again for the Reserve Corps, Army of the Gulf, in December, 1864, out of which on February 18, 1865, a new Thirteenth Army Corps was created, which, under command of General Gordon Granger, took part in the capture of Mobile, in April, 1865. The corps was discontinued at Galveston, Texas, July 20, 1865.

Brigadier - General George Washington Morgan was born in Washington County, Pennsylvania, September 20, 1820. He did not graduate from West Point, which he entered in 1841, but took up the practice of law in Mount Vernon, Ohio. But he went to the Mexican War and was brevetted brigadier-general. Entering the diplomatic service, he was consul at Marseilles and minister to Portugal. When the Civil War broke

JOSEPH CONRAD
Noted Brigade Commander.

EGBERT B. BROWN
Originally of the 7th
Regiment.

JOHN D. STEVENSON
Originally Colonel of the
7th Regiment.

ISAAC F. SHEPHARD
Originally Colonel of the
3d Regiment.

GABRIEL R. PAUL
Gallant Figure at Gettysburg.

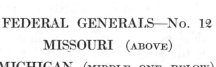

JOHN ELISHA PHELPS
Originally Colonel of the
2d Kansas Cavalry.

CLINTON B. FISK
Originally Colonel of
the 33d Regiment.

LEWIS B. PARSONS
Promoted at the Close
of the War.

FEDERAL GENERALS—No. 12

MISSOURI (ABOVE)

MICHIGAN (MIDDLE ONE BELOW)

MINNESOTA (FOUR REMAINING BELOW)

JOHN McNEIL
Originally Colonel of the 3d
Infantry.

ALEXANDER ASBOTH
Promoted at the End of
the War.

NAPOLEON J. T. DANA
Commander of a Brigade
in the Peninsula.

C. C. ANDREWS
Organizer and Division
Commander.

WILLIAM SANBORN
Promoted for Conspicuous
Gallantry.

STEPHEN MILLER
Colonel of the 7th Regiment;
Governor in 1863.

WILLIS A. GORMAN
First Commander of
the 1st Minnesota.

out he returned, and was made brigadier-general of volunteers in November, 1861. He served first under Buell and then as division commander in the Department of the Tennessee (Thirteenth Army Corps). He commanded a division in the Yazoo Expedition, and was the first commander of the reorganized Thirteenth Corps which he led at the capture of Arkansas Post (January, 1863). Ill-health compelled him to resign from the service in June, 1863. In 1868 and 1870, he was a member of Congress. He died at Old Point Comfort, Virginia, July 26, 1893.

MAJOR-GENERAL JOHN ALEXANDER McCLERNAND was born in Breckinridge County, Kentucky, May 30, 1812. He became a lawyer and served in the Black Hawk War as private. He was a member of Congress when the Civil War broke out and resigned to enter it, being made brigadier-general of volunteers in May, 1861. He first distinguished himself at Belmont, November 7, 1861. After Fort Donelson, he was made major-general of volunteers in the Army of West Tennessee, and commanded a division at Shiloh. On January 4, 1863, he replaced Sherman in command of the Yazoo Expedition which, under the name of McClernand's Army of the Mississippi, together with the Mississippi Squadron, captured Arkansas Post, January 11th. Grant removed McClernand from the command, and he was placed at the head of the Thirteenth Army Corps, of which he was in turn relieved on June 19th, during the siege of Vicksburg. He commanded this corps again for a short time in 1864, while it was serving in the Army of the Gulf. He resigned his commission on November 30, 1864, and resumed the practice of law. He died at Springfield, Illinois, September 20, 1900.

MAJOR-GENERAL CADWALLADER COLDEN WASHBURN was born in Livermore, Maine, April 22, 1818. He settled in Wisconsin as a lawyer and financier. At the outbreak of the war he raised the Second Wisconsin Cavalry, and as its colonel was successful under Major-General Curtis in Arkansas. He rose to the rank of major-general of volunteers in November, 1862, and later headed divisions in the Army of the Tennessee. He was the first commander of the reorganized Thirteenth Army Corps, and went with it from the Army of the Tennessee to that of the Gulf. After that, he was at the head of the District of West Tennessee, and resigned from the volunteer service in May, 1865. Later on, he was member of Congress and governor of Wisconsin. He died at Eureka Springs, Arkansas, May 14, 1882.

BREVET MAJOR-GENERAL THOMAS EDWARD GREENFIELD RANSOM was born in Norwich, Vermont, November 29, 1834. He became a captain in an Illinois regiment in April, 1861, and was made brigadier-general of volunteers in November, 1862. He fought at Fort Donelson and Shiloh, and was for a time on Grant's staff. He commanded a brigade in the Seventeenth Army Corps during the Vicksburg campaign, and a detachment of the Thirteenth Army Corps on the Red River expedition, in 1864. He was wounded at Sabine Cross Roads. In the Atlanta campaign, he commanded a division of the Sixteenth Army Corps and headed that and the Seventeenth for short periods. On October 10th, he was obliged to give up the Seventeenth Corps on account of illness, and he died, October 29th, near Rome, Georgia. The brevet of major-general of volunteers had been conferred on him in September, a few weeks before his death.

Fourteenth Army Corps

THE ORGANIZATION of the Army of the Ohio into three corps, in September, 1862, was changed on October 24th, when this force became the Army of the Cumberland, and consisted of the Fourteenth Army Corps, with Major-General Rosecrans at its head. In November, the Fourteenth Corps was divided into the Right Wing, Center, and Left Wing, and on January 9, 1863, the Center was designated the Fourteenth Army Corps, with Major-General George H. Thomas in command.

The corps fought at Stone's River and won its greatest fame at Chickamauga. It also distinguished itself at Missionary Ridge. It was prominent in the Atlanta campaign, and was one of the two corps of the Army of Georgia in the march to the sea and the campaign through the Carolinas. It was discontinued August 1, 1865. Besides Thomas, it was commanded by Major-Generals John M. Palmer, Jeff. C. Davis, and Brigadier-General R. W. Johnson.

| Gilman Marston, Colonel of the 10th Regiment. | Simon G. Griffin, Leader at the Crater Battle. | Joab N. Patterson, Colonel of the 2d Regiment. | Joseph H. Potter, Promoted for Gallantry. | John L. Thompson, Colonel of the 1st Cavalry. |

FEDERAL GENERALS—No. 13—NEW HAMPSHIRE (ABOVE) NEW JERSEY (BELOW)

Joseph W. Revere, Originally Colonel of the 7th Regiment. Promoted in 1862.

Gershom Mott, Active as a Division Commander in the Wilderness Campaign.

Ranald S. Mackenzie, Dashing Cavalry Leader in the Army of the Potomac.

Horatio P. VanCleve, Division Leader at Stone's River and Chickamauga.

Geo. W. Mindil, Originally Colonel of the 33d New Jersey.

Lewis C. Arnold, Active Commander in Florida.

William Birney, Brevetted for Gallantry in Action.

Edward Burd Grubb, Brevetted at the Close of the War.

Fifteenth Army Corps

MAJOR-GENERAL JOHN McAULEY PALMER was born at Eagle Creek, Kentucky, September 13, 1817, and became a lawyer and politician. He entered the Civil War as colonel of volunteers and was major-general of volunteers before the end of 1862. His first service was with Fremont and Pope in Missouri, and later he was given a division of the Army of the Cumberland. For a short time during the Tullahoma campaign he headed the Twenty-first Corps. During the Atlanta campaign he was in command of the Fourteenth Corps until August, 1864. Later, he was in charge of the Department of Kentucky. After the war, he was governor of Illinois, United States senator, and candidate of the Gold Democrats for President, in 1896. He died in Springfield, Illinois, September 25, 1900.

BREVET MAJOR-GENERAL JEFFERSON COLUMBUS DAVIS was born in Clarke County, Indiana, March 2, 1828, and served as a volunteer in the Mexican War. After this he entered the regular army. He was a lieutenant at Fort Sumter when the Civil War broke out. Later on, he became captain and then colonel of an Indiana Regiment, and led a division in the Army of the Southwest at Pea Ridge. As brigadier-general of volunteers, he served as division commander in Pope's Army of the Mississippi and also in that of the Cumberland, and took command of the Fourteenth Army Corps, August 22, 1864, and led it through Georgia and the Carolinas until the close of the war. He remained in the regular army as colonel,

and was at one time commander of the United States troops in Alaska, and also was at the head of the troops that quelled the Modoc uprising of 1873, after the murder of Canby. He received the brevet of major-general in 1865. He died in Chicago, November 30, 1879.

BREVET MAJOR-GENERAL RICHARD W. JOHNSON (U.S.M.A. 1849) was born in Livingston County, Kentucky, February 7, 1827, and saw his first service on the frontier. He entered the Civil War as captain of cavalry, becoming colonel of a Kentucky regiment. He served in the Army of the Cumberland and its prior organizations. His commission as brigadier-general of volunteers was dated October 19, 1861. As cavalry commander, he was captured by Morgan in August, 1862. He commanded a division at Stone's River, Chickamauga, and Chattanooga, and was severely wounded at New Hope Church. For a short time in August, 1864, he headed the Fourteenth Army Corps. Then he took charge of the cavalry forces in the Army of the Cumberland, and headed a division at Nashville, for which service he received a brevet of major-general in the regular army. After the war he entered the regular army as major in the Fourth Cavalry, also serving as provost-marshal-general and judge advocate in several departments. He was professor of military science in the University of Minnesota, 1869-71. He retired as major-general in 1867, and after 1875 had the rank of brigadier-general. He died in St. Paul, Minnesota, April 21, 1897.

Fifteenth Army Corps

Two DIVISIONS and some district troops of the Thirteenth Corps, Army of the Tennessee, were constituted the Fifteenth, on December 18, 1862. In two divisions, it was on Sherman's Yazoo Expedition and was also known as the Second Corps, McClernand's Army of the Mississippi, from January 4 to January 12, 1863. The commanders of the Fifteenth Corps were Major-Generals W. T. Sherman, F. P. Blair, Jr., John A. Logan, Brigadier-General M. L. Smith, and Major-Generals P. J. Osterhaus and W. B. Hazen. The corps took part in the Vicksburg campaign, the battle of Chattanooga, the relief of Knoxville, the Atlanta campaign, and the last campaigns of Sherman. After the Grand Review of May 24, 1865, the corps

went to Louisville, Kentucky, and one division served with the army of occupation at Little Rock, Arkansas. The corps was discontinued August 1, 1865.

MAJOR-GENERAL PETER JOSEPH OSTERHAUS was born in Coblenz, Germany, in 1823, and served as an officer in the Prussian army. He came to St. Louis, and in 1861 entered the Union army as major of volunteers. Later, as colonel, he had a brigade in the Army of the Southwest, and at Pea Ridge he commanded a division. Passing into the Army of the Tennessee as brigadier-general of volunteers, he commanded divisions in the Thirteenth and Fifteenth corps, taking part in the

FEDERAL GENERALS
No. 14
NEW MEXICO
(LEFT)
NEBRASKA
(RIGHT)
NEW YORK
(BELOW)

Christopher Carson (Kit Carson), of New Mexico, Famous Rocky Mountain Scout.

John M. Thayer, of Nebraska, an Important Division Commander.

Henry M. Judah, Conspicuous During Morgan's Raid of 1863.

J. J. Bartlett Received the Arms of Lee's Troops at Appomattox.

Gustavus A. De Russy, who was Brevetted for Gallantry.

Charles K. Graham Led a Brigade at Chancellorsville.

N. Martin Curtis, Promoted for Gallantry at Fort Fisher.

Romeyn B. Ayres, Active as a Division Commander.

Abram Duryee, First Colonel of Duryee's Zouaves.

John P. Hatch, Dashing Leader of Cavalry.

Henry A. Barnum, Conspicuous Brigade Leader.

Vicksburg campaign and assisting Hooker in the capture of Lookout Mountain. During the Atlanta campaign, he was made major-general of volunteers (July, 1864), and he commanded the Fifteenth Army Corps on the march to the sea. He was Major-General Canby's chief-of-staff in 1865. After the war he resigned from the service, and was American consul at Lyons, France. Thereafter, remaining in Europe, he made his home in Mannheim, Germany.

Sixteenth Army Corps

CREATED from three divisions and troops of several districts of the Thirteenth Army Corps on December 18, 1862, with Major-General S. A. Hurlbut in command. The corps was much divided during its existence, and divisions were several times exchanged for others in the Seventeenth Corps. Some of it saw service at Vicksburg, but little active fighting at that place. A division went with Sherman to Chattanooga. Two divisions were in the Atlanta campaign, and two on the Red River expedition of 1864. Some troops were sent to the Seventh Corps in Arkansas. The corps was officially discontinued on November 1, 1864, but the right wing, under Major-General A. J. Smith, known as "Detachment, Army of the Tennessee," assisted Thomas at Nashville. Besides Hurlbut, the command was held by Brigadier-General C. S. Hamilton and Major-General N. J. T. Dana. The left wing was commanded from time to time by Major-Generals C. S. Hamilton, R. J. Oglesby, Brigadier-General G. M. Dodge, Colonel A. Mersey, and Brigadier-Generals E. A. Carr and T. E. G. Ransom. The "Detachment," which included a division of the Seventeenth Army Corps, was, on February 18, 1865, designated the Sixteenth Corps, with Smith in command. The corps was now in the Military Division of West Mississippi and assisted in the last operations around Mobile. It was discontinued July 20, 1865.

MAJOR-GENERAL STEPHEN AUGUSTUS HURLBUT was born in Charleston, South Carolina, November 29, 1815, and was admitted to the bar in 1837. In 1845, he removed to Illinois and attained considerable prominence in politics. At the opening of the Civil War he was appointed a brigadier-general of volunteers, and commanded a division at Shiloh. Later, he was at the head of several districts in the department and was given command of the reorganized Sixteenth Corps, Army of the Tennessee, in December, 1862. In September, 1862, he was promoted to major-general of volunteers. He succeeded Major-General N. P. Banks in command of the Army and Department of the Gulf. He left the volunteer service at the end of the war, and at the time of his death, March 27, 1882, was United States minister to Peru.

MAJOR-GENERAL GRENVILLE MELLEN DODGE was born in Danvers, Massachusetts, April 12, 1831. He was a member of the Government survey in the West until the Civil War broke out, when he went to the front as colonel of the Fourth Iowa Infantry, in July, 1861. He fought with the Army of the Southwest, and, being transferred to the Department of Tennessee, he commanded the troops in several districts thereof, as well as divisions of the Thirteenth and Sixteenth corps, having been made brigadier-general of volunteers in March, 1862. In the summer of 1863, he was put in command of the left wing of the Sixteenth Army Corps as major-general of volunteers, and was wounded on August 19, 1864, at Jonesboro, Georgia, in the Atlanta campaign. In December, 1864, he succeeded Major-General Rosecrans in the Department of Missouri, and remained there until the close of the war. He resigned from the service in May, 1866, and became chief engineer of the Union Pacific and Texas Pacific railways. In 1866-67, he was member of Congress from Iowa. In 1898, he was at the head of the commission appointed to investigate the conduct of the Spanish-American war.

MAJOR-GENERAL ANDREW JACKSON SMITH (U. S.M.A. 1838) was born in Berks County, Pennsylvania, April 28, 1815, and served in the Mexican War and in the West. He was made major in the cavalry when the Civil War broke out. His appointment of brigadier-general of volunteers was dated March 17, 1862. He had a division in the Army of the Ohio, but his name is chiefly associated with the Army of the Tennessee. He commanded a division in the Thirteenth Corps and was with the Yazoo Expedition and McClernand's Army of the Mississippi, and took part in

William Dwight, Originally
Colonel of the 70th
Regiment.

Morgan H. Chrysler, Bre-
vetted for Meritorious
Services.

Hiram Berdan, Celebrated
Commander of Sharp-
shooters.

Schuyler Hamilton, Con-
spicuous at Island
No. 10.

Wladimir Krzyzanowski,
Originally Colonel of
the 58th Regiment.

Henry E. Davies, Daring
Cavalry Leader
in the East.

Joseph E. Hamblin, Origi-
nally Colonel of the
65th Volunteers.

John Cochrane, Originally
Colonel of the 65th
Regiment.

FEDERAL   GENERALS

No. 15

NEW   YORK

(CONTINUED)

Philip Regis De Trobriand,
Prominent Brigade
Commander.

Thomas W. Egan, Prominent
Brigade Commander
in the East.

the siege of Vicksburg. He commanded the right wing of the Sixteenth Army Corps on the Red River expedition, and, as major-general of volunteers, in various operations in Tennessee and Mississippi during the Atlanta campaign. He took part in the battle of Nashville, and became commander of the reorganized Sixteenth Corps on February 18, 1865, participating in the closing operations around Mobile. He became Colonel of the Seventh U. S. Cavalry in 1866, and was retired in 1869. For a time he was postmaster of St. Louis. He died in St. Louis, January 30, 1897.

Seventeenth Army Corps

CREATED December 18, 1862, from troops in the Thirteenth Corps, Army of the Tennessee, and the command given to Major-General J. B. McPherson, with whose name it is closely linked. Divisions were exchanged with the Sixteenth Corps. It was prominent in the operations on the Mississippi before and after the fall of Vicksburg, and was a member of Sherman's Meridian expedition. After this the corps was divided: half remained in the Mississippi valley; the other two divisions went with Sherman to Atlanta. The Mississippi section was on the Red River expedition with Brigadier-General A. J. Smith and formed part of the detachment that fought at Nashville. It never rejoined the rest of the corps, which followed Sherman through Georgia and the Carolinas. On August 1, 1865, the corps was discontinued. Besides McPherson, it was commanded by Major-Generals F. P. Blair, Jr., J. A. Mower, Brigadier-Generals T. E. G. Ransom, M. D. Leggett, and W. W. Belknap.

MAJOR-GENERAL FRANCIS PRESTON BLAIR, JR., was born in Lexington, Kentucky, February 19, 1821, and became a lawyer and editor in St. Louis. He was a member of Congress for several years, and at the outbreak of the Civil War he was instrumental in saving Missouri to the Union. Entering the army as colonel, his commission of major-general of volunteers was dated November 29, 1862. He commanded a brigade on the Yazoo expedition, and afterward was division commander in the Fifteenth Army Corps, and headed it for a short time. In Sherman's campaigns to Atlanta and through Georgia and the Carolinas, he commanded the Seventeenth Army Corps. Resigning from the volunteer service in November, 1865, he was Democratic nominee for vice-president in 1868, and senator from Missouri, 1871-73. He died in St. Louis, July 8, 1875.

MAJOR-GENERAL JOSEPH ANTHONY MOWER was born in Woodstock, Vermont, August 22, 1827. He served as a private in the Mexican War and reentered the army as second lieutenant in 1855. After the Civil War broke out, he was promoted to a captaincy, became colonel of a Missouri regiment in May, 1862, and brigadier-general of volunteers in November of that year. He led his regiment in the attacks on Island No. 10, in other activities in Kentucky and Tennessee, and headed a brigade in the Army of the Mississippi at the time it was discontinued, passing thence to brigades in the Thirteenth, Sixteenth, and Fifteenth corps (Army of the Tennessee). With the latter, he served at the siege of Vicksburg. From December, 1863, to October, 1864, he commanded a brigade and then a division in the right wing of the Sixteenth Corps, and took part in the Red River expedition and in the operations in Mississippi and Tennessee while Sherman was fighting his way to Atlanta. In October, he joined Sherman's army at the head of a division of the Seventeenth Army Corps, and was its commander for a short time. In the closing days of the Carolina campaign he had command of the Twentieth Army Corps. Mower was appointed major-general of volunteers in August, 1864. After leaving the volunteer service he continued as colonel in the regular army, serving with the Thirty-ninth and Twenty-fifth infantry. He commanded the Department of Louisiana. He died in New Orleans, January 6, 1870.

Eighteenth Army Corps

ON DECEMBER 24, 1862, the troops in the Department of North Carolina were designated the Eighteenth Army Corps, and Major-General J. G. Foster was placed at its head. There were five divisions, at first. Two divisions were detached in February, 1863, and sent to the Tenth Corps,

John J. Peck, Commander on the Peninsula.

Charles H. Tompkins, Promoted in 1865.

Edward E. Potter, Brevetted for Gallantry.

William H. Morris, Colonel of the 6th Artillery.

Elisha G. Marshall Led a Brigade in the Crater Battle.

Robert Nugent, Originally Colonel of the 69th Regiment.

John C. Robinson Commanded a Division at Gettysburg.

James R. O'Beirne, Promoted from Major for Gallantry.

FEDERAL GENERALS

No. 16

NEW YORK (CONTINUED)

Rush C. Hawkins, Colonel of "Hawkins' Zouaves," 9th Infantry.

R. B. Potter, Commander of a Division at Crater Battle.

operating around Charleston Harbor. On July 15th, the Departments of Virginia and North Carolina were united, and on August 1st, the Seventh Corps, including Getty's division of the Ninth, was merged in the Eighteenth. The other commanders of the corps were Brigadier-General I. N. Palmer, Major-Generals B. F. Butler, W. F. Smith, Brigadier-General J. H. Martindale, Major-Generals E. O. C. Ord, John Gibbon, Brigadier-General C. A. Heckman, and Brevet Major-General Godfrey Weitzel. In April, 1864, this corps, with the Tenth, formed the Army of the James. It fought a series of battles after reaching Bermuda Hundred—especially that at Drewry's Bluff. Later in May, the corps joined the Army of the Potomac at Cold Harbor, in which battle it was very prominent. Then it returned to Bermuda Hundred and was very active in numerous engagements around Petersburg until December 3, 1864, when it was discontinued. The white troops were merged in the Twenty-fourth and the colored ones in the Twenty-fifth Corps.

MAJOR-GENERAL JOHN GRAY FOSTER (U.S. M.A. 1846) was born in Whitefield, New Hampshire, May 27, 1823. He rendered able service in the Mexican War, taught engineering at West Point, superintended Government works, and was one of the officers garrisoned at Fort Sumter during the siege. He distinguished himself at the capture of Roanoke Island and at New Berne; assumed chief command of the Department of North Carolina, the Department of Virginia and North Carolina, the Department and Army of the Ohio, and the Department of the South. He became major-general of volunteers in July, 1862. Being mustered out of the volunteer service in 1866, he, with the rank of lieutenant-colonel of engineers, continued his work on important engineering projects of the Government. He died in Nashua, New Hampshire, September 2, 1874.

BREVET MAJOR-GENERAL JOHN HENRY MARTINDALE (U.S.M.A. 1835) was born at Sandy Hill, New York, March 20, 1815. He resigned from the army the year after leaving West Point, but, offering his services at the outbreak of the Civil War, he was made brigadier-general of volunteers in August, 1861. He was brigade commander in several corps of the Army of the Potomac, and in February, 1863, took charge of the troops in the District of Washington—a portion of the Twenty-second Army Corps. In May, 1864, he was assigned to a division in the Eighteenth Army Corps, and for a short period in July, during the early operations against Petersburg, he had command of the corps itself. On September 13th, he resigned from the service. The brevet of major-general of volunteers was conferred upon him on March 13, 1865, in recognition of his services at the battle of Malvern Hill (1862). He became attorney-general of the State of New York, and died at Nice, France, December 13, 1881.

MAJOR-GENERAL WILLIAM FARRAR SMITH (U. S.M.A. 1845) was born in St. Albans, Vermont, February 17, 1824, and taught mathematics at West Point. In the early days of the Civil War he served on the staffs of Major-Generals Butler and McDowell. His commission as major-general of volunteers was dated July 4, 1862, to which rank he was recommissioned March 9, 1864. After leading a brigade and division in the early organization of the Army of the Potomac, he had divisions in the Fourth and Sixth corps, and commanded the latter in the battle of Fredericksburg. After heading the Ninth Corps for a short time, he went to the Department of the Susquehanna and later—in 1863—became chief engineer of the Army of the Cumberland, where he rendered valuable assistance in the relief of Chattanooga. In May, 1864, he took command of the Eighteenth Corps in the Army of the James and led it at the battle of Cold Harbor, where it had joined the Army of the Potomac. He resigned from the volunteer service in 1865, and from the regular army in 1867, with the brevet of major-general. He became president of the International Telegraph Company, and was president of the board of Police Commissioners in New York City, 1877. After that, he practised civil engineering. He died in Philadelphia, February 28, 1903.

BRIGADIER-GENERAL CHARLES ADAMS HECKMAN was born in Easton, Pennsylvania, December 3, 1822. He served in the Mexican War, and went to the Civil War as lieutenant-colonel of the Ninth New Jersey Infantry. He became a colonel and had a brigade in the Department of North Carolina, where, after being made brigadier-general of volunteers, he had a division in the Eighteenth Army Corps. Later, he had charge of the District of Beaufort and the defenses of New Berne and at Newport News. On May 16, 1864, at the head of a brigade he was captured at Drewry's Bluff. He had temporary command of the Eighteenth Corps in September, 1864, and was temporary commander of the Twenty-fifth Army Corps, January-February, 1865. He resigned from the service in May, 1865, and died in Philadelphia, January 14, 1896.

Nelson Taylor, Originally Colonel
of the 72d Regiment.

John H. H. Ward, Originally Colonel
of the 38th Regiment.

Daniel Ullmann, Originally Colonel
of the 78th Regiment.

FEDERAL

GENERALS

No. 17

NEW YORK

(CONTINUED)

Adolph Von Steinwehr, Originally
Colonel of the 29th Infantry.

Emory Upton Led a Storming Column
at Spotsylvania.

Egbert L. Viele, Engaged at Fort
Pulaski and Norfolk.

Alexander Shaler Commanded a Brigade at Spotsylvania.

Nineteenth Army Corps

On January 5, 1863, the troops in the Department of the Gulf were constituted the Nineteenth Army Corps, with Major-General N. P. Banks in command. Its other leaders were Major-General W. B. Franklin, Brigadier-Generals W. H. Emory, B. S. Roberts, M. K. Lawler, and Major-General J. J. Reynolds. It operated in Louisiana, took part in the investment of Port Hudson, and did garrison duty until it went on the Red River expedition in March, 1864, where it was prominent at Sabine Cross Roads and in other engagements. In July, the First and Second divisions, under Emory, went to Virginia, and entered the Army of the Shenandoah and fought at the Opequon, Fisher's Hill, and Cedar Creek. This "detachment," as it was called until November 7th, was commanded by Brigadier-Generals W. H. Emory and Cuvier Grover, and after the campaign in the Shenandoah, it went, in different sections, to Savannah. Some of the troops were afterward attached to the Tenth Corps; others remained in Savannah until the corps was discontinued on March 20, 1865, and even longer. On November 7, 1864, the portion of the corps that had remained in Louisiana was discontinued, and the designation, Nineteenth Army Corps, passed to the divisions operating in the Shenandoah valley. Most of the troops in Louisiana were put in the Gulf Reserve Corps, which, in February, 1865, became the new Thirteenth Corps, and assisted at the capture of Mobile.

Major-General William Hemsley Emory (U.S.M.A. 1831) was born in Queen Anne's County, Maryland, September 9, 1811. He served in the Mexican War, and later was appointed astronomer to the commission which determined the boundary between Mexico and the United States. As colonel, he entered the Civil War in the cavalry of the Army of the Potomac, and, as brigadier-general of volunteers, had a brigade in the Fourth Army Corps after the Peninsula campaign. In 1863, he was sent to the Department of the Gulf, where, for a time, he was in charge of the defenses of New Orleans, and in May, 1864, he assumed command of the Nineteenth Army Corps. In July, with two divisions, he went to Washington and the Shenandoah valley to assist in the campaign against Early. He received the rank of major-general of volunteers in September, 1865, and commanded several departments after the war, being retired in 1876, as brigadier-general. He died in Washington, December 1, 1887.

Twentieth Army Corps

The right wing of the Army of the Cumberland was made the Twentieth Army Corps on January 9, 1863, under Brigadier-General A. McD. McCook, who held it until October 9, 1863, when it was merged in the Fourth Corps, which had been created on September 28th. It was prominent in the engagement at Liberty Gap, Tennessee, June 25th, during the advance of the army to Tullahoma, and eight of its brigades were in the battle of Chickamauga.

Major-General Alexander McDowell McCook (U.S.M.A. 1863) was born in Columbiana County, Ohio, April 22, 1831, and was the son of Major Daniel McCook, whose eight other sons also served in the Civil War. He did garrison duty in the West and was an instructor at West Point. He was colonel of the First Ohio at Bull Run, and then, as brigadier-general of volunteers, went to the Department of the Ohio, where he had a command, and, later, a division at Shiloh and elsewhere, until he headed the First Corps, Army of the Ohio, in the Kentucky campaign against Bragg. He had been made major-general of volunteers in July. He had command of the right wing (Army of the Cumberland), which bore the brunt of the attack at Stone's River. In the new organization of the army, he commanded the Twentieth Corps until after the battle of Chickamauga. Later, he had command of the northern defenses of Washington, and the District of Eastern Kansas. Retiring from the volunteer service, he resumed his rank of lieutenant-colonel in the regular army, serving with the Twenty-sixth and other infantry regiments. He was aide-de-camp to General Sherman from 1875 to 1880. In 1890 he was made brigadier-general, and became major-general, in 1894. He held several public positions of honor, and was retired in 1895. General McCook served on a commission to investigate the administration of the War Department during the Spanish war. He died in Dayton, Ohio, June 12, 1903.

John H. Ketcham, Promoted for
Gallantry During the War.

George W. Von Schaack Led the
Seventh New York in the Charge
against the Stonewall at
Fredericksburg.

Max Weber, in Command at Harper's
Ferry in 1864.

Charles G. Halpine
(Miles O'Reilly),
Poet and Author;
Assistant Adju-
tant-General.

Charles H. Morgan,
Promoted to Reg-
ular Rank for
Gallantry in
the Field.

Patrick H. Jones, Originally Colonel
of the 154th Regiment.

Charles H. Van Wyck, Originally
Colonel of the 56th Regiment.

Hiram C. Rogers, Chief of Staff to
General H. W. Slocum.

FEDERAL GENERALS
No. 18

NEW YORK
(Continued)

Guy V. Henry, Originally Colonel
of the 40th Regiment.

Twentieth Army Corps

A CORPS with the designation of Twentieth was created on April 4, 1864, from the troops of the Eleventh and Twelfth corps which, under Hooker, had joined the Army of the Cumberland in October, 1863. One division never joined the main body and finally engaged in Thomas' campaign against Hood in Tennessee, but the remainder followed the fortunes of the Atlanta campaign, and one of its brigades was the first to enter that city. On the march to the sea and the campaign through the Carolinas, the Twentieth Corps was part of Slocum's Army of Georgia. The corps commanders were Major-Generals Joseph Hooker, Henry W. Slocum, Joseph A. Mower, and Brigadier-General Alpheus S. Williams. The corps was discontinued on June 1, 1865.

Twenty-first Army Corps

THE LEFT WING of the Army of the Cumberland was made the Twenty-first Army Corps on January 9, 1863, and the command was given to Major-General T. L. Crittenden. Its other commanders were Brigadier-Generals T. J. Wood and Major-General J. M. Palmer. On October 9th, it was consolidated with the original Twentieth Corps and merged in the new Fourth Corps. The only battle the Twenty-first Corps participated in as an organization was Chickamauga, where one division fought with Thomas throughout the entire battle.

MAJOR-GENERAL THOMAS LEONIDAS CRITTENDEN was born in Russellville, Kentucky, May 15, 1815, and became a lawyer. He served in the Mexican War and later was United States consul at Liverpool, until 1853. In September, 1861, he was given a division in the Army of the Ohio under Buell, and was made major-general of volunteers for his conduct at Shiloh. In the campaign against Bragg, in Kentucky, he commanded the Second Corps, Army of the Ohio; the Left Wing, Army of the Cumberland, at Stone's River and the Twenty-first Army Corps at Chickamauga. For a short period, May–June, 1864, he led a division in the Ninth Corps. He resigned from the volunteer service in December, 1864, and after the war reentered the regular army as colonel. He received the brevet of brigadier-general in 1867, was retired in 1881, and died on Staten Island, New York, October 23, 1893.

Twenty-second Army Corps

CREATED February 2, 1863, and consisted of the troops occuping the defenses of Washington. It was first headed by Major-General S. P. Heintzelman, and he was succeeded by Major-Generals C. C. Augur and J. G. Parke. This corps saw active service only when it held the outer line of works during Lieutenant-General Early's attack on Washington, July 12, 1864. The roster of this corps was constantly changing as the troops were sent to reenforce other corps, so that it had no strong organization.

MAJOR-GENERAL CHRISTOPHER COLON AUGUR (U.S.M.A. 1843) was born in New York, July 10, 1821. He served in the Mexican War, and the campaign against the Oregon Indians. He entered the Civil War as major in the infantry, and was made brigadier of volunteers in November, 1861. He was severely wounded at Cedar Mountain, August 9, 1862, where he commanded a division in the Second Corps, Army of Virginia. He subsequently, as major-general of volunteers, had a division in the Nineteenth Corps, Army of the Gulf, from January to July, 1863, and in October was put in command of the Twenty-second Army Corps (Department of Washington) where he remained until the close of the war. He returned to the regular army in 1866, as colonel, and was made brigadier-general in 1869. He commanded several departments in the West and South and was retired in July, 1885. He died in Washington, D. C., January 16, 1898.

Samuel H. Hurst, Colonel of the 73d Regiment.

John W. Sprague, Originally Colonel of the 63d Regiment.

Charles F. Manderson, Originally Colonel of the 19th Infantry.

Eliakim P. Scammon, Colonel of the 23d Regiment.

Americus V. Rice, Originally Colonel of the 57th Regiment.

Thomas C. H. Smith, Promoted from the 1st Cavalry in 1862.

FEDERAL

GENERALS

No. 19—OHIO

Nathaniel C. McLean, Originally Colonel of the 7th Infantry.

E. B. Tyler, Originally Colonel of the 7th Infantry.

Twenty-third Army Corps

CREATED April 27, 1863, out of troops in the Department of the Ohio, then headed by Major-General A. E. Burnside. The regiments forming it had been stationed in Kentucky, and Major-General G. L. Hartsuff was placed in command. He was succeeded by Brigadier-Generals M. D. Manson, J. D. Cox, Major-Generals George Stoneman, and J. M. Schofield. The corps fought in Eastern Tennessee and was besieged in Knoxville. As the Army of the Ohio, it went on the Atlanta campaign and after the capture of that city, it returned to Tennessee and was prominent at Franklin and Nashville. The corps was then (except two divisions) moved to North Carolina and captured Wilmington in February, 1865. It joined Sherman's army at Goldsboro and marched with it to Washington. The corps was discontinued, August 1, 1865.

MAJOR-GENERAL GEORGE LUCAS HARTSUFF (U. S.M.A. 1852) was born in Tyre, New York, May 28, 1830, and served in Texas and Florida. He was at Fort Pickens from April to July, 1861, and then under Rosecrans. At Cedar Mountain, Manassas, and Antietam, he commanded a brigade, and in the last battle was severely wounded. In November, he was made major-general of volunteers, and after May, 1863, he was in command of the new Twenty-third Army Corps until September 24, 1863. Toward the end of the siege of Petersburg, he commanded the works at Bermuda Hundred. After leaving the volunteer service at the conclusion of the war he continued in the regular army, and was retired with the rank of major-general in June, 1871, on account of his wounds. He died in New York, May 16, 1874.

Twenty-fourth Army Corps

CREATED December 3, 1864, to consist of white troops of the Tenth and Eighteenth corps, Army of the James. Its first commander, Major-General E. O. C. Ord, headed it for only three days, and he was followed by Brevet Major-General A. H. Terry, Brigadier-General Charles Devens, Jr., Major-General John Gibbon, and Brevet Major-General John W. Turner. One division was sent to the operations against Fort Fisher, and its place was taken by one from the Eighth Army Corps. It was present at the final operations around Petersburg, and the pursuit of Lee. The corps was discontinued August 1, 1865.

MAJOR-GENERAL EDWARD OTHO CRESAP ORD (U.S.M.A. 1839) was born in Cumberland, Maryland, October 18, 1818. He served in the Seminole War and in various Indian expeditions in the far West. In 1859, he took part in the capture of

John Brown at Harper's Ferry. As brigadier-general of volunteers, he commanded a brigade in Buell's Division and the First Corps of the Army of the Potomac from October, 1861, to April, 1862, and had a division in the Department of the Rappahannock until June 10th. As major-general of volunteers, he commanded a division in the Army of West Tennessee. Then he assumed command of the Thirteenth Army Corps in the Armies of the Tennessee, and of the Gulf; of the Eighteenth Army Corps in the Department of Virginia and North Carolina, and of the Twenty-fourth Army Corps in the Army of the James, to the command of which army he succeeded Major-General B. F. Butler in January, 1865. He was wounded in the assault on Fort Harrison, but did not give up his command. Ord was retired with full rank of major-general in 1880, and died July 22, 1883, in Havana, Cuba.

Twenty-fifth Army Corps

CREATED December 3, 1864, to consist of the colored troops of the Tenth and Eighteenth corps, Army of the James. Its commanders were Major-General Godfrey Weitzel and Brigadier-General C.

A. Heckman. One division went with Terry to Fort Fisher; the others remained in Virginia, taking part in the final operations around Petersburg, and then formed the army of occupation in Texas.

James S. Robinson, Originally
Colonel of the 82d Regiment.

John G. Mitchell, Originally Colonel
of the 113th Regiment.

George W. Morgan, Commander of a
Division at Chickasaw Bluffs.

James W. Forsyth, Origi-
nally Colonel of the
18th U. S. Infantry.

FEDERAL GENERALS—

No. 20

OHIO

Ralph P. Buckland, Origi-
nally Colonel of the 72d
Regiment.

Benjamin Potts, Originally
Colonel of the 32d
Regiment.

Charles G. Gilbert, Corps
Commander at Perry-
ville under Gen. Buell.

Jacob Ammen, Originally
Colonel of the 24th Ohio;
Led a Brigade at Shiloh.

Thomas Smith, Originally
Colonel of the 54th
Regiment.

Its last regiments were mustered out on January 8, 1866. In February, 1865, it numbered about fourteen thousand troops.

MAJOR-GENERAL GODFREY WEITZEL (U.S.M. A. 1855) was born in Cincinnati, Ohio, November 1, 1835, and entered the Engineer Corps. At the opening of the Civil War, as first lieutenant, he served at the defense of Fort Pickens and was chief engineer of Butler's expedition to New Orleans, the capture of which city he planned and the acting mayor of which he became. As brigadier-general of volunteers, he had a brigade in the Department of the Gulf, and a brigade and division in the Nineteenth Army Corps at the siege of Port Hudson, where he commanded the right wing of Major-General Banks' forces. In May, 1864, he was given a division in the Eighteenth Army Corps, and later was chief engineer of the Army of the James, and constructed the fortifications at Bermuda Hundred and Deep Bottom. He was in command of the Eighteenth Army Corps from October to December, 1864, having been made major-general of volunteers. On the formation of the Twenty-fifth Army Corps (December, 1864) he was placed at its head and remained so, except for one short interval, until it was discontinued in January, 1866. He occupied Richmond, in April, 1865. After commanding a district in Texas, he was mustered out of the service, and returned to engineering work in the army. He became lieutenant-colonel of engineers in 1882. He had been brevetted major-general in the regular army in 1865. He died in Philadelphia, March 19, 1884.

First Corps—Army of the Ohio

THE ARMY OF THE OHIO was organized into three corps on September 29, 1862. The First was commanded by Major-General A. McDowell McCook. It bore the chief part in the battle of Perryville, Kentucky (October 8, 1862), and the campaign against Bragg in Kentucky. On October 24th, it was merged in the Fourteenth Corps, known as the Army of the Cumberland.

Second Corps—Army of the Ohio

THIS CORPS fought at Bardstown in the campaign against Bragg. It was headed by Major-General T. L. Crittenden. It constituted the right wing of the army, and was accompanied by Major-General George H. Thomas, who was second in command in the Army of the Ohio. Like the First Corps it had a brief existence, and it was merged in the Fourteenth Corps, October 24, 1862.

Third Corps—Army of the Ohio

THIS CORPS was commanded by Major-General C. C. Gilbert. It took part in the Kentucky campaign, but was only slightly engaged in Perryville. Its three divisions were commanded by Brigadier-Generals Schoepff, Mitchell, and Sheridan and Colonel Kennett. It was merged in the Fourteenth Corps, October 24, 1862.

Cavalry Corps—Military Division of the Mississippi

THE FIRST CAVALRY CORPS in the West was organized in October, 1864, with Brevet Major-General J. H. Wilson at its head. There were seven divisions, of which four took part in the battle of Nashville, December 15th and 16th. Wilson entered Alabama in March, 1865, and the corps fought its last engagement with Forrest at Columbus, Georgia, on April 16th. One division of this corps, under Brigadier-General Judson Kilpatrick, consisting of four brigades, accompanied Sherman's army through Georgia and the Carolinas, and was present at Bentonville and Johnston's surrender.

Emerson Opdycke, Brevetted for
Gallantry at the Battle of Franklin.

Henry Van Ness Boynton, Decorated for Gallantry in Action.

Joseph Warren Keifer, Originally
Colonel of the 110th Regiment.

FEDERAL GENERALS

No. 21

OHIO (CONTINUED)

John Beatty, Originally Colonel
of the 3d Regiment of Infantry.

Joel A. Dewey, Originally Colonel
of the 111th U. S. Colored Troops.

Hugh Ewing, Brevetted for Gallantry in 1865.

George P. Este, Originally Colonel
of the 14th Infantry.

Catherinus P. Buckingham, Appointed in 1862.

Cavalry Forces—Department of the Cumberland

THE CAVALRY was a separate command in the Army of the Cumberland after the reorganization of January 9, 1863. It was headed in turn by Major-General D. S. Stanley and Brigadier-Generals R. B. Mitchell, W. L. Elliott, and R. W. Johnson. In October, 1864, this force was included in the newly formed Cavalry Corps of the Military Division of the Mississippi.

Reserve Corps—Army of the Cumberland

ORGANIZED June 8, 1863, and discontinued October 9th, when the troops were merged in the reorganized Fourth and Fourteenth corps. Major-General Gordon Granger was its commander. It served through the Tullahoma campaign, and went to the assistance of Thomas at Chickamauga.

Reserve Corps—Army of the Gulf

THE TROOPS of the Nineteenth Corps that were not sent to Washington and the Shenandoah valley were organized into the Reserve Corps of the Army of the Gulf, on December 5, 1864. It was commanded by Major-Generals J. J. Reynolds and Gordon Granger, and was merged in the reorganized Thirteenth Army Corps, February 18, 1865.

South Carolina Expeditional Corps

ORGANIZED under the command of Brigadier-General T. W. Sherman in September and October, 1861. It consisted of three brigades. This was the force that assisted the navy at the capture of Port Royal, occupying the abandoned works and garrisoning the base thus secured. It formed the nucleus of the Department of the South and the Tenth Army Corps.

BRIGADIER-GENERAL THOMAS WEST SHERMAN (U.S.M.A. 1836) was born at Newport, Rhode Island, March 26, 1813. He served in the Seminole War and as captain in the War with Mexico. At the opening of the Civil War, he was lieutenant in the artillery, and was promoted to brigadier-general of volunteers, May 17, 1861. He was placed at the head of the South Carolina Expeditional Corps and commanded the land forces in the operations around Port Royal. After that, he commanded a division in Grant's Army of West Tennessee. In September, 1862, he was put at the head of the Federal troops at Carrollton, Louisiana, in the Department of the Gulf, and in January, 1863, took charge of the defenses of New Orleans. He went with Banks to Port Hudson, in May, 1863, as division commander in the Nineteenth Army Corps. After that, he was again stationed at New Orleans with the reserve artillery and at the defenses of the city. After leaving the volunteer service at the close of the war, he was colonel of the Third Artillery, at Fort Adams, Rhode Island. On December 31, 1870, he was retired with full rank, of major-general. He died in Newport, March 16, 1879.

First Corps—Army of Virginia

CREATED June 26, 1862, from troops in the Mountain Department under Major-General Fremont, who, refusing to serve under Major-General Pope, was replaced by Major-General Franz Sigel. Brigadier-General R. C. Schenck headed the corps for short periods. After the close of Pope's Virginia campaign, it was merged in the Eleventh Corps, Army of the Potomac, September 12, 1862.

Franklin Sawyer, Orig-
inally Colonel of the
8th Regiment.

Anson G. McCook,
Colonel of the 194th
Regiment.

Henry M. Cist, Pro-
moted for Gallantry
at Stone's River.

Charles H. Grosve-
nor, Colonel of the
18th Veteran.

Timothy Stanley, Orig-
inally Colonel of the
18th Regiment.

Anson Stager, Conspicuous in the
Telegraph Corps.

Henry C. Corbin, Colonel of Colored
Infantry; Later Lieutenant-General of the United States Army.

William S. Smith, Originally Colonel
of the 13th Regiment.

FEDERAL

GENERALS

—No. 22—

OHIO

William B. Woods, Originally Colonel of
the 76th Regiment.

Robert K. Scott, Originally Colonel of
the 68th Regiment.

Second Corps—Army of Virginia

CREATED June 26, 1862, from the troops in the Department of the Shenandoah. It was commanded by Major-General N. P. Banks, and later by Brigadier-General A. S. Williams. It defeated Jackson at Cedar Mountain and fought in the other battles of the campaign. When the Army of Virginia was discontinued it was merged in the Twelfth Corps, Army of the Potomac.

Third Corps—Army of Virginia

CREATED June 26, 1862, from the troops in the Department of the Rappahannock, previously the First Corps of the Army of the Potomac. It was commanded by Major-General Irvin McDowell and later by Brigadier-General J. B. Ricketts and Major-General Joseph Hooker. On the discontinuation of the Army of Virginia, it became again the First Corps of the Army of the Potomac.

Cavalry Corps—Army of the Potomac

A CAVALRY DIVISION under Brigadier-General A. Pleasonton was organized in July, 1862, and was with the Army of the Potomac, until February, 1863, when the Cavalry Corps was created with Major-General George Stoneman at its head. Its other commanders were Brigadier-Generals A. Pleasonton, D. McM. Gregg, Major-General P. H. Sheridan, Brigadier-General A. T. A. Torbert, Brevet Brigadier-General William Wells, Major-Generals Wesley Merritt and George Crook. Two divisions were transferred to the Army of the Shenandoah in August, 1864, and remained with it until til March, 1865. At first, the corps numbered over eleven thousand men. It saw constant active service; its most important battle being the one at Beverly Ford, Virginia, on June 9, 1863. Its hardest fighting took place in the Wilderness campaign of 1864. The corps was broken up in May, 1865.

MAJOR-GENERAL PHILIP HENRY SHERIDAN (U.S.M.A. 1853) was born in Albany, New York, March 6, 1831. After service in the West he became captain in May, 1861. He was on the staff of Halleck at Corinth, and in May, 1862, was made colonel of the Second Michigan Cavalry. Defeating Forrest's and repulsing Chalmer's superior force at Booneville, he was made brigadier-general of volunteers. In August, he defeated Falkner in Mississippi, and in September commanded a division in the Army of the Ohio, at Perryville and another in the Army of the Cumberland at Stone's River, for which service he was made major-general of volunteers and fought with great ability at Chickamauga and Missionary Ridge. In April, 1864, he was transferred to the command of the Cavalry Corps, Army of the Potomac, and in August he was put at the head of the Army of the Shenandoah and defeated Early at Cedar Creek. In December, 1864, he was made major-general in the regular army, lieutenant-general in March, 1869, and general June 1, 1888. He died in Nonquit, Massachusetts, August 5, 1888.

BREVET MAJOR-GENERAL ALFRED THOMAS ARCHIMEDES TORBERT (U.S.M.A. 1855) was born in Georgetown, Delaware, July 1, 1833. He entered the Civil War as colonel of the First New Jersey Volunteers, and commanded a brigade in the Sixth Army Corps. He had command of a division in the Sixth Corps, March–April, 1864, after which he had a division in the Cavalry Corps, and was given command of the Corps on August 6, 1864. He resigned in 1866, with the brevet of major-general of volunteers and served as United States consul-general at Havana in 1871. September 30, 1880, he was drowned in the wreck of the ill-fated steamer *Vera Cruz* off the Florida coast.

MAJOR-GENERAL WESLEY MERRITT (U.S.M.A. 1860) was born in New York, June 16, 1836. In 1861, he was at first, second and then first lieutenant of cavalry. He served throughout the Civil War, for the most part in the cavalry of the Army of the Potomac, where he rose to the command of the Cavalry Corps in the Shenandoah on January 26, 1865, and in the Army of the Potomac from March 25–May 22, 1865. After the war he served in various Indian campaigns, was superintendent of the United States Military Academy at West Point, and in May, 1898, was given command of the United States forces to be sent to the Philippines. He was first American military governor of those islands. He retired from the army in 1900 and died December 3, 1910.

VII

CONFEDERATE
ARMIES
AND
GENERALS

CONFEDERATES OF '61—AT THE BIRTH OF THE SOUTHERN ARMY, WHEN "GUARDS," "GRAYS," AND "RIFLES" ABOUNDED—THESE ARE THE "PELICAN RIFLES" OF BATON ROUGE, LOUISIANA, LATER MERGED INTO THE SEVENTH LOUISIANA VOLUNTEERS WHICH SUFFERED THE HEAVIEST LOSS OF ANY CONFEDERATE REGIMENT ENGAGED IN THE FIGHT AT PORT REPUBLIC, JUNE 9, 1862

The Armies of the Confederate States

THE permanent Constitution of the Confederate States of America provided that the President should be commander-in-chief of the army and navy, and of the militia of the several States when called into actual service. Accordingly, in any consideration of the Confederate army, the part played by President Davis must be borne in mind; also the fact that he previously had seen service in the United States army and that he had been Secretary of War of the United States. As Secretaries of War in the Confederate States Government there were associated with President Davis, the following: LeRoy Pope Walker, of Alabama, February 21, 1861, to September 17, 1861; Judah P. Benjamin, of Louisiana, September 17, 1861, to March 17, 1862; George W. Randolph, of Virginia, March 17, 1862, to November 17, 1862; Major-General Gustavus W. Smith, of Kentucky, November 17, 1862, to November 21, 1862; James A. Seddon, of Virginia, from November 21, 1862, to February 6, 1865; and Major-General John C. Breckinridge, of Kentucky, February 6, 1865, to the close of the war.

Unlike the Union army there were generals, both regular and of the provisional army, as well as lieutenant-generals; it being the intention that every commander of an army should rank as general, and every commander of a corps should rank as lieutenant-general. Such was the case with the generals mentioned in the biographical matter following in connection with the various armies and other organizations. An exception to this statement was General Samuel Cooper, who served at Richmond as adjutant and inspector-general.

GENERAL SAMUEL COOPER (U.S.M.A. 1815) was born in Hackensack, New Jersey, June 12, 1798, and served in the army, receiving the brevet of colonel for his services in the Mexican War. He resigned in March, 1861, to enter the service of the Confederacy. He was appointed general on May 16th, but, owing to his age, took no active part in the field. He was adjutant and inspector-general of the Confederate States army throughout the entire war, performing his duties with great thoroughness and ability. He died at Cameron, Virginia, December 3, 1876.

Army of the Shenandoah

MAJOR-GENERAL KENTON HARPER, of the Virginia State forces, had collected about two thousand Virginia volunteers at Harper's Ferry as early as April 21, 1861. He was relieved on the 28th by Colonel Thomas J. Jackson, and the mustering in of volunteers went rapidly on. On May 24th, Brigadier-General Joseph E. Johnston assumed command of the troops, and on June 30th, there were 10,654 present for duty, in four brigades and cavalry. This was the force that opposed Major-General Patterson in the Valley, and it was known as the Army of the Shenandoah. It took part in the engagement at Falling Waters, July 2d, and the skirmishes near Bunker Hill and Charlestown. Strengthened with eight Southern regiments, this army started for Manassas, on July 18th, and took part in the first battle of Bull Run. After this, it formed a part of the Confederate Army of the Potomac.

GENERAL JOSEPH EGGLESTON JOHNSTON (U.S. M.A. 1829) was born in Cherry Grove, near Farmville, Virginia, February 3, 1807. He served in the Black Hawk, Seminole, and Mexican wars, in the last of which he was twice severely wounded. He resigned his rank of brigadier-general to enter the Confederate service on April 20, 1861, and was given the rank of general in August. He was in command at Harper's Ferry after May 24th, and headed the Army of the Shenandoah. He brought his troops to Manassas and superseded Beauregard in the command, at Bull Run, joining his force to the Army of the Potomac. In command of the Army of Northern Virginia, he was severely wounded at Fair Oaks. In November, 1862, he was assigned to the head of the Department of Tennessee, but outside of an attempt to relieve Pemberton at Vicksburg in May, 1863, he saw no active service until he assumed command of the Army of Tennessee in December, 1863. He opposed Sherman during the Atlanta campaign of 1864, being superseded by General Hood on July 18th. His strategy was much criticised at the time, but it is now recognized that he displayed great ability during the campaign. In February, 1865, he was again given command of the Army of Tennessee,

CONFEDERATE
GENERALS
FULL RANK
BEAUREGARD
AND
JOHNSTON

Pierre Gustave Tou-
tant Beauregard re-
ceived the Surrender
of the First Federal
Citadel — Fort Sum-
ter; Fought in De-
fense of the Last Con-
federate Citadel—the
City of Petersburg.

All the officers who
held the rank of Gen-
eral in the Confed-
erate States Army are
shown here, except-
ing Robert E. Lee,
whose portrait has
already appeared in
this volume, and
Albert Sidney John-
ston, whose portrait
appears among those
killed in battle.

Joseph Eggleston
Johnston commanded
the First and the Last
Great Aggressive
Movements of Con-
federate Armies—Bull
Run and Bentonville.

and attempted to prevent Sherman's advance through the Carolinas. Johnston's capitulation was agreed upon near Durham's Station, North Carolina, April 26, 1865. He was United States commissioner of railroads from 1885 to 1889. He died in Washington, March 21, 1891.

Army of the Peninsula

THE DEPARTMENT OF THE PENINSULA was established on May 26, 1861, and Colonel John B. Magruder was put in command. The troops therein were organized into divisions in November, and denominated the Army of the Peninsula. In December, the aggregate present was about sixteen thousand. On April 12, 1862, it was merged in the Army of Northern Virginia—constituting, under Major-General Magruder, the right wing of that army.

MAJOR-GENERAL JOHN BANKHEAD MAGRUDER (U.S.M.A. 1830) was born at Winchester, Virginia, August 15, 1810, and served in the Seminole and Mexican wars. He was stationed in Washington in 1861, and resigned in April to enter the Confederate service as colonel. He had charge of the artillery in and around Richmond, and after May 21st, a division in the Department of the Peninsula, the troops of which were later designated the Army of the Peninsula. On June 10th, his division repelled the attack of Major-General B. F. Butler at Big Bethel, for which feat he was made brigadier-general. In October, he was promoted to major-general. Having fortified the Peninsula, he kept McClellan's army in check in April, 1862. On April 18th, his forces became the Right Wing of the Army of Northern Virginia, and he commanded it during the Peninsula campaign. Magruder was then appointed to the Trans-Mississippi Department, in order to prosecute the war more vigorously in the West, but the assignment was changed, and in October, 1862, he was given the District of Texas, which was afterward enlarged to include New Mexico and Arizona. Magruder recaptured Galveston, January 1, 1863, and kept the port open. After the war he served in the army of Maximilian, and after the fall of the Mexican empire settled in Houston, Texas, where he died, February 19, 1871.

Army of the Northwest

THE TROOPS assigned to operate in northwestern Virginia were placed under the command of Brigadier-General R. S. Garnett on June 8, 1861, and were subsequently known as the Army of the Northwest. This was the force that opposed McClellan and Rosecrans in West Virginia, and was defeated at Rich Mountain and other places. On July 13th, Garnett was killed while retreating, and Brigadier-General Henry R. Jackson was put in command, to be superseded, within a week, by Brigadier-General W. W. Loring. Early in 1862, dissension arose between Loring and T. J. Jackson, commanding the Valley District (Department of Northern Virginia), which led to the latter preferring charges against the commander of the Army of the Northwest. As a result, the Secretary of War, on February 9, 1862, divided the army, sending some of the regiments to Knoxville, some to the Aquia District, and the remainder to the Army of the Potomac (Department of Northern Virginia). After this, the forces under Brigadier-General Edward Johnson stationed at Camp Alleghany, and sometimes called the Army of the Alleghany, continued to be called the Army of the Northwest. Its aggregate strength in March, 1862, was about four thousand. It finally came under Jackson in the Valley District and passed into the Army of Northern Virginia.

BRIGADIER-GENERAL ROBERT SELDEN GARNETT (U.S.M.A. 1841) was born in Essex County, Virginia, December 16, 1819, and served in the Mexican War as aide to General Taylor. At the outbreak of the Civil War he entered the Confederate service, and in June, 1861, was appointed brigadier-general, with command of the Army of the Northwest. In the action at Carrick's Ford he was killed, June 13, 1861.

BRIGADIER-GENERAL HENRY ROOTES JACKSON was born in Athens, Georgia, June 24, 1820, and became a lawyer. He served in the Mexican War as colonel of the First Georgia Volunteers, and was *chargé d'affaires* at Vienna, in 1863. As United States district attorney for Georgia he aided in trying slave-trading cases. At the outbreak of the

JOHN BELL HOOD
To Paraphrase a Classic Eulogy, "None Led with More Glory
than Hood, yet Many Led and There Was Much Glory."

EDMUND KIRBY SMITH
Skilful and Persistent Fighter Against Odds and Ever
Indomitable in the Face of Reverses in the Field.

BRAXTON BRAGG
Leader in Three of the Fiercest Battles of the War and
Carried the Southern Battle Line to Its Farthest North
in the West; A Record of Four Years in the Field.

SAMUEL COOPER
Ranking Officer of the Army. All Commanding Generals Re-
ported to Cooper and Received All Orders from Him. His
Post and Duties were those of a Modern Chief of Staff.

CONFEDERATE GENERALS—FULL RANK
HOOD, KIRBY SMITH, BRAGG AND COOPER

Civil War he entered the Confederate Army as a brigadier-general, succeeding to temporary command of the Army of the Northwest after Brigadier-General Garnett was killed. He resigned his commission because he could not obtain leave of absence to take charge of the Georgia coast defenses, to which post he was called by the Governor of Georgia, who made him a major-general in command of the State troops. After these became part of the Confederate army, in 1862, Jackson received no commission until July, 1864, when he was assigned a brigade in the Army of Tennessee. During the battle of Nashville he was made prisoner and not released until the close of the war, when he returned to Savannah to practise law. He was United States minister to Mexico in 1885, and died in Savannah, May 23, 1898.

MAJOR-GENERAL WILLIAM WING LORING was born in Wilmington, North Carolina, December 4, 1818, and served in the Seminole and Mexican wars. In the latter he lost an arm. Later, he was colonel of a regiment sent against the Indians in New Mexico. He resigned from the army to enter the Confederate service, and came into command of the Army of the Northwest, July 20, 1861. He was made major-general in February, 1862. His chief active service was in Kentucky, and in Mississippi, before and during the Vicksburg campaign; in that same State under Polk, and as division commander in the Army of Mississippi in the Atlanta campaign, and in the Army of Tennessee at Franklin and Nashville, and under Johnston in the Carolinas. After the war he went to Egypt, where he served as general in command of a division in the army of the Khedive. He died in New York city, December 30, 1886.

MAJOR-GENERAL EDWARD JOHNSON (U.S.M. A. 1838) was born in Chesterfield County, Virginia, April 16, 1816, and served in the Mexican War. He entered the Confederate army and was made a brigadier-general, commanding the Northwest forces directly under Major-General T. J. Jackson, in May, 1862. The next year (February, 1863), he was made major-general. He had a division in the Second Corps, Army of Northern Virginia, and in September, 1864, was assigned to the division of the Second Corps, Army of Tennessee. He died in Richmond, Virginia, March 2, 1873.

Army of the Potomac

ON MAY 24, 1861, Brigadier-General M. L. Bonham was placed in command of the troops on the line of Alexandria. On the 31st, he was relieved by Brigadier-General P. G. T. Beauregard. The forces here gathered were denominated the Army of the Potomac (afterward First Corps, Army of the Potomac) and consisted of six brigades, some unattached troops, and artillery, by the date of the battle of Bull Run. The Army of the Shenandoah joined this force on July 20th, when Johnston superseded Beauregard. The Department of Northern Virginia was created October 22, 1861, with Johnston at its head. It included the District of the Potomac (Beauregard); Valley District (T. J. Jackson), and Aquia District (T. H. Holmes.) In February, 1862, some of the troops in the Army of the Northwest came under Johnston's control, giving his entire command a strength of over eighty-two thousand. Beauregard had been sent to Kentucky on January 29th, and the troops in the Potomac district were now divided into four divisions with several separate detachments. On March 14th, the Army of the Potomac was denominated the Army of Northern Virginia. The total force then amounted to about fifty-five thousand.

GENERAL PIERRE GUSTAVE TOUTANT BEAUREGARD (U.S.M.A. 1838) was born near New Orleans, May 28, 1818, and entered the Engineer Corps. He served with distinction in the Mexican War, and at the outbreak of the Civil War resigned his commission (February 20, 1861), to enter the Confederate army as a brigadier-general, being given command of the Confederate forces bombarding Fort Sumter. He took command of the Army of the Potomac on June 20th. After Bull Run he was made general. He was given the command of the Army of the Mississippi in March, 1862, and was second in command after A. S. Johnston joined his forces with it. After the latter's death at Shiloh, Beauregard remained at the head of the army until after the withdrawal from Corinth at the end of May. In 1863, he defended Charleston, and after May, 1364, cooperated with Lee in the defense of Petersburg and Richmond. He commanded the Confederate forces in the Carolinas in 1865, merging them with those under General J. E. Johnston, and surrendered his army to Sherman. After the war, he was a railroad president, adjutant-general of Louisiana, and manager of the State lottery. He died in New Orleans, February 20, 1893.

RICHARD STODDERT EWELL
A Battle Record from July 21, 1861, to April 6, 1865.
Fought Nearly Three Years on a Wooden Leg.

JAMES LONGSTREET
None Knew Better than Longstreet's Opponents How and
Where He Earned the Sobriquet "Lee's Warhorse."

JUBAL ANDERSON EARLY
Modest in Victory, Undaunted by Defeat, He Defended the
Shenandoah Against Enormous Odds.

DANIEL HARVEY HILL
Had No Superior as the Marshal of a Division in
Assault or Defense.

LIEUTENANT–GENERALS OF THE CONFEDERACY—GROUP No. 1

On this and the two pages following appear portraits of all officers who held the rank of Lieutenant-
General in the Confederate States Army, with the exception of "Stonewall" Jackson and
A. P. Hill, whose portraits have appeared among the general officers killed in battle.

Army of Northern Virginia

GENERAL J. E. JOHNSTON was wounded at Seven Pines, May 31, 1862, and Major-General G. W. Smith took command of the Army of Northern Virginia. On June 1st, General Robert E. Lee assumed command. In April, the forces on the Peninsula had been included in this army, and now the troops in eastern Virginia and North Carolina were made part of it. By the end of July, 1862, the division organization had been further concentrated into three commands, or corps, headed by Major-Generals T. J. Jackson, James Longstreet, and D. H. Hill, with cavalry under Brigadier-General J. E. B. Stuart, and artillery under Brigadier-General W. N. Pendleton. There was an aggregate present of about ninety-five thousand. Subsequently, the army took a more permanent form in two corps commanded by Jackson and Longstreet, with cavalry corps and artillery separate. Lieutenant-General A. P. Hill was given the Second Corps after Jackson's death, and on

May 30, 1863, this was divided, with additions from the First Corps, into the Second and Third corps, commanded by Lieutenant-Generals R. S. Ewell and A. P. Hill respectively. The army numbered about seventy thousand in the Gettysburg campaign. This organization of the main body of the army continued throughout the war, although other generals, for various reasons, commanded the corps from time to time. A new corps of North Carolina and Virginia troops under Lieutenant-General R. H. Anderson was added at the end of 1864. Longstreet's corps, with the exception of Pickett's division, was with the Army of Tennessee, and in eastern Tennessee, for a short period in 1863 and 1864, at and after the battle of Chickamauga. The last report of the army, February, 1865, showed an aggregate present of over seventy-three thousand. The Army of Northern Virginia laid down its arms at Appomattox Court House, April 9, 1865.

First Corps—Army of Northern Virginia

THE ORGANIZATION of the volunteer Confederate forces under Brigadier-General Beauregard into the First Corps, Army of the Potomac, was announced on June 20, 1861. There were then six brigades, which number was increased later to eight. The strength of the corps was about thirty thousand. A division organization was afterward adopted, and one of these divisions, commanded by Major-General Longstreet, was denominated the Center of Position, Army of Northern Virginia, at the opening of the Peninsula campaign. It contained about fourteen thousand men. As the Second Division (or Corps) of the army, the troops fought from Fair Oaks, where they were known as the Right Wing, through the Seven Days' battles. Toward the end of July, the army was further concentrated into commands of which one, consisting of six divisions, was headed by Longstreet, and this, during the campaign against Pope, was called the Right Wing or Longstreet's Corps. After the battle of Antietam, the corps was designated the First Corps, Army of Northern Virginia. In September, 1863, Lee sent the corps, with the exception of Pickett's division, to assist Bragg, and, as Longstreet's Corps, fought in the Army of Tennessee at Chickamauga and remained in East Tennessee until April, 1864, when it rejoined the Army of Virginia. Major-

General R. H. Anderson succeeded to the command of the corps after Longstreet was wounded at the battle of the Wilderness, May 6th. The latter returned to his corps, October 19th, and continued at the head until the surrender at Appomattox.

LIEUTENANT-GENERAL JAMES LONGSTREET (U. S.M.A. 1842) was born in Edgefield District, South Carolina, January 8, 1821, and served in the Mexican War, where he was severely wounded. In June, 1861, he resigned as major in the army and was appointed brigadier-general in the Confederate service. As major-general, he had a division, and, later, as lieutenant-general, the First Corps of the Army of Northern Virginia. In September, 1863, he was sent with part of his corps to Tennessee and took command of the left wing at the battle of Chickamauga. He was then placed at the head of the Department of East Tennessee and returned to Virginia in April, 1864. He was severely wounded at the battle of the Wilderness, May 6, 1864, but resumed command of the corps in October. After the war, he engaged in business in New Orleans and held several political offices. In 1880-81 he was American minister to Turkey, and in 1898 he was appointed United States railway commissioner. He died at Gainesville, Georgia, January 2, 1904.

Wade Hampton Fought from Bull Run to Bentonville. With J. E. B. Stuart's Cavalry he "Stood in the Way" of Sheridan at Trevilian Station in 1864.

Richard Henry Anderson Commanded a Brigade on the Peninsula; Later He Commanded a Division and, after the Wilderness, Longstreet's Corps.

John Brown Gordon. This Intrepid Leader of Forlorn Hope Assaults Rose from a Civilian Captain to the Second Highest Rank in the Army.

Leonidas Polk, Bishop and Soldier Both, to the End; He Fell on the Battlefield of Pine Mountain in the Defense of Atlanta.

William Joseph Hardee, On the Front Line for Four Years; Last Commander of the Defense of Charleston and Savannah.

Stephen Dill Lee Fought in Five States; with Beauregard at Charleston, April, 1861, and with Hood at Nashville, December, 1864.

LIEUTENANT-GENERALS OF THE CONFEDERACY—GROUP No. 2

Second Corps—Army of Northern Virginia

On September 25, 1861, Major-General G. W. Smith was assigned to the command of the Second Corps, Army of the Potomac, which was organized to consist of all the troops not hitherto assigned to the First Corps. After October 22d, the force was known as the Second Division and contained five brigades. It numbered almost twenty thousand men, and passed into the Reserve, Second Division, and D. H. Hill's Division of the Army of Northern Virginia. Most of these troops finally came under the command of Lieutenant-General T. J. Jackson and became known as the Second Corps of the Army of Northern Virginia, after the battle of Antietam. After Jackson's death, Lieutenant-General R. S. Ewell succeeded to the corps, after it had been temporarily headed by Stuart and A. P. Hill. On May 30, 1863, two divisions were detached to enter the Third Army Corps. The corps was commanded by Lieutenant-General J. A. Early in the Shenandoah campaign of 1864, and in the closing months of the war around Petersburg, by Lieutenant-General John B. Gordon.

Major-General Gustavus Woodson Smith (U.S.M.A. 1842) was born in Georgetown, Kentucky, January 1, 1822, and served in the Mexican War. He resigned from the army in 1854 to enter upon a Cuban expedition under Quitman, and afterward settled in New York City. At the outbreak of the Civil War he joined the Confederate forces at New Orleans, under Lovell. In September, 1861, he was appointed major-general and was given command of the Second Corps, Army of the Potomac, which was continued in the Army of Northern Virginia, until March 23, 1862, when he was put at the head of the Reserves. After Johnston was wounded at Fair Oaks, May 31st, Major-General Smith, who was leading the left wing, took command of the whole army, but was stricken by illness the following day and was succeeded by General Lee. In August, he took charge of the defenses of Richmond and was acting Secretary of War in November. In February, 1863, he resigned from the service, and on June 1, 1864, took command of the Georgia Militia. He was captured by Major-General J. H. Wilson at Marion in April, 1865. He died in New York, June 24, 1896.

Lieutenant-General Richard Stoddert Ewell (U.S.M.A. 1840) was born in Georgetown, District of Columbia, February 8, 1817, and served with distinction in the Mexican War. He joined the Confederate army in 1861, and was made major-general the following year. He fought as bri-gade and division commander with the Army of Northern Virginia, and was given command of the Second Corps after the death of Lieutenant-General T. J. Jackson, being made lieutenant-general in May, 1863. He was prominent in all its battles, and at Groveton he lost a leg. After June, 1864, when his corps was sent to the Shenandoah valley under Lieutenant-General J. A. Early, he was in command of the defenses of Richmond until the evacuation of that city. He died at Spring Hill, Tennessee, January 25, 1872.

Lieutenant-General Jubal Anderson Early (U.S.M.A. 1837) was born in Franklin County, Virginia, November 3, 1816, and served in the Seminole War of 1837, after which he resigned to take up the practice of law. In the Mexican War, he served as major of Virginia volunteers, and at the outbreak of the Civil War he entered the Confederate army as colonel, rising to the rank of lieutenant-general in May, 1864. He commanded a brigade at Bull Run, was wounded at Williamsburg, and had a division at Antietam and afterward. He had temporary command of both the Second and Third corps, Army of Northern Virginia, during the Wilderness campaign, and in June, 1864, was sent with the Second Army Corps to the Shenandoah valley, whence he made his way to Washington and attacked the city on July 12th. His forces were finally routed at Cedar Creek, October 19th, by Sheridan. He was relieved of the command of the Trans-Alleghany Department in March, 1865, after a defeat by Custer. After the war he practised law. He refused to take the oath of allegiance to the United States, and died in Lynchburg, Virginia, March 2, 1894. He is recognized as one of the ablest of the Confederate generals.

Lieutenant-General John Brown Gordon was born in Upson County, Georgia, February 6, 1832. He became a lawyer, but entered the Confederate service as lieutenant-colonel of an Alabama regiment, and rose to the rank of lieutenant-general before the close of the war. He was brigade and division commander in the Army of Northern Virginia, and was prominent in the Second Army Corps during Early's campaign in the Shenandoah valley. He was at the head of the Second Corps after January 31, 1865, and was in command of the left wing at the time of Lee's surrender. After the war, he became prominent in Georgia politics and was United States senator from that State, 1873–1880, and in 1891–1897.

ALEXANDER PETER STEWART

A Leader in Every Great Campaign
from Shiloh to Bentonville.

NATHAN BEDFORD FORREST

The American Murat and the King
of Mounted Raiders.

JOSEPH WHEELER

Masterful as Well as Indefatigable
and Indomitable Leader of Cavalry.

LIEUTENANT–GENERALS OF THE CONFEDERACY—GROUP No. 3

SIMON BOLIVAR
BUCKNER

Defender of His Native Kentucky in 1861 and in 1865;
Led a Corps to Victory
at Chickamauga.

RICHARD
TAYLOR

Skillful Defender of the
Trans-Mississippi
Territory.

THEOPHILUS HUNTER
HOLMES

Defender of the James River
in 1862 and Arkansas
in 1863.

JOHN CLIFFORD
PEMBERTON

Baffled the Assailants of
Vicksburg Through Three
Campaigns, Yielding to
only Heavy Odds.

From 1887 to 1890, he was governor of Georgia. He was commander-in-chief of the United Confederate Veterans after 1900. He died at Miami, Florida, January 9, 1904.

Third Corps—Army of Northern Virginia

CREATED from three divisions of the First and Second corps, Army of Northern Virginia, on May 30, 1863, and put under the command of Lieutenant-General A. P. Hill. Its first battle was Gettysburg. Hill was killed in front of Petersburg, April 2, 1865, and the corps was united with the First until the surrender at Appomattox.

LIEUTENANT-GENERAL AMBROSE POWELL HILL (U.S.M.A. 1847) was born in Culpeper County, Virginia, November 9, 1825, and served in the Mexican and Seminole wars. In 1861, he resigned from the army to enter the Confederate volunteers. He was appointed brigadier-general February 26, 1862, major-general in the following May and was one of the most efficient officers in the Confederate army, and rose to the command of the Third Corps, Army of Northern Virginia, when it was created in May, 1863, being made lieutenant-general at the same time. He was killed April 2, 1865.

Anderson's Corps—Army of Northern Virginia

ORGANIZED late in 1864 to consist of the divisions of Major-Generals R. F. Hoke and Bushrod R. Johnson, and a battalion of artillery under Colonel H. P. Jones. It contained an aggregate strength of about fourteen thousand. Hoke's division served with the First Army Corps and was sent to Wilmington, North Carolina, on December, 20, 1864. Johnson's division remained with the Army of Northern Virginia until the surrender at Appomattox.

LIEUTENANT-GENERAL RICHARD HERRON ANDERSON (U.S.M.A. 1842) was born in South Carolina, October 27, 1821, and served with distinction in the Mexican War. He resigned from the army in March, 1861, to enter the Confederate service. As colonel, he commanded the First South Carolina Infantry in the attack on Fort Sumter, and became brigadier-general in July, 1861. He destroyed a Union camp near Pensacola, in October, and in February, 1862, was assigned to a brigade in Longstreet's Division in the Department of Northern Virginia. This he led with great distinction through the Peninsula campaign, being made major-general in July, 1862. He had a division in the First Corps, Army of Northern Virginia, at Second Bull Run and after. At Antietam, he was severely wounded, but he fought at Fredericksburg and Chancellorsville, and at Gettysburg he was in the Third Army Corps. After the wounding of Longstreet, in the battle of the Wilderness, Anderson was given command of the First Army Corps, receiving the appointment of lieutenant-general on June 1, 1864. In August, he was sent with an infantry division, one of cavalry, and a battalion of artillery to the assistance of Lieutenant-General Early in the Shenandoah, remaining there about a month. After the return of Longstreet to his corps, Anderson's Corps, consisting of two divisions, was organized, with Lieutenant-General Anderson at its head. He died at Beaufort, South Carolina, June 26, 1879.

Cavalry Corps—Army of Northern Virginia

THE VARIOUS TROOPS of cavalry in this army were finally gathered into a division of several brigades under the command of Brigadier-General J. E. B. Stuart. By the date of the battle of Gettysburg, July, 1863, the cavalry was organized in divisions and the organization was known as the Cavalry Corps. After the death of Major-General J. E. B. Stuart, May, 1864, Major-General (later Lieutenant-General) Wade Hampton took command. Major-General Fitzhugh Lee also

Gustavus Woodson Smith, Defender of Yorktown and Richmond.

John Bankhead Magruder, Defender of the Virginia Peninsula in 1861.

William Wing Loring, with Robert E. Lee in West Virginia in 1861.

Samuel Jones, Commander Florida, Georgia and South Carolina.

Sterling Price Fought on Both Sides of the Mississippi River.

Benjamin Franklin Cheatham, Brigade, Division and Corps Commander.

Dabney Herndon Maury, Defender of the Lower Mississippi in 1862-4.

John Cabel Breckinridge, Defender of the Mississippi in 1861.

CONFEDERATE MAJOR–GENERALS

Earl Van Dorn, a Daring and Resourceful Army Commander.

CONSPICUOUS AS COMMANDERS OF ARMIES OR ARMY CORPS

commanded several divisions at one time and was in command of the corps at Appomattox.

MAJOR-GENERAL JAMES EWELL BROWN STUART (U.S.M.A. 1854) was born in Patrick County, Virginia, February 6, 1833, and entered the Cavalry Corps of the United States army, serving in Kansas and against the Cheyenne Indians. He resigned his commission as captain in the army in May, 1861, to enter the Confederate service, as colonel of the First Virginia Cavalry, with which he fought under Johnston at Bull Run. He was made brigadier-general in September and major-general the following July. He had a brigade, and a division, and was placed at the head of the Cavalry Corps, Army of Northern Virginia, when it was organized, in the summer of 1863. Stuart proved himself to be a great cavalry leader, and his exploits won him much renown. Among his famous deeds were the ride around McClellan's army in June, 1862; the dash on Pope's headquarters at Catlett's Station, Virginia, and the raid on Manassas Junction in August; the expedition into Pennsylvania after Antietam, and the cooperation with Jackson at Chancellorsville. After the wounding of Jackson in that battle, he had temporary command of the Second Corps, Army of Northern Virginia. In the Wilderness campaign of 1864, he was very active, but was mortally wounded in an encounter with Sheridan's cavalry at Yellow Tavern. He died May 12, 1864.

LIEUTENANT-GENERAL WADE HAMPTON was born in Charleston, South Carolina, March 28, 1818. He was one of the largest slave-owners in the South. At the outbreak of the Civil War, he raised and equipped, in part, Hampton's South Carolina Legion, of which he was colonel. He was wounded at Fair Oaks, as brigadier-general at the head of a brigade, and thrice at Gettysburg, where he commanded a cavalry brigade. In August, 1863, he was made major-general with a division in the cavalry, and after the death of Stuart, he became head of the Cavalry Corps, Army of Northern Virginia. He made a famous raid on General Grant's commissariat, capturing some twenty-five hundred head of cattle. In February, 1865, he was made lieutenant-general, and commanded the cavalry in the Army of Tennessee, as well as a division of that of the Army of Northern Virginia. After the war, he strongly advocated the policy of conciliation. In 1876, he was governor of South Carolina; from 1878 to 1891, United States senator, and from 1893 to 1897, United States commissioner of railroads. He died in Columbia, South Carolina, April 11, 1902.

MAJOR-GENERAL FITZHUGH LEE (U.S.M.A. 1856) was born in Clermont, Virginia, November 19, 1835. He served against the Indians, and was cavalry instructor at West Point until he resigned his commission in May, 1861, to enter the Confederate service, becoming adjutant-general in Ewell's brigade. He was made major-general September 3, 1863. He had a brigade and division in the cavalry of the Army of Northern Virginia through all its campaigns, including that of Early in the Shenandoah in 1864, where he was wounded at the Opequon. He was in command of the Cavalry Corps, Army of Northern Virginia, from March, 1865, until the surrender, replacing Wade Hampton, who went to the Army of Tennessee. From 1886 to 1890 he was governor of Virginia, and, under appointment of President Cleveland, consul-general at Havana from 1896 to the outbreak of the Spanish-American War. President McKinley appointed him major-general of volunteers in 1898 and placed him at the head of the Seventh Army Corps. He was made military governor of Havana in 1899. Later, he commanded the Department of the Missouri. He received the rank of brigadier-general in February, 1901, and was retired the following month. He died in Washington, April 28, 1905.

Army of the Kanawha

THE CONFEDERATE FORCES assigned to operate in the Kanawha valley, West Virginia, were placed under the command of Brigadier-General John B. Floyd on August 11, 1861, and denominated the Army of the Kanawha. This force and one under Brigadier-General Henry A. Wise were its chief constituents. The troops took part in the engagement at Carnifex Ferry. The strength of the command was about thirty-five hundred. Some of the troops were sent with Floyd to the Central Army of Kentucky, early in 1862, and formed one of its divisions. Several of the regiments were captured at Fort Donelson when this post capitulated to General Grant.

James T. Holtzclaw Led a Brigade of Alabamians.

John H. Kelly, a Gallant Boy General.

Cullen A. Battle Led a Brigade in Virginia.

CONFEDERATE GENERALS
No. 1—ALABAMA

This is the first of 25 groups embracing representative general officers of 14 States. On preceding pages of this volume appear portraits of all generals and lieutenant-generals, all generals killed in battle, also commanders of armies and army corps. Many appear in preceding volumes of this History as identified with particular events or special branches of the service, as cavalry and artillery. Information concerning every general officer may be found through the roster and index concluding this volume.

Jonas M. Withers, Originally Colonel of the 3d Infantry.

Edmund W. Pettus Became a Noted United States Senator.

James H. Clanton Led a Cavalry Brigade in Mississippi.

Charles M. Shelley Led a Brigade with Stewart.

Philip D. Roddey, Conspicuous Cavalry Leader.

Henry De Lamar Clayton, Originally Colonel of Infantry.

Army of Eastern Kentucky

BRIGADIER-GENERAL JOHN BUCHANAN FLOYD was born at Blacksburg, Virginia, June 1, 1807, and became a lawyer, practising in Arkansas and Virginia. He entered politics, and served in the Virginia legislature, and as governor of the State in 1850. He was Secretary of War in the Buchanan cabinet, where owing to his administrative methods he was requested to resign in 1860. At the opening of the Civil War he entered the Confederate army and was appointed brigadier-general in May, 1861.

He headed the force known as the Army of the Kanawha, and in February, 1862, was in command of Fort Donelson, Tennessee. He and Brigadier-General Gideon J. Pillow fled therefrom the night before the capitulation, leaving Brigadier-General Simon Bolivar Buckner to conduct the negotiations and surrender to General Grant. For this General Floyd was relieved of his command. In November, 1862, he was in command of the Virginia State Line, and died at Abingdon, Virginia, August 26, 1863.

Army of Eastern Kentucky

A TITLE applied to the troops under Brigadier-General Humphrey Marshall, consisting of the militia of Wise, Scott and Lee counties, in 1861. It was a small force of about fifteen hundred men, and was scattered by Federal troops under Brigadier-General James A. Garfield. Its chief action was at Pound Gap, March 16, 1862.

BRIGADIER-GENERAL HUMPHREY MARSHALL (U.S.M.A. 1832) was born in Frankfort, Kentucky, January 13, 1812. He resigned from the army the year after his graduation and became a lawyer. He went to the Mexican War as colonel of

cavalry, and led a charge at Buena Vista. In 1849, he became a member of Congress, and, after being commissioner to China in 1852, served again until 1859. He entered the Confederate service, being made brigadier-general in October, 1861. At the head of a small force, sometimes called the Army of Eastern Kentucky, he undertook the conquest of that region, but was driven from it by Brigadier-General James A. Garfield in March, 1862. After this, he had several commands in Virginia and resigned from the service in June, 1863. He resumed his practice of law and was elected member of the Confederate Congress from Kentucky. He died in Louisville, March 28, 1872.

Army of New Mexico

ORGANIZED December 14, 1861, to embrace all the forces on the Rio Grande above Fort Quitman, and those in the territories of New Mexico and Arizona. Its main object was the conquest of California. Brigadier-General H. H. Sibley was placed in command. He had about thirty-seven hundred men. His troops won the battle of Valverde, occupied Santa Fé and fought at Glorieta (or Apache Cañon). The army was forced to retreat into Texas, in April, 1862, by Federal troops under Colonel E. R. S. Canby. Sibley was relieved of the command in December, 1862.

BRIGADIER-GENERAL HENRY HOPKINS SIBLEY (U.S.M.A. 1838) was born at Natchitoches, Louis-

iana, May 23, 1816, and served in the Seminole and Mexican wars. He was the inventor of the famous Sibley tent. The outbreak of the Civil War found him on an Indian campaign in New Mexico, serving as a major of dragoons, but he accepted a commission as brigadier-general in the Confederate army and became commander of the Army of New Mexico. After his repulse at Glorieta, March 28, 1862, he was driven back into Texas. He continued his service at the head of various commands in Louisiana, south of the Red River. After the war he entered the service of the Khedive of Egypt, where he was, from 1869 to 1873, engaged in building coast and river defenses. He died at Fredericksburg, Virginia, August 23, 1886.

Army of Louisiana

AT THE BEGINNING of the war, the Louisiana State troops, commanded by Major-General Braxton Bragg and later by Colonel P. O. Hébert, were sometimes designated the Army of Louisiana.

BRIGADIER-GENERAL PAUL OCTAVE HÉBERT (U.S.M.A. 1840) was born in Bayou Goula, Herville Parish, Louisiana, November 12, 1818. He resigned from the army in 1845, reentering as

Young M. Moody, Commander of the District of Florida.

Isham W. Garrott, Original Colonel of 20th Regiment.

William F. Perry Led a Noted Brigade under Longstreet.

William H. Forney Led an Alabama Brigade in Hill's Corps.

CONFEDERATE

GENERALS

No. 2

ALABAMA

William W. Allen Led a Cavalry Division in Wheeler's Corps.

John H. Forney, One of the Defenders of Vicksburg in 1863.

LeRoy P. Walker, First Confederate Secretary of War.

Sterling A. M. Wood Led a Brigade at Chickamauga.

James Cantey Commanded the Garrison at Mobile.

Zachary C. Deas Led a Brigade of Alabamians in Tennessee.

lieutenant-colonel in the Mexican War, where he received the brevet of colonel for his gallant conduct at Molino del Rey. While governor of Louisiana, 1853 to 1856, he appointed his classmate, W. T. Sherman, to the head of the Louisiana Military Academy. When the Civil War broke out he succeeded Bragg in command of the Confederate forces in Louisiana, and was appointed brigadier-general August 17, 1861. He was in special command of the defenses of New Orleans. Later, he commanded in turn the Department and District of Texas in the Trans-Mississippi. After the war he became state engineer of Louisiana. He died in New Orleans, August 29, 1880.

Army of Pensacola

THE FORCES at or near Pensacola, Florida, under Major-General Braxton Bragg, were designated the Army of Pensacola on October 22, 1861. Brigadier-General A. H. Gladden had temporary command in December, and Brigadier-General Samuel Jones took charge on January 27, 1862. The force then numbered eighty-one hundred men, divided among regiments from Alabama, Florida, Georgia, Louisiana, and Mississippi. On March 13th, the army was discontinued, the regiments entering the Army of the Mississippi or assigned for duty elsewhere. Pensacola was evacuated by the Confederate troops on the 9th of May.

BRIGADIER-GENERAL ADLEY H. GLADDEN was born in South Carolina. He entered the Confederate army and was appointed a brigadier-general from Louisiana in September, 1861. He had a brigade at Pensacola, and was in temporary command of the Army of Pensacola in December, 1861, and was given command of a brigade in the Second Corps, Army of the Mississippi. He was mortally wounded at Shiloh April 6, 1862.

MAJOR-GENERAL SAMUEL JONES (U.S.M.A. 1841) was born in Virginia, in 1820, and resigned his commission of captain in April, 1861, to enter the Confederate service. He was made major of artillery. He was acting adjutant-general of the Virginia forces in May and chief of artillery and ordnance in the Army of the Potomac from May to July, 1861. Appointed brigadier-general after the battle of Bull Run, he was assigned to the Army of Pensacola, in January, 1862, and the following month to the head of the Department of Alabama and West Florida. In April, he was given a division in the Army of the West, and in June, after having been appointed major-general in May, he was put at the head of a division in the Second Corps, Army of the Mississippi. After September, 1862, he commanded various departments in Tennessee and Virginia, being placed at the head of the Department of South Carolina, Georgia, and Florida, in April, 1864. At the close of the war he was in charge of the Department of Florida and South Georgia. He died in Washington, D. C., April 1, 1887.

Army of Mobile

ON JANUARY 27, 1862, the command of Brigadier-General Jones M. Withers, consisting of Alabama troops in and around the city of Mobile, was designated the Army of Mobile. Its strength was about ten thousand. It was subsequently commanded by Colonel J. B. Villepigue, temporarily, and Brigadier-General Samuel Jones, after March 15th. Many of the regiments entered the Army of the Mississippi and fought at Shiloh under Withers. More regiments were sent to that army, and on June 27, the Army of Mobile was discontinued.

MAJOR-GENERAL JONES MITCHELL WITHERS (U.S.M.A. 1835) was born in Madison County, Alabama, January 12, 1814, and resigned from the army in 1848. He entered the Confederate service and received an appointment as brigadier-general in July, 1861. He was promoted to major-general after the battle of Shiloh. From January 27th to February 28, 1862, he was in command of the Army of Mobile. He then had a division in the Second Corps, Army of the Mississippi, and also the Reserve Corps for a time, and passed into the Right Wing and Polk's Corps, Army of Tennessee. He resigned his commission July 13, 1863, but his rank was restored within a few days, after which he assumed various commands in Alabama. He surrendered at Merid-

Thomas Churchill Commanded a Division in the Army of the West; Defender of Arkansas and Red River Region.

Thomas C. Hindman Commanded the Trans-Mississippi District in 1863; Led Troops at Shiloh and Chickamauga.

John F. Fagan, Originally Colonel of the 1st Arkansas Infantry; Conspicuous in the Attack on Helena, July 4, 1863.

CONFEDERATE

GENERALS

No. 3

ARKANSAS

Lucius E. Polk, Leader of a Charge at Murfreesboro.

Albert Pike, Commander of Indian Troops at Pea Ridge.

Albert Rust Led a Brigade in the Army of the West.

James C. Tappan Led a Brigade West of the Mississippi.

William L. Cabell Led a Brigade of Arkansas Cavalry.

John S. Roane, in Commission at Little Rock, Ark.

ian, Mississippi, May 11, 1865, and died March 13, 1890.

BRIGADIER-GENERAL JOHN BORDENAVE VILLE-PIGUE (U.S.M.A. 1854) was born in Camden, South Carolina, July 2, 1830, and resigned from the army in March, 1861, to enter the Confederate service. As colonel, he was temporarily in command of the Army of Mobile. He was appointed brigadier-general, March 18, 1862. He was in command at Fort Pillow at the time of Flag-Officer Davis's attack, May-June, 1862, and commanded a brigade at the battle of Corinth, October 4th. He died at Port Hudson, Louisiana, November 9, 1862, as the result of illness. Ville-pigue was considered one of the most promising young officers in the Confederate service, and his untimely death was greatly deplored.

Central Army of Kentucky

BRIGADIER-GENERAL S. B. BUCKNER assumed command of the forces in central Kentucky, September, 1861, and he was followed October 28th, by General Albert Sidney Johnston. The troops were organized in two divisions with a reserve, and a third division, under Brigadier-General John B. Floyd, was added later on. Major-General Hardee had temporary command, December, 1861-February, 1862. On March 29, 1862, the Central Army of Kentucky, whose strength was about twenty-three thousand, was consolidated with the Army of the Mississippi, under the latter designation, with General Johnston in command and General P. G. T. Beauregard second.

LIEUTENANT-GENERAL SIMON BOLIVAR BUCKNER (U.S.M.A. 1841) was born in Kentucky, April 1, 1823. He served in the Mexican War and taught at West Point. He resigned from the army in 1855, and returned to Kentucky to practise law. He entered the Confederate service in September, 1861, taking command in central Kentucky. He commanded a division of the Central Army of Kentucky at Bowling Green and at Fort Donelson. On February 16, 1862, he surrendered the fort and garrison of Fort Donelson and was sent to Fort Warren as a prisoner of war, being exchanged in August. He was then made major-general and had a division in Bragg's army and was given a temporary corps at Chickamauga. He was made lieutenant-general in September, 1864, and was commander in several districts of the Trans-Mississippi Department. He was elected governor of Kentucky in 1887, and in 1896 was the candidate of the Gold Democrats for Vice-President.

Army of East Tennessee—Army of Kentucky

IN FEBRUARY, 1862, Major-General E. Kirby Smith was sent to Knoxville to assume command of the troops in East Tennessee. With the army thus organized, it was intended to create a diversion in favor of General A. S. Johnston's operations with the Army of the Mississippi. The Army of East Tennessee was engaged in many minor engagements. On August 25th, the organization was designated the Army of Kentucky and was composed of three divisions. It led the advance in Bragg's invasion of Kentucky and was successful at the battle of Richmond, August 30th, raising great hopes for the Confederate conquest of Kentucky. On November 20, 1862, the Army of Kentucky was merged as Smith's Corps in the Army of Tennessee.

GENERAL EDMUND KIRBY SMITH (U.S.M.A. 1845) was born in St. Augustine, Florida, May 16, 1824, and served in the Mexican War, after which he was professor of mathematics at West Point. In April, 1861, he resigned his commission as captain to join the Confederates, becoming a brigadier-general in June. He was chief-of-staff to and had a brigade under General Joseph E. Johnston. He was seriously wounded at Bull Run. Early in 1862, as major-general, he was placed in command of the Army of East Tennessee (afterward Kentucky). In October of the same year he was made lieutenant-general and continued in the Department of East Tennessee. He was made general, and assumed command of the Trans-Mississippi Department in February, 1863. He surrendered his troops to Major-General Canby at Baton Rouge, May 26, 1865, having, the year before, defeated Major-General Banks in the Red

William N. R. Beall, District Commander in Mississippi and Louisiana.

Dandridge McRae Led a Brigade in Battles West of the Mississippi.

Alexander T. Hawthorne Led a Brigade in the Army of the Mississippi.

Daniel H. Reynolds Fought with Hood at Nashville.

Daniel C. Govan Commanded a Noted Brigade.

Evander McNair, Important Leader in the Army of Tennessee.

CONFEDERATE GENERALS

No. 4

ARKANSAS

Thomas P. Dockery Led a Cavalry Brigade.

Frank C. Armstrong, Brilliant Cavalry Commander.

River campaign. After the war, he devoted himself largely to education, becoming chancellor of the University of Nashville from 1870 to 1875, and later professor of mathematics at the University of the South. He died in Sewanee, Tennessee, March 28, 1893.

Army of the Mississippi

FROM TROOPS in the Western Department (Department No. 2) was created the Army of the Mississippi on March 5, 1862, and to General P. G. T. Beauregard was given the command. The army was divided into two corps headed by Major-Generals Leonidas Polk and Braxton Bragg. On March 29th, the army was joined to the Central Army of Kentucky with its three divisions, reserve corps, and cavalry. General A. S. Johnston, of the latter, took command of the Army of the Mississippi, that name having been preserved. Beauregard was second in command. The whole body was gathered at Corinth (except a force at Fort Pillow) in three corps, a reserve corps, and cavalry, and this was the organization that fought at Shiloh, when its strength was about forty thousand. The death of General Johnston placed the chief command upon General Beauregard, who was relieved June 27, 1862, by Major-General Hardee, and he, on August 15th, by Major-General Bragg. The army was transferred to Chattanooga in July. Major-General Polk had temporary command from September 28th to November 7, 1862, when, on the return of Bragg, the organization was called the Army of Tennessee.

GENERAL ALBERT SIDNEY JOHNSTON (U.S.M. A. 1826) was born in Washington, Mason County, Kentucky, February 3, 1803. He served in the Black Hawk War and resigned his commission in 1834. Two years later, he entered the army of the Texan Republic as a private, soon becoming a brigadier-general, and in 1838 was commander-in-chief of the army of Texas and Secretary of War. Later, he reentered the United States Army and served in the Mexican War with distinction. As colonel, he conducted an expedition against the Mormons in Utah in 1857, which won him a brevet of brigadier-general. He remained in command in Utah until February, 1860. At the outbreak of the Civil War, he was in command of the Department of the Pacific, but, by reason of his Southern sympathies, he resigned his commission to enter the Confederate service with the rank of general. He assumed command of Department No. 2, or Western Department, on September 15, 1861. In October he took immediate control of the Central Army of Kentucky, holding the line of Bowling Green, Kentucky, until February, 1862, against vastly superior numbers. On March 29, 1862, this army united with the Army of the Mississippi and Johnston took command of the new organization. He was killed on the battlefield of Shiloh, April 6, 1862, and his death was a stunning blow to the new Confederacy.

Third Corps—Army of the Mississippi

MAJOR-GENERAL W. J. HARDEE, who had been commander in northwestern Arkansas, was placed at the head of the Third Corps of the Army of the Mississippi on its reorganization, March 29, 1862. In August, the corps was merged in the Left Wing of the Army of the Mississippi.

Reserve Corps—Army of the Mississippi

COMMANDED by Major-General George B. Crittenden on March 29, 1862, and by Major-General J. C. Breckinridge after April 6th, and, later, by Brigadier-General Jones M. Withers. After Shiloh, and the siege of Corinth, the corps went to Louisiana and fought the battle of Baton Rouge, August 6, 1862, with the Federal troops under Brigadier-General Thomas Williams. Then it returned with Breckinridge to form the Army of Middle Tennessee and was merged in Hardee's (Second) Corps, Army of Tennessee, as the First Division, in November, 1862.

Jesse J. Finley Commanded a Brigade.

William G. M. Davis Led a Brigade of Cavalry.

Robert Bullock, Colonel of the 7th Regiment.

William Miller Commanded Reserve Forces in Florida.

CONFEDERATE
GENERALS

No. 5

FLORIDA

J. Patton Anderson, Active Division
Commander in the West.

Martin L. Smith, One of the Defenders of Vicksburg.

Francis A. Shaup, Chief of Artillery, Army of Tennessee.

William S. Walker Commanded a South Carolina Brigade.

Theodore W. Brevard, Colonel of the 11th Regiment.

Army of Tennessee

THE JOINING of the Army of Kentucky with the Army of the Mississippi, on November 20, 1862, was the origin of the Army of Tennessee—the great Confederate army of the West. There were three corps and a division of cavalry, with an effective total of forty-seven thousand. General Braxton Bragg was in command. This army fought the battle of Stone's River, went through the Tullahoma campaign, and fought the battle of Chickamauga, assisted by Longstreet's Corps from the Army of Northern Virginia. It was driven from Chattanooga in November, 1863, by Grant's forces. After the battle of Chickamauga, the corps were reorganized several times. Bragg was removed from the command on December 2, 1863, and until General Johnston assumed it, on December 27th, both Hardee and Polk were in temporary command. Polk was sent to the Department of Alabama, Mississippi and East Louisiana before the end of December. The army spent the winter around Dalton, Georgia, and faced Sherman's advance in May, 1864, in two infantry and one cavalry corps. Polk brought back his divisions, which he called the Army of Mississippi, and these forces were consolidated with the Army of Tennessee on July 26th, after Polk had been killed. On July 18th, Johnston was replaced by General John B. Hood. After the capture of Atlanta, the army returned to Tennessee, and, failing to cut off Major-General Schofield's command at Franklin, was routed by Major-General Thomas at Nashville (December 15-16, 1864). In February, 1865, General Johnston was again placed in command of the Army of Tennessee, as well as the troops in South Carolina, Georgia, and Florida. The army had greatly dwindled. Lieutenant-General A. P. Stewart was at the actual head of the Army of Tennessee after March 16th, and Johnston's enlarged command included troops from the far South under Hardee, which, in February, had been organized in a corps, and those in North Carolina under Bragg. The aggregate present of the old Army of Tennessee was about twenty thousand. The army surrendered to Sherman in North Carolina, April 26, 1865.

GENERAL BRAXTON BRAGG (U.S.M.A. 1837) was born in Warren County, North Carolina, March 22, 1817, and served in the Seminole and Mexican wars. He resigned from the army in 1859, and became an extensive planter in Louisiana. On the secession of Louisiana, he was made a brigadier-general in the Confederate provisional army, and was the first commander of the military forces of Louisiana. After being appointed major-general in September, he took command of the forces in Alabama and West Florida from October, 1861, to February, 1862. He commanded the right wing of the Army of the Mississippi at Shiloh, and was made general after the death of Albert Sidney Johnston. He succeeded Beauregard as commander of the Army of the Mississippi (or Tennessee), and led it into Kentucky in September, 1862, and after his retreat therefrom, was defeated by Rosecrans at Stone's River (January, 1863). He in turn defeated Rosecrans at Chickamauga, but was driven from Chattanooga by Grant in November, 1863. Bragg was now relieved of the Army of Tennessee, and, later, was given control of the Confederate army's military operations at Richmond. As commander of the Department of North Carolina, he failed in attempts to check Sherman and prevent the fall of Wilmington. After February, 1865, he cooperated with Johnston and surrendered with the latter. Later on, he was state engineer of Alabama, and died in Galveston, Texas, September 27, 1876.

GENERAL JOHN BELL HOOD (U.S.M.A. 1853) was born in Owingsville, Kentucky, June 1, 1831, and fought against the Comanche Indians in Texas. He resigned from the army in April, 1861, to enter the Confederate service. After serving as captain in the cavalry and colonel of a Texas regiment, he received the appointment of brigadier-general in March, 1862. He was made major-general in October, 1862, after taking a conspicuous part in the Virginia campaigns. At Gettysburg, he commanded the largest division in Longstreet's Corps. In September, he went to Tennessee with Longstreet's Corps, which he commanded at Chickamauga, where he lost a leg. After the battle, he was given the rank of lieutenant-general, and at the head of the Second Corps in the Army of Tennessee, took part in the Atlanta campaign from May to July 18, 1864, when he succeeded Johnston in the command of the army with the temporary rank of general. He lost Atlanta, and, returning to Tennessee, was driven into Alabama by Major-General Thomas in the middle of December. In January, 1865, he was relieved of his command and was ordered to Richmond. After the war, he went to New Orleans, where he died, August 30, 1879.

Howell Cobb, Leader of Cobb's Georgia Legion.　G. T. Anderson Commanded a Brigade in Longstreet's Corps.　David E. Twiggs, in Command in East Louisiana in 1861.　Pierce M. B. Young, Brilliant Cavalry Leader.

Goode Bryan Led a Georgia Brigade in Longstreet's Corps.　Hugh W. Mercer Led a Georgia Brigade in the Army of Tennessee.　David R. Jones, Active Leader at Second Manassas and Sharpsburg.　William M. Brown, Defender of Savannah, December, 1864.

CONFEDERATE

GENERALS

No. 6

GEORGIA

Clement A. Evans, Leader in the Army of Northern Virginia.

Robert Toombs, Defender of Lee's Right Flank at Antietam.

First Corps—Army of the Mississippi and of Tennessee

MAJOR-GENERAL LEONIDAS POLK commanded from June, 1861, to March, 1862, the First Division in the Western Department (No. 2), the troops of which were scattered along the Mississippi from Columbus, Kentucky, to Memphis, and in the interior of Tennessee and Mississippi. It numbered about twenty-five thousand men. On the organization of the Army of the Mississippi in March, 1862, this division was called the First Grand Division, and after the consolidation with the Central Army of Kentucky, on March 29th, the First Corps, Army of the Mississippi. On August 15th, Polk's Corps was reorganized as the Right Wing in ten divisions, with over fifteen thousand present for duty. In the Army of Tennessee, the Right Wing became the First, or Polk's Corps. After the battle of Chickamauga, Polk was relieved of the command, and both corps of the army underwent reorganization. The leading corps was thereafter known as Hardee's, or Cheatham's Corps, from the names of its commanders.

LIEUTENANT-GENERAL LEONIDAS POLK (U.S. M.A. 1827) was born in Raleigh, North Carolina, April 10, 1806. He left the army for the church, and eventually became the first Protestant Episcopal Bishop of Louisiana, in 1841. In 1861, he entered the Confederate army and was made major-general in June. He was assigned to the command of the Western Department (No. 2); and in September he was replaced by General A. S. Johnston and given the First Division, Army of the Mississippi, with which he won the battle of Belmont in November. He led the First Corps at Shiloh, and later had temporary command of the army itself. In October, 1862, he was given the rank of lieutenant-general, and accompanied the Western Confederate army until after Chickamauga, where he commanded the Right Wing when he was temporarily suspended, but the charge of delay on his part was dismissed by President Davis. In the winter of 1863–64, he was in command of the Department of Alabama, Mississippi, and East Louisiana, and brought his forces, which he called the Army of Mississippi, to Georgia in May, 1864, to assist Johnston in opposing Sherman's advance to Atlanta. On Pine Mountain, near Marietta, Georgia, he was killed by a cannon-ball, June 14, 1864.

MAJOR-GENERAL BENJAMIN FRANKLIN CHEATHAM was born in Nashville, Tennessee, October 20, 1820. He entered the Mexican War, rising to the rank of colonel after distinguished service at Monterey and elsewhere. At the close of this war he became major-general of the Tennessee militia, and when the Civil War broke out he attached himself to the Confederate cause and organized the entire supply department for the Western troops. As brigadier-general, he served under Polk at Belmont, and had a division of the First Corps, Army of the Mississippi, at Shiloh, and was commander of the Right Wing of the same army during Bragg's invasion of Kentucky in 1862. He led his division at Stone's River, through the Tullahoma campaign, and at Chickamauga, and after that battle was head of Cheatham's Corps, an organization formed upon the departure of Polk from the army, and of which Hardee shortly afterward took command. In the Atlanta campaign he led a division in Hardee's Corps, and assumed command of the corps, which later was known as Cheatham's Corps, after the departure of Hardee for Savannah in October, 1864, with which he continued until the surrender at Durham Station. After the war he became a farmer in Tennessee, and was appointed postmaster of Nashville in 1885. He died there September 4, 1886.

MAJOR-GENERAL PATRICK ROMAYNE CLEBURNE was born in County Cork, Ireland, March 17, 1828. He ran away from Trinity College, Dublin, and enlisted in the Forty-first Foot. In 1855 he came to America, settling in Helena, Arkansas, where he practised law until the opening of the war. He entered the Confederate service as private, and rose to the rank of major-general, in 1862. He planned the capture of the United States arsenal in Arkansas, March, 1861. He was colonel of an Arkansas regiment, and at Shiloh, as brigadier-general, he commanded a brigade in the Third Corps, Army of the Mississippi. He was wounded at Perryville. At Murfreesboro and Chickamauga he commanded a division, and his troops formed the rear guard at Missionary Ridge. For his defense of Ringgold Gap, in the Atlanta campaign, he received the thanks of the Confederate Congress. Cleburne covered Hood's retreat at Jonesboro, and had temporary command of Hardee's Corps. He continued to hold his division in Cheatham's Corps, and at the battle of Franklin was killed, November 30, 1864. A brilliant charge at Chickamauga earned him the title of " Stonewall of the West," and it was he who initiated the Order of the Southern Cross and was among the first to urge the advantages to the Confederates of colored troops.

PHILIP COOK
Leader in Gordon's Attack
on Fort Stedman.

WILLIAM M. GARDNER
Commander of the Post of
Richmond, Va., in 1865.

JOHN K. JACKSON
Commanded a Reserve Corps
Army of the Mississippi.

CLAUDIUS C. WILSON
Led a Brigade in the
Army of Tennessee.

ISAAC M. ST. JOHN
Commissary General,
1865,

CONFEDERATE

GENERALS

No. 7—GEORGIA

(CONTINUED)

BRYAN M. THOMAS
Led a Brigade of Alabamians.

G. MOXLEY SORRELL
Staff Officer with Longstreet.

DUDLEY M. DUBOIS
Led a Brigade in Longstreet's Corps.

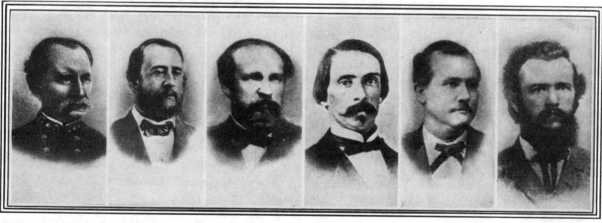

MARCELLUS A. STOVALL
Led a Brigade in
Hood's Corps.

LUCIUS J. GARTRELL
Led a Brigade in
Georgia Reserves.

HENRY C. WAYNE
Adjutant-General and
Inspector-General of
Georgia.

ALFRED CUMMING
Led a Brigade of
Georgians in the West.

JAMES P. SIMMS
Led a Georgia Brigade in
Longstreet's Corps.

WILLIAM R. BOGGS
Chief of Staff to Gen.
E. Kirby Smith.

Second Corps—Army of the Mississippi and of Tennessee

MAJOR-GENERAL BRAXTON BRAGG was given command of the Second Corps of the Army of the Mississippi on its organization, March 29, 1862. There were ten divisions, composed chiefly of Alabama, Mississippi, and Louisiana troops. In July, Major-General Samuel Jones had command, and on August 15th, when General Bragg resumed command of the whole army, his former corps passed to the control of Major-General Hardee. There was an aggregate present of about sixteen thousand men. On November 7th, the Left Wing, in an organization that had a short existence after August 15th, again became the Second (or Hardee's) Corps. In July, 1863, Lieutenant-General Hardee was relieved by Lieutenant-General D. H. Hill, who commanded at Chickamauga, and the later commanders were Major-Generals J. C. Breckinridge, T. C. Hindman, Lieutenant-General J. B. Hood, Major-General C. L. Stevenson and Lieutenant-General S. D. Lee. After 1864, the corps was known as Hood's, or Lee's Corps, Hardee having assumed command of the other corps.

LIEUTENANT-GENERAL WILLIAM JOSEPH HARDEE (U.S.M.A. 1838) was born in Savannah, Georgia, October 10, 1815, and served in the Seminole and Mexican wars. He resigned his commission of lieutenant-colonel in January, 1861, to join the Confederate forces, in which he was appointed a brigadier-general in June. He was given command of Fort Morgan, Mobile Bay, in March, and later, as major-general, was transferred to the Central Army of Kentucky, of which he had command from December, 1861, to February, 1862. He was given the Second Corps in the Army of the Mississippi and led the advance at Shiloh. He took part with this army as corps or wing commander in Bragg's invasion of Kentucky, at Stone's River, and at Chattanooga, having been made lieutenant-general in October, 1862. In the summer of 1863 he had charge of the defenses of Mississippi and Alabama. He had temporary command of the Army of Tennessee after Bragg was removed in December, 1863. He had a corps during the Atlanta campaign, and in October, 1864, he was placed in command of the Department of South Carolina, Georgia, and Florida. He was unable to prevent the capture of Savannah, and, in February, 1865, joined Johnston, serving in the Army of Tennessee, at the head of a corps formed from the troops in his department, until its surrender. After the war, he lived at Selma, Alabama, and died at Wytheville, Virginia, November 6, 1873.

LIEUTENANT-GENERAL DANIEL HARVEY HILL (U.S.M.A. 1842) was born at Hill's Iron Works, York District, South Carolina, July 12, 1821. He resigned from the army after the Mexican War, in which he had received the brevet of major, and was engaged in teaching until he entered the Confederate army, in 1861. As colonel of the First North Carolina Infantry, he showed marked talent at Big Bethel, June 10th, and was made brigadier-general the following month. As major-general, he had a division and later a command, or corps, in the Army of Northern Virginia, and fought through the Peninsula campaign. He was assigned to the Department of North Carolina in July, but fought with his division at South Mountain, where he held the Federal forces in check, and at Antietam. In July, 1863, he was made lieutenant-general, and replaced Lieutenant-General Hardee in command of the Second Corps, Army of Tennessee, which he led at Chickamauga, and of which he was relieved in November. With the rank of major-general, he took command of a division in Lee's Corps, Army of Tennessee, in March, 1865, and at the battle of Bentonville he led the corps itself. After the war, he became an editor, and from 1877 to 1884 was president of the Arkansas Industrial University. He died at Charlotte, North Carolina, September 25, 1889.

MAJOR-GENERAL CARTER LITTLEPAGE STEVENSON (U.S.M.A. 1838) was born near Fredericksburg, Virginia, September 21, 1817. He was dismissed from the army in June, 1861, having entered the Confederate service as lieutenant-colonel. He did duty at Cumberland Gap, from which he drove Brigadier-General G. W. Morgan away, and commanded a division in the Army of Tennessee. He rose to the rank of major-general in October, 1862. His division was with Pemberton's forces in the battle of Chickasaw Bayou, December 26, 1862. He fought at Chickamauga and in the Atlanta campaign onward with the Army of Tennessee, having on July, 1864, temporary command of Hood's Corps, before the appointment of Lieutenant-General S. D. Lee. He also assumed command of Lee's Corps, when the latter was wounded after the battle of Nashville, until the army had crossed the Tennessee. He died August 15, 1888.

MAJOR-GENERAL THOMAS CARMICHAEL HINDMAN was born in Tennessee, November, 1818. He became a lawyer and served in Congress. He fought in the Mexican War, and in 1860 was a

John S. Williams Commanded
a Cavalry Brigade.

INDIAN

TERRITORY

(ONE TO RIGHT)

KENTUCKY

(FIVE REMAINING)

Stand Watie, Indian Leader of Troops
at Pea Ridge.

Thomas H. Taylor Led a
Brigade in the Army of
Tennessee.

William Preston Led a Division
at the Battle of
Chickamauga.

James M. Hawes Com-
manded a Brigade West
of the Mississippi.

CONFEDERATE

GENERALS

No. 8

Humphrey Marshall, Confederate
Defender of Kentucky.

member of the Charleston Convention. He went to the Civil War as colonel of an Arkansas regiment, and served in the armies of the West and of the Mississippi. For his conduct at Shiloh he was made major-general. He was, at different times, division commander in the Army of Tennessee, and a temporary commander of the Second Corps, and was also at the head of the Trans-Mississippi District and that of Arkansas. He was defeated at Prairie Grove and at Newtonia. After the war, he went to Mexico, but returned to Arkansas and was murdered by one of his former soldiers at Helena, September 28, 1863.

LIEUTENANT-GENERAL STEPHEN DILL LEE (U. S.M.A. 1854) was born in Charleston, South Carolina, September 22, 1833. He resigned from the army in February, 1861, to enter the Confederate service as captain in the artillery, and rose to the rank of lieutenant-general June, 1864. He was one of the three men who called on Major Anderson, April 12, 1861, and demanded the surrender of Fort Sumter. He had a battalion in the Washington Artillery, and was prominent at Second Bull Run and at Antietam. He was then sent to the West and commanded a division at the battle of Chickasaw Bayou, December 27, 1862, driving back the Federal troops with great slaughter. He was among those who surrendered at Vicksburg, July 4, 1863, and in August was put at the head of the cavalry in the Department of Alabama, Mississippi, and East Louisiana, and fought at Tupelo and other places. In May, 1864, he succeeded Lieutenant-General Polk at the head of this department, remaining there until July, when he was assigned to the command of Hood's Corps, Army of Tennessee, General Hood having been placed at the head of the whole army. Henceforth it was known as Lee's Corps. He was wounded December 17, 1864, while protecting the rear of the army in the retreat from Nashville. After the war he became a planter in Mississippi; a member of the State legislature; and in 1880 he became president of the Mississippi Agricultural and Mechanical College. He was also at the head of the Vicksburg National Park, and was commander-in-chief of the United Confederate Veterans, after the death of Lieutenant-General John B. Gordon, in 1904. He died at Vicksburg, Mississippi, May 28, 1908.

Wheeler's Cavalry Corps—Army of Tennessee

ON JANUARY 22, 1863, Major-General Joseph Wheeler was assigned to command all the cavalry in Middle Tennessee. On March 16th, the cavalry divisions in the Army of Tennessee were designated as corps, and were given the names of their respective commanders, Wheeler and Van Dorn. The corps were organized into divisions and brigades, and Wheeler's Corps, sometimes known as the Second Corps, had an aggregate present of nearly twelve thousand. It displayed great activity in Tennessee, making numerous raids and guarding the flanks of the army. After the battle of Chickamauga, it made a famous raid on Rosecrans' communications, October, 1863. It also operated on the flanks of the army during the Atlanta and other campaigns until the close of the war.

LIEUTENANT-GENERAL JOSEPH WHEELER (U. S.M.A. 1859) was born in Augusta, Georgia, September 10, 1836, and entered the mounted infantry, resigning, in 1861, to join the Confederate army, in which he reached the rank of major-general (January, 1863), and commander of the Second Cavalry Corps, Army of Tennessee. He was conspicuous as a raider, and was constantly employed in guarding the flanks of the army, cutting the Federal communications, covering retreats, and obtaining information for the army commanders. He was appointed lieutenant-general, February 28, 1865. After the war, he was a member of Congress from 1881 to 1899. He was commissioned major-general of volunteers in 1898, and went to the Spanish War, commanding the troops at Las Guasimas, and was senior field-officer at the battle of San Juan Hill. He was senior member of the commission which negotiated the surrender of Santiago. He served with the American troops during the insurrection in the Philippines from August, 1899, to January 24, 1900, and on June 13, 1900, was appointed brigadier-general of the United States army, being retired the following September. He died in Brooklyn, New York, January 25, 1906. General Wheeler made a unique reputation for himself as a cavalry leader, and in the Spanish war his services won universal acknowledgment as typical of the complete reunion of the North and South.

George B. Crosby Led a Brigade in Mississippi and Louisiana.

Abraham Buford, Active Leader of Cavalry.

Adam R. Johnson Led a Brigade of Morgan's Cavalry.

CONFEDERATE GENERALS—No. 9—KENTUCKY (Continued)

Hyland B. Lyon Led a Brigade of Cavalry in Forrest's Division.

Joseph H. Lewis Led a Brigade in the Army of Tennessee.

George B. Hodge Commanded a Brigade of Cavalry.

Van Dorn's Cavalry Corps—Army of Tennessee

On March 16, 1863, Major-General Van Dorn's Cavalry Division in the Army of Tennessee was called Van Dorn's, or the First Cavalry Corps. It had an average aggregate present of about eight thousand, and was a valuable adjunct to General Bragg's army.

Army of Middle Tennessee

When Major-General John C. Breckinridge assumed command of the forces around Murfreesboro on October 28, 1862, they were denominated the Army of Middle Tennessee. There were three brigades, with cavalry under Brigadier-General Forrest, who was shortly relieved by Brigadier-General Wheeler. When Bragg advanced from Chattanooga to oppose Rosecrans, the Army of Middle Tennessee became identified with a division of Hardee's Corps, Army of Tennessee.

Major-General John Cabell Breckinridge was born near Lexington, Kentucky, January 21, 1821, and became a lawyer. He served as major in the Mexican War. From 1857 to 1861, he was vice-president of the United States. In 1860, he was a candidate for the. presidency, receiving the electoral votes of the Southern States, with the exception of Virginia, Kentucky, Tennessee, and Missouri. He was sent to the Senate, but left that body to join the Confederates. He was made brigadier-general in November, 1861, and major-general in April, 1862, after the battle of Shiloh. He had a command under General A. S. Johnston in the Central Army of Kentucky, and Army of the Mississippi, and led the reserve corps at Shiloh. After the siege of Corinth he took his force to Louisiana, and fought the battle of Baton Rouge, August 6, 1862. Later, he headed the Department and Army of Middle Tennessee. Rejoining the Army of Tennessee at the end of 1862, he fought at Stone's River, Chickamauga, and Chattanooga, at the head of a division in Hardee's Corps, and was its temporary commander for a period before the battle of Chattanooga. He was brought East after the opening of the Wilderness campaign, fought at Cold Harbor, and was second in command under Early in the Shenandoah. From February 6, 1865, to the downfall of the Confederacy, he was Secretary of War. He then went to Europe, but returned in 1868, and resumed the practice of law. He died in Lexington, Kentucky, May 17, 1875.

Missouri State Guard

On June 12, 1861, Governor C. F. Jackson of Missouri, in defiance of the United States military government, issued a call for fifty thousand of the State militia for active service. At the time of the flight of the governor and his followers to the extreme southwestern corner of the State, he was joined by Price. At that time, the whole Confederate State force amounted to about three thousand men. This Missouri State Guard was in command of Brigadier-Generals Sterling Price and M. M. Parsons from October 29, 1861, to March 17, 1862, when it merged in the Army of the West.

Army of the West

Major-General Earl Van Dorn assumed command of the troops in the Trans-Mississippi District of Western Department (No. 2), on January 29, 1862. Out of the force grew the Army of the West, so called after March 4th. It was largely composed of the Missouri State Guard. This army fought at Pea Ridge and elsewhere in Arkansas, and, being transferred across the Mississippi, was present at the siege of Corinth. The First Division was commanded by Major-General Sterling Price after March 22d, and the Second by Major-General Samuel Jones. It had three divisions after May, and a strength of over twenty thousand. On June 20th, Van Dorn was replaced by Major-General John P. McCown, who had commanded the Third Division, and he in turn by Major-General Price, on July 3d. The transfer of the Army of the Mississippi to Chattanooga at

Paul O. Hébert Commanded the Army of Lousiana Defending New Orleans.

Louis Hébert, Active Commander in the Southwest.

Thomas M. Scott, Originally Colonel of the 12th Regiment.

Franklin Gardner, Defender of Port Hudson against Banks in 1863.

CONFED–

ERATE

GENERALS

No. 10

LOUISI–

ANA

James P. Major Led a Cavalry Brigade in Louisiana.

Edward Higgins, Conspicuous at New Orleans in 1862.

Henry H. Sibley, Conspicuous Leader in New Mexico.

Albert G. Blanchard Led a Brigade in the Army of Northern Virginia.

Zebulon York Commanded a Brigade.

Allan Thomas Led a Brigade in the Army of Northern Virginia.

the end of July, left the Army of the West in control of western Tennessee, and northern Mississippi. One division of the army fought the battle of Iuka, September 10th. On September 28th, a junction was made with Van Dorn's new command of troops in Mississippi, and the new organization was denominated the Army of West Tennessee. To Price was assigned a corps, which continued to be called, sometimes, the Army of the West.

MAJOR-GENERAL EARL VAN DORN (U.S.M.A. 1842) was born near Port Gibson, Mississippi, September 17, 1820, and served in the Mexican War and in several Indian campaigns. He resigned from the army, and was commissioned a colonel in the Confederate States army in March, 1861. His first commands were at New Orleans, and in the Department of Texas, where he forced the surrender of United States troops under Major Sibley and Colonel Reeve. He was made brigadier-general in June and major-general in September. In October and November, 1861, he commanded a division in the Army of the Potomac, and was assigned, in January, 1862, to the Trans-Mississippi District (Department No. 2), in which he had command of the Army of the West. He was defeated at Pea Ridge in March, and, with the Army of West Tennessee, at Corinth in October. After Pemberton assumed control of this force in the department in which Van Dorn was operating, he continued to command a cavalry division, at the head of which he made a brilliant raid in Mississippi in December, 1862. In March, 1863, Van Dorn's cavalry division was designated a corps in the Army of Tennessee. On May 8, 1863, he was shot and killed by Doctor Peters, at Spring Hill, Tennessee, the result of a private quarrel.

MAJOR-GENERAL JOHN PORTER McCOWN (U.S.M.A. 1840) was born in Tennessee, in 1815, and served in the Mexican war, being brevetted captain for gallant conduct at Cerro Gordo. He resigned from the service in May, 1861, and entered the Confederate army, taking charge of the artillery in the provisional army of the State of Tennessee. As brigadier-general, he commanded a division of Polk's army at the battle of Belmont, November 7, 1861. After commanding at New Madrid, he had a division in the Army of the West, and was temporarily at the head of that force in June, 1862. He was placed in command of the Department of East Tennessee in September. Subsequently, he commanded a division of the Army of Kentucky, which fought with the Second Corps, Army of Tennessee, at the battle of Stone's River. In February, 1863, he was arrested on charges of conduct prejudicial to good order and military discipline and sent to Chattanooga, but was released. At the end of the war he fought with the Army of Tennessee in North Carolina. He died, January 22, 1879.

Army of West Tennessee—Army of Mississippi

MAJOR-GENERAL VAN DORN was transferred June 20, 1862, from the Army of the West to the Department of Southern Mississippi and East Louisiana. His troops occupied Vicksburg, and a force from the Reserve Corps of the Army of the Mississippi, under Major-General Breckinridge, fought the battle of Baton Rouge, August 6th. On September 28th, Van Dorn's troops joined the Army of the West to oppose Rosecrans' activities in northern Mississippi, and the combined force was denominated the Army of West Tennessee, with Van Dorn at the head. It fought the battle of Corinth (October 4th), and on December 7th its name was changed to the Army of Mississippi. It consisted of two corps, headed by Van Dorn and Price, the chief control having passed to Lieutenant-General John C. Pemberton, at the head of the Department of Mississippi and East Louisiana. Van Dorn, with his cavalry, made a famous raid in northern Mississippi in December, capturing the Federal supply depot at Holly Springs. In January, 1863, the corps were changed into divisions. The title, Army of Mississippi, ceased to be used shortly after this date. The chief force under Pemberton surrendered at Vicksburg. Meanwhile, Van Dorn had been killed in Tennessee, May 8, 1863, and Price had been ordered to the Trans-Mississippi Department, February 27, 1863.

LIEUTENANT-GENERAL JOHN CLIFFORD PEMBERTON (U.S.M.A. 1837) was born in Philadelphia, August 10, 1814, and served in the Seminole and Mexican wars, making a noteworthy record in the artillery service. He entered the Confederate army in April, 1861, as major and chief of the Virginia artillery, being made brigadier-general in June. In November, 1861, he was transferred to South Carolina, and appointed major-general in

Johnson K. Duncan Commanded the
River Defenses below New Orleans.

Randall L. Gibson, Active Leader
in many Western Battles.

William R. Peck Commanded 9th Louisiana; Led a Charge at Appomattox.

CONFEDERATE

GENERALS—No. 11

LOUISIANA AND

MARYLAND

(Two Below.)

Daniel W. Adams, Noted Commander
in the Southwest.

St. John Lidell Led a Brigade in the
Army of the Mississippi.

Mansfield Lovell, Defender of the
Lower Mississippi in 1862.

William W. Mackall, Chief of Staff,
Army of Tennessee.

January, 1862, when his command was enlarged to include Georgia and East Florida. In October, he was advanced to the rank of lieutenant-general and sent to the Department of Mississippi and East Louisiana, where he took chief command of all the troops therein, including the Army of West Tennessee (or Mississippi) under Van Dorn and Price. He surrendered Vicksburg to Major-General Grant, July 4, 1863, and after exchange resigned his commission on account of criticism resulting from the surrender. In May, 1864, with the rank of lieutenant-colonel, he was given command of the artillery defenses at Richmond where he served until the close of the war. He became a farmer in Virginia, and died in Penllyn, Pennsylvania, July 13, 1881.

Southern Army—Trans-Mississippi Army

THE FORCES in the Department of West Louisiana and Texas were constituted the Southwestern Army, January 14, 1863, and the command was given to Lieutenant-General E. Kirby Smith. On February 9th, the command was enlarged so as to embrace the whole Trans-Mississippi Department, which, on May 26, 1862, had been separated from the Western Department (Department No. 2). Major-General T. H. Holmes had previously commanded in the Trans-Mississippi. Smith had about thirty thousand men, widely scattered from Fort Smith, Arkansas, to the Rio Grande. Major-General Holmes was defeated at Helena, July 4, 1863. The various portions of the army were constantly occupied in small engagements. These forces opposed the Federal Red River expedition in 1864. At the latest returns, in 1865, the aggregate present of the force was about forty-three thousand. They were the last Confederate troops to surrender, May 26, 1865.

LIEUTENANT-GENERAL THEOPHILUS HUNTER HOLMES (U.S.M.A. 1829) was born in Sampson County, North Carolina, in 1804, and fought in the Florida and Mexican wars. He resigned his commission of major in April, 1861, and entered the Confederate service, rising to the rank of lieutenant-general on October 10, 1862. On account of his age he saw little active service, but was placed at the head of various districts and departments throughout the Confederacy. On July 4, 1863, while in command of the District of Arkansas, Trans-Mississippi Department, he led an unsuccessful attack on Helena. He died in Fayetteville, North Carolina, June 20, 1880.

LIEUTENANT-GENERAL RICHARD TAYLOR, son of Zachary Taylor, was born in New Orleans, Louisiana, January 27, 1826. He was a Yale graduate and went to the Mexican War with General Taylor. He joined the Confederate army in 1861, serving first as colonel of the Ninth Louisiana Volunteers in the Army of the Potomac. He was promoted to brigadier-general in October, and served under " Stonewall " Jackson in the Shenandoah valley and in the Peninsula campaign. He was made major-general in July, 1862, and the following month was assigned to the command of the District of West Louisiana (Trans-Mississippi Department), where he remained until June, 1864. It was hoped that he would recover New Orleans. He occupied the Teche country during the winter of 1862–63. In the following spring and summer he fought against Weitzel and captured Brashear City. He reached the west bank of the Mississippi near New Orleans in July, but was driven back by Weitzel and Franklin. The following year he was instrumental in defeating the Red River expedition. In September, 1864, he was sent to command the Department of Alabama, Mississippi and East Louisiana, and surrendered to Major-General Canby, May 4, 1865. He died in New York City, April 12, 1879.

Army of Missouri

IN AUGUST, 1864, General E. Kirby Smith ordered Major-General Sterling Price to move into Missouri. It was expected that the various independent bands could be organized and bring at least twenty thousand recruits into the Confederate army. Price's force, consisting of the divisions of Fagan, Marmaduke, and Shelby, amounted to nearly twelve thousand men, and is variously called the Army of the Missouri, Price's Expeditionary Corps, and the Army in the Field. After a

John W. Frazer Commanded a Brigade.   Samuel J. Gholson Commanded a Brigade.   William F. Tucker Led a Brigade under Hood.   Benjamin G. Humphries Led a Brigade in Virginia.

CONFEDERATE

GENERALS

No. 12

MISSISSIPPI

William E. Baldwin, Commander of a Brigade at Mobile.

Jacob H. Sharp Led a Brigade in General Polk's Corps.

Claudius W. Sears, Originally Colonel of the 46th Regt.   Robert Lowry, Commander of a Brigade.   William F. Brantly Commanded a Brigade in Tennessee.   Douglas H. Cooper, Leader of Indian Troops.

very active campaign, Price was driven into Arkansas at the end of November by Major-Generals Rosecrans and Pleasanton, and the Army of the Missouri again became identified with the forces in the Trans-Mississippi Department.

MAJOR-GENERAL STERLING PRICE was born in Prince Edward County, Virginia, September 14, 1809. He settled in Missouri in 1830, and was a member of Congress in 1845, when he went to the Mexican War, in which he was made brigadier-general of volunteers. From 1853 to 1857, he was governor of the State, and president of the State Convention of 1853. He was made major-general of the Missouri militia in May, and assumed command of the Missouri State Guard, July 30, 1861. As major-general of the Confederate Army he commanded the Army of the West from July 2 to September 28, 1862, and later a corps of Van Dorn's Army of Mississippi. In February, 1863, he was ordered to the Trans-Mississippi Department, where he held various commands in Arkansas and elsewhere. His most noteworthy effort was the expedition into Missouri, August-December, 1864, in an attempt to gather a large number of recruits from the independent bands in that State. But Rosecrans drove him back to Arkansas. After the war he became interested in a colonization scheme in Mexico, but returned to the United States in 1866, and died in St. Louis, September 29, 1867.

Army of Mississippi

IN DECEMBER, 1863, Lieutenant-General Leonidas Polk, succeeding Pemberton, was put in command of the force of the Department of Alabama, Mississippi and East Louisiana. It had two divisions of cavalry and a strength of about twenty thousand. This is the force that contended with Major-General Sherman in Mississippi during the winter of 1864. In May, Polk joined the Army of Tennessee to oppose Sherman's advance to Atlanta, and he then denominated his troops the Army of Mississippi. Polk was killed on Pine Mountain, Georgia, June 14th, and was succeeded by Lieutenant-General A. P. Stewart. On July 26th, the Army of Mississippi was joined to the Army of Tennessee as Stewart's Corps.

LIEUTENANT-GENERAL ALEXANDER PETER STEWART (U.S.M.A. 1842) was born in Rogersville, Tennessee, October 12, 1821. He resigned from the army in 1845. He entered the Confederate service from Tennessee, rising to the rank of lieutenant-general in June, 1864, which rank was confirmed the following year. He had a brigade in Polk's command in the Western Department, and later a division in the Army of Tennessee. He was wounded at Ezra Church in the Atlanta campaign, and after Polk's death, he succeeded to the command of the Army of Mississippi, which later became a corps of the Army of Tennessee. On March 16, 1865, he was assigned to the command of the infantry and artillery in that army. He died at Biloxi, Mississippi, August 30, 1908.

MAJOR-GENERAL EDWARD CARY WALTHALL was born in Richmond, Virginia, April 4, 1831. He became a lawyer, practising in Coffeyville, Mississippi. He entered the Confederate service, in 1861, as lieutenant of the Fifteenth Mississippi Infantry, and in December, 1862, became brigadier-general, and major-general in June, 1864. He fought gallantly at Missionary Ridge and covered Hood's retreat at Nashville, where he prevented the capture of the Army of Tennessee by Thomas. In March, 1865, he had command of Stewart's Corps, Army of Tennessee, until the reorganization of April 9th, when he returned to the head of his division. After the war he became United States senator from Mississippi. He died in Washington, April 21, 1898.

Confederate Generals

MAJOR-GENERAL WILLIAM DORSEY PENDER (U. S.M.A. 1854) was born in Edgecombe County, North Carolina, February 6, 1834. He resigned from the army in March, 1861, to enter the Confederate service as colonel of the Sixth North Carolina Infantry. In June, 1862, he became brigadier-general and was made major-general in May, 1863. He was brigade and division commander in

Mark B. Lowrey Led a Brigade in Cleburne's Division in the Army of Tennessee.

Edward Cary Walthall, Conspicuous at Franklin; Later United States Senator.

Charles Clark Commanded a Division under General J. C. Breckinridge.

Samuel G. French, Leader of the Assault on Alatoona Pass in 1864.

CONFEDERATE GENERALS—

No. 13—MISSISSIPPI

William L. Brandon Commanded a Cavalry Brigade.

Nathaniel H. Harris, Colonel of the 19th Regiment.

Peter B. Stark Led a Cavalry Brigade in Forrest's Corps.

Samuel W. Ferguson Commanded a Cavalry Brigade.

George D. Johnston Led a Brigade under Bragg.

Joseph R. Davis Led a Brigade in R. E. Lee's Army.

Wirt Adams, a Conspicuous Cavalry Commander.

the Army of Northern Virginia, receiving his division on the organization of the Third Army Corps. He died in Staunton, Virginia, July 18, 1863, from wounds received upon the field of Gettysburg.

MAJOR-GENERAL STEPHEN DODSON RAMSEUR (U.S.M.A. 1860) was born in Lincolnton, North Carolina, May 31, 1837, and was assigned to the artillery at Fort Monroe. He resigned in April, 1861, to enter the Confederate service. He was made major in the North Carolina State artillery. He was present at the siege of Yorktown, and was placed at the head of a North Carolina regiment in April. He was severely wounded at Malvern Hill, but returned to the army during the winter of 1862-63, having been made brigadier-general in October. He led a brigade with great ability in the Second Army Corps at Chancellorsville and at Gettysburg. In the latter battle he was prominent in the capture of the town. The following year he was again wounded at Spotsylvania, and as major-general he succeeded to Early's division, when the latter was placed at the head of the Second Army Corps. He went to the Shenandoah valley with Early, and after taking a prominent part in all the principal engagements, he was captured, mortally wounded, at Cedar Creek on October 19, 1864.

MAJOR-GENERAL WILLIAM HENRY TALBOT WALKER (U.S.M.A. 1837) was born in Georgia in October, 1816. While serving in Florida he was thrice wounded in the battle of Okeechobee, December 25, 1837. He fought with great distinction in the Mexican War. Early in 1861, he joined the Confederate army, in which he rose to the rank of major-general in May, 1863. He had a brigade in the Second Corps, Army of the Mississippi, and later a command in the District of Georgia, under Beauregard. He was sent with a brigade to the assistance of Johnston in the latter's attempt to keep Grant from Vicksburg, in May, 1863. In August, he was given a division in Hill's Corps, Army of Tennessee, and commanded the reserves at Chickamauga, after which he was in Hardee's Corps in the Chattanooga and Atlanta campaigns until he was killed at Decatur, near Atlanta, July 22, 1864.

LIEUTENANT-GENERAL NATHAN BEDFORD FORREST was born near the site of Chapel Hill, Tennessee, July 13, 1821, and became a slave-trader at Memphis. In the summer of 1861, he joined the Tennessee mounted rifles as private, and a month later raised and equipped a force of Confederate cavalry. He escaped with his battalion from Fort Donelson, and by the middle of 1862 he had become brigadier-general and was one of the most important officers in the Confederate army. At the head of his independent cavalry organization, he was active during Bragg's invasion of Kentucky and remained there some time. He was with the Army of Tennessee at Chickamauga, and in November, 1863, was made major-general and assigned to the command of all the cavalry in western Tennessee and northern Mississippi. In March and April, 1864, he advanced from Mississippi with a large force. He captured Union City with its garrison, and attacked Paducah, Kentucky. He fought with Sooy Smith, and retreating to Fort Pillow, captured the garrison there, amid great slaughter on April 12th. He then returned to Mississippi and began to operate against Sherman's lines of communication. He defeated Sturgis, at Guntown, on June 10th, but was put to rout by A. J. Smith, at Tupelo, on July 14th. In January, 1865, he was placed in command of the District of Mississippi and East Louisiana, and on February 28th was made lieutenant-general. He was defeated at Selma, Alabama, by the Federal cavalry-leader, J. H. Wilson, and surrendered his forces with those of Lieutenant-General Richard Taylor in May. After the war he conducted several large plantations. He died in Memphis, Tennessee, October 29, 1877.

MAJOR-GENERAL DABNEY HERNDON MAURY (U.S.M.A. 1846) was born in Fredericksburg, Virginia, May 20, 1822, and served in the Mexican War with distinction. He taught at West Point, and served in the West, being assistant adjutant-general in New Mexico when the Civil War broke out. He was dismissed from the service in June, 1861, having enlisted as captain in the Confederate cavalry. He served with the forces that later became the Army of the West, and after the battle of Pea Ridge was made brigadier-general. He had a division in the Army of the West, and commanded the whole force temporarily in June, 1862. As major-general, he had a division with Pemberton's forces in the battle with Sherman at Chickasaw Bayou, December 26, 1862. In 1863, he was placed at the head of the Department of East Tennessee, and in 1864-65, he was in command of the Department of the Gulf, surrendering at Meridian, Mississippi, May 11, 1865. He was the founder of the Southern Historical Society, and from 1886 to 1889 was American minister to Colombia. He died in Peoria, Illinois, January 11, 1900.

John B. Clark Com-
manded a Cavalry
Brigade; Engaged
at Pea Ridge.

John G. Walker, a Dar-
ing Leader in the
Army of Northern
Virginia.

Joseph O. Shelby, Cav-
alry Commander in
Arkansas and Mis-
souri Battles.

M. M. Parsons Led a
Brigade in Price's
Division; Defender
of Red River.

Francis M. Cockrell, Dis-
tinguished in Missouri
Campaigns; Later
U. S. Senator.

CONFEDERATE

GENERALS—No. 14

MISSOURI

(ABOVE AND TO RIGHT)

NORTH CAROLINA

(BELOW)

John S. Marmaduke, Leader
of Cavalry West of the
Mississippi.

Daniel M. Frost Led a Brigade of State Guard
under General Price.

John S. Bowen, Conspicuous
at Port Gibson and
Vicksburg in 1863.

James G. Martin Led a
Brigade Defending Rich-
mond in 1864–5.

Robert Ransom, Jr., One of
the Defenders of Marye's
Heights in 1862.

Richard C. Gatlin, Colonel
of a Corps of Infantry,
C. S. A., in 1861.

Bryan Grimes Led a Di-
vision in the Army of
Northern Virginia.

Confederate Generals

BRIGADIER-GENERAL JOHN HUNT MORGAN was born in Huntsville, Alabama, June 1, 1826. He served in the Mexican War and joined the Confederate army in command of the Lexington Rifles, of Kentucky. He did scouting duty, and, as colonel, organized three cavalry companies known as Morgan's Squadron, which operated in Tennessee and Kentucky and fought at Shiloh. His invasion of Kentucky in July, 1862, prepared the way for Bragg. At Lexington, he routed a Union force and his frequent raids, especially the famous Christmas raid of 1862, were among the boldest Confederate exploits. His ability won him promotion to brigadier-general. In July, 1863, he made another raid into Kentucky. At Buffington Ford, about seven hundred of his men, hemmed in by Shackelton and Hobson, were forced to surrender, but Morgan escaped. At last he was captured by Shackelton at New Lisbon, July 26, 1863, but he and six fellow prisoners escaped from the Ohio State Penitentiary at Columbus, on November 27th, and joined the Confederate army in northern Georgia. In April, 1864, he was put at the head of the Department of Southwestern Virginia. Late in May, Morgan, with a few followers, went over into Kentucky, making a raid upon Lexington and dashing toward Frankfort, but Burbridge struck him a severe blow at Cynthiana, June 12th, and Morgan lost seven hundred men and one thousand horses. The early part of September found him in Greenville. While there the town was surprised and surrounded by Gillem's troops, and in attempting to escape Morgan was shot and killed September 4, 1864.

MAJOR-GENERAL LAFAYETTE McLAWS (U.S. M.A. 1842) was born in Augusta, Georgia, January 15, 1821. In March, 1861, he resigned from the army to enter the Confederate service, in which he reached the rank of major-general in May, 1862. He commanded a division in Magruder's command, Army of Northern Virginia, through the Seven Days' battle, and was then transferred to Longstreet's command, being identified as division commander with the First Army Corps through the Maryland campaign of 1862, and all the succeeding campaigns of the Army of Northern Virginia (including Chancellorsville) until September, 1863, when he went West with Longstreet and fought at Chickamauga and Knoxville. In May, 1864, he was sent to Georgia and South Carolina and being under Lieutenant-General Hardee eventually had a division in Hardee's Corps, when in February, 1865, the latter united his forces with the Army of Tennessee. After the war he

was collector of internal revenue and postmaster at Savannah, where he died, July 24, 1897.

BRIGADIER-GENERAL FELIX KIRK ZOLLICOFFER was born in Maury County, Tennessee, May 19, 1812. He became a printer and editor, interrupting the pursuit of this calling to serve in the Seminole War. In 1841, he was made associate editor of the Nashville *Banner*, was State comptroller from 1844 to 1849, and continued his political career in the State senate. He was a member of Congress from 1853 to 1859, and also a delegate to the Peace Conference held at Washington, 1861. In May of that year he was appointed major-general of the provisional army of Tennessee, and in July, after commanding an instruction camp, was made brigadier-general of the Confederate army and assigned to the District of East Tennessee. His forces were defeated by Brigadier-General Schoepf at Camp Wildcat, Kentucky, October 21st, and in an encounter with Brigadier-General Thomas at Logan's Cross Roads, or Mill Springs, Kentucky, January 19, 1862, he was killed.

MAJOR-GENERAL HENRY HETH (U.S.M.A. 1847) was born in Chesterfield County, Virginia, December 16, 1825. He rose to the rank of captain in the Tenth Infantry, from which he resigned, April 25, 1861, to enter the Confederate Army. He was made colonel of the Forty-fifth Virginia Infantry, June 17, 1861. He was commissioned brigadier-general, January 6, 1862, and major-general, May 24, 1863. After serving with his brigade in West Virginia under General Humphrey Marshall, and in the invasion of Kentucky under General Bragg, where he commanded a division of infantry and a brigade of cavalry, he came East, and commanded a division in the Gettysburg campaign. He was also in various campaigns with the Army of Northern Virginia, commanding a division in A. P. Hill's Third Army Corps. He surrendered at Appomattox, and died at Washington, D. C., September 26, 1899.

MAJOR-GENERAL JOSEPH B. KERSHAW was born at Camden, South Carolina, January 5, 1822. He was a member of the State Senate, 1852–57. He entered the Confederate service and was soon made colonel of the Second South Carolina regiment, and on February 15, 1862, he was appointed a brigadier-general. In that capacity he served on the Peninsula and in the Seven Days' battle. He also fought at Antietam, Fred-

Alfred M. Scales Led a North Carolina Brigade in Hill's Corps.

William P. Roberts Led a Brigade of Cavalry in Virginia.

John D. Barry, Colonel of the 18th North Carolina Regiment.

William McRae Led a North Carolina Brigade in Lee's Army.

William R. Cox Led a North Carolina Brigade in Ewell's Corps.

CONFED–
ERATE
GENERALS

No. 15

NORTH

CAROLINA

R. Leventhorpe, Defender of Fort Fisher.

Lawrence S. Baker, Colonel of the 1st Cavalry.

Thomas F. Toon Led a North Carolina Brigade in Lee's Army.

John R. Cooke, Engaged in Repelling Burnside at Fredericksburg.

Rufus Barringer Led a Brigade of Cavalry in Virginia.

Thomas L. Clingman Led a North Carolina Brigade in Lee's Army.

ericksburg, and Gettysburg, and with General Longstreet's Corps. He was engaged at the battle of Chickamauga, commanding a brigade in McLaws' Division of the Left Wing. Returning to the East he was prominent in the Wilderness campaign, and in the Shenandoah he was with Ewell's Corps at Sailors' Creek, when his command was captured on April 6, 1865, and he was released from Fort Warren, Mass., July 24, of the same year. He was elected President of the State Senate and later became a judge of the Circuit Court of South Carolina. General Kershaw died at Camden, South Carolina, April 13, 1894.

MAJOR-GENERAL CHARLES WILLIAM FIELD (U.S.M.A. 1849) was born in Woodford County, Kentucky, in 1818. He served in the Second Dragoons until May, 1861, when he resigned to enter the Confederate service, and was appointed brigadier-general on March 14, 1862. On February 12, 1864, he was appointed major-general. He served at Gaines' Mill, the Second Bull Run, the Wilderness, Spotsylvania, Drewry's Bluff, and in the campaign around Petersburg; being in command of Field's Division of the First Army Corps. General Field died in Washington, D. C., April 9, 1892.

MAJOR-GENERAL CADMUS MARCELLUS WILCOX (U.S.M.A. 1846) was born in Wayne County, North Carolina, May 29, 1826. He served with distinguished bravery in the Mexican War and was brevetted for gallantry and meritorious conduct at Chapultepec, acting as assistant instructor at West Point (1852–57) and becoming a Captain in 1860. On June 8, 1861, he resigned to enter the Confederate service. He was made a brigadier-general October 21, 1861, and served at Seven Pines, the Second Bull Run, and in the Antietam campaign; his name being associated with a brigade that achieved notable reputation during the war. It was composed of the Eighth, Ninth, Tenth, and Eleventh Alabama regiments and Thomas' Artillery, and was in Longstreet's division of the Army of Northern Virginia. It made a striking record in the Seven Days' battles, where it sustained a loss of 1055, or 57 per cent. of its entire number. Later this brigade was in General R. H. Anderson's division, to the command of which General Wilcox succeeded. He also participated at the battle of Gettysburg and served through a number of campaigns in the Army of Northern Virginia until the final surrender at Ap-

pomattox. He was appointed a major-general in 1863. From 1886 until his death, on December 2, 1890, he was chief of the Railroad Division of the General Land Office at Washington, D. C. He wrote a "History of the Mexican War," which is regarded as the standard military work on the subject.

MAJOR-GENERAL ROBERT E. RODES was born at Lynchburg, Virginia, March 29, 1829. He was graduated at the Virginia Military Institute at Lexington in 1848, and was a professor there until appointed captain of the Mobile Cadets early in 1861. He was made colonel of the Fifth Alabama and in October, 1861, was appointed brigadier-general. He served at the First Battle of Bull Run and at the battles of Seven Pines and Gaines' Mills, and distinguished himself in command of Rodes' Brigade, which was composed of Alabama troops in Hill's Division of Jackson's Corps, Army of Northern Virginia. On May 7, 1863, General Rodes was appointed major-general and he commanded a division at Chancellorsville and Gettysburg in Ewell's Second Corps of the Army of Northern Virginia. He also participated in the Wilderness campaign and in the operations in the Shenandoah valley, where he was killed in action at Winchester, September 19, 1864.

MAJOR-GENERAL GEORGE EDWARD PICKETT (U.S.M.A. 1846) was born at Richmond, Virginia, June 28, 1828. He served in the Mexican War, receiving the brevet of first lieutenant for gallant service at Contreras and Churubusco, and also the brevet of lieutenant for distinguished service at Chapultepec. He served with the regular army in the Territory of Washington, and at various posts in the West until June 25, 1861, when he resigned. He was appointed a colonel in the Confederate army, on July 23, and on January 14, 1862, he was appointed as brigadier-general. He served in command of a brigade in Longstreet's division of General Joseph E. Johnston's Army, and on October 11 he was made major-general, commanding a division in the Army of Northern Virginia. General Pickett made a memorable charge against the Federal front at Cemetery Hill on the third day of Gettysburg, his division having reached the field on that day. In September, 1863, General Pickett commanded the Department of North Carolina and operated against Drewry's Bluff in the following year, after his return to Virginia. He was defeated at Lynchburg in an attempt to

James H. Trapier, Commander at Fort Moultrie and Sullivan's Island.

Benjamin Huger, Commander of a Division at Seven Pines.

William H. Wallace, Originally Colonel of the 18th Regiment.

CONFEDERATE

GENERALS

No. 16

SOUTH CAROLINA

Milledge L. Bonham Became Governor of South Carolina.

Thomas F. Drayton Commanded a Military District in South Carolina.

James Chestnut, Aide to Beauregard at Fort Sumter.

Johnson Hagood, Defender of Richmond and Petersburg.

Arthur M. Manigault, Colonel 10th Regiment.

oppose Sheridan's cavalry in March, 1865, and also at Dinwiddie Court House and Five Forks. He surrendered with the Army of Northern Virginia and at the conclusion of the war he settled in Richmond, where he died in 1875.

MAJOR-GENERAL WILLIAM HENRY FITZHUGH LEE was born at Arlington, Virginia, May 31, 1837, the second son of General Robert E. Lee. For two years he served as second lieutenant with the Sixth U. S. Infantry, resigning in May, 1859. At the outbreak of the Civil War he entered the Confederate Army in a Virginia cavalry regiment, was made a brigadier-general to rank from September 15, 1862, being promoted to major-general, April 23, 1864. During the Peninsula campaign General Lee, then colonel commanding the Ninth Virginia Cavalry, participated in Stuart's ride around McClellan's army. In the Chancellorsville campaign General Lee was in command of a body of cavalry which fought with the Union Cavalry of General Stoneman under the immediate command of General Averell. General Lee's brigade also participated in the Gettysburg campaign, forming one of the six brigades commanded by Major-General J. E. B. Stuart. General Lee with his cavalry opposed the advances of General Sheridan in his Trevilian raid when Wilson was sent out to cut the Weldon and South Side Road; and at the Petersburg campaign his cavalry participated actively, making many valiant assaults on the Federal lines. Before the surrender of Appomattox, General Lee with his cavalry aided General Gordon in keeping back the Union advances and protecting the wagon-trains of the Confederate army. He was paroled at Appomattox Court House, April 9, 1865, and died at Ravensworth, Fairfax County, Virginia, October 15, 1891.

MAJOR-GENERAL GEORGE WASHINGTON CUSTIS LEE (U.S.M.A. 1854) was born at Fortress Monroe, Virginia, September 16, 1832, and was the eldest son of General Robert E. Lee. Upon graduation from the United States Military Academy he joined the corps of engineers, in which he served until May 2, 1861, when he resigned to enter the Confederate Army. The greater part of his service was as aide to President Jefferson Davis. He was appointed major-general serving with the volunteer troops with temporary rank on February 7, 1865, the commission dating from October 20, 1864. On the same date he was also made full major-general. He was captured at Sailor's Creek, April 6, 1865, and was paroled six days later, which parole was extended until April 23, 1865.

In addition to serving as aide to President Davis, General Lee was in command of military forces in the city of Richmond. In the latter part of the war he commanded a division of Ewell's corps, and it was at this time that his division was captured along with that of General Kershaw. After the war he became professor of civil engineering at the Virginia Military Institute, and in 1871 he succeeded his father,—General Robert E. Lee,—as president of the Washington & Lee University. This position he held until 1897, when he became president emeritus.

MAJOR-GENERAL MATTHEW CALBRAITH BUTLER was born near Greenville, South Carolina, March 8, 1836. He was admitted to the South Carolina bar in 1856, and in addition to practising law was elected to the State legislature in 1859. At the outbreak of the Civil War he entered the Confederate Army as captain, and rose to the command of the Second South Carolina Cavalry, which fought a notable action at Brandy Station on June 10, 1863, in which Colonel Butler lost his right leg. He was appointed brigadier-general, September 2, 1863. In the following year General Butler had command of a brigade consisting of the Fourth, Fifth, and Sixth South Carolina Cavalry, which was included in General Wade Hampton's division and operated with the Army of Northern Virginia. General Butler participated in the battle of Trevilian Station on June 12, 1864, commanding General Hampton's division, where he was engaged with the cavalry of General Sheridan, and later broke through General J. H. Wilson's lines. General Butler was sent to resist the onward march of Sherman through North Carolina, and he participated in the battle of Bentonville. He had previously, December 7, 1864, been appointed major-general. After the surrender at Greensboro, General Butler was paroled, May 1, 1865. Entering politics again after the war, General Butler met with rapid advancement, and was United States Senator from South Carolina from 1877 to 1889. At the outbreak of the Spanish War he was made a major-general of volunteers, May 28, 1898, and served until honorably discharged, April 15, 1899. He was a member of the commission appointed by President McKinley to arrange for the evacuation of Cuba by the Spaniards. General Butler died at Columbus, S. C., April 14, 1909.

MAJOR-GENERAL WILLIAM MAHONE was born at Monroe, Southampton County, Virginia, December 1, 1826. Graduating from the Virginia Military Institute in 1847, he followed the profes-

John Bratton Led a Brigade in Long-street's Corps.

Thomas M. Logan Led a Cavalry Brigade in Lee's Army.

Nathan G. Evans, Commander of a District on the Atlantic Coast.

CONFEDERATE

GENERALS

No. 17

SOUTH CAROLINA

Martin W. Gary, Originally Colonel in Hampton's Legion.

James Connor Commanded a Brigade in Lee's Army.

Ellison Capers Led a Brigade in the Army of Tennessee.

John D. Kennedy Led a Brigade in Longstreet's Corps.

John S. Preston, Chief of the Bureau of Conscription.

sion of civil engineering until the outbreak of the Civil War, when he entered the Confederate Army. He participated in the capture of the Norfolk Navy Yard by the Virginia volunteers, raised and commanded the Sixth Virginia regiment and on November 16, 1861, he was appointed brigadier-general in the Confederate Army in March, 1864. In the battle of Seven Pines, General Mahone commanded a brigade in Huger's Division, while at Malvern Hill also his troops were engaged. General Mahone also fought in the Chancellorsville and Gettysburg campaigns, as well as in the Wilderness. At the North Anna on May 24th, General Mahone made a desperate attack on Warren's Corps, driving it back. On August 3, 1864, General Mahone was promoted to be major-general. He was active in the brilliant repulse of the Federal attack after the explosion of the mine at Petersburg and in the various operations about the Weldon Railroad. General Mahone was present at the last struggles of the war, and was paroled at Appomattox Court House, April 9, 1865. After the war he was made president of the Norfolk and Tennessee Railroad and became a leading figure in Virginia politics, being elected to the United States Senate in 1880, where he acted with the Republican party. He failed of re-election on the expiration of his term in 1887, and died at Washington, D. C., October 9, 1893.

VIII

THE ORGANIZATIONS
OF THE
VETERANS

THE GERM OF THE "G. A. R." IDEA

William W. Silkworth, of Long Branch, New Jersey, a veteran who had an opportunity to inspect some of the pictures reproduced in the Photographic History, recognized this group as Company B, 170th Regiment, New York Volunteers. "You cannot appreciate or understand fully my amazement and joy in the discovery," he wrote to the editors. "There right in the front of the picture sits my brother playing cards (You will note that he is left handed. We laid him away in front of Petersburg). With him is John Vandewater, Geo. Thomas and Wash. Keating. There is Charlie Thomas and all the rest as true as life. With the exception of two, I have not seen any of the boys for thirty years." It was at such moments as this, when the Federal soldiers played games and chatted and became

UNION RESERVES ON PICKET DUTY

acquainted, that the organization was being evolved which has grown into a leading national institution since its formation at Decatur, Illinois, on April 6, 1866.   Between the men who had fought and marched and suffered together, who time out of mind had shared their last crust and saved each others' lives, who had nursed each other and cheered each other on when another step forward seemed to mean certain death, there arose a great love that extended to the widows and orphans of those whose dying words they had heard on the field of battle.   Ever since that time the organization has lent assistance to those reduced to need by the inexorable war.   It admits to membership any soldier or sailor of the United States Army, Navy or Marine Corps, who served between April 12, 1861, and April 9, 1865.

The Grand Army of the Republic

By John E. Gilman, Commander-in-Chief, Grand Army of the Republic

AT the close of the Civil War, there were over a million men in the Union armies. Nearly two and a half million had served under the Stars and Stripes during the four long years of warfare, of whom three hundred and fifty-nine thousand had died. It was essential that those still in the service should disband and retire to civilian life. This was effected after a grand parade of the armies of the Potomac, the Tennessee, and of Georgia, on May 23 and 24, 1865, when one hundred and fifty thousand men marched through the wide avenues of Washington in review before the President and the commanding generals. From the glare and glory, the power and prestige of the soldier's career, they went into the obscurity of the peaceful pursuits of American citizenship, and in a few short months the vast armies of the United States had disappeared.

The great war was ended, but it would have been strange indeed if the memories of those years of storm and stress, the sacrifices of those who had fallen, the experiences of the march, the battlefield, and the camp, and the needs of their disabled comrades, and of the widows and the orphans had been forgotten.

Even before the war had ended, organizations of veterans of the Union armies had begun to be formed. The first veteran society formed, The Third Army Corps Union, was organized at the headquarters of General D. B. Birney, commander of the Third Army Corps, at a meeting of the officers of the corps, September 2, 1863. The main object, at that time, was to secure funds for embalming and sending home for burial the bodies of officers killed in battle or dying in hospitals at the front. General D. E. Sickles was its first president.

In April, 1865, the Society of the Army of the Tennessee was formed at Raleigh, North Carolina, membership being restricted to officers who had served with the old Army of the Tennessee. The object was declared to be " to keep alive that kindly and cordial feeling which has been one of the characteristics of this army during its career in the service." General Sherman was elected president in 1869, and continued to hold the office for many years.

After the war, many other veteran societies were formed, composed not only of officers but of enlisted men of the various armies, corps, and regiments, as well as many naval organizations. Among them, the Military Order of the Loyal Legion of the United States was the first society formed by officers honorably discharged from the service. It was first thought of at a meeting of a group of officers who had met the day after the assassination of President Lincoln for the purpose of passing resolutions on his death. These resolutions were subsequently adopted, and it was determined to effect a permanent organization. This was done May 3, 1865, and a constitution and by-laws were, in part, adopted the same month. The titles of officers, the constitution, and general plan, were, in part, afterward adopted by the Grand Army of the Republic. The essential difference was that first-class membership of the Loyal Legion was restricted to officers.

Besides the foregoing organizations of veterans, there were others formed of a political nature, such as the Boys in Blue and other similar societies, and there were held in September, 1866, two political conventions of veterans of the army and navy. These political soldiers' clubs were the result of the times, for the controversy between Congress and President Johnson was at its height. In the East, after the fall elections of 1866, most of these political clubs of veterans were ready to disband. The desire for a permanent organization of veterans became strong. No post of the Grand Army had been organized east of Ohio prior to October, 1866. Posts were started, and inasmuch as eligibility to membership in the Grand Army was possessed by those who composed the membership of these political clubs, the Boys in Blue and similar clubs formed, in many places, the nucleus of the Grand Army posts.

This fact gave, in good part, a political tinge to the Grand Army during the first year or two of its existence, and to it was due, chiefly, the severe losses in membership that the order sustained for a short period. But, eventually, the political character was wholly eradicated, and the order recovered its standing and its losses.

During the winter of 1865–66, Major B. F. Stephenson, surgeon of the Fourteenth Illinois regiment, discussed with friends the matter of the

Galusha Pennypacker, Colonel of the 97th Regiment.

Joshua T. Owens, Colonel of the 69th Regiment.

James A. Beaver, Colonel of the 148th Regiment.

Isaac J. Wistar, Originally Colonel of the 71st Reg't.

FEDERAL GENERALS

No. 23

PENNSYLVANIA

Joshua K. Sigfried, Originally Colonel of the 48th Regiment.

David H. Williams, Originally Colonel of the 82d Infantry.

John B. McIntosh, Originally Colonel of the 3d Cavalry.

Frederick S. Stumbaugh, Originally Colonel of the 2d Infantry.

Thomas J. McKean Led a Division at Corinth.

Montgomery C. Meigs, Quartermaster-General of the Army.

formation of an organization of veteran soldiers. He had, previously, while the war was still continuing, talked over the formation of such an organization with his tent-mate, Chaplain William J. Rutledge of the same regiment, and both had agreed to undertake the work of starting such a project after the war was ended, if they survived.

At the national encampment in St. Louis, in 1887, it was stated by Fred. J. Dean, of Fort Scott, Arkansas, that in February, 1866, he, with Doctors Hamilton and George H. Allen, assisted Doctor Stephenson in compiling ritualistic work, constitution, and by-laws at Springfield, Illinois, and these four assumed the obligations of the Grand Army of the Republic at that time. It is conceded that the initiatory steps to constitute the order were taken in Illinois, and Doctor Stephenson's name is the first one connected with the systematic organization of the Grand Army. He and his co-workers were obligated in the work. Several other veterans joined with them, and a ritual was prepared.

The question of printing this ritual occasioned some anxiety on account of the desire to keep it secret, but this difficulty was solved by having it printed at the office of the Decatur (Illinois) *Tribune*, the proprietor of which, together with his compositors, were veterans. They were accordingly obligated, and the ritual was printed by them. Captain John S. Phelps, one of the active associates of Doctor Stephenson, who had gone to Decatur to supervise the work of printing the ritual, had met several of his comrades of the Forty-first Illinois and had sought their cooperation. One of them, Doctor J. W. Routh, who was acquainted with Doctor Stephenson, went to Springfield to consult the latter about organizing, and, with Captain M. F. Kanan, called upon Doctor Stephenson. They returned to Decatur to organize a post there, and at once set to work and secured a sufficient number of signatures to an application for a charter. They returned to Springfield to present the application in person. On April 6, 1866, Doctor Stephenson issued the charter, signing it as department commander of Illinois, thus creating the first post of the Grand Army of the Republic. The ritual was revised and a constitution written by a committee from this post, at the suggestion of Doctor Stephenson. The committee reported that the regulations and ritual had been presented to department headquarters and accepted. The plan of organization consisted of post, district, department, and national organizations, to be known as the Grand Army of the Republic.

The declaration of principles in the constitution, written by Adjutant-General Robert M. Woods, set forth that the soldiers of the volunteer army of the United States, during the war of 1861–65, actuated by patriotism and combined in fellowship, felt called upon to declare those principles and rules which should guide the patriotic freeman and Christian citizen, and to agree upon plans and laws which should govern them in a united and systematic working method to effect the preservation of the grand results of the war. These results included the preservation of fraternal feelings, the making of these ties advantageous to those in need of assistance, the providing for the support, care, and education of soldiers' orphans, and maintenance of their widows, the protection and assistance of disabled soldiers, and the " establishment and defense of the late soldiery of the United States, morally, socially, and politically, with a view to inculcate a proper appreciation of their services to the country, and to a recognition of such services and claims by the American people."

To this last section, the national encampment in Philadelphia, in 1868, added, " But this association does not design to make nominations for office or to use its influence as a secret organization for partisan purposes." The word " sailors " was added by the Indianapolis encampment. In May, 1869, the present form of rules and regulations was adopted.

Post No. 2 of the Department of Illinois was organized at Springfield, as stated by General Webber, in April, 1866.

In 1865, in Indiana, correspondence relating to the continuance of the Army Club, a society of veterans, had come to the hands of Governor Oliver P. Morton, of Indiana. He sent General R. S. Foster, of Indianapolis, to Springfield, to examine into Doctor Stephenson's plan of organization. General Foster met the latter, and was obligated by him. On his return, he obligated a number of his intimate comrades, and these he constituted as a department organization. The first post of this department was organized at Indianapolis, on the 22d of August, 1866.

Doctor Stephenson had issued, as department commander, General Orders No. 1, on April 1, 1866, at Springfield, in which he announced the following officers: General Jules C. Webber, aide-de-camp and chief of staff; Major Robert M. Woods, adjutant-general; Colonel John M. Snyder, quartermaster-general; Captain John S. Phelps, aide-de-camp, and Captain John A. Lightfoot, assistant adjutant-general, on duty at the de-

Charles T. Campbell, Originally
Colonel of the 1st Regiment
of Artillery.

Thomas R. Rowley, Originally Colonel of the 102d Regiment.

James Nagle, Originally Colonel of
the 48th Regiment.

FEDERAL GENERALS–
No. 24

PENNSYLVANIA
(CONTINUED)

Alexander Schimmelpfennig, Originally
Colonel of the 14th Infantry.

George A. McCall, Commander of the
Pennsylvania Reserves in
the Seven Days.

Albert L. Lee Led a Cavalry
Column in the Red River
Campaign.

Joshua B. Howell, Originally
Colonel of the 85th
Regiment.

partment headquarters. On June 26, 1866, a call had been issued for a convention, to be held at Springfield, Illinois, July 12, 1866. The convention was held on this date and the Department of Illinois organized, General John M. Palmer being elected department commander. Doctor Stephenson was recognized, however, in the adoption of a resolution which proclaimed him as " the head and front of the organization." He continued to act as commander-in-chief.

In October, 1866, departments had been formed in Illinois, Wisconsin, Indiana, Iowa, and Minnesota, and posts had been organized in Ohio, Missouri, Kentucky, Arkansas, District of Columbia, Massachusetts, New York, and Pennsylvania. On October 31, 1866, Doctor Stephenson issued General Orders No. 13, directing a national convention to be held at Indianapolis, November 20, 1866, signing this order as commander-in-chief. In accordance with this order, the First National Encampment of the Grand Army of the Republic convened at Indianapolis on the date appointed, and was called to order by Commander-in-Chief Stephenson. A committee on permanent organization was appointed and its report nominating the officers of the convention was adopted, and General John M. Palmer became the presiding officer of the convention. The committee on constitution submitted a revised form of the constitution which, with a few amendments, was adopted. Resolutions were adopted calling the attention of Congress to the laws in regard to bounties, recommending the passage of a law making it obligatory for every citizen to give actual service when called upon in time of war, instead of providing a substitute, and suggesting, for the consideration of those in authority, the bestowal of positions of honor and profit upon worthy and competent soldiers and sailors. General S. A. Hurlbut, of Illinois, was elected commander-in-chief and Doctor Stephenson, adjutant-general.

The national organization of the Grand Army of the Republic was thus fairly started. The Second National Encampment was held at Philadelphia, January 15, 16, and 17, 1868, when General John A. Logan was elected commander-in-chief. At the Third National Encampment at Cincinnati, May 12 and 13, 1869, General Logan was reelected commander-in-chief. It appears from Adjutant-General Chipman's report at this encampment that, at the Philadelphia encampment in 1868, there were represented twenty-one departments, which claimed a total membership of over two hundred thousand. But there had been very few records kept, either in departments or at national headquarters, and there seems to have been very little communication between posts and headquarters. At the Cincinnati encampment, the adjutant-general reported that the aggregate number of departments was thirty-seven, and that the number of posts, reported and estimated, was 2050. At the encampment at Cincinnati, in 1869, the grade system of membership was adopted, establishing three grades of recruit, soldier, and veteran. This system met with serious opposition and was finally abandoned at the encampment at Boston, in 1871. It was claimed that to this system much of the great falling-off in membership was due. It is a fact that, at this period, there had been a large decrease in the numbers in the order, particularly in the West. But the cause of this may be laid to a variety of reasons. The order, at first, seems to have had a rapid growth. Because of the incompleteness of the records, it is impossible even to estimate what the strength of the membership in those early days was. But the real solidity of the order was not established until some years had passed.

On May 5, 1868, Commander-in-Chief Logan, by General Orders No. 11, had assigned May 30, 1868, as a memorial day which was to be devoted to the strewing of flowers on the graves of deceased comrades who had died in the defense of their country during the Civil War. The idea of Memorial Day had been suggested to Adjutant-General Chipman in a letter from some comrade then living in Cincinnati, whose name has been lost. At the encampment at Washington, in 1870, Memorial Day was established by an amendment to the rules and regulations. It has been made a holiday in many of the States, and is now observed throughout the country, not only by the Grand Army but by the people generally, for the decoration of the graves of the soldiers.

The first badge of the order was adopted in 1866. A change was made in October, 1868, in its design, and a further change in October, 1869. At the national encampment of 1873, the badge was adopted which is substantially the one that exists to-day, a few minor changes being made in 1886. It is now made from captured cannon purchased from the Government. The bronze button worn on the lapel of the coat was adopted in 1884.

The matter of pensions has, in the nature of things, occupied much of the time of the Grand Army encampments, both national and departmental. The order has kept careful watch over pension legislation; its recommendations have been conservative, and of late years have been adopted by Congress to a very great extent. Aid

William A. Quarles, Wounded in
Hood's Charge at Franklin.

George G. Dibrell, Leader of Cavalry
Opposing Sherman's March.

Alfred E. Jackson Commanded a
District of East Tennessee.

CONFEDERATE

GENERALS

No. 18

TENNESSEE

George Maney, Active Organizer and
Leader of Tennessee.

Bushrod R. Johnson, Conspicuous
in the West and in the East.

John P. McCown; At Belmont, in 1861.
Later Led a Division.

John C. Brown Led a Division in the
Army of Tennessee.

William H. Jackson Led a Brigade
of Forrest's Cavalry.

has been given to veterans and widows entitled to pensions, by cooperation with the Pension Office in obtaining and furnishing information for the adjudication of claims.

The Grand Army has been assisted in carrying out its purposes by its allied orders, the Woman's Relief Corps, the Sons of Veterans, the Daughters of Veterans, and the Ladies of the G. A. R. These organizations have adopted the principles and purposes that have actuated the Grand Army and have given much valued aid in the achievement of the results obtained.

The Grand Army of the Republic before the end of the nineteenth century had passed the zenith of its career. Its membership remained about the same in numbers after its first great leap and subsequent subsidence, varying between 25,000 and 50,000 from 1870 to 1880. During the decade between 1880 and 1890 it rose to its highest number of 409,-489. Since then it has decreased, through death, in very great part, until, at the national encampment of 1910, at Atlantic City, it had diminished to 213,901. Its posts exist throughout the length and breadth of the country, and even outside, and nearly every State has a department organization. Its influence is felt in every city, town, and village, and it has earned the good-will and support of the entire American people. Among its leaders have been some of the most prominent men of the country. Its commanders-in-chief have been:

B. F. Stephenson,	Illinois,	1866
S. A. Hurlbut,	Illinois,	1866-67
John A. Logan,	Illinois,	1868-70
Ambrose E. Burnside,	Rhode Island,	1871-72
Charles Devens,	Massachusetts,	1873-74
John F. Hartranft,	Pennsylvania,	1875-76
John C. Robinson,	New York,	1877-78
William Earnshaw,	Ohio,	1879
Louis Wagner,	Pennsylvania,	1880
George S. Merrill,	Massachusetts,	1881
Paul Van Dervoort,	Nebraska,	1882
Robert B. Beath,	Pennsylvania,	1883
John S. Kountz,	Ohio,	1884
S. S. Burdett,	Dist. of Columbia,	1885
Lucius Fairchild,	Wisconsin,	1886
John P. Rea,	Minnesota,	1887
William Warner,	Missouri,	1888
Russell A. Alger,	Michigan,	1889
Wheelock G. Veazey,	Vermont,	1890
John Palmer,	New York,	1891
A. G. Weissert,	Wisconsin,	1892
John G. B. Adams,	Massachusetts,	1893
Thomas G. Lawler,	Illinois,	1894
Ivan N. Walker,	Indiana,	1895
T. S. Clarkson,	Nebraska,	1896
John P. S. Gobin,	Pennsylvania,	1897
James A. Sexton,	Illinois,	1898
W. C. Johnson,	Ohio,	1899
Albert D. Shaw,	New York,	1899
Leo Rassieur,	Missouri,	1900
Ell Torrence,	Minnesota,	1901
Thomas J. Stewart,	Pennsylvania,	1902
John C. Black,	Illinois,	1903
Wilmon W. Blackmar,	Massachusetts,	1904
John R. King,	Maryland,	1904
James Tanner,	Dist. of Columbia,	1905
Robert B. Brown,	Ohio,	1906
Charles G. Burton,	Missouri,	1907
Henry M. Nevius,	New Jersey,	1908
Samuel R. Van Sant,	Minnesota,	1909
John E. Gilman,	Massachusetts,	1910
Hiram M. Trimble,	Illinois,	1911

The United Confederate Veterans

By S. A. Cunningham, Late Sergeant-Major, Confederate States Army, and Founder and Editor of "The Confederate Veteran"

THE organization known as the United Confederate Veterans was formed in New Orleans, June 10, 1889. The inception of the idea for a large and united association is credited to Colonel J. F. Shipp, a gallant Confederate, commander of N. B. Forrest Camp, of Chattanooga, Tennessee—the third organized—who was in successful business for years with a Union veteran. Colonel Shipp had gone to New Orleans in the interest of the Chattanooga and Chickamauga Military Park, and there proposed a general organization of Confederates on the order of the Grand Army of the Republic, his idea being to bring into a general association the State organizations, one of which in Virginia, and another in Tennessee, had already been organized.

Following these suggestions, a circular was sent out from New Orleans in regard to the proposed organization, and the first meeting was held in that city on June 10, 1889, the organization being

ROBERT V. RICHARDSON
Commanded a Tennessee
Brigade.

SAMUEL R. ANDERSON
Commander of a Tennessee
Brigade.

BENJAMIN J. HILL
Provost-Marshal-General Army
of Tennessee.

JAMES A. SMITH
Led a Brigade in Cleburne's
Division.

ROBERT C. TYLER
Commander of the Garrison at West
Point, Georgia.

THOMAS B. SMITH
Led a Brigade in the Army of
Tennessee.

WILLIAM Y. C. HUMES
Commanded a Division of Wheeler's
Cavalry.

CONFEDERATE
GENERALS
No. 19
TENNESSEE

LUCIUS M. WALKER
Led a Calvary Brigade in the Army of the West.

ALEXANDER W. CAMPBELL
Led a Brigade of Forrest's Cavalry.

perfected under the name of United Confederate Veterans, with F. S. Washington, of New Orleans, as president, and J. A. Chalaron, secretary. A constitution was adopted, and Lieutenant-General John B. Gordon, of Georgia, was elected general and commander-in-chief. At this meeting there were representatives from the different Confederate organizations already in existence in the States of Louisiana, Mississippi and Tennessee.

While giving Colonel Shipp credit for suggesting the general organization of the United Confederate Veterans, the important part played by the Louisiana camps in furthering the association must be emphasized. The previously existing organizations became the first numbers in the larger association. The Army of Northern Virginia, of New Orleans, became Camp No. 1; Army of Tennessee, New Orleans, No. 2; and LeRoy Stafford Camp, Shreveport, No. 3. The N. B. Forrest Camp, of Chattanooga, Tennessee, became No. 4; while Fred. Ault Camp, of Knoxville, is No. 5. There are other camps, not among the first in the list, which are among the most prominent in the organization. For instance, Tennessee had an organization of bivouacs, the first and largest of which was Frank Cheatham, No. 1, of Nashville, but which is Camp No. 35, U. C. V. Then, Richmond, Virginia, had its R. E. Lee Camp, which has ever been of the most prominent, and was the leader in a great soldiers' home movement. In the U. C. V. camp-list, the R. E. Lee, of Richmond, is No. 181. The camps increased to a maximum of more than fifteen hundred, but with the passage of years many have ceased to be active.

While the organization was perfected in New Orleans, the first reunion of United Confederate Veterans was held in Chattanooga, Tennessee, July 3 to 5, 1890. To this reunion invitations were extended "to veterans of both armies and to citizens of the Republic," and the dates purposely included Independence Day.

The first comment both in the North and South was, "Why keep up the strife or the memory of it?" but it was realized that such utterances were from those who did not comprehend the scope of the organization of United Confederate Veterans, which, from the very outset, was clear in the minds of its founders. It was created on high lines, and its first commander was the gallant soldier, General John B. Gordon, at the time governor of Georgia, and later was United States senator. General Gordon was continued as commander-in-chief until his death.

The nature and object of the organization can-

not be explained better than by quoting from its constitution.

The first article declares:

"The object and purpose of this organization will be strictly social, literary, historical, and benevolent. It will endeavor to unite in a general federation all associations of the Confederate veterans, soldiers and sailors, now in existence or hereafter to be formed; to gather authentic data for an impartial history of the War between the States; to preserve the relics or memories of the same; to cherish the ties of friendship that exist among the men who have shared common dangers, common suffering and privations; to care for the disabled and extend a helping hand to the needy; to protect the widow and orphan, and to make and preserve the record of the services of every member and, as far as possible, of those of our comrades who have preceded us in eternity."

Likewise, the last article provides that neither discussion of political or religious subjects nor any political action shall be permitted in the organization, and that any association violating that provision shall forfeit its membership.

The notes thus struck in the constitution of the United Confederate Veterans were reechoed in the opening speech of the first commander-in-chief. General Gordon, addressing the Veterans and the public, said:

"Comrades, no argument is needed to secure for those objects your enthusiastic endorsement. They have burdened your thoughts for many years. You have cherished them in sorrow, poverty, and humiliation. In the face of misconstruction, you have held them in your hearts with the strength of religious convictions. No misjudgments can defeat your peaceful purposes for the future. Your aspirations have been lifted by the mere force and urgency of surrounding conditions to a plane far above the paltry consideration of partisan triumphs. The honor of the American Government, the just powers of the Federal Government, the equal rights of States, the integrity of the Constitutional Union, the sanctions of law, and the enforcement of order have no class of defenders more true and devoted than the ex-soldiers of the South and their worthy descendants. But you realize the great truth that a people without the memories of heroic suffering or sacrifice are a people without a history.

"To cherish such memories and recall such a past, whether crowned with success or consecrated in defeat, is to idealize principle and strengthen character, intensify love of country, and convert defeat and disaster into pillars of support for

Gideon J. Pillow, Opponent of Grant
in Grant's First Battle—Belmont.

William H. Carroll
Led a Brigade in
East Tennessee.

John C. Carter, Orig-
inally Colonel of the
38th Regiment.

John C. Vaughn, Com-
mander of a Cav-
alry Brigade.

George W. Gordon
Led a Brigade in
Army of Tennessee.

Alfred J. Vaughan Led
a Brigade in Gen-
eral Polk's Corps.

Henry B. Davidson
Led a Brigade of
Wheeler's Cavalry.

CONFEDERATE GENERALS

No. 20—TENNESSEE

Tyree H. Bell Led a Cavalry Command under Forrest.

William McComb Led a Brigade
in R. E. Lee's Army.

Joseph B. Palmer Led a Brigade in
General Polk's Corps.

future manhood and noble womanhood. Whether the Southern people, under their changed conditions, may ever hope to witness another civilization which shall equal that which began with their Washington and ended with their Lee, it is certainly true that devotion to their glorious past is not only the surest guarantee of future progress and the holiest bond of unity, but is also the strongest claim they can present to the confidence and respect of the other sections of the Union."

Referring to the new organization, General Gordon said:

" It is political in no sense, except so far as the word ' political ' is a synonym of the word ' patriotic.' It is a brotherhood over which the genius of philanthropy and patriotism, of truth and justice will preside; of philanthropy, because it will succor the disabled, help the needy, strengthen the weak, and cheer the disconsolate; of patriotism, because it will cherish the past glories of the dead Confederacy and transmute them into living inspirations for future service to the living Republic; of truth, because it will seek to gather and preserve, as witnesses for history, the unimpeachable facts which shall doom falsehood to die that truth may live; of justice, because it will cultivate national as well as Southern fraternity, and will condemn narrow-mindedness and prejudice and passion, and cultivate that broader and higher and nobler sentiment which would write on the grave of every soldier who fell on our side, ' Here lies an American hero, a martyr to the right as his conscience conceived it.' "

The reunions, thus happily inaugurated, became at once popular and have been held every year except the first appointment at Birmingham, Alabama, which was postponed from 1893 to 1894. No event in the South is comparable in widespread interest to these reunions. Only the large cities have been able to entertain the visitors, which range in number between fifty thousand and one hundred thousand.

The greatest of all gatherings was at Richmond, Virginia, June 30, 1907, when the superb monument to the only President of the Confederacy was unveiled. There were probably a hundred thousand people at the dedication. An idea of the magnitude of these reunion conventions and the interest in them may be had by reference to that held in Little Rock, Arkansas, in May, 1911, a city of a little more than thirty thousand inhabitants, wherein over a hundred thousand visitors were entertained during the three days.

No finer evidences of genuine patriotism can be found than in the proceedings of these conventions. In fact, there are no more faithful patriots. The Gray line of 1911 is not yet so thin as the press contributions make it. True, the veterans are growing feeble, but the joy of meeting comrades with whom they served in camp and battle for four years—many of whom had not seen one another in the interim—is insuppressible. It is not given to men in this life to become more attached to each other than are the Confederates. They had no pay-roll to look to, and often but scant rations, which they divided unstintedly. And their defeat increased their mutual sympathy.

Yet, on the other hand, there is a just appreciation of their adversaries. The great body of Confederate veterans esteem the men who fought them, far above the politician. They look confidently to the better class of Union veterans to cooperate with them in maintaining a truthful history. Maybe the time will come when the remnant of the soldiers, North and South, will confer together for the good of the country.

The Confederates have not pursued the excellent method of rotation in office in their organization, as have the Grand Army comrades. General John B. Gordon sought to retire repeatedly, but his comrades would not consent. At his death General Stephen D. Lee, next in rank, became commander-in-chief. It was a difficult place to fill, for there never was a more capable and charming man in any place than was General Gordon as commander-in-chief. However, General Lee was so loyal, so just, and so zealous a Christian that he grew rapidly in favor, and at his death there was widespread sorrow. He was succeeded by General Clement A. Evans, of Georgia, who possessed the same high qualities of Christian manhood, and he would have been continued through life, as were his predecessors, but a severe illness, which affected his throat, made a substitute necessary, so he and General W. L. Cabell, commander of the Trans-Mississippi Department from the beginning—their rank being about equal—were made honorary commanders-in-chief for life, and General George W. Gordon, a member of Congress from Tennessee, was chosen as active commander-in-chief in 1910. Generals Gordon, Cabell, and Evans died in 1911. Each had a military funeral in which U. S. Army officials took part.

Within a score of years there had developed a close and cordial cooperation between the veterans and such representative Southern organizations as the Confederated Southern Memorial Association, the United Sons of Confederate Veterans, and the United Daughters of the Confederacy. All are devoted to the highest patriotic ideals.

IX

ROSTER
OF
GENERAL OFFICERS

BOTH UNION
AND CONFEDERATE

THE GENERAL-IN-CHIEF OF THE ARMIES OF THE UNITED STATES A
PICTURE OF GRANT WITH HIS FAVORITE CHARGER "CINCINNATI"
TAKEN AT COLD HARBOR ON JUNE 4, 1864, IN THE MIDST OF THE
"HAMMERING POLICY" THAT IN TEN MONTHS TERMINATED THE WAR

General Officers of the Union Army

This roster includes in alphabetical order under the various grades the names of all general officers either of full rank or by brevet in the United States (Regular) Army and in the United States Volunteers during the Civil War. The highest rank attained, whether full or by brevet, only is given, in order to avoid duplications. It is, of course, understood that in most cases the actual rank next below that conferred by brevet was held either in the United States Army or the Volunteers. In some cases for distinguished gallantry or marked efficiency brevet rank higher than the next grade above was given. The date is that of the appointment.

LIEUTENANT-GENERAL
UNITED STATES ARMY
(*Full Rank*)

Grant, Ulysses S., Mar. 2, '64.

LIEUTENANT-GENERAL
UNITED STATES ARMY
(*By Brevet*)

Scott, Winfield, Mar. 29, '47.

MAJOR-GENERALS
UNITED STATES ARMY
(*Full Rank*)

Fremont, J. C., May 14, '61.
Halleck, H. W., Aug. 19, '61.
Hancock, W. S., July 26, '66.
McClellan, G. B., May 14, '61.
Meade, G. G., Aug. 18, '64.
Sheridan, P. H., Nov. 8, '64.
Sherman, Wm. T., Aug. 12, '64.
Thomas, Geo. H., Dec. 15, '64.
Wool, John E., May 16, '62.

MAJOR-GENERALS
UNITED STATES ARMY
(*By Brevet*)

Allen, Robert, Mar. 13, '65.
Ames, Adelbert, Mar. 13, '65.
Anderson, Robert, Feb. 3, '65.
Arnold, Richard, Mar. 13, '65.
Augur, Chris. C., Mar. 13, '65.
Averell, Wm. W., Mar. 13, '65.
Ayres, R. B., Mar. 13, '65.
Baird, Absalom, Mar. 13, '65.
Barnard, John G., Mar. 13, '65.
Barnes, Joseph K., Mar. 13, '65.
Barry, Wm. F., Mar. 13, '65.
Beckwith, Amos, Mar. 13, '65.
Benham, H. W., Mar. 13, '65.
Brannan, J. M., Mar. 13, '65.
Brice, Benj. W., Mar. 13, '65.
Brown, Harvey, Aug. 2, '66.
Buchanan, R. C., Mar. 13, '65.
Butterfield, D., Mar. 13, '65.
Canby, Ed. S. R., Mar. 13, '65.
Carleton, J. H., Mar. 13, '65.
Carlin, Wm. P., Mar. 13, '65.
Carr, Eugene A., Mar. 13, '65.
Carroll, Sam. S., Mar. 13, '65.
Casey, Silas, Mar. 13, '65.

Clarke, Henry F., Mar. 13, '65.
Cook, P. St. G., Mar. 13, '65.
Cram, Thomas J., Jan 13, '66.
Crawford, S. W., Mar. 13, '65.
Crook, George, Mar. 13, '65.
Crossman, G. H., Mar. 13, '65.
Cullum, Geo. W., Mar. 13, '65.
Custer, Geo. A., Mar. 13, '65.
Davidson, J. W., Mar. 13, '65.
Davis, Jef. C., Mar. 13, '65.
Delafield, Rich., Mar. 13, '65.
Donaldson, J. L., Mar. 13, '65.
Doubleday, A., Mar. 13, '65.
Dyer, Alex. B., Mar. 13, '65.
Easton, L. E., Mar. 13, '65.
Eaton, Amos B., Mar. 13, '65.
Elliott, W. L., Nov. 13, '65.
Emory, Wm. H., Mar. 13, '65.
Fessenden, F., Mar. 13, '65.
Foster, John G., Mar. 13, '65.
Franklin, Wm. B., Mar. 13, '65.
French, Wm. H., Mar. 13, '65.
Fry, James B., Mar. 13, '65.
Garrard, Kenner, Mar. 13, '65.
Getty, Geo. W., Mar. 13, '65.
Gibbon, John, Mar. 13, '65.
Gibbs, Alfred, Mar. 13, '65.
Gibson, Geo., May 30, '48.
Gillem, Alvan G., April 12, '65.
Gilmore, Q. A., Mar. 13, '65.
Granger, Gordon, Mar. 13, '65.
Granger, Robt. S., Mar. 13, '65.
Grierson, B. H., Mar. 2, '67.
Griffin, Charles, Mar. 13, '65.
Grover, Cuvier, Mar. 13, '65.
Hardie, James A., Mar. 13, '65.
Harney, Wm. S., Mar. 13, '65.
Hartsuff, G. L., Mar. 13, '65
Hatch, Edward, Mar. 2, '67.
Hawkins, J. P., Mar. 13, '65.
Hazen, Wm. B., Mar. 13, '65.
Heintzelman, S. P., Mar. 13, '65.
Hoffman, Wm. Mar. 13, '65.
Holt, Joseph, Mar. 13, '65.
Hooker, Joseph, Mar. 13, '65.
Howard, O. O., Mar. 13, '65.
Howe, A. P., Mar. 13, '65.
Humphreys, A. A., Mar. 13, '65.
Hunt, Henry J., Mar. 13, '65.
Hunter, David, Mar. 13, '65.
Ingalls, Rufus, Mar. 13, '65.
Johnson, R. W., Mar. 13, '65.
Kautz, August V., Mar. 13, '65.
Ketchum, Wm. S., Mar. 13, '65.

Kilpatrick, Judson, Mar. 13, '65.
King, John H., Mar. 13, '65.
Long, Eli, Mar. 13, '65.
McCook, A. McD., Mar. 13, '65.
McDowell, Irvin, Mar. 13,'65.
McIntosh, John B., Aug. 5, '62.
Marcy, R. B., Mar. 13, '65.
Meigs, Mont. C., July 5, '64.
Merritt, Wesley, Mar. 13, '65.
Miles, Nelson A., Mar. 2, '67.
Morris, Wm. W., Mar. 13, '65.
Mower, J. A., Mar. 13, '65.
Newton, John, Mar. 13, '65.
Nichols, Wm. A., Mar. 13, '65.
Ord, Ed. O. C., Mar. 13, '65.
Parke, John G., Mar. 13, '65.
Pennypacker, G., Mar. 2, '67.
Pleasonton, A., Mar. 13, '65.
Pope, John, Mar. 13, '65.
Ramsey, Geo. D., Mar. 13, '65.
Rawlins, John A., April 9, '65.
Reynolds, J. J., Mar. 2, '67.
Ricketts, J. B., Mar. 13, '65.
Ripley, Jas. W., Mar. 13, '65.
Robinson, J. C., Mar. 13, '65.
Rosecrans, W. S., Mar. 13, '65.
Rousseau, L. H., Mar. 28, '67.
Rucker, D. H., Mar. 13, '65.
Russell, David A., Sept. 19, '64.
Sackett, Delos B., Mar. 13, '65.
Schofield, J. M., Mar. 13, '65.
Schriver, E., Mar. 13, '65.
Seymour, T., Mar. 13, '65.
Sherman, T. W., Mar. 13, '65.
Shiras, Alex., Mar. 13, '65.
Sickles, Daniel E., Mar. 2, '67.
Simpson, M. D. L., Mar. 13, '65.
Smith, Andrew J., Mar. 13, '65.
Smith, Chas. H., Mar. 21, '67.
Smith, John E., Mar. 2, '67.
Smith, W. F., Mar. 13, '65.
Stanley, David S., Mar. 13, '65.
Steele, Frederick, Mar. 13, '65.
Stoneman, Geo., Mar. 13, '65.
Sturgis, S. D., Mar. 13, '65.
Sumner, Edwin V., May 6, '64.
Swayne, Wager, Mar. 2, '67.
Swords, Thomas, Mar. 13, '65.
Sykes, George, Mar. 13, '65.
Terry, Alfred H., Mar. 13, '65.
Thomas, Charles, Mar. 13, '65.
Thomas, Lorenzo, Mar. 13, '65.

Torbert, A. T. A., Mar. 13, '65.
Totten, J. G., April 21, '64.
Tower, Z. B., Mar. 13, '65.
Townsend, E. D., Mar. 13, '65.
Turner, J. W., Mar. 13, '65.
Tyler, Robt. O., Mar. 13, '65.
Upton, Emory, Mar. 13, '65.
Van Vliet, S., Mar. 13, '65.
Vinton, D. H., Mar. 13, '65.
Warren, G. K., Mar. 13, '65.
Webb, Alex. S., Mar. 13, '65.
Weitzel, G., Mar. 13, '65.
Wheaton, Frank, Mar. 13, '65.
Whipple, A. W., May 7, '63.
Whipple, Wm. D., Mar. 13, '65.
Willcox, O. B., Mar. 2, '67.
Williams, Seth, Mar. 13, '65.
Wilson, James H., Mar. 13, '65.
Wood, Thos. J., Mar. 13, '65.
Woodbury, D. P., Aug. 15, '64.
Woods, Chas. R., Mar. 13, '65.
Wright, H. G., Mar. 13, '65.

MAJOR-GENERALS
U. S. VOLUNTEERS
(*Full Rank*)

Banks, N. P., May 16, '61.
Barlow, F. C., May 25, '65.
Berry, H. G., Nov. 29, '62.
Birney, David D., May 3, '63.
Blair, Frank P., Nov. 29, '62.
Blunt, James G., Nov. 29, '62.
Brooks, W. T. H., June 10, '63.
Buell, Don Carlos, Mar. 21, '62.
Buford, John, July 1, '63.
Buford, N. B., Mar. 13, '65.
Burnside, A. E., Mar. 18, '62.
Butler, Benj. F., May 16, '61.
Cadwalader, G. B., Apr. 25, '62.
Clay, Cassius M., April 11, '62.
Couch, Darius N., July 4, '62.
Cox, Jacob Dolson, Oct. 6, '62.
Crittenden, T. L., July 17, '62.
Curtis, S. R., Nov. 21, '62.
Dana, N. J. T., Nov. 29, '62.
Davies, Henry E., May 4, '65.
Dix, John A., May 16, '61.
Dodge, G. M., June 7, '64.
Doubleday, A., Nov. 29, '62.
Garfield, J. A., Sept. 19, '63.
Hamilton, C. S., Sept. 18, '62.
Hamilton, S., Sept. 17, '62.
Herron, F. J., Nov. 29, '62.
Hitchcock, E. A., Feb. 10, '62.

Samuel P. Spear, Originally
Colonel of the 11th
Cavalry.

Roy Stone, Commander
of the "Bucktail
Brigade."

William A. Nichols, Promoted
for Faithful Services
in the War.

Israel Vogdes, Promoted
for Gallantry in the
Field.

S. B. M. Young, Originally
Colonel 4th Cavalry; Later
Commander of the U. S. Army.

John R. Brooke, Originally
Colonel of the 54th Reg't,
Army of the Potomac.

Pennock Huey, Originally
Colonel of the 8th Cavalry,
Army of the Potomac.

Henry J. Madill, Originally
Colonel of the 141st Reg't,
Noted at Gettysburg.

FEDERAL GENERALS—No. 25—PENNSYLVANIA

Andrew Porter, Commanded
a Brigade at First
Bull Run.

Thomas Welsh, Originally
Colonel of the 45th
Regiment.

Charles F. Smith, Originally
Colonel of the 3d
Infantry.

Thomas L. Kane, Organizer
and Leader of "Kane's
Bucktails."

The Union Generals

Hurlbut, Stephen, Sept. 17, '62.
Kearny, Philip, July 4, '62.
Keyes, Erasmus D., May 5, '62.
Leggett, M. D., Aug. 21, '65.
Logan, John A., Nov. 29, '62.
McClernand, J. A., Mar. 21, '62.
McPherson, J. B., Oct. 8, '62.
Mansfield, J. K. F., July 18, '62.
Milroy, Robt. H., Nov. 29, '62.
Mitchell, Ormsby, April 11, '62.
Morell, Geo. W., July 4, '62.
Morgan, E. D., Sept. 28, '61.
Morris, Thos. A., Oct. 25, '62.
Mott, Gersham, May 26, '65.
Mower, Joseph A., Aug. 12, '64.
Negley, James S., Nov. 29, '62.
Nelson, William, July 17, '62.
Oglesby, R. J., Nov. 29, '62.
Osterhaus, P. J., July 23, '64.
Palmer, John M., Nov. 29, '62.
Peck, John J., July 4, '62.
Porter, Fitz John, July 4, '62.
Potter, Rbt. B., Sept. 29, '65.
Prentiss, B. M., Nov. 29, '62.
Reno, Jesse L., July 18, '62.
Reynolds, J. F., Nov. 29, '62.
Reynolds, Jos. J., Nov. 29, '62.
Richardson, I. B., July 4, '62.
Schenck, Robt. C. Aug. 30, '62.
Schurz, Carl, March 14, '63.
Sedgwick, John, July 4, '62.
Sigel, Franz, March 21, '62.
Slocum, Henry W., July 4, '62.
Smith, Chas. F., Mar. 21, '62.
Smith, Giles A., Nov. 24, '65.
Stahel, Julius H., Mar. 14, '63.
Steedman, Jas. B., April 30, '64.
Stevens, Isaac I., July 18, '62.
Strong, Geo. C., July 18, '63.
Wallace, Lewis, March 21, '62.
Washburn, C. C., Nov. 29, '62.

MAJOR-GENERALS
U. S. Volunteers
(By Brevet)

Abbott, Henry L., Mar. 13, '65.
Allen, Robert, Mar. 13, '65.
Alger, Russell A., June 11, '65.
Anderson, N. L., Mar. 13, '65.
Andrews, C. C., Mar. 9, '65.
Andrews, G. L., Mar. 26, '65.
Asboth, Alex., Mar. 13, '65.
Atkins, Smith D., Mar. 13, '65.
Avery, Robert, Mar. 13, '65.
Ayres, R. B., Aug. 1, '64.
Bailey, Joseph, Mar. 13, '65.
Baker, Benj. F., Mar. 13, '65.
Banning, H. B., Mar. 13, '65.
Barnes, James, Mar. 13, '65.
Barney, Lewis T., Mar. 13, '65.
Barnum, H. A., Mar. 13, '65.
Barry, H. W., Mar. 13, '65.
Bartlett, Jos. J., Aug. 1, '64.
Bartlett, Wm. F., Mar. 13, '65.
Baxter, Henry, April 1, '65.
Beal, Geo. L., Mar. 13, '65.
Beatty, Samuel, Mar. 13, '65.
Belknap, Wm. W., Mar. 13, '65.
Benton, Wm. P., Mar. 26, '65.
Birge, H. W., Feb. 25, '65.

Birney, Wm., Mar. 13, '65.
Bowen, James, Mar. 13, '65.
Brayman, Mason, Mar. 13, '65.
Brisbin, James, Mar. 13, '65.
Brooke, John R., Aug. 1, '64.
Buckland, R. P., Mar. 13, '64.
Bussey, Cyrus, Mar. 13, '65.
Byrne, James J., Mar. 13, '65.
Caldwell, John C., Aug. 19, '65.
Cameron, R. A., Mar. 13, '65.
Capehart, Henry, June 17, '65.
Carr, Joseph B., Mar. 13, '65.
Carter, Samuel P., Mar. 13, '65.
Catlin, Isaac S., Mar. 13, '65.
Chamberlain, J. L., Mar. 29, '65.
Chapin, Daniel, Aug. 17, '64.
Chapman, G. H., Mar. 13, '65.
Chetlain, A. L., June 18, '65.
Chrysler, M. H., Mar. 13, '65.
Clark, Wm. T., Nov. 24, '65.
Comstock, C. B., Nov. 26, '65.
Connor, P. E., Mar. 13, '65.
Cooke, John, Aug. 24, '65.
Cooper, Jos. A., Mar. 13, '65.
Cole, Geo. W., Mar. 13, '65.
Collis, C. H. T., Mar. 13, '65.
Corse, John M., Oct. 5, '64.
Coulter, Richard, April 6, '65.
Crawford, S. W., Aug. 1, '64.
Cross, Nelson, Mar. 13, '65.
Croxton, John T., April 27, '65.
Cruft, Charles, March 5, '65.
Curtis, N. M., Mar. 13, '65.
Cutler, Lys., Aug. 19, '64.
Davies, Thos. A., July 11, '65.
Dennis, Elias S., April 13, '65.
Dennison, A. W., Mar. 31, '65.
De Trobriand, P. R., Apr. 9, '65.
Devens, Chas., April 3, '65.
Devin, Thos. C., Mar. 13, '65.
Doolittle, C. C., June 13, '65.
Dornblazer, B., Mar. 13, '65.
Duncan, Sam'l A., Mar. 13, '65.
Duryee, Abram, Mar. 13, '65.
Duval, Isaac H., Mar. 13, '65.
Edwards, Oliver, April 5, '65.
Egan, Thos. W., Oct. 27, '64.
Ely, John, April 15, '65.
Ewing, Hugh, Mar. 13, 1865.
Ewing, Thos. Jr., Mar. 13, '65.
Ferrero, Edward, Dec. 2, '64.
Ferry, Orris S., May 23, '65.
Fessenden, J. D., Mar. 13, '65.
Fisk, Clinton B., Mar. 13, '65.
Force, M. F., Mar. 13, '65.
Foster, R. S., Mar. 31, '65.
Fuller, John W., Mar. 13, '65.
Geary, John W., Jan. 12, '65.
Gilbert, Jas. J., Mar. 26, '65.
Gleason, John H., Mar. 13, '65.
Gooding, O. P., Mar. 13, '65.
Gordon, Geo. H., April 9, '65.
Graham, C. K., Mar. 13, '65.
Grant, Lewis A., Oct. 19, '64.
Greene, George S., Mar. 13, '65.
Gregg, D. McM., Aug. 1, '64.
Gregg, John I., Mar. 13, '65.
Gregory, E. M., April 9, '66.
Gresham, W. Q., Mar. 13, '65.
Griffin, S. G., April 2, '65.
Grose, Wm., Aug. 15, '65.

Guss, Henry R., Mar. 13, '65.
Gwyn, James, April 1, '65.
Hamblin, J. E., April 5, '65.
Hamlin, Cyrus, Mar. 13, '65.
Harris, T. M., April 2, '65.
Hartranft, John F., Mar. 25, '65.
Hatch, John P., Mar. 13, '65.
Hawley, Jos. R., Sept. 28, '65.
Hayes, Joseph, Mar. 13, '65.
Hayes, Ruth. B., Mar. 13, '65.
Hays, Alex., May 5, '65.
Heath, H. H., Mar. 13, '65.
Hill, Chas. W., Mar. 13, '65.
Hinks, Edw. W., Mar. 13, '65.
Hovey, Chas. E., Mar. 13, '65.
Howe, Al. P., July 13, '65.
Jackson, N. J., Mar. 13, '65.
Jackson, R. H., Nov. 24, '65.
Jourdan, Jas., Mar. 13, '65.
Kane, Thos. L., Mar. 13, '65.
Keifer, J. W., April 9, '65.
Kelly, Benj. F., Mar. 13, '65.
Kenly, John R., Mar. 13, '65.
Ketcham, J. H., Mar. 13, '65.
Kiddoo, Jos. B., Sept. 4, '65.
Kimball, Nathan, Feb. 1, '65.
Kingsman, J. B., Mar. 13, '65.
Lanman, J. G., Mar. 13, '65.
Lawler, M. K., Mar. 13, '65.
Long, Eli, Mar. 13, '65.
Loring, Chas. G., July 17, '65.
Lucas, Thos. J., Mar. 26, '65.
Ludlow, Wm. H., Mar. 13, '65.
McAllister, Rbt., Mar. 13, '65.
McArthur, John, Dec. 15, '64.
McCallum, D. C., Mar. 13, '65.
McCook, E. M., Mar. 13, '65.
McCook, E. S., Mar. 13, '65.
McIvor, Jas. P., Mar. 13, '65.
McIntosh, J. B., Mar. 13, '65.
McKean, T. J., Mar. 13, '65.
McMahon, M. T., Mar. 13, '65.
McMillan, J. W., Mar. 5, '65.
McMillan, W. L., Mar. 13, '65.
McNeil, John, April 12, '65.
McQuade, Jas., Mar. 13, '65.
Mackenzie, R. S., Mar. 31, '65.
Macy, Geo. A., April 9, '65.
Madill, Henry J., Mar. 13, '65.
Marshall, E. G., Mar. 13, '65.
Martindale, J. H., Mar. 13, '65.
Maynadier, H. E., Mar. 13, '65.
Meredith, Sol., Aug. 14, '65.
Miller, John F., Mar. 13, '65.
Mindil, Geo. W., Mar. 13, '65.
Minty, R. H. G., Mar. 13, '65.
Mitchell, J. G., Mar. 13, '65.
Molineux, E. L., Mar. 13, '65.
Moore, M. F., Mar. 13, '65.
Morgan, Jas. D., Mar. 19, '65.
Morris, Wm. H., Mar. 13, '65.
Morrow, H. A., Mar. 13, '65.
Mulholland, St. C., Mar. 13, '65.
Neil, Thos. H., Mar. 13, '65.
Nye, Geo. H., Mar. 13, '65.
Oliver, John M., Mar. 13, '65.
Opdyke, Emer., Nov. 30, '64.
Osborn, Thos. O., Apr. 2, '65.
Paine, Chas. J., Jan. 15, '65.
Paine, Hal. E., Mar. 13, '65.
Palmer, I. M., Mar. 13, '65.
Parsons, L. B., Apr. 30, '65.

Patrick, M. R., Mar. 13, '65.
Pearson, A. L., May 1, '65.
Peck, Lewis M., Mar. 13, '65.
Pierce, B. R., Mar. 13, '65.
Pile, Wm. A., April 9, '65.
Plaisted, H. M., Mar. 13, '65.
Potter, Edw. E., Mar. 13, '65.
Potts, B. F., March 13, '65.
Powell, Wm. H., Mar. 13, '65.
Powers, Chas. J., Mar. 13, '65.
Ramsey, John, Mar. 13, '65.
Ransom, T. E. S., Sept. 1, '64.
Rice, Eliot W., Mar. 13, '65.
Runkle, Benj. P., Nov. 9, '65.
Roberts, Benj. S., Mar. 13, '65.
Robinson, J. C., June 27, '64.
Robinson, J. S., Mar. 13, '65.
Root, Adrian R., Mar. 13, '65.
Ruger, Thos. H., Nov. 30, '64.
Salomon, Fred'k, Mar. 13, '65.
Sanborn, John B., Feb. 10, '65.
Saxton, Rufus, Jan. 12, '65.
Scott, R. K., Dec. 5, '65.
Sewell, Wm. J., Mar. 13, '65.
Shaler, Alex., July 27, '65.
Shanks, J. P. C., Mar. 13, '65.
Sharpe, Geo. H., Mar. 13, '65.
Sibley, Henry H., Nov. 29, '65.
Sickle, H. G., Mar. 31, '65.
Slack, Jas. R., Mar. 13, '65.
Smith, G. C., Mar. 13, '65.
Smith, T. K., Mar. 13, '65.
Smyth, T. A., April 7, '65.
Spooner, B. U., Mar. 13, '65.
Sprague, J. W., Mar. 13, '65.
Stannard, Geo. J,, Oct. 28, '64.
Stevenson, J. D., Mar. 13, '65.
Stoughton, W. L., Mar. 13, '65.
Sully, Alfred, Mar. 8, '65.
Thayer, John M., Mar. 13, '65.
Thomas, H. G., Mar. 13, '65.
Tibbetts, Wm. B., Mar. 13, '65.
Tidball, John C., April 2, '65.
Tillison, Davis, Mar. 13, '65.
Trowbridge, L. S., Mar. 13, '65.
Tyler, E. B., Mar. 13, '65.
Tyler, Robt. O., Aug. 1, '64.
Tyndale, Hector, Mar. 13, '65.
Ullman, Daniel, Mar. 13, '65.
Underwood, A. B., Aug. 13, '65.
Van Cleve, H. P., Mar. 13, '65.
Vandever, Wm., June 7, '65.
Veatch, Jas. C., Mar. 26, '65.
Voris, Alvin C., Nov. 15, '65.
Wadsworth, Jas. S., May 6, '64.
Walcutt, C. C., Mar. 13, '65.
Ward, Wm. T., Feb. 24, '65.
Warner Willard, Mar. 13, '65.
Warren, FitzH., Aug. 24, '65.
Washburn, H. D., July 26, '65.
Webster, Jos. D., Mar. 13, '65.
Wells, Wm., Mar. 13, '65.
West, Jas. R., Jan. 4, '66.
Wheaton, Frank, Oct. 19, '64.
Whitaker, W. C., Mar. 13, '65.
White, Julius, Mar. 13, '65.
Williams, A. S., Jan. 12, '65.
Williamson, J. A., Mar. 13, '65.
Willich, Aug., Oct. 21, '65.
Winthrop, Fred., April 1, '65.
Wood, Jas., Jr., Mar. 13, '65.
Woods, Wm. B., Mar. 13, '65.
Zook, S. K., July 2, '64.

Frank Wheaten, Brigade and Division Commander in the Army of the Potomac.

Richard Arnold, Originally Colonel of the 5th Regiment, U. S. Artillery.

George S. Greene Commanded a Brigade at Antietam and Gettysburg.

John G. Hazard, Originally Major of the 1st Regiment of Light Artillery.

FEDERAL GENERALS

No. 26

RHODE ISLAND

(ABOVE AND TO LEFT)

TENNESSEE

(BELOW AND TO RIGHT)

William Hays, Brevetted for Gallantry on the Field.

Samuel P. Carter, Originally Colonel 2d Regiment.

James A. Cooper, Originally Colonel of the 6th Regiment.

James G. Spears, Brevetted Brigadier-General in 1862.

Robert Johnson, Originally Colonel of the 1st Cavalry.

William B. Campbell, Commissioned in 1862; Resigned in 1863.

The Union Generals

BRIGADIER–GENERALS
U. S. ARMY
(Full Rank)
Hammond, W. A., April 25, '62.
Taylor, Jos. P., Feb. 9, '63.

BRIGADIER–GENERALS
U. S. ARMY
(By Brevet)
Abercrombie, J. J., Mar. 13, '65.
Alexander, A. J., April 16, '65.
Alexander, B. S., Mar. 13, '65.
Alexander, E. B., Oct. '65.
Alvord, Ben., April 9, '65.
Arnold, Lewis G., Mar. 13, '65.
Babbitt, E. B., Mar. 13, '65.
Babcock, O. E., Mar. 13, '65.
Bache, H., Mar. 13, '65.
Badeau, Adam, Mar. 2, '67.
Barriger, J. W., Mar. 13, '65.
Beckwith, E. G., Mar. 13, '65.
Bell, George, April 9, '65.
Bingham, J. D., April 9, '65.
Blake, Geo. A. H., Mar. 13, '65.
Bomford, Jas. V., Mar. 13, '65.
Bonneville, B. L. E., Mar. 13, '65.
Bowers, Theo. S., April 9, '65.
Bradley, L. P., Mar. 2. '67.
Breck, Samuel, Mar. 13, '65.
Brewerton, H., Mar. 13, '65.
Brooks, Horace, Mar. 13, '65.
Brown, N. W., Oct. 15, '67.
Buell, Geo. P., Mar. 2, '67.
Burbank, Sid., Mar. 13, '65.
Burke, Martin, Mar. 13, '65.
Burns, Wm. W., Mar. 13, '65.
Burton, H. S., Mar. 13, '65.
Cady, Al., Mar. 13, '65.
Callender, F. D., April 9, '65.
Card, Benj. C., Mar. 13, '65.
Carrington, H. B., April 9, '65.
Churchill, Syl., Feb. 23, '47.
Clary, Rbt. E., Mar. 13, '65.
Clitz, Henry B., Mar. 13, '65.
Craig, Henry K., Mar. 13, '65.
Crane, Chas. H., Mar. 13, '65.
Crawford, S. W., Mar. 13, 65.
Cross, Osborn, Mar. 13, '65.
Cuyler, John M., April 9, '65.
Dana, James J., Mar. 13, '65.
Dandy, Geo. B., Mar. 13, '65.
Davis, N. H., Mar. 13, '65.
Dawson, Sam. K., Mar. 13, '65.
Day, Hannibal, Mar. 13, '65.
Dent, Fred. T., Mar. 13, '65.
DeRussey, R. E., Mar. 13, '65.
De Russy, G. A., Mar. 13, '65.
Dimick, Justin, Mar. 13, '65.
Drum, Rich. C., Mar. 13, '65.
Duane, Jas. C., Mar. 13, '65.
Duncan, Thos., Mar. 13, '65.
Dunn, W. McK., Mar. 13, '65.
Eastman, Seth, Aug. 9, '66.
Eaton, Joseph H., Mar. 13, '65.
Ekin, James A., Mar. 13, '65.
Finley, Clement, Mar. 13, '65.
Fitzhugh, C. L., Mar. 13, '65.
Forsyth, Jas. W., April 9, '65.
Fry, Cary H., Oct. 15, '67.

Gardner, John L., Mar. 13, '65.
Garland, John, Aug. 20, '47.
Gates, Wm., Mar. 13, '65.
Graham, L. P., Mar. 13, '65.
Graham, W. M., Mar. 13, '65.
Greene, James D., Mar. 13, '65.
Greene, Oliver D., Mar. 13, '65.
Grier, Wm. N., Mar. 13, '65.
Hagner, Peter V., Mar. 13, '65.
Haines, Thos. J., Mar. 13, '65.
Hardin, M. D., Mar. 13, '65.
Haskin, Jos. A., Mar. 13, '65.
Hayden, Julius, Mar. 13, '65.
Hays, William, Mar. 13, '65.
Hill, Bennett H., Jan. 31, '65.
Holabird, S. B., Mar. 13, '65.
Hunt, Lewis C., Mar. 13, '65.
Ibrie, George P., Mar. 2, '65.
Kelton, John C., Mar. 13, '65.
Kilburn, C. L., Mar. 13, '65.
Kingsbury, C. P., Mar. 13, '65.
Kirkham, R. W., Mar. 13, '65.
Leonard, H., Mar. 13, '65.
Leslie, Thos. J., Mar. 13, '65.
Loomis, Gus., Mar. 13, '65.
Lovell, Chas. S., Mar. 13, '65.
Lowe, Wm. W., Mar. 13, '65.
McAlester, M. D., April 9, '65.
McDougall, C., Mar. 13, '65.
McFerran, J. C., Mar. 13, '65.
McKeever, C., Mar. 13, '65.
McKibbin, D. B., Mar. 13, '65.
McLaughlin, N. B., Mar. 13, '65.
Mason, John S., Mar. 13, '65.
Maynadier, W., Mar. 13, '65.
Merchant, C. S., Mar. 13, '65.
Meyer, Albert J., Mar. 13, '65.
Michler, Nat., April 2, '65.
Miller, M. S., Mar. 13, '65.
Mills, Madison, Mar. 13, '65.
Moore, Tred., Mar. 13, '65.
Morgan, Chas. H., Mar. 13, '65.
Morgan, M. R., April 3, '65.
Morrison, P., Mar. 13, '65.
Morton, J. St. C., June, 17, '64.
Myers, Fred., Mar. 13, '65.
Myers, William, Mar. 13, '65.
Oakes, James, Mar. 30, '65.
Palfrey, John C., Mar. 26, '65.
Parker, Ely S., Mar. 2, '67.
Paul, G. R., Feb. 23, '65.
Pelouze, L. H., Mar. 13, '65.
Penrose, Wm. H., April 9, '65.
Perry, Alex. J., Mar. 13, '65.
Pitcher, Thos. G., Mar. 13, '65.
Poe, Orlando M., Mar. 13, '65.
Porter, Horace, Mar. 13, '65.
Potter, Jos. A., Mar. 13, '65.
Potter, Jos. H., Mar. 13, '65.
Prime, Fred'k E., Mar. 13, '65.
Prince, Henry, Mar. 13, '65.
Raynolds, Wm. F., Mar. 13, '65.
Reese, C. B., Mar. 13, '65.
Reeve, I. V. D., Mar. 13, '65.
Roberts, Jos., Mar. 13, '65.
Robertson, J. M., Mar. 13, '65.
Rodenbough, T. F., Mar. 13, '65.
Rodman, Thos. J., Mar. 13, '65.
Ruff, Chas. F., Mar. 13, '65.
Ruggles, Geo. D., Mar. 13, '65.

Satterlee, R. S., Sept. 2, '64.
Sawtelle, C. G., Mar. 13, '65.
Seawell, Wash., Mar. 13, '65.
Shepherd, O. L., Mar. 13, '65.
Sibley, Caleb C., Mar. 13, '65.
Sidell, Wm. H., Mar. 13, '65.
Simonson, J. S., Mar. 13, '65.
Simpson, J. H., Mar. 13, '65.
Slemmer, A. J., Mar. 13, '65.
Small, M. P., April 9, '65.
Smith, Joseph R., April 9, '65.
Sweitzer, N. B., Mar. 13, '65.
Thayer, Syl., May 31, '63.
Thom, George, Mar. 13, '65.
Thornton, W. A., Mar. 13, '65.
Tompkins, C. H., Mar. 13, '65.
Totten, James, Mar. 13, '65.
Townsend, Fred., Mar. 13, '65.
Trippler, Chas. S., Mar. 13, '65.
Vincent, T. M., Mar. 13, '65.
Vogdes, Israel B., April 9, '65.
Waite, C. A., Mar. 13, '65.
Wallen, Henry D., Mar. 13, '62.
Warner, Jas. M., April 9, '65.
Watkins, L. D., Mar. 13, '65.
Wessells, H. W., Mar. 13, '65.
Whiteley, R. H. K., Mar. 13, '65.
Williams, Rbt., Mar. 13, '65.
Wilson, Thos., Mar. 13, '65.
Wood, Rbt. C., Mar. 13, '65.
Woodruff, I. C., Mar. 13, '65.
Wright, George, Dec. 10, '64.
Wright, Jas. J. B., Mar. 13, '65.

BRIGADIER–GENERALS
U. S. VOLUNTEERS
(Full Rank)
Ammen, Jacob, July 16, '62.
Baker, Edw. D., May 17. '61.
Baker, L. C., April 26, '65.
Bayard, Geo. D., April 28, '62.
Beatty, John, Nov. 29, '62.
Biddle, Chas. J., Aug. 31, '61.
Bidwell, D. D., Aug. 11, '64.
Blenker, Louis, Aug. 9, '61.
Bohlen, Henry, April 28, '62.
Boyle, J. T., Nov. 4, '61.
Bragg, Edw. S., June 25, '64.
Bramlette, T. E., April 24, '63.
Briggs, Henry S., July 17, '62.
Brown, Egbert B., Nov. 29, '62.
Buckingham, C. P., July 16, '62.
Burbridge, S. G., June 9, '62.
Burnham, H., April 27, '64.
Busteed, Rich., Aug. 7, '62.
Campbell, C. T., Nov. 29, '62.
Campbell, W. B., June 30, '62.
Catterson, R. F., May 31, '65.
Chambers, Alex., Aug. 11, '63.
Champlin, S. G., Nov. 29, '62.
Chapin, Edw. P., June 27, '63.
Clayton, Powell, Aug. 1, '64.
Cluseret, G. P., Oct. 14, '62.
Cochrane, John, July 17, '62.
Conner, Seldon, June 11, '64.
Cooper, James, May 17, '61.
Cooper, Jos. A., July 21, '64.
Copeland, Jos. T., Nov. 29, '62.
Corcoran, M., July 21, '61.

Cowdin, Robt., Sept. 26, '62.
Craig, James, Mar. 21, '62.
Crittenden, T. T., April 28, '62.
Crocker, M. M., Nov. 29, '62.
Davis, E. J., Nov. 10, '64.
Deitzler, Geo. W., Nov. 29, '62.
Denver, Jas. W., Aug. 14, '61.
Dewey, J. A., Nov. 20, '65.
Dodge, Chas. C., Nov. 29, '62.
Dow, Neal, April 28, '62.
Duffie, Alfred N., June 23, '63.
Dumont, E., Sept. 3, '61.
Dwight, Wm., Nov. 29, '62.
Edwards, John, Sept. 26, '64.
Ellett, Alfred W., Nov. 1, '62.
Este, Geo. P., May 31, '65.
Eustis, H. L., Sept. 12, '63.
Ewing, Charles, Mar. 8, '65.
Fairchild, Lucius, Oct. 19, '65.
Farnsworth, E. J., June 29, '63.
Farnsworth, J. F., Nov. 29, '62.
Fry, Speed S., Mar. 21, '62.
Gamble, Wm., Sept. 25, '65.
Garrard, Th. T., Nov. 29, '62.
Gilbert, Chas. C., Sept. 9, '62.
Gorman, W. A., Sept. 7, '61.
Hackleman, P. A., April 28, '62.
Hamilton, A. J., Nov. 14, '62.
Harding, A. C., Mar. 13, '63.
Harker, Chas. G., Sept. 20, '63.
Harland, Edw., Nov. 29, '62.
Harrow, William, Nov. 29, '62.
Hascall, Milo S., April 25, '62.
Haupt, Herman, Sept. 5, '62.
Haynie, I. N., Nov. 29, '62.
Heckman, C. A., Nov. 29, '62.
Hicks, Thos. H., July 22, '62.
Hobson, Edw. H., Nov. 29, '62.
Hovey, A. P., April 28, '62.
Howell, J. B., Sept. 12, '64.
Jackson, C. F., July 17, '62.
Jackson, Jas. S., July 16, '62.
Jamison, C. D., Sept. 3, '61.
Johnson, Andrew, Mar. 4, '62.
Jones, Patrick H., Dec. 6, '64.
Judah, H. M., Mar. 21, '62.
Kaemerling, Guitar, Jan. 5, '64.
Keim, Wm. H., Dec. 20, '61.
Kiernan, James L., Aug. 1, '63.
King, Rufus, May 17, '61.
Kirby, Edmund, May 23, '63.
Kirk, E. N., Nov. 29, '62.
Knipe, Joseph F., Nov. 29, '62.
Krzyanowski, W., Nov. 29, '62.
Lander, F. W., May 17, '61.
Ledlie, James H., Dec. 24, '62.
Lee, Albert L., Nov. 29, '62.
Lightburn, J. A. J., Mar.14, '63.
Lockwood, H. H., Aug. 8, '61.
Lowell, Chas. R., Oct. 19, '64.
Lyon, Nath'l., May 17, '61.
Lytle, William H., Nov. 29, '62.
McCall, G. A., May 17, '61.
McCandless, W., July 21, '64.
McCook, Daniel, July 16, '64.
McCook, R. L., Mar. 21, '62.
McGinnis, G. P., Nov. 29, '62.
McKinstry, J., Sept. 12, '61.
McLean, N. C., Nov. 29, '62.
Maltby, J. A., Aug. 4, '63.
Manson, M. D., Mar. 24, '62.
Marston, G., Nov. 29, '62.
Matthies, C. L., Nov. 29, '62.

[306]

TRUMAN SEYMOUR
Captain at Fort Sumter in 1861;
Later a Brigade Commander
in Army of the Potomac.

EDWIN H. STOUGHTON
Originally Colonel of the 4th
Vermont; Later commanded
the Second Vermont Brigade.

EDWARD H. RIPLEY
Commanded a Brigade in the
24th Corps.

ANDREW J. HAMILTON
Brigadier-General, 1862; Resigned, 1865.

GEORGE J. STANNARD
Led his Brigade against the
Flank of Pickett's Column
at Gettysburg.

JAMES M. WARNER
Colonel of the 1st Regiment
of Artillery.

JOHN W. PHELPS
Commander of a New England
Brigade in Operations on
the Gulf in 1861–2.

EDMUND J. DAVIS
Colonel 1st Texas Cavalry,
1862; Brigadier-General,
1864.

FEDERAL

GENERALS

No. 27—TEXAS

(TWO ABOVE)

VERMONT

(NINE TO LEFT)

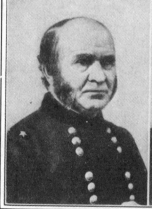

B. S. ROBERTS
Colonel 4th Regiment.

GEORGE WRIGHT
Colonel 9th U. S. Infantry.

STEPHEN THOMAS
Colonel of the 8th Regiment.

Meagher, T. F., Feb. 3, '62.
Meredith, S. A., Nov. 29, '62.
Miller, Stephen, Oct. 26, '63.
Mitchell, R. B., April 8, '62.
Montgomery, W. R., May 17, '61.
Morgan, Geo. W., Nov. 12, '61.
Nagle, James, Sept. 10, '62.
Naglee, H. M., Feb. 4, '62.
Nickerson, F. S., Nov. 29, '62.
Orme, Wm. W., Nov. 29, '62.
Owens, Joshua T., Nov. 29, '62.
Paine, Eleazer, Sept. 3, '61.
Patterson, F. E., April 11, '62.
Phelps, John S., July 19, '62.
Phelps, John W., May 17, '61.
Piatt, Abraham, April 28, '62.
Plummer, J. B., Oct. 22, '61.
Porter, Andrew, May 17, '61.
Pratt, Calvin E., Sept. 10, '62.
Quinby, Isaac F., Mar. 17, '62.
Raum, Green B., Feb. 15, '65.
Reid, Hugh T., Mar. 13, '63.
Reilly, James W., July 30, '64.
Revere, J. W., Oct. 25, '62.
Rodman, Isaac P., April 28, '62.
Ross, Leonard F., April 25, '62.
Rowley, T. A., Nov. 29, '62.
Rice, Americus V., May 31, '65.
Rice, James C., Aug. 17, '63.
Rice, Samuel A., Aug. 4, '63.
Richardson, W. A., Sept. 3, '61.
Rutherford, F. S., June 27, '64.
Sanders, Wm. P., Oct. 18, '63.
Scammon, E. P., Oct. 15, '62.
Schimmelpfennig, Alex., Nov. 29, '62.
Schoepf, Albin, Sept. 30, '61.
Seward, W. H., Jr., Sept. 13, '64.
Shackelford, J. M., Jan. 2, '63.
Shepard, Isaac F., Oct. 27, '63.
Shepley, Geo. F., July 18, '62.
Sherman, F. T., July 21, '65.
Shields, James, Aug. 19, '61.
Sill, Joshua W., July 16, '62.
Slough, John B., Aug. 25, '62.
Smith, G. A., Sept. 19, '62.
Smith, Morgan L., July 16, 62.
Smith, T. C. H., Nov. 29, '62.
Smith, Wm. S., April 15, '62.
Spears, James G., Mar. 5, '62.
Spinola, F. B., June 8, '65.
Sprague, John W., July 21, '64.
Sprague, Wm., May 17, '61.
Starkweather, J. C., July 17, '63.
Stevenson, T. G., Mar. 14, '63.
Stokes, James H., July 20, '65.
Stolbrand, C. J., Feb. 18, '65.
Stone, C. P., May 17, '61.
Stoughton, E. H., Nov. 5, '62.
Strong, Wm. K., Sept. 28, '61.
Stuart, D., Nov. 29, '62.
Stumbaugh, F. S., Nov. 29, '62.
Sullivan, J. C., April 28, '62.
Sweeney, T. W., Nov. 29, '62.
Taylor, Geo. W., May 9, '62.
Taylor, Nelson, Sept. 7, '62.
Terrill, Wm. R., Sept. 9, '62.
Terry, Henry D., July 17, '62.
Thomas, Stephen, Feb. 1, '65.
Thurston, C. M., Sept. 7, '61.

Todd, John B. S., Sept. 19, '65.
Turchin, John B., July 17, '62.
Tuttle, James M., June 9, '62.
Tyler, Daniel, Mar. 13, '62.
Van Allen, J. H., April 15, '62.
Van Derveer, F., Oct. 4, '64.
Van Wyck, C. H., Sept. 27, '65.
Viele, Egbert L., Aug. 17, '61.
Vincent, Strong, July 3, '63.
Vinton, F. L., Sept. 19, '62.
Vogdes, Israel, Nov. 29, '62.
Von Steinwehr, Adolph, Oct. 12, '61.
Wade, M. S., Oct. 1, '61.
Wagner, Geo. D., Nov. 29, '62.
Wallace, W. H. L., Mar. 21, '62.
Ward, John H. H., Oct. 4, '62.
Weber, Max, April 28, '62.
Weed, Stephen H., June 6, '63.
Welsh, Thomas, Mar. 13, '63.
Wild, Edw. A., April 24, '63.
Williams, D. H., Nov. 29, '62.
Williams Thos., Sept. 28, '61.
Wistar, Isaac, Nov. 29, '62.

BRIGADIER–GENERALS
U. S. Volunteers
(By Brevet)

Abbott, Ira C., Mar. 13, '65.
Abbott, J. C., Jan. 5, '65.
Abert, Wm. S., Mar. 13, '65.
Acker, Geo. S., Mar. 13, '65.
Adams, A. W., Mar. 13, '65.
Adams, Chas. F., Mar. 13, '65.
Adams, Chas. P., Mar. 13, '65.
Adams, Chas. W., Feb. 13, '65.
Adams, Robt. N., Mar. 13, '65.
Adams, Will. A., Mar. 13, '65.
Agnus, Felix, Mar. 13, '65.
Albright, Chas., Mar. 7, '65.
Alden, Alonzo, Jan. 15, '65.
Allaire, A. J., June 28, '65.
Allcock, Thos. R., Mar. 13, '65.
Allen, Harrison, Mar. 13, '65.
Allen, Thos. S., Mar. 13, '65.
Ames, John W., Jan. 15, '65.
Ames, William, Mar. 13, '65.
Amory, Thos. J. C., Oct. 7, '64.
Anderson, A. L., Mar. 13, '65.
Anderson, J. F., April 2, '65.
Anderson, W. B., Mar. 13, '65.
Anthony, DeW. C., Mar. 13, '65.
Appleton, J. F., Mar. 13, '65.
Armstrong, S. C., Mar. 13, '65.
Askew, Franklin, July 14, '65.
Astor, John J., Jr., Mar. 13, '65.
Aukeny, Rollin V., Mar. 13, '65.
Averill, John T., Oct. 18, '65.
Avery, Mat. H., Mar. 13, '65.
Babcock, W., Sept. 19, '65.
Bailey, Silas M., Mar. 13, '65.
Baker, James H., Mar. 13, '65.
Balch, Joseph P., Mar. 13, '65.
Baldey, George, Mar. 13, '65.
Baldwin, Chas. P., April 1, '65.
Baldwin, Wm. H., Aug. 22, '65.
Ball, Wm. H., Oct. 19, '64.
Ballier, John F., July 13, '64.
Ballock, G. W., Mar. 13, '65.
Bangs, Isaac S., Mar. 13, '65.
Bankhead, H. C., April 1, '65.

Barber, G. M., Mar. 13, '65.
Barnes, Charles, Sept. 28, '65.
Barney, A. M., Mar. 11, '65.
Barney, B. G., Mar. 13, '65.
Barnett, James, Mar. 13, '65.
Barrett, Theo. H., Mar. 13, '65.
Barrett, W. W., Mar. 13, '65.
Barstow, Wilson, April 2, '65.
Barstow, S. F., Mar. 13, '65.
Bartholomew, O. A., Mar. 13, '65.
Bartlett, C. G., Mar. 13, '65.
Bartlett, Wm. C., Mar. 13, '65.
Barton, Wm. B., Mar. 13, '65.
Bassett, Isaac C., Dec. 12, '64.
Batchelder, R. N., Mar. 13, '65.
Bates, Delavan, July 30, '64.
Bates, Erastus N., Mar. 13, '65.
Baxter, D. W. C., Mar. 13, '65.
Beadis, John E., Mar. 13, '65.
Beadle, W. H. H., Mar. 16, '66.
Beaver, James A., Aug. 1, '64.
Bedel, John, Jan. 5, '65.
Beecher, James C., Mar. 13, '65.
Bell, John H., Nov. 30, '65.
Bell, J. W., Feb. 13, '65.
Bendix, John E., Mar. 13, '65.
Benedict, Lewis, April 9, '64.
Benjamin, W. H., Mar. 13, '65.
Bennett, John E., April 6, '65.
Bennett, T. W., Mar. 5, '65.
Bennett, Wm. T., May 25, '65.
Bentley, R. H., Mar. 13, '65.
Bentley, R. C., Mar. 13, '65.
Benton, Jr., T. H., Dec. 15, '64.
Berdan, Hiram, Mar. 13, '65.
Bertram, Henry, Mar. 13, '65.
Beveridge, J. L., Feb. 7, '65.
Biddle, James, Mar. 13, '65.
Biggs, Herman, Mar. 8, '65.
Biggs, Jonathan, Mar. 13, '65.
Biles, E. R., Mar. 13, '65.
Bingham, H. H., April 9, '65.
Bintliff, James, April 2, '65.
Bishop, J. W., June 7, '65.
Black, J. C., Mar. 13, '65.
Blackman, A. M., Oct. 27, '64.
Blair, C. W., Feb. 13, '65.
Blair, Louis J., Mar. 13, '65.
Blair, W. H., Mar. 13, '65.
Blaisdell, W., Jan. 23, '64.
Blakeslee, E., Mar. 13, '65.
Blanchard, J. W., Mar. 13, '65.
Blanden, L., Mar. 26, '65.
Bloomfield, Ira J., Mar. 13, '65.
Blunt, Asa P., Mar. 13, '65.
Bodine, R. L., Mar. 13, '65.
Bolinger, H. C., Mar. 13, '65.
Bolles, John A., July 17, '65.
Bolton, Wm. J., Mar. 13, '65.
Bond, John R., Mar. 13, '65.
Bonham, Edw., Mar. 13, '65.
Boughton, H., Mar. 11, '65.
Bouton, Edw., Feb. 28, '65.
Bowen, T. M., Feb. 13, '65.
Bowerman, R. N., April 1, '65.
Bowie, Geo. W., Mar. 13, '65.
Bowman, S. M., Mar. 13, '65.
Bowyer, Eli, Mar. 13, '65.
Boyd, Joseph F., Mar. 13, '65.
Boynton, H. V. N., Mar. 13, '65.

Boynton, H., Mar. 13, '65.
Bradshaw, R. C., Mar. 13, '65.
Brady, T. J., Mar. 13, '65.
Brailey, M. R., Mar. 13, '65.
Brayton, C. R., Mar. 13, '65.
Brewster, W. R., Dec. 2, '64.
Brinkerhoff, R., Sept. 20, '65.
Briscoe, Jas. C., Mar. 13, '65.
Broadhead, T. F., Aug. 30, '62.
Bronson, S., Sept. 28, '65.
Browne, T. M., Mar. 13, '65.
Browne, W. H., Mar. 13, '65.
Brown, C. E., Mar. 13, '65.
Brown, H. L., Sept. 3, '64.
Brown, J. M., Mar. 13, '65.
Brown, L. G., Mar. 13, '65.
Brown, O., Jan. 6, '66.
Brown, P. P., Mar. 13, '65.
Brown, S. B., Jr., Mar. 13, '65.
Brown, S. L., Mar. 13, '65.
Brown, T. F., Mar. 13, '65.
Brown, Wm. R., Mar. 13, '65.
Brownlow, J. P., Mar. 13, '65.
Bruce, John, Mar. 13, '65.
Brumback, J., Mar. 13, '65.
Brush, D. H., Mar. 13, '65.
Bukey, Van H., Mar. 13, '65.
Burke, J. W., Mar. 13, '65.
Burling, G. C., Mar. 13, '65.
Burnett, H. L., Mar. 13, '65.
Busey, S. T., April 9, '65.
Butler, T. H., Mar. 13, '65.
Callis, J. B., Mar. 13, '65.
Cameron, D., Mar. 13, '65.
Cameron, Hugh, Mar. 13, '65.
Campbell, C. J., Mar. 13, '65.
Campbell, E. L., June 2, '65.
Campbell, J. M., Mar. 13, '65.
Campbell, J. A., Mar. 13 '65.
Candy, Charles, Mar. 13, '65.
Capron, Horace, Feb. 13, '65.
Carle, James, Mar. 13, '65.
Carleton, C. A., Mar. 13, '65.
Carman, Ezra A., Mar. 13, '65.
Carnahan, R. H., Oct. 28, '65.
Carruth, Sumner, April 2, '65.
Carson, Chris., Mar. 13, '65.
Case, Henry, Mar. 16, '65.
Casement, J. S., Jan. 25, '65.
Cassidy, A. L., Mar. 13, '65.
Cavender, J. S., Mar. 13, '65.
Chamberlain, S. E., Feb. 24, '65.
Champion, T. E., Feb. 20, '65.
Chickering, T. E., Mar. 13, '65.
Chipman, H. L., Mar. 13, '65.
Chipman, N. P., Mar. 13, '65.
Christ, B. C., Aug. 1, '64.
Christensen, C. T., Mar. 13, '65.
Christian, W. H., Mar. 13, '65.
Churchill, M., Mar. 13, '65.
Cilly, J. P., June 2, '65.
Cist, H. M., Mar. 13, '65.
Clapp, D. E., Mar. 13, '65.
Clark, G. W., Mar. 13, '65.
Clark, J. S., Mar. 13, '65.
Clarke, Gideon, Mar. 13, '65.
Clarke, Wm. H., Mar. 13, '65.
Clay, Cecil, Mar. 13, '65.
Clendenin, D. R., Feb. 20, '65.
Clough, J. M., Mar. 13, '65.
Coates, B. F., Mar. 13, '65.

Edward S. Bragg Commanded the Iron Brigade.

Lysander Cutler Commanded a Brigade at Gettysburg.

Lucius Fairchild, Colonel of the 2d Regiment.

FEDERAL

GENERALS

No. 28

WISCONSIN

Frederick Salomon, Originally Colonel of the 9th Regiment of Infantry.

Jeremiah M. Rusk, Originally Lieut.-Colonel of the 25th Regiment

Charles S. Hamilton Commanded a Division at Corinth.

John C. Starkweather Commanded a Brigade at Perryville.

Halbert E. Paine Commanded a Division at Port Hudson.

Rufus King Commanded a Division in the Army of the Potomac.

Coates, J. H., Mar. 13, '65.
Cobb, Amasa, Mar. 13, '65.
Cobham, G. A., Jr., July 19, '64.
Coburn, J., Mar. 13, '65.
Cockerill, J. R., Mar. 13, '65.
Coggswell, W., Dec. 15, '64.
Coit, J. B., Mar. 13, '65.
Colgrove, Silas, Aug. 4, '64.
Collier, F. H., Mar. 13, '65.
Colville, Jr., W., Mar. 3, '65.
Comly, J. M., Mar. 13, '65.
Commager, H. S., Mar. 13, '65.
Congdon, J. A., Mar. 13, '65.
Conklin, J. T., Mar. 13, '65.
Conrad, J., Mar. 13, '65.
Cook, Edw. F., Mar. 13, '65.
Coon, D. E., Mar. 8, '65.
Corbin, H. C., Mar. 13, '65.
Coughlin, John, April 9, '65.
Cowan, B. R., Mar. 13, '65.
Cox, John C., July 4, '63.
Cox, Rob't C., April 2, '65.
Cram, Geo. H., Mar. 13, '62.
Cramer, F. L., Mar. 13, '65.
Crandal, F. M., Oct. 24, '65.
Crane, M. M., Mar. 13, '65.
Cranor, Jonathan, Mar. 3, '65.
Crawford, S. J., Mar. 13, '65.
Crocker, J. S., Mar. 13, '65.
Crowinshield, C., Mar. 13, '65.
Cummings, Alex., Apr. 19, '65.
Cummings, G. W., Mar. 13, '65.
Cummins, J. E., Mar. 13, '65.
Cunningham, J. A., Apr. 1, '65.
Curly, Thos., Mar. 13, '65.
Curtin, John J., Oct. 12, '64.
Curtis, A. R., Mar. 13, '65.
Curtis, G. S., Mar. 13, '65.
Curtis, J. F., Mar. 13, '65.
Curtis, Wm. B., Mar. 13, '65.
Curtiss, J. E., Mar. 13, '65.
Cutcheon, B. M., Mar. 13, '65.
Cutting, Wm., April 2, '65.
Cutts, R. D., Mar. 13, '65.
Daggett, A. S., Mar. 13, '65.
Daggett, Rufus, Jan. 15, '65.
Dana, E. L., July 26, '65.
Darr, Francis, Mar. 13, '65.
Dawson, A. R. Z., Nov. 21, '65.
Davis, E. P., Oct. 19, '64.
Davis, Hasbrook, Feb. 13, '65.
Davis, H. G., Mar. 13, '65.
Davis, W. W. H., Mar. 13, '65.
Day, Henry M., Mar. 26, '65.
Day, Nich. W., Mar. 13, '65.
Dayton, Oscar V., Mar. 13, '65.
Dawes, R. R., Mar. 18, '65.
Deems, J. M., Mar. 13, '65.
De Groat, C. H., Mar. 13, '65.
De Hart, R. P., Mar. 13, '65.
De Lacey, Wm., Mar. 13, '65.
De Land, C. V., Mar. 13, '65.
Dennis, John B., Mar. 13, '65.
Devereux, A. F., Mar. 13, '65.
De Witt, D. P., Mar. 13, '65.
Dick, Geo. F., Mar. 13, '65.
Dickerson, C. J., Mar. 13, '65.
Dickey, Wm. H., Mar. 13, '65.
Dickinson, Jos., Mar. 13, '65.
Dilworth, C. J., Mar. 13, '65.
Dimon, C. A. R., Mar. 13, '65.
Diven, Alex. S., Aug. 30, '64.
Diven, C. W., Mar. 25, '65.

Dixon, Wm. D., Mar. 13, '65.
Doan, A. W., Mar. 13, '65.
Dodd, Levi A., April 2, '65.
Dodge, Geo. S., Jan. 15, '65.
Donohue, M. T., Mar. 13, '65.
Doster, Wm. E., Mar. 13, '65.
Doubleday, U., Mar. 11, '65.
Dox, Ham. B., Feb. 13, '65.
Drake, Francis M., Feb. 22, '65.
Drake, Geo. B., Mar. 13, '65.
Draper, Alonzo G., Oct. 28, '64.
Draper, W. F., Mar. 13, '65.
Drew, C. W., Mar. 13, '65.
Ducat, A. C., Mar. 13, '65.
Dudley, N. A. M., Jan. 19, '65.
Dudley, Wm. W., Mar. 13, '65.
Duer, John O., July 12, '65.
Duff, Wm. L., Mar. 13, '65.
Dunham, T. H., Jr., Mar. 13, '65.
Dunlap, H. C., Mar. 13, '62.
Dunlap, James, Mar. 13, '65.
Duryea, Hiram, Mar. 13, '65.
Duryee, J. E., Mar. 13, '65.
Dustin, Daniel, Mar. 13, '65.
Dutton, A. H., May 16, '64.
Dutton, E. F., Mar. 16, '65.
Duval, Hiram F., Mar. 13, '65.
Dye, Wm. McE., Mar. 13, '65.
Dyer, Isaac, Mar. 13, '65.
Eaton, Chas. G., Mar. 13, '65.
Eaton, John, Jr., Mar. 13, '65.
Eckert, Thos. T., Mar. 13, '65.
Edgerton, A. J., Mar. 13, '65.
Edmonds, J. C., Mar. 13, '65.
Edwards, C. S., Mar. 13, '65.
Eggleston, B. B., Mar. 13, '62.
Eldridge, H. N., Mar. 13, '65.
Elliott, I. H., Mar. 13, '65.
Elliott, S. M., Mar. 13, '65.
Ellis, A. VanHorn, July 2, '63.
Ellis, Theo. G., Mar. 13, '65.
Elstner, G. R., Aug. 8, '64.
Elwell, J. J., Mar. 13, '65.
Ely, Ralph, April 2, '65.
Ely, Wm. C., April 13, '65.
Engleman, A., Mar. 13, '65.
Enochs, Wm. H., Mar. 13, '65.
Ent, W. H., Mar. 13, '65.
Enyart, D. A., Mar. 13, '62.
Erskine, Albert, Feb. 13, '65.
Estes, L. G., Mar. 13, '65.
Evans, George S., Mar. 13, '65.
Everett, Charles, Mar. 13, '65.
Fairchild, C., Mar. 13, '65.
Fairchild, H. S., Mar. 13, '65.
Fallows, Samuel, Oct. 24, '65.
Fardella, Enrico, Mar. 13, '65.
Farnum, J. E., Jan. 3, '66.
Farnsworth, A., Sept. 27, '65.
Farrar, B. G., Mar. 9, '65.
Fearing, Benj. D., Dec. 2, '64.
Fisher, Benj. F., Mar. 13, '65.
Fisher, Joseph W., Nov. 4, '65.
Fisk, Henry C., April 6, '65.
Fiske, Frank S., Mar. 13, '65.
Fiske, Wm. O., Mar. 13, '65.
Fitzsimmons, C., Mar. 13, '65.
Flanigan, Mark, Mar. 13, '65.
Fleming, R. E., Mar. 13, '64.
Fletcher, T. C., Mar. 13, '65.
Flood, Martin, Mar. 13, '65.
Flynn, John, Mar. 13, '65.

Fonda, John G., June 28, '65.
Ford, James H., Dec. 10, '65.
Forsyth, Geo. A., Feb. 13, '65.
Foster, Geo. P., Aug. 1, '64.
Foster, John A., Sept. 28, '65.
Foust, B. F., Mar. 13, '65.
Fowler, Edw. B., Mar. 13, '65.
Franchot, R., Mar. 13, '65.
Francine, Louis R., July 2, '63.
Frank, Paul, Mar. 13, '65.
Frankle, Jones, Sept. 3, '65.
Frazer, D., Mar. 13, '65.
Frazer, John, Mar. 13, '65.
Frederick, C. H., Mar. 13, '65.
French, W. B., Mar. 13, '65.
Frink, Henry A., Oct. 4, '65.
Frisbie, H. N., Mar. 13, '65.
Fritz, Peter, Jr., Mar. 13, '65.
Frizell, J. W., Mar. 13, '65.
Frohock, Wm. T., Mar. 13, '65.
Fuller, H. W., Mar. 13, '65.
Fullerton, J. S., Mar. 13, '65.
Funke, Otto, Feb. 13, '65.
Fyffe, Edw. P., Mar. 13, '65.
Gage, Joseph S., June 15, '65.
Gallagher, T. F., Mar. 13, '65.
Gallup, Geo. W., Mar. 13, '62.
Gansevoort, H. S., June 24, '64.
Gardiner, Alex., Sept. 19, '64.
Garrard, Israel, June 20, '65.
Garrard, Jephtha, Mar. 13, '65.
Gates, Theo. B., Mar. 13, '65.
Geddes, James L., June 5, '65.
Gerhardt, Joseph, Mar. 13, '65.
Gibson, H. G., Mar. 13, '65.
Gibson, Wm. H., Mar. 13, '65.
Giesy, Henry H., May 28, '64.
Gilbert, S. A., Mar. 13, '65.
Gilchrist, C. A., Mar. 26, '65.
Gile, Geo. W., May 6, '65.
Ginty, Geo. C., Sept. 28, '65.
Given, Josiah, Mar. 13, '65.
Given, William, Mar. 13, '65.
Glasgow, S. L., Dec. 19, '64.
Gleason, Newell, Mar. 13, '65.
Glenny, Wm., Mar. 13, '65.
Gobin, J. P. S., Mar. 13, '65.
Goddard, Wm., Mar. 13, '65.
Godman, J. H., Mar. 13, '65.
Goff, Nathan, Jr., Mar. 13, '65.
Goodell, A. A., Mar. 13, '65.
Goodyear, E. D. S., April 2, '65.
Gowan, Geo. W., April 2, '65.
Graham, Harvey, July 25, '65.
Graham, Samuel, Mar. 13, '65.
Granger, Geo. F., June 12, '65.
Greeley, Edwin S., Mar. 13, '65.
Green, Wm. M., May 14, '64.
Gregg, Wm. M., April 2, '65.
Grier, D. P., Mar. 26, '65.
Griffin, Dan'l F., Mar. 13, '65.
Grindlay, James, Mar. 13, '65.
Grosvenor, C. H., Mar. 13, '65.
Grosvenor, T. W., Feb. 13, '65.
Grover, Ira G., Mar. 13, '65.
Grubb, E. Burd, Mar. 13, '65.
Guiney, P. R., Mar. 13, '65.
Guppy, Joshua J., Mar. 13, '65.
Gurney, William, May 19, '65.
Hall, Caldwell K., Mar. 13, '65.
Hall, Cyrus, Mar. 13, '65.
Hall, H. Seymour, Mar. 13, '65.
Hall, Jas. A., Mar. 3, '65.

Hall, James F., Feb. 24, '65.
Hall, Jarius W., Mar. 13, '65.
Hall, Rob't M., Mar. 13, '65.
Hallowell, E. N., June 27, '65.
Halpine, C. G., Mar. 13, '65.
Hamilton, W. D., April 9, '65.
Hamlin, Chas., Mar. 13, '65.
Hammell, John S., Mar. 13, '65.
Hammond, J. H., Oct. 31, '64.
Hammond, John, Mar. 13, '65.
Hanbreght, H. A., June 7, '65
Hanna, Wm., Mar. 13, '65.
Hardenbergh, J. B., Mar. 13, '65.
Harding, C., Jr., May 27, '65.
Harlin, E. B., Mar. 13, '65.
Harnden, Henry, Mar. 13, '65.
Harriman, Sam'l, April 2, '65.
Harriman, W., Mar. 13, '65.
Harris, A. L., Mar. 13, '65.
Harris, Benj. F., Mar. 13, '65.
Harris, Chas. L., Mar. 13, '65.
Harrison, Benj., Jan. 23, '65.
Harrison, M. LaRue, Mar. 13, '65.
Harrison, T. J., Jan. 31, '65.
Hart, James H., Mar. 13, '65.
Hart, O. H., Mar. 13, '65.
Hartshorne, W. R., Mar. 13, '65.
Hartsuff, Wm., Jan. 24, '64.
Hartwell, A. S., Dec. 30, '64.
Hartwell, C. A., Dec. 2, '65.
Haskill, L. F., Mar. 13, '65.
Hastings, R., Mar. 13, '65.
Haughton, Nath'l, Mar. 13, '65.
Hawkes, Geo. P., Mar. 13, '65.
Hawkins, I. R., Mar. 13, '65.
Hawkins, R. C., Mar. 13, '65.
Hawley, William, Mar. 16, '65.
Hayes, P. C., Mar. 13, '65.
Hayman, S. B., Mar. 13, '65.
Hays, E. L., Jan. 12, '65.
Hazard, J. G., Mar. 13, '65.
Healy, R. W., Mar. 13, '65.
Heath, Francis, Mar. 13, '65.
Heath, Thomas T., Dec. 15, '64.
Hedrick, J. M., Mar. 13, '65.
Heine, Wm., Mar. 13, '65.
Heinrichs, Gus., Mar. 13, '65.
Henderson, R. M., Mar. 13, '65.
Henderson, T. J., Nov. 30, '64.
Hendrickson, J. A., Mar. 13, '65.
Hennessey, J. A., Mar. 13, '65.
Henry, Guy V., Oct. 28, '64.
Henry, Wm. W., Mar. 7, '65.
Herrick, W. F., May 13, '65.
Herring, Chas. P., Mar. 13, '65.
Hickenlooper, A., Mar. 13, '65.
Hill, Jonathan A., April 9, '65.
Hill, Sylvester G., Dec. 15, '64.
Hillis, David B., Mar. 13, '65.
Hillyer, W. S., Mar. 13, '65.
Hitchcock, G. H., Mar. 13, '65.
Hobart, J. B., Jan. 12, '65.
Hobson, Wm., April 6, '65.
Hoffman, H. C., Mar. 13, '65.
Hoffman, Wm. J., Aug. 1, '64.
Hoge, Geo. B., Mar. 13, '65.
Hoge, George W., Mar. 13, '65.
Holbrook, M. T., Mar. 13, '65.
Holloway, E. S., Mar. 13, '65.

David H. Strother, of Virginia, Originally Colonel 3d West Virginia Cavalry.

Thomas M. Harris, of West Virginia, Originally Colonel of the 10th Infantry.

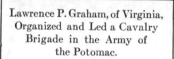

Lawrence P. Graham, of Virginia, Organized and Led a Cavalry Brigade in the Army of the Potomac.

FEDERAL GENERALS

No. 29

VIRGINIA AND WEST VIRGINIA

Henry Capehart, of West Virginia, Colonel 1st Cavalry.

John W. Davidson, of Virginia, Promoted for the Capture of Little Rock.

James A. Hardie, of West Virginia, Brevetted for Distinguished Services.

Robert C. Buchanan, of District of Columbia, Brevetted for Gallantry.

Henry B. Carrington, Originally Colonel of the 18th West Virginia Infantry.

WEST VIRGINIA AND DISTRICT OF COLUMBIA

Richard H. Jackson, of District of Columbia, Brevetted for Gallantry During the War.

Holman, J. H., Mar. 13, '65.
Holt, Thomas, Mar. 13, '65.
Holter, M. J. W., Mar. 13, '65.
Hooker, A. E., Mar. 13, '65.
Horn, John W., Oct. 19, '64.
Hotchkiss, C. T., Mar. 13, '65.
Hough, John, March 13, '65.
Houghtaling, Chas., Feb. 13, '65.
Houghton, M. B., Mar. 13, '65.
Howard, Chas. H., Aug. 15, '65.
Howe, John H., Mar. 13, '65.
Howland, H. N., Mar. 13, '62.
Howland, Joseph, Mar. 13, '65.
Hoyt, Chas. H., Mar. 13, '65.
Hoyt, Geo. H., Mar. 13, '65.
Hoyt, Henry M., Mar. 13, '65.
Hubbard, James, April 6, '65.
Hubbard, L. F., Dec. 16, '64.
Hubbard, T. H., June 30, '65.
Hudnutt, Jos. O., Mar. 13, '65.
Hudson, John G., Mar. 13, '65.
Huey, Pennock, Mar. 13, '65.
Hugunin, J. R., Mar. 13, '65.
Humphrey, T. W., June 10, '65.
Humphrey, Wm., Aug. 1, '64.
Hunt, Lewis C., Mar. 13, '65.
Hunter, M. C., Mar. 13, '65.
Hurd, John R., Mar. 13, '65.
Hurst, Samuel H., Mar. 13, '65.
Hutchins, Rue P., Mar. 13, '65.
Hutchinson, F. S., May 24, '65.
Hyde, Thomas W., April 2, '65.
Ingraham, T., Oct. 2, '65.
Innes, Wm. P., Mar. 13, '65.
Irvine, Wm., March 13, '65.
Irvin, William H., Mar. 13, '65.
Ives, Brayton, March 13, '65.
Jacobs, Ferris, Jr., Mar. 13, '65.
Jackson, S. M., March 13, '64.
Jackson, Jos. C., Mar. 13, '65.
James, W. L., March 1, '66.
Jardine, Edw., Nov. 2, '65.
Jarvis, Dwight, Jr., Mar. 13, '65.
Jeffries, Noah L., Mar. 30, '65.
Jenkins, H., Jr., March 13, '65.
Jennison, S. P., March 13, '65.
Johnson, Chas. A., Mar. 13, '65.
Johnson, G. M. L., Mar. 13, '65.
Johnson, J. M., March 13, '65.
Johnson, Lewis, March 13, '65.
Johnson, Robert, Mar. 13, '65.
Johns, Thos. D., March 13, '65.
Jones, J. B., March 13, '65.
Jones, Edward F., Mar. 13, '65.
Jones, Fielder A., Mar. 13, '65.
Jones, John S., March 13, '65.
Jones, Samuel B., Mar. 31, '65.
Jones, Theodore, Mar. 13, '65.
Jones, Wells S., Mar. 13, '65.
Jones, Wm. P., March 13, '65.
Jordan, Thos. J., Feb. 25, '65.
Judson, R. W., July 28, '66.
Judson, Wm. R., Mar. 13, '65.
Karge, Jonah, March 13, '65.
Keily, D. J., March 13, '65.
Kellogg, John A., April 9, '65.
Kelly, John H., Feb. 13, '65.
Kennedy, R. P., March 13, '65.
Kent, Loren, March 22, '65.
Kennett, H. G., March 13, '65.
Ketner, James, March 13, '65.

Kidd, James H., Mar. 13, '65.
Kilgour, Wm. M., June 20, '65.
Kimball, John W., Mar. 13, '65.
Kimball, Wm. R., Mar. 13, '65.
Kimberly, R. L., Mar. 13, '65.
King, Adam E., Mar. 13, '65.
King, John F., March 13, '65.
King, Wm. S., March 13, '65.
Kingsbury, H. D., Mar. 10, '65.
Kinney, T. J., March 26, '65.
Kinsey, Wm. B., Mar. 13, '65.
Kirby, Byron, Sept. 6, '65.
Kirby, Dennis T., Mar. 13, '65.
Kirby, Isaac M., Jan. 12, '65.
Kise, Reuben C., Mar. 13, '65.
Kitchell, Edward, Mar. 13, '65.
Kitching, J. H., Aug. 1, '64.
Kneffner, Wm. C., Mar. 13, '65.
Knefler, Fred'k, Mar. 13, '65.
Knowles, Oliv. B., Mar. 13, '65.
Kozlay, E. A., March 13, '65.
Krez, Conrad, March 26, '65.
Lafflin, Byron, March 13, '65.
Lagow, C. B., March 13, '65.
La Grange, O. H., Mar. 13, '65.
La Motte, C. E., Mar. 13, '65.
Landram, Wm. J., Mar. 13, '62.
Lane, John Q., March 13, '65.
Langdon, E. Bassett, Mar. 13, '65.
Lansing, H. S., Mar. 13, '65.
Laselle, Wm. P., Mar. 13, '65.
Laughlin, R. G., Mar. 13, '65.
Latham, Geo. R., Mar. 13, '65.
Lawrence, A. G., Mar. 25, '65.
Lawrence, Wm. Henry, Mar. 13, '65.
Lawrence, Wm. Hudson, Mar. 13, '65.
Leake, Jos. B., March 13, '65.
Le Duc, Wm. G., Mar. 13, '65.
Lee, Horace C., Mar. 13, '65.
Lee, Edward M., Mar. 13, '65.
Lee, John C., March 13, '65.
Lee, Wm. R., March 13, '65.
Le Favour, H., March 13, '65.
Le Gendre, C. W., Mar. 13, '65.
Leech, Wm. A., Mar. 13, '65.
Leib, Herman, March 13, '65.
Leiper, Chas. L., Mar. 13, '65.
Lewis, Chas. W., Mar. 13, '65.
Lewis, John R., March 13, '65.
Lewis, W. D., Jr., Mar. 13, '65.
Lincoln, Wm. S., June 23, '65.
Locke, Fred'k. T., April 1, '65.
Lockman, J. T., March 13, '65.
Loomis, Cyrus O., June 20, '65.
Lord, T. Ellery, Mar. 13, '65.
Love, George M., Mar. 7, '65.
Lovell, Fred'k S., Oct. 11, '65.
Lindley, J. M., March 13, '65.
Lippincott, C. E., Feb. 17, '65.
Lippitt, Francis J., Mar. 3, '65.
Lister, Fred. W., Mar. 13, '65.
Litchfield, A. C., Mar. 13, '65.
Littell, John S., Jan. 15, '65.
Littlejohn, De Witt C., Mar. 13, '65.
Littlefield, M. S., Nov. 26, '65.
Livingston, R. R., June 21, '65.
Ludington, M. J., Mar. 13, '65.
Ludlow, Benj. C., Oct. 28, '64.
Lyle, Peter, Mar. 13, '65.

Lyman, Luke, Mar. 13, '65.
Lynch, Jas. C., Mar. 13, '65.
Lynch, Wm. F., Jan. 31, '65.
Lyon, Wm. P., Oct. 26, '65.
McArthur, W. M., Mar. 13, '65.
McBride, J. D., Mar. 13, '65.
McCall, W. H. H., April 2, '65.
McCalmont, A. B., Mar. 13, '65.
McCleery, Jas., Mar. 13, '65.
McCleunen, M. R., April 2, '65.
McClurg, A. C., Sept. 18, '65.
McConihe, John, June 1, '64.
McConihe, Sam., Mar. 13, '65.
McConnell, H. K., Mar. 13, '65.
McConnell, John, Mar. 13, '65.
McCook, A. G., Mar. 13, '65.
McCormick, Chas. C., Mar. 13, '65.
McCoy, Daniel, Mar. 13, '65.
McCoy, Rob't A., Mar. 13, '65.
McCoy, Thos. F., April 1, '65.
McCreary, D. B., Mar. 13, '65.
McCrillis, L., Sept. 4, '64.
McDougall, C. D., Feb. 25, '65.
McEwen, Matt., Mar. 13, '65.
McGarry, Ed., Mar. 13, '65.
McGowan, J. E., Mar. 13, '65.
McGregor, J. D., Mar. 13, '65.
McGroarty, S. J., May 1, '65.
McKenny, T. J., Mar. 13, '65.
McKibbin, G. H., Dec. 2, '64.
McLaren, R. N., Dec. 14, '65.
McMahon, J., June 30, '65.
McNary, Wm. H., Mar. 13, '65.
McNaught, T. A., Aug. 4, '65.
McNett, A. J., July 28, '66.
McNulta, John, Mar. 13, '65.
McQueen, A. G., Mar. 13, '65.
McQueston, J. C., Mar. 13, '65.
Mackey, A. J., Mar. 13, '65.
Macauley, Dan., Mar. 13, '65.
Magee, David W., Mar. 13, '65.
Malloy, Adam G., Mar. 13, '65.
Manderson, C. F., Mar. 13, '65.
Mank, Wm. G., Mar. 13, '65.
Mann, Orrin L., Mar. 13, '65.
Manning, S. H., Mar. 13, '65.
Mansfield, John, Mar. 13, '65.
Markoe, John, Mar. 13, '65.
Marple, Wm. W., Mar. 13, '65.
Marshall, W. R., Mar. 13, '65.
Martin, Jas. S., Feb. 28, '65.
Martin, John A., Mar. 13, '65.
Martin, Wm. H., June 8, '65.
Mason, Ed. C., June 3, '65.
Mather, T. S., Sept. 28, '65.
Matthews, J. A., April 2, '65.
Matthews, Sol. S., Mar. 13, '65.
Mattocks, C. P., Mar. 13, '65.
Maxwell, N. J., April 18, '65.
Maxwell, O. C., Mar. 13, '65.
May, Dwight, Mar. 13, '65.
Mehringer, John, Mar. 13, '65.
Merrill, Lewis, Mar. 13, '65.
Mersey, August, Mar. 13, '65.
Messer, John, Mar. 13, '65.
Meyers, Edw. S., Mar. 13, '65.
Michie, Peter S., Jan. 1, '65.
Miller, A. O., Mar. 13, '65.
Miller, Madison, Mar. 13, '65.
Mills, Jas. K., Mar. 13, '65.
Mintzer, Wm. M., Mar. 13, '65.
Mitchell, G. M., Aug. 22, '65.

Mitchell, W. G., Mar. 13, '65.
Mix, Elisha, Mar. 13, '65.
Mizner, H. R., Mar. 13, '65.
Mizner, John K., Mar. 13, '65.
Moffitt, Stephen, Mar. 13, '65.
Monroe, Geo. W., Mar. 13, '62.
Montgomery, M., Mar. 13, '65.
Moody, G., Jan. 12, '65.
Moon, John C., Nov. 21, '65.
Moonlight, Thos., Feb. 13, '65.
Moor, Augustus, Mar. 13, '65.
Moore, David, Feb. 21, '65.
Moore, Fred'k W., Mar. 26, '65.
Moore, Jesse H., May 15, '65.
Moore, Jon. B., Mar. 26, '65.
Moore, Tim. C., Mar. 13, '65.
Morehead, T. G., Mar. 13, '65.
Morgan, G. N., Mar. 13, '65.
Morgan, Thos. J., Mar. 13, '65.
Morgan, Wm. H., April 20, '65.
Morgan, Wm. H., Mar. 13, '65.
Morrill, John, Mar. 13, '65.
Morrison, D., Mar. 13, '65.
Morrison, Jos. J., Mar. 13, '65.
Morse, Henry B., Mar. 13, '65.
Mott, Sam'l R., Mar. 13, '65.
Mudgett, Wm. S., Mar. 13, '65.
Mulcahey, Thos., Mar. 13, '65.
Mulford, J. E., July 4, '64.
Mulligan, J. A., July 23, '65.
Mundee, Chas., April 2, '65.
Murphy, John K., Mar. 13, '65.
Murray, Benj. B., Mar. 13, '65.
Murray, Edw., Mar. 13, '65.
Murray, Ely H., Mar. 25, '65.
Murray, John B., Mar. 13, '65.
Mussey, R. D., Mar. 13, '65.
Myers, Geo. R., Mar. 13, '65.
Nase, Adam, Mar. 13, '65.
Neafie, Alfred, Mar. 13, '65.
Neff, Andrew J., Mar. 13, '65.
Neff, Geo. W., Mar. 13, '65.
Neide, Horace, Mar. 13, '65.
Nettleton, A. B., Mar. 13, '62.
Newbury, W. C., Mar. 31, '65.
Newport, R. M., Mar. 13, '65.
Nichols, Geo. F., Mar. 13, '65.
Nichols, Geo. S., Mar. 13, '65.
Niles, Nat., Mar. 13, '65.
Noble, John W., Mar. 13, '65.
Noble, Wm. H., Mar. 13, '65.
Northcott, R. S., Mar. 13, '65.
Norton, Chas. B., Mar. 13, '65.
Noyes, Edw. F., Mar. 13, '65.
Nugent, Robert, Mar. 13, '65.
O'Beirne, J. R., Sept. 26, '65.
O'Brien, Geo. M., Mar. 13, '65.
O'Dowd, John, Mar. 13, '65.
Oley, John H., Mar. 13, '65.
Oliphant, S. D., June 27, '65.
Oliver, Paul A., Mar. 8, '65.
Olmstead, W. A., April 9, '65.
Ordway, Albert, Mar. 13, '65.
Osband, E. D., Oct. 5, '64.
Osborn, F. A., Mar. 13, '65.
Otis, Calvin N., Mar. 13, '65.
Otis, Elwell S., Mar. 13, '65.
Otis, John L., Mar. 13, '65.
Ozburn, Lyndorf, Mar. 13, '65.
Packard, Jasper, Mar. 13, '65.
Painter, Wm., Mar. 13, '65.
Palfrey, F. W., Mar. 13, '65.
Palmer, Oliver H., Mar. 13, '65.

Walter P. Lane Led a Brigade of Cavalry West of the Mississippi.

William P. Hardeman Led a Brigade in Magruder's Army.

Lawrence S. Ross Commanded a Brigade in Wheeler's Cavalry.

Walter H. Stevens, Chief Engineer, Army of Northern Virginia.

Elkanah Greer Commanded the Reserve Corps, Trans-Mississippi Department.

A. P. Bagby, Originally Colonel of the 7th Cavalry; Later Led a Division.

John A. Wharton Commanded a Division of Wheeler's Cavalry in Tennessee.

James E. Harrison Commanded a Brigade of Polignac's Division in Louisiana.

William H. Young Led a Brigade in the Army of Tennessee.

John W. Whitfield Commanded a Brigade of Texas Cavalry.

Joseph L. Hogg Led a Brigade in the Army of the West.

Samuel Bell Maxcy, Originally Colonel of the 9th Infantry.

William Steele Led a Brigade at Shreveport in 1864.

CONFEDERATE GENERALS—No. 21—TEXAS

The Union Generals

Palmer, Wm. J., Nov. 6, '64.
Partridge, F. W., Mar. 13, '65.
Partridge, B. F., Mar. 31, '65.
Parish, Chas. S., Mar. 13, '65.
Parrott, Jas. C., Mar. 13, '65.
Park, Sidney W., Mar. 13, '65.
Parkhurst, J. G., May 22, '65.
Pardee, D. A., Mar. 13, '65.
Pardee, Ario, Jr., Jan. 12, '65.
Parry, Aug. C., Mar. 13, '65.
Pattee, John, Mar. 13, '65.
Pattee, Jos. B., April 9, '65.
Patterson, R. F., Mar. 13, '65.
Patterson, R. E., Mar. 13, '65.
Patterson, J. N., Mar. 13, '65.
Patten, H. L., Sept. 10, '64.
Paul, Frank, Mar. 13, '65.
Payne, Eugene B., Mar. 13, '65.
Payne, Oliver H., Mar. 13, '65.
Pearsall, Uri B., Mar. 13, '65.
Pearson, Rbt. N., Mar. 13, '65.
Pearce, John S., Mar. 13, '65.
Pease, Phineas, Mar. 13, '65.
Pease, Wm. R., Mar. 13, '65.
Peck, Frank H., Sept. 19, '65.
Pennington, A. C. M., July16, '65.
Perkins, H. W., Mar. 13, '65.
PerLee, Sam'l R., Mar. 13, '65.
Phelps, Chas. E., Mar. 13, '65.
Phelps, John E., Mar. 13, '65.
Phelps, W., Jr., Mar. 13, '65.
Phillips, Jesse L., Mar. 13, '65.
Pickett, Josiah, Mar. 13, '65.
Pierson, Chas. L., Mar. 13, '65.
Pierson, J. Fred., Mar. 13, '65.
Pierson, Wm. S., Mar. 13, '65.
Pierce, F. E., Mar. 13, '65.
Pinckney, Jos. C., Mar. 13, '65.
Pinto, F. E., Mar. 13, '64.
Platner, John S., Mar. 13, '65.
Pleasants, H., Mar. 13, '65.
Pollock, S. M., Mar. 13, '65.
Pomutz, Geo., Mar. 13, '65.
Pope, Ed. M., Mar. 13, '65.
Porter, Sam'l A., Mar. 13, '65.
Post, P. Sidney, Dec. 16, '64.
Potter, Carroll H., Mar. 13, '65.
Powell, Eugene, Mar. 13, '65.
Price, Francis, Mar. 13, '65.
Price, W. R., Mar. 13, '65.
Price, S. W., Mar. 13, '62.
Price, Rich'd B., Mar. 13, '65.
Pritchard, B. D., May 10, '65.
Proudfit, J. L., Mar. 13, '65.
Pratt, Benj. F., Mar. 13, '65.
Preston, S. M., Dec. 30, '65.
Prescott, Geo. L., June 18, '64.
Prevost, C. M., Mar. 13, '65.
Pugh, Isaac C., Mar. 10, '65.
Pulford, John, Mar. 13, '65.
Quincy, S. M., Mar. 13, '65.
Randall, Geo. W., Mar. 13, '65.
Randol, A. M., June 24, '65.
Ratliff, Rbt. W., Mar. 13, '65.
Raynor, Wm. H., Mar. 13, '65.
Read, S. Tyler, Mar. 13, '65.
Read, Theo., Sept. 29, '64.
Remick, D., Mar. 13, '65.
Reno, M. A., Mar. 13, '65.
Revere, W. R., Jr., Mar. 13, '65.
Revere, P. J., July 2, '65.

Reynolds, Jos. S., July 11, '65.
Richardson, H., Mar. 13, '65.
Richardson, W. P., Dec. 7, '64.
Richmond, Lewis, Mar. 13, '65.
Riggin, John, Mar. 13, '65.
Rinaker, J. I., Mar. 13, '65.
Ripley, Edw. H., Aug. 1, '64.
Ripley, Theo. A., Mar. 13, '65.
Risdon, O. C., Mar. 13, '65.
Ritchie, John, Feb. 21, '65.
Robbins, W. R., Mar. 13, '65.
Roberts, Chas. W., Mar. 13,'65.
Roberts, S. H., Oct. 28, '64.
Robeson, W. P., Jr., April 1, '65.
Robinson, G. D., Mar. 13, '65.
Robinson, H. L., Mar. 13, '65.
Robinson, M. S., Mar. 13, '65.
Robinson, W. A., Mar. 13, '65.
Robison, J. K., Mar. 13, '65.
Rockwell, A. P., Mar. 13, '65.
Rodgers, H., Jr., Mar. 13, '65.
Rodgers, H. C., Mar. 13, '65.
Rogers, Jas. C., Mar. 13, '65.
Rogers, George, Mar. 13, '65.
Rogers, Geo. C., Mar. 13, '65.
Rogers, Wm. F., Mar. 13, '65.
Roome, Chas., Mar. 13, '65.
Rose, Thos. E., July 22, '65.
Ross, Samuel, April 13, '65.
Ross, W. E. W., Mar. 11, '65.
Rowett, Rich'd, Mar. 13, '65.
Rowley, Wm. R., Mar. 13, '65.
Ruggles, Jas. M., Mar. 13, '65.
Rusk, Jer. M., Mar. 13, '65.
Rusling, Jas. F., Feb. 16, '66.
Russell, Chas. S., July 30, '64.
Russell, Hy. S., Mar. 13, '65.
Rust, John D., Mar. 13, '65.
Rust, H., Jr., Mar. 13, '65.
Rutherford, Allen, Mar. 13,'65.
Rutherford, G. V., Mar. 13, '65.
Rutherford, R. C., Mar. 13,'65.
Sackett, Wm. H., June 10,·'64.
Salm Salm, F. P., April 13, '65.
Salomon, C. E., Mar. 13, '65.
Salomon, E. S., Mar. 13, '65.
Sanborn, Wm., Mar. 13, '65.
Sanders, A. H., Mar. 13, '65.
Sanders, H. T., April 19, '65.
Sanderson, T. W., Mar. 13, '65.
Sanford, E. S., Mar. 13, '65.
Sargent, H. B., Mar. 21, '64.
Sawyer, Frank, Mar. 13, '65.
Scates, W. B., Mar. 13, '65.
Schmitt, Wm. A., Mar. 13, '65.
Schneider, E. F., Mar. 13, '65.
Schofield, H., Mar. 13, '65.
Schofield, Geo. W., Jan. 26,'65.
Schwenk, S. K., July 24, '65.
Scribner, B. F., Aug. 8, '64.
Scott, Geo. W., Mar. 13, '65.
Scott, Rufus, Mar. 13, '65.
Seaver, Joel J., Mar. 13, '65.
Seawall, Thos. D., Mar. 13,'65.
Selfridge, J. L., Mar. 16, '65.
Serrell, Edw. W., Mar. 13, '65.
Sewall, F. D., July 21, '65.
Shaffer, G. T., Mar. 13, '65.
Shaffer, J. W., Mar. 13, '65.
Shafter, Wm. R., Mar. 13, '65.
Sharpe, Jacob, Mar. 13, '65.
Shaurman, N., Mar. 13, '65.

Shaw, Jas., Jr., Mar. 13, '65.
Shedd, Warren, Mar. 13, '65.
Sheets, Benj. F., Mar. 13, '65.
Sheets, Josiah A., Mar. 13, '65.
Sheldon, Chas. S., Mar. 13, '65.
Sheldon, L. A., Mar. 13, '65.
Shepherd, R. B., Mar. 13, '65.
Sherwood, I. R., Feb. 27, '65.
Sherwin, T., Jr., Mar. 13, '65.
Shoup, Sam'l, Mar. 13, '65.
Shunk, David, Feb. 9, '65.
Shurtleff, G. W., Mar. 13, '65.
Sickles, H. F., Mar. 13, '65.
Sigfried, J. K., Aug. 1, '64.
Simpson, S. P., Mar. 13, '65.
Sleven, P. S., Mar. 13, '65.
Slocum, Willard, Mar. 13, '65.
Smith, Arthur A., Mar. 13, '65.
Smith, Al. B., Mar. 13, '65.
Smith, Benj. F., Mar. 26, '65.
Smith, Chas. E., Mar. 13, '65.
Smith, E. W., Mar. 13, '65.
Smith, F. C., Mar. 13, '65.
Smith, Geo. W., Mar. 13, '65.
Smith, Gus. A., Mar. 13, '65.
Smith, Israel C., Mar. 13, '65.
Smith, James, Mar. 13, '65.
Smith, John C., June 20, '65.
Smith, Jos. S., July 11, '65.
Smith, Orlando, Mar. 13, '65.
Smith, Orlow, Mar. 13, '65.
Smith, Robert F., Mar. 13, '65.
Smith, Rbt. W., Feb. 13, '65.
Smith, Wm. J., July 16, '65.
Sniper, Gustavus, Mar. 13, '65.
Sowers, Edgar, Mar. 13, '65.
Sprague, A. B. R., Mar. 13, '65.
Sprague, Ezra T., June 20, '65.
Spalding, George, Mar. 21, '65.
Spaulding, Ira, April 9, '65.
Spaulding, O. L., June 25, '65.
Spencer, Geo. E., Mar. 13, '65.
Spear, Ellis, Mar. 13, '65.
Spear, Sam'l P., Mar. 13, '65.
Spicely, Wm. T., Aug. 26, '65.
Spurling, A. B., Mar. 26, '65.
Spofford, John P., Mar. 13, '65.
Stafford, Jacob A., Mar. 13, '65.
Stager, Anson, Mar. 13, '65.
Stagg, Peter, Mar. 30, '65.
Stanley, Tim. L., Mar. 13, '65.
Stanton, David L., April 1, '65.
Starbird, I. W., Mar. 13, '65.
Starring, F. A., Mar. 13, '65.
Stedman, G. A., Jr., Aug. 5, '64.
Stedman, Wm., Mar. 13, '65.
Steers, Wm. H. P., Mar. 13, '65.
Steiner, John A., Mar. 13, '65.
Stephenson, L., Jr., Mar. 13, '64.
Stevens, Aaron F., Dec. 8, '64.
Stevens, A. A., Mar. 7, '65.
Stevens, Hazard, April 2, '65.
Stevenson, R. H., Mar. 13, '65.
Stewart, Jas., Jr., Mar. 13, '65.
Stewart, W. S., Mar. 13, '65.
Stewart, Wm. W., Mar. 13, '65.
Stibbs, John H., Mar. 13, '65.
Stiles, Israel N., Jan. 31, '64.
Stockton, Jos., Mar. 13, '65.
Stokes, Wm. B., Mar. 13, '65.
Stone, Geo. A., Mar. 13, '65.

Stone, Roy, Sept. 7, '64.
Stone, Wm. M., Mar. 13, '65.
Stough, Wm., Mar. 13, '65.
Stoughton, C. B., Mar. 13, '65.
Stout, Alex. W., Mar. 13, '62.
Stratton, F. A., Mar. 13, '65.
Streight, Abel D., Mar. 13, '65.
Strickland, S. A., Mar. 13, '65.
Strong, Jas. C., Mar. 13, '65.
Strong, Thos. J., Mar. 13, '65.
Strong, Wm. E., Mar. 21, '65.
Strother, D. H., Aug. 23, '65.
Sumner, E. V., Jr., Mar. 13, '65.
Sullivan, P. J., Mar. 13, '65.
Sweet, Benj., Dec. 20, '64.
Sweitzer, J. B., Mar. 13, '65.
Swift, Fred. W., Mar. 13, '65.
Switzler, T. A., Mar. 13, '65.
Sypher, J. Hale, Mar. 13, '65.
Talbot, Thos. H., Mar. 13, '65.
Talley, Wm. C., Mar. 13, '65.
Tarbell, Jon., Mar. 13, '65.
Taylor, Ezra, Feb. 13, '65.
Taylor, J. E., Mar. 13, '65.
Taylor, John P., Aug. 4, '65.
Taylor, Thos. T., Mar. 13, '65.
Tevis, W. Carroll, Mar. 13, '65.
Tew, Geo. W., Mar. 13, '65.
Thomas, De Witt C., Mar. 13, '65.
Thomas, M. T., Feb. 10, '65.
Thomas, Samuel, Mar. 13, '65.
Thompson, C. R., April 13, '65.
Thompson, D., Mar. 13, '65.
Thompson, H. E., Mar. 13, '65.
Thompson, J. L., Mar. 13, '65.
Thompson, J. M., Mar. 13, '65.
Thompson, R., Mar. 13, '65.
Thompson, Wm., Mar. 13, '65.
Thorp, Thos. J., Mar. 13, '65.
Throop, Wm. A., Mar. 13, '65.
Thruston, G. P., Mar. 13, '65.
Thurston, W. H., Mar. 13, '65.
Tilden, Chas. W., Mar. 13, '65.
Tilghman, B. C., April 13, '65.
Tillson, John, Mar. 10, '65.
Tilton, Wm. S., Sept. 9, '64.
Titus, Herbert B., Mar. 13, '65.
Tompkins, C. H., Aug. 1, '64.
Tourtelotte, J. E., Mar. 13, '65.
Tracy, B. F., Mar. 13, '65.
Trauernicht, T., Mar. 13, '65.
Tremaine, H. E., Nov. 30, '65.
Trotter, F. E., Mar. 13, '65.
True, Jas. M., Mar. 6, '65.
Truex, William S., April 2, '65.
Trumbull, M. M., Mar. 13, '65.
Turley, John A., Mar. 13, '65.
Turner, Charles, Mar. 26, '65.
Van Antwerp, V., Feb. 13, '65.
VanBuren, D. T., Mar. 13, '65.
VanBuren, J. L., April 2, '65.
VanBuren, T. B., Mar. 13, '65.
Van Schrader, A., Mar. 13, '65.
Varney, Geo., Mar. 13, '65.
Van Petten, J. V., Mar. 13, '65.
Van Shaak, G. W., Mar. 13, '65.
Vail, Jacob G., Mar. 13, '65.
Vail, Nicholas J., Mar. 13, '65.
Vaughn, Sam'l K., Aug. 9, '65.
Vickers, David, Mar. 13, '65.
Vifquain, V., Mar. 13, '65.
Von Blessingh, L., Mar. 13, '65.

Richard M. Gano Led a Brigade of Morgan's Cavalry.

Matthew D. Ector Led a Brigade in the Army of Tennessee.

Richard Waterhouse Led a Brigade of Infantry and Cavalry.

Thomas Harrison Led a Brigade in the Army of Tennessee.

Felix H. Robertson Led a Brigade of Cavalry in the Army of Tennessee.

John C. Moore Led a Brigade in the Army of the West.

John R. Baylor, Conspicuous in Operations in Texas and New Mexico in 1861–62.

Henry E. McCulloch, Texas Brigade and District Commander.

Louis T. Wigfall, Bearer of a Flag of Truce at Fort Sumter.

Thomas N. Waul, Colonel of Waul's Texas Legion.

Jerome B. Robertson Led a Brigade in Hood's Division.

CONFEDERATE GENERALS

—No. 22—

TEXAS (CONTINUED)

The Union Generals

Von Egloffstein, F. W., Mar. 13, '65.
Von Vegesack, E., Mar. 13, '65.
Vreeland, M. J., Mar. 13, '65.
Wade, Jas. F., Feb. 13, '64.
Wagner, Louis, Mar. 13, '65.
Waite, Charles, April 2, '65.
Waite, John M., Feb. 13, '65.
Wainwright, C. S., Aug. 1, '64.
Wainwright, W. P., Mar. 13, '65.
Walcutt, C. F., April 9, '65.
Walker, D. S., Mar. 13, '65.
Walker, F. A., Mar. 31, '65.
Walker, M. B., Mar. 27, '65.
Walker, Samuel, Mar. 13, '65.
Walker, Thos. M., July 5, '65.
Wallace, M. R. M., Mar. 13, '65.
Wangelin, Hugo, Mar. 13, '65.
Warner, D. B., Feb. 13, '65.
Ward, Durbin, Oct. 18, '65.
Ward, Geo. H., July 2, '63.
Ward, Henry C., Nov. 29, '65.
Ward, Lyman M., Mar. 13, '65.
Warner, A. J., Mar. 13, '65.
Warner, Edw. R., April 9, '65.
Warren, L. H., Mar. 13, '65.
Washburn, F., April 6, '65.
Washburn, G. A., Mar. 13, '65.

Wass, Ansell D., Mar. 13, '65.
Waters, L. H., June 18, '65.
Weaver, Jas. B., Mar. 13, '65.
Webber, Jules C., Mar. 13, '65.
Webber, A. W., Mar. 26, '65.
Weld, S. M., Jr., Mar. 13, '65.
Welles, Geo. E., Mar. 13, '65.
Wells, Geo. D., Oct. 12, '64.
Wells, Henry H., June 3, '65.
Wells, Milton, Mar. 13, '65.
Wentworth, M. F., Mar. 13, '65.
Welsh, William, Mar. 13, '65.
West, Edward W., Mar. 13, '65.
West, Francis H., Mar. 13, '65.
West, Geo. W., Dec. 2, '64.
West, Henry R., July 13, '65.
West, Robert M., April 1, '65.
Wever, Clark R., Feb. 9, '65.
Wheelock, Charles, Aug. 9, '64.
Wherry, Wm. M., April 2, '65.
White, Daniel, Mar. 13, '65.
Whitaker, E. W., Mar. 13, '65.
Whistler, J. N. G., Mar. 13, '65.
Whitbeck, H. N., Mar. 13, '65.
White, Carr B., Mar. 13, '65.
White, David B., Mar. 13, '65.
White, Frank, Mar. 13, '65.
White, Frank J., Mar. 13, '65.
White, Harry, Mar. 2, '65.

Whittier, Chas. A., April 9, '65.
Whittier, F. H., Mar. 13, '65.
Whittlesey, C. H., Mar. 13, '65.
Whittlesey, E., Mar. 13, '65.
Whittlesey, H. M., Mar. 13, '65.
Wilcox, Jas. A., Feb. 13, '65.
Wilcox, John S., Mar. 13, '65.
Wilder, John T., Aug. 7, '64.
Wildes, Thos. F., Mar. 11, '65.
Wildrick, A. C., April 2, '65.
Wiles, G. F., Mar. 13, '65.
Wiley, Aquila, Mar. 13, '65.
Wiley, Dan'l D., Mar. 13, '65.
Williams, A. W., Mar. 13, '65.
Williams, Jas. M., July 13, '65.
Williams, John, Mar. 13, '65.
Williams, R., Mar. 13, '65.
Williams, T. J., Sept. 22, '62.
Willian, John, April 9, '65.
Wilson, J. G., Mar. 13, '65.
Wilson, James, Mar. 13, '65.
Wilson, Lester S., Mar. 13, '65.
Wilson, Thomas, Mar. 13, '65.
Wilson, Wm. T., Mar. 13, '65.
Wilson, Wm., Nov. 13, '65.
Winkler, Fred. C., June 15, '65.
Winslow, Bradley, April 2, '65.
Winslow, E. F., Dec. 12, '64.
Winslow, R. E., Mar. 13, '65.

Wise, Geo. D., Mar. 13, '65.
Wisewell, M. N., Mar. 13, '65.
Wister, L., Mar. 13, '65.
Witcher, John S., Mar. 13, '65.
Withington, W. H., Mar. 13, '65.
Wolfe, Edw. H., Mar. 13, '65.
Wood, Oliver, Mar. 13, '65.
Wood, Wm. D., Mar. 13, '65.
Woodall, Daniel, June 15,'65.
Woodford, S. L., May 12, '65.
Woodhull, M. V. L., Mar. 13, '65.
Woodward, O. S., Mar. 13, '65.
Woolley, John, Mar. 13, '65.
Wormer, G. S., Mar. 13, '65.
Wright, Ed., Mar. 13, '65.
Wright, Elias, Jan. 15, '65.
Wright, John G., Mar. 13, '65.
Wright, Thos. F., Mar. 13, '65.
Yates, Henry, Jr., Mar. 13, '65.
Yeoman, S. B., Mar. 13, '65.
Yorke, Louis E., Mar. 13, '65.
Young, S. B. M., April 9, '65.
Young, Thos. L., Mar. 13, '65.
Zahm, Louis, Mar. 13, '62.
Ziegler, Geo. M., Mar. 13, '65.
Zinn, Geo., April 6, '65.
Zulick, Sam'l M., Mar. 13, '65.

D. B. Harris, Colonel in the Engineer Corps; Chief Engineer at Charleston.

Armstead L. Long, Staff Officer to Lee and His Authorized Biographer.

John B. Floyd, in Command in West Virginia in 1861, later at Fort Donelson.

William L. Jackson, Originally Colonel of the 31st Regiment.

CONFEDERATE

GENERALS

No. 23

VIRGINIA

Albert G. Jenkins Led a Command in Southwest Virginia; Wounded at Cloyd's Mountain.

Daniel Ruggles Commanded a Division in General Breckinridge's Army.

Camille J. Pol'gnac, Defender of the Red River Country, Leading in many Battles.

Montgomery D. Corse Battled Heroically at Five Forks and Petersburg.

Richard L. T. Beale Led a Brigade in Lee's Army.

Henry H. Walker Led a Virginia Brigade in Lee's Army.

Joseph R. Anderson Led a Brigade in Lee's Army.

Thomas Jordan, Beauregard's Chief of Staff; Later Fought for "Cuba Libre."

General Officers of the Confederate Army

A FULL ROSTER COMPILED FROM THE OFFICIAL RECORDS

The Confederate titles below derive authority through verification by General Marcus J. Wright, for many years in charge of Confederate records at the United States War Department, Washington. Some ranks appropriate to high commands, and fully justified, were never legally confirmed. In such cases, as those of Joseph Wheeler and John B. Gordon, General Wright has followed the strictest interpretation of the Confederate records below. As for the body of this History it has been thought best to employ the titles most commonly used, and found in the popular reference works. The highest rank attained is given in every case together with the date of the commission conferring such rank.

GENERALS

REGULAR

Beauregard, P. G. T., July 21, '61.
Bragg, Braxton, April 6, '62.
Cooper, Samuel, May 16, '61.
Johnston, A. S., May 30, '61.
Johnston, J. E., July 4, '61.
Lee, Robert E., June 14, '61.

GENERAL

PROVISIONAL ARMY

Smith, E. Kirby, Feb. 19, '64.

GENERALS

PROVISIONAL ARMY

(With Temporary Rank)

Hood, John B., July 18, '64.

LIEUTENANT-GENERALS

PROVISIONAL ARMY

Buckner, S. B., Sept. 20, '64.
Ewell, Richard S., May 23, '63.
Forrest, N. B., Feb. 28, '65.
Hampton, Wade, Feb. 14, '65.
Hardee, Wm. J., Oct. 10, '62.
Hill, Ambrose P., May 24, '63.
Hill, Daniel H., July 11, '63.
Holmes, T. H., Oct. 13, '62.
Jackson, T. J., Oct. 10, '62.
Lee, Stephen D., June 23, '64.
Longstreet, James, Oct. 9, '62.
Pemberton, J. C., Oct. 10, '62.
Polk, Leonidas, Oct. 10, '62.
Taylor, Richard, April 8, '64.

LIEUTENANT-GENERALS

PROVISIONAL ARMY

(With Temporary Rank)

Anderson, R. H., May 31, '64.
Early, Jubal A., May 31, '64.
Stewart, A. P., June 23, '64.

MAJOR-GENERALS

PROVISIONAL ARMY

Anderson, J. P., Feb. 17, '64.
Bate, William B., Feb. 23, '64.
Bowen, John S., May 25, '63.

Breckinridge, J. C., Apr. 14, '62.
Butler, M. C., Sept. 19, '64.
Cheatham, B. F., Mar. 10, '62.
Churchill, T. J., Mar. 17, '65.
Crittenden, G. B., Nov. 9, '61.
Cleburne, P. R., Dec. 13, '62.
Cobb, Howell, Sept. 9, '63.
Donelson, D. S., Jan. 17, '63.
Elzey, Arnold, Dec. 4, '62.
Fagan, James F., April 25, '64.
Field, Chas. W., Feb. 12, '64.
Forney, John H., Oct. 27, '62.
French, S. G., Aug. 31, '62.
Gardner, F., Dec. 13, '62.
Grimes, Bryan, Feb. 15, '65.
Gordon, John B., May 14, '64.
Heth, Henry, Oct. 10, '62.
Hindman, T. C., April 14, '62.
Hoke, Robert F., April 20, '64.
Huger, Benj., Oct. 7, '61.
Johnson, B. R., May 21, '64.
Johnson, Edward, Feb. 28, '63.
Jones, David R., Oct. 11, '62.
Jones, Samuel, Mar. 10, '62.
Kemper, J. L., Sept. 19, '64.
Kershaw, J. B., May 18, '64.
Lee, Fitzhugh, Aug. 3, '63.
Lee, G. W. Custis, Oct. 20, '64.
Lee, W. H. F., Apr. 23, '64.
Loring, W. W., Feb. 17, '62.
Lovell, Mansfield, Oct. 7, '61.
McCown, John P., Mar. 10, '62.
McLaws, L., May 23, '62.
Magruder, J. B., Oct. 7, '61.
Mahone, William, July 30, '64.
Marmaduke, J. S., Mar. 17, '65.
Martin, Will T., Nov. 10, '63.
Maury, D. H., Nov. 4, '62.
Polignac, C. J., April 8, '64.
Pender, W. D., May 27, '63.
Pickett, George E., Oct. 10, '62.
Price, Sterling, Mar. 6, '62.
Ransom, R., Jr., May 26, '63.
Rodes, Robert E., May 2, '63.
Smith, G. W., Sept. 19, '61.
Smith, Martin L., Nov. 4, '62.
Smith, William, Aug. 12, '63.
Stevenson, C. L., Oct. 10, '62.
Stuart, J. E. B., July 25, '62.
Taylor, Richard, July 28, '62.
Trimble, Isaac R., Jan. 17, '63.
Twiggs, D. E., May 22, '61.
Van Dorn, Earl, Sept. 19, '61.
Walker, John G., Nov. 8, '62.
Walker, W. H. T., May 23, '63.
Wharton, John A., Nov. 10, '63.
Wheeler, Joseph, Jan. 20, '64.
Whiting, W. H. C., Apr. 22, '63.
Withers, Jones M., April 6, '62.
Wilcox, C. M., Aug. 3, '63.

MAJOR-GENERALS

PROVISIONAL ARMY

(With Temporary Rank)

Allen, William W., Mar. 4, '65.
Brown, John C., Aug. 4, '64.
Clayton, Henry D., July 7, '64.
Lomax, L. L., Aug. 10, '64.
Ramseur, S. D., June 1, '64.
Rosser, T. L., Nov. 1, '64.
Walthall, E. C., July 6, '64.
Wright, A. R., Nov. 26, '64.
Young, P. M. B., Dec. 20, '64.

MAJOR-GENERAL

FOR SERVICE WITH VOLUNTEER TROOPS

(With Temporary Rank)

Gilmer, J. F., Aug. 25, '63.

BRIGADIER-GENERALS

PROVISIONAL ARMY

Adams, Daniel W., May 23, '62.
Adams, John, Dec. 29, '62.
Adams, Wirt, Sept. 25, '63.
Allen, Henry W., Aug. 19, '63.
Anderson, G. B., June 9, '62.
Anderson, J. R., Sept. 3, '61.
Anderson, S. R., July 9, '61.
Armistead, L. A., April 1, '62.
Armstrong, F. C., April 20, '63.
Anderson, G. T., Nov. 1, '62.
Archer, James J., June 3, '62.
Ashby, Turner, May 23, '62.
Baker, Alpheus, May 5, '64.
Baker, L. S., July 23, '63.
Baldwin, W. E., Sept. 19, '62.
Barksdale, W., Aug. 12, '62.
Barringer, Rufus, June 1, '64.
Barton, Seth M., Mar. 11, '62.
Battle, Cullen A., Aug. 20, '63.
Beall, W. N. R., April 11, '62.
Beale, R. L. T., Jan. 6, '65.
Bee, Barnard E., June 17, '61.
Bee, Hamilton P., Mar. 4, '62.
Bell, Tyree H., Feb. 28, '65.
Benning, H. L., Jan. 17, '63.
Boggs, William R., Nov. 4, '62.
Bonham, M. L., April 23, '61.
Blanchard, A. G., Sept. 21, '61.
Buford, Abraham, Sept. 2, '62.
Branch, L. O. B., Nov. 16, '61.
Brandon, Wm. L., June 18, '64.
Bratton, John, May 6, '64.
Brevard, T. W., Mar. 22, '65.
Bryan, Goode, Aug. 29, '63.
Cabell, Wm. A., Jan. 20, '63.
Campbell, A. W., Mar. 1, '65.
Cantey, James, Jan. 8, '63.

Capers, Ellison, Mar. 1, '65.
Carroll, Wm. H., Oct. 26, '61.
Chalmers, J. R., Feb. 13, '62.
Chestnut, J., Jr., April 23, '64.
Clark, Charles, May 22, '61.
Clark, John B., Mar. 8, '64.
Clanton, J. H., Nov. 16, '63.
Clingman, T. L., May 17, '62.
Cobb, T. R. R., Nov. 1, '62.
Cockrell, F. M., July 18, '63.
Cocke, P. St. G., Oct. 21, '61.
Colston, R. E., Dec. 24, '61.
Cook, Philip, Aug. 5, '64.
Cooke, John R., Nov. 1, '62.
Cooper, D. H., May 2, '63.
Colquitt, A. H., Sept. 1, '62.
Corse, M. D., Nov. 1, '62.
Cosby, Geo. B., Jan. 20, '63.
Cumming, Alfred, Oct. 29, '62.
Daniel, Junius, Sept. 1, '62.
Davidson, H. B., Aug. 18, '63.
Davis, Wm. G. M., Nov. 4, '62.
Davis, J. R., Sept. 15, '62.
Deas, Z. C., Dec. 13, '62.
De Lagnel, J. A., April 15, '62.
Deshler, James, July 28, '63.
Dibrell, Geo. G., July 26, '64.
Dockery, T. P., Aug. 10, '63.
Doles, George, Nov. 1, '62.
Drayton, T. F., Sept. 25, '61.
Duke, Basil W., Sept. 15, '64.
Duncan, J. K., Jan. 7, 62.
Echols, John, April 16, '62.
Ector, M. D., Aug. 23, '62.
Evans, C. A., May 19, '64.
Evans, Nathan G., Oct. 21, '61.
Farney, Wm. H., Feb. 15, '65.
Featherson, W. S., Mar. 4, '62.
Ferguson, S. W., July 23, '63.
Finegan, Joseph, April 5, '62.
Finley, Jesse J., Nov. 16, '63.
Floyd, John B., May 23, '61.
Forney, John H., Mar. 10, '62.
Frazer, John W., May 19, '63.
Frost, Daniel M., Mar. 3, '62.
Gano, Rich. M., Mar. 17, '65.
Gardner, Wm. M., Nov. 14, '61.
Garland, Sam., Jr., May 23, '62.
Garnett, Rich. B., Nov. 14, '61.
Garnett, Robt. S., June 6, '61.
Garrott, I. W., May 28, '63.
Gartrell, Lucius J., Aug. 22, '64.
Gary, Martin W., May 19, '64.
Gatlin, Richard C., July 8, '61.
Gholson, S. J., May 6, '64.
Gist, States R., Mar. 20, '62.
Gladden, A. H., Sept. 30, '61.
Godwin, Arch. C., Aug. 5, '64.
Gordon, James B., Sept. 28, '63.
Govan, Dan'l C., Dec. 29, '63.

David A. Weisinger, Defender of the Petersburg Crater.

Gabriel C. Wharton, in the Shenandoah Valley in 1864.

Philip St. G. Cocke, First Defender of Virginia, in 1861.

Patrick T. Moore, in Command of Reserves Defending Richmond.

CONFEDERATE

GENERALS

No. 24

VIRGINIA

Edwin G. Lee, On Special Service.

James B. Terrell Led Pegram's Old Brigade at the Wilderness.

Robert H. Chilton, Lee's Adjutant-General.

Seth M. Barton Led a Brigade in Lee's Army.

George W. Randolph, Secretary of War in 1862.

William C. Wickham Fought Sheridan Before Richmond.

Eppa Hunton Led a Brigade in Pickett's Division.

Gracie, Arch., Jr., Nov. 4, '63.
Gray, Henry, Mar. 17, '65.
Grayson, John B., Aug. 15, '61.
Green, Martin E., July 21, '62.
Green, Thomas, May 20, '63.
Greer, Elkanah, Oct. 8, '62.
Gregg, John, Aug. 29, '62.
Gregg, Maxcy, Dec. 14, '61.
Griffith, Rich., Nov. 2, '61.
Hagood, Johnson, July 21,'62.
Hanson, Roger W., Dec. 13, '62.
Hardeman, W. P., Mar. 17, '65.
Harris, Nat. H., Jan. 20, '64.
Harrison, J. E., Dec. 22, '64.
Hays, Harry T., July 25, '62.
Hatton, Robert, May 23, '62.
Hawes, James M., Mar. 5, '62.
Hawthorne, A. T., Feb. 18, '64.
Helm, Ben. H., Mar. 14, '62.
Hebert, Louis, May 26, '62.
Hebert, Paul O., Aug. 17, '61.
Higgins, Edward, Oct. 29, '63.
Hodge, Geo. B., Nov. 20, '63.
Hogg, Joseph L., Feb. 14, '62.
Hoke, Robert F., Jan. 17, '63.
Hood, John B., Mar. 3, '62.
Huger, Benjamin, June 17,'61.
Humes, W. Y. C., Nov. 16, '63.
Humphreys, B. G., Aug. 12, '63.
Hunton, Eppa, Aug. 9, '63.
Iverson, Alfred, Nov. 1, '62.
Jackson, Alfred E., Feb. 9, '63.
Jackson, H. R., June 4, '61.
Jackson, John K., Feb. 13, '62.
Jackson, Wm. A., Dec. 19, '64.
Jackson, Wm. H., Dec. 29, '62.
Jenkins, Albert G., Aug. 5, '62.
Jenkins, Micah, July 22, '62.
Johnston, R. D., Sept. 1, '63.
Jones, John M., May 15, '63.
Jones, John R., June 23, '62.
Jones, William E., Sept. 19, '62.
Jordan, Thomas, April 14, '62.
Kelly, John H., Nov. 16, '63.
Kirkland, W. W., Aug. 29, '63.
Lane, James H., Nov. 1, '62.
Lane, Walter P., Mar. 17, '65.
Law, Evander M., Oct. 3, '62.
Lawton, Alex. R., April 13, '61.
Leadbetter, D., Feb. 27, '62.
Lee, Edwin G., Sept. 20, '64.
Lewis, Joseph H., Sept. 30, '63.
Liddell, St. J. R., July 12, '62.
Little, Henry, April 16, '62.
Logan, T. M., Feb. 15, '65.
Lowrey, Mark. P., Oct. 4, '63.
Lowry, Robert, Feb. 4, '65.
Lyon, Hylan B., June 14, '64.
McCausland, J., May 18, '64.
McComb, Wm., June 30, '65.
McCulloch, H. E., Mar. 14, '62.
McCullough, Ben., May 11, '61.
McGowan, S., Jan. 17, '63.
McIntosh, James, Jan. 24, '62.
McNair, Evander, Nov. 4, '62.
McRae, Dandridge, Nov. 5, '62.
Mackall, Wm. W., Feb. 27, '62.
Major, James P., July 21, '63.
Maney, George, April 16, '62.
Manigault, A. M., April 26, '63.
Marshall, H., Oct. 30, '61.
Martin, James G., May 15, '62.
Maxey, S. B., Mar. 4, '62.

Mercer, Hugh W., Oct. 29, '61.
Moody, Young M., Mar. 4, '65.
Moore, John C., May 26, '62.
Moore, P. T., Sept. 20, '64.
Morgan, John H., Dec. 11, '62.
Morgan, John T., June 6, '63.
Mouton, Alfred, April 16, '62.
Nelson, Allison, Sept. 12, '62.
Nicholls, F. T., Oct. 14, '62.
O'Neal, Ed. A., June 6, '63.
Parsons, M. M., Nov. 5, '62.
Paxton, E. F., Nov. 1, '61.
Peck, Wm. R., Feb. 18, '65.
Pegram, John, Nov. 7, '62.
Pendleton, W. N., Mar. 26, '62.
Perrin, Abner, Sept. 10, '63.
Perry, Ed. A., Aug. 28, '62.
Perry, Wm. F., Feb. 21, '65.
Pettigrew, J. J., Feb. 26, '62.
Pettus, E. W., Sept. 18, '63.
Pike, Albert, Aug. 15, '61.
Pillow, Gideon J., July 9, '61.
Polk, Lucius E., Dec. 13, '62.
Preston, William, April 14, '62.
Pryor, Roger A., April 16, '62.
Quarles, Wm. A., Aug. 25, '63.
Rains, G. J., Sept. 23, '61.
Rains, James E., Nov. 4, '62.
Randolph, G. W., Feb. 12, '62.
Ransom, M. W., June 13, '63.
Reynolds, A. W., Sept. 14, '63.
Richardson, R. V., Dec. 1, '63.
Ripley, Roswell S., Aug. 15, '61.
Roberts, Wm. P., Feb. 21, '65.
Robertson, B. H., June 9, '62.
Robertson, J. B., Nov. 1, '62.
Roddy, Philip D., Aug. 3, '63.
Roane, John S., Nov. 20, '62.
Ross, Lawrence S., Dec. 21, '63.
Ruggles, Daniel, Aug. 9, '61.
Rust, Albert, Mar. 4, '62.
Scales, Alfred M., June 3, '63.
Scott, T. M., May 10, '64.
Scurry, Wm. R., Sept. 12, '62.
Sears, Claudius W., Mar. 1, '64.
Semmes, Paul J., Mar. 11, '62.
Shelby, Joseph O., Dec. 15, '63.
Shoup, Francis A., Sept. 12, '62.
Sibley, H. H., June 17, '61.
Simms, James P., Dec. 4, '64.
Slack, William Y., April 12,'62.
Slaughter, J. E., Mar. 8, '62.
Smith, James A., Sept. 30, '63.
Smith, Preston, Oct. 27, '62.
Smith, Wm. D., Mar. 7, '62.
Stafford, Leroy A., Oct. 8, '63.
Starke, Peter B., Nov. 4, '64.
Starke, Wm. E., Aug. 6, '62.
Steele, William, Sept. 12, '62.
Sterling, A. M. W., Jan. 7, '62.
Steuart, Geo. H., Mar. 6, '62.
Stevens, C. H., Jan. 20, '64.
Stovall, M. A., April 23, '63.
Strahl, Otho F., July 28, '63.
Taliaferro, Wm. B., Mar. 4, '62.
Tappan, James C., Nov. 5, '62.
Taylor, T. H., Nov. 4, '62.
Thomas, Allen, Feb. 4, '64.
Thomas, Ed. L., Nov. 1, '62.
Toombs, Robert, July 19, '61.
Tilghman, Lloyd, Oct. 18, '61.
Tracy, Edward D., Aug. 16, '62.
Trapier, James H., Oct. 21, '61.

Tucker, Wm. F., Mar. 1, '64.
Tyler, Robert C., Feb. 23, '64.
Vance, Robert B., Mar. 4, '63.
Vaughn, A. J., Jr., Nov. 18, '63.
Vaughn, J. C., Sept. 22, '62.
Villepigue, J. B., Mar. 13, '62.
Walker, H. H., July 1, '63.
Walker, James A., May 15, '63.
Walker, Leroy P., Sept. 17, '61.
Walker, L. M., April 11, '62.
Walker, Wm. S., Oct. 30, '62.
Waterhouse, R., Mar. 17, '65.
Watie, Stand, May 6, '64.
Waul, Thomas N., Sept. 18, '63.
Wayne, Henry C., Dec. 16, '61.
Weisiger, D. A., July 30, '64.
Wharton, G. C., July 8, '63.
Whitfield, John W., May 9, '63.
Wickham, W. C., Sept. 1, '63.
Wigfall, Louis T., Oct. 2, '61.
Williams, John S., April 16,'62.
Wilson, C. C., Nov. 16, '63.
Winder, Chas. S., Mar. 1, '62.
Winder, John H., June 21, '61.
Wise, Henry A., June 5, '61.
Woffard, Wm. T., Jan. 17, '63.
Wood, S. A. M., Jan. 7, '62.
Wright, Marcus J., Dec. 13, '62.
Zollicoffer, Felix K., July 9,'61.

BRIGADIER-GENERALS OF ARTILLERY
PROVISIONAL ARMY

Alexander, Ed. P., Feb. 26, '64.
Long, A. L., Sept. 21, '63.
Walker, R. L., Feb. 18, '65.

BRIGADIER-GENERAL
(COMMISSARY GENERAL)
PROVISIONAL ARMY

St. John, Isaac M., Feb. 16, '65.

BRIGADIER-GENERALS
(Special Appointments)
PROVISIONAL ARMY

Imboden, John D., Jan. 28, '63.
Johnson, Adam R., June 1, '64.

BRIGADIER-GENERALS
(Special)
PROVISIONAL ARMY

Benton, Samuel, July 26, '64.
Chambliss, J. R., Jr., Dec. 19, '63.
Chilton, R. H., Oct. 20, '62.
Connor, James, June 1, '64.
Elliott, S., Jr., May 24, '64.
Fry, Birkett D., May 24, '64.
Gibson, R. L., Jan. 11, '64.
Goggin, James M., Dec. 4, '64.
Gorgas, Josiah, Nov. 10, '64.
Granberry, H. B., Feb. 29, '64.
Hodge, Geo. B., Aug. 2, '64.
Leventhorpe, C., Feb. 3, '65.
McRae, William, Nov. 4, '64.
Northrop, L. B., Nov. 26, '64.
Page, Richard L., Mar. 1, '64.
Payne, Wm. H., Nov. 1, '64.

Posey, Carnot, Nov. 1, '62.
Preston, John S., June 10, '64.
Reynolds, D. H., Mar. 5, '64.
Stevens, W. H., Aug. 28, '64.
Terry, William, May 19, '64.

BRIGADIER-GENERALS
PROVISIONAL ARMY
(With Temporary Rank)

Anderson, R. H., July 26, '64.
Barry, John D., Aug. 3, '64.
Brantly, Wm. F., July 26, '64.
Browne, Wm. M., Nov. 11, '64.
Bullock, Robert, Nov. 29, '64.
Carter, John C., July 7, '64.
Cox, William R., May 31, '64.
Dubose, D. M., Nov. 16, '64.
Dunnovant, John, Aug. 22, '64.
Girardey, V. J. B., July 30, '64.
Gordon, Geo. W., Aug. 15, '64.
Harrison, T., Jan. 14, '65.
Hill, Benjamin J., Nov. 30, '64.
Holtzclaw, J. T., July 7, '64.
Johnson, B. T., June 28, '64.
Johnson, G. D., July 26, '64.
Kennedy, J. D., Dec. 22, '64.
Lewis, Wm. G., May 31, '64.
Lilley, Robt. D., May 31, '64.
Miller, William, Aug. 2, '64.
Palmer, Joseph B., Nov. 15, '64.
Robertson, F. H., July 26, '64.
Sanders, J. C. C., May 31, '64.
Sharp, Jacob H., July 26, '64.
Shelley, Chas. M., Sept. 17, '64.
Smith, T. B., July 29, '64.
Sorrell, G. Moxley, Oct. 27, '64.
Terrill, James B., May 31, '64.
Terry, Wm. R., May 31, '64.
Toon, Thomas F., May 31, '64.
Wallace, Wm. H., Sept. 20, '64.
York, Zebulon, May 31, '64.
Young, Wm. H., Aug. 15, '64.

BRIGADIER-GENERALS
FOR SERVICE WITH VOLUNTEER TROOPS
(With Temporary Rank)

Armstrong, F. C., Jan. 20, '63.
Dearing, James, April 29, '64.
Thomas, Bryan M., Aug. 4, '64.

The following were assigned to duty as general officers by Gen. E. Kirby Smith commanding the Trans-Mississippi Department, and served as such.

Green, Cullen.
Gordon, B. Frank.
Harrison, G. P. J.
Jackman, S. D.
Lewis, Leven M.
Maclay, Robt. P.
Munford, Thomas T.
Pearce, N. B.
Randall, Horace.

Assigned to duty as brigadier-general by Major-General Fitzhugh Lee and served as such though not appointed by the President or confirmed.

Terrell, Alex. W., May 16, '65.

Richard L. Page Commanded the Defenses of Mobile Bay.

Carter L. Stevenson, Active Division Leader in the West.

Henry A. Wise, Defender of Petersburg in 1864.

CONFEDERATE GENERALS

No. 25

VIRGINIA (CONTINUED)

William Terry Led a Brigade in Lee's Army.

James E. Slaughter, Inspector-General of the Army of Tennessee.

John McCausland, Cavalry Leader in the Shenandoah Valley.

William H. Payne, Leader of the Black Horse Cavalry.

Alexander W. Reynolds Led a Brigade in the Army of Tennessee.

SELECTED PORTRAITS
OF
CIVIL WAR LEADERS AND TROOPS

THE LEADER OF THE CHARGE

The Hero of the Federal Attack. General Samuel W. Crawford, here seen with his staff, at Cedar Mountain led a charge on the left flank of the Confederate forces that came near being disastrous for Jackson. At about six o'clock the brigade was in line. General Williams reported: "At this time this brigade occupied the interior line of a strip of woods. A field, varying from 250 to 500 yards in width, lay between it and the next strip of woods. In moving across this field the three right regiments and the six companies of the Third Wisconsin were received by a terrific fire of musketry. The Third Wisconsin especially fell under a partial flank fire under which Lieut.-Colonel Crane fell and the regiment was obliged to give way. Of the three remaining regiments which continued the charge (Twenty-eighth New York, Forty-sixth Pennsylvania, and Fifth Connecticut) every field-officer and every adjutant was killed or disabled. In the Twenty-eighth New York every company officer was killed or wounded; in the Forty-sixth Pennsylvania all but five; in the Fifth Connecticut all but eight." It was one of the most heroic combats of the war.

COL. ALFRED N. DUFFIÉ

A Leader of Cavalry. Colonel Alfred N. Duffié was in command of the First Rhode Island Cavalry, in the Cavalry Brigade of the Second Division of McDowell's (Third) Corps in Pope's Army of Virginia. The cavalry had been used pretty well during Pope's advance. On the 8th of August, the day before the battle of Cedar Mountain, the cavalry had proceeded south to the house of Dr. Slaughter. That night Duffié was on picket in advance of General Crawford's troops, which had come up during the day and pitched camp. The whole division came to his support on the next day. When the infantry fell back to the protection of the batteries, the cavalry was ordered to charge the advancing Confederates. "Officers and men behaved admirably, and I cannot speak too highly of the good conduct of all of the brigade," reported General Bayard. After the battle the cavalry covered the retreat of the artillery and ambulances. On August 18th, when the retreat behind the Rappahannoc was ordered, the cavalry again checked the Confederate advance. During the entire campaign the regiment of Colonel Duffié did yeoman's service.

A START TOO LONG DELAYED

Where the troops of General McClellan, waiting near the round-house at Alexandria, were hurried forward to the scene of action where Pope was struggling with Jackson and Ewell. Pope had counted upon the assistance of these reënforcements in making the forward movement by which he expected to hold Lee back. The old bogey of leaving the National Capital defenseless set up a vacillation in General Halleck's mind and the troops were held overlong at Alexandria. Had they been promptly forwarded, "Stonewall" Jackson's blow at Manassas Junction could not have been struck. At the news of that disaster the troops were hurriedly despatched down the railroad toward Manassas. But Pope was already in retreat in three columns toward that point, McDowell had failed to intercept the Confederate reënforcements coming through Thoroughfare Gap, and the situation had become critical. General Taylor, with his brigade of New Jersey troops, was the first of McClellan's forces to be moved forward to the aid of Pope. At Union

BRIGADIER–GENERAL
GEORGE W. TAYLOR

Mills, Colonel Scammon, commanding the First Brigade, driven back from Manassas Junction, was further pressed by the Confederates on the morning of August 27th. Later in the day General Taylor's brigade arrived by the Fairfax road and, crossing the railroad bridge, met the Confederates drawn up and waiting near Manassas Station. A severe artillery fire greeted the Federals as they emerged from the woods. As General Taylor had no artillery, he was obliged either to retire or charge. He chose the latter. When the Confederate cavalry threatened to surround his small force, however, Taylor fell back in good order across the bridge, where two Ohio regiments assisted in holding the Confederates in check. At this point, General Taylor, who had been wounded in the retreat, was borne past in a litter. Though suffering much, he appealed to the officers to prevent another Bull Run. The brigade retired in good order to Fairfax Court House, where General Taylor died of his wounds a short time afterward.

A REGIMENT THAT FOUGHT AT SOUTH MOUNTAIN—THE THIRTY-FIFTH NEW YORK

Here sits Colonel T. G. Morehead, who commanded the 106th Pennsylvania, of the Second Corps. At 7.20 A.M. the order came to advance, and with a cheer the Second Corps—men who for over two years had never lost a gun nor struck a color—pressed forward. But again they were halted. It was almost an hour later when Sedgwick's division, with Sumner at the head, crossed the Antietam. Arriving nearly opposite the Dunker church, it swept out over the cornfields. On it went, by Greene's right, through the West Woods; here it met the awful counter-stroke of Early's reënforced division and, stubbornly resisting, was hurled back with frightful loss.

COLONEL T. G. MOREHEAD
A HERO OF SEDGWICK'S CHARGE

Early in the morning of September 17, 1862, Knap's battery (shown below) got into the thick of the action of Antietam. General Mansfield had posted it opposite the north end of the West Woods, close to the Confederate line. The guns opened fire at seven o'clock. Practically unsupported, the battery was twice charged upon during the morning; but quickly substituting canister for shot and shell, the men held their ground and stemmed the Confederate advance. Near this spot General Mansfield was mortally wounded while deploying his troops. About noon a section of Knap's battery was detached to the assistance of General Greene, in the East Woods.

KNAP'S BATTERY, JUST AFTER THE BLOODY WORK AT ANTIETAM

THE MEDIATOR

President Lincoln's Visit to the Camps at Antietam, October 8, 1862.   Yearning for the speedy termination of the war, Lincoln came to view the Army of the Potomac, as he had done at Harrison's Landing.   Puzzled to understand how Lee could have circumvented a superior force on the Peninsula, he was now anxious to learn why a crushing blow had not been struck.   Lincoln (after Gettysburg) expressed the same thought: "Our army held the war in the hollow of their hand and they would not close it!"   On Lincoln's right stands Allan Pinkerton, the famous detective and organizer of the Secret Service of the army.   At the President's left is General John A. McClernand, soon to be entrusted by Lincoln with reorganizing military operations in the West.

THE SECOND LEADER AGAINST RICHMOND

Major-General Ambrose Everett Burnside was a West Point graduate, inventor of a breech-loading rifle, commander of a brigade in the first battle of Bull Run, captor of Roanoke Island and Newberne (North Carolina), and commander of the Federal left at Antietam. He was appointed to the command of the Army of the Potomac and succeeded General George B. McClellan on November 8, 1862. He was a brave soldier, but was an impatient leader and inclined to be somewhat reckless. He pressed rapidly his advance against Lee and massed his entire army along Stafford Heights, on the east bank of the Rappahannock, opposite Fredericksburg. According to General W. B. Franklin (who commanded the left grand division of the army), the notion that a serious battle was necessary to Federal control of the town "was not entertained by any one." General Sumner (who led the advance of Burnside's army) held this opinion but he had not received orders to cross the river. Crossing was delayed nearly a month and this delay resulted in the Federal disaster on December 13th. This put an abrupt end to active operations by Burnside against Lee. This picture was taken at Warrenton, November 24th, on the eve of the departure of the army for its march to Fredericksburg.

A MAN OF WHOM MUCH WAS EXPECTED

General Joseph Hooker.   A daring and experienced veteran of the Mexican War, Hooker had risen in the Civil War from brigade commander to be the commander of a grand division of the Army of the Potomac, and had never been found wanting.   His advancement to the head of the Army of the Potomac, on January 26, 1863, was a tragic episode in his own career and in that of the Federal arms. Gloom hung heavy over the North after Fredericksburg.   Upon Hooker fell the difficult task of redeeming the unfulfilled political pledges for a speedy lifting of that gloom.   It was his fortune only to deepen it.

"STONEWALL" JACKSON—TWO WEEKS BEFORE HIS MORTAL WOUND

The austere, determined features of the victor of Chancellorsville, just as they appeared two weeks before the tragic shot that cost the Confederacy its greatest Lieutenant-General—and, in the opinion of sound historians, its chief hope for independence.   Only once had a war photograph of Jackson been taken up to April, 1863, when, just before the movement toward Chancellorsville, he was persuaded to enter a photographer's tent at Hamilton's Crossing, some three miles below Fredericksburg, and to sit for his last portrait.   At a glance one can feel the self-expression and power in this stern worshiper of the God of Battles; one can understand the eulogy written by the British military historian, Henderson: "The fame of 'Stonewall' Jackson is no longer the exclusive property of Virginia and the South: it has become the birthright of every man privileged to call himself an American."

ROBERT E. LEE IN 1863

It was with the gravest misgivings that Lee began his invasion of the North in 1863. He was too wise a general not to realize that a crushing defeat was possible. Yet, with Vicksburg already doomed, the effort to win a decisive victory in the East was imperative in its importance. Magnificent was the courage and fortitude of Lee's maneuvering during that long march which was to end in failure. Hitherto he had made every one of his veterans count for two of their antagonists, but at Gettysburg the odds had fallen heavily against him. Jackson, his resourceful ally, was no more. Longstreet advised strongly against giving battle, but Lee unwaveringly made the tragic effort which sacrificed more than a third of his splendid army.

HANCOCK, "THE SUPERB"

Every man in this picture was wounded at Gettysburg. Seated, is Winfield Scott Hancock; the boy-general, Francis C. Barlow (who was struck almost mortally), leans against the tree. The other two are General John Gibbon and General David B. Birney. About four o'clock on the afternoon of July 1st a foam-flecked charger dashed up Cemetery Hill bearing General Hancock. He had galloped thirteen miles to take command. Apprised of the loss of Reynolds, his main dependence, Meade knew that only a man of vigor and judgment could save the situation. He chose wisely, for Hancock was one of the best all-round soldiers that the Army of the Potomac had developed. It was he who re-formed the shattered corps and chose the position to be held for the decisive struggle.

THE MAN WHO HELD THE CENTER

Headquarters of Brigadier-General Alexander S. Webb. It devolved upon the man pictured here (booted and in full uniform, before his headquarters tent to the left of the picture) to meet the shock of Pickett's great charge. With four Pennsylvania regiments (the Sixty-Ninth, Seventy-First, Seventy-Second, and One Hundred and Sixth) of Hancock's Second Corps, Webb was equal to the emergency. Stirred to great deeds by the example of a patriotic ancestry, he felt that upon his holding his position depended the outcome of the day. His front had been the focus of the Confederate artillery fire. Batteries to right and left of his line were practically silenced. Young Lieutenant Cushing, mortally wounded, fired the last serviceable gun and fell dead as Pickett's men came on. Cowan's First New York Battery on the left of Cushing's used canister on the assailants at less than ten yards. Webb at the head of the Seventy-Second Pennsylvania fought back the on-rush, posting a line of slightly wounded in his rear. Webb himself fell wounded but his command checked the assault till Hall's brilliant charge turned the tide at this point.

THE MEN WHO COMPLETED THE VICTORY

General Hooker and Staff at Lookout Mountain. Hooker's forces of about 9,700 men had been sent from the East to reënforce Rosecrans, but until the arrival of Grant they were simply so many more mouths to feed in the besieged city. In the battle of Wauhatchie, on the night of October 20th, they drove back the Confederates and established the new line of communication. On November 24th they, too, had a surprise in store for Grant. Their part in the triple conflict was also ordered merely as a "demonstration," but they astounded the eyes and ears of their comrades with the spectacular fight by which they made their way up Lookout Mountain. The next day, pushing on to Rossville, the daring Hooker attacked one of Bragg's divisions and forced it into precipitate retreat.

HOOKER'S CAMP AT THE BASE OF LOOKOUT MOUNTAIN

The Photographic History of The Civil War

The Cavalry

"STAND TO HORSE!"—AN AMERICAN VOLUNTEER CAVALRYMAN, OCTOBER, 1862

"He's not a regular—but he's 'smart.'" This tribute to the soldierly bearing of the trooper above was bestowed, forty-nine years after the taking of the picture, by an officer of the U. S. cavalry, himself a Civil War veteran. The recipient of such high praise is seen as he "stood to horse" a month after the battle of Antietam. The war was only in its second year, but his drill is quite according to army regulations— hand to bridle, six inches from the bit. His steady glance as he peers from beneath his hat into the sun- light tells its own story. Days and nights in the saddle without food or sleep, sometimes riding along the 60-mile picket-line in front of the Army of the Potomac, sometimes faced by sudden encounters with the Southern raiders, have all taught him the needed confidence in himself, his horse, and his equipment.

The Photographic History of The Civil War

The Cavalry

THEO. F. RODENBOUGH

Brigadier-General United States Army (Retired)

Contributors

THEO. F. RODENBOUGH
Brigadier-General United States Army (Retired)

CHARLES D. RHODES
Captain, General Staff, United States Army

HOLMES CONRAD
Major Cavalry Corps, Army of Northern Virginia

JOHN A. WYETH, M.D., LL.D.
Captain Quirk's Scouts, Confederate States Army

CONTENTS

PAGE

FRONTISPIECE —*"Stand to Horse"—An American Volunteer Cavalryman.* . . . 4

FOREWORD 8

PREFACE 11

INTRODUCTION —*The Evolution of the American Cavalryman* 13
    Theo. F. Rodenbough

THE FEDERAL CAVALRY—ITS ORGANIZATION AND EQUIPMENT 39
    Charles D. Rhodes

THE CONFEDERATE CAVALRY IN THE EAST 71
    Holmes Conrad

FEDERAL RAIDS AND EXPEDITIONS IN THE EAST 115
    Charles D. Rhodes

FEDERAL RAIDS AND EXPEDITIONS IN THE WEST 129
    Charles D. Rhodes

MORGAN'S CHRISTMAS RAID, 1862–63 141
    John Allan Wyeth

THE DESTRUCTION OF ROSECRANS' GREAT WAGON-TRAIN 158
    John Allan Wyeth

PARTISAN RANGERS OF THE CONFEDERACY 165
    Charles D. Rhodes

OUTPOSTS, SCOUTS, AND COURIERS 181
    Charles D. Rhodes

A RIDE THROUGH THE FEDERAL LINES AT NIGHT 204
    John Allan Wyeth

CAVALRY BATTLES AND CHARGES 215
    Charles D. Rhodes

CAVALRY LEADERS—NORTH AND SOUTH 259
    Theo. F. Rodenbough

FAMOUS CHARGERS 289
    Theo. F. Rodenbough

MOUNTING THE CAVALRY OF THE UNION ARMY 319
    Charles D. Rhodes

PHOTOGRAPHIC DESCRIPTIONS THROUGHOUT THIS BOOK
    Roy Mason

FOREWORD

ON April 14, 1861, Fort Sumter underwent a thirty-four-hour bombardment by the Confederate Army. As the fighting drew to a close, Union officer Major Robert Anderson lowered the flag and turned the fort over to the Confederacy. The American Civil War had begun. It would be four long, hard-fought years before the guns would finally be silenced.

The Photographic History of the Civil War: The Cavalry captures the images of both intense drama and horror created by this internal national conflict. This unique collection of black-and-white photographs takes the reader into the campsites and onto the battlefields where victories were won and lives were lost. The superb text and photograph descriptions present an authoritative yet sensitive portrayal of the War Between the States.

The cavalry was an important fighting force for both the North and South during the Civil War. The main objectives of these mounted men included the destruction of supply centers, the cutting of railroads and lines of communication between these centers and the enemy, and engaging in battle. The cavalry also provided guides, orderlies, and grooms for staff officers. Scouting was another important role assigned to the cavalryman. *The Photographic History of the Civil War: The Cavalry* outlines the makeup of both the Federal and Confederate cavalries, their contributions to the war effort, and profiles such important cavalry leaders as Major-General James Ewell Brown Stuart, Major-General George Armstrong Custer, and Lieutenant-General Wade Hampton, C.S.A.

By the 1860s the camera was on its way to becoming an important medium for communication. The method used during this period was known as daguereotype, named after its inventor Frenchman Louis Jacques Mandé Daguerre. By using this wet-plate process, however, the Civil War photographer was unable to capture action shots. Yet this disadvantage did not prevent him from capturing on film the human and material wreckage created by the war—the wistful face of the dying young soldier or the sabotaged railroad. The Battle of Bull Run marked the beginning of American military photography.

The Civil War photographers risked constant danger of battle and worked under the most difficult conditions—the bitter cold during the winters of 1862 and 1863 and the blistering heat in the summer. Important Civil War photographers—including Mathew B. Brady, Timothy O'Sullivan and Alexander Gardner as well as other combat photographers—provided the American people with an inside look at this war through their work. These poignant photographs stirred the hearts of Americans on both sides of the Mason-Dixon line then and will continue to do so today.

K.M.B.

"SIR—THE GUARD IS FORMED!"

This picture of guard-mounting is one of the earliest Civil War cavalry photographs. It was taken in 1861 at the Cavalry School of Practice and Recruiting Depot, at Carlisle barracks, Pennsylvania. The guard wears full-dress uniform. The adjutant is presenting it to the new Officer of the Day, on the right.

PREFACE

TO the public at large, the volume prepared by General Rodenbough and his associates will be not only instructive but decidedly novel in its view-point. In the popular conception the cavalryman figures as the most dashing and care-free among soldiers. He is associated primarily with charges at a gallop to the sound of clashing sabers and bugle calls, and with thrilling rescues on the field.

Adventurous, indeed, are the exploits of "Jeb" Stuart, Custer, and others recounted in the pages that follow, together with the typical reminiscences from Dr. Wyeth.

The characteristic that stands dominant, however, throughout this volume shows that the soldiers in the cavalry branch were peculiarly responsible. Not only must they maintain a highly trained militant organization, ready to fight with equal efficiency either mounted or on foot, but to them fell the care of valuable, and frequently scarce, animals, the protection of the armies' supplies, the transmission of important messages, and dozens more special duties which must usually be performed on the cavalryman's own initiative. On such detached duty there was lacking the shoulder to shoulder comradeship that large masses of troops enjoy. Confronted by darkness, distance, and danger, the trooper must carry out his orders with few companions, or alone.

The discussion of organization and equipment is most important to an understanding of the cavalryman as he actually worked. The Federal methods, described at length in this volume, naturally involved a larger system and a more elaborate growth than those of the South with its waning resources. In other respects, however, the Confederate organization differed from that of the Union. The feeling for locality in the South manifested itself at the beginning of the war through the formation of companies and regiments on a geographical basis, and the election of officers by the men of the companies themselves. Thus, in spite of the want of military arms and ordnance stores, and the later disastrous scarcity of horses, the Confederates "hung together" in a manner that recalls the English yeomen archers who fought so sturdily, county by county.

Altogether it was a gallant and devoted part that the American cavalryman, Federal or Confederate, played on his hard-riding raids and his outpost duty, as well as his better-known battles and charges, from 1861 to 1865.

CHAPTER

ONE

———

THE EVOLUTION
OF THE
AMERICAN CAVALRYMAN

———

THE FIRST EXPERIMENT

The men on dress parade here, in 1862, are much smarter, with their band and white gloves, their immaculate uniforms and horses all of one color, than the troopers in the field a year later. It was not known at that time how important a part the cavalry was to play in the great war. The organization of this three months' regiment was reluctantly authorized by the War Department in Washington. These are the Seventh New York Cavalry, the "Black Horse," organized at Troy, mustered in November 6, 1861, and mustered out

SEVENTH NEW YORK CAVALRY, 1862

March 31, 1862. They were designated by the State authorities Second Regiment Cavalry on November 18, 1861, but the designation was changed by the War Department to the Seventh New York Cavalry. The seven companies left for Washington, D. C., November 23, 1861, and remained on duty there till the following March. The regiment was honorably discharged, and many of its members saw real service later. General I. N. Palmer, appears in the foreground with his staff, third from the left.

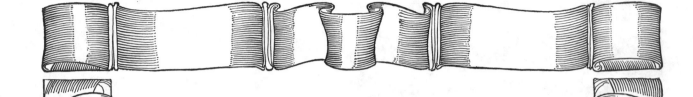

CAVALRY OF THE CIVIL WAR
ITS EVOLUTION AND INFLUENCE

By Theo. F. Rodenbough
Brigadier-General, United States Army (Retired)

IT may surprise non-military readers to learn that the United States, unprepared as it is for war, and unmilitary as are its people, has yet become a model for the most powerful armies of Europe, at least in one respect. The leading generals and teachers in the art and science of war now admit that our grand struggle of 1861–65 was rich in examples of the varied use of mounted troops in the field, which are worthy of imitation.

Lieutenant-General von Pelet-Narbonne, in a lecture before the Royal United Service Institution of Great Britain, emphatically maintains that "in any case one must remember that, from the days of Napoleon until the present time, in no single campaign has cavalry exercised so vast an influence over the operations as they did in this war, wherein, of a truth, the personality of the leaders has been very striking; such men as, in the South, the God-inspired Stuart, and later the redoubtable Fitzhugh Lee, and on the Northern side, Sheridan and Pleasonton."

For a long time after our Civil War, except as to its political or commercial bearing, that conflict attracted but little attention abroad. A great German strategist was reported to have said that "the war between the States was largely an affair of armed mobs "—a report, by the way, unverified, but which doubtless had its effect upon military students. In the meantime other wars came to pass in succession—Austro-Prussian (1866), Franco-German (1870), Russo-Turkish (1877), and later the Boer War and that between Russia and Japan.

THE AMERICAN CAVALRYMAN—1864

The type of American cavalryman developed by the conditions during the war fought equally well on foot and on horseback. In fact, he found during the latter part of the war that his horse was chiefly useful in carrying him expeditiously from one part of the battlefield to the other. Except when a mounted charge was ordered, the horses were far too valuable to be exposed to the enemy's fire, be he Confederate or Federal. It was only when cavalry was fighting cavalry that the trooper kept continually mounted. The Federal sabers issued at the beginning of the war were of long, straight Prussian pattern, but these were afterward replaced by a light cavalry saber with curved blade. A carbine and revolver completed the Federal trooper's equipment.

In none of these campaigns were the cavalry operations conspicuous for originality or importance as auxiliary to the main forces engaged.

Meanwhile, the literature of the American war—official and personal—began to be studied, and its campaigns were made subjects for text-books and monographs by British authors, which found ready publishers. Nevertheless, the American cavalry method has not gained ground abroad without a struggle. On the one hand, the failure of cavalry in recent European wars to achieve success has been made use of by one class of critics, who hold that " the cavalry has had its day "; that " the improved rifle has made cavalry charges impracticable "; that it has degenerated into mere mounted infantry, and that its value as an arm of service has been greatly impaired.

On the other hand it is held by the principal cavalry leaders who have seen service in the field—Field-Marshal Lord Roberts, Generals French, Hamilton, and Baden-Powell (of Boer War fame), De Negrier and Langlois of France, and Von Bernhardi of Germany, and others, (1) that while the method of using modern cavalry has changed, the arm itself is more important in war than ever; (2) that its scope is broadened; (3) that its duties require a higher order of intelligence and training of its personnel—officers and men, and (4), above all, that it is quite possible to turn out a modern horse-soldier, armed with saber and rifle, who will be equally efficient, mounted or dismounted.

Still the battle of the pens goes merrily on—the champions of the *arme blanche* or of the rifle alone, on the one side, and the defenders of the combination of those weapons on the other. The next great war will demonstrate, beyond peradventure, the practical value of " the American idea," as it is sometimes called.

A glance at the conditions affecting the use of mounted troops in this country prior to our Civil War may be instructive;

THE *ARME BLANCHE* OR THE RIFLE

The eternal question that has confronted cavalry experts ever since long-range firearms became effective, is whether the modern cavalry-man should use the saber—the *arme blanche*—or the rifle, or both the arms together. The failure of cavalry to achieve success in recent European wars has been used by one class of critics to prove that "the cavalry has had its day" and that "the improved rifle had made cavalry charges impracticable." On the other hand, many of the experienced cavalry leaders of the present day hold that it is quite possible to turn out a modern horse-soldier, armed with saber and rifle, who will be equally efficient, mounted or dismounted. In 1911 an American board of officers recommended, however, that the United States troopers should give up their revolvers on the principle that two arms suffice—the carbine for long distance, the saber for hand-to-hand fighting.

it will show that eighty-five years of great and small wars, Indian fighting, and frontier service, proved to be a training school in which the methods followed by Sheridan, Stuart, Forrest, and others of their time had been really initiated by their famous predecessors—Marion, the "Swamp Fox," and "Light Horse Harry" Lee of the War for Independence, Charlie May and Phil Kearny of the Mexican War, and those old-time dragoons and Indian fighters, Harney and Cooke.

Before the Revolution of 1776, the colonists were generally armed with, and proficient in the use of, the rifle—of long barrel and generous bore—and familiarity with the broken and wooded surface of the country made them formidable opponents of the British from the start, who both in tactical methods and armament were very inferior to the American patriots. Fortescue, an English writer, records the fact that " at the time of the Lexington fight there was not a rifle in the whole of the British army, whereas there were plenty in the hands of the Americans, who understood perfectly how to use them."

In the mountains of Kentucky and Tennessee, bodies of horsemen, similarly armed, were readily formed, who, if ignorant of cavalry maneuvers, yet with little preparation became the finest mounted infantry the world has ever seen; distinguishing themselves in numerous affairs, notably at King's Mountain, South Carolina, September 25, 1780, where two thousand sturdy "Mountain Men," hastily assembled under Colonels Sevier, Shelby, and Campbell, surrounded and almost annihilated a force of twelve hundred men (one hundred and twenty being regulars) under Major Ferguson, of the British army. Marion, the partisan, led a small brigade of mounted infantry, who generally fought on foot, although at times charging and firing from the saddle. There were also small bodies of cavalry proper, using the saber and pistol, with effect, against the British cavalry in many dashing combats.

The War of 1812 was not conspicuous for mounted operations, but the irregular warfare which preceded and followed

GRADUATES OF "THE ROUGH SCHOOL OF WAR"

The photograph reproduced above through the courtesy of Captain Noble D. Preston, who served with the Tenth New York Cavalry here represented, shows to what stage the troopers had progressed in the rough school of war by the winter of 1862–3. The Tenth New York was organized at Elmira, N. Y., September 27, 1861, and moved to Gettysburg, Penn., December 24th, where it remained till March, 1862. It took part in the battle of Fredericksburg in December, 1862, and participated in the famous "mud march," January, 1863, about the time this photograph was taken. The men had ample time for schooling and training in the Middle Department, in Maryland and the vicinity of Washington. They proved their efficiency in Stoneman's raid in April, 1863, and at Brandy Station and Warrenton. Later they accompanied Sheridan on his Richmond raid in May, 1864, in the course of which Stuart met his death, and they were still "on duty" with Grant at Appomattox.

that "difference" with the mother country, further demonstrated the value of the dual armament of saber and rifle. The cavalry particularly distinguished itself in General Wayne's campaign of 1794 against the Northwestern Indians, and again under Harrison in the historic battle of Tippecanoe, November 7, 1811. At the battle of the Thames, October 5, 1813, a decisive charge made by a regiment of Kentucky cavalry against a large force of British and Indians was successful, resulting in the defeat of the enemy and death of the famous chieftain, Tecumseh. General Jackson's campaigns (1813–14) against the Creek Indians were marked by effective work on the part of the mounted volunteers.

In 1833, Congress reorganized the regular cavalry by creating one regiment, followed in 1836 by another, called respectively, the First and Second United States Dragoons. The First Dragoons were sent to the Southwest to watch the Pawnees and Comanches. On this expedition, it was accompanied by Catlin, the artist, who made many of his Indian sketches then. These regiments have been in continuous service ever since.

The first service of the Second Dragoons was against the Seminole Indians, in Florida, and for seven years the regiment illustrated the adaptability of the American soldier to service in the field under the most trying circumstances. "There was at one time to be seen in the Everglades, the dragoon (dismounted) in water from three to four feet deep; the sailor and marine wading in the mud in the midst of cypress stumps; and the infantry and artillery alternately on the land, in the water, or in boats." Here again, the combined mounted and dismounted action of cavalry was tested in many sharp encounters with the Indians.

It was but a step from the close of the Florida war to the war with Mexico, 1846–47. The available American cavalry comprised the two regiments of dragoons and seven new regiments of volunteers. The regular regiments were in splendid

THE FIRST UNITED STATES REGULAR CAVALRY

The sturdy self-reliance of these *sabreurs*, standing at ease though without a trace of slouchiness, stamps them as the direct successors of Marion, the "Swamp Fox," and of "Light-Horse Harry" Lee of the War for Independence. The regiment has been in continuous service from 1833 to the present day. Organized as the First Dragoons and sent to the southwest to watch the Pawnees and Comanches at the time it began its existence, the regiment had its name changed to the First United States Regular Cavalry on July 27, 1861, when McClellan assumed command of the Eastern army. This photograph was taken at Brandy Station in February, 1864. The regiment at this time was attached to the Reserve Brigade under General Wesley Merritt. The troopers took part in the first battle of Bull Run, were at the siege of Yorktown, fought at Gaines' Mill and Beverly Ford, served under Merritt on the right at Gettysburg, and did their duty at Yellow Tavern, Trevilian Station, and in the Shenandoah Valley under Sheridan; and they were present at Appomattox.

condition. The most brilliant exploit was the charge made
by May's squadron of the Second Dragoons upon a Mexican
light battery at Resaca de la Palma, May 9, 1846, which resulted in the capture of the battery and of General La Vega,
of the Mexican artillery. This dashing affair was afterward
to be repeated many times in the great struggle between the
North and South.

The sphere of action, however, which had the most direct
bearing upon the cavalry operations of the war was that known
as "the Plains." The experience gained in the twelve years
from 1848 to 1860, in frequent encounters with the restless
Indian tribes of the Southwest, the long marches over arid
wastes, the handling of supply trains, the construction of military roads, the exercise of command, the treatment of cavalry
horses and draught animals, and the numerous other duties
falling to officers at frontier posts, far distant from railroad
or telegraph, all tended to temper and sharpen the blades that
were to point the "path of glory" to thousands destined to
ride under the war-guidons of Sheridan, Stuart, Buford, Pleasonton, Fitzhugh Lee, Stanley, Wilson, Merritt, Gregg, and
others—all graduates of the service school of "the Plains."

At the outbreak of the Civil War, the military conditions
in the two sections were very unequal. The South began the
struggle under a commander-in-chief who was a graduate of
West Point, had seen service in the regular army, had been a
Secretary of War (possessing much inside information as to
the disposition of the United States forces) and who, in the
beginning at least, was supreme in the selection of his military
lieutenants and in all matters relating to the organization and
equipment of the Confederate troops.

On the other hand the North lacked similar advantages.
Its new President was without military training, embarrassed
rather than aided by a cabinet of lawyers and politicians as
military advisers, captains of the pen rather than of the sword,
and "blind leading the blind." Mr. Lincoln found himself

AMERICAN LANCERS—THE SIXTH PENNSYLVANIA

Few people have heard that there was an American regiment of lancers in '61–'63. Colonel Richard Rush's regiment, the Sixth Pennsylvania, attempted to fight in this European fashion during the great conflict in which so much was discovered about the art of war. The Pennsylvanians carried the lance from December, 1861, until May, 1863, when it was discarded for the carbine, as being unsuited to the wooded country of Virginia through which the command operated. The regiment was organized in Philadelphia by Colonel Richard H. Rush, August to October, 1861, and was composed of the best blood in that aristocratic city. The usual armament of Federal volunteer cavalry regiments at the outset of the war consisted of a saber and a revolver. At least two squadrons, consisting of four troops of from eighty-two to a hundred men, were armed with rifles and carbines. Later, all cavalry regiments were supplied with single-shot carbines, the decreased length and weight of the shorter arm being a decided advantage to a soldier on horseback.

surrounded by office-seekers—especially those claiming high
military command as a reward for political services. It is true
that the Federal Government possessed a small, well-trained
army, with a large proportion of the officers and nearly all of
the enlisted men loyal to their colors, which, together with a
few thousand organized militia, would have formed a valuable
nucleus for war had it been properly utilized at the start.
From its ranks some were selected who achieved distinction as
leaders when not hampered by association with incompetent
" generals." For at least one year, the inexhaustible resources
of the North were wasted for want of competent military direction and training.

If these field conditions marked the genesis of the Civil
War in all arms of service, they were especially true of the
mounted troops. In 1860, the " athletic wave " had not made
its appearance in the United States, and out-of-door amuse-
ments had not become popular above the Mason and Dixon
line. In the more thickly settled North, the young men of
cities and towns took rather to commercial and indoor pursuits;
in the South, the sports of a country life appealed to young
and middle-aged alike, and the rifle and the saddle furnished
particular attractions to a large majority. So it happened
that the Confederates (their President an erstwhile dragoon)
had only to mobilize the cavalry companies of the militia scattered through the seceding States, and muster, arm, and equip
the thousands of young horsemen, each bringing his own horse
and eager to serve the Confederacy.

The trials of many of the newly recruited organizations,
until the beginning of the third year of the war, are illustrated
in the following extract from a typical regimental history:*
Captain Vanderbilt describes in graphic terms his first experience in escort duty (December 10, 1862) :

Please remember that my company had been mustered into the service only about six weeks before, and had received horses less than a

* "History of the Tenth New York Cavalry." (Preston, N. Y.)

VOLUNTEERS AT DRILL—A NEW YORK REGIMENT

It was New York State that furnished the first volunteer cavalry regiment to the Union—Autumn, 1861. The fleet horsemen of the Confederacy soon taught the North the need of improving that arm of the service. But it requires time to train an efficient trooper, and the Union cavalrymen were helpless at first when opposed to the natural horsemen of the South. After a purgatory of training they were hurried into the field, often to fall victims to some roving body of Confederates who welcomed the opportunity to appropriate superior arms and equipment. The regiment in this photograph is the Thirteenth New York Cavalry at Prospect Hill, Virginia. They are no longer raw troopers but have become the "eyes" of Washington and its chief protection against the swift-riding Mosby and his men. The troopers were drilled on foot as well as mounted.

month prior to this march; and in the issue we drew everything on the list—watering-bridles, lariat ropes, and pins—in fact, there was nothing on the printed list of supplies that we did not get. Many men had extra blankets, nice large quilts presented by some fond mother or maiden aunt (dear souls), sabers and belts, together with the straps that pass over the shoulders, carbines and slings, pockets full of cartridges, nose bags and extra little bags for carrying oats, haversacks, canteens, and spurs—some of them of the Mexican pattern as large as small windmills, and more in the way than the spurs of a young rooster, catching in the grass when they walked, carrying up briers, vines, and weeds, and catching their pants, and in the way generally—curry-combs, brushes, ponchos, button tents, overcoats, frying-pans, cups, coffee-pots, etc. Now the old companies had become used to these things and had got down to light-marching condition gradually, had learned how to wear the uniform, saber, carbine, etc.; but my company had hardly time to get into proper shape when "the general" was sounded, "boots and saddles" blown.

Such a rattling, jingling, jerking, scrabbling, cursing, I never heard before. Green horses—some of them had never been ridden—turned round and round, backed against each other, jumped up or stood up like trained circus-horses. Some of the boys had a pile in front on their saddles, and one in the rear, so high and heavy it took two men to saddle one horse and two men to help the fellow into his place. The horses sheered out, going sidewise, pushing the well-disposed animals out of position, etc. Some of the boys had never ridden anything since they galloped on a hobby horse, and they clasped their legs close together, thus unconsciously sticking the spurs into their horses' sides.

Well, this was the crowd I commanded to mount on the morning I was ordered by General Smith to follow him. We got in line near headquarters, and when we got ready to start we started all over. He left no doubt about his starting! He went like greased lightning! In less than ten minutes Tenth New York cavalrymen might have been seen on every hill for two miles rearward. Poor fellows! I wanted to help them, but the general was "On to Richmond"; and I hardly dared look back for fear of losing him. I didn't have the remotest idea where he was going, and didn't know but he was going to keep it up all day. It was my first Virginia ride as a warrior in the field. My uneasi-

A CAVALRY LEADER AT GETTYSBURG—GENERAL DAVID McM. GREGG AND STAFF

The Federal army at Gettysburg owed much to the cavalry. As Gettysburg was the turning-point in the fortunes of the Union army, it also marked an epoch in the development of the cavalry, trained in methods which were evolved from no foreign text-books, but from stern experience on the battlefields of America. The Second Cavalry Division under Gregg patrolled the right flank of the Federal army, with occasional skirmishing, until Stuart's arrival July 3d with the Confederate horse. Gregg's division and Custer's brigade were then on the right of the line. The ensuing cavalry battle was one of the fiercest of the war. W. H. F. Lee's brigade made the first charge for Stuart, as did the First Michigan Cavalry for Gregg. Countercharge followed upon charge. In a dash for a Confederate battleflag, Captain Newhall was received by its bearer upon the point of the spear-head and hurled to the ground. Finally the Confederate brigades withdrew behind their artillery, and the danger that Stuart would strike the rear of the Union army simultaneously with Pickett's charge was passed. This photograph shows Gregg with the officers of his staff.

ness may be imagined. I was wondering what in the mischief I should say to the general when we halted and none of the company there but me. He was the first real live general I had seen who was going out to fight. Talk about the Flying Dutchman! Blankets slipped from under saddles and hung from one corner; saddles slipped back until they were on the rumps of horses; others turned and were on the under side of the animals; horses running and kicking; tin pans, mess-kettles, patent sheet-iron stoves the boys had seen advertised in the illustrated papers and sold by the sutlers of Alexandria—about as useful as a piano or folding bed—flying through the air; and all I could do was to give a hasty glance to the rear and sing out at the top of my voice, " C-l-o-s-e u-p! " But they couldn't " close." Poor boys! Their eyes stuck out like those of maniacs. We went only a few miles, but the boys didn't all get up till noon.

It was not until May, 1861, that the War Department at Washington reluctantly authorized the organization of a regiment of volunteer cavalry from New York with the proviso that the men furnish the horses, an allowance being made for use and maintenance. This system applied in the South, but was soon abandoned in the North. The door once open, other regiments were speedily formed, containing at least the crude elements of efficient cavalry. As a rule, the men regarded the horses with mingled curiosity and respect, and passed through a purgatory of training—" breaking in," it was sometimes called—before they had acquired the requisite confidence in themselves, plus horses and arms. All too soon they were " pitchforked " into the field, often to fall victims to some roving body of Confederates who were eager to appropriate the superior arms and equipment of the Federals.

Within a year in the rough school of war, these same helpless recruits became fairly efficient cavalry, at home in the saddle, able to deliver telling blows with the saber, and to ride boot-to-boot in battle charges. During the first two years of the war the Confederate cavalry exercised a tremendous moral effect. Beginning with the cry of " The Black Horse

THIRTEENTH NEW YORK CAVALRY—RESERVES AT GETTYSBURG

These were some of the few men who would have stood between Lee and the Northern Capital if the tide of battle which hung in the balance three days at Gettysburg had rolled with the line in gray. The organization of the Thirteenth New York Cavalry was not completed till June 20, 1863, ten days before Gettysburg. Six companies left New York State for Washington on June 23d, and took their part in patrolling the rear of the Army of the Potomac during the three fateful days. They were more than raw recruits; the regiment had been made up by the consolidation of several incomplete organizations. Had the troopers arrived a few days earlier they probably would have been brigaded with Pleasonton's cavalry. A week after Gettysburg they were back in New York quelling the draft riots. Thereafter they spent their time guarding Washington, when this photograph was taken, and scouting near the armies in the Virginia hills.

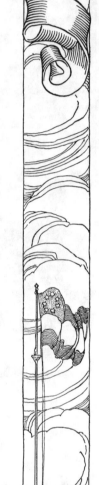

Cavalry," at the First Bull Run, so terrible to the panic-stricken Federal troops in their race to Washington and safety; Mosby's frequent dashes at poorly guarded Union trains and careless outposts; and Stuart's picturesque and gallant promenade around McClellan's unguarded encampment on the Chickahominy, in 1862, the war record of the Southern horse notwithstanding its subsequent decline and the final disasters of 1864–65 will always illumine one of the brightest pages of cavalry history.

The Gettysburg campaign, June 1 to July 4, 1863, was exceptionally full of examples of the effective use of mounted troops. They began with the great combat of Beverly Ford, Virginia, June 9th, in which for twelve hours, eighteen thousand of the flower of the horsemen of the armies of the Potomac and Northern Virginia, in nearly equal proportions, struggled for supremacy, with many casualties,* parting by mutual consent at the close of the day. This was followed by a series of daily skirmishes during the remainder of the month, in efforts to penetrate the cavalry screen which protected each army in its northward progress, culminating on the first day of July at Gettysburg in the masterly handling of two small brigades of cavalry.

It was here that General Buford delayed the advance of a division of Confederate infantry for more than two hours, winning for himself, in the opinion of a foreign military critic,† the honor of having " with the inspiration of a cavalry officer and a true soldier selected the battlefield where the two armies were about to measure their strength." The important actions on the third day comprised that in which Gregg prevented Stuart from penetrating the right rear of the Union line (largely a mounted combat with saber and pistol), and the affair on the Emmittsburg Road on the same day where

* The Second U. S. Cavalry alone losing 57 per cent. killed and wounded of its officers engaged.

† The Comte de Paris in " The Civil War in America."

STABLES FOR SIX THOUSAND HORSES

GIESBORO—ONE OF THE BUSIEST SPOTS OF THE WAR

The cavalry depot at Giesboro, D. C., established in July, 1863, was the place where remounts were furnished to the cavalry and artillery of the Army of the Potomac during the last two years of the war.   The tents in the lower photograph are those of the officers in charge of that immense establishment, where they received and issued thousands of horses.   Convalescents who had lost their mounts, with men to be remounted, were drawn upon to help take care of the horses, until their departure for the front.   This photograph was taken in May, 1864, when Grant and Lee were grappling in the Wilderness and at Spottsylvania, only seventy miles distant.   The inspection of horses for remounting was made by experienced cavalry officers, while the purchasing was under the Quartermaster's Department.

Merritt and Farnsworth menaced the Confederate left and, according to General Law,* neutralized the action of Hood's infantry division of Longstreet's corps by bold use of mounted and dismounted men, contributing in no small degree to the Federal success.

In the West, during the same period, the cavalry conditions were not unlike those in the East, except that the field of operations extended over five States instead of two and that numerous bands of independent cavalry or mounted riflemen under enterprising leaders like Forrest, Morgan, Wharton, Chalmers, and Wheeler of the Confederate army, for two years had their own way. The Union generals, Lyon, Sigel, Pope, Rosecrans, and others, loudly called for more cavalry, or in lieu thereof, for horses to mount infantry. Otherwise, they agreed, "it was difficult to oppose the frequent raids of the enemy on communications and supply trains."

Ultimately, Generals Grant and Rosecrans initiated a system of cavalry concentration under Granger and Stanley, and greater efficiency became manifest. About the time of the battle of Stone's River, or Murfreesboro, the Federal horse began to show confidence in itself, and in numerous encounters with the Confederates—mounted and dismounted—acquitted itself with credit, fairly dividing the honors of the campaign. The names of Grierson, Streight, Wilder, and Minty became famous not only as raiders but as important factors in great battles, as at Chickamauga, where the "obstinate stand of two brigades of [Rosecrans'] cavalry against the Confederate infantry gave time for the formation of the Union lines."

The most conspicuous cavalry operations of the war were those of 1864–65: Sheridan's Richmond raid, in which the South lost the brilliant and resourceful Stuart, and the harassing flank attacks on Lee's army in advance of Grant's infantry, which, ending in the campaign at Appomattox, simultaneously with Wilson's successful Selma raid, marked

* "Battles and Leaders of the Civil War."

THE CAVALRY DEPOT IN THE DISTRICT OF COLUMBIA

This photograph of the cavalry depot at Giesboro is peaceful and orderly enough with the Stars and Stripes drooping lazily in the wind, but it does not betray the hectic activity "behind the scenes." Not long after the depot was established the entire Second United States Cavalry was sent there to be remounted, recruited, and refitted. This operation took about a month, and they were ordered to rejoin the army in October, 1863. Every company had a special color of horse at the outset, but this effect was speedily lost in the field, except for the grays. "These were easily recruited," said an old cavalryman, "because nobody wanted grays. They were too conspicuous. No, I don't mean that they attracted the enemy's fire, but a gray horse that lies down in muddy places is very apt to get dirty. If you were coming in from a night of picket duty, would you rather take a rest, or spend your time getting your horse ready for inspection? The dark-coated animals did not show the dirt so much."

EVER–BUSY TROOPERS AT DRILL

The swiftly moving Confederate troopers, under dashing leaders like Stuart and Wheeler, allowed the heads of the Union cavalry not a moment of peace. When infantry went into winter quarters they could live in comparative comfort and freedom from actual campaigning until the roads became passable again for their heavy wagon-trains in the spring. But Confederate raiders knew neither times nor seasons, and there were many points when the damage they might do would be incalculable. So the Federal cavalry's winter task

UNION CAVALRY IN WINTER QUARTERS

was to discover, if possible, the Confederates' next move, and to forestall it. This photograph shows three troops drilling on the plain beside their winter quarters. The stark trees and absence of grass indicate clearly the time of the year, and the long shadows show as truly as a watch that the time of day was late afternoon. A swift night-march may be in store for the troopers on the plain, or they may return to the shelter of their wooden huts. It is probable, however, that they cannot enjoy their comfort for more than a week or two.

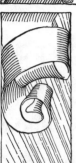

the collapse of the war. Under most discouraging conditions the Confederate cavalry disputed every inch of territory and won the sincere admiration of their opponents.

Major McClelland, of Stuart's staff, thus impartially summarizes the situation: *

"During the last two years no branch of the Army of the Potomac contributed so much to the overthrow of Lee's army as the cavalry, both that which operated in the Valley of Virginia and that which remained at Petersburg. But for the efficiency of this force it is safe to say that the war would have been indefinitely prolonged. From the time that the cavalry was concentrated into a corps until the close of the war, a steady progress was made in discipline. Nothing was spared to render this arm complete. Breech-loading arms of the most approved pattern were provided; horses and accouterments were never wanting, and during the last year of the war Sheridan commanded as fine a body of troops as ever drew sabers.

"On the other hand, two causes contributed steadily to diminish the numbers and efficiency of the Confederate cavalry. The Government committed the fatal error of allowing the men to own their horses, paying them a *per diem* for their use, and the muster valuation in cases where they were killed in action; but giving no compensation for horses lost by any other casualties of a campaign. . . . Toward the close of the war many were unable to remount themselves, and hundreds of such dismounted men were collected in a useless crowd, which was dubbed 'Company Q.' The second cause was the failure or inability of the Government to supply good arms and accouterments. Our breech-loading arms were nearly all captured from the enemy and the same may be said of the best of our saddles and bridles. From these causes, which were beyond the power of any commander to remedy, there was a steady decline in the numbers of the Confederate cavalry and, as compared with the Federal cavalry, a decline in efficiency."

* "Life and Campaigns of Major-General J. E. B. Stuart."

CHAPTER TWO

THE FEDERAL CAVALRY
ITS ORGANIZATION
AND EQUIPMENT

"BOOTS AND SADDLES"—THIRD DIVISION, CAVALRY
CORPS, ARMY OF THE POTOMAC, 1864

A SPREADING SECTION OF THE FEDERAL CAVALRY ORGANIZATION IN 1864

At Belle Plain Landing on the Potomac lay a chief base of supplies for Grant's armies in the spring of 1864. On April 4th Sheridan had been given charge of all the cavalry. He had found the corps much run down and the horses in poor condition. In a month he had effected a decided change for the better in the condition and *morale* of his ten thousand men, and was begging to be allowed to use them as an independent corps to fight the Confederate cavalry. Though they had been relieved of much of the arduous picket duty that they formerly performed, they were still considered as auxiliaries, to protect the flanks and front of the infantry. On May 7th Grant's army advanced with a view to taking Spotsylvania Court House.

CAVALRY IN CLOVER AT THE BELLE PLAIN LANDING

Thus was precipitated the cavalry battle at Todd's Tavern, and in part at least Sheridan's earnest desire became fulfilled.   The battle was between Hampton's and Fitzhugh Lee's commands of Stuart's cavalry and Gregg's division, assisted by two brigades of Torbert's division under the command of General Merritt. After a severe engagement the Confederate cavalry broke and were pursued almost to Spotsylvania Court House.   This photograph shows some of the Federal horses recuperating at Belle Plain Landing before this cavalry engagement on a large scale.   The cavalry were in clover here near the tents and ships that meant a good supply of forage.   There was no such loafing for horses and men a little later in that decisive year.

THE BELLE PLAIN CAVALRY

A CLOSER VIEW

This photograph brings the eye a little nearer to the cavalry at Belle Plain landing than the picture preceding. One can see the horses grazing by the side of the beautiful river. A group of cavalrymen have ridden their mounts into the water. The test of the efficient trooper was his skill in caring for his horse. Under ordinary circumstances, in a quiet camp like the above, it might be safe to turn horses out to graze and let them drink their fill at the river. But when on the march a staggering animal with parched throat and fast-glazing eyes whinnied eagerly at the smell of water, it was the trooper who had to judge its proper allowance. One swallow too many for a heated horse on a long march, multiplied by the number of troopers still ignorant of horsemanship, meant millions of dollars loss to the Union Government in the early stages of the war. Comparatively few horses were destroyed by wounds on the battlefield as compared with those lost through the ignorance of the troopers as to the proper methods of resting a horse, and as to the science of how, when, and what to feed him, and when to allow him to drink his fill. The Southern horsemen, as a rule more experienced, needed no such training, and their superior knowledge enabled the Confederate cavalry, with little "organization" in the strict sense of the word, to prove nevertheless a mighty weapon for their cause.

NEARER STILL

AT THE RIVER'S BRINK

This view brings us to the very edge of the water, where Sheridan's troopers were getting their mounts into shape for the arduous duties of the summer and fall. They are sitting at ease on the barebacked horses which have walked out into the cool river to slake their thirst. The wagon with the four-mule team bears the insignia of the Sixth Army Corps, commanded by Sedgwick. The canvas top is somewhat wrinkled, so it is impossible to see the entire device, which was in the shape of a Greek cross. It was during the campaign which followed these preparations that Sheridan had his famous interview with Meade, in which the former told his senior that he could whip Stuart if allowed to do so. General Grant determined to give Sheridan the opportunity that he sought, and on the very day of the interview Meade directed that the cavalry be immediately concentrated and that Sheridan proceed against the Confederate cavalry. On May 9th the expedition started with a column thirteen miles long. Stuart, however, was nothing loth to try conclusions with the Federal cavalry once more. He finally overtook it on May 11th at Yellow Tavern. The Confederate horse, depleted in numbers and equipment alike, was no longer its former brilliant self, and in this engagement the Confederacy lost James B. Gordon and Stuart, the leader without a peer.

WITH THE FARRIERS

OF THE

FEDERAL CAVALRY

These photographs were made at the headquarters of the Army of the Potomac in August, 1863, the month following the battle of Gettysburg, where the cavalry had fully demonstrated its value as an essential and efficient branch of the service. Every company of cavalry had its own farrier, enlisted as such. These men not only had to know all about the shoeing of horses, but also had to be skilled veterinary surgeons, such as each regiment has at the present day, coming next in pay to a second lieutenant. Plainly visible are the small portable anvil on an overturned bucket and the business-like leather aprons of the men. An army "marches upon its stomach," but cavalry marches upon its horses' feet, which must be cared for. In the larger photograph the men have evidently just become aware that their pictures are being taken. In the smaller exposure in the corner, the man holding the horse on the right has faced about to show off his horse to the best advantage; the horse holder on the left is facing the camera, arms akimbo, and a cavalryman in the rear has led up his white-faced mount to insure his inclusion in the picture.

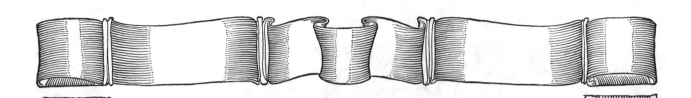

THE FEDERAL CAVALRY
ITS ORGANIZATION AND EQUIPMENT

By Charles D. Rhodes

Captain, General Staff, United States Army

AT the outbreak of the great Civil War in America, the regular cavalry at the disposal of the Federal Government consisted of the First and Second Regiments of Dragoons, one regiment of Mounted Rifles, and the First and Second Regiments of Cavalry. Early in the year 1861, the Third Cavalry was added to the others, and soon after, all six regiments were designated as cavalry and numbered serially from one to six.

The old regiments had been composed of ten troops, subdivided into five squadrons of two troops each, but the organization of the Sixth Cavalry Regiment called for twelve troops. In July, 1861, this organization was extended to all regular regiments, and in September of the same year the volunteer regiments, which had started out with ten troops each, were organized in a like manner. As the war progressed, the squadron organization was abandoned. When a regiment was subdivided for detached service, it was usually into battalions of four troops each.

The early war organization of cavalry troops called for one hundred enlisted men to a troop, officered by a captain, a first lieutenant, a second lieutenant, and a supernumerary second lieutenant. But in 1863, troops were given an elastic strength, varying between eighty-two and one hundred enlisted men, and the supernumerary lieutenant was dropped. Each regiment, commanded by a colonel, had a lieutenant-colonel and three majors, with a regimental commissioned and

THE FIRST EXTENSIVE FEDERAL CAVALRY CAMP—1862

This photograph shows the cavalry camp at Cumberland Landing just before McClellan advanced up the Peninsula. The entire strength of the cavalry the previous autumn had aggregated 8,125 men, of which but 4,753 are reported as "present for duty, equipped." It was constantly drilled during the fall and winter of 1861, with enough scouting and outpost duty in the Virginia hills to give the cavalry regiments a foretaste of actual service. In the lower photograph we get a bird's-eye view of Cumberland Landing where McClellan's forces were concentrated after the siege of Yorktown and the affair at Williamsburgh, preparatory to moving on Richmond. The cavalry reserve with the Peninsular army under that veteran horseman Philip St. George Cooke, was organized as two brigades under General Emry and Colonel Blake, and consisted of six regiments. Emry's brigade comprised the Fifth United States Cavalry, Sixth United States Cavalry, and Rush's Lancers—the Sixth Pennsylvania Cavalry. Blake's brigade consisted of the First United States Cavalry, the Eighth Pennsylvania Cavalry, and Barker's squadron of Illinois Cavalry.

AT CUMBERLAND LANDING

non-commissioned staff, which included two regimental surgeons, an adjutant, quartermaster, commissary, and their
subordinates.

Owing, however, to losses by reason of casualities in action,
sickness, and detached service, and through the lack of an efficient system of recruiting, whereby losses could be promptly
and automatically made good with trained men, the cavalry
strength, in common with that of other arms, always showed
an absurd and oftentimes alarming discrepancy between the
troopers actually in ranks and the theoretical organization provided by the existing law. Again, the losses in horse-flesh were
so tremendous in the first years of the war, and the channels
for replacing those losses were so inadequate and unsystem-
atized, that regiments oftentimes represented a mixed force
of mounted and unmounted men. Although the value of the
dismounted action of cavalry was one of the greatest developments of the war, its most valuable asset, mobility, was wholly
lacking when its horses were dead or disabled.

Cavalry is a most difficult force to organize, arm, equip,
and instruct at the outbreak of war. Not only must men be
found who have some knowledge of the use and handling of
horses, but the horses themselves must be selected, inspected,
purchased, and assembled. Then, after all the delays usually
attending the organizing, arming, and equipping of a mounted
force, many months of patient training, dismounted and
mounted, are necessary before cavalry is qualified to take the
field as an efficient arm. It is an invariable rule in militant
Europe to keep cavalry at all times at war strength, for it is
the first force needed to invade or to repel invasion, and, except
perhaps the light artillery, the slowest to "lick into shape"
after war has begun. In the regular cavalry service, it was a
common statement that a cavalryman was of little real value
until he had had two years of service.

It is, therefore, small wonder that during the first two
years of the great struggle, the Federal cavalry made only a

BEEF FOR THE CAVALRY AT COMMISSARY HEADQUARTERS

So seldom did the cavalry get a chance to enjoy the luxuries to be had at commissary headquarters that they took advantage of every opportunity. It is February, 1864, and the cavalry officer in the picture can look forward to a month or two more of fresh beef for his men. Then he will find his troop pounding by the desolate farmhouses and war-ridden fields, as the army advances on Richmond under Grant. While the infantry lay snug in winter-quarters, the troopers were busy scouring the Virginia hills for signs of the Confederates, or raiding their lines of communication and destroying their supplies. It took a large part of the time of the Northern and Southern infantry to repair the damage done by the cavalry. The cavalry often had to live by foraging, or go without food. Miles of railroad destroyed, bridges burned, telegraph wires cut, a sudden cessation of the source of supplies caused hundreds of miles of marching and counter-marching, beside the actual work of repairing by the engineering corps. It was Van Dorn's capture of Holly Springs that forced Grant to abandon his overland march against Vicksburg and return to Memphis in December, 1862.

poor showing. The regular cavalry was but a handful, and when President Lincoln issued his call for volunteers, little or no cavalry was accepted. Even when need for it was forced on the North, it took the Federal War Department a long time to realize that an efficient cavalry ready for field service could not be extemporized in a day.

Strange as it may now seem, the Federal authorities intended, in the beginning, to limit the cavalry force of the Union army to the six regular regiments; and even such a veteran soldier as General Scott gave it as his opinion that, owing to the broken and wooded character of the field of operations between the North and South, and the improvements in rifled cannon, the duties of cavalry would be unimportant and secondary.

Only seven troops of regular cavalry were available for the first battle of Bull Run, in 1861, but the firm front which they displayed in covering the confused and precipitate retreat of the Federal army, probably saved a large part of the main body from capture; but they never received the recognition that was deserved. However, the importance of cavalry was not altogether unappreciated, for we find, at Gettysburg, the Union cavalry of the Army of the Potomac aggregating nearly thirteen thousand officers and men. The close of the war saw Sheridan at Appomattox with fifteen thousand cavalrymen, while Wilson, in the South, was sweeping Mississippi and Alabama with an army of horsemen. But the evolution of this vast host from insignificant beginnings was a slow process, fraught with tremendous labor.

In the South, lack of good highways forced the Southerner to ride from boyhood, while contemporaneously the Northerner, with his improved roads, employed wheeled vehicles as a means of transportation. But aside from this positive advantage to Southern organization, the Confederate leaders seemed, from the very beginning of the Civil War, to appraise cavalry and its uses at its true valuation; while the Northern

[50]

AT THE BUSY OFFICE OF A CAVALRY QUARTERMASTER

This photograph was taken at Brandy Station in the spring of 1864. The sign on the wooden door of the little tent tells where "A. Q. M." held forth. The cavalrymen are evidently at ease. They have not yet met Stuart in the Wilderness. The quartermaster of a cavalry corps was the nearest approach to perpetual motion discovered during the war. His wagon-train could receive only the most general directions. He could never be certain where the men he was to supply with food could be found at any given time. He had to go exploring for his own regiments, and watch vigilantly that he did not incidentally feed the Confederates. He had to give precedence to ammunition-trains; dark often found his wagons struggling and floundering in the wake of their vanished friends. The quartermaster was responsible for their movements and arrivals. Besides carrying a map of the country in his head, he assumed immense responsibilities.

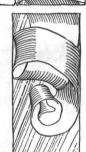

cavalry, even when finally mounted and equipped, was so mis-used and mishandled by those in control of military operations, that it was almost always at a disadvantage.

One of the first efforts of the War Department looking to the organization of Federal cavalry, is seen in the following circular letter, addressed by the Secretary of War to the Governors of the States:

> WAR DEPARTMENT, WASHINGTON,
> May 1, 1861.
>
> To the Governors of the Several States,
>   And All Whom it may Concern:
>
> I have authorized Colonel Carl Schurz to raise and organize a vol-unteer regiment of cavalry. For the purpose of rendering it as efficient as possible, he is instructed to enlist principally such men as have served in the same arm before. The Government will provide the regiment with arms, but cannot provide the horses and equipments. For these neces-saries we rely upon the patriotism of the States and the citizens, and for this purpose I take the liberty of requesting you to afford Colonel Schurz your aid in the execution of this plan.
>
> (Signed)   SIMON CAMERON,
>   *Secretary of War.*

Yet, in his report of preliminary operations in the first year of the war, General McClellan says:

> Cavalry was absolutely refused, but the governors of the States com-plied with my request and organized a few companies, which were finally mustered into the United States service and proved very useful.

The armament of the volunteer cavalry regiments, organ-ized with some show of interest after the battle of Bull Run, was along the same general lines as that of the regular regi-ments. Though suffering from a general deficiency in the number which could be purchased from private manufacturers—there being no reserve stock on hand—each trooper was armed with a saber and a revolver as soon as circumstances per-mitted. At least two squadrons (four troops) in each regi-

A WELL-EQUIPPED HORSE OF THE FIRST MASSACHUSETTS CAVALRY—1864

The saddle-bags and hooded stirrup of Captain E. A. Flint's horse shown in this photograph are "regulation," but the outfit of a regular cavalry horse did not call for a breast-strap. It was more apt to be used among the volunteers. The regulars as a rule preferred a single rein, curb bit, and no breast-strap or martingale. No breast-straps were issued, but they were found useful when cavalry was pounding up a slope, leaping fences, walls, and ditches, and otherwise putting unusual strain on the belly-band. The hooded stirrup was useful both to keep out rain and to keep the foot warm in winter. The saddle and blanket equipment in the photograph also conform to regulations. This is one of the horses and men that charged Stuart's cavalry so fiercely on the night of the third day at Gettysburg. The First Massachusetts was in the second division, under General David McM. Gregg. The photograph was taken in November, 1864, at the headquarters of the Army of the Potomac, then thoroughly in touch with its ample "supply trains."

JUST BEFORE SHERIDAN CAME, 1864

This photograph shows the Eighteenth Pennsylvania in winter-quarters near Brandy Station in March, 1864, a month before the most important event in the history of the Federal cavalry—the unifying of the cavalry branch under the aggressive Sheridan. After Kilpatrick's raid on Richmond, ending the 2d of March, these troopers rested in camp until Sheridan left for his Richmond raid on May 9th. A month in camp is a long time for cavalry, and here one has a good opportunity to see with what rapidity and ease a trooper had learned to make himself comfortable. Barrels have been placed upon the chimneys in order to

THE EIGHTEENTH PENNSYLVANIA CAVALRY

increase their draft. Light enclosures of poles have been thrown up for the horses, and fodder has been stacked up on the hill. With stumps and cross-pieces the McClellan saddles are kept out of the wet and mud. The saddles were covered with rawhide instead of leather, and were more uncomfortable when they split than an ill-fitting shoe. The troopers themselves look fairly contented, and some of them are not so lean and angular as in the days of scouting and hard riding. There is plenty of work ahead of them, however, nearer Richmond, which will quickly enable them to rid themselves of any superfluous flesh.

ment were armed with rifles or carbines. Later, all cavalry regiments were supplied with single-shot carbines, the decreased length and weight of the shorter arm being a decided advantage to a soldier on horseback. One volunteer regiment, the Sixth Pennsylvania Cavalry (Rush's Lancers), was armed with the lance in addition to the pistol, twelve carbines being afterwards added to the equipment of each troop for picket and scouting duty. But in May, 1863, all the lances were discarded for carbines as being unsuited for the heavily wooded battle-grounds of Virginia.

The carbines issued were of various pattern—the Sharp's carbine being succeeded by the Spencer, which fired seven rounds with more or less rapidity but which was difficult to reload quickly. In the later years of the war, certain regiments were armed with the Henry rifle, an improved weapon firing sixteen shots with great accuracy. A Colt's rifle, firing six rounds, and a light, simple carbine called the Howard, were also in evidence among cavalry regiments at the close of the war. Previous to, and during the first year of the war, the Burnside was favorably thought of by the Federal officers. This carbine was the invention of General Ambrose E. Burnside, and was manufactured in Bristol, Rhode Island. Its chief value lay in its strength and the waterproof cartridges used. But its chief objection also lay in the high cost and the difficulty in obtaining this cartridge, which was manufactured of sheet brass, an expensive metal at that time. Another arm, similar to Burnside's and made with a tapering steel barrel, was the Maynard, which was manufactured by the Maynard's Arms Company, Washington, District of Columbia.

At the beginning, the sabers issued were of the long, straight, Prussian pattern, but these were afterwards replaced by a light cavalry saber with curved blade. Many of these were fitted with attachments so as to be fastened to the end of the carbines in the form of a bayonet. There also was an ordinary saber handle which allowed of their being carried at the

CAVALRY STABLES AT GRANT'S HEADQUARTERS, CITY POINT, IN 1864

City Point was Grant's base of supplies during the operations about Petersburg, in 1864. Sheridan at last was handling his cavalry as a separate command, and was soon to go to the Shenandoah. Brigadier-General David McM. Gregg was in command of the cavalry which remained with Grant. The First Massachusetts, First New Jersey, Tenth New York, Sixth Ohio, and Twenty-first Pennsylvania formed the First Brigade, and the First Maine, Second Pennsylvania, Fourth Pennsylvania, Eighth Pennsylvania, Thirteenth Pennsylvania, and Sixteenth Pennsylvania were the Second Brigade. Some of these men had been on Sheridan's Richmond and Trevilian raids. This shows the comparative comfort of City Point. To the left is a grindstone, where sabers might be made keen.

hip, as a side-arm, for which purpose it was well adapted, having a curved edge with a sharp point.

The standard pistol was the Colt's revolver, army or navy pattern, loaded with powder and ball and fired with percussion caps. Within its limitations, it was a very efficient weapon.

The saddle was the McClellan, so-called because adopted through recommendations made by General McClellan after his official European tour, in 1860, although it was in reality a modification of the Mexican or Texan tree. It was an excellent saddle, and in an improved pattern is, after fifty years of trial, still the standard saddle of the United States regular cavalry. In its original form it was covered with rawhide instead of leather, and when this covering split, the seat became very uncomfortable for the rider.

Although the original recruiting regulations required cavalry troopers to furnish their own horses and equipments, this requirement was later modified, and the Government furnished everything to the recruit, in volunteer as well as in regular regiments. Many troopers sold their private horses to the Government and then rode them in ranks. It was argued by some cavalry officers of that period that this system was eminently successful in securing men for the cavalry who could ride and who would care for horses.

As is usual in a country weak in trained cavalry and utterly unprepared for war, vexatious delays occurred in receiving the equipment of newly organized cavalry regiments. Long after the Western regiments were organized, they were kept inactive from lack of equipment, for which the Federal Government had made no provision in the way of reserve supplies. In some instances months elapsed before saddles were received, and in several cases arms were even longer in putting in an appearance. The interim was employed by the commanders in teaching their men to ride and drill, to use their arms, and to care for their horses. In the absence of saddles,

THE FAR-REACHING FEDERAL CAVALRY ORGANIZATION—WATER-TANK AT THE LOUISIANA DEPOT

Water—that word alone spells half the miseries and difficulties of the cavalry, especially in the parched Southern country. Although an infantry column could camp beside a little spring, cavalry horses had to plod wearily on till they reached a river, a stream, or at least a fair-sized pool. Even then, some officer grown wise in war might pronounce the water unfit for drinking, and the troopers must rein up their thirsty, impatient steeds, wild to plunge their noses in the cool morass, and ride patiently on again till good water was found. The place is Green-ville in Louisiana, where one of the six great Union cavalry depots was located. The site of the camp was selected by General Richard Arnold, Chief of Cavalry, Department of the Gulf. On June 8, 1864, from New Orleans, he requested permission to move his camping ground. "Present camping-ground of the First and Fifth Brigades of my command near Banks is entirely unsuitable, and I ask permission to move to this side of the river, at or near Greenville. I can find no more suitable place on either side of the river within twenty miles of the city." Permission to move was granted June 14, 1864.

various makeshifts were used on the horses' backs, and the troopers were even drilled bareback.

This probationary period was a wearisome one for the cavalry recruit. A trooper must perforce learn much of what his comrade of the infantry knows, and in addition must be taught all that pertains to horses and horsemanship. Those who had been fascinated by the glamour and dash of the cavalry life doubtless wished many times, during those laborious days, that they had the more frequent hours of recreation granted their neighbors of the infantry. The reward of the Federal cavalry came in those later days when, after painstaking and unremitting instruction covering many months and enlightening experiences in the field, they gained that confidence in themselves and their leaders, which resulted in the ultimate destruction of the opposing cavalry, and the decisive triumph of the Federal arms.

But good cavalry cannot be made in a month, or even in a year. The first year of the war saw the Confederate cavalry plainly superior in every way, and there were humiliating instances of the capture by the *corps d'élite* of the South, of whole squadrons of Northern horsemen. The second year of the tremendous struggle passed with much improvement in the Federal cavalry, but with a still marked lack of confidence in itself. It was not until the third year of its organization and training that the Union cavalry really found itself, and was able to vindicate its reputation in the eyes of those who in the preceding period were wont to sneeringly remark that "no one ever sees a dead cavalryman!

The drill regulations of the period, called tactics in those days, were the "'41 Tactics" or "Poinsett Tactics," authorized for dragoon regiments in the year 1841, by the Honorable J. R. Poinsett, Secretary of War. These drill regulations were in the main a translation from the French, and although occasional attempts were made to improve them, they continued in use by the Eastern cavalry of the Union armies throughout the

WELL-GROOMED OFFICERS OF THE THIRTEENTH NEW YORK CAVALRY

Many of the Federal cavalry officers were extremely precise in the matter of dress, paying equal attention to their horses' equipment, in order to set a good example to their men. Custer was a notable example. This photograph shows full dress, fatigue dress, a properly equipped charger, an orderly, sentry, cavalry sabres and the short cavalry carbine. Except for the absence of revolvers, it is an epitome of the dress and equipment which the Federal Government supplied lavishly to its troopers during the latter half of the war. At the outset, the volunteer cavalrymen were required to supply their own horses, a proper allowance being made for food and maintenance. In 1861, the Confederate cavalry had no Colt's revolvers, no Chicopee sabers, and no carbines that were worth carrying. Their arms were of the homeliest type and of infinite variety. This photograph was taken in July, 1865, when Washington no longer needed watching.

war. The Western cavalry used the " '41 Tactics " until late in the year 1864, and thereafter a system of drill formulated by General Philip St. George Cooke, which was published in 1862 by the War Department and prescribed a single-rank formation for the cavalry.

After all the months of drill, how different were those days of actual service in the field—weary marches in mud, rain, and even snow; short rations for men and for horses when the trains were delayed or when there were no trains; bivouacs on the soggy ground with saddles for pillows; gruesome night rides when troopers threw reins on the necks of horses and slept in their saddles; nerve-racking picket duty in contact with the foe's lines, where the whinny of a horse meant the wicked " ping " of a hostile bullet.

Like all soldiers new to the rigors of actual service in war, the Union volunteer cavalry, in those early days, loaded themselves and their horses with an amount of superfluous baggage which provoked sarcasm from the seasoned soldier and which later experience taught them wholly to discard. Some articles were absolutely necessary; much was entirely useless and oftentimes unauthorized.

In addition to his arms, which weighed not a little, the volunteer cavalryman carried a huge box of cartridges and another of percussion caps; from his shoulder depended a haversack filled with rations, and to which was often attached not only a tin cup but a coffee-pot. A canteen of water, a nose-bag of corn, a shelter tent, a lariat and picket pin, extra horseshoes and nails, a curry-comb and brush, a set of gun-tools and cleaning materials, and saddle-bags filled with extra clothing brought the weight of the trooper and his kit to a figure which was burdensome to an animal in even the best of condition. When to these articles of equipment were added an overcoat, extra blankets, additional boots, and the odds and ends of luxuries, which the recruit is wont to stow away surreptitiously, the result was a lame and broken-down horse, hundreds of troopers

BREAD AND COFFEE FOR THE CAVALRYMAN

The mess-house for cavalry ordered to Washington.—In the field the cavalrymen were glad when they could get the regular rations—bacon and hard bread. During the winter, in permanent camp, they occasionally enjoyed the luxury of soft bread. But they were kept so constantly employed, reconnoitering the enemy's position, watching the fords of the Rappahannock, and engaged in almost constant skirmishing, even in severe winter weather while the infantry was being made comfortable in winter-quarters, that this mess-house was regarded as a sort of Mecca by the troopers sent to Washington to be organized and remounted. Soft bread was not the only luxury here, and when they rejoined their commands their comrades would listen with bated breath to their thrilling stories of soup and eggs and other Lucullan delicacies. There was an army saying that it takes a good trooper to appreciate a good meal.

afoot, and the whole cavalry service rendered inefficient and almost useless.

As an evidence of the lack of discipline and of the ignorance of things military, which marked those early days of the cavalry service, it may be mentioned that many credulous troopers purchased so-called invulnerable vests, formed of thin steel plates and warranted by the makers to ward off a saber stroke or stop a leaden bullet. Dents in the armor were pointed out as evidence of this remarkable quality. Of course the vests were sooner or later discarded, but while retained they added about ten pounds to the burden of the already overloaded horse.

It is stated that the first time the Confederate cavalrymen, who rode light, met some of these remarkably equipped troopers, they wondered with amazement whether the Union horsemen were lifted into the saddle after the latter was packed, or whether the riders mounted first, and then had the numberless odds and ends of their equipment packed around them.

An anecdote is related of a humane Irish recruit, who, when he found his horse was unable to carry the heavy load allotted him, decided as an act of mercy to share the load with his charger. So, unloading nearly a hundred pounds from the horse, he strapped the mass to his own broad shoulders; and remounting his steed, rode off, quite jubilant over his act of unselfishness.

But it did not take long for cavalrymen in the field to learn with how little equipment the soldier may live and fight efficiently, and with how much greater zest the horses can withstand the long marches when the load is cut down to the limit of actual needs. There was danger then of the opposite extreme, and that absolutely necessary articles would be conveniently dropped and reported as "lost in action" or as "stolen." The net result, however, was that after one or two campaigns, the Federal cavalrymen learned to travel light, and, better than anything else, learned that quality of discipline

THE HAY BUSINESS OF THE GOVERNMENT

The matter of proper feed for cavalry horses was a constant perplexity to the Federal Government until the men had learned how to care for their mounts.   During the first two years of the war two hundred and eighty-four thousand horses were furnished to the cavalry, although the maximum number of cavalrymen in the field at any time during this period did not exceed sixty thousand.   The enormous number of casualties among the horses was due to many causes, among which were poor horsemanship on the part of the raw troopers mustered in at the beginning of the war, and the ignorance and gross inefficiency on the part of many officers and men as to the condition of the horses' backs and feet, care as to food and cleanliness, and the proper treatment of the many diseases to which horses on active service are subject.   In such a tremendous machine as the quartermaster's department of the Army of the Potomac, containing at the beginning of the war many officers with absolutely no experience as quartermasters, there were necessarily many vexatious delays in purchasing and forwarding supplies, and many disappointments in the quality of supplies, furnished too often by scheming contractors.   By the time the photograph above reproduced was taken, 1864, the business of transporting hay to the army in the field had been thoroughly systematized, as the swarming laborers in the picture attest.

AT THE HAY WHARF, ALEXANDRIA

GOVERNMENT HAY–WHARF AT ALEXANDRIA, VIRGINIA

The army which McClellan took to the Peninsula had to be created from the very foundation. The regular army was too small to furnish more than a portion of the general officers and a very small portion of the staff, so that the staff departments and staff officers had to be fashioned out of perfectly raw material. Artillery, small-arms, and ammunition were to be manufactured, or purchased from abroad; wagons, ambulances, bridge-trains, camp equipage, hospital stores, and all the vast impedimenta and material indispensable for an army in the field were to be manufactured. The tardiness with which cavalry remounts were forwarded to the regiments was a frequent subject of complaint. General McClellan complained that many of the horses furnished were "totally unfitted for the service and should never have been re-

SENTRY GUARDING FEED FOR FEDERAL HORSES, 1864

ceived." General Pope had in fact reported that "our cavalry numbered on paper about four thousand men, but their horses were completely broken down, and there were not five hundred men, all told, capable of doing such service as should be expected of cavalry." The demand for horses was so great that in many cases they were sent on active service before recovering sufficiently from the fatigue incident to a long railway journey. One case was reported of horses left on the cars fifty hours without food or water, and then being taken out, issued, and used for immediate service. Aside, too, from the ordinary diseases to which horses are subject, the Virginia soil seemed to be particularly productive of diseases of the feet. That known as "scratches" disabled thousands of horses during the Peninsula campaign and the march of Pope.

MEN WHO SHOD A MILLION HORSES

This photograph presents another aspect of the gigantic system whereby the Union cavalry became organized and equipped so as to prove irresistible after 1863. In the fiscal year 1864 the Union Government bought and captured nearly 210,000 horses. The army in the field required about 500 new horses every day. Sheridan's force alone required 150 new horses a day during the Shenandoah campaign. At Giesboro, the big remount depot near Washington, they handled 170,622 horses in 1864, and in June, 1866, they had

PART OF THE GIGANTIC ORGANIZATION OF THE FEDERAL CAVALRY

only 32 left. This was exclusive of 12,000 or 13,000 artillery horses handled at the same depot. All these animals had to be shod. This photograph shows some of the men who did it, with the implements of their trade. The army in the field kept this army at home busy supplying its manifold needs. The Southerners' only array of men was at the front. At home, they had only an army of women, knitting, weaving, and sewing for the ragged soldiers in the field. The men wholesale had left their businesses and enlisted.

which subordinates the comfort and pleasure of the individual to the greatest good of the greatest number.

The trouble was that upon the organization of so many regiments of volunteer cavalry, both officers and men were naturally uninstructed and therefore inefficient. Horses were overloaded, marches were prolonged beyond endurance and without proper halts for rest, forage was not always regularly provided, and troopers were not held down to those many little things which, whether in the saddle or in camp, make for the endurance of the horse and for the mobility of mounted troops.

Tactically, both officers and men of the newly made cavalry had everything to learn. In spite of the splendid natural material which was attracted to the mounted service, and the lavish expenditures of the Federal Government in its behalf, the first period of the war only emphasized the fact that, given unlimited resources in the way of men, horses, and equipment, efficient cavalry cannot be developed inside of two years or more.

To be fully prepared at the outbreak of war, regular cavalry should be kept during peace at its war strength; while if reserves of militia cavalry cannot be conveniently maintained during peace, ample reserve supplies of arms and equipment should be laid by, and such encouragement given to the breeding and rearing of saddle-horses as will enable the Government to place cavalry in the field without all the vexatious and humiliating delays which attended the fitting out of the Federal cavalry force in 1861 and 1862.

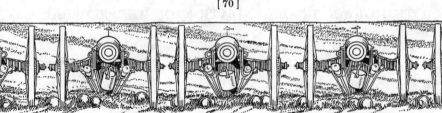

CHAPTER

THREE

————

THE CONFEDERATE CAVALRY
IN THE EAST

————

GENERAL "JEB" STUART
LEADER OF
THE VIRGINIA CAVALRY

BRIGADIER–GENERAL
BEVERLY H. ROBERTSON
C.S.A.

SUCCESSOR TO ASHBY
AS COMMANDER OF
THE "VALLEY" CAVALRY
IN 1862

MAJOR–GENERAL
W. H. F. LEE,
C.S.A.

IN 1862 COLONEL OF
THE NINTH VIRGINIA CAVALRY
IN "FITZ" LEE'S BRIGADE
UNDER STUART

CONFEDERATE
CAVALRY
LEADERS

MAJOR–GENERAL
THOMAS L. ROSSER,
C.S.A.

IN 1862 COLONEL OF THE
FIFTH VIRGINIA CAVALRY
IN "FITZ" LEE'S BRIGADE
UNDER STUART

BRIGADIER–GENERAL
WILLIAM E. JONES,
C.S.A.

IN 1862 COLONEL OF
THE SEVENTH VIRGINIA
CAVALRY IN THE ARMY
OF THE VALLEY

ACTIVE IN THE
EARLY VIRGINIA
CAMPAIGNS

ONE OF THE REGIMENTS THAT STUART ELUDED

A glance at the gallant and hardy bearing of Rush's Lancers as they looked in 1862, and at their curious weapons, suggestive more of Continental than of American warfare, brings sufficient testimony to the high quality of the men who endeavored to curb the Confederate leader, Stuart, and the resources behind them. The usual armament of the Union volunteer cavalry regiments consisted of a saber, a revolver, and a single-shot carbine. The Sixth Pennsylvania was provided with lances in addition to the pistol, twelve carbines being afterwards added to the equipment of each troop for picket and scouting duty. A clean cut, smart-looking lot they are by the streaming pennants—the privates, recruited from the fashionable athletic set of the day in Philadelphia, no less than the officer, so intent upon the coffee that his orderly is pouring out. But it was vainly that in North or South, in Pennsylvania or in Virginia, in Federal territory or along the banks of the Chickahominy, the men of this crack Pennsylvania regiment tried to catch Stuart and his

LANCERS IN THE FEDERAL CAVALRY

fleet command. At Tunstall's Station, Virginia, they were two hours late; at Emmittsburg, Maryland, an hour early. On the occasion of Stuart's famous raid on Chambersburg, in October, 1862, General Pleasonton, irritated by the audacity of the daring Southerner, had made every disposition to head off the raiders before they reached the Potomac. General Pleasonton himself, with eight hundred men; Colonel Richard H. Rush, with his unique lancers, and General Stoneman, with his command, were all scouring the country in search of Stuart, who was encumbered with many captured horses, but was moving steadily toward the Potomac. A march of thirty-two miles from Chambersburg brought the wily Stuart to Emmittsburg about seven o'clock on the evening of the 11th. One hour before their arrival six companies of the Lancers, at that time attached to the Third Brigade, had passed through the town on their way to Gettysburg. But until the day of his death, Stuart often managed so that the Union cavalry came too early or too late.

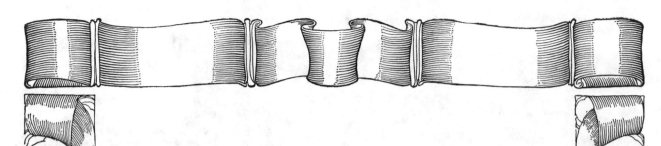

THE CAVALRY CORPS OF THE ARMY OF NORTHERN VIRGINIA

By Holmes Conrad
Major Cavalry Corps, Army of Northern Virginia

THE Cavalry Corps of the Army of Northern Virginia was a growth, not a creation. Its nucleus was formed of three cavalry companies, at Harper's Ferry, in April, 1861. "Clarke's Cavalry" was stationed at the bridge over the Shenandoah River near Harper's Ferry; Ashby's company was at the bridge over the Potomac River at the Point of Rocks, and Drake's company was at the bridge at Brunswick. J. E. B. Stuart was commissioned as lieutenant-colonel and assigned to the command of the cavalry in the district then commanded by Colonel T. J. Jackson. When General Joseph E. Johnston relieved Colonel Jackson, the forces were withdrawn from Harper's Ferry, and the headquarters of that army were at Winchester, in the Shenandoah valley.

On July 1, 1861, General Patterson crossed the Potomac at Williamsport with the intention of operating against General Johnston, and preventing him from reenforcing Beauregard at Manassas. The first engagement of any kind between these opposing forces is known as "the affair at Falling Waters," in which Jackson, with three hundred and eighty infantry and one piece of artillery, detained the advance of Patterson's army for some days. Colonel Stuart, with his cavalry, was reconnoitering on Patterson's right flank. While passing along the edge of a piece of woods, he came suddenly upon a company of Pennsylvania infantry, separated from him by a high rail fence. Stuart, dressed in a blue-flannel coat and corduroy trousers, rode to the fence and in peremptory tones

ONE OF THE EARLIEST CONFEDERATE CAVALRY EXPLOITS

A month before the first battle of Bull Run, the bridge at Berlin, Md., six miles below Harper's Ferry, was thoroughly destroyed in one of the first exploits of the Confederate cavalry. It was not yet organized. A few detached bands here and there—the Clarke company at the bridge over the Shenandoah River near Harper's Ferry, Ashby's company at the bridge over the Potomac River at the Point of Rocks, and Drake's company at the bridge at Brunswick—were operating along the first Confederate line of defense. But they had already begun to demonstrate their daring and effectiveness. This was the prelude to the bold rides of Stuart and Forrest, to the swift raids of Morgan and the terror-inspiring Mosby. It was acts like this that hampered the Union leaders, and detained an army between Washington and the Confederates. Not until the Union cavalry had learned to retaliate, and to meet and fight the exhausted Confederate horsemen on their own ground and in their own way, did the Union generals get complete possession of their infantry.

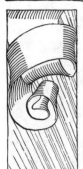

ordered the Federals to pull down the fence at once, which they did. The cavalry rode into their midst, and without the firing of a pistol took the entire company of thirty or forty men.

On the 18th of July, Johnston withdrew his army from Winchester, and moved toward Manassas. Stuart's entire command consisted of twenty-one officers and three hundred and thirteen men. All were well mounted and at home on horseback. Yet for arms they could muster but few sabers of regulation make and still fewer revolvers, although double-barreled shotguns and rifles were prevalent.

This command reached Manassas on the evening of the 20th of July, and went into camp. The next morning, at early dawn, it was aroused by the firing of a signal gun by the Federals. In the afternoon, General T. J. Jackson's brigade, while fully occupied in front, was threatened by the advance of a heavy attacking column on its left. Stuart was sent to its relief, and moving in column on Jackson's left, he soon came in view of a formidable line of Zouaves moving upon Jackson. The appearance of the head of Stuart's column arrested the movement of the opponents, attracted their fire, and finally caused their withdrawal, for which Jackson, in his report, made grateful acknowledgment.

During the summer and fall, the cavalry occupied and held Mason's and Munson's hills and picketed as far as Falls Church and at points along the Potomac. With the exception of an affair at Lewinsville, in September, the period was uneventful and free from striking incidents. In September, 1861, Stuart was commissioned brigadier-general, and in December occurred the battle of Dranesville, in which he commanded the Confederate forces, but the result of the engagement afforded him no ground for congratulation.

In March, 1862, the Confederates evacuated Manassas, and moved below Richmond. The advance of McClellan up the Peninsula toward Williamsburg, afforded but little opportunity for cavalry operations other than protecting the flanks

FALLS CHURCH, ON THE CONFEDERATE PICKET LINE IN '61—NEARLY THREE MILES FROM WASHINGTON

This typical cross-roads Virginia church, less than three miles from Washington, lay on the end of the line patroled by the Confederate cavalry pickets in the summer and fall of '61. Strange-looking soldiers were those riders in Colonel J. E. B. Stuart's command, without uniforms, armed with rifles and double-barreled shot-guns, with hardly a saber or a revolver. While McClellan was drilling his army in Washington and metamorphosing it from an "armed mob" into an efficient fighting machine, the Confederate horsemen occupied and held Mason's and Munson's Hill and picketed at points along the Potomac. With the exception of an affair at Lewinsville in September there was little actual fighting. In that month Stuart was commissioned brigadier-general, and in December occurred the battle of Dranesville, in which he commanded the Confederate forces, but failed to carry the day. Soon, however, he leaped into fame.

and rear of the army as it withdrew within the lines around
Richmond. Toward the middle of June was effected that brilliant movement which so distinctly illustrates the daring and
skill of Stuart and the unfailing endurance of his men. He
passed around the entire Federal army, obtaining the information he sought and returning to camp with the substantial
rewards of his prowess.

During the Seven Days' battles around Richmond, but little opportunity was afforded for cavalry operations beyond the
ordinary work of obtaining information on the front and
flanks, but in the latter part of June, Stuart reached White
House, where a Federal gunboat had been seen on the Pamunkey. Seventy-five dismounted cavalrymen, armed with
carbines and deployed as skirmishers, approached the vessel,
whereupon a body of sharpshooters was landed from the gunboat and advanced to meet them. A single howitzer of the
Stuart horse artillery opened on the war-ship from a position
on which her guns could not be brought to bear. The shells
from the howitzer greatly distressed her, and withdrawing her
sharpshooters, she disappeared down the river.

On no occasion was the audacity of Stuart and the temper
of his men more severely tested than in October, when there
was carried through the movement to Chambersburg, Pennsylvania, which was reached on the 10th. The advance was
bold and perilous enough, but it was tame in comparison with
the return. The Union forces had been thoroughly aroused,
and dispositions had been ordered, intended and calculated to
head off the invaders before they could recross the Potomac.
Leaving Chambersburg, a march of nearly thirty-two miles
brought Stuart and his men to Emmittsburg at about seven
o'clock on the evening of the 11th. One hour before their arrival, four companies of the Sixth Pennsylvania Cavalry had
passed through the town on their way to Gettysburg. General
Pleasonton with eight hundred men, Colonel Rush with his regiment, and General Stoneman with his command were scouring

A CONFEDERATE HORSE AT AN HISTORIC VIRGINIA SPOT, IN MAY, 1862

When '61 came, the young men in the North were to be found rather at commercial and indoor pursuits, as compared to those in the South. There the sports of country life appealed in preference, and the rifle and saddle were more familiar than the counting-house. Thus the Confederate cavalrymen saw nothing wrong in the proposition that they should furnish their own mounts throughout the war. The name of the beautiful horse in this photograph was "Secesh." Its upraised ears and alert expression of interest in the man who is waving his hat in the foreground, to make it look at the camera, proves it a "well-bred" animal. "Secesh" was captured by the Federals in 1862 at Yorktown, and the spot where the photograph was taken is historic. It is the cave excavated in the marl bluff by Cornwallis in 1781, for secret councils.

the country in search of Stuart, who was encumbered with many captured horses in his march toward the Potomac. Pleasonton had so interpreted Stuart's movements as to make it clear to his mind that Stuart must cross the river at the mouth of the Monocacy, but, as a matter of fact, White's Ferry was the point at which the Confederate purposed to get over. Colonel W. H. F. Lee commanded the advance, and as he approached the ferry, he found it guarded by a force of Federal infantry.

Lee had arranged his plan of attack upon these troops when it occurred to him to try a milder method. He sent a flag of truce to the Union commander and demanded the unconditional surrender of his men within fifteen minutes. To this there was no response, and Colonel Lee then opened with one gun, which fire was not returned. In a few moments the Union infantry quit their impregnable position and withdrew down the river. Stuart and his returning legions, with all their plunder, then crossed the Potomac in safety.

Several companies in the Virginia cavalry regiments were mounted on thoroughbred racers, sired by horses whose names are as household words in racing annals. One experience, in the summer of 1861, demonstrated their unfitness for cavalry service. After General Patterson had crossed the Potomac at Williamsport and occupied Martinsburg, the First Virginia Cavalry was in camp in an apple orchard, about two miles south of that town. A section of a Federal battery of two rifled guns advanced and took position a few hundred yards from the orchard, and threw some percussion shells over the cavalrymen. The missiles struck soft earth beyond and did not explode, but their screams, as they passed over the camp, were appalling. One of the companies, mounted on thoroughbreds, had no more control over their steeds than they had over the shells that frightened them. The commander of the company sought to divert attention from the noise by keeping the horses in motion, but no sooner were they brought into line than they broke and ran. A hundred yards distant was a fence, eight

A SOUTHERN ROADSTER IN 1862, AT THE SPOT WHERE STUART ON HIS FAMOUS
RAID ESCAPED FROM DANGER

The spring, the rangy endurance of this Virginia riding-horse, halted on the highway near Charles City
Court House, illustrates one factor in the dismay the Confederate cavalrymen were able to implant in the
hearts of their Northern opponents during the first two years of the war. This horse, by the way, is tread-
ing the very road where Stuart, two years before, had escaped across the Chickahominy from the vengeful
army riding in his wake after he had ridden completely around its rear. Such raids, until the North had
created an efficient cavalry force, destroyed millions of dollars' worth of Federal property and exercised a
tremendous moral effect. The cry of "The Black Horse Cavalry" terrified still further the panic-stricken
Federal troops at Bull Run; Mosby's brilliant dashes at poorly guarded Union wagon trains and careless
outposts taught the Northern leaders many a lesson, and Stuart's two raids around McClellan's army, on
the Peninsula and in Maryland, resulted in the systematic upbuilding of a Federal cavalry. In the
latter years of the war, when the South was exhausted of such horses, their cavalry became less efficient,
but nothing can dim the luster of their performances in those first two hopeful and momentous years.

rails high. They cleared this like deer, and moved to the northwest. The rifled guns returned to Martinsburg, and the regiment remained in the orchard, but it was two days before all
those race-horses found their way back to the regiment.
Blooded horses proved unfit for the service; they fretted and
exhausted themselves on a quiet march, and proved to be unmanageable in field engagements.

June, 1863, witnessed the most spectacular tournament
in which the cavalry of the opposing armies in Virginia ever
engaged. The Army of Northern Virginia was entering upon
the campaign that was to culminate in the three days' battle
of Gettysburg, and the entire cavalry force had been assembled
for review, at Brandy Station. General Pleasonton, commander of the Union Cavalry Corps, wished to cross the Rappahannock to ascertain the disposition of General Lee's army.
Two fords led across the river in that vicinity, Beverly and
Kelly's, and these were promptly approached by the inquisi-
tive Northerners. The second and third divisions of cavalry
and a brigade of infantry were ordered to cross at Kelly's
Ford; the first cavalry division, with another brigade of
infantry, was ordered to cross at Beverly Ford. Several batteries of artillery accompanied each column, and never were
batteries more gallantly served or skilfully commanded. On
the morning of the 9th of June, the Eighth New York Cavalry
crossed at Beverly Ford. One company of the Sixth Virginia,
under Captain Gibson, formed the picket at this point. Stuart's
headquarters had been on Fleetwood Hill from which, however, he had, luckily, removed his baggage at an early hour.

General Buford's force of Federal cavalry which crossed
at Beverly Ford was, in the opinion of all of us, quite enough
to satisfy the wishes of reasonable men, and Stuart had not
reckoned on a further assault on his rear. But General Gregg,
with another division of Federal cavalry, crossed at Kelly's
Ford, and thus had Fleetwood Hill, which was the key to
the situation between the two hostile forces. A disabled

THE BANKS OF THE CHICKAHOMINY IN '62—WHEN STUART CROSSED IT IN THE

FIRST GREAT RAID OF THE WAR

This small but quick-rising little stream came nearer than the entire Union army to stopping Stuart in his famous "ride around McClellan" on the Peninsula, June 13–15, 1862. This was the first of the great Confederate raids that served to startle the Union into a recognition of the maladministration of its cavalry. After a brush with a squadron the Fifth United States Cavalry, commanded by Captain W. B. Royall, and a short halt at Old Church, he marched with only twelve hundred cavalrymen, by night, down through New Kent to Sycamore Ford on the Chickahominy, thence straight back to Richmond along the James River road. His entire loss was one man killed and a few wounded; yet he brought prisoners and plunder from under McClellan's very nose. Of most importance, he discovered the exact location of the Federal right wing, so that Jackson attacked it a few days later successfully. The cavalry gained confidence in itself, and the Confederacy rang with praises of its daring. The one really dangerous moment to the adventurous party came when the Chickahominy was reached on the homeward journey and was found to be swollen suddenly, and impassable even by swimming. Only Stuart's promptness in tearing down a mill and building a bridge with its timbers got his men across before the Federals hove in sight.

6-pounder howitzer had been left on Fleetwood Hill, under charge of Lieutenant Carter, and with this disabled gun and a very limited amount of ammunition, General Gregg was held in check until aid from General W. E. Jones' brigade could be sent. Gregg very naturally supposed that so important a position would not have been left unprotected, and that a stronger protection than one howitzer would have been afforded it. One dash by him with but a single regiment would have taken the position, and placed Stuart in a very uncomfortable situation.

From early morn till the stars arose did the battle of Brandy Station rage. The full cavalry forces of both armies were engaged, and neither could claim the advantage in gallantry or skill. The greater credit is due, perhaps, to the Federals, because they were the attacking party, and their assault had to be made by crossing a swollen river in the face of a cavalry corps that had the advantage of being on its own ground, and had the means of concentrating at each of the fords, which were the only ways the Federals had of getting access to the field. In no engagement between these two cavalry corps were sabers used so freely, or charges by regiments in line made so frequently and furiously.

General Lee was then advancing toward Pennsylvania; Stuart was screening this movement by keeping to the east of the Blue Ridge, and marching northward. The country was checkered with stone fences, strongly built and in good condition. Along the turnpike from Washington to Winchester, passing through Aldie, Middleburg, Upperville, and Paris there was continuous and severe fighting in which the cavalry alone participated. A Federal force, formed of the second cavalry division under General Gregg, with Kilpatrick's brigade and a battery of artillery, moved swiftly and with determination. Captain Reuben Boston had been placed with his Confederate squadron on the right of the road, with instructions to hold it. It appeared later that this little band had been

BRIGADIER–GENERAL THOMAS T. MUNFORD, C.S.A.

From the Peninsula to the last stand of the Confederate cavalry at Sailor's Creek, General Munford did his duty both gallantly and well. As colonel of the Second Virginia Cavalry he masked the placing of a battery of thirty-one field pieces upon the bluff at White Oak swamp, June 30, 1862. When the screen of cavalry was removed, the gunners opened up and drove a Union battery of artillery and a brigade of McClellan's infantry rearguard from a large field just across the White Oak stream. His was the regiment which picketed the roads leading in the direction of the Federal forces upon the occasion of Jackson's famous raid around Pope's army to Manassas Junction. At Antietam he commanded a brigade of dismounted cavalry, comprising the Second and Twelfth Virginia regiments and eight guns, and he was with Longstreet and Hill at South Mountain. General Munford and General Rosser were two brigadiers of Fitzhugh Lee when the latter assumed command of all the cavalry of the Army of Northern Virginia in March, 1865. Munford's diminished brigade was swept before the Federal infantry fighting bravely at Five Forks, but with undiminished courage it drove back Crook on the north side of the Appomattox River only two days before Lee's surrender to Grant.

stationed too far to the front to receive aid from the rest of the regiment, and hence, after receiving and repulsing several attacks, Boston fell, with a remnant of his squadron, into the hands of the Sixth Ohio Cavalry.

Peremptory orders were frequently given without due consideration, and they were as frequently obeyed, even when the person so ordered knew that they were destructive. In this same campaign, Colonel Duffié, of the First Rhode Island Cavalry, was ordered to encamp at Middleburg on the night of June 17th, and his line of march was prescribed. He followed that line and it disclosed to him the presence of the Confederates at many points along its course. He reached Middleburg, and despatched an officer to General Kilpatrick, at Aldie, to advise him of the situation, but Kilpatrick's troops were too exhausted to go to Duffié's relief, and the latter's regiment was attacked in the morning by Robertson's Confederate brigade, and two hundred of his men fell into Robertson's hands.

Many brilliant incidents of the Gettysburg campaign testify to the efficiency of the cavalry on both sides. While Stuart was off on the left of the Confederate army, Robertson's brigade was on the right. General W. E. Jones was sent, with three regiments, to protect the wagon train near Fairfield. Near that place, the Sixth United States Cavalry, under Major Starr, met the Seventh Virginia, and decidedly worsted that gallant regiment; but the Sixth Virginia, under Major Flournoy, took its place, and the tide was turned. The Sixth United States was routed, its brave commander was wounded and captured, with one hundred and eighty-four of his command.

As Lee fell back from Gettysburg, the Potomac River was much swollen. From the 8th to the 11th of July, Stuart was engaged in guarding the front of the Confederate army, waiting for the waters to fall. Cavalry engagements, of more or less severity, with the divisions of Buford and Kilpatrick, took place at Boonesboro, Beaver Creek, Funkstown, and in

A RESTFUL SCENE AT GENERAL McDOWELL'S HEADQUARTERS—TAKEN WHILE
STUART'S CAVALRY WAS EXTREMELY BUSY

The Federals were camping in peaceful and luxurious fashion, August, 1862, quite unconscious that Jackson with Stuart's cavalry, was cutting in between them and Washington. It would have seemed madness to the Union generals in command of one hundred thousand men, with potential reinforcements of fifty thousand more, that the Confederate leaders should split their army of only fifty-five thousand and separate the parts by two days' march. It turned out that the Confederate generals were "mad," but that there was brilliant method in their madness. Twice they had attempted to turn the Federal right, when Pope lay across the Rappahannock waiting for McClellan's return from the Peninsula, and twice the watchful Pope had foiled the attempt. It was not until Jackson left Early's brigade in an exposed position across the hastily repaired bridge at Rappahannock Station that he managed to delude the Union general into accepting this point as his real objective. Leaving Early quite as mystified as his opponent, Jackson dispatched Stuart with all the cavalry to Catlett's Station, on the Orange & Alexandria Railroad, where Pope's supply trains were parked. The night of August 23d was pitchy black, and the rain was descending in torrents, when the Confederate horsemen burst into Pope's camp. A few hours later they rode away with the Federal general's uniform and horses, his treasure-chest and personal effects, a member of his staff, and some three hundred prisoners, leaving the blazing camp behind them. The retreat of the cavalry was the final indication that there would be no more efforts to turn his right. Two days later Jackson, with twenty thousand men, marched around the Union right and, joined by Stuart's cavalry, captured the immense supply-department depot at Manassas Junction.

REPAIRING AFTER STUART'S RAID

In a single night Stuart's cavalry, falling upon the Orange & Alexandria Railroad at Catlett's Station, thirty-five miles from Washington, had done damage to Pope's railroad connection which it took days to repair. This was on August 22d, and only the heavy rainstorm prevented the burning of a large quantity of army stores at Catlett's. Stuart's troopers got away with two hundred and twenty horses from the wagon trains and all the personal baggage of General Pope and his staff. The superior railroad facilities of the Federals were in this instance turned into a means of danger and delay, necessitating the detachment of a large repair force and enabling Lee's army to seize advantage elsewhere.

A MILITARY TRAIN UPSET BY CONFEDERATES

This is part of the result of General Pope's too rapid advance to head off Lee's army south of the Rappahannock River. Although overtaking the advance of the Confederates at Cedar Mountain, Pope had arrived too late to close the river passes against them. Meanwhile he had left the Orange & Alexandria Railroad uncovered, and Jackson pushed a large force under General Ewell forward across the Bull Run Mountains. On the night of August 26, 1862, Ewell's forces captured Manassas Junction, while four miles above the Confederate cavalry fell upon an empty railroad train returning from the transfer of Federal troops. The train was destroyed. Here we see how well the work was done.

front of Sharpsburg. Thus was the advance of Meade's army delayed until the Confederates had recrossed the river.

In September, 1863, the Cavalry Corps of the Army of Northern Virginia was reorganized, and Stuart's headquarters were at Culpeper Court House. On the 18th, Kilpatrick's division crossed the Rappahannock, and pressing its way with celerity and vigor toward Culpeper, captured three guns of the Confederate horse artillery. On the 22d, Buford encountered Stuart at Jack's shop, in Madison County, and a fierce engagement occupied the divisions of both Buford and Kilpatrick, with the result that Stuart withdrew across the Rapidan.

In October, General Lee entered upon what is known as the Bristoe campaign, which aimed at turning the right flank of the Federal army in Culpeper County. To cover this movement, Stuart distributed his command over a wide extent of country and along the Rapidan. On the 10th, Stuart was ordered to make a reconnaissance toward Catlett's Station. He sent Lomax forward, who moved to Auburn, and there learned that the Federals were in force at Warrenton Junction. He further discovered that the entire Federal wagon train was parked in a position easy of access. It was most desirable that its commissary supplies should be so applied as to appease the hunger of his half-starved cavalrymen. Stuart consequently moved in that direction, and on reaching a piece of woods there was plainly seen, about half a mile beyond, the vast park of wagons. Stuart gazed long and ardently at this coveted prize, but as he gazed, the hopeful expression on his countenance faded away and was succeeded by one of vexation and disappointment. Beyond the park of wagons, his practised eye discerned a moving cloud of dust, which appeared to be passing on the left of the wagons. It was growing dusk; tidings from his rear seemed to disconcert him, and he appeared to those who were near to be anxiously awaiting something. He rearranged his column; some pieces of artillery were put in front, and behind these a medical transport wagon, and then

THE TRAIN "STONEWALL" JACKSON AND STUART STOPPED AT BRISTOE

By a move of unparalleled boldness, "Stonewall" Jackson, with twenty thousand men, captured the immense Union supplies at Manassas Junction, August 26, 1862. His was a perilous position. Washington lay one day's march to the north; Warrenton, Pope's headquarters, but twelve miles distant to the southwest; and along the Rappahannock, between "Stonewall" Jackson and Lee, stood the tents of another host which outnumbered the whole Confederate army. "Stonewall" Jackson had seized Bristoe Station in order to break down the railway bridge over Broad Run, and to proceed at his leisure with the destruction of the stores. A train returning empty from Warrenton Junction to Alexandria darted through the station under heavy fire. The line was promptly torn up. Two trains which followed in the same direction as the first went crashing down a high embankment. The report received at Alexandria from the train which escaped ran as fol-

lows: "No. 6 train, engine Secretary, was fired into at Bristoe by a party of cavalry some five hundred strong. They had piled ties on the track, but the engine threw them off. Secretary is completely riddled by bullets." It was a full day before the Federals realized that "Stonewall" Jackson was really there with a large force. Here, in abundance, was all that had been absent for some time; besides commissary stores of all sorts, there were two trains loaded with new clothing, to say nothing of sutler's stores, replete with "extras" not enumerated in the regulations, and also the camp of a cavalry regiment which had vacated in favor of Jackson's men. It was an interesting sight to see the hungry, travel-worn men attacking this profusion and rewarding themselves for all their fatigues and deprivations of the preceding few days, and their enjoyment of it and of the day's rest allowed them. There was a great deal of difficulty for a time in finding what each man needed most, but this was overcome through a crude barter of belongings as the day wore on.

the cavalry. Thus formed, he moved to the front, leaving wagons and moving dust far to our right.

At some distance ahead, there rose from the plain a wooded ridge, extending northeast and southwest. Toward the end nearest to us we headed, and began its ascent, in the order in which we were formed. The front of the column reached the top and moved on to the further end, from which the ridge fell with more precipitousness than the end which we had ascended. When the last file of the rear regiment was well up on the ridge and protected by the trees, no room remained for more. We were dismounted and lay down, holding the bridle-reins in our hands.

In less than an hour a heavy column of infantry approached the ridge from the direction in which we had come. It passed to the left and moved along very close to the ridge and toward its further end. Almost at once, another column, like unto the first and moving by its side, passed to the right of the ridge, and at about the same distance from it, in a parallel line toward the same end of the ridge. So near were these moving columns, and so still were we, that all night long we could hear the conversation carried on among our foemen on either side of us.

The hours seemed interminable, but those marching columns seemed even longer. Daylight came, but still they marched. Should sunrise find us still so beleaguered, our chances of escape would be small. As the earliest rays of the sun routed the mists, the long-hoped-for rear of these columns went by, and halted but a few rods beyond the further end of our ridge. During the night, Stuart had sent messengers to General Lee, telling him of our situation and asking for relief. That relief was sent, but it miscarried. As the sun rose higher, Stuart opened on the rear of these two columns, which had halted for breakfast, had made their fires, and were boiling their coffee. The four guns did some execution, and the Federals, startled by this " bolt from the blue," ran—not, as we hoped,

MANASSAS JUNCTION, WHERE THE FEDERAL WAR DEPARTMENT ENTERTAINED
UNEXPECTED GUESTS

"Stonewall" Jackson and twenty thousand men were the unexpected guests of the North at Manassas Junction on August 26, 1862. The ragged and famished Confederates, who had marched over fifty miles in the last two days, had such a feast as they never knew before. The North had been lavish in its expenditures for the army. No effort had been spared to feed, clothe, and equip them, and for the comfort of the individual soldier the purse-strings of the nation were freely loosed. Streets of warehouses, crammed to the doors, a line of freight cars two miles in length, thousands of barrels of flour, pork, and biscuit, ambulances, field-wagons, and pyramids of shot and shell, met the wondering gaze of the Confederate soldiery. The sutlers' stores contained a wealth of plunder. "Here," says General George H. Gordon, describing the scene that followed, "a long, yellow-haired, barefooted son of the South claimed as prizes a tooth-brush, a box of candies, and a barrel of coffee, while another, whose butternut homespun hung round him in tatters, crammed himself with lobster salad, sardines, potted game, and sweetmeats, and washed them down with Rhenish wine. Nor was the outer man neglected. From piles of new clothing, the Southerners arrayed themselves in the blue uniforms of the Federals. The naked were clad, the barefooted were shod, and the sick provided with luxuries to which they had long been strangers." All unportable stores were destroyed.

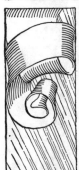

from the danger that presented itself, but ran, and with intrepid force, toward us. They charged the steep ascent, struck down the commander of a North Carolina regiment, and only desisted when the fire from our guns repelled them. Stuart withdrew from the ridge. He had extricated himself in safety, and what would have been stigmatized as his folly, had we been routed, became a proof of his genius and heroic courage.

The object of the Bristoe campaign was accomplished as far as such objects are generally accomplished, but, on the 18th of October, Stuart was at Buckland, with Kilpatrick in front of him. A device suggested by Fitzhugh Lee proved successful. Stuart withdrew and Kilpatrick followed him hopefully, but Fitzhugh Lee had taken a position which threw him in Kilpatrick's rear. Upon an agreed signal, Stuart turned on Kilpatrick in front and Lee struck his rear, and a rout ensued in which Davies' brigade bore the brunt. It ran, and the race extended over five miles. Custer, however, saved his artillery and crossed Broad Run in safety.

On the 28th of February following, Custer made a brilliant, and in the main successful, foray from Madison Court House into Charlottesville, with about fifteen hundred cavalry. Near Charlottesville were four battalions of artillery, resting in fond security in winter quarters. The guns were all saved but horses were taken, and some of the quarters were burned, with the loss of clothing and blankets.

Kilpatrick was moving on Richmond with about thirty-five hundred cavalry. Colonel Ulric Dahlgren and about four hundred and fifty men were pushed rapidly toward the Virginia Central Railroad, which they struck at Frederick's Hall, where they captured eight officers who were sitting on a court martial, and moved toward the James River. Thence they moved down on the north side of the James to Richmond, where they attacked the outer entrenchments. Hampton attacked Kilpatrick's camp and drove him from it, compelling his return to Fredericksburg. Colonel Dahlgren made a wide

OUT OF REACH   U. S. MILITARY

OF THE   ENGINES STORED

CONFEDERATE CAVALRY   IN ALEXANDRIA, 1863

By the middle of 1863 the Federal generals had learned the wisdom of storing in a safe place, under a heavy guard, anything they wanted to keep. Of especial value was the rolling stock of the military railroads, which when not in use was ordered out of the danger zone. General J. E. B. Stuart with his tireless troopers had proved himself so ignorant of the meaning of the words "danger" or "distance" that the Federals had lost their confidence of the previous year, when they believed that the mere interposition of an army of a hundred thousand men was sufficient to protect a base of supplies. This photograph was taken about the time the battle of Gettysburg was raging, and Stuart was causing a diversion by throwing shells near Washington. It was not until the Army of the Potomac returned to Virginia, with headquarters established at Brandy Station, that any great number of these iron horses were allowed out of their stables. By that time the Union cavalry had received the experience and equipment to meet the Confederate troopers in their own way, and threatened the railroads running into Richmond. Organization and numbers had begun to tell.

circuit, crossing the Pamunkey and the Mattapony, but at length he fell into an ambuscade near King and Queen Court House where he lost his life, as did many of his command.

We have reached now, in the order of time, the Wilderness campaign which opened May 4, 1864. General Grant's object was to interpose his army between Lee and Richmond. Sheridan, with about ten thousand cavalry and several batteries, had moved to Hamilton's Crossing and thence toward Richmond, on the Telegraph road. General Wickham, with his brigade, followed in pursuit. Near Mitchell's shop he was joined by Fitzhugh Lee, with about five thousand cavalry. Stuart, now in command, moved toward Yellow Tavern, which he reached before the appearance of Sheridan's troopers. They did appear, however, and attempted to drive Stuart from the Telegraph road. A severe fight ensued, in which Stuart lost heavily in officers, but maintained his position.

About four o'clock in the afternoon, a brigade of Federal cavalry attacked Stuart's extreme left, and he, after his fashion, hurried to the point of danger. One company of the First Virginia Cavalry was bearing the entire burden. Stuart joined himself to this little band and attacked the flank of the Union cavalry. The First Virginia drove the Federals back. Many of the latter, having lost their horses in the fight, were keeping up on foot. One of these dismounted men turned, as he ran, and firing at the general with his pistol, inflicted the wound from which he shortly afterward died.

Now, to turn back, when General Johnston, on the 18th of July, 1861, moved from the Shenandoah valley to Manassas, he left a body of cavalry, under Colonel McDonald, scattered throughout the country between the Shenandoah River and the North Mountains. In this body was a company from Fauquier County, commanded by Turner Ashby. Later on, this company was organized into a huge regiment of which McDonald was colonel; Turner Ashby, lieutenant-colonel, and Oliver Funsten, major. The duty assigned to this regiment

[98]

COVERING LEE'S RETREAT FROM PENNSYLVANIA

This photograph is an excellent illustration of the cavalry's method of destroying the railroads between the two capitals. The light rails were placed across piles of ties. The ties were lighted and the rails heated until of their own weight they bent out of shape. Mile upon mile of railroad could thus be destroyed in a day. New rails had to be brought before it was possible to rebuild the line. Note the tangle of telegraph wires. The telegraph lines were also destroyed wherever the Confederate position was known and it was therefore impossible to tap them and read the Union leaders' messages. The Army of Northern Virginia and the Army of the Potomac spent the month of October, 1863, when this photograph was taken, maneuvering for position along the Rappahannock. On October 20th the Army of the Potomac was occupying Warrenton and Lee had retired to the north bank of the Rappahannock, having destroyed the Orange and Alexandria Railroad from Bristoe Station to the river, and by the 22d, both armies were again in camp.

THE PRIZE THAT IMPERILLED STUART ON HIS DARING RAID INTO THE
FEDERAL LINES

In this striking photograph of 1863 appears the prize at which General J. E. B. Stuart gazed long and ardently during his reconnaissance to Warrenton Station on the 10th of October, 1863, after Lee's Bristoe campaign. His half-starved cavalrymen urgently needed just such a wagon-train as that. But, as they peered from their ambush, the hopeful expressions faded away. Beyond the park of wagons Stuart's practiced eye had discerned a moving cloud of dust. That night he was confined to a little ridge, with the Union columns moving to the right and left of his isolated force. By dawn the rear of the passing columns were cooking their breakfasts at the foot of the ridge. By the bold device of firing into them and

PART OF THE "VAST PARK OF WAGONS" ON WHICH THE CONFEDERATES GAZED
FROM AMBUSH, OCTOBER 10, 1863

repelling their first attack, Stuart disconcerted the pursuit and made good his escape. This view of the wagons "in park," or gathered in one large body in an open field, represents a train of the Sixth Corps, Army of the Potomac, near Brandy Station, during the autumn days of 1863, after the Gettysburg campaign. The wagons in the foreground are ambulances, while immediately in their rear stand the large army wagons used for subsistence and quartermaster's stores. The horses are harnessed to the vehicles preparatory to the forward movement. It took this train across the Rappahannock River toward Culpeper and the Rapidan, where history indicates that they formed part of those upon which Stuart gazed so covetously.

was the guarding of the Potomac River on a line nearly one hundred and twenty-five miles in length. No more striking and picturesque figure than Ashby ever won the confidence and affections of his followers. Since his boyhood he had been famed as a horseman, even in that land of centaurs. Throughout all those marvelous campaigns in the Valley, which have made Jackson immortal, Turner Ashby, as brigadier-general, commanded the cavalry that formed an impenetrable screen between Jackson and the Federal armies in his front.

In May and June, 1862, Jackson moved up the Shenandoah valley, Generals Banks and Saxton following with fourteen thousand troops. General Fremont, with his army, was approaching Strasburg from the direction of Moorefield, while General Shields, who had crossed the Blue Ridge from the east, was moving up Luray Valley on Jackson's left flank, with still another division. Jackson waited at Strasburg nearly twenty-four hours for one of his regiments, which he had left below him, to rejoin his command. Meanwhile Fremont approached within ten miles, was met by General Richard Taylor, and held in check until Jackson, starting his wagon trains off before him, had followed in a leisurely manner, while Ashby, with his cavalry, kept back Fremont, who was pressing Jackson's rear. Shields was moving rapidly in the hope of intercepting Jackson before he could cross the Blue Ridge, which Shields supposed he was striving to do. A few miles south of Harrisonburg, Jackson turned toward Port Republic, encountered Fremont's cavalry, under Colonel Percy Wyndham, which Ashby quickly routed, capturing Colonel Wyndham and a large part of his command. Fremont sent forward General Bayard and his command, which met the Fifty-eighth Virginia, near Cross Keys. General Ashby dismounted, and placing himself at the head of this infantry regiment, received the bullet which ended his career.

His former regiment, with certain additions, was organized into a brigade consisting of the Second, Sixth, Seventh,

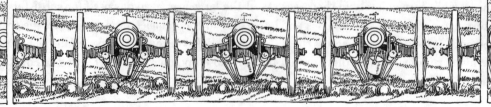

A SAD SIGHT FOR THE CAVALRYMAN

This pitiful scene after the battle of Gettysburg illustrates the losses of mounts after each engagement, which told heaviest on the Southern cavalry. Up to the next winter, 1863–4, it was well organized and had proved its efficiency on many fields. But from that period its weakness increased rapidly. The sources of supplies of both men and horses had been exhausted simultaneously; many of the best and bravest of men and officers had fallen in battle. From then onward it was a struggle for bare existence, until at Appomattox the large-hearted Lee pointed out to Grant that the only mounts left to the Confederacy were those that his men were actually riding. Be it recorded to the Northern general's credit that he gave immediate instructions that every Confederate who owned his horse should be allowed to take it home for plowing and putting in his crop. This photograph shows staff officers' horses killed at Gettysburg.

and Twelfth Virginia regiments, and the Seventeenth Battalion which soon afterward became the Eleventh Virginia Cavalry. After Ashby's death, this brigade was, for a time, commanded by Colonel Munford. General Shields reached the village of Port Republic, where Jackson encountered him and drove him back down Luray Valley, and thus ended the Valley campaign of that year.

General Beverly Robertson was now assigned to the command of the old Ashby brigade. On the 2d of August, a sharp hand-to-hand encounter took place in the streets of Orange Court House, between the Seventh Virginia, and the Fifth New York and First Vermont, both commanded by General Crawford, in which Colonel Jones and Lieutenant-Colonel Marshall, of the Seventh Virginia, were wounded. The Sixth Virginia coming up, the Federals reluctantly gave way, and were pursued as far as Rapidan Station.

On December 29th, 1862, General W. E. Jones was assigned to the command of the Valley District, and in March, 1863, he moved to Moorefield Valley, with the view of gathering much-needed supplies of food, and also with the intention of destroying the Cheat River viaduct, on the Baltimore and Ohio Railroad. The south branch, at Petersburg in Hardy County, West Virginia, was high, and the fords were almost impassable. The artillery and the loaded wagon trains were sent back to Harrisonburg, and Jones, with his cavalry alone, undertook the invasion of West Virginia. At Greenland Gap, on the summit of the Alleghany Mountains, a body of Federal infantry held a blockhouse, strongly built and gallantly defended. This was taken only after the loss of several men, and the wounding of Colonel Dulany of the Seventh Virginia. It was repeatedly charged by the dismounted cavalry, and was finally taken by stratagem rather than assault.

The Cheat River viaduct was reached on the 26th of April, and found to be guarded by three hundred infantry entrenched in a blockhouse, too strong to be taken in a moment, and time

HORSES KILLED IN BATTLE—A SERIOUS LOSS

The number of horses killed in battle was, after all, but a small fraction of those destroyed by exhaustion, starvation, and disease during the Civil War. When Lee's army marched into Pennsylvania he had issued stringent orders against plundering. The orders were almost implicitly obeyed except when it came to the question of horses. The quartermasters, especially of artillery battalions, could seldom report their commands completely equipped. The Confederacy had no great cavalry depots like Giesboro, or those at St. Louis or Greenville in Louisiana. When a mount was exhausted he had to be replaced. Some of the farmers actually concealed their horses in their own houses, but a horseless trooper was a veritable sleuth in running down a horse, whether concealed in the parlor or in the attic. The Confederates offered to pay for the horses, but in Confederate currency. The owners occasionally accepted it on the principle that it was "better than nothing." The animals thus impressed in Pennsylvania were for the most part great, clumsy, flabby Percherons and Conestogas, which required more than twice the feed of the compact, hard-muscled little Virginia horses. It was pitiable to see these great brutes suffer when they were compelled to dash off at full gallop with a field-piece after pasturing on dry broom-sedge and eating a quarter of a feed of weevil-infested corn.

A CAVALRY HORSE PICKETED
AT THE EVENING BIVOUAC

did not allow of tarrying. On April 28th, the command reached Morgantown, where it crossed on a suspension bridge to the west side of the Monongahela, and after dark moved on Fairmont. Here the Federals were found in considerable force, which, after some fighting, was dispersed, and the object of the visit to that point being the destruction of the fine iron bridge, of three spans of three hundred feet each, that work was entered upon and continued until the bridge was destroyed.

Oiltown, near Elizabeth Court House, on the Little Kanawha River, was owned mainly by Southern men who had first engaged in the oil industry. There were found thousands of gallons of oil, in barrels, tanks, and in deep flatboats then on the water. All was burned, and Dante might have gained some new impressions of the regions described by him, from the scenes that presented themselves to the destroyers. The dense, black smoke rose to the heights of hundreds of feet; the intense heat caused by the burning oil excited a breeze, and the flatboats filled with burning oil, floated down the river toward Elizabeth. After thirty days incessant marching, without supplies of food, save what was taken from the people, without artillery or wagons of any kind, the expedition returned with seven hundred prisoners, one thousand cattle and twelve hundred horses, and with a loss of ten killed and forty-two wounded.

Jones was back in the Valley the last week of May, and, by crossing the mountains, joined Stuart near Culpeper Court House. A little later he took conspicuous part in the battle of Brandy Station and the ensuing campaign. The events and incidents of that and the following campaigns to the death of General Stuart, have been already related.

General Thomas L. Rosser had been assigned to the command of the old Ashby brigade, and soon proved himself a most efficient cavalry commander. In January, 1864, then under General Early in the Valley District, he was in command of the cavalry. On January 29th, Rosser crossed the

A SECOND "ARMY" OPPOSED TO THE CONFEDERATE CAVALRY—A FEDERAL CAVALRY MESS-HOUSE

The Confederate cavalry, like the Confederacy itself, was hastened to its fall because of the exhaustion of resources. While horseflesh was growing scarcer and poorer in quality in Virginia, and proper fodder had become little but a memory since Sheridan's devastation of the Shenandoah Valley, the Union Government, with its immense resources, was able to systematize the handling of supplies for its cavalry corps, establishing half a dozen huge cavalry remount depots, and devoting the proper amount of attention to every branch of the work. This photograph shows the mess-house at the Government stables in Washington. The Confederacy barely supplied food for the troopers themselves, while the Union Government was able to build mess-houses for those who were engaged in caring for the troopers' wants.

mountains to Moorefield, in Hardy County, West Virginia, and there learning that a large wagon train of supplies was moving from New Creek to Petersburg, moved forward to take it. He found parked at Medley a train of ninety-five wagons, guarded by three hundred infantry and a small body of cavalry. He moved one regiment toward the rear of this body, placed others on the flank, and then opened with one gun on its front. The effect was to stampede the teamsters, and the infantry were unable to withstand the attack by dismounted cavalry, so that in a short time the wagons, with some prisoners, fell into Rosser's hands. On the 1st of February, moving upon the Baltimore and Ohio Railroad, at Patterson's Creek, he captured the guard there, and brought out about twelve hundred cattle and some sheep.

On the 7th of June, Sheridan was sent with two divisions to communicate with Hunter, and to break up the Virginia Central Railroad and the James River Canal. He started on this mission with eighty-nine hundred cavalry. On the morning of the 8th, Hampton, who had succeeded Stuart in the command of the Cavalry Corps of the Army of Northern Virginia, moved with two divisions and some batteries of horse artillery to look after this movement. His first step was to intercept Sheridan before he reached the railroad. On the night of the 10th, he had reached Green Spring Valley, three miles from Trevilian Station, and there encamped. At this time General Fitzhugh Lee was at Louisa Court House, and Custer, with his characteristic boldness, took an unguarded road around Hampton's right and essayed to reach Trevilian. He captured ambulances, caissons, and many led horses. Near at hand was Thompson's battery, wholly unmindful of danger, and this Custer essayed to take. But Colonel Chew, commander of the battalion of artillery to which this belonged, deployed a South Carolina regiment to hold Custer in check until he could get another battery into position. This he soon did, and Rosser, coming up with his brigade at the moment,

A WAR–TIME VIEW OF STUART'S GRAVE

"Gen'l Stuart—wounded May 11, 1864—died May 12, 1864." This simple head-slab on its wooded hill near Richmond toward the close of the war spelt a heavy blow to the Confederate cause. In that struggle against heavier and heavier odds, every man counted. And when destroying Fate chose for its victim the leader whose spirit had never fallen, whose courage had never failed, no matter how dangerous the raid, how fierce the charge and counter-charge—well might the Confederacy mourn. To the memory of this American chevalier, tributes came not only from comrades but from opponents. One of these, Theophilus F. Rodenbough—a Federal captain at the time of Stuart's death, later a cavalry historian and a contributor to other pages of this volume—wrote, twenty years after the tragedy, this fitting epitaph: "Deep in the hearts of all true cavalrymen, North and South, will ever burn a sentiment of admiration mingled with regret for this knightly soldier and generous man."

compelled Custer to relinquish his well-earned gains and betake himself to flight, while all his plunder fell into Rosser's hands.

Custer, however, remained that night near Trevilian, from which Rosser strove to drive him, but his reward was a severe wound which disabled him from further action that day. Desperately did Sheridan endeavor to drive Hampton from his path, and the fight continued through three days, but the result was the withdrawal of Sheridan's forces, and his rejoining Grant. General Grant, in his " Memoirs," states of this withdrawal that " Sheridan went back because the enemy had taken possession of a crossing by which he proposed to go west, and because he heard that Hunter was not at Charlottesville."

In September, Lee's army was sorely in need of beef. Scouts reported at Coggin's Point a large but well-guarded herd of cattle, and on the morning of the 11th, Hampton, with his cavalry, started to capture it. Notice of this movement had got abroad, and near Sycamore Church a regiment of Federal cavalry was awaiting the assault. The cattle were protected by a strong abatis, through which cavalry could not pass, and a deliberate attack was required. Accordingly the Seventh Virginia was dismounted and moved forward, while other regiments were sent around the obstruction. The herders then broke down the fence of the corral, and tried by firing pistols to stampede the cattle, and thus get them beyond Hampton's reach. But Hampton's cavalry were born cowboys, and, heading off the frightened cattle, soon rounded them up, so that the expedition returned with twenty-five hundred cattle to Lee's starving soldiers. On the 17th, General B. F. Butler informed General Grant that " three brigades of Hampton's cavalry turned our left and captured about two thousand cattle, and our telegraph construction party."

Rosser returned to the Valley with his brigade, and on November 27th started on the " New Creek raid," so called from a village on the Baltimore and Ohio Railroad, about

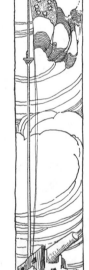

BRIGADIER–GEN-
ERAL JAMES B.
GORDON, C.S.A.

KILLED DURING
SHERIDAN'S RAID ON
RICHMOND,
MAY 11, 1864

MAJOR–GENERAL
LENSFORD L.
LOMAX, C.S.A.

WITH THE
CONFEDERATE CAVALRY
IN THE
SHENANDOAH

twenty-two miles west from Cumberland. A Federal scouting party had been sent out from New Creek on the 26th, and Rosser, marching all night, arrived within six miles of New Creek at daylight on the morning of the 27th. The village was strongly fortified, with one heavy gun enfilading the road on which Rosser was moving toward it. General W. H. Payne's brigade was put in front, with about twenty men in blue overcoats. The column moved slowly toward its object, and citizens along the road, and travelers at that early hour thought it was the returning party that had gone out the night before on a scout. Less than a mile from the two, the first picket was reached. These men jocularly mocked the empty-handed returning party, but they were silently surrounded and taken along with the column. New Creek was reached and entered. On the left was a high hill, not steep, on which an infantry force of twelve hundred men was encamped. The Federal troops were engaged in drying their blankets and preparing their breakfast, when the mounted column of Confederates, suddenly breaking into line, charged the hill, and, without the loss of a single life, took eight hundred of these infantry. The Confederates then proceeded to destroy the railroad bridge, and gather as much as they could carry away of the large supplies they found stored at that point. Rosser, encumbered with many hundred cattle and sheep, and a long train of captured stores, turned his column homeward.

At Beverly, a village seventy-five miles west from Staunton, there were stored large supplies, guarded by a Federal garrison that did not exceed one thousand men. Rosser, learning of this fact, took three hundred men from the several brigades and started before daylight from Swoope's Depot, on January 10th. He spent that night, or a part of it, on a mountainside, without fires. The snow was deep, and the weather bitterly cold. Before daylight on the morning of the 11th, he was on a hill west of Beverly, overlooking the garrison of Federal infantry in their wooden huts on the plain below. The moon

BRIGADIER–GENERAL M. C. BUTLER, C. S. A.

General Butler was a leader under Wade Hampton, who played an important part in the defeat of Sheridan with eight thousand men at Trevilian Station, June 12, 1864, just one month after the death of Stuart. Between 2 P.M. and dark, Butler, in command of Hampton's division of cavalry, repulsed seven determined assaults of Sheridan's men. During the day Butler was unable to keep his batteries in exposed positions entirely manned, but between sunset and dark, when the Federal cavalrymen made their last desperate effort, the howitzers were remanned and double-shotted with canister. The Federals emerged from the woods a stone's throw from the Confederate lines, and the canister tore great holes in their lines. It was at this engagement that General Butler lost his leg.

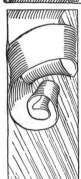

was full and shining brilliantly on snow over a foot in depth. Dismounting a part of his command, and moving them in line in front, with the mounted men behind, Rosser moved upon the sleeping host. Had they remained in their strong huts and used their rifles, the disaster might have been averted, but as the result, five hundred and eighty prisoners, and ten thousand rations fell into the hands of the invaders.

On the morning of February 21, 1865, a portion of McNeill's command, under Lieutenant Jesse McNeill, entered the city of Cumberland, Maryland, an hour before daylight. Major-General Crook, the commander of the Department of West Virginia, and Brigadier-General Kelley, his able lieutenant, were quietly sleeping, the one at the St. Nicholas Hotel, and the other at the Revere House. Six thousand troops, of all arms, occupied the city. Sergeant Vandiver called on General Crook, while some other member of the command performed the like civility to General Kelley. These two officers were persuaded to accompany their ill-timed callers on their return to Dixie, and were entertained in Richmond at an official hostelry there. Rosser and his command were present at Appomattox, but did not participate in the surrender, but while that ceremony was in progress, this command passed on to Lynchburg, and dissolved into their individual elements.

Up to the winter of 1863–64, the Confederate cavalry was well organized and had proven its efficiency on many fields, but its weakness from that period grew rapidly. The sources of supplies of both men and horses had been exhausted, and the best and the bravest of men and officers had fallen in battle.

On the other hand, when General Sheridan took command of the Federal cavalry, a new and far more vigorous life was imparted to it. Armed with repeating carbines and fighting on foot, as well as mounted, it became the most formidable arm of the Federal service. When the war ended, it was but reasonable to aver that the cavalry of the Army of the Potomac was the most efficient body of soldiers on earth.

CHAPTER
FOUR

—————

RAIDS OF THE
FEDERAL CAVALRY

—————

WELL-CONDITIONED MOUNTS, EQUIPPED FOR A LONG RAID
1862

FEDERAL CAVALRY LEAVING CAMP

The well-filled bags before and behind each trooper indicate a long and hard trip in store. Both the Confederate and Federal cavalry distinguished themselves by their endurance on their arduous and brilliant raids. The amount of destruction accomplished by this arm of the service was well-nigh incalculable. Stuart, Mosby, Forrest on one side—Sheridan, Grierson, Kilpatrick on the other—each in turn upset the opponents' calculations and forced them to change their plans. It was Van Dorn's capture at Holly Springs that caused Grant's first failure against Vicksburg. It was not until after the surrender at Appomattox that Lee learned

THE ARM THAT DEALT A FINAL BLOW TO THE CONFEDERACY

the final crushing blow—that the rations destined for his men had been captured by Sheridan.   Up and down the Rappahannock the cavalry rode and scouted and fought by day and by night, sometimes saddled for sixty hours, often sleeping by regiments on the slowly moving columns of horses.   It was Grierson who reported, after his ride from Vicksburg to Baton Rouge, that the Confederacy was but a hollow shell—all of its men were on the battle-line.   It was Stuart who twice circled McClellan's army, on the Peninsula and in Maryland, and who caused Lincoln to recall the schoolboy game: " Three times round and out."

REPAIRING CONFEDERATE DAMAGE

The busy Federal engineers are rebuilding the railroad bridge across Cedar Run, near Catlett's Station, destroyed by the Confederates on the previous day, October 13th, when they fell back before the Army of the Potomac under General Meade. The fall of 1863 was a period of small cavalry battles. On September 16th the Army of the Potomac crossed the Rappahannock and took position near Culpeper Court House. During the next few weeks the cavalry was actively engaged in reconnoitering duty. On October 10th General John Buford was sent across the Rappahannock with the First Cavalry Division (consisting of the Eighth Illinois, Twelfth Illinois, four companies Third Indiana, six companies Eighth New York, Sixth New York, Ninth New York, Seventeenth Pennsylvania, and

[118]

FEDERAL ENGINEERS AT WORK OCTOBER 14, 1863

Third West Virginia, two companies) to uncover, if possible, the upper fords of the river. Buford forced a passage over the Germanna Ford, and bivouacked that night at Morton's Ford, where he recrossed the Rapidan and engaged a body of the enemy. At daylight on October 14th, the Confederates attacked Gregg's Second Cavalry Division, but he held his position tenaciously while General Warren got the Second Corps across Cedar Run. It seldom took over a few hours to rebuild one of these bridges. Sometimes the troops tore down the nearest wooden houses to get boards and timber. This wrecking of houses was very arduous work. The trees in the foreground have been sacrificed for construction purposes.

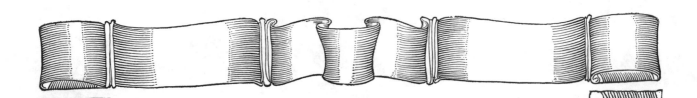

FEDERAL RAIDS AND EXPEDITIONS
IN THE EAST

By Charles D. Rhodes

Captain, General Staff, United States Army

CAVALRY operations known as raids, were a distinct product of the Civil War, and although many other tactical and strategical lessons have since been deduced by European experts from this great war, it was the raid which first excited comment abroad and created interest, as something new in the handling of mounted men.

As early as June, 1862, General "Jeb" Stuart had demonstrated to both armies the possibilities of independent operations by well-mounted cavalry boldly handled by a resourceful leader, when, with twelve hundred Confederate troopers, he rode entirely around the Federal army on the Peninsula of Virginia. And again, in October of the same year, his raid into Pennsylvania proved that good cavalry can move with impunity through a well-supplied hostile country. This raid had the effect of causing consternation in the National capital, and of drawing off many Federal troops for the protection of Washington.

Stuart's successful raids caused some modification of the previous short-sighted policy of always attaching Union cavalry to infantry commands, and although until Sheridan's time, the raids made by the Federal cavalry in the East were not remarkably successful and the time for their initiation not well chosen, the Federal cavalry constantly increased in powers of mobility and independence of action.

Early in 1863, General Hooker detached Stoneman with the Cavalry Corps from the main operations of the Army of

[120]

COLONEL ULRIC DAHL-GREN, WHO MET HIS DEATH IN THE RAID UPON RICHMOND

As Stuart threatened Washington, so Kilpatrick in turn threatened the Capital of the South. He was accompanied by Colonel Ulric Dahlgren who was to leave him near Spotsylvania with five hundred picked men, to cross the James, enter Richmond on the south side, after liberating the prisoners at Belle Isle, and unite with Kilpatrick's main force March 1, 1864. The latter left Stevensburg with four thousand cavalry and a battery of horse artillery on the night of Sunday, the

28th of February, crossed the Rapidan at Ely's Ford, surprised and captured the picket there, and marched rapidly toward Richmond. On March 1st the column was within five miles of the city. Failing to connect with Dahlgren, Kilpatrick finally withdrew, but not until he had driven in the force sent to oppose him to the inner lines of the Richmond defenses. This was the nearest that any body of Union troops got to Richmond before its fall. Colonel Dahlgren met his death upon this raid, and part of his command was captured, the rest escaping to Kilpatrick, March 2d, at Tunstall's Station, near White House.

UNION CAVALRYMEN IN RICHMOND—NOT UNTIL 1865

the Potomac, with orders to cross the Rappahannock for a raid on the communications with Richmond—turning Lee's left flank and inflicting on him every possible injury.

During Stoneman's absence the sanguinary battle of Chancellorsville was fought by the Army of the Potomac, and as the success of the raid depended in great measure upon a Federal victory at Chancellorsville, it was not, strategically at least, a success. The detachment of the Union troopers deprived General Hooker of cavalry at a time when he particularly needed a screening force to conceal his movements by the right flank; and it is probable that if Stoneman's cavalry had been present with the Army of the Potomac, it would have given ample warning of "Stonewall" Jackson's secret concentration opposite the Union right, which well nigh caused a decisive defeat for the Union army.

But Stoneman's raid destroyed millions of dollars' worth of Confederate property, and although it cut Lee's communications for a short time only, its moral effect was considerable, as shown by the Confederate correspondence since published.

The Stoneman raid was followed in February, 1864, by the famous raid of General Judson Kilpatrick, having as its objective the taking of the city of Richmond and the liberation of the Union prisoners confined therein. General Meade assisted the raid by demonstrations against Lee's left and by sending Custer on a minor raid into Albemarle County. It was supposed, at the time, that Richmond was comparatively defenseless, and that Kilpatrick's force might take the city before reenforcements from either Petersburg or Lee's army on the Rapidan could reach it.

Kilpatrick's force consisted of nearly four thousand men. Near Spotsylvania, about five hundred men under Colonel Ulric Dahlgren were detached for the purpose of crossing the James River, and, after liberating the Union prisoners at Belle Isle, attacking Richmond from the south.

Dahlgren's little command destroyed considerable

TROOPERS OF THE FIRST MASSACHUSETTS JUST AFTER THEIR ATTEMPT TO RAID RICHMOND IN 1864

A GROUP OF OFFICERS, FIRST MASSACHUSETTS CAVALRY

The officers and men of the First Massachusetts Cavalry formed part of General Judson Kilpatrick's force in his Richmond raid. The men look gaunt and hungry because they are down to "fighting weight." Starvation, fatigue, exposure, and nights in the saddle soon disposed of any superfluous flesh a trooper might carry. These men heard the laugh of the Confederate sentries inside the fortifications of the Southern Capital, and turned back only when success seemed impossible. Kilpatrick's object had been to move past the Confederate right flank, enter Richmond, and release the Union captives in its military prisons. This bold project had grown out of President Lincoln's desire to have his proclamation of amnesty circulated within the Confederate lines. The plan included also a raid upon communications and supplies. A joint expedition, under Dahlgren, met defeat, and Kilpatrick, not hearing from it, turned back.

Confederate property, but through the alleged treachery of a guide, the raiders were led out of their course. A portion of the command became separated; Dahlgren, with about one hundred and fifty troopers, was ambushed near Walkerton, and the leader killed and most of his force captured. The remainder of Dahlgren's command, under Captain Mitchell, managed to rejoin Kilpatrick, who had meanwhile threatened Richmond from the north, and who, finding the city prepared for his attack, finally withdrew across the Chickahominy and joined General Butler on the Peninsula, March 3, 1864.

The Kilpatrick raid failed in its main object, but that it might easily have succeeded seems evident from Confederate correspondence, which shows that the interception of a despatch from Dahlgren to Kilpatrick, asking what hour the latter had fixed for a simultaneous attack upon Richmond, alone made it possible for the Confederates successfully to defend the city.

When, early in 1864, General Grant gave Sheridan the long hoped for opportunity to " whip Stuart," and until the final end at Appomattox, this peerless cavalry leader never missed an opportunity to cut loose from the main army, drawing off from Grant's flanks and rear the enterprising and oftentimes dangerous Confederate cavalry, cutting Lee's communications with the South and Southwest time and again, and destroying immense quantities of the precious and carefully husbanded supplies of the Army of Northern Virginia.

Sheridan's Richmond raid, probably the most daring and sensational of these more or less independent operations, had for its object, not so much the destruction of Confederate property, as to draw Stuart and his cavalry away from the Union army's long lines of supply-trains, and then to defeat the great Confederate trooper.

In May, 1864, Sheridan's splendid body of horsemen, ten thousand in number and forming a column thirteen miles in length, moved out from the vicinity of Spotsylvania, through Chilesburg and Glen Allen Station. At Yellow Tavern the

A STILL SMOKING WRECK ON THE PATH OF THE FEDERAL RAIDERS

This photograph shows the ruins of the bridge over the North Anna, which were still smoking when the photographer arrived with the Union troops at the end of Sheridan's raid. He had ridden nearer to Richmond than any other Union leader before its fall. On the night of May 11, 1864, his column of cavalry could see the lights of the city and hear the dogs barking, and the following day an enterprising newsboy slipped through the lines and sold copies of the Richmond *Inquirer*. Sheridan declared that he could have taken Richmond, but that he couldn't hold it. The prisoners told him that every house was loopholed and the streets barricaded, and he did not think it worth the sacrifice in men. But in the death of Stuart at Yellow Tavern, Sheridan had dealt a blow severer than a raid into the Capital would have been.

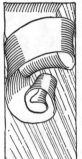

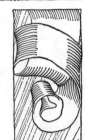

decisive conflict which Sheridan had sought with the Confederate cavalry took place. The latter were driven back upon Richmond; the gallant and knightly Stuart received his mortal wound, and the Union cavalry gained complete control of the highway leading to the Confederate capital. The casualties on both sides were severe.

Pushing on rapidly by way of the Meadow Bridge, Sheridan actually found himself and his force within the outer fortifications of the city of Richmond, and in imminent peril of annihilation. In fact, a portion of the command was in such close proximity to the city proper, that officers could plainly discern its lights and hear the dogs barking a warning to the city's defenders of the presence of an army of invaders.

But with his usual genius for overcoming difficulties, Sheridan quickly extricated his command from its hazardous and uncomfortable position, and pressing on over Bottom's Bridge and past Malvern Hill successfully reached Haxall's Landing on the James River, where the command was furnished much needed supplies. On May 17th, the raiding force began its retrograde movement to rejoin Grant, which was successfully accomplished on the 24th near Chesterfield Station, Virginia. Sheridan's casualties suffered on the raid were six hundred and twenty-five men killed, wounded, and captured, and three hundred horses.

General Grant describes the results attained in this famous raid as follows:

Sheridan, in this memorable raid, passed entirely around Lee's army, encountered his cavalry in four engagements, and defeated them in all; recaptured four hundred Union prisoners, and killed and captured many of the enemy; destroyed miles of railroad and telegraph, and freed us from annoyance by the cavalry for more than two weeks.

This brilliant success by the Cavalry Corps of the Army of the Potomac, was followed in June by one scarcely less important in its moral and material effect upon the Confederacy

THE RETURN OF SHERIDAN'S TROOPERS—MAY 25, 1864

After their ride of sixteen days to the very gates of Richmond, Sheridan and his men rejoined Grant near Chesterfield Station. The photographer caught the returning column just as they were riding over the Chesterfield bridge. On the 21st they had crossed the Pamunkey near White House on the ruins of the railroad bridge, which they took only six hours to repair. Two regiments at a time, working as pioneers, wrecked a neighboring house, and with its timbers soon had the bridge ready to bear the weight of horses and artillery. The only mishap was the fall of a pack-mule from the bridge into the water thirty feet below. It takes much, however, to disturb the equanimity of an army mule. It turned a somersault in the air, struck an abutment, disappeared under water, came up, and swam tranquilly ashore without disturbing its pack. This speaks well for the ability as saddle-packers of Sheridan's men. The total results of this important raid were the destruction of an immense quantity of supplies, damage to Confederate communications, the death of Stuart, and the saving to the Union Government of the subsistence of ten thousand horses and men for three weeks. It perfected the *morale* of the cavalry corps, with incalculable benefit to the Union cause. The casualties on the raid were six hundred and twenty-five men killed and wounded.

—Sheridan's Trevilian raid, in which, at Trevilian Station, the Confederate cavalry was again seriously defeated.

The purpose of the raid was to injure Lee's lines of supply, and to draw off the Southern cavalry during Grant's movement forward by the left flank, following his unsuccessful attempt to take the strong Confederate position at Cold Harbor by direct assault.

Sheridan started on June 7, 1864, with about eight thousand cavalrymen, the trains and supplies being cut down to the absolute minimum. Wilson's division remained with the Army of the Potomac. By June 11th, the command was in the vicinity of Trevilian Station, where the enemy was encountered. Here, Torbert's division, pressing back the Confederate's pickets, found the foe in force about three miles from Trevilian, posted behind heavy timber. At about the same time, Custer was sent by a wood road to destroy Trevilian Station, where he captured the Confederate wagons, caissons, and led horses.

Assured of Custer's position, Sheridan dismounted Torbert's two remaining brigades, and aided by one of Gregg's, carried the Confederate works, driving Hampton's division back on Custer, and even through his lines. Gregg's other brigade had meanwhile attacked Fitzhugh Lee, causing the entire opposing cavalry to retire on Gordonsville.

Following this victory, Sheridan continued his raid and finally reached White House on the Pamunkey, on June 20th, where he found orders directing him to break up the supply depot there and conduct the nine hundred wagons to Petersburg. This was successfully accomplished.

It is interesting to note that in this period of great activity for the Cavalry Corps (May 5th to August 1, 1864) the casualties in the corps were nearly forty-nine hundred men, and the loss in horses from all causes about fifteen hundred. The captures by the cavalry exceeded two thousand men and five hundred horses, besides many guns and colors.

[128]

CHAPTER
FIVE

FEDERAL RAIDS
IN THE WEST

A BLOCKHOUSE ON THE TENNESSEE

SIX HUNDRED MILES IN SIXTEEN DAYS

Seventeen hundred men who marched 600 miles in sixteen days, from Vicksburg to Baton Rouge. On April 17, 1863, Grant despatched Grierson on a raid from LaGrange, Tennessee, southward as a means of diverting attention from his own movements against Vicksburg, and to disturb the Confederate line of supplies from the East. Grierson destroyed sixty miles of tracks and telegraph, numberless stores and munitions of war, and brought his command safely through to Baton Rouge. These two pictures by Lytle, the Confederate Secret Service agent at Baton Rouge, form one of the most remarkable feats of wet-plate photography. The action continued as he moved his camera a trifle to the right, and the result is a veritable "moving picture." In the photograph on the left-hand page, only the first troop is dismounted and unsaddled. In the photo-

HOW GRIERSON'S RAIDERS LOOKED TO THE CONFEDERATE SECRET SERVICE CAMERA

graph on the right-hand page two troops are already on foot.   Note the officers in front of their troops.   The photograph was evidently a long time exposure, as is shown by the progress of the covered wagon which has driven into the picture on the left-hand page.   It was at the conclusion of this remarkable raid that Grierson reported that "the Confederacy was a hollow shell."   All of its population able to carry arms was on the line of defense.   Captain John A. Wyeth, the veteran Confederate cavalryman who contributes to other pages of this volume, wrote when he saw these photographs: "I knew General Grierson personally, and have always had the highest regard for his skill and courage as shown more particularly in this raid than in anything else that he did, although he was always doing well."

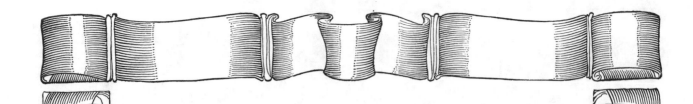

FEDERAL RAIDS AND EXPEDITIONS IN THE WEST

By Charles D. Rhodes
Captain, General Staff, United States Army

THE military operations of the Union armies in the South and West were not lacking in famous raids, having for their main objects the destruction of the supply centers of the Confederacy, the cutting of railroads and lines of communication between these centers and the Southern troops, and the drawing away from important strategic operations of large bodies of the foe. One of the most famous of these raids was that made by Colonel B. H. Grierson in the spring of 1863.

Starting from La Grange, Tennessee, on April 17th, with three cavalry regiments of about seventeen hundred men, Grierson made a wonderful march through the State of Mississippi, and finally reached the Union lines at Baton Rouge, Louisiana, on May 2d.

On April 21st, Grierson had detached a regiment under Colonel Hatch, Second Iowa Cavalry, to destroy the railroad bridge between Columbus and Macon, and then return to La Grange. At Palo Alto, Hatch had a sharp fight with Confederate troops under General Gholson, defeating them without the loss of a man. Much of Hatch's success during his entire raid was due to the fact that his regiment was armed with Colt's revolving rifles. Hatch then retreated along the railroad, destroying it at Okolona and Tupelo, and arriving at La Grange on April 26th, with the loss of but ten troopers. The principal object of his movement—to decoy the Confederate troops to the east, and thus give Grierson ample opportunity to get well under way, was fully attained.

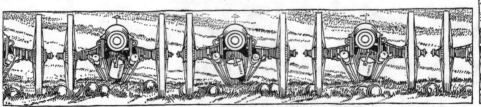

GRIERSON—THE RAIDER WHO PUZZLED PEMBERTON

To the enterprise of Lytle, the Confederate Secret Service photographer, we owe this portrait of Colonel
B. H. Grierson, at rest after his famous raid. He sits chin in hand among his officers, justly proud of having
executed one of the most thoroughly successful feats in the entire war. It was highly important, if Grant was
to carry out his maneuver of crossing the Mississippi at Grand Gulf and advance upon Vicksburg from the
south, that Pemberton's attention should be distracted in other directions. The morning after Admiral
Porter ran the batteries, Grierson left La Grange, Tennessee, to penetrate the heart of the Confederacy,
sweeping entirely through Mississippi from north to south, and reaching Baton Rouge on May 2d. Exaggerated reports flowed in on Pemberton as to Grierson's numbers and whereabouts. The Confederate
defender of Vicksburg was obliged to send out expeditions in all directions to try to intercept him. This was
one of the numerous instances where a small body of cavalry interfered with the movements of a much larger
force. It was Van Dorn, the Confederate cavalryman, who had upset Grant's calculations four months before.

Meanwhile Grierson had continued his raid with less than one thousand horsemen, breaking the Southern Mississippi, and the New Orleans, Jackson, and Great Northern railroads. Near Newton the raiders burned several bridges, and destroyed engines and cars loaded with commissary stores, guns, and ammunition; at Hazelhurst, cars and ammunition; and at Brookhaven, the railroad depot and cars.

Having no cavalry available to watch Grierson's movements, the Confederates were kept in a state of excitement and alarm. Rumors exaggerated his numbers, and he was reported in many different places at the same time. Several brigades of Confederate infantry were detached to intercept him, but he evaded them all.

In sixteen days, Grierson marched six hundred miles—nearly thirty-eight miles a day—destroying miles of railroad, telegraph, and other property; but most of all, he distracted the Confederates' attention from Grant's operations against Vicksburg at the critical time when the latter was preparing to cross the Mississippi River near Grand Gulf. In its entirety, the Grierson raid was probably the most successful operation of its kind during the Civil War.

The appearance of Morgan's men on the north bank of the Ohio River (July, 1863) created great consternation in Indiana and Ohio. The Governor of Indiana called out the "Home Guards" to the number of fifty thousand, and as Morgan's advance turned toward Ohio, the Governor of the "Buckeye State" called out fifty thousand "Home Guards" from his State. At Corydon, Indiana, the "Home Guards" gave the invaders a brisk little battle, and delayed their advance for a brief time.

On July 1, 1864, General A. J. Smith assembled a large force at La Grange, Tennessee, for a raid on Tupelo, Mississippi, in which a cavalry division under General Grierson took a prominent part in defeating the formidable General Forrest as he had probably never been defeated before. The raid

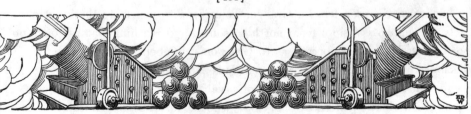

A FEDERAL CAVALRY CAMP AT BATON ROUGE

This photograph of an Illinois regiment's camp at Baton Rouge was taken in 1863, just before the Port Hudson campaign upon which Grierson and his men accompanied General Banks. The troopers have found fairly comfortable quarters. The smoke rising from their camp-fires lends a peaceful touch to the scene. A cavalry camp ccupied more space than an infantry camp. The horses are tethered in long lines between the tents, about the width of a street-way. They are plainly visible in this photograph, tethered in this fashion, a few of them grazing about the plain. In the foreground by the officers' quarters, a charger stands saddled, ready for his master. This is an excellent illustration of a camp laid out according to Federal army regulations.

resulted in the burning of all bridges and trestles north and south of Tupelo, and the destruction of the railroad.

During the raid, a portion of the cavalry division was newly armed with seven-shot Spencer carbines, capable of firing fourteen shots per minute. The Confederates were astonished and dismayed by the tremendous amount of lead poured into their ranks, and after the Tupelo fight one of the Confederate prisoners wonderingly asked a cavalryman, "Say, do you all load those guns you all fight with on Sunday, and then fire 'em all the week?"

In the spring of the following year, 1865, General James H. Wilson, who had commanded a division in Sheridan's Army of the Shenandoah, began, under the direction of General Thomas, an important demonstration against Selma and Tuscaloosa, Alabama, in favor of General Canby's operations against Mobile and central Alabama. This great raid, which severed the main arteries supplying life-blood to the Confederacy, was destined to be the culminating blow by the Federal cavalry inflicted on the already tottering military structure of the Southern Confederacy.

Starting on March 22, 1865, and marching in three separate columns on a wide front, because of the devastated condition of the country, Wilson began his movement by keeping the Confederate leaders completely in ignorance as to whether Columbus, Selma, or Tuscaloosa, was his real objective. At Selma, April 2d, a division of Wilson's dismounted cavalry, facing odds in position, gallantly carried the Confederate semipermanent works surrounding the city, in an assault which swept all before it.

General Wilson's report says:

The fortifications assaulted and carried consisted of a bastioned line, on a radius of nearly three miles, extending from the Alabama River below to the same above the city. The part west of the city is covered by a miry, deep, and almost impassable creek; that on the east side by a swamp, extending from the river almost to the Summerfield

[136]

A DESTRUCTIVE RAID IN MISSISSIPPI

The burning of all bridges and trestles north and south of Tupelo and the destruction of the railroad was the result of General A. J. Smith's raid on that point in 1864. General Smith started from Lagrange, Tenn., on July 1st, accompanied by a cavalry division under General Grierson, who took a prominent part in defeating the formidable General Forrest as he had probably never been defeated before. The Union cavalry raids in the West were more uniformly successful than the raids of the cavalry with the Army of the Potomac. The greater part of the Confederate cavalry was busy attacking the supply-trains of the armies in the North or striking at the long lines of communication. The story of the campaigns in the West, where there were fewer photographers and communication was slower is not so well-known as that of the more immediate East, but the deeds performed there were of quite equal dash and daring and importance to the result.

GENERAL A. J. SMITH

road, and entirely impracticable for mounted men at all times. General Upton ascertained by a personal reconnaissance that dismounted men might with great difficulty work through it on the left of the Range Line road. The profile of that part of the line assaulted is as follows: Height of parapet, six to eight feet; thickness, eight feet; depth of ditch, five feet; width, from ten to fifteen feet; height of stockade on the glacis, five feet; sunk into the earth, four feet. . . . The distance which the troops charged, exposed to the fire of artillery and musketry, was six hundred yards. . . . General Long's report states . . . that the number actually engaged in the charge was 1550 officers and men. The portion of the line assaulted was manned by Armstrong's brigade, regarded as the best in Forrest's corps, and reported by him at more than 1500 men. The loss from Long's division was 40 killed, 260 wounded, and 7 missing. . . . The immediate fruits of our victory were 31 field-guns, and one 30-pounder Parrott, which had been used against us; 2700 prisoners, including 150 officers; a number of colors and immense quantities of stores of every kind. . . . I estimate the entire garrison, including the militia of the city and surrounding country, at 7000 men. The entire force under my command, engaged and in supporting distance, was 9000 men and eight guns.

On April 8th and 9th, Wilson's entire cavalry corps, excepting Croxton's brigade, crossed the Alabama River, and having rendered Selma practically valueless to the Confederacy by his thorough destruction of its railroads and supplies, Wilson marched into Georgia by way of Montgomery. On April 12th, the mayor of Montgomery surrendered that city to the cavalry advance guard, and after destroying great quantities of military stores, small arms, and cotton, the cavalry corps moved, on April 14th, with General Upton in advance, and on the 16th captured the cities of Columbus and West Point.

The capture of Columbus lost to the South 1200 prisoners, fifty-two field-guns, the ram *Jackson* (six 7-inch guns), nearly ready for sea, together with such tremendously valuable aids in prolonging the war as fifteen locomotives and two hundred and fifty cars, one hundred and fifteen thousand bales of cot-

FLEET STEAMING UP THE ALABAMA RIVER IN WAR-TIME

The sight of the stern-wheelers splashing up the Alabama River into the heart of the threatened Confederacy has been preserved by a curious chance. This photograph was secured by a Scotch visitor to the States on his wedding-trip in 1865. He took it home. A generation later his son came to America, bringing his father's collection of pictures. He settled in New Orleans. An editor of the PHOTOGRAPHIC HISTORY, traveling in search of photographs to round out the collection, perceived this to be unique as a war-time scene on the river where Wilson and Forrest were making history. The Alabama River was not only one of the great arteries of the South along which it conveyed its supplies, but it was also the scene of much of its naval construction which the blockade precluded on the coast. Wilson's raid resulted in the capture at Columbus of the Confederate ram *Jackson* with six 7-inch guns, when she was nearly ready for the sea. Just a year previous, in April, 1864, the hull of the Confederate iron-clad ram *Tennessee* was constructed on the Alabama River, just above Selma. Admiral Buchanan sent James M. Johnston, C. S. N., with two steamers to tow her down to Mobile. The work was all done at high pressure for fear of just such a raid as Wilson's. The incident is somewhat similar to the saving of Admiral Porter's Red River fleet in May, 1864.

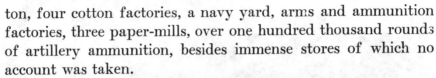

ton, four cotton factories, a navy yard, arms and ammunition factories, three paper-mills, over one hundred thousand rounds of artillery ammunition, besides immense stores of which no account was taken.

This great and decisive blow to the material resources of the Confederacy, was followed by the surrender of the cities of Macon and Tuscaloosa, and other successes, until, on April 21st, Wilson's victorious progress was ordered suspended by General Sherman, pending the result of peace negotiations between the Federal and Confederate Governments.

This great movement was made in a hostile country which had been stripped of supplies except at railroad centers, and in which no aid or assistance could be expected from the inhabitants of the country. As an evidence of some of the hardships attending the operations of separate columns composing Wilson's corps, General Croxton states in an official report that from Elyton (March 30th) through Trion and Tuscaloosa, Alabama, to Carrollton, Georgia (April 25th), his command marched six hundred and fifty-three miles through a mountainous country so destitute of supplies that the troops could only be subsisted and foraged with the greatest effort. The brigade swam four rivers and destroyed five large iron works (the last remaining in the cotton States), three factories, numerous mills, and quantities of supplies. The losses of the brigade during this important movement, were but four officers and one hundred and sixty-eight men, half of whom were made prisoners by the Confederates while straggling from the command.

CHAPTER
SIX

_____

CONFEDERATE RAIDS
IN THE WEST

_____

THE PRIZE OF THE CONFEDERATE RAIDER—
A FEDERAL COMMISSARY CAMP
ON THE TENNESSEE

CAMP IN THE TENNESSEE MOUNTAINS, 1863

The soldiers leaning on their sabers by the mountain path would have smiled in grim amusement at the suggestion that a life like theirs in "the merry greenwood" must be as care-free, picturesque, and delightful as the career of Robin Hood, according to old English ballads. These raiders of 1863 could have drawn sharp contrasts between the beauty of the scene in this photograph—the bright sunshine dappling the trees, the mountain wind murmuring through the leaves, the horse with his box of fodder, the troopers at ease in the shade—and the hardships that became every-day matters with the cavalry commands whose paths led them up and down the arduous western frontier. On such a pleasant summer day the Civil War photographer was able to make an exposure.
[142]

A PLEASANT INTERLUDE FOR THE WESTERN CAVALRYMAN

But the cavalryman's duty called at all hours and at all seasons; and the photographer could not portray the dreary night rides over rocks made slippery with rain, through forests hanging like a damp pall over the troopers rocking with sleep in their saddles, every moment likely to be awakened by the bark of the enemy's carbines. It is undoubtedly true that there is something more dashing about the lot of a cavalryman, but on account of his greater mobility he was ordered over more territory and ran more frequent if not greater risks than the infantryman. But this was the sort of day the cavalryman laughed and sang. Though the storm-clouds and war-clouds, the cloud of death itself, lay waiting, the trooper's popular song ran: "If you want to have a good time, jine the cavalry."

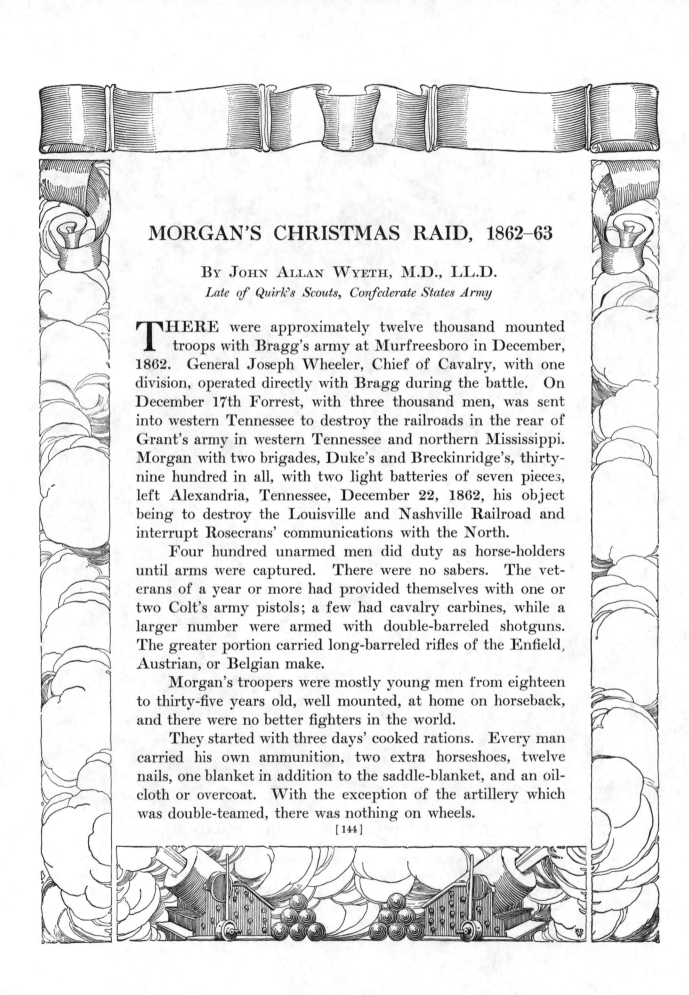

MORGAN'S CHRISTMAS RAID, 1862–63

By John Allan Wyeth, M.D., LL.D.
Late of Quirk's Scouts, Confederate States Army

THERE were approximately twelve thousand mounted troops with Bragg's army at Murfreesboro in December, 1862. General Joseph Wheeler, Chief of Cavalry, with one division, operated directly with Bragg during the battle. On December 17th Forrest, with three thousand men, was sent into western Tennessee to destroy the railroads in the rear of Grant's army in western Tennessee and northern Mississippi. Morgan with two brigades, Duke's and Breckinridge's, thirty-nine hundred in all, with two light batteries of seven pieces, left Alexandria, Tennessee, December 22, 1862, his object being to destroy the Louisville and Nashville Railroad and interrupt Rosecrans' communications with the North.

Four hundred unarmed men did duty as horse-holders until arms were captured. There were no sabers. The veterans of a year or more had provided themselves with one or two Colt's army pistols; a few had cavalry carbines, while a larger number were armed with double-barreled shotguns. The greater portion carried long-barreled rifles of the Enfield, Austrian, or Belgian make.

Morgan's troopers were mostly young men from eighteen to thirty-five years old, well mounted, at home on horseback, and there were no better fighters in the world.

They started with three days' cooked rations. Every man carried his own ammunition, two extra horseshoes, twelve nails, one blanket in addition to the saddle-blanket, and an oil-cloth or overcoat. With the exception of the artillery which was double-teamed, there was nothing on wheels.

A GROUP OF
CONFEDERATE CAVALRY
IN THE WEST

Old cavalrymen find this photograph absorbing; it brings to life again the varied equipment of the Confederate cavalrymen in the West. The only uniformity is found with respect to carbines, which are carried by all except the officers. Three of the men in the center have pistols thrust in their belts, ready for a fight at close quarters. Some have belts crossed over their chests, some a single belt, still others none at all. One of the single belts acts as a carbine sling, the other as a canteen strap. Horse holders have fallen out with the chargers visible behind the line of men. The Western photographers, Armstead & Carter, were the artists enterprising enough to secure this photograph. The territory their travels covered in Mississippi and Tennessee changed hands so frequently that fortunately for posterity an opportunity at last did come to photograph a troop of the swift-traveling and little interviewed warriors that composed the Confederate cavalry. They did important service in the West.

AN OFFICER

Under Forrest and Wheeler they helped Bragg to defeat Rosecrans at Chickamauga, and their swift raids were a constant menace to the Union supplies. This photograph was probably taken late in the war, as up to the third year the Confederate troopers could not boast equipments even so complete as shown in this photograph. In 1861 the Confederate cavalry had no Colt revolvers, no Chicopee sabers, and no carbines that were worth carrying. Their arms were of the homeliest type and of infinite variety. At the battle of Brandy Station, in 1863, every man was armed with at least one, and sometimes several, Army and Navy revolvers and excellent sabers. The civilian saddles had given place to McClellans, and that man was conspicuous who could not boast a complete outfit of saddle, bridle, blankets—woolen and rubber—and arms, all taken from the generous foe. The Confederate cavalry in the West failed to secure equally complete outfits, although they looked to the same source of supply.

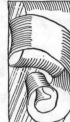

In three short winter days, over little-used highways through a rough and hilly country, they rode a distance of ninety miles to Glasgow, Kentucky, arriving at dark, December 24th. The order was to start at daylight, stop from eleven to twelve to feed, unsaddle, curry, and rest, then on until night. As the advance guard reached one corner of the public square, several companies of the Second Michigan Cavalry with no idea that Morgan's men were near, rode into sight a few yards away. In the *mêlée* which ensued, one Federal was killed and two wounded, and a Confederate captain and one soldier were mortally and one lieutenant slightly wounded. Twenty prisoners were captured, among them the adjutant of the regiment, whose equipment the writer appropriated. A number of Christmas turkeys which these excellent foragers had strapped to their saddles were also taken by us.

Ten miles north of Glasgow, on December 25th, with our company of fifty men a mile in advance of the main column, the vedette reported the Federals in line of battle in our front. We were ordered to load and cap our guns, and then rode briskly forward. When about two hundred yards from the Federal lines, Captain Quirk halted us, called off horse-holders, and we advanced on foot. Reaching the top of a rise in the lane with a high worm-fence on either side, the Federals gave us a lively volley, which we returned from the fence corners. The fight had scarcely opened, when a second detachment of Federals (Company C, Fifth Indiana), which had been in ambush to our right, charged to within a few yards of the road abreast of and in the rear of our position, and fired into us at practically muzzle range. Several of our men were wounded, our captain being twice hit. The fusillade stampeded the horses and horse-holders who fled in panic to the rear, leaving us on foot in the presence of a superior force. Five members of our company were captured. The rest of us scrambled over the opposite fence and ran for a scrub-oak thicket, one or two hundred yards across a field.

FEDERAL CAVALRY GUARDING THE CHATTANOOGA STATION

General Rosecrans looked narrowly to his line of communications when he set out from Nashville to attack General Braxton Bragg in the latter part of December, 1862. The Confederate cavalry leader, General Wheeler, was abroad. At daylight on December 30th he swooped down at Jefferson on Starkweather's brigade of Rousseau's division, in an attempt to destroy his wagon-train. From Jefferson, Wheeler proceeded to La Vergne, where he succeeded in capturing the immense supply trains of McCook's Corps. Seven hundred prisoners and nearly a million dollars' worth of property was the Union Government's penalty for not heeding the requests of the commanding general for more cavalry. A train at Rock Spring and another at Nolensville shared the same fate at Wheeler's hands, and at two o'clock on the morning of the 31st Wheeler completed the entire circuit of Rosecrans' army, having ridden in forty-eight hours.

By this time the leading regiment of the main column came in sight, caught our horses, and rescued us. We remounted at once, and joined in the charge which drove the Federals from the field. In the pursuit Captain Quirk, despite two scalp wounds, killed one of the Northerners with his pistol. Two others surrendered.

On the further march to Green River and Hammondsville that day, we captured a sutler's huge outfit, the contents of which were appropriated. That night we camped in the woods between Hammondsville and Upton Station on the Louisville and Nashville Railroad. We had had a merry Christmas.

Early December 26th, we struck the road at Upton, capturing a number of Union soldiers guarding the track. Here General Morgan overtook the scouts. Attached to his staff was a telegraph operator, a quick-witted young man named Ellsworth, better known by the nickname of "Lightning." After the wire was tapped, I sat within a few feet of General Morgan and heard him dictate messages to General Boyle, in Louisville, and other Federal commanders, making inquiries as to the disposition of the Federal forces, and telling some tall stories in regard to the large size of his own command and its movements. While thus engaged, a train with artillery and other material came in sight from the north, but the wary engineer saw us in time to reverse his engine and escape. Heavy cannonading was now heard at Bacon Creek Bridge stockade, which after a stout resistance surrendered, and the bridge was destroyed. That same afternoon before dark, the stockade at Nolin was taken by Duke and another bridge burned.

We camped that night, December 26th, a few miles from Elizabethtown, which place, guarded by eight companies of an Illinois regiment, six hundred and fifty-two men and officers, we captured on the 27th. A number of brick warehouses near the railroad station had been loopholed and otherwise strengthened for defense. The town was surrounded, the artillery

LIEUTENANT–GENERAL

JOSEPH WHEELER,

C. S. A.

After his exploits in Tennessee, and the days of Chickamauga, Chattanooga, and Knoxville, where his cavalry were a constant menace to the Union lines of communication, so much so that the railroads were guarded by blockhouses at vulnerable points, Wheeler joined Johnston with the remnant of his men. Their swift movements went far to make it possible for Johnston to pursue his Fabian policy of constantly striking and retreating before Sherman's superior force, harassing it to the point of desperation. Wheeler operated on Sherman's flank later in the Carolinas, but the power of the Confederate cavalry was on the wane, and the end was soon to come.

ONE OF THE BLOCKHOUSES ON THE NASHVILLE AND CHATTANOOGA RAILROAD IN 1864

brought up, and after the raiders fired a number of shells and solid shot, which knocked great holes in the houses, the garrison surrendered.

On the 28th, the two great trestles on the Louisville and Nashville Railroad at Muldraugh's Hill were destroyed. They were each from sixty to seventy-five feet high, and nine hundred feet long, constructed entirely of wood. They were guarded by two strong stockade forts, garrisoned by an Indiana regiment of infantry. Both strongholds were assailed at the same time, the artillery doing effective work, and in less than two hours, the two garrisons of seven hundred men were prisoners. They were armed with new Enfield rifles, one of the most effective weapons of that day.

After burning the trestles, the command moved to Rolling Fork River. The greater portion crossed that night and proceeded toward Bardstown. Five hundred men under Colonel Cluke, with one piece of artillery, attacked the stockade at the bridge over Rolling Fork River, but before it could be battered down, a column three thousand strong under Colonel Harlan (later a Justice of the Supreme Court), compelled his withdrawal. A sharp engagement between our rear guard and Harlan's command took place at Rolling Fork. Colonel Basil W. Duke recrossed to take command and led Cluke's five hundred men and Quirk's scouts in such a vigorous attack that the Federal commander hesitated to press his advantage.

At this moment, Duke was wounded by a fragment of a well-aimed shrapnel which struck him on the head and stunned him. The same shell killed several horses. Captain Quirk and two of the scouts placed Duke astride the pommel of the saddle on which our captain was seated, who, with one arm around the limp body, guided his faithful horse into the swollen stream. Quirk and Duke were both small in stature, and the powerful big bay carried his double load safely across. A carriage was impressed, filled with soft bedding, and in this our wounded colonel was placed, and carried safely along with the command.

BLOCKHOUSES GARRISONED

AGAINST

WHEELER'S CAVALRY

In 1863 an attempt to supplement his lack of cavalry for the guarding of his line of communications was made by Rosecrans, through the building of blockhouses along the railroad, garrisoned by small forces of infantry. The attempt was not uniformly successful. The Confederate horsemen under Wheeler sometimes advanced on foot and succeeded in carrying the blockhouses and enforcing the surrender of its garrison. The cavalry were the real trouble-makers for the generals in the field who were attempting to victual their armies. The problem became less complex in the last two years of the war, when the Federal cavalry was trained to higher efficiency and the power of the Confederates had dwindled following the exhaustion of their supply of horses.

Colonel Harlan reported his loss as three killed and one wounded. We did not lose a man, and with the exception of Duke, our wounded rode out on their horses.

We reached Bardstown at dusk on the 29th. Between daylight and sunrise, December 30th, I witnessed one of the frequent incidents in all warfare—the pillaging of the largest general store in this town. The men who had crowded in through the doors they had battered down, found difficulty in getting out with their plunder through the surging crowd, which was pressing to get in before everything was gone. One trooper induced the others to let him out by holding an ax in front of him, cutting edge forward. His arm clasped a bundle of a dozen pairs of shoes and other plunder, while on his head was a pyramid of eight or ten soft hats, telescoped one into the other just as they had come out of the packing-box.

About midday a chilling rain set in, which soon turned into sleet. Reaching Springfield in the gloom of December 30th, we were ordered on to Lebanon, nine miles further, to drive in the pickets there and build fires in order to give the foe the impression that we were up in force and were only awaiting daylight to attack. We piled rails and made fires until late at night, while Morgan was making a detour along a narrow and little-used country road around Lebanon. Later we overtook the command, and acted as rear guard throughout that awful night. Between the bitter, penetrating cold, the fatigue, the overwhelming desire to sleep, so difficult to overcome and under the conditions we were experiencing so fatal if yielded to, the numerous halts to get the artillery out of bad places, the impenetrable darkness, and the inevitable confusion which attends the moving of troops and artillery along a narrow country road, we endured a night of misery never to be forgotten.

As morning neared, it became our chief duty to keep each other awake. All through the night the sleet pelted us unmercifully, and covered our coats and oilcloths with a sheet of ice. Time and time again we dismounted, and holding on to the

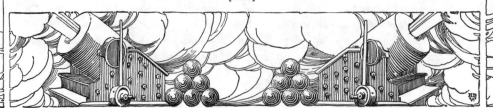

General Chalmers was the right-hand man of General Forrest. His first service was at Shiloh. During Bragg's invasion of Kentucky he attacked Munfordville, September 14, 1862, but was repulsed. He took part in a Confederate charge at Murfreesboro, December 31st of the same year, and was so severely wounded as to disqualify him for further duty on that field. He commanded two brigades on Forrest's expedition of April 12, 1864, when the latter captured Fort Pillow and was unable to restrain the massacre. He served with Forrest at Nashville and led Hood's cavalry at the battle of Franklin, delaying the Federal cavalry long enough to enable the Confederate army to make good its escape. He was with Forrest when the latter was defeated by Wilson on the famous Wilson raid through Alabama and Georgia in the spring of 1865, and remained with the cavalry until it crumbled with the Confederacy to nothing. The lower photograph of the rails laid across the piles of ties shows how the Confederate cavalry, east and west, destroyed millions of dollars' worth of property. While Generals Lee and Bragg and Hood were wrestling with the Union armies, the Confederate cavalry were dealing blow after blow to the material resources of the North. But in vain; the magnificently equipped Union pioneer corps was able to lay rails nearly as fast as they were destroyed by the Confederates, and when the Army of Northern Virginia shot its weight in men from the ranks of Grant's army in the fearful campaign of 1864, the ranks were as constantly replenished.

BRIGADIER–GENERAL JAMES R. CHALMERS

IN THE WAKE OF THE RAIDERS

stirrup leather, trudged on through the slush and ice to keep from freezing.

Daylight found us several miles south of Lebanon and the strong Federal command concentrated there to catch us, but we kept on without halting, for another heavy column was reported moving out from Mumfordville and Glasgow to intercept us at Columbia or Burkesville, before we could recross the Cumberland River.

About ten o'clock on the morning of December 31st, as the rear guard was crossing Rolling Fork some five or six miles south of Lebanon, there occurred an incident of more than ordinary interest. Captain Alexander Tribble, Lieutenant George B. Eastin, and a private soldier were sent on a detour to New Market, four or five miles from the line of march, to secure a supply of shoes which were reported stored at that point. As they were returning to overtake the command, they were pursued by a squad of Federal cavalry. Being well mounted, the three kept a safe distance ahead of their pursuers. Glancing backward over a long, straight stretch of road, they observed, as the chase proceeded, that all but three of their pursuers had checked up, and they determined at the first favorable place to ride to one side and await the approach of their pursuers and attack them. The place selected was the ford at the river. At this point Eastin checked his horse and turned sharply to the right, concealing himself under the bank. Tribble continued into the middle of the stream, which here was about fifty yards wide, and stopped his horse where the water was about two feet deep. For reasons satisfactory to himself, the private soldier kept on, leaving the two officers to confront the three Federals, who now were in sight, coming at full speed toward the river and from fifty to one hundred yards apart. The leading Federal was Colonel Dennis J. Halisy of the Sixth Kentucky Cavalry. As he came near Eastin, the latter fired at him with his six-shooter, which fire Halisy returned. Both missed, and as Eastin now had the drop on his adversary,

[154]

"By all means," telegraphed Grant to Thomas, "avoid a foot-race to see which, you or Hood, can beat to the Ohio." This was the voicing of the Union general's fear in December, 1864, that Hood would cross the Cumberland River in the vicinity of Nashville and repeat Bragg's march to the Ohio. A cavalry corps was stationed near the Louisville and Nashville Railroad fortified bridge, and a regiment of pickets kept guard along the banks of the stream, while on the water, gunboats, ironclads, and "tinclads" kept up a constant patrol. The year before the Confederate raider, John H. Morgan, had evaded the Union guards of the Cumberland and reached the border of Pennsylvania, before he was forced to surrender. On December 8th a widespread report had the Confederates across the Cumberland, but it proved that only a small detachment had been sent out to reconnoiter—sufficient, however, to occasion Grant's telegram. Note the huge gates at the end of the bridge ready to be rushed shut in a moment.

THE VALLEY OF THE CUMBERLAND, FROM THE TOP OF THE NASHVILLE MILITARY ACADEMY

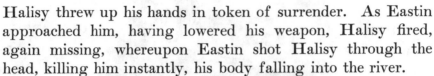

Halisy threw up his hands in token of surrender. As Eastin approached him, having lowered his weapon, Halisy fired, again missing, whereupon Eastin shot Halisy through the head, killing him instantly, his body falling into the river.

While this combat was taking place, the next in order of the Federals had closed with Captain Tribble. These two opened fire without effect when Tribble spurred his horse toward his adversary, threw his arm around him, and dragged him with himself from the saddle into the river. Tribble fell on top, and strangled his foe into surrendering. At this moment, the third Union trooper came on the scene, only to throw up his hands and deliver himself to the two Confederates.

Midday, December 31st, we rested an hour, and then on to Campbellsville where we arrived at dark, having been thirty-six hours in the saddle. That night we slept eight hours, and New Year's Day, 1863, left for Columbia, and thence on throughout the whole bitter cold night without stopping, passing through Burkesville on the morning of January 2d, where we recrossed the Cumberland.

This was Morgan's most successful expedition. The Louisville and Nashville Railroad was a wreck from Bacon Creek to Shepherdsville, a distance of sixty miles. We had captured about nineteen hundred prisoners, destroyed a vast amount of Government property, with a loss of only two men killed, twenty-four wounded, and sixty-four missing. The command returned well armed and better mounted than when it set out. The country had been stripped of horses. Every man in my company led out an extra mount.

During our absence the battle of Murfreesboro had been fought. The Confederates had captured twenty-eight pieces of artillery, and lost four—and although Bragg retreated, he had hammered his opponent so hard, that it was nearly six months before he was ready to advance. Morgan's destruction of the Louisville and Nashville Railroad was an important factor in this enforced delay.

RUINS OF SALTPETRE WORKS

IN TENNESSEE

1863

Saltpetre being one of the necessary ingredients of powder, it was inevitable that when cotton-mills, iron-works, and every useful industry were suffering destruction by the Union cavalry in Tennessee, the salt-petre factory should share the same fate. The works were foredoomed, whether by the Union cavalry or by the Confederate cavalry, in order to prevent them from falling into Union hands. The enterprising photographer seized a moment when the cavalry was at hand. A dejected charger is hanging his head by the side of the ruined mill. Two men are standing at the left of the house, of which nothing remains but the framework and chimney. The importance of destroying these works could hardly have been over-estimated. It was the case half a century later, as stated by Hudson Maxim and other military authorities, that collision between America and a foreign country with a powerful navy would bring, as that country's first move, the cutting off of our saltpetre supply from South America and thus the crippling of our ability to manufacture powder.

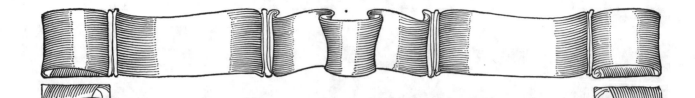

THE DESTRUCTION OF ROSECRANS' GREAT WAGON TRAIN

By John Allan Wyeth, M.D., LL.D.
(Late of Quirk's Scouts, Confederate States Army)

THE Confederate cavalry was an important factor in Bragg's defeat of Rosecrans' army at Chickamauga. Forrest was in full command on the right, while Wheeler, six miles away, covered the Confederate left wing.

Bragg had placed them thus wide apart for the reason that Forrest had flatly refused to serve under his chief of cavalry. After Wheeler's disastrous assault on Fort Donelson, February 3, 1863, where Forrest had two horses shot under him, and his command lost heavily, he bluntly told his superior in rank he would never serve under him again, and he never did.

The records of these two days of slaughter at Chickamauga—for twenty-six per cent. of all engaged were either killed or wounded—show how these great soldiers acquitted themselves. Forrest's guns fired the first and last shots on this bloody field. It was Wheeler's vigilance and courage which checked every move and defeated every advance on the Federal right, and finally in his last great charge on Sunday, pursued the scattered legions of McCook and Crittenden through the cedar brakes and blackjack thickets in their wild flight toward Chattanooga. And it was this alert soldier who on Monday, September 21st, in the Chattanooga valley, five miles from the field of battle, made an additional capture of a train of ninety wagons and some four hundred prisoners. The success of his operations at Chickamauga may be judged from his official report:

THE PRECARIOUS MILITARY RAIL-
ROAD IN 1864

A close look down the line will convince the beholder that this is no modern railroad with rock-ballasted road-bed and heavy rails, but a precarious construction of the Civil War, with light, easily bent iron which hundreds of lives were sacrificed to keep approximately straight. In order to supply an army it is absolutely necessary to keep open the lines of communication. An extract from General Rosecrans' letter to General Halleck, written October 16, 1863, brings out this necessity most vividly: "Evidence increases that the enemy intend a desperate effort to destroy this army. They are bringing up troops to our front. They have prepared pontoons, and will probably operate on our left flank, either to cross the river and force us to quit this place and fight them, or lose our communication. They will thus separate us from Burnside. We cannot feed Hooker's troops on our left, nor can we spare them from our right depots and communications, nor has he transportation. . . . Had we the railroad from here to Bridgeport, the whole of Sherman's and Hooker's troops brought up, we should not probably outnumber the enemy. This army, with its back to the barren mountains, roads narrow and difficult, while the enemy has the railroad and the corn in his rear, is at much disadvantage." The railway repairs of Sherman's army in the Atlanta campaign were under the management of Colonel Wright, a civil engineer, with a corps of two thousand men. They often had to work under a galling fire until the Confederates had been driven away, but their efficiency and skill was beyond praise. The ordinary wooden railway bridges were reconstructed with a standard pattern of truss, of which the parts were interchangeable, safely in the rear.

"During the battle, with the available force (which never exceeded 2000 men) not on other duty (such as guarding the flanks), we fought the enemy vigorously and successfully, capturing 2000 prisoners, 100 wagons and teams, a large amount of other property, and 18 stands of colors, all of which were turned over to the proper authorities."

After Rosecrans' army had sheltered itself behind the fortifications of Chattanooga, Forrest was ordered in the direction of Loudon and Knoxville to watch Burnside, whose corps occupied the latter place, while Wheeler remained in command of the cavalry with Bragg in front of Chattanooga.

When Bragg consulted Wheeler in regard to an expedition north of the Tennessee to break Rosecrans' lines of communications, Wheeler informed him that few of the horses were able to stand the strain of such an expedition. He was, however, ordered to do the best he could, and a few days after the battle all the best mounts were assembled for the raid.

We reached the Tennessee River on September 30th, at or near Cottonport, about forty miles east of Chattanooga, and although our crossing was opposed by some squadrons of the Fourth Ohio Cavalry, posted in the timber which lined the north bank, under cover of two 6-pounder Parrott guns, we succeeded in fording the river, which here was not more than two or three feet deep at this dry season of the year. From this point, without meeting with any material opposition, we made our way rapidly across Walden's Ridge and descending into the Sequatchie valley at Anderson's Cross Roads, early on the morning of October 2d, encountered the advance guard of an infantry escort to an enormous wagon train loaded with supplies for the army in Chattanooga. Parts of two regiments under Colonel John T. Morgan were ordered to charge the escort of the train, which they did, but were repulsed, and came back in disorder. I was standing near Colonel A. A. Russell who commanded the Fourth Alabama Cavalry, when General Wheeler rode up and ordered him to lead his regiment in. As soon as our line could be formed, we rode forward at

THE INADEQUATE REDOUBT

AT

JOHNSONVILLE

When, most unexpectedly, the Confederate General Nathan B. Forrest appeared on the bank opposite Johnsonville, Tennessee, November 4, 1864, and began firing across the Tennessee River, a distance of about four hundred yards, the fortifications of the post were quite inadequate.   They consisted only of a redoubt for six guns on the spur of the hill overlooking the town and depot (seen clearly in the distance above), and two advanced batteries and rifle-pits.   Three gunboats were in the river.   Their commander, afraid of falling into the hands of the enemy, ordered his gunboats set afire and abandoned.   The ranking officer of the troops ashore followed his example and ordered all transports and barges destroyed in the same way. A terrible conflagration which consumed between one and two million dollars' worth of Federal property ensued.   On the 30th of November the few remaining stores not burned or captured by Forrest having been removed by railroad to Nashville, the post was evacuated.

full speed, and receiving a volley at close quarters, were successful in riding over and capturing the entire escort within a few minutes. We found ourselves in possession of an enormous wagon train, and such a scene of panic and confusion I had never witnessed. Our appearance directly in the rear of Rosecrans' army, which was not more than twenty miles away, was wholly unexpected. As a matter of precaution, the Federal general had directed Colonel E. M. McCook with a division of cavalry, then near Bridgeport, to move up the Sequatchie valley, and be within supporting distance of this train, but he failed to be in position at the critical moment.

When the fighting with the escort began, the teamsters had turned about in the hope of escape in the direction of Bridgeport. As we came nearer, they became panic-stricken and took to their heels for safety, leaving their uncontrolled teams to run wild. Some of the wagons were overturned, blocking the road in places with anywhere from ten to fifty teams, some of the mules still standing, some fallen and tangled in the harness, and all in inextricable confusion. For six or eight miles we followed this line of wagons, with every half-mile or so a repetition of this scene. As we proceeded, men were detailed to set fire to the wagons and to kill the mules, since it was impossible to escape with the livestock. After a run of six or seven miles, I ventured to stop for a few minutes to help myself to a tempting piece of cheese and some crackers which I saw in one of the wagons. Filling my haversack, I was on the point of remounting, when General Wheeler rode up and ordered me to " get out of that wagon and go on after the enemy," which order I obeyed, and had the honor of riding side by side with my commander for some distance further among the captured wagons. As he turned back, he ordered the small squadron that was in advance, to go on until the last wagon had been destroyed, which order was fully executed.

By this time the smoke of the burning train was visible for many miles, and soon the explosions of fixed ammunition, with

THE EVACUATION OF JOHNSONVILLE AFTER FORREST'S SUCCESSFUL RAID

When General Forrest swooped down on Johnsonville the landings and banks, several acres in extent, were piled high with freight for Sherman's army. There were several boats and barges yet unloaded for want of room. Forrest captured *U. S. Gunboat 55* and three transports and barges. Owing to a misunderstanding of Forrest's orders to a prize-crew, two Union gunboats recaptured the transport *Venus*, loaded with stores which Forrest had transferred from the steamer *Mazeppa*, captured at Fort Heiman, and also some of Forrest's 20-pounder Parrott guns, which his exhausted horses could no longer draw. Colonel R. D. Mussey U. S. A., reports that the Thirteenth U. S. Colored Infantry and a section of Meig's battery stood their ground well. This was one of Forrest's swift raids which imperiled the stores of the Union armies.

which a number of wagons were loaded, sounded along the valley road, not unlike the firing of artillery in action. General Rosecrans expressed the opinion that the Confederates were bombarding his depot of supplies at Bridgeport.

General Rosecrans, in his official report, admitted the loss of five hundred wagons, so that there must have been from one to two thousand mules destroyed. While the wagons were still burning, and before those of us who had gone to the extreme limit of the train could return to the main column, Colonel McCook, in command of the Federal cavalry, arrived on the scene and formed his line of battle between us and our main column.

The capture and destruction of this immense train was one of the greatest achievements of General Wheeler's cavalry, and I was proud of the fact that the Fourth Alabama, unaided, did the fighting which took it. Its loss was keenly felt by the Federals, for it added to the precarious situation of the army in Chattanooga, and reduced rations to a cracker a day per man for several days in succession. General Wheeler reported:

"The number of wagons was variously estimated from eight hundred to fifteen hundred. . . . The quartermaster in charge of the train stated that there were eight hundred six-mule wagons, besides a great number of sutler's wagons. The train was guarded by a brigade of cavalry in front and a brigade of cavalry in rear, and on the flank, where we attacked, were stationed two regiments of infantry." General Rosecrans in a despatch to General Burnside dated October 5, 1863, said, "Your failure to close your troops down to our left has cost five hundred wagons loaded with essentials, the post of McMinnville, and heaven only knows where the mischief will end." From my own observation, I believe that five hundred would not be very far from correct. We missed about thirty wagons which had turned off in a narrow and little-used roadway, and were already partly toward Walden's Ridge.

CHAPTER
SEVEN

PARTISAN RANGERS
OF THE CONFEDERACY

AFTER A VISIT BY THE CONFEDERATE RAIDERS—ON THE FEDERAL
LINE OF COMMUNICATION IN VIRGINIA, 1862

COLONEL JOHN S. MOSBY AND SOME OF HIS MEN

Speaking likenesses of Colonel John S. Mosby, the famous Confederate independent leader and his followers—chiefly sons of gentlemen attracted to his standard by the daring nature of his operations. His almost uniform success, with the spirit of romance which surrounded his exploits, drew thousands of recruits to his leadership. Usually his detachments were small—twenty to eighty men. The names and locations in the group are as follows: Top row, left to right: Lee Herverson, Ben Palmer, John Puryear, Tom Booker, Norman Randolph, Frank Raham; second row: Parrott, John Troop, John W. Munson, Colonel John S. Mosby, Newell, Necly, Quarles; third row: Walter Gosden, Harry T. Sinnott, Butler, Gentry.

FAIRFAX COURT HOUSE, AFTER MOSBY'S CAPTURE OF STOUGHTON

If you had said "Mosby" to the Federal cavalrymen that this picture shows loitering before Fairfax Court House in June, 1863, they might have gnashed their teeth in mortification; for only a couple of months before, the daring Confederate partisan had entered the nearby headquarters of General Edwin H. Stoughton, and had "captured" him from the very midst of the army. When Lee retired behind the Blue Ridge and began to advance up the Shenandoah in the summer of 1863, Hooker's line was spread out from Fairfax Court House on the north to Culpeper on the south. Hooker followed up Lee closely on the other side of the Blue Ridge, leaving three corps, the Second, Fifth, and Twelfth, held in reserve at Fairfax Court House within twenty miles of Washington, for the protection of the Capital. The Federal cavalry sought and scouted in vain to locate the elusive partisan. It was at this time that Mosby performed one of the most audacious feats of his career. On March 8, 1863, with a small band of carefully picked men, he rode safely through the Union picket lines, where the sentries mistook him for their own scouts returning from one of their vain searches for himself. Upon reaching the vicinity of Fairfax Court House, Mosby entered the house used as headquarters by General Stoughton, woke the general and demanded his person. Believing that the town had surrendered, Stoughton made no resistance.

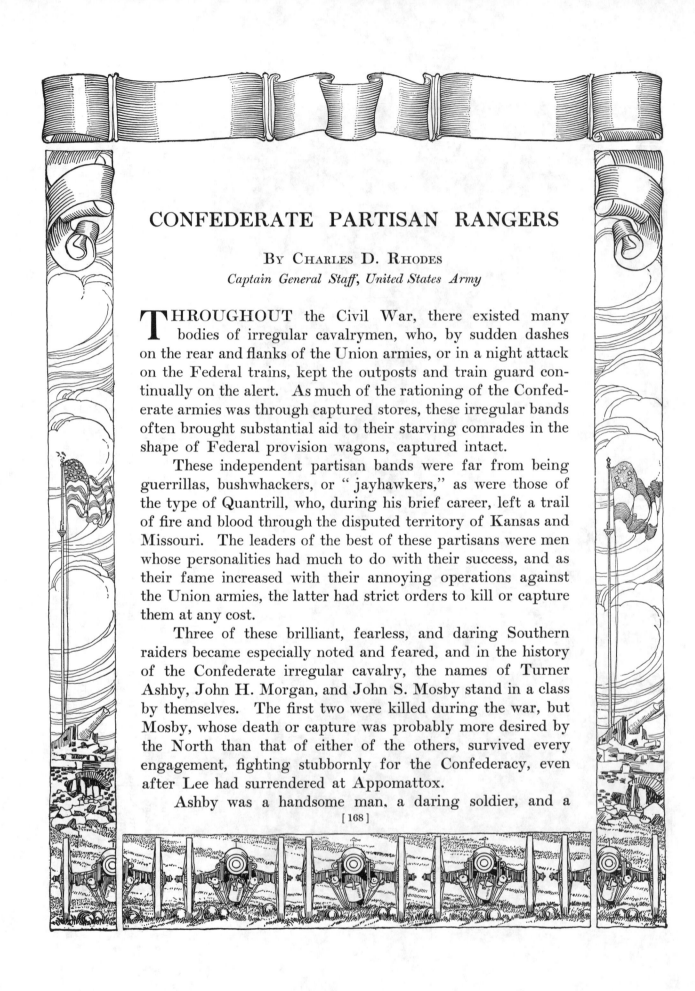

CONFEDERATE PARTISAN RANGERS

By Charles D. Rhodes
Captain General Staff, United States Army

THROUGHOUT the Civil War, there existed many bodies of irregular cavalrymen, who, by sudden dashes on the rear and flanks of the Union armies, or in a night attack on the Federal trains, kept the outposts and train guard continually on the alert. As much of the rationing of the Confederate armies was through captured stores, these irregular bands often brought substantial aid to their starving comrades in the shape of Federal provision wagons, captured intact.

These independent partisan bands were far from being guerrillas, bushwhackers, or "jayhawkers," as were those of the type of Quantrill, who, during his brief career, left a trail of fire and blood through the disputed territory of Kansas and Missouri. The leaders of the best of these partisans were men whose personalities had much to do with their success, and as their fame increased with their annoying operations against the Union armies, the latter had strict orders to kill or capture them at any cost.

Three of these brilliant, fearless, and daring Southern raiders became especially noted and feared, and in the history of the Confederate irregular cavalry, the names of Turner Ashby, John H. Morgan, and John S. Mosby stand in a class by themselves. The first two were killed during the war, but Mosby, whose death or capture was probably more desired by the North than that of either of the others, survived every engagement, fighting stubbornly for the Confederacy, even after Lee had surrendered at Appomattox.

Ashby was a handsome man, a daring soldier, and a

THE WORK OF THE RANGER—RAILROAD IRON ON THE FIRE

A pile of bent and twisted railroad iron across a heap of smouldering ties was often the only indication found by the Union soldiers that Mosby had paid them another visit. The daring Confederate ranger himself seemed to have a charmed life. Even after he became well-established as a partisan, his men were never organized as a tactical fighting body, and had no established camp. His expeditions often led him far within the Union lines, and when the command was nearly surrounded and the situation apparently hopeless, Mosby would give the word and the detachment would suddenly disintegrate, so that there was no longer any "Mosby and his band,"—until the next time.

superb horseman. At the outbreak of the war, he received a commission as captain of a band of picked rangers, working in conjunction with the main operations of the Confederate armies, but unhampered by specific instructions from a superior. He was rapidly promoted. As colonel of a partisan band he was a continual menace to the Federal trains, and moved with such rapidity as oftentimes to create the impression that several bodies of mounted troops were in the field instead of but one. Falling upon an isolated column of army wagons at dawn, he would strike a Federal camp thirty miles away by twilight of the same day. His men were picked by their leader with great care, and although there is reason to believe that Southern writers surrounded these troopers with a halo of romance, there is no disputing that they were brave, daring, and self-sacrificing.

Ashby himself was looked upon by many officers and men in the Union armies as a purely mythical character. It was said that no such man existed, and that the feats accredited to Ashby's rangers were in reality the work of several separate forces. Much of the mystery surrounding this officer was due to his beautiful white horse, strong, swift, and a splendid jumper. He and his horse, standing alone on a hill or ridge, would draw the Union troops on. When the latter had reached a point where capture seemed assured, Ashby would slowly mount and canter leisurely out of sight. When his pursuers reached the spot where he had last been seen, Ashby and his white charger would again be observed on the crest of a still more distant hill.

Only once during his spectacular career in the Confederate army was Ashby outwitted and captured, but even then he made his escape before being taken a mile by his captors—a detachment of the First Michigan Cavalry.

The Confederate leader was surrounded before he was aware of the presence of the Union troops, and the latter were within fifty rods of him when he saw several of them pushing

COLONEL JOHN SINGLETON MOSBY

It is hard to reconcile Mosby's peaceful profession of a lawyer at Bristol, Washington County, Louisiana, before the war with the series of exploits that subsequently made him one of the most famous of the partisan leaders in the war. After serving under General Joseph E. Johnston in the Shenandoah in 1861–62, he was appointed by General E. B. Stuart as an independent scout. His independent operations were chiefly in Virginia and Maryland. His most brilliant exploit was the capture in March, 1863, of Brigadier-General Stoughton at Fairfax Courthouse, far inside the Federal lines. He followed Lee's army into Pennsylvania in June, 1863, and worried the flanks of the Federal army as it moved southward after Gettysburg. In January, 1864, he was repulsed in a night attack on Harper's Ferry; in May he harassed the rear of Grant's army as it advanced on Fredericksburg; a little later he made a long raid into Maryland, and in August he surprised and captured Sheridan's entire supply-train near Berryville. In September he was wounded at Falls Church, but the following month he captured two Federal paymasters with $168,000, tore up the Baltimore & Ohio Railroad tracks, destroyed rolling-stock, and made a prisoner of Brigadier-General Alfred Duffié. In December, 1864, he was promoted to be a colonel, and at the close of the war was paroled by the intercession of no less a person than Grant himself.

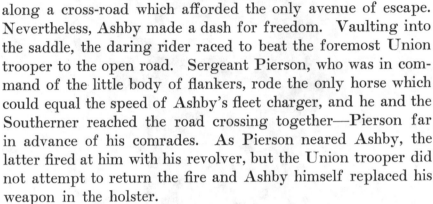

along a cross-road which afforded the only avenue of escape. Nevertheless, Ashby made a dash for freedom. Vaulting into the saddle, the daring rider raced to beat the foremost Union trooper to the open road. Sergeant Pierson, who was in command of the little body of flankers, rode the only horse which could equal the speed of Ashby's fleet charger, and he and the Southerner reached the road crossing together—Pierson far in advance of his comrades. As Pierson neared Ashby, the latter fired at him with his revolver, but the Union trooper did not attempt to return the fire and Ashby himself replaced his weapon in the holster.

As the two men, magnificently mounted, came together, Ashby drew a large knife and raised it to strike. Pierson was a bigger and stronger man than Ashby, and reaching over, he seized Ashby's wrist with one hand while with the other he grasped the partisan leader's long black beard. Then, throwing himself from his horse, Pierson dragged the Confederate officer to the ground, and held him until the remaining Union troopers reached the scene of the struggle and disarmed Ashby.

The white horse had instantly stopped when Ashby was pulled from his back, and the captive was allowed to ride him back to the Union lines, slightly in advance of his captors, Sergeant Pierson at his side. The detachment had gone but a short distance when the mysterious white horse wheeled suddenly to one side, bounded over the high plantation fence which lined the roadside, and dashed away across the fields. Before the Union troops could recover from their surprise, Ashby was again free, and it was not long before he was once more reported by the Federal scouts as standing on a distant hill, engaged in caressing his faithful horse.

Only a few weeks later, this famous horse, which had become so familiar to the Union troops, was shot and killed by a sharpshooter belonging to the Fifth Michigan, who was attempting to bring down Ashby. Not long after, while leading his men in a cavalry skirmish, at Harrisonburg, during

MEN WHO TRIED TO CATCH MOSBY

GUARDING THE CAPITAL—CAMP OF THE THIRTEENTH NEW YORK CAVALRY

The Thirteenth New York horsemen were constantly held in the vicinity of Washington endeavoring to cross swords with the elusive Mosby, when he came too near, and scouting in the Virginia hills. This shows their camp at Prospect Hill at the close of the war. During most of their service they were attached to the Twenty-second Army Corps. The Administration policy of always keeping a large army between the Confederates and Washington resulted in the turning of the National Capital into a vast military camp. Prospect Hill became the chief center of cavalry camps during the latter part of the war.

"Stonewall" Jackson's famous Valley campaign, Ashby met his own death, on June 6, 1862. As he fell, his last words to his troopers were: "Charge men! For God's sake, charge!"

Next to the gallant Ashby there was no partisan leader whose death created a greater loss to the South than John Hunt Morgan. He was a slightly older man than Ashby and had seen service in the Mexican War. When the call to arms sounded, he was one of the first to organize a company of cavalry and pledge his support to the Southern cause. He was fearless and tireless, a hard rider, and a man of no mean ability as a tactician and strategist. Morgan's men were picked for their daring and their horsemanship, and until the day of his death, he was a thorn in the flesh of the Union commanders.

Starting before daybreak, Morgan and his troopers would rush along through the day, scarcely halting to rest their weary and jaded horses. When, worn to the very limit of endurance, the exhausted animals refused to go farther, the cavalrymen would quickly tear off saddle and bridle, and leaving the horse to live or die, would hurry along to the nearest farm or plantation and secure a fresh mount.

At night, far from their starting-point, the dust-covered troopers threw themselves, yelling and cheering, on the Union outposts, riding them down and creating consternation in the camp or bivouac. Then, with prisoners or perhaps captured wagon trains, the rangers rode, ghostlike, back through the night, while calls for reenforcements were being passed through the Federal lines. By dawn, Morgan and his weary horsemen would have safely regained their own lines, while oftentimes the Union troops were still waiting an attack at the spot where the unexpected night raid had been made. Morgan's famous raid through the State of Ohio exerted a moral and political influence which was felt throughout the entire North.

On their raids, Morgan's men were usually accompanied by an expert telegraph operator. They would charge an isolated telegraph office on the railroad communications of the

GENERAL JOHN H. MORGAN, C.S.A.

Morgan was a partisan leader who differed in method from Mosby. His command remained on a permanent basis. In the summer of 1863 Bragg decided, on account of his exposed condition and the condition of his army, weakened by detachments sent to the defense of Vicksburg, to fall back from Tullahoma to Chattanooga. To cover the retreat he ordered Morgan to ride into Kentucky with a picked force, breaking up the railroad, attacking Rosecrans' detachments, and threatening Louisville. Morgan left Burkesville July 2d, with 2,640 men and four guns. Ten thousand soldiers were watching the Cumberland but Morgan, exceeding his instructions, effected a crossing and rode northward. After a disastrous encounter with the Twenty-fifth Michigan at a bridge over the Green River, he drew off and marched to Brandenburg, capturing Lebanon on the way. By this time Indiana and Ohio were alive with the aroused militia, and Morgan fled eastward, burned bridges and impressed horses, marched by night unmolested through the suburbs of Cincinnati, and was finally forced to surrender near New Lisbon, Ohio, on July 26th. He escaped from the State Penitentiary at Columbus, Ohio, by tunneling on November 27, 1863, and took the field again.

Union army, and, capturing the operator, would place their own man at the telegraph key. In this way they gained much valuable and entirely authentic information, which, as soon as known, was rushed away to the headquarters of the army.

At other times, Morgan's operator would "cut in" on the Federal telegraph lines at some distant point, and seated on the ground by his instrument, would read the Union messages for many hours at a time. This service to the Confederate leaders was of inestimable value, and created a feeling among the Union signal-men that even cipher messages were not entirely safe from Morgan's men.

As Morgan was promoted from grade to grade, and the size of his command increased accordingly, he became more and more of an annoyance and even a terror to the North. His troopers were no longer mere rangers, but developed into more or less trained cavalry. Yet even then, his command showed a partiality for sudden and highly successful attacks upon Union outposts and wagon trains. The death of Morgan occurred near Greeneville, Tennessee, on September 4, 1864, when, being surrounded, he was shot down in a dash for life.

Colonel John S. Mosby, with his raiding detachments of varying size, was probably the best known and the most anxiously sought by the Union forces of any of the partisan leaders. Mosby's absolute fearlessness, his ingenious methods of operating, as well as his innate love of danger and excitement, all combined to make his sudden descents upon the Federal lines of communication spectacular in the extreme.

His almost uniform success and the spirit of romance which surrounded his exploits, drew thousands of recruits to his leadership, and had he desired, he could have commanded a hundred men for every one who usually accompanied him on his forays. But he continued throughout the war using small detachments of from twenty to eighty men, and much of his success was probably due to this fact, which permitted sudden appearances and disappearances. From beginning to end

BRIGADIER–GENERAL TURNER ASHBY, C. S. A.

Such a will-o'-the-wisp was Turner Ashby, the audacious Confederate cavalryman, that he was looked upon by many officers and men in the Union armies as a purely mythological character. It was widely declared that no such man existed, and that the feats accredited to Ashby's rangers were in reality the work of many different partisan bands. His habit of striking at different and widely divergent points in rapid succession went far toward substantiating this rumor. He would fall upon an isolated wagon-train at dawn, and by twilight of the same day would strike a Federal camp thirty miles or more away. But Ashby was a real character, a daring soldier, a superb horseman, and the right-hand man of "Stonewall" Jackson. Careless of the additional danger, he customarily rode a beautiful white horse. After he was captured by the First Michigan cavalry, it was due to the courage and splendid jumping ability of this animal that he was able to make good his escape. Ashby met his death in a "Valley" cavalry skirmish at Harrisonburg on June 6, 1862, crying to his troopers in his last words: "Charge, men! For God's sake, charge!"

of the war, Mosby's raiders were a constant menace to the Union troops, and the most constant vigilance was necessary to meet successfully his skilfully planned stratagems.

On March 8, 1863, Mosby performed one of the most daring and effective feats of his career. In this case, as well as in others, it was the supreme boldness of the act which alone made it possible. Even with their knowledge of Mosby's methods, the Union officers could hardly conceive of such an apparently rash and unheard-of exploit being successful.

With a small band of carefully picked men, Mosby rode safely through the Union picket-lines, where the sentries believed the party to be Federal scouts returning from a raid. Upon reaching the vicinity of Fairfax Court House, Mosby entered the house used as headquarters by General Edwin H. Stoughton, woke the general, and demanded his surrender. Believing that the town had surrendered, the Union leader made no resistance. Meanwhile, each trooper in Mosby's little command had quietly secured several prisoners. Stoughton was forced to mount a horse, and with their prisoners Mosby and his cavalcade galloped safely back to their lines.

It was with similar strokes, original in conception and daring in execution, that Mosby kept thousands of Federal cavalry and infantry away from much-needed service at the front. After he became well established as a partisan ranger, his men were never organized as a tactical fighting body, and never had, as with other troops, an established camp. Through his trusty lieutenants, the call would be sent out for a designated number of men "for Mosby." This was the most definite information as to their mission that these volunteers ever received. In fact, they always moved out with sealed orders, but at the appointed time and place the rangers would assemble without fail. That Mosby wanted them was sufficient.

Many of these men were members of regular cavalry regiments home on furlough, others were farmers who had been duly enlisted in the rangers, and were always subject to call,

PROTECTION AGAINST THE "JAYHAWKERS" OF LOUISIANA

The lookout tower in the midst of this Federal cavalry camp in the northwest part of Baton Rouge, Louisiana, is a compliment to the "jayhawkers"—soldiers not affiliated with any command—and nondescript guerilla bands which infested this region along the banks of the Mississippi. Here the land is so level that lookout towers were built wherever a command stopped for more than a few hours. The soldiers found it safer also to clear away the brush and obstructing trees for several hundred yards on all sides of their camps, in order to prevent the roving Confederate sharpshooters from creeping up and picking off a sentry, or having a shot at an officer. The guerilla bands along the Mississippi even had some pieces of ordnance, and used to amuse themselves by dropping shells on the Union "tin-clad" gunboats from lofty and distant bluffs.

still others were troopers whose mounts were worn out, and whose principal object was to secure Northern horses. The Union cavalry always claimed that among Mosby's men were a number who performed acts for which they were given short shrift when caught. Of course, the nature of the service performed by these rangers was subversive of discipline, and it is quite possible that many deeds were committed which the leader himself had absolutely nothing to do with and would not have sanctioned. But this is true with all warfare.

Mosby's expeditions often led him far within the Union lines, and the command was often nearly surrounded. On such occasions Mosby would give the word and the detachment would suddenly disintegrate, each trooper making his way back to his own lines through forests and over mountains as best he could. Frequently his men were captured. But Mosby seemed to bear a charmed life, and in spite of rewards for his capture and all manner of plans to entrap him, he continued his operations as a valuable ally to the main Confederate army.

Of course much of his success was due to the fact that he was ever operating in a friendly country. He could always be assured of authentic information, and wherever he went was certain of food, fresh horses, and means of concealment.

In 1864, Mosby was shot during one of his forays, and was left, apparently dying, by the Union troops, who failed to recognize him, in the house where he had been surprised. Learning soon after that the wounded Confederate was the famous leader of Mosby's rangers, the troops hastily returned to capture him or secure his dead body. But in the meantime, Mosby's men had spirited him away, and within a short time he and his men were again raiding Federal trains and outposts.

Until the very end of the war he kept up his indefatigable border warfare, and it was not until after the surrender at Appomattox, that Mosby gathered his men about him for the last time, and telling them that the war was over, pronounced his command disbanded for all time.

CHAPTER
EIGHT

CAVALRY
PICKETS, SCOUTS
AND COURIERS

A VETERAN SCOUT
OF THE
THIRTEENTH NEW YORK CAVALRY

WHY FEDERAL

CAVALRY HISTORY

BEGAN LATE

These four Federal troopers holding their horses, side by side with an equal number of infantry, are typical of the small detachments that split up the cavalry into units of little value during the first two years of the war. The cavalry also furnished guides, orderlies, and grooms for staff officers. The authorities divided it up so minutely among corps, division, and brigade commanders as completely to subvert its true value. It was assigned to accompany the slow-moving wagon-trains, which could have been equally well guarded by an infantry detail, and was practically never used as a coherent whole. "Detachments

CAVALRY WITH INFANTRY

ON

PROVOST–GUARD DUTY

from its strength were constantly increased, and it was hampered by instructions which crippled it for all useful purposes." This photograph was taken in February, 1865, after the cavalry had proved itself. The companies attached at that time to the provost-guard were Company K of the First Indiana Cavalry, Companies C and D of the First Massachusetts Cavalry, and the Third Pennsylvania Cavalry. The officer is inspecting the arms of the Zouaves at the right, and the troopers with their white gauntlets are much more spick and span than if they were assigned to the long rides and open air life of active campaigning.

CAVALRY GUARDING THE ORANGE & ALEXANDRIA RAILROAD, 1864

Here it is apparent why the Northern generals found it necessary to detach large portions of their armies along their lines of communication, to guard against the impending raids of the Confederate cavalry. The destruction of the bridge in this photograph, part of Grant's line of communication in the Wilderness campaign, would have delayed his movements for days and have compelled him to detach a strong body to recapture the railroad, and another to rebuild the bridge. Hence this strong force detailed as a guard. Cavalry boots

READY TO FORESTALL A CONFEDERATE RAID

and sabers are visible in the photograph, with the revolver, distinctive of that branch of the service. The photographer evidently posed his men. Note the hands thrust into the breasts of their jackets, or clasped in front of them, the folded arms, and the jaunty attitudes. The two boys at the left of the picture seem hardly old enough to be real soldiers. The tangle of underbrush along the banks suggest the mazes of the Wilderness where Grant was baffled in his overland campaign.

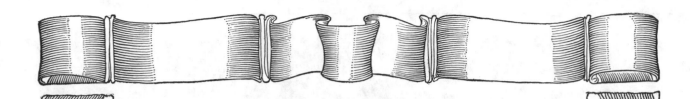

OUTPOSTS, SCOUTS AND COURIERS

By Charles D. Rhodes
Captain, General Staff, United States Army

AN army on the march is protected from surprise and annoyance by advance, rear, and flank guards, or by independent cavalry scouting far to the front until contact with the enemy is established. When it halts, its security is maintained through outposts, instructed to observe the front and flanks while it sleeps, and to act as a barrier to the entrance of patrols and spies, or to resist strenuously any sudden and unexpected advance of a hostile force.

Outpost duty, therefore, is most important, not alone as a protective measure, but because deductions from many campaigns have shown that troops which suffer continuously from many night alarms either lose nerve or become indifferent, so that, in either case, discipline and efficiency suffer.

In the Federal armies, outpost or picket duty in the presence of their enterprising adversaries was ever fatiguing, nerve-racking, and dangerous. Organizations went on picket for twenty-four continuous hours, and, in the cavalry, horses at the advanced posts remained saddled and bridled for hours at a time, ready for instant use. Except by the supports and reserves, the lighting of fires and cooking of food, when in close contact with the Confederates, were forbidden, but many a strip of bacon and occasionally a stolen chicken were fried surreptitiously in a safe hiding-place. Although a farmhouse was oftentimes available, horses and troopers were usually without shelter, and this, in rainy or freezing weather, made outpost duty an uncomfortable, if not a thrilling, experience.

The nervous period for the vedette was between midnight

CAVALRY AT SUDLEY'S FORD
BULL RUN

Not until the time this photograph was taken—March, 1862—did the Union cavalrymen revisit this little ford after the disastrous rout of the inchoate Federal army the July previous. The following March, the Confederate commander Johnston left his works at Centerville for the Peninsula, having learned that McClellan's move on Richmond would take that direction. This group of cavalrymen is advancing across the stream near the ford where they had so gallantly protected the Federal flight only a few months before. At the time this was taken, the Federal Government had already changed its first absurd decision to limit its cavalry to six regiments of regulars, and from the various States were pouring in the regiments that finally enabled the Union cavalry to outnumber and outwear the exhausted Southern horse in 1864 and 1865.

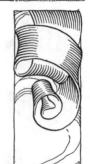

and daybreak, when all was still and dark and mysterious. For the inexperienced soldier, with eyes and ears at extraordinary tension, the grunting of a predatory hog or the browsing of a calf was quite sufficient to create alarm.

Again, when the excitement had subsided, and eyes had grown drowsy from lack of sleep, steps among the trees would bring the sharp challenge and colloquy:

" Halt! Who comes there? "

" A friend."

" Advance, friend, with the countersign."

Sometimes the " friend " was an officer, making his rounds of inspection; sometimes a countryman who had never heard of the countersign. Occasionally the answer to the countersign was a rush of feet, a blow, and the driving-in of the outpost by a force of the foe, or by guerrillas.

The tendency of the raw recruit was to see a gray uniform behind every stump, tree, or bush, and in the early period of the Civil War, the rifle-firing by opposing pickets, especially at night, was constant and uninterrupted. Many a time, too, the lone sentinel or vedette was shot down in cold blood.

A member of one of the first organized companies of Union sharpshooters tells a story of creeping with his comrades, in the early morning hours, upon a Confederate outpost. The break of a lovely day was just showing red in the eastern sky. The range to the hostile picket was considerable, but the rifles of the sharpshooters were equipped with telescopic sights.

Through the glass, a tall, soldierly-looking cavalry officer in Confederate gray could be seen through the morning mist, sitting motionless on his black charger, admiring the dawn. The rifles were leveled; the telescopic sights were adjusted on the poor fellow's chest; the triggers were pulled in unison, and although too distant to hear a sound from the outpost, the cavalryman was seen to fall dead from his horse. To the narrator, an inexperienced New England lad, such deeds were wanton murder, and he made haste to transfer to a cavalry command,

GUARDING A PONTOON-BRIDGE

These cavalrymen posted at the strategic point known as Varuna Landing, across the James River, in 1864, are engaged in no unimportant task. The Federals were by no means sure that Lee's veterans would not again make a daring move northward. However, by this time (1864) the true value of the Federal cavalry had been appreciated by the authorities; it was being used in mass on important raids, and had been given a chance to show its prowess in battle. But not until after Hooker reorganized the Army of the Potomac in 1863 was the policy definitely abandoned of splitting up the cavalry into small detachments for minor duties, and of regarding it merely as an adjunct of the infantry.

not equipped with telescopic sights and hair-trigger rifles. But as the war progressed, this constant firing by sentinels and vedettes disappeared, and opposing pickets began to comprehend that this was not war. To the guerrillas, who killed to rob and loot, it was, of course, a different matter.

The time came when the " Yankee " troopers exchanged newspapers, bacon, or hardtack with the " Johnny Rebs," for tobacco or its equivalent, or they banteringly invited each other to come out and meet half-way between the lines of outposts.

It was two years before the true rôle of cavalry was understood by the Federal commanders. During that early period, the constant use of the mounted branch as outposts for infantry divisions and army corps, was largely responsible for cavalry inefficiency, and for the tremendous breaking-down of horse-flesh. Indeed, it was not until 1864 that Sheridan impressed upon Meade the wastefulness of thus rendering thousands of cavalry mounts unserviceable through unnecessary picket duty, which could be as well performed by infantry.

But many opportunities for brave and gallant deeds occurred on outpost duty, albeit many such were performed in obscurity, and were thus never lauded to the world as heroic.

One such deed, which fortunately did not escape recognition, was that of Sergeant Martin Hagan, of the Second United States Cavalry. When the city of Fredericksburg was evacuated by the Union army on December 13, 1862, Sergeant Hagan was left behind in charge of an outpost detachment of seven troopers, with orders to remain until relieved.

For some reason or other, Hagan was not relieved, and remained at his post with his pitiably small force until the Confederate Army of Northern Virginia began entering the town. Then Hagan and his troopers succeeded in delaying the advanced troops by skirmishing. Subsequently learning that the bridges over the Rappahannock behind him had been removed, and that his outpost was the only Union force in Fredericksburg, he retired, stubbornly disputing every foot of his

A FEDERAL CAVALRY "DETAIL" GUARDING A WAGON–TRAIN, 1862

These troopers bending over their saddles in the cold autumn wind, as the wagon-train jolts along the Rappahannock bank, are one of the many "details" which dissipated the strength and impaired the efficiency of the cavalry as a distinct arm of the service during the first two years of the war. They carried revolvers, as well as their sabers and carbines, for they had to be ready for sudden attack, an ambush, a night rush, or the dash of the swift Southern raiders who helped provision the Confederate armies from Northern wagon-trains.

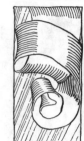

way with a brigade of Confederate cavalry, until the banks of the Rappahannock were reached. Here, seeing his men and their horses well over the river, he plunged in himself under a shower of balls, and swam across without the loss of a man, horse, or article of equipment. For this gallant act of " valor and fidelity," this cavalry sergeant was awarded the Congressional Medal of Honor.

SCOUTING

At the beginning of the Civil War, what is now known as military information or intelligence was not appreciated as it was later. The organization of the scout service was not perfected; accurate military maps of the theater of operations were almost wholly lacking, and many commanders accepted the gage of battle with no very comprehensive idea of the foe's numbers, position, and *morale*, and with no accurate conception of the topography of the battlefield.

As the military organization of the Union armies was perfected, however, and the newly made officers learned their lesson in the stern school of experience, the importance of scouting became apparent, and this use of cavalry developed into a necessary preliminary to every serious encounter.

Perhaps no branch of the military operations of the Civil War gave such opportunities for individual intelligence, initiative, nerve, daring, resourcefulness, tact, and physical endurance, as the constant scouting by the cavalry of the opposing armies between the great battles of the war. It required bold riding combined with caution, keen eyesight and ready wit, undaunted courage—not recklessness—an appreciation of locality amounting to a sixth sense, and above all other things a mind able to differentiate between useful and useless information.

The increased importance given to scouting, as the cavalry of the Federal armies gained in experience and efficiency, by no means did away with the use of paid civilian spies. But the

WATCHING AT RAPPAHANNOCK STATION

A FEDERAL CAVALRY PICKET IN '62

IN DANGER AT THE TIME

THIS PHOTOGRAPH WAS TAKEN

This picture of August, 1862, shows one of the small cavalry details posted to guard the railroad at Rappahannock Station. The Confederate cavalry, operating in force, could overcome these details as easily as they could drive away an equal number of infantry, and unless it was on account of their superior facilities for flight, there was little use in using the mounted branch of the service instead of the infantry. On the other hand the Union cavalry was so constantly crippled by having its strength dissipated in such details that it was unable to pursue the Confederate raiders. Before this scene, the summer and fall of 1862, Pope and Lee had been maneuvering for position along each side of the Rappahannock River. Pope had established a *tête-de-pont* at this railroad station, and on August 22d Longstreet feinted strongly against it in order to divert Pope's attention from Jackson's efforts to turn his right flank. Longstreet and Stuart burned the railroad bridge, and drove the Federals from the *tête-de-pont*, after a contest of several hours' duration.

information furnished by soldier scouts served as a check upon untrustworthy civilians—sometimes employed as spies by both sides—and enabled the Union commanders to substantiate valuable information secured from prisoners, newspapers, and former slaves. As in a great many other things, the Confederate cavalry excelled in the use of trained officers as scouts—officers' patrols, as they are called nowadays—men whose opinion of what they observed was worth something to their commanders; while the Federal leaders were very slow to appreciate that false or faulty military information, in that it is misleading, is worse than no information at all.

In many cases loyal inhabitants of the border States were utilized as scouts, men who knew each trail and by-path, and who were more or less familiar with Confederate sentiment in their own and adjoining counties. These men were placed in a most uncomfortable position, suspected by their friends and neighbors at home, and looked upon with suspicion by their military employers. Their service to their country was oftentimes heroic, and they frequently laid down their lives in her cause.

General Sheridan was one of the first of the Union commanders who appreciated, at its true value, the importance of the information service—a part of headquarters which should be systematically organized and disciplined, and whose reports as to topography and the location of the foe could be absolutely relied upon. Indeed, this was one of the secrets of Sheridan's almost uniform success. He was always well informed as to his opponent's movements, strength, and probable intentions.

After Sheridan's engagements in the Shenandoah valley at Clifton and Berryville, he decided to dispense almost entirely with the use of civilians and alleged Confederate deserters, and to depend entirely on Union scouts. For this purpose he organized a scout battalion recruited entirely from soldiers who volunteered for this dangerous duty. These troopers were disguised in the Confederate uniform when necessary, and were paid from secret-service funds.

CAVALRY TO KEEP THE PEACE—THE "ONEIDA" COMPANY

Cavalrymen playing cards, washing, smoking pipes, whittling sticks, indolently leaning against a tree, do not fulfill the usual conception of that dashing arm of the service. These are the Oneida Cavalry, used as provost-guards and orderlies throughout the war. Not a man of them was killed in battle, and the company lost only ten by disease. This does not mean that they did not do their full share of the work, but merely that they exemplified the indifference or ignorance on the part of many military powers as to the proper rôle of the cavalry. The "Oneidas" were attached to Stoneman's cavalry command with the Army of the Potomac from the time of their organization in September, 1861, to April, 1862. They did patrol duty and took care of the prisoners during several months in the latter year. Thereafter they acted as head-quarters escort until they were mustered out, June 13, 1865, and honorably discharged from the service.

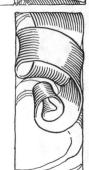

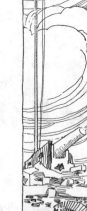

This assumption of the Confederate uniform, giving these soldiers the character of spies, caused Sheridan's scouts to be more or less disliked by the Cavalry Corps, and it has been stated on good authority that they were frequently fired upon deliberately by their own side, under the pretense of being taken for the foe. These scouts literally took their lives in their hands, and it required all their ready wit to escape being killed or captured by either the one side or the other. But the independence of the service, its constant risk, as well as patriotic impulses in the case of many, fascinated and appealed to a certain class of men, and they kept Sheridan well informed at all times.

The specially selected scouts of the Federal armies usually were mounted on the best available horses, and were furnished fresh remounts whenever occasion required—or they helped themselves to what the country afforded. The best scouting was done by cavalry troopers working in pairs, on the principle that two pairs of eyes are better than one pair. So in case of surprise, at least one scout might escape.

Sheridan's scouts were usually excellent pistol shots, and were encouraged to carry several revolvers in their belts or saddle holsters. They carried no sabers lest the rattle of scabbards or the gleam of bright metal attract the attention of the Southern scouts and betray their presence. The most experienced scouts traveled light. Many times they were forced to ride for their lives, and an extra pound or two made a difference in the weight-carrying speed of their horses. They usually left their grain and clothing in the headquarters' wagons, and managed to live off the country.

Sheridan's disguised scouts became expert in picking up the stragglers of the opposing army and in questioning them, and even went to the extent of riding around the Confederate columns and wagon trains. If detected, their fleet horses usually put considerable distance between them and their pursuers, but they were ever ready to shoot, and instances have been recorded of one of their number holding off four men.

BUILDING A CAVALRY CAMP

Waving sabers in battle, as the cavalryman soon learned, consumed but a small part of his time as compared with handling pickaxes and felling trees. In this photograph the cavalry detail at the head-quarters of General Adelbert Ames is breaking ground to build a camp. The men have just arrived, and the horses are still saddled. A barrel is supplying draft for a temporary fireplace, and even the dog is alert and excited. The faces gazing out of the photograph below are of men who more than once have looked death in the face and have earned their comparative rest. A pleasant change from active service is this camp of Companies C and D of the First Massachusetts Cavalry. They had served at Antietam, at Kelly's Ford, at Brandy Station, at Gettysburg, in the Wilderness, at Spotsylvania, and in a host of minor operations before they were assigned to provost duty near the end of the war.

A REST IN THE WOODS

COURIERS

The risk taken by the despatch bearers of both armies, when occasion demanded, is well illustrated in the story of the fate of private William Spicer, of the Tenth Missouri Cavalry, who undertook to carry an order through the Confederate lines while Sherman was conducting his campaign in Mississippi. The cavalry of General Smith, numbering nearly seven thousand men, had been detached from the remainder of the army and sent away along the Mobile and Ohio Railroad, with orders to join the army near Meridian, on February 10, 1864.

Meanwhile, the main body had marched to Meridian, and there Sherman waited for Smith until the 18th, without receiving any tidings of the missing troopers. Then the remainder of the Federal cavalry, under Winslow, was ordered to scout twenty miles toward the direction from which Smith was expected, and to convey new orders to him. Winslow's forces reached their objective point at Lauderdale Springs, and still no news had been heard of Smith.

Scouts that traveled far into the surrounding country obtained no further news. As Winslow's orders allowed him to go no farther, he abandoned the search, but it was necessary that Smith receive Sherman's orders, and a volunteer was called for to carry the despatch through a country occupied by Forrest's cavalry, and other portions of Polk's army. The messenger would be forced to locate Smith in whatever manner he could, and then to reach him as quickly as possible.

From many volunteers, Private Spicer was finally chosen. He was an Arkansas man, and as many Confederate troops had been enlisted there, he was less likely to be suspected than a man from any of the Northern States. Spicer considered all the features of the case, and his final decision was to risk detection in the gray uniform of a Confederate. The Federals were supplied with uniforms taken from prisoners and captured wagons, which were kept for use in such an emergency

KEEPING FODDER DRY

Fodder and equipment were scarcer in the field than men. Whether the trooper slept in the open or not, he took advantage of any and every facility to keep the fodder dry and protect his horses. This photograph shows a half-ruined and deserted house utilized for these two purposes. The saddles were laid beneath the shelter; those covered with rawhide instead of leather soon split if wet, and when cracked were far from comfortable. This, like the scene below, was taken near City Point in 1864.

A HOME BECOMES A CAVALRY STABLE

QUICKLY IMPROVISED STALLS

QUARTERS FOR HORSES

The trooper's first regard was for the comfort of his horse, not only in the matter of feeding and watering, but also in respect to providing him with comfortable quarters. Along the crest of the hill stretches a row of stalls improvised with poles, to afford each horse room enough to lie down and not be walked on or kicked by his neighbor—room was essential for the hard-worked horses. The haze in the distance indicates the Virginia summer of 1864—a trying one for members of the mounted service.

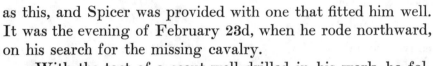

as this, and Spicer was provided with one that fitted him well. It was the evening of February 23d, when he rode northward, on his search for the missing cavalry.

With the tact of a scout well drilled in his work, he followed each little clue on his northward ride, until he had learned where Smith could be found. On the morning following his exit from his camp, he met several bodies of Confederates, who passed him with little notice.

Then another band was met. Spicer saluted; the salute was returned, and the Confederates were passing him, as the others had. But suddenly one of the party stopped and looked closely at the lone rider. The Confederates halted and Spicer was ordered to dismount. The man who had called the commander's attention to the courier stepped before Spicer. The courier recognized him as a neighbor in Arkansas.

With all the ingenuity at his command the courier fought to allay the suspicions of the Confederates, but slowly and surely the case against him was built up. Then a drumhead court martial was held in the middle of the road. The verdict was soon reached, and Spicer was hanged to a near-by tree.

One of the swiftest and most daring courier trips of the war was made, immediately after the second battle of Bull Run, by Colonel Lafayette C. Baker, a special agent of the War Department, acting as courier for Secretary Stanton. He was sent from Washington with a message to General Banks, whose troops were at Bristoe Station, and, as was then believed, cut off from Pope's main army. Riding all night, making his way cautiously along, Baker passed through the entire Confederate army, and at daylight had reached Banks.

Waiting only for a response to the message, the despatch bearer remounted his horse and started the return trip to Washington in broad daylight. For a time he eluded the Confederates, but finally, as he attempted to pass between certain lines, he was seen, and a party of cavalrymen started in pursuit of him. In spite of the distance traveled, his horse

CAVALRY SCOUTS NEAR GETTYSBURG—1863

Nothing could illustrate better than this vivid photograph of scouts at White's house, near Gettysburg, a typical episode in the life of a cavalry scout. The young soldier and his companions are evidently stopping for directions, or for a drink of water or milk. The Pennsylvania farmers were hospitable. The man of the family has come to the front gate. His empty right sleeve seems to betoken an old soldier, greeting old friends, and asking for news from the front. The lady in her hoop-skirt remains on the porch with her little boy. His chubby legs are visible beneath his frock, and he seems to be hanging back in some awe of the troopers who are but boys themselves. The lady's hair is drawn down around her face after the fashion of the day, and the whole picture is redolent of the stirring times of '63.

raced away at a speed that soon left a number of the cavalrymen in the rear. Finally, the number of pursuers dwindled
to three, and the courier, crossing the brow of a small hill,
turned his horse into the woods bordering the turnpike.

The ruse was successful, and the three Confederate cavalrymen dashed on down the hill. A short distance farther
along one of the horsemen abandoned the chase and started to
return. As he came abreast of Stanton's courier, a movement
of Baker's horse attracted the Confederate's attention and he
stopped. The cavalryman saw the courier and started to cover
him with his rifle, but Baker was prepared. The Federal's
revolver cracked, and the Southerner fell from his saddle.

The other Confederates had given up the chase and were
returning when they heard the shot. They rushed back in
time to see Baker's steed galloping across an open field to
reach the road in front of them, and dashed to intercept him.
The Federal was the first to reach the road, and again the pursuit commenced. Baker turned into the fields, and with the
pursuers close behind him started a last race for Bull Run.

The despatch bearer's horse was panting and exhausted,
but, with the grit of a blooded racer it struggled on, holding the
pursuers almost at the same distance. With a final dash Baker
reached the bank, leaped into the stream and started for the
opposite shore. The creek was little more than twelve yards
wide at that point and the horse soon reached the other side,
but there a steep bank several feet high confronted it, and it
could not climb out. With revolver ready the courier waited,
prepared to offer his last resistance, when a shot rang out. It
was the pickets of the Federal army firing on the Confederates, who abandoned their pursuit at the first shot. The
messenger made his way into Centreville, and mounting another horse dashed on toward Washington.

It was late afternoon when he delivered the messages
from Banks to the Secretary. In twenty-four hours the courier had ridden nearly one hundred miles.

A CHANGE OF BASE—THE CAVALRY SCREEN

This photograph of May 30, 1864, shows the Federal cavalry in actual operation of a most important function—the "screening" of the army's movements. The troopers are guarding the evacuation of Port Royal
on the Rappahannock, May 30, 1864. After the reverse to the Union arms at Spottsylvania, Grant ordered the change of base from the Rappahannock to McClellan's former starting-point, White House on
the Pamunkey. The control of the waterways, combined with Sheridan's efficient use of the cavalry, made
this an easy matter. Torbert's division encountered Gordon's brigade of Confederate cavalry at Hanovertown and drove it in the direction of Hanover Court House. Gregg's division moved up to this line; Russell's division of infantry encamped near the river-crossing in support, and behind the mask thus formed
the Army of the Potomac crossed the Pamunkey on May 28th unimpeded. Gregg was then ordered to reconnoiter towards Mechanicsville, and after a severe fight at Hawes' shop he succeeded (with the assistance of
Custer's brigade) in driving Hampton's and Fitzhugh Lee's cavalry divisions and Butler's brigade from the
field. Although the battle took place immediately in front of the Federal infantry, General Meade declined
to put the latter into action, and the battle was won by the cavalry alone. It was not to be the last time.

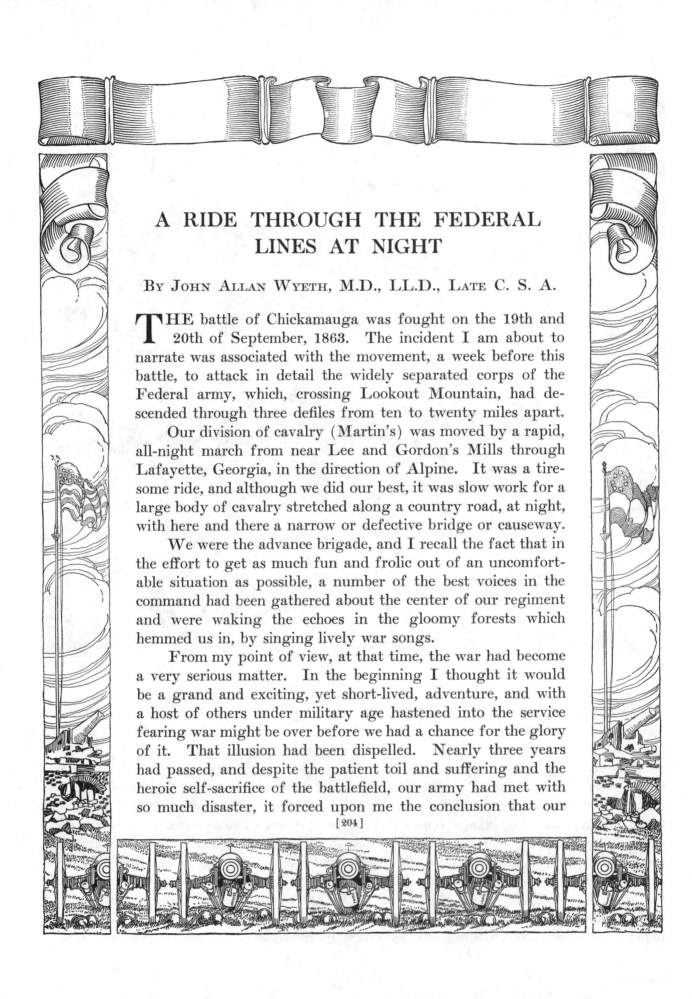

A RIDE THROUGH THE FEDERAL
LINES AT NIGHT

By John Allan Wyeth, M.D., LL.D., Late C. S. A.

THE battle of Chickamauga was fought on the 19th and
20th of September, 1863. The incident I am about to
narrate was associated with the movement, a week before this
battle, to attack in detail the widely separated corps of the
Federal army, which, crossing Lookout Mountain, had de-
scended through three defiles from ten to twenty miles apart.

Our division of cavalry (Martin's) was moved by a rapid,
all-night march from near Lee and Gordon's Mills through
Lafayette, Georgia, in the direction of Alpine. It was a tiresome ride, and although we did our best, it was slow work for a
large body of cavalry stretched along a country road, at night,
with here and there a narrow or defective bridge or causeway.

We were the advance brigade, and I recall the fact that in
the effort to get as much fun and frolic out of an uncomfortable situation as possible, a number of the best voices in the
command had been gathered about the center of our regiment
and were waking the echoes in the gloomy forests which
hemmed us in, by singing lively war songs.

From my point of view, at that time, the war had become
a very serious matter. In the beginning I thought it would
be a grand and exciting, yet short-lived, adventure, and with
a host of others under military age hastened into the service
fearing war might be over before we had a chance for the glory
of it. That illusion had been dispelled. Nearly three years
had passed, and despite the patient toil and suffering and the
heroic self-sacrifice of the battlefield, our army had met with
so much disaster, it forced upon me the conclusion that our

[204]

THE EVACUATION OF PORT ROYAL NEARLY COMPLETED

This photograph, taken shortly after the one preceding, witnesses how quickly an army accomplishes its movements. The pontoon-bridge leading out to the boats has been practically cleared; all but a few of the group of cavalrymen have ridden away, and the transports are whistling "all aboard," as can plainly be seen from the sharp jets of steam. A few of the cavalry remain with the headquarters wagon which stands near the head of the pontoon. Sterner work awaits the troopers after this peaceful maneuver. Grant needs every man to screen his infantry in its attempt to outflank the brilliantly maneuvered army of Lee.

struggle was hopeless, and that if we fought on as we had determined to do, death was the inevitable end. That was my conviction, and I believe it accounts for the fact that I volunteered to go on the errand which I undertook that night.

About two o'clock word was passed down from the head of the column to stop the singing, and for the entire column to move in silence. When we heard the order, we knew we were coming close to the foe. About four o'clock we were again halted, and another message was started at the head of the column and came back down the line in a low tone, for it was the custom on night marches, on account of the darkness and the crowded condition of the roadway, to transmit orders in this fashion. An aide or courier could not get through the crowded highway or ride through the thick underbrush and woods on either side. The message was, in effect, a call for a volunteer to go on a special errand.

My messmate, Lieutenant Jack Weatherley, who was killed soon after at Big Shanty, rode with me to the head of the column where, in the darkness, I made out a number of men, presumably officers and aides, some mounted and some on the ground. The general in command—Wheeler or Martin—asked if I were willing to go inside the foe's lines. I replied I would go provided I could wear my uniform, but not as a spy. He said: "You can go as you are. I want you to find a detachment of cavalry which has been sent around the right of the enemy's lines, and which by this time should be in their rear, about opposite our present position. It is important that they be found and ordered not to attack, but to rejoin this column by the route which they have already traveled. In order to reach them," he added, "you will proceed upon a road which leads through the enemy's lines, and should bring you in contact with their pickets about one mile from this point."

The message was entirely verbal. I carried nothing but one army six-shooter. Lieutenant Weatherley, Colonel Hambrick, in command of our regiment at the time, and a guide

COURIERS AT BEVERLY HOUSE—WARREN'S HEADQUARTERS AT
SPOTSYLVANIA

The couriers doing duty before this farmhouse, headquarters of General G. K.
Warren, are kept riding day and night at breakneck speed. The Fifth Army
Corps, of which he was in command, occupied a position northwest of Spotsylvania Court House on the right of the Federal line, where it remained from May
9th to May 13th. On the evening of May 10th Warren made two assaults on the
position at his front, at a loss of six thousand men. Again, on the 12th, the dogged
Grant persisted in his hammering tactics and ordered heavy assaults at different
points. The Federal loss on that day was approximately seven thousand men
all told. For another week Grant made partial attacks all along the line,
but Lee's veterans withstood every onset. In two weeks Grant lost thirty-
six thousand men. The Fifth Corps bore the brunt of much of the heavy
work. One can imagine with what rapidity the couriers gathered around
Beverly's house wore out their horses in transmitting all-important commands.

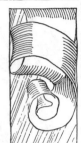

accompanied me a few hundred yards down the road. As I started, our colonel said: " This is an important matter, and I hope you will succeed. If you do, I will see that you have a furlough for as long a period as you wish."

The officers soon left me, and the guide accompanied me half a mile further to where the road forked. He indicated the route I should travel which was to the right, as we were going, and then telling me that the Federal pickets were at a point half a mile beyond, he turned back. By this time, it must have been nearly five o'clock.

To the normal human being in times of peace and quiet, the love of life is so natural and so strong that it is difficult to appreciate, until one has passed into and through it, that strange and unusual mental condition in which the value of existence becomes a minor consideration. I look back upon this occasion as the one supreme moment when I came nearest to the elimination of every selfish consideration from the motive with which I was then actuated. I do not overstate the case in saying that death was preferable to life with failure in the accomplishment of my errand.

I had determined, if halted, to ride over every obstacle at full speed, and not to fire my pistol unless in dire extremity, although I had taken it from the holster and had it cocked and ready for quick use. I was riding a splendid horse, strong, swift, and mettlesome, and so alert that nothing escaped his quick observation.

I have no means of knowing how far I had gone, probably half a mile or more, when suddenly I felt my horse check himself as if he were about to change his gait. This movement told me that he had seen something more than the ordinary inanimate object. At the same instant he lifted his head, and in such a knowing way, that I was convinced the moment had come, and that the Federal outposts were here. Without waiting to be halted, I tightened the reins, and crouching down close to the saddle and the horse's neck, touched him with the spurs, and

A COURIER AT HEADQUARTERS

Located as they were near the Orange and Alexandria Railroad and at times between the hostile lines, the dwellings near Fairfax Court House passed time and again from the hands of one army to the other. The home in this photograph was used at different times by General Beauregard and General McClellan as headquarters. Even now a Union orderly is waiting to dash off on one of the powerful chargers. The assigning of troopers to such duties as these was part of the system which crippled the Federal cavalry till it passed under the control of efficient and aggressive Sheridan. The details of the picture indicate a hurried departure of the former occupants. The house itself is a fine example of the old Colonial Southern architecture—white columns in front of red brick. The white stucco has fallen away in places from the brick of the columns—a melancholy appearance for a home.

HORSES THAT CARRIED THE ORDERS OF THE GENERAL–IN–CHIEF

Crack horses were a first requisite for Grant's staff, escort, and couriers. This photograph shows several at Bethseda Church, the little Virginia meeting-house where the staff had halted the day before Cold Harbor. The staff consisted of fourteen officers only, and was not larger than that of some division commanders. Brigadier-General John A. Rawlins was the chief. Grant's instructions to his staff showed the value that he placed upon celerity and the overcoming of delays in communicating orders. He urged his

WAITING ON GRANT AT BETHESDA CHURCH, JUNE, 1864

officers to discuss his orders with him freely whenever it was possible in the course of an engagement or battle, to learn his views as fully as possible, and in great emergencies, where there was no time to communicate with headquarters, to act on their own initiative along the lines laid down by him without his specific orders. The result was an eager, confident, hard-riding staff that stopped at no danger, whether to horse or man. What was even more important, its members did not hesitate to assume responsibility.

AN ESCORT THAT MADE HISTORY

These men and boys formed part of the escort of General Grant during the Appomattox campaign. The same companies (B, F, and K of the Fifth United States Cavalry, under Captain Julius W. Mason) were with him at the fall of Petersburg. Perhaps they won this high distinction by their intrepid charge at Gaines' Mill, when they lost fifty-five of the two hundred and twenty men who participated. With such gallant troopers on guard, the North felt reassured as to the safety of its general-in-chief. The little boy

MEN OF THE FIFTH "REGULAR" CAVALRY

buglers, in the very forefront of the making of American history, stand with calm and professional bearing. Although but fifteen and sixteen years old, they rode with the troopers, and not less bravely. One boy of similar age was severely wounded in one of the numerous fights between Stuart and the Second United States Cavalry near Gettysburg. His captain, whom he was faithfully following, left him for dead upon the field. Many years after the young man sent the captain his photograph to prove that he was whole and sound.

he bounded forward like the wind. His clear vision was not at fault, for as I flew by, I saw two men leap up in front of me from the edge of the roadway and jump into the shadows of the woods and undergrowth at one side. They said something to me, and I replied, but my excitement was so intense, expecting every moment the crack of their rifles, that no part of the picture which flashed through my mind remains clearly registered except the forms of two men and the swift scurry of the horse.

Fortunately they did not fire. It may be that they felt something of the excitement and fright I was experiencing, but more than likely they were drowsy or asleep, and the soft, sandy road enabled me to approach them so closely without being heard (for in the darkness they could not have seen farther than a few feet), that they were taken by surprise, and moreover, they may have thought I was a Federal picket, since I was riding into their lines. In any event, in less time than it takes to tell it, I had scurried away beyond their vision and out of range of their guns. Although I believed a large body of Federals was on either side of the road, I was riding along at such a rapid gait, that in the darkness I saw no sign of troops. I cannot even now estimate how far I went at the speed I was making—probably two or three miles. I know I had slowed up, and was riding again at a canter when daylight came, and with it I noticed in the valley below a cloud of dust not more than half a mile away. This told me of the moving cavalry, and in a few minutes more I had the great good fortune of riding into the column I was sent to intercept.

A few days after the battle of Chickamauga, all of the good mounts in the cavalry were organized to cross the Tennessee River and break up General Rosecrans' communications, and I went with this flying column. We took the great wagon train in the Sequatchie valley on the 2d of October, and on the 4th I was captured and taken to the military prison at Camp Morton, Indiana, where I remained until the latter part of February, 1865.

CHAPTER
NINE

CAVALRY BATTLES
AND CHARGES

ON THE WAY TO THE BATTLE OF GETTYSBURG
COMPANY L, SECOND "REGULARS"

The "Second" fought in the reserve brigade under General Merritt, during the second day of the battle. The leading figures in the picture are First-Sergeant Painter and First-Lieutenant Dewees. Few photographs show cavalry thus, in column.

THE WAGONS WITH THE RIGHT OF WAY

The ammunition-train had the right of way over everything else in the army, short of actual guns and soldiers, when there was any possibility of a fight. The long, cumbrous lines of commissary wagons were forced to draw off into the fields to the right and left of the road, or scatter any way they could, to make way for the ammunition-train. Its wagons were always marked, and were supposed to be kept as near the troops as possible. Soldiers could go without food for a day or two if necessary; but it might spell defeat

AMMUNITION–TRAIN OF THE THIRD DIVISION, CAVALRY CORPS

and capture to lack ammunition for an hour.   This is a photograph of the ammunition wagons of the Third Cavalry Division commanded by General James H. Wilson.   They are going into bivouac for the night. The wagons on the right are being formed in a semi-circle, and one of the escort has already dismounted. A led mule is attached to the wagon on the right, for even mule power is fallible, and if one dies in the traces he must be promptly replaced.   The men with these trains often held the fate of armies in their hands.

THE BATTLE–LINE—AN ENTIRE CAVALRY REGIMENT IN FORMATION

This stirring picture shows some of the splendid cavalry that was finally developed in the North arrayed in battle-line. Thus they looked before the bugle sounded the charge. One can almost imagine them breaking into a trot, increasing gradually to a gallop, and finally, within a score of yards of the Confederates' roaring guns, into a mad dash that carried them in clusters flashing with sabers through the struggling, writhing line. This regiment is the Thirteenth New York Cavalry, organized June 20, 1863. Two weeks after the regiment was organized these men were patroling the rear of the Army of the Potomac at Gettysburg. The following month they were quelling the draft riots in New York, and thereafter they were engaged

THE THIRTEENTH NEW YORK CAVALRY DRILLING NEAR WASHINGTON

in pursuing the redoubtable and evanescent Mosby, and keeping a watchful eye on Washington. They participated in many minor engagements in the vicinity of the Capital, and lost 128 enlisted men and officers. The photograph is proof enough that they were a well-drilled body of men. The ranks are straight and unbroken, and the company officers are keeping their proper distances. The colonel, to the extreme right in the foreground, has good reason to sit proudly erect. Note the white-horse troop in the rear, where the war chargers can be seen gracefully arching their necks. This is a triumph of wet-plate photography. Only by the highest skill could such restless animals as horses be caught with the camera of '65.

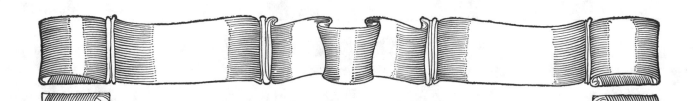

CAVALRY BATTLES AND CHARGES

By Charles D. Rhodes
Captain, General Staff, United States Army

DURING the first two years of the Civil War, the Federal cavalry was subordinated in every way to its true rôle, and one of the common mistakes in those early days of the war was to use cavalry with infantry support, so that the latter used to shout derisively: "There's going to be a fight, boys! The cavalry's coming back!"

One of the early cavalry actions which excited attention, took place during the Peninsula campaign, at the close of the battle of Gaines' Mill, June 27, 1862. General Fitz John Porter with his Fifth Corps was covering the communications of the Army of the Potomac on the Chickahominy line with the base at White House Landing on the Pamunkey. The Confederate army had made four desperate assaults on the Union lines, and every available infantryman had been brought into action, so that there was not a single reserve in rear of the line of battle, save the cavalry and some artillery.

The day was fast drawing to a close, when the Confederates made a final effort to force Porter's left flank and cut it off from the bridge. The cavalry commander, General P. St. George Cooke, directed the artillery to hold its precarious position, and ordered Captain Whiting, commanding the Fifth United States Cavalry, to charge the advancing infantry.

Numbering but two hundred and twenty sabers, the little force moved out under heavy fire, and striking the foe intact with a portion of its line, the charging troopers were only stopped by the woods at the bottom of the slope. The casualties of the charging force were fifty-five, with twenty-four

GENERAL

PHILIP ST. GEORGE

COOKE

COMMANDING

THE FIRST GREAT

FEDERAL

CAVALRY CHARGE OF THE

CIVIL WAR

Had it not been for General Philip St. George Cooke and his cavalry, Major-General Fitz-John Porter and his staff would not be enjoying the luxuries portrayed in the lower photograph, taken nineteen days after the battle of Gaines' Mill. The typical old-time Virginia cook, and the pleasant camping-ground on the banks of the river, suggest little of the deadly peril that faced the Federals June 27, 1862. The line of battle formed the arc of a circle, almost parallel to the Chickahominy. During the day the Confederate forces made four desperate assaults on the Union lines, and every available infantryman was brought into action. The only reserve on the left of the line was the cavalry and considerable artillery. As night was falling, the Confederates made a final effort to force the left flank and cut it off from the bridge across the Chickahominy. The artillery was directed to maintain its position, and General Cooke ordered Captain Whiting, commanding the Fifth United States Cavalry, to charge with his troopers. The little force of 220 sabers charged the advancing lines of Confederate infantry; a portion of the line struck the enemy intact and were stopped only by the woods at the bottom of the slope. Their casualties were fifty-five men—but under cover of the charge the artillery was safely withdrawn, and the sacrifice was well worth the results attained.

GENERAL FITZ–JOHN PORTER AND STAFF, JUNE, 1862

horses killed—a sacrifice well worth the results attained. Of this action, the Comte de Paris wrote fifteen years later: " The sacrifice of some of the bravest of the cavalry certainly saved a part of the artillery, as did, on a larger scale, the Austrian cavalry on the evening of Sadowa."

General Wesley Merritt, U. S. A., one of the ablest cavalry officers of his time, who was present at Gaines' Mill as an aide-de-camp to General Cooke, thus described this affair: *

During the early part of this battle the Union army held its ground and gained from time to time some material success. But it was only temporary. In the afternoon the writer of this, by General Cooke's direction, reported at the headquarters of the commanding general on the field, Fitz John Porter, and during his attendance there heard read a despatch from General McClellan congratulating Porter on his success. It closed with directions to drive the rebels off the field, and to take from them their artillery. At the time this despatch was being read, the enemy were forcing our troops to the rear. Hasty preparations were made for the retreat of the headquarters, and everything was in the most wretched confusion. No orders could be obtained, and I returned to my chief reporting the condition of affairs. It was apparent from movements in our front that the Confederates would make a supreme effort to force the left flank of Fitz John Porter's command, and cutting it off from the bridge over the Chickahominy, sever it from McClellan's army, and capture or disperse it.

It was growing late. Both armies were exhausted by the exertions of the day. But the prize at hand was well worth the effort, and the Confederates with renewed strength were fighting to make their victory complete. The Union cavalry commander seized the situation at a glance. The cavalry had been posted behind a plateau on the left bank of the Chickahominy, with ground to its front free of obstacles and suitable for cavalry action. To the right front of the cavalry the batteries of the reserve artillery were stationed. . . .

The events of that day at Gaines' Mill are pictured on the mind of the writer of this imperfect sketch as on a never fading photograph. The details of the battle are as vivid as if they had occurred yesterday. As

* Journal United States Cavalry Association, March, 1895.

MECHANICSVILLE, IN 1862, WHERE THE TROUBLE STARTED

At this sleepy Virginia hamlet the series of engagements that preceded the struggles along the Chickahominy in front of Richmond began. Early in June, 1862, as the Army of the Potomac extended its wings along both banks of the Chickahominy, Mechanicsville fell into its possession. There was a struggle at Beaver Dam Creek and on the neighboring fields, the defenders finally retreating in disorder down the pike and over the bridge toward Richmond, only three and a half miles away. The pickets of the opposing armies watched the bridge with jealous eyes till the Union lines were withdrawn on the 26th of June, and the Confederates retook the village.

OFFICERS OF THE FIFTH UNITED STATES CAVALRY, IN THE FAMOUS CHARGE

the Confederates came rushing across the open in front of the batteries, bent on their capture, one battery nearest our position was seen to limber up with a view to retreating. I rode hurriedly, by direction of General Cooke, to its captain, Robinson, and ordered him to unlimber and commence firing at short range, canister. He complied willingly, and said, as if in extenuation of his intended withdrawal, that he had no support. I told him the cavalry were there, and would support his and the other batteries. The rapid fire at short range of the artillery, and the daring charge of the cavalry in the face of an exhausted foe, prevented, without doubt, the enemy seizing the Chickahominy bridge and the capture or dispersion of Fitz John Porter's command. No farther advance was made by the Confederates, and the tired and beaten forces of Porter withdrew to the farther side of the Chickahominy and joined the Army of the Potomac in front of Richmond. The cavalry withdrew last as a rear guard, after having furnished torch and litter bearers to the surgeons of our army, who did what was possible to care for our wounded left on the field.

But it was not until a year later (March 17, 1863), at Kelly's Ford on the Rappahannock, that the Union cavalry first gained real confidence in itself and in its leaders.

In this engagement, following the forcing of the river crossing, two regiments of cavalry dismounted, with a section of artillery, and held the foe in front, while mounted regiments rolled up the Confederate flanks; their entire line was thrown into confusion and finally driven from the field.

The decisive cavalry battle at Brandy Station, or Beverly Ford, on June 9th, following, having for its object a reconnaissance in force of the Confederate troops on the Culpeper-Fredericksburg road, was the first great cavalry combat of the war. It virtually "made" the Union cavalry.

Buford's division of the Federal cavalry corps accompanied by Ames' infantry brigade, had been directed to cross the Rappahannock at Beverly Ford, and move by way of St. James' Church to Brandy Station. A second column composed of Gregg's and Duffié's divisions, with Russell's infantry

MAJOR CHARLES JARVIS WHITING

Major (then Captain) Whiting was the man who led the charge of the Fifth United States Cavalry upon the advancing Confederate infantry ordered by General Philip St. George Cooke at Gaines' Mill, June 27, 1862. He could entertain no hope of victory. The Confederates were already too near to allow of an effective charge. It was practically a command to die in order to check the Confederate column until infantry reenforcements could be rushed forward to save some imperiled batteries. Over twenty-five per cent. of the troopers who rode through the Confederate lines were killed, wounded, or missing.

GAINES' MILL

From this rural Virginia spot the battle of June 27th took its name. At the close of that fearful day the building fell into use as a hospital. It was later burned during a Federal raid, and nothing but the gaunt walls remain. The skull that lies in front of the mill evidently belonged to one of those brave cavalrymen who gave up their lives to save their comrades. He may have received a soldier's hasty burial, but it was by no means unusual for the heavy rains to wash away the shallow covering of soil, and to have exposed to view the remains of the men who had gone to their reward.

brigade, was to cross the river at Kelly's Ford—Gregg to push on by way of Mount Dumpling to Brandy Station, and Duffié to proceed to Stevensburg. By a strange coincidence, that brilliant cavalry leader, Stuart, planned on the same day to cross the Rappahannock at Beverly and the upper fords, for the purpose of diverting the attention of the Army of the Potomac from General Lee's northward dash into Maryland.

Under cover of a heavy fog, Buford's column crossed the river at four o'clock in the morning, surprising the Southern outposts and nearly capturing the Confederate artillery. Here, in spite of superior numbers, the Union commander, General Pleasonton, formed his cavalry in line of battle, covering the ford in less than an hour, but he could make no perceptible movement forward until Gregg's guns on the extreme left had made a general advance possible.

The Confederates fell rapidly back, and the headquarters of Stuart's chief of artillery, with all his papers and Lee's order for the intended movement, were captured. A junction was soon formed with Gregg, and with heavy losses on both sides, the foe was pushed back to Fleetwood Ridge. Of this part of the action General Stuart's biographer says:

A part of the First New Jersey Cavalry came thundering down the narrow ridge, striking McGregor's and Hart's unsupported batteries in the flank, and riding through and between guns and caissons from right to left, but were met by a determined hand-to-hand contest from the cannoneers with pistols, sponge-staffs, and whatever else came handy to fight with. The charge was repulsed by artillerists alone, not a single friendly trooper being within reach of us.

On Fleetwood Ridge the Confederate infantry rallied to the support of Stuart's cavalry, and the object of the reconnaissance having been gained, a general withdrawal of the Union cavalry was ordered, Gregg by way of the ford at Rappahannock Bridge, and Buford by Beverly Ford. But as the order was about to be executed, the Confederates fiercely

A BRIDGE OVER THE MUDDY CHICKAHOMINY—1862

This is a photograph of the insignificant stream that figured so largely in the calculations of the opposing generals before Richmond. Under the effect of the almost tropical rains, in a day luxuriant meadows would become transformed into lakes, and surging floods appear where before were stagnant pools. Thus it became doubtful in June whether the struggling Union army could depend upon the little bridges. It was said by some of the Union engineers that it was only the weight of the troops passing over them that held some in place. One was swept away immediately after a column had crossed. The muddy banks show more plainly than words what the little Chickahominy could do when it was thoroughly aroused.

attacked the Union right, and the most serious fighting of the day resulted. At four o'clock in the afternoon, a large Confederate infantry force being reported at Brandy Station, General Pleasonton began a general withdrawal of the Union cavalry, a movement which was executed in good order and completed by seven o'clock in the evening without molestation by the Confederates.

This great cavalry battle lasted for over ten hours, and was preeminently a mounted combat, the charges and countercharges of the opposing horsemen being of the most desperate character. During the day, the First New Jersey Cavalry, alone, made six regimental charges, besides a number of smaller ones; the fighting and charging of the regular and Sixth Pennsylvania Cavalry was kept up for over twelve hours; and the other regiments were almost equally engaged through the eventful day.

Commenting on this defeat of the Confederate cavalry at Brandy Station, the *Richmond Examiner* of that period said:

The surprise of this occasion was the most complete that has occurred. The Confederate cavalry was carelessly strewn over the country, with the Rappahannock only between it and an enemy who has already proven his enterprise to our cost. It is said that their camp was supposed to be secure because the Rappahannock was not supposed to be fordable at the point where it actually was forded. What! Do the Yankees then know more about this river than our own soldiers, who have done nothing but ride up and down its banks for the past six months?

Brandy Station was really the turning-point in the evolution of the Federal cavalry, which had heretofore been dominated by a sense of its own inferiority to Stuart's bold horsemen. Even the Confederate writer, McClellan, has this to say of Brandy Station and its effect on the *morale* of the Union cavalry:

Up to this time, confessedly inferior to the Southern horsemen, they gained on this day that confidence in themselves and their commanders

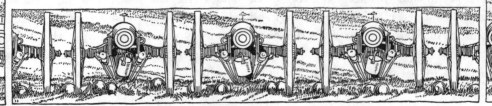

REUNION OF OFFICERS

OF THE THIRD AND FOURTH PENNSYLVANIA

CAVALRY

The soldiers in a great war-game make merry while they can. This photograph shows the officers of the Third and Fourth Pennsylvania Cavalry picknicking on the banks of the river at Westover Landing in August, 1862. The Fourth Pennsylvania had taken part in the actions on the upper Chickahominy hardly a month before, when the Fifth United States Cavalry made their daring charge at Gaines' Mill. Both regiments had been active in the Peninsula campaign, although the Third Pennsylvania had been split up into detachments and on headquarters duty, and they were to be together on the bloody days at Antietam the middle of the following month. They have snatched a brief moment together now, and are hopefully pledging each other long lives. Neither the Union nor the Confederacy realized that the war was to stretch out over four terrible years.

which enabled them to contest so fiercely the subsequent battlefields of June, July, and October.

Passing by without comment the splendid stand of Buford's dismounted troops covering the approaches to the town of Gettysburg, in which less than three thousand cavalrymen and Calef's battery made possible the occupation by the delayed Union army of the dominating position along Cemetery Ridge and the Round Tops, the desperate battles of the cavalry on the right and left flanks at Gettysburg, are history.

On the Union left flank, Pleasonton had ordered Kilpatrick to move from Emmittsburg with his entire force to prevent a Confederate turning movement on the Round Tops, and, if practicable, to attack the Confederate flank and rear. Late on July 3, 1863, the reserve cavalry brigade under Merritt moved up and took position to the left of Kilpatrick. Custer's brigade had been detached to report to Gregg on the Union right. The fight which ensued on this third and last day of the great battle, was severe in the extreme.

Merritt's position on the left caused the Confederate general, Law, to detach a large force from his main line to protect his flank and rear. This so weakened the Confederate line in front of General Farnsworth, that Kilpatrick ordered the latter to charge the center of Law's line of infantry. The ground was most unfavorable for a mounted charge, being broken, covered with stone, and intersected by fences and stone walls.

Writing of this charge in "Battles and Leaders of the Civil War," Captain H. C. Parsons of the First Vermont Cavalry, says:

I was near Kilpatrick when he impetuously gave the order to Farnsworth to make the last charge. Farnsworth spoke with emotion: "General, do you mean it? Shall I throw my handful of men over rough ground, through timber, against a brigade of infantry? The First Vermont has already been fought half to pieces; these are too good men to kill." Kilpatrick said: "Do you refuse to obey my orders? If you are afraid to lead this charge, I will lead it."

HELD BY THE CAVALRY AT ANTIETAM

The Federal cavalry bore its share of the work on the bloodiest single day of the war, September 17, 1862, at Antietam. At this bridge on the Keedysville road the gallant cavalry leader General Pleasonton had a most important part to play in the plan of attack on the Confederate positions west of Antietam Creek. In spite of galling cross-fire from the Confederate batteries, Pleasonton threw forward his mounted skirmishers, who held their ground until Tidball's batteries of the regular artillery were advanced piece by piece across the bridge. Opening with canister, the guns routed the sharpshooters, and soon four batteries were in position on the ridge beyond the creek. Here they held their ground till nightfall, at times running short of ammunition, but giving needed aid to Sumner's advance to their right and in Burnside's desperate struggle to cross the bridge below to their left. To the left of the bridge where Pleasonton's successful crossing on the morning of the 17th was accomplished stands Newcomers' Mill. On the ridge above, the cavalry and artillery held their positions, keeping open a way for reenforcements. These were much needed when the ammunition of the batteries ran low. More regular troops were sent forward, together with two more batteries from Sykes' division, under command of Captain Dryer. These reenforcements threw themselves splendidly into the fight. The cavalry had scored again.

NEWCOMERS' MILL ON ANTIETAM CREEK

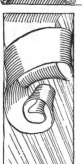

Farnsworth rose in his stirrups—he looked magnificent in his passion—and cried, "Take that back!" Kilpatrick returned his defiance, but, soon repenting, said, "I did not mean it; forget it."

For a moment there was silence, when Farnsworth spoke calmly, "General, if you order the charge, I will lead it, but you must take the responsibility."

I did not hear the low conversation that followed, but as Farnsworth turned away, he said, "I will obey your order." Kilpatrick said earnestly, "I take the responsibility."

The charge was a daring and spectacular one. The First West Virginia, and Eighteenth Pennsylvania moved through the woods first, closely followed by the First Vermont and Fifth New York Cavalry, all mounted, and drove the foe before them until heavy stone walls and fences were reached. Two regiments cleared the obstacles, charged a second line of infantry, and were stopped by another stone wall, covering a third line of infantry. The First West Virginia was for a time entirely surrounded, but succeeded in cutting its way back with a loss of but five killed and four wounded, bringing with it a number of prisoners. When the body of Farnsworth was afterwards recovered, it was found to have received five mortal wounds.

General W. M. Graham, U. S. A. (Retired), says: *

The following is the account of Farnsworth's death as seen by a Confederate officer and by him related to me in the winter of 1876–77 at Columbia, South Carolina: I was introduced to Captain Bachman, who commanded the "Hampton Legion Battery," with which I was engaged (Battery K, First United States Artillery), at Gettysburg on July 3d. Naturally our conversation drifted to the war, and he remarked: "One of the most gallant incidents of the war witnessed by me was a cavalry charge at the battle of Gettysburg, on July 3d, made by a General Farnsworth of the Yankee army. He led his brigade, riding well ahead of his men, in a charge against my battery and the infantry supports; we were so filled with admiration of his bravery that we were reluctant

*Journal Military Service Institution for March, 1910, p. 343.

DUFFIÉ, WHO LED THE CHARGE AT KELLY'S FORD

Led by Colonel Alfred Duffié, the dashing cavalryman whose portrait is above, Federal cavalry had its first opportunity to measure itself in a real trial of strength with the hardy horsemen of the South at Kelly's Ford on March 17, 1863. Brigadier-General William W. Averell, in command of the Second Division, Cavalry Corps, Army of the Potomac, received orders to cross the river with 3,000 cavalry and six pieces of artillery, and attack and destroy the forces of General Fitzhugh Lee, supposed to be near Culpeper Court House. Starting from Morrisville with about 2,100 men, General Averell found the crossing at Kelly's Ford obstructed by abatis and defended by sharpshooters. The First Rhode Island Cavalry effected a crossing, and the battle-line was formed on the farther side of the river. Colonel Duffié on the Federal left flank, and Colonel McIntosh on the right led almost simultaneous charges. The entire body of Confederate cavalry was driven back in confusion. The Confederates made another stand three-quarters of a mile farther back in the woods, but when the Federal cavalry finally withdrew, their killed and wounded were 78, and those of the Confederates 133.

to kill him, and so called out to him to 'surrender,' as his position was hopeless. He replied by emptying his revolver and then hurling it at us and drawing his saber, when we shot him through the body, killing him. His men were nearly all killed, wounded, or captured, very few escaping to their own lines."

General Graham adds, " Bachman was a fine fellow who, like *all* those who *fought* on each side, had buried all bitterness of feeling."

All things considered, it seems wonderful that these four regiments did not suffer more severely (sixty-five casualties out of three hundred men in the charge). This fact can best be accounted for by the moral effect of the charge, the fearless troopers leaping the obstacles and sabering many of the Confederate infantry in their positions. The Confederate general, Law, said of this:

It was impossible to use our artillery to any advantage, owing to the close quarters of the attacking cavalry with our own men, the leading squadrons forcing their horses up to the very muzzles of the rifles of our infantry.

But while this was taking place on the Federal left flank, a great cavalry battle, fraught with tremendous responsibilities, was being waged on the right flank.

On July 3d, the Second Cavalry Division, under Gregg, had been ordered to the right of the line with orders to make a demonstration against the Confederates. About noon, a despatch reached Gregg that a large body of the Southern cavalry was observed from Cemetery Hill, moving against the right of the Union line. In consequence of this important information, Custer's brigade, which had been ordered back to Kilpatrick's command, was held by Gregg.

This Confederate column moving to the attack was Stuart's cavalry, which, belated by many obstacles, was advancing toward the lines of Ewell's corps. Stuart took position on a ridge, which commanded a wide area of open ground, and

THE HOLLOW SQUARE IN THE CIVIL WAR—A FORMATION USED AT GETTYSBURG

Many authorities doubted that the formation portrayed in this picture was used at the battle of Gettysburg. Not until the meeting of the survivors of the First Corps at Gettysburg in May, 1885, were these doubts finally dispelled. Late in the afternoon of July 1st General Buford had received orders from General Howard to go to General Doubleday's support. Buford's cavalry lay at that time a little west of the cemetery. Though vastly outnumbered by the advancing Confederate infantry, Buford formed his men for the charge. The Confederates immediately set to forming squares in echelon. This consumed time, however, and the respite materially aided in the escape of the First Corps, if it did not save the remnant from capture. Cavalry in the Civil War was not wont to charge unbroken infantry, the latter being better able to withstand a cavalry charge than cavalry itself. In such a charge the cavalry ranks become somewhat blended, and arrive in clusters on the opposing lines. The horses avoid trampling on the fallen and wounded, and jump over them if possible. Buford's threatened charge was a successful ruse.

TWO LEADERS OF THE FEDERAL CAVALRY AT GETTYSBURG

This martial photograph portrays two of the men who prevented the success of the Confederate General Stuart's charge on the third day at Gettysburg, when the tide of battle between the long lines of infantry had been wavering to and fro, and Pickett was advancing on Cemetery Ridge. Had the brilliant Stuart with his veteran cavalry gained the rear of the Federal line, the natural panic following might have been more than sufficient to win the day for the Confederate cause. About noon on July 3d, General Gregg was informed that a large body of Confederate cavalry was moving against the right of the line. General

PLEASONTON AND CUSTER, THREE MONTHS BEFORE THE BATTLE

Gregg held Custer's brigade, which had been ordered back to the left of the line, in order to help meet the attack. The Seventh Michigan Cavalry met the charge of a regiment of W. H. F. Lee's brigade, and this was followed by a charge of the First Michigan, driving back the Confederate line. Then followed counter-charges by the Confederates until a large part of both commands were fighting desperately. In this terrible cavalry combat every possible weapon was utilized. This photograph of Pleasonton on the right, who commanded all the cavalry at Gettysburg, and of the dashing Custer, was taken three months before.

SOME OF PLEASONTON'S MEN

AT GETTYSBURG

These men and mere boys stood seriously before the camera. Without a trace of swagger they leaned upon their flashing sabers; yet they had seen all the important cavalry fighting in the East before their final supreme test at Gettysburg. They had fought at Fair Oaks and the Seven Days around Richmond. They had played their part at Kelly's Ford and in the great cavalry battle at Brandy Station. They came to Gettysburg seasoned troopers, with poise and confidence in themselves. On the first day Gregg's Second Cavalry Division, of which they formed part, fought the Second Virginia on foot with carbines. On the second day they were deployed as dismounted skirmishers to meet Stuart's men. The Confederate cavalry leader hoped to charge at the opportune moment when Pickett was advancing, but Pleasonton's men frus-

COMPANY D

THIRD PENNSYLVANIA CAVALRY

trated this attempt. The desperate charges and counter-charges on the Union right on that third decisive day were the fiercest of the entire war. This photograph was taken seven months later at Brandy Station, a few weeks before the Third Pennsylvania went into the Wilderness. Their time intervening since the battle of Gettysburg has been spent scouting and picketing along the Rappahannock, including many a skirmish with their active adversaries. They have had time to spruce up a bit during one of their short rests, but their quiet veteran bearing reflects the scenes they have passed through. Their swords that gleam so brilliantly are the regulation light curved cavalry sabers. With these and all other needed articles of equipment they and most of the Federal cavalry are now thoroughly equipped.

his plan of attack was to engage the Federal troops in his front with sharpshooters, while he moved the Confederate brigades of Jenkins and W. F. H. Lee secretly through the woods in an effort to reach the Union rear. Stuart hoped to strike at the psychological moment when Pickett's famous infantry charge, on the center of the Union line of battle, would engage the entire attention of the Army of the Potomac.

The cavalry combat which followed was probably as desperate and as stubbornly contested as any in which the cavalry took part during the entire period of the war. A mounted charge by a regiment of W. F. H. Lee's brigade, was met by a countercharge of the Seventh Michigan Cavalry, the two regiments meeting face to face on opposite sides of a stone wall, and discharging their carbines point blank. The First Michigan Cavalry, aided by Chester's battery made a charge which, followed by a hand-to-hand fight, drove the Confederate lines back in confusion. Then followed charges and counter-charges by each opponent, until a large part of both commands was involved in a general mêlée.

In this terrible cavalry combat every possible weapon was utilized, and after it was over, men were found interlocked in each other's arms, with fingers so firmly imbedded in the flesh as to require force to remove them. The casualties were heavy for both Stuart and Gregg, but the latter was able to stop the Confederate cavalry leader's critical turning movement. Had Stuart with his veteran cavalry been able to strike the rear of the Federal army simultaneously with Pickett's infantry charge in front, the result of this decisive battle of the war might have been different.

On April 4, 1864, General Sheridan assumed command of the cavalry of the Army of the Potomac, and thereafter a new order of things was inaugurated for the Union cavalry in the Eastern theater of operations.

Sheridan insisted that his cavalry should not be separated into fragments, but should be concentrated " to fight the

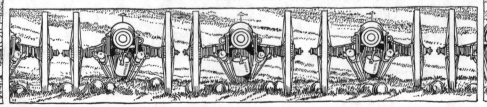

CAVALRY FROM INDIANA—A FIGHTING REGIMENT AT GETTYSBURG AND ELSEWHERE

Looking at the resolute faces and confident mien of these boys from what was then the far-western State of Indiana, the reader, even of a later generation, understands instantly how it was that the Western cavalry of the Federal army earned such an enviable reputation from '61 to '65. Not only did it protect the fast-spreading Federal frontier in the West; not only did it bear the brunt of the raids conducted by the dashing leaders Grierson, Smith, Wilson, and others, whereby the more southern portions of the Confederacy were cut off from their supplies and deprived of their stores; but States like Indiana also provided several of the most conspicuously gallant regiments that served with the Eastern armies. This Third Indiana, for instance, was busy East and West. At Nashville, at Shiloh, at Stone's River, at Chattanooga, at Atlanta, and on Sherman's march to the sea, it did its duty in the West, while six companies of the regiment participated in Buford's stand at Gettysburg.

enemy's cavalry," and in deference to Sheridan's wishes, General Meade promptly relieved the cavalry from much of the arduous picket duty which it was performing at the time. But he gave little encouragement as yet to Sheridan's plans for an *independent* cavalry corps—a corps in fact as well as in name. By the end of July, the Cavalry Corps had succeeded in almost annihilating the Confederate cavalry and had accomplished the destruction of millions of dollars' worth of property useful to the Confederate Government. In all the important movements of the Army of the Potomac, the cavalry had acted as a screen, and by its hostile demonstrations against the Southern flanks and rear, had more than once forced General Lee to detach much-needed troops from his hard-pressed front.

On May 11th, at Yellow Tavern, Sheridan had fought an engagement which gave him complete control of the road to Richmond and resulted in the loss to the Confederates of Generals Stuart and James B. Gordon. Merritt's brigade first entered Yellow Tavern and secured possession of the turnpike. The other Union divisions being brought up, Custer with his own brigade, supported by Chapman's brigade of Wilson's division, made a mounted charge which was brilliantly executed, followed by a dash at the Southern line which received the charge in a stationary position. This charge resulted in the capture of two guns. Then, while Gibbs and Devin forced the Confederate right and center, Gregg charged in the rear and the battle was won.

At Deep Bottom, too, July 28th, occurred a brilliant fight which is worthy of more than passing notice.

The Second United States Cavalry led the advance on the 27th and took the New Market road in the direction of Richmond. When close to the Confederate pickets a dashing charge was made, forcing the foe back rapidly. On the afternoon of the following day the Union cavalry pickets were furiously attacked, and before the leading troops could dismount and conduct the led horses to the rear, an entire brigade of

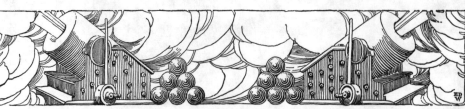

WHERE THE CAVALRY RESTED—CASTLE MURRAY, NEAR AUBURN, VIRGINIA

In the fall of 1863 the headquarters of the Army of the Potomac were pitched for some days on the Warrentown Railroad near Auburn, Virginia. Near-by lay Dr. Murray's house, called the Castle, a picturesque gray stone edifice, beautifully contrasting with the dark green ivy which had partly overgrown it, and situated in a grove on an eminence known as Rockhill. Here General Pleasonton, commanding the cavalry, had his camp, his tents forming an effective picture when silhouetted by the setting sun against the gray walls of the Castle. At night the green lamps that showed the position of the general's camp would shine mysteriously over the trees, and the band of the Sixth United States Cavalry would make the stone walls echo to its martial music. The cavalry was resting after its desperate encounters at Gettysburg and its fights along the Rappahannock. But there remained much yet for the troopers to do.

Confederate infantry broke from the woods, and with colors flying advanced in splendid alignment across an open field. So closely were the advanced Union troops pressed, that despite the destruction wrought in the Southern ranks by the breech-loading carbines, there was danger of losing the led horses.

The following is quoted from the graphic description of this fight by Lieutenant (afterwards Colonel U. S. V.) William H. Harrison, Second United States Cavalry:

With a cheer which makes our hearts bound, the First New York Dragoons, the First United States, and the Sixth Pennsylvania on the run, dismount, and form themselves on the shattered lines of the Second and Fifth. A few volleys from our carbines make the line of the enemy's infantry waver, and in an instant the cry is heard along our entire line, "Charge! Charge!" We rush forward, firing as we advance; the Confederate colors fall, and so furious is our charge that the North Carolina brigade breaks in complete rout, leaving three stands of colors, all their killed and wounded, and many prisoners in our hands. The enemy did not renew the fight, and we remained in possession of the field until relieved by our infantry.

It was, however, in the fall of the year (1864) that under Sheridan's brilliant leadership the Union cavalry won its greatest laurels. On September 19th, at Opequon Creek, Sheridan's infantry and cavalry achieved a victory which sent the Confederates under Early "whirling through Winchester," as Sheridan tersely stated in a telegram which electrified the people of the North.

While essentially a battle participated in by all arms, the brilliant part taken by Wilson's division in a mounted charge which gained possession of the Winchester-Berryville turnpike, and the subsequent demoralizing attack of Averell's and Merritt's cavalry divisions on the Confederate rear, had much to do with the Union victory.

The most severe fighting on the part of the cavalry took place in the afternoon. Breckinridge's Confederate corps had

BURNETT'S HOUSE, NEAR COLD HARBOR

A CLOSER VIEW

Three days before these photographs were taken Brigadier-General Alfred T. A. Torbert, with an isolated command of cavalry, was holding the breastworks at Cold Harbor in face of a magnificent attack by a brigade of Confederate infantry. The troopers busy beneath the trees are some of the very men who stood off the long gray lines blazing with fire. In the lower photograph they have moved forward, so that we can study them more closely. They seem quite nonchalant, considering their recent experience, but that is a veteran's way. Burnett's house, here pictured, stood not far from the road leading from Old Church Hotel to Old Cold Harbor. It was along this road that Torbert pursued the Confederates in the afternoon of May 30th, and it was near this house that his division of Sheridan's Cavalry Corps bivouacked that night. The following morning he continued his pursuit, first driving the Confederates into their breastworks at Cold Harbor, and then executing a flank movement to the left, which forced the Southern infantry to fall back three-quarters of a mile farther. Sheridan ordered him to withdraw from this isolated position, and he returned to the scene of his bivouac near Burnett's house,

OLD CHURCH HOTEL NEAR COLD HARBOR

The very attitude of the rough and ready cavalryman with his curved saber shows the new confidence in itself of the Federal cavalry as reorganized by Sheridan in April, 1864. Here the photographer has caught a cavalry detail at one of the typical cross-roads taverns that played so important a part in the Virginia campaigns of that year. So successful is the picture that even the rude lettering "Old Church Hotel" on the quaint, old fashioned swinging sign can be made out. The scene is typical of the times. The reorganized Federal cavalry was proving of the greatest help to Grant in locating the enemy, particularly ahead of the main column as in the case of the fight at Old Church. In Grant's advance toward Richmond from North Anna, Sheridan's cavalry corps served as an advance

FOUR DAYS AFTER THE CAVALRY CLASH OF MAY 30, 1864

guard.   Torbert and Gregg with the First and Second Divisions formed the guard for the left flank.   On May 27th Torbert crossed the Pamunkey at Hanover Ferry, captured Hanover Town, took part the following day in the sanguinary struggle at Hawes' Shop, and on the 29th picketed the country about Old Church Hotel seen in the picture, and toward Cold Harbor.   At 4 P.M. on May 30th, the clash at Old Church took place, and it was necessary to put in General Merritt with the Reserve Brigade.   The photograph was taken on June 4th, the day after the battle of Cold Harbor where the Federal loss was so severe.   The horses look sleek and well-conditioned in spite of the constant marching and fighting.

fallen back on Winchester, leaving General Early's flank protected by his cavalry, which was successfully attacked by General Devin's Second Brigade and driven in confusion toward Winchester. Then within easy supporting distance of each other, the First Brigade, the Second Brigade, and the Reserve Brigade moved forward without opposition until the open fields near Winchester were reached.

What followed is well described in Lieutenant Harrison's recollections: *

While awaiting in suspense our next movement the enemy's infantry was distinctly seen attempting to change front to meet our anticipated charge. Instantly, and while in the confusion incident to their maneuver, the Second Brigade burst upon them, the enemy's infantry breaking into complete rout and falling back a confused and broken mass.

Immediately after, the Union reserve brigade under the gallant Lowell, formed to the left of the position from which the Second Brigade, under Devin, had just charged. They rode out fearlessly within five hundred yards of the Confederate line of battle, on the left of which, resting on an old earthwork was a two-gun battery. The order was given to charge the line and get the guns. Lieutenant Harrison continues:

At the sound of the bugle we took the trot, the gallop, and then the charge. As we neared their line we were welcomed by a fearful musketry fire, which temporarily confused the leading squadron, and caused the entire brigade to oblique slightly to the right. Instantly, officers cried out, "Forward! Forward!" The men raised their sabers, and responded to the command with deafening cheers. Within a hundred yards of the enemy's line we struck a blind ditch, but crossed it without breaking our front. In a moment we were face to face with the enemy. They stood as if awed by the heroism of the brigade, and in an instant broke in complete rout, our men sabering them as they vainly sought safety in flight.

* Everglade to Cañon, N. Y., 1873.

[248]

A CUSTER FAMILY GROUP

Two Union cavalrymen distinguished in the final "Valley" campaigns appear here—George A. Custer and his brother, Thomas W. The lady whose presence adds such charm to the striking group had become Mrs. George A. Custer just before Grant's campaign opened—in February, 1864. The September following, her husband took command of the Third Cavalry Division in Sheridan's army. In April, 1865, he recalled to his men an astonishing record for the division while serving under him. It had captured every piece of artillery that had opened upon it! A worthy brother to such a leader was "Colonel Tom." Having enlisted at sixteen, fought in the West, and served as aide-de-camp on his brother's staff, he became second lieutenant of Co. B., Sixth Michigan Cavalry, in November, 1864, when only nineteen. At Namozine Church, April 2, 1865, he captured a stand of colors, and four days later, at Sailor's Creek, performed the remarkable feat of leaping his horse over the Confederate works, and seizing another stand of colors. His horse was shot under him. He was severely wounded, but refused to go to the rear for treatment until his brother placed him under arrest. This record of two flag-captures is believed to have been held by no other officer in the Federal army. After the war, the daring *sabreur* entered the regular cavalry and rose to the rank of lieutenant-colonel. He served under his brother, and fell at his side on that fatal day in Montana, June 25, 1876—the "Custer Massacre."

The charging force emerged from the fight with two guns, three stands of colors, and over three hundred Confederate prisoners. Altogether there had been six distinct charges by parts of the First Cavalry Division—two by the Second Brigade and one by the First Brigade; one by the Second Brigade and one by the Reserve Brigade against Early's infantry; and one, the final charge, in which all three of the brigades joined. General Custer describes the scene in graphic language:

At this time five brigades of cavalry were moving on parallel lines; most, if not all, of the brigades moved by brigade front, regiments being in parallel columns of squadrons. One continuous and heavy line of skirmishers covered the advance, using only the carbine, while the line of brigades, as they advanced across the country, the bands playing the national airs, presented in the sunlight one moving mass of glittering sabers. This, combined with the various and bright-colored banners and battle-flags, intermingled here and there with the plain blue uniforms of the troops, furnished one of the most inspiring as well as imposing scenes of martial grandeur ever witnessed upon a battlefield.

The Union victory at Opequon came at a time when its moral effect was most needed in the North, and restored the fertile Shenandoah valley to the Union armies, after a long series of humiliating reverses in that granary of the Confederacy.

A month later Custer encountered three brigades of Confederate cavalry under Rosser near Tom's Brook Crossing. Merrit at about the same time struck the cavalry of Lomax and Johnson on the Valley pike, the Federal line of battle extending across the Valley. The fighting was desperate on both sides, being essentially a saber contest. For two hours charges were given and received in solid masses, boot-to-boot, the honors being almost equally divided—the Confederates successfully holding the center while the Federal cavalry pushed back the flanks.

This finally weakened the Confederates, and as both their

GENERAL TORBERT IN THE SHENANDOAH

This photograph, made in the Shenandoah Valley in the fall of 1864, shows General Alfred T. A. Torbert, immaculately clad in a natty uniform, on the steps of a beautiful vine-clad cottage. Virginia homes such as this fared but badly in that terrible October. The black shame of war spread over the valley and rose in the smoke from burning barns. Grant had resolved that Shenandoah should no longer be allowed to act as a granary for the armies of the Confederacy. Sheridan and his men had orders ruthlessly to destroy all supplies that could not be carried away. The Confederate cavalry clung desperately to his rear, and gave so much annoyance that on October 8th Sheridan directed Torbert "to give Rosser a drubbing next morning or get whipped himself." The saber contest that ensued at Tom's Brook was the last attempt of the Confederate cavalry to reestablish their former supremacy. The sight of the devastated valley spurred the Southern troopers to the most valiant attacks, in spite of their inferior equipment. Again and again were charges made and returned on both sides. For two hours the honors were almost even, the Confederates holding the center, while the Federal cavalry pushed back the flanks. Finally Merritt and Custer ordered a charge along the whole line, and at last the Confederates broke.

flanks gave way, Merritt and Custer ordered a charge along their entire line. The retreat of Rosser's force became a panic-stricken rout, which continued for twenty-six miles up the Shenandoah valley. Eleven pieces of artillery, three hundred and thirty prisoners, ambulances, caissons, and even the headquarters' wagons of the Confederate commanders were captured by the Federal troops.

Early ascribed his defeat to Sheridan's superiority in numbers and equipment, and to the fact that Lomax's cavalry was armed entirely with rifles and had no sabers; that as a consequence they could not fight on horseback, and in open country could not successfully fight on foot with large bodies of well-trained cavalry.

In the brilliant part taken by Sheridan's cavalry in retrieving the misfortunes of the morning of October 19, 1864, when the Union camp at Cedar Creek was surprised and routed—with " Sheridan only twenty miles away "—resulting in the final defeat and pursuit of the Confederate army, the Federal cavalry alone captured 45 pieces of artillery, 32 caissons, 46 army wagons, 672 prisoners, and an enormous quantity of other property.

This battle, which Sheridan's magnetic presence turned into a great victory, was followed by a number of small but highly successful cavalry movements, culminating on March 27, 1865, in Sheridan's veteran cavalry corps joining the Army of the Potomac in front of Petersburg for the final campaign against Lee.

In the Valley campaign Sheridan's cavalry captured 2556 prisoners, 71 guns, 29 battle-flags, 52 caissons, 105 army wagons, 2557 horses, 1000 horse equipments, and 7152 beef cattle. It destroyed, among other things, 420,742 bushels of wheat, 780 barns, and over 700,000 rounds of ammunition.

Meanwhile, during the years of vicissitudes which marked the evolution of the cavalry of the East, from a multitude of weak detachments lacking organization, equipment,

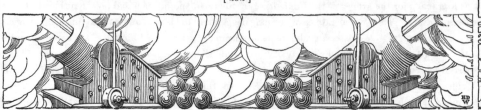

CAVALRY THAT CLOSED IN ON RICHMOND

While Sheridan's troopers were distinguishing themselves in the Shenandoah, the cavalry of the Army of the James, which was closing around Richmond, were doing their part. This photograph shows the Fifth Pennsylvania Cavalry, or "Cameron Dragoons," part of the second brigade, in winter-quarters. It was taken in the fall of 1864, on the scene of the engagement at Fair Oaks and Darbytown Road, October 29th of that year. Brigadier-General August V. Kautz had led them on a raid on the Petersburg and Weldon Railroad May 5th to 11th, and on the Richmond and Danville Railroad May 12th to 17th. On June 9th they went to Petersburg and remained there during the siege operations until the Southern Capital fell. During all this time they reversed the situation of the early part of the war, and incessantly harassed the Army of Northern Virginia by constant raids, cutting its communications, and attacking its supply trains.

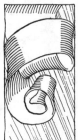

and training to a veteran army, filled with confidence in itself and in its commanders, the cavalry of the West had been equally unfortunate in its slow and discouraging development of fighting efficiency.

Under General Rosecrans, as early as 1862, the cavalry of the Army of the Cumberland was organized into three brigades under General David S. Stanley, but the mounted force actually at the disposal of its commander was but four thousand effective men. Although actively engaged, particularly in curbing the depredations of the Confederate cavalry under Forrest, its operations were not especially important. Nevertheless, at Stone's River, at Knoxville, at Chickamauga, and at other important battles, the cavalry of the West did desperate fighting and, considering its numbers, was not lacking in efficiency.

The cavalry which General Sherman assembled for his Atlanta campaign numbered about fifteen thousand sabers, organized into four divisions, and it participated with credit in all the celebrated movements and engagements of Sherman's army between May and August, 1864. Protecting the rear and preventing the destruction of the Nashville and Chattanooga Railroad by Wheeler's enterprising cavalry, some Union cavalry under Rousseau remained at Decatur until by a rapid and circuitous march around Johnston's Confederate army, in which he destroyed immense quantities of stores and damaged several railroads, Rousseau joined Sherman near Atlanta. After the fall of the latter city, a cavalry division of over five thousand men under Kilpatrick, accompanied Sherman on his famous march to the sea.

Up to this time the activities of the Union cavalry in the Southwest, while noted for boldness and celerity of movement, for endurance, and for accomplishment of results, though hampered by many drawbacks, were not yet distinguished by any of those great cavalry combats which marked the development of the cavalry of the Army of the Potomac.

RICHMOND AT LAST—APRIL, 1865

There is no need now for the troopers' carbines which can be seen projecting beside their saddles just as the cavalry rode into Richmond. The smoke still rising from the city's ruins seems to be the last great shuddering sigh of the Confederacy. The sight of the stark, blackened walls rising around them in the noonday sun brings but little joy to the hearts of the troopers. These ruined piles of brick and mortar are the homes of their brothers who fought a good fight. A few days from now, in the fullness of their hearts, the Union soldiers will be cheering their erstwhile foes at Appomattox. One more cavalry exploit, the capture of Lee's provision trains by Sheridan, which Grant in his delicacy did not reveal to the stricken commander, and the cavalry operations are over. Horses and men go back to the pursuits of peace.

Towards the close of October, 1864, however, General James H. Wilson, who had commanded a cavalry division in Sheridan's Army of the Shenandoah, and who had been instrumental in raising the efficiency of the cavalry service through the Cavalry Bureau, reported to Sherman, in Alabama, and began a thorough reorganization, a remounting and re-equipping of the cavalry corps of Sherman's army.

Wilson's cavalry corps speedily made itself felt as an integral part of the army, taking a prominent part in the battle of Franklin, scoring a decisive victory over Forrest's cavalry under Chalmers, and pressing the foe so closely that the Confederate troopers were actually driven into the Harpeth River. This decisive action of the Union cavalry prevented Forrest from turning Schofield's left flank and cutting his line of retreat.

In the battle of Nashville, which followed (December 15–16, 1864), Wilson's dismounted cavalry gallantly stormed the strong Confederate earthworks side by side with their comrades of the infantry. General Thomas mentions the part taken by this cavalry as follows:

Whilst slightly swinging to the left, [the cavalry] came upon a redoubt containing four guns, which was splendidly carried by assault, at 1 P.M., by a portion of Hatch's division, dismounted, and the captured guns turned upon the enemy. A second redoubt, stronger than the first, was next assailed and carried by the same troops that carried the first position, taking four more guns and about three hundred prisoners. The infantry, McArthur's division, on the left of the cavalry, . . . participated in both of the assaults; and, indeed, the dismounted cavalry seemed to vie with the infantry who should first gain the works; as they reached the position nearly simultaneously, both lay claim to the artillery and prisoners captured.

But the gallant part taken by Wilson's cavalry in these operations is best exemplified by the spoils of war. During and after the battle of Nashville, and including prisoners taken in the hospitals at Franklin, the Union cavalry captured 2 strong redoubts, 32 field guns, 11 caissons, 12 colors, 3232

THE FEDERAL CAVALRY AND THEIR REWARD—MAY, 1865

Shoulders squared, accouterments shining, all of the troops in perfect alignment, a unified, splendidly equipped and disciplined body, the Federal cavalry marched up Pennsylvania Avenue on that glorious sunshiny day in May when the Union armies held their grand review in Washington.   What a change from the long night rides and the terrible moments of the crashing charge was this holiday parade, when not a trooper thought of sleeping in the saddle which had often proved his only bed.   The battles are over now. Never again will their ears be riven by the agonized shriek of a wounded horse, said by many a cavalryman to be the most horrible sound in the field of battle.   Never again will they bend over the silent body of a wounded friend.   Men die more quietly than their mounts.   This is an arm of the service that proved itself. From early disappointments and disasters, and dissipation of energy in useless details, it emerged a wonderfully effective fighting force that did much to hasten the surrender of the exhausted Confederacy.

prisoners (including 1 general officer), 1 bridge train of 80 pontoons, and 125 wagons. Its own losses were 122 officers and men killed, 1 field-gun, 521 wounded, and 259 missing.

The following spring, while Wilson and his horsemen were sapping the very life blood of the Confederacy, Sheridan and his cavalry of the Army of the Potomac had been playing a most important part in the grand operations of that remarkable army, now under the direction of the inexorable Grant.

After joining Grant in front of Petersburg on March 27, 1865, Sheridan received instruction from his chief to move with his three cavalry divisions of nine thousand men near or through Dinwiddie, reaching the right and rear of the Confederate army, without attempting to attack the Confederates in position. Should the latter remain entrenched, Sheridan was to destroy the Danville and South Side railroads, Lee's only avenues of supply; and then either return to the Army of the Potomac, or to join Sherman in North Carolina. History shows that two of the Confederate infantry divisions and all of Lee's cavalry failed to push back five brigades of Sheridan's cavalry, fighting dismounted, in an effort to cut off the Confederate retreat.

In the desperate fighting which took place in the days following, it was the same splendid cavalry at Five Forks, which dashed dismounted over the Southern entrenchments, carrying all before them.

And finally, on April 6th, at Sailor's Creek, after desperate and exhausting fighting by Custer's and Devin's divisions, it was Crook with his cavalry which intercepted the Confederate line of retreat, cut off three of Lee's hard-pressed infantry divisions, and made possible the surrender at Appomattox of the gallant but exhausted Army of Northern Virginia.

CHAPTER
TEN

———

CAVALRY LEADERS
NORTH AND SOUTH

———

CUSTER AND HIS DOG

SHERIDAN AND HIS RIGHT-HAND MEN

This photograph shows Sheridan and his leaders, who drove Early and the Confederate cavalry from the Shenandoah Valley, and brought the Federal cavalry to the zenith of its power. Sheridan stands at the extreme left of the picture. Next to him is General Forsyth, and General Merritt is seated at the table. General

Devin stands with his hand on his hip, and Custer leans easily back in his chair. This is a ceremonious photograph; each leader wears the uniform of his rank. Even Custer has abandoned his favorite velvet suit. Together with the facing photograph, this offers an interesting study in the temperament of the Union cavalry leaders.

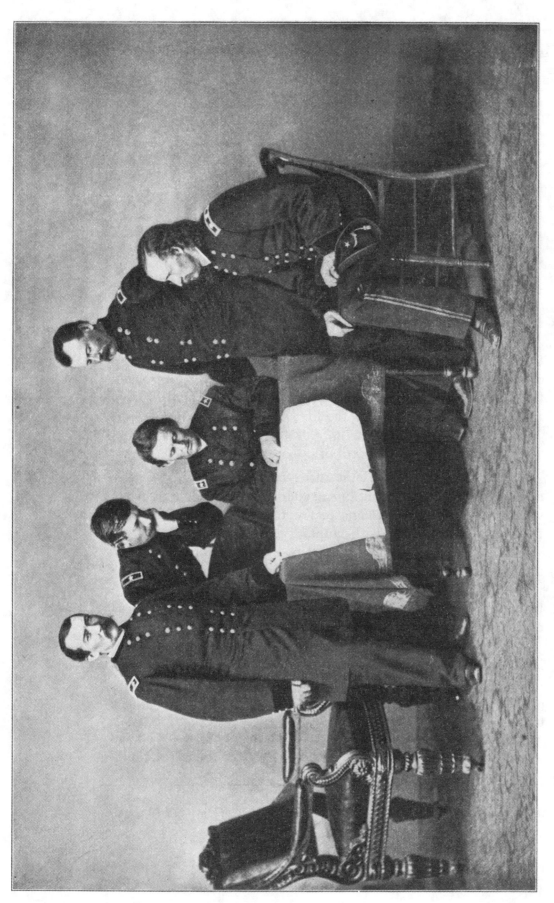

A STUDY IN TEMPERAMENT OF THE MEN WHO LED THE FEDERAL CAVALRY

The photographer has evidently requested the distinguished sitters to inspect a map, as if they were planning some actual movement such as that which "sent Early whirling through Winchester." All but Sheridan have been obliging. General Forsyth is leaning over, hand on chin, one foot on a rung of Merritt's chair. Merritt has cast down his eyes and bowed his head above the map. General Devin is leaning slightly forward in an attentive position. Custer alertly surveys his chief. But Sheridan, his hand clenched beside him, still gazes resolutely at the camera. These were the leaders who stood between the Confederate army and Washington, the capture of which might have meant foreign intervention.

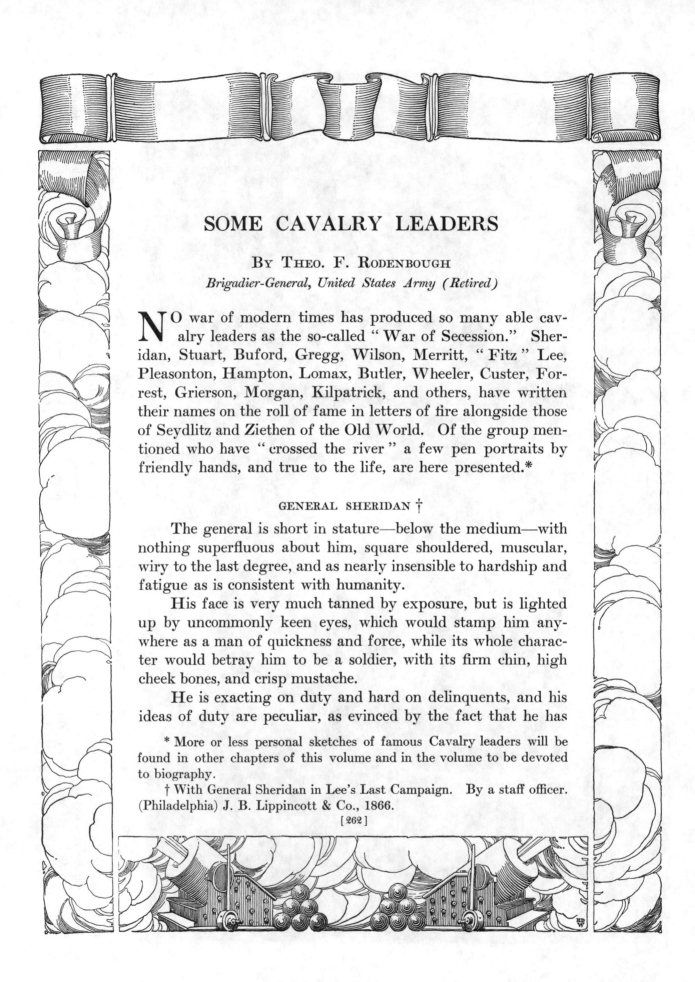

SOME CAVALRY LEADERS

BY THEO. F. RODENBOUGH
Brigadier-General, United States Army (Retired)

NO war of modern times has produced so many able cavalry leaders as the so-called "War of Secession." Sheridan, Stuart, Buford, Gregg, Wilson, Merritt, "Fitz" Lee, Pleasonton, Hampton, Lomax, Butler, Wheeler, Custer, Forrest, Grierson, Morgan, Kilpatrick, and others, have written their names on the roll of fame in letters of fire alongside those of Seydlitz and Ziethen of the Old World. Of the group mentioned who have "crossed the river" a few pen portraits by friendly hands, and true to the life, are here presented.*

GENERAL SHERIDAN †

The general is short in stature—below the medium—with nothing superfluous about him, square shouldered, muscular, wiry to the last degree, and as nearly insensible to hardship and fatigue as is consistent with humanity.

His face is very much tanned by exposure, but is lighted up by uncommonly keen eyes, which would stamp him anywhere as a man of quickness and force, while its whole character would betray him to be a soldier, with its firm chin, high cheek bones, and crisp mustache.

He is exacting on duty and hard on delinquents, and his ideas of duty are peculiar, as evinced by the fact that he has

* More or less personal sketches of famous Cavalry leaders will be found in other chapters of this volume and in the volume to be devoted to biography.

† With General Sheridan in Lee's Last Campaign. By a staff officer. (Philadelphia) J. B. Lippincott & Co., 1866.

MAJOR–GENERAL PHILIP HENRY SHERIDAN

General Sheridan was the leader who relieved the Union cavalry from waste of energy and restored it an arm of the service as effective and terrible to the Confederacy as the Southern cavalry had been to the North at the outset of the war. He was born at Albany, N. Y., 1831, and graduated at West Point in 1853. In May, 1862, he was appointed colonel of the Second Michigan Cavalry, and served in northern Mississippi. In July he was appointed brigadier-general of volunteers and distinguished himself on October 8th at the battle of Perryville. He commanded a division of the Army of the Cumberland at Stone's River, and was appointed major-general of volunteers early in 1863. He took part in the pursuit of General Van Dorn, afterwards aided in the capture of Manchester, Tennessee, on June 27th, and was in the battle of Chickamauga. In the battles around Chattanooga he attracted the attention of General Grant. In April, 1864, he was placed in command of the cavalry corps of the Army of the Potomac, and its brilliant exploits under his leadership culminated in the death of General J. E. B. Stuart at Yellow Tavern, where the Confederates were defeated. In August, 1864, he was placed in command of the Army of the Shenandoah. He defeated General Early at Opequon Creek, Fisher's Hill, and Cedar Creek, and captured 5,000 of his men and several guns. He drove the Confederates from the valley and laid it waste. On September 10th he was made brigadier-general, and in November major-general. In July, 1865, he received the thanks of Congress for his distinguished services. He died at Nonquitt, Mass., on August 5, 1888.

THE LEADER'S EYES

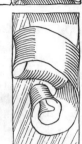

never issued orders of encouragement or congratulations to his troops before or after campaigns or battles. He has apparently taken it for granted that all under his command would do as well as they could, and they did so quite as a matter of course. And to this soldierly view the troops always responded. Understanding so well what they were fighting for and the issues at stake, they would not fight harder to accomplish results simply for the satisfaction of having them recounted. . . .

Though always easy of approach, the general has little to say in busy times. Set teeth and a quick way tell when things do not go as they ought, and he has a manner on such occasions that stirs to activity all within sight, for a row seems brewing that nobody wants to be under when it bursts. Notwithstanding his handsome reputation for cursing, he is rather remarkably low-voiced, particularly on the field, where, as sometimes happens, almost everybody else is screaming. "Damn you, sir, don't yell at me," he once said to an officer who came galloping up with some bad news, and was roaring it out above the din of battle. In such moments the general leans forward on his horse's neck, and hunching his shoulders up to his ears, gives most softly spoken orders in a slow, deliberate way, as though there were niches for all the words in his hearer's memory, and they must be measured very carefully to fit exactly, that none of them be lost in the carrying. . . .

The general has a remarkable eye for topography, not only in using to the best advantage the peculiarities of the country through which he is campaigning, either for purposes of marching, assaults, or defense, but he can foresee with accuracy, by studying a map, how far the country will be available for these purposes.

He has been called ruthless and cruel because, in obedience to the orders of the officers appointed over him, he was compelled, by the stern necessities of war, to destroy property in the Shenandoah valley, and to take from the war-ridden people

MAJOR–GENERAL JAMES EWELL BROWN STUART, C.S.A.

In the hat on General Stuart's knee appears the plume which grew to symbolize the dash and gallantry of the man himself. Plume and hat were captured, and Stuart himself narrowly escaped, at Verdiersville, August 17, 1862. "I intend," he wrote, " to make the Yankees pay for that hat." Less than a week later he captured Pope's personal baggage and horses, and for many days thereafter the Federal general's uniform was on exhibition in a Richmond store window—a picturesque and characteristic reprisal. Born in Virginia in 1833, Stuart graduated at the United States Military Academy in 1854. He saw service on the Texas frontier, in Kansas, and against the Cheyenne Indians before the outbreak of the war. On April, 1861, he resigned from the United States Army and joined the Confederacy in his native State. He won distinction at Bull Run, and also the rank of brigadier-general. Stuart rode twice around the Army of the Potomac when McClellan was in command, and played a conspicuous part in the Seven Days before Richmond. At the second Bull Run, at Antietam, by a destructive raid into Pennsylvania, at Fredericksburg, and at Chancellorsville Stuart added to his laurels. He was too late for anything except the last day of Gettysburg, where the strengthened Union cavalry proved his match. He was mortally wounded at Yellow Tavern May 11, 1864, in a pitched battle with Sheridan's cavalry.

there what their friends had left them of supplies for man and beast. As he rode down the Martinsburg pike in his four-horse wagon, heels on the front seat, and smoking a cigar, while behind him his cavalry was destroying the provender that could not be carried away, the inhabitants of the Valley doubtless regarded him as history regards the emperor who fiddled while Rome was burning, and would not now believe, what is the simple truth, that this destruction was distasteful to him, and that he was moved by the distress he was obliged to multiply upon these unfortunate people, whose evil fate had left them in the ruinous track of war so long. But the Shenandoah valley was the well-worn pathway of invasion, and it became necessary that this long avenue leading to our homes should be stripped of the sustenance that rendered it possible to subsist an army there.

GENERAL STUART

Stuart was undoubtedly the most brilliant and widely known *sabreur* of his time. The term is used advisedly to describe the accomplished horseman who, while often fighting dismounted, yet by training and the influence of his environment was at his best as a leader of mounted men.

Stuart as a cadet at the Military Academy is thus described by General Fitzhugh Lee:

"I recall his distinguishing characteristics, which were a strict attention to his military duties, an erect, soldierly bearing, an immediate and almost thankful acceptance of a challenge to fight from any cadet who might in any way feel himself aggrieved, and a clear, metallic ringing voice."

In the Indian country as a subaltern in the cavalry, his commanding officer, Major Simonson, thus wrote of him:

"Lieutenant Stuart was brave and gallant, always prompt in the execution of orders, and reckless of danger or exposure. I considered him at that time one of the most promising young officers in the United States army."

MAJOR–GENERAL JOHN BUFORD

General Buford was one of the foremost cavalry leaders of the North. He is credited by many with having chosen the field on which the battle of Gettysburg was fought. He was born in 1826 in Woodford County, Kentucky, graduated at West Point in 1848, and saw service against the Indians. In November, 1861, he attained to the rank of major, and in July, 1862, he was made brigadier-general of volunteers. While in command of a cavalry brigade in 1862, Buford was wounded in the second battle of Bull Run. In McClellan's Maryland campaign, at Fredericksburg, and in the spirited cavalry engagements at Brandy Station, he played his part nobly. In Pennsylvania he displayed remarkable ability and opened the battle of Gettysburg before the arrival of Reynolds' infantry on July 1st. The Comte de Paris says in his "History of the Civil War in America": "It was Buford who selected the battlefield where the two armies were about to measure their strength." After taking part in the pursuit of Lee and subsequent operations in central Virginia, he withdrew on sick leave in November, 1863, and died in Washington on December 16th, receiving a commission as major-general only on the day of his death.

As a Confederate colonel at the first Bull Run battle, General Early reported:

"Stuart did as much toward saving the battle of First Manassas as any subordinate who participated in it; and yet he has never received any credit for it, in the official reports or otherwise. His own report is very brief and indefinite."

In a letter to President Davis, General J. E. Johnston recommended Stuart's promotion, which was made September 24, 1861:

"He is a rare man, wonderfully endowed by nature with the qualities necessary for an officer of light cavalry. Calm, firm, acute, active, and enterprising, I know of no one more competent than he to estimate the occurrences before him at their true value. If you add a real brigade of cavalry to this army, you can find no better brigadier-general to command it."

In an account of the raid into Pennsylvania (October, 1862) Colonel Alexander K. McClure speaks of the behavior of Stuart's command in passing through Chambersburg:

"General Stuart sat on his horse in the center of the town, surrounded by his staff, and his command was coming in from the country in large squads, leading their old horses and riding the new ones they had found in the stables hereabouts. General Stuart is of medium size, has a keen eye, and wears immense sandy whiskers and mustache. His demeanor to our people was that of a humane soldier. In several instances his men commenced to take private property from stores, but they were arrested by General Stuart's provost-guard. In a single instance only, that I heard of, did they enter a store by intimidating the proprietor. All of our stores and shops were closed, and with very few exceptions were not disturbed." *

General John B. Gordon, in his "Reminiscences" relates:

"An incident during the battle of Chancellorsville [illustrates] the bounding spirits of that great cavalry leader, General 'Jeb' Stuart. After Jackson's fall, Stuart was

* Campaigns of Stuart's Cavalry.

[268]

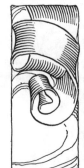

LIEUTENANT–GENERAL WADE HAMPTON, C.S.A.

General Hampton was the leader selected three months after Stuart's death to command all of Lee's cavalry. Although it had become sadly decimated, Hampton lived up to his reputation, and fought effectively to the very end of the war. His last command was the cavalry in Johnston's army, which opposed Sherman's advance from Savannah in 1865. Hampton was born in Columbia, S. C., in 1818. After graduating in law at the University of South Carolina, he gave up his time to the management of his extensive estates. At the outbreak of the war he raised and equipped from his private means the "Hampton's Legion," which did good service throughout the war. He fought at the head of his Legion at Bull Run and in the Peninsula campaign, was wounded at Fair Oaks, and soon afterward was commissioned brigadier-general. He served brilliantly at Gettysburg, where he was wounded three times, and was made major-general on August 3d following. He was engaged in opposing the advance of Sheridan toward Lynchburg in 1864, and showed such high qualities as a cavalry commander that he was commissioned lieutenant-general in August of that year, and placed in command of all of Lee's cavalry. He was Governor of South Carolina from 1876 to 1878; then United States Senator until 1891. He was United States Commissioner of Railroads, 1893 to 1897. His death occurred in 1902.

designated to lead Jackson's troops in the final charge. The
soul of this brilliant cavalry commander was as full of sentiment as it was of the spirit of self-sacrifice. He was as musical
as he was brave. He sang as he fought. Placing himself at
the head of Jackson's advancing lines and shouting to them
' Forward,' he at once led off in that song, ' Won't you come
out of the Wilderness?' He changed the words to suit the
occasion. Through the dense woodland, blending in strange
harmony with the rattle of rifles, could be distinctly heard
that song and words, ' Now, Joe Hooker, won't you come
out of the Wilderness?' "

GENERAL BUFORD *

But something more than West Point and frontier service
was needed to produce a Buford. He was "no sapling chance-
sown by the fountain." He had had years of training and experience in his profession, and although they were precious and
indispensable, they could not have produced the same results
which were realized in him, had it not been for the honorable
deeds of his ancestors and the hereditary traits developed and
transmitted by them. Such men as Buford are not the fruit
of chance. Springing, as he did, from a sturdy Anglo-Nor-
man family long settled in the " debatable land " on the bor-
ders of England and Scotland, he came by the virtues of the
strong hand through inheritance. His kinsmen, as far back
as they can be traced, were stout soldiers, rough fighters, and
hard riders, accustomed to lives of vicissitude, and holding what
they had under the good old rule, the simple plan, " Those to
take who have the power, and those to keep who can." Men of
his name were the counsellors and companions of kings, and
gained renown in the War of the Roses, and in the struggle for

* Major-General John Buford. By Major-General James H. Wilson,
U. S. V., Brevet Major-General, U. S. A. Oration delivered at Gettysburg on July 1, 1895.

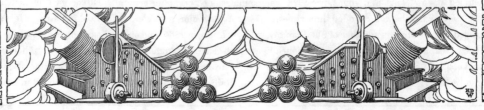

MAJOR–GENERAL WESLEY MERRITT

General Merritt did his share toward achieving the momentous results of Gettysburg. With his reserve brigade of cavalry on the Federal left, he caused Law to detach a large force from the Confederate main line in order to protect his flank and rear. Merritt served with distinction throughout the Civil War and later in the Spanish-American War. He was born in New York City in 1836, graduated at West Point in 1860, and was assigned to the Second Dragoons. In April, 1862, he was promoted to be captain. He rode with Stoneman on his famous Richmond raid in April and May, 1863, and was in command of the cavalry reserve at Gettysburg. Merritt commanded a cavalry division in the Shenandoah Valley campaign under Sheridan from August, 1864, to March, 1865, and in the final Richmond campaign the cavalry corps. After rendering service in the Spanish-American War, and commanding the forces in the Philippines, he was retired from active service in June, 1900. He died December 3, 1910.

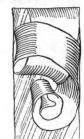

dominion over France. In the wars between the Stuarts and the Commonwealth they were "king's men." . . .

A distinguished officer of the same arm of the service, said of him that as a captain of dragoons "he was considered," in a regiment famed for its dashing and accomplished officers, "as the soldier *par excellence*." He adds in loving admiration, that "no man could be more popular or sincerely beloved by his fellow officers, nor could any officer be more thoroughly respected by his men, than he was. His company had no superior in the service." The same distinguished officer, writing after his career had closed in death, says, "He was a splendid cavalry officer, and one of the most successful in the service; was modest, yet brave; unostentatious, but prompt and persevering; ever ready to go where duty called him, and never shrinking from action however fraught with peril." . . .

Speaking many years after of the part taken in this great day's work * by Buford's cavalry, General F. A. Walker, in the "History of the Second Army Corps," uses the following language: "When last it was my privilege to see General Hancock in November, 1885, he pointed out to me from Cemetery Hill the position occupied by Buford at this critical juncture, and assured me that among the most inspiring sights of his military career was the splendid spectacle of that gallant cavalry as it stood there, unshaken and undaunted, in the face of the advancing Confederate infantry." No higher commendation for the cavalry can be found. Its services have been generally minimized, if not entirely ignored, by popular historians, but no competent critic can read the official reports or the Comte de Paris' "History of the Civil War in America" without giving the cavalry the highest praise for its work on this day, and throughout this campaign. "To Buford was assigned the post of danger and responsibility. He, and he alone, selected the ground," says that trustworthy historian, "upon which unforeseen circumstances were about to bring the two armies into

* The First Day, Gettysburg, July 1, 1863.

MAJOR–GENERAL NATHAN BEDFORD FORREST, C.S.A.

General Forrest was one of the born cavalry leaders. Daring and resourceful in every situation, he and his hard-riding raiders became a source of terror throughout the Mississippi Valley. He was born near the site of Chapel Hill, Tennessee, on July 31, 1821, attended school for about six months, became a horse and cattle trader, and slave trader at Memphis. He cast in his lot with the Confederacy and entered the army as a private in June, 1861. In July he organized a battalion of cavalry, of which he became lieutenant-colonel. He escaped from Fort Donelson when it surrendered to Grant, and as brigadier-general served in Kentucky under Bragg. Transferred to Northern Mississippi in November, 1863, Forrest was made major-general on December 4th of that year, and at the close of the following year was placed in command of all the cavalry with the Army of the Tennessee. On January 24, 1865, he was put in command of the cavalry in Alabama, Mississippi, and east Louisiana, and was appointed lieutenant-general on February 28th. He met defeat at the hands of General James H. Wilson at Selma, Ala., in March, 1865, and surrendered to General Canby at Gainesville the following May. He remained in business in Tennessee until he died in 1877—one of the most striking characters developed by the war.

hostile contact. Neither Meade nor Lee had any knowledge of it. . . . Buford, who, when he arrived on the evening of [June] 30th, had guessed at one glance the advantages to be derived from these positions, did not have time to give a description of them to Meade and receive his instructions. The unfailing indications to an officer of so much experience, revealed to Buford the approach of the enemy. Knowing that Reynolds was within supporting distance of him, he boldly resolved to risk everything in order to allow the latter time to reach Gettysburg in advance of the Confederate army. This first inspiration of a cavalry officer and a true soldier decided, in every respect, the fate of the campaign. It was Buford who selected the battlefield where the two armies were about to measure their strength."

GENERAL WADE HAMPTON *

Wade Hampton entered the military service of the Confederate States as colonel of the Hampton Legion, South Carolina Volunteers, June 12, 1861, said legion consisting of eight companies of infantry, four companies of cavalry, and two companies of artillery. With the infantry of his command, Colonel Hampton participated in the first battle of Bull Run, July 21, 1861, where he was wounded. He bore a part as a brigade commander in the subsequent battles on the Peninsula of Virginia, from the beginning of operations at Yorktown until the battle of Seven Pines, where he was again wounded. . . .

I have been often asked if General Hampton was a good tactician. If in a minor, technical sense, I answer to the best of my judgment, " No." I doubt if he ever read a technical book on tactics. He knew how to maneuver the units of his command so as to occupy for offensive or defensive action the strongest points of the battlefield, and that is about all there

* Butler and His Cavalry, 1861–1865. By U. R. Brooks (Columbia S. C.). The State Company, 1909.

MAJOR–GENERAL GEORGE ARMSTRONG CUSTER WITH GENERAL PLEASONTON

The *beau sabreur* of the Federal service is pictured here in his favorite velvet suit, with General Alfred Pleasonton, who commanded the cavalry at Gettysburg. This photograph was taken at Warrenton, Va., three months after that battle. At the time this picture was taken, Custer was a brigadier-general in command of the second brigade of the third division of General Pleasonton's cavalry. General Custer's impetuosity finally cost him his own life and the lives of his entire command at the hands of the Sioux Indians June 25, 1876. Custer was born in 1839 and graduated at West Point in 1861. As captain of volunteers he served with McClellan on the Peninsula. In June, 1863, he was made brigadier-general of volunteers and as the head of a brigade of cavalry distinguished himself at Gettysburg. Later he served with Sheridan in the Shenandoah, won honor at Cedar Creek, and was brevetted major-general of volunteers on October 19, 1864. Under Sheridan he participated in the battles of Five Forks, Dinwiddie Court House, and other important cavalry engagements of Grant's last campaign.

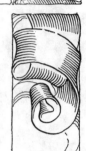
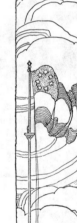

is in tactics. A successful strategist has a broader field for the employment of his military qualities. General Hampton appeared possessed of almost an instinctive topographical talent. He could take in the strong strategic points in the field of his operations with an accuracy of judgment that was surprising to his comrades. It was not necessary for him to study Jomini, Napoleon's "Campaigns," and other high authorities in the art of war. He was a law unto himself on such matters. According to the rules laid down in the books, he would do the most unmilitary things. He would hunt his antagonist as he would hunt big game in the forest. The celerity and audacity of his movements against the front, sometimes on the flank, then again in the rear, kept his enemies in a constant state of uncertainty and anxiety as to where and when they might expect him. With his wonderful powers of physical endurance, his alert, vigilant mind, his matchless horsemanship, no obstacles seemed to baffle his audacity or thwart his purpose.

GENERAL MERRITT *

Merritt was graduated in the class of 1860 at the Military Academy. He was twenty-four years of age. In scholarship he was rated at the middle of his class, and in the other soldierly qualities he was near the head. . . .

At the battle of the Opequon (Winchester), on September 19th, his division gave the most effective instance in a hundred years of war, of the use of a cavalry division in a pitched battle. He rode over Breckinridge's infantry and Fitzhugh Lee's cavalry and effectually broke the Confederate left. At this time Sheridan wrote to a friend, " I claim nothing for myself; my boys Merritt and Custer did it all.". . .

On the disastrous morning of October 19th, at Cedar

* General Wesley Merritt. By Lieutenant-Colonel Eben Swift, Eighth Cavalry. From the (March, 1911) Journal of the United States Cavalry Association.

MAJOR–GENERAL FITZHUGH LEE, C.S.A.

A nephew of the South's greatest commander, General Fitzhugh Lee did honor to his famous family. Along the Rappahannock and in the Shenandoah he measured swords with the Federal cavalry, and over thirty years later he was leading American forces in Cuba. He was born at Clermont, Va., in 1835, graduated at West Point in 1856, and from May, 1860, until the outbreak of the Civil War was instructor of cavalry at West Point. He resigned from the United States Army, and entered the Confederate service in 1861. He fought with Stuart's cavalry in almost all of the important engagements of the Army of Northern Virginia, first as colonel, from July, 1862, as brigadier-general, and from September, 1863, as major-general. He was severely wounded at Winchester, on September 19, 1864, and from March, 1865, until his surrender to General Meade at Farmville, was in command of all the cavalry of the Army of Northern Virginia. In 1896 he was sent to Cuba by President Cleveland as consul-general at Havana, and in May, 1898, when war with Spain seemed inevitable, was appointed major-general of volunteers, and placed in command of the Seventh Army Corps. He returned to Havana as Military Governor in January, 1899. He died in 1905.

Creek, Merritt's division blocked the way of Gordon's victorious Confederates, held its position north of Middletown all day, without assistance, then charged and, crossing the stream below the bridge, joined Custer in the pursuit to Fisher's Hill. In that campaign Merritt's division captured fourteen battle-flags, twenty-nine pieces of artillery, and more than three thousand prisoners. . . .

Merritt at his high prime was the embodiment of force. He was one of those rare men whose faculties are sharpened and whose view is cleared on the battlefield. His decisions were delivered with the rapidity of thought and were as clear as if they had been studied for weeks. He always said that he never found that his first judgment gained by time and reflection. In him a fiery soul was held in thrall to will. Never disturbed by doubt, or moved by fear, neither circumspect nor rash, he never missed an opportunity or made a mistake.

These were the qualities that recommended him to the confidence of that commander whose ideals were higher and more exacting than any other in our history. To his troops he was always a leader who commanded their confidence by his brave appearance, and his calmness in action, while his constant thoughtfulness and care inspired a devotion that was felt for few leaders of his rank.

GENERAL FORREST *

When the war broke out, Forrest was in the prime of his mental and physical powers. Over six feet in stature, of powerful frame, and of great activity and daring, with a personal prowess proved in many fierce encounters, he was a king among the bravest men of his time and country. He was among the first to volunteer when war broke out, and it was a matter of

* Recollections of a Virginian in the Mexican, Indian, and Civil Wars. By General Dabney Herndon Maury. (New York) Charles Scribner's Sons, 1894.

LIEUTENANT–GENERAL JOSEPH WHEELER, C.S.A.

Commander of Confederate forces in more than a hundred cavalry battles, General Wheeler well deserved the tribute of his erstwhile opponent, General Sherman, who once said: "In the event of war with a foreign country, Joe Wheeler is the man to command the cavalry of our army." He was born in 1836, and graduated at West Point in 1859. He served in the regular army until April, 1861, then entered the Confederate service. He commanded a brigade of infantry at Shiloh in April, 1862, and later in the year was transferred to the cavalry. He fought under Bragg in Kentucky at Perryville and in other engagements, and covered the retreat of Bragg's army to the southward. In January, 1863, he was commissioned major-general. In the Chattanooga campaigns Wheeler showed himself a brave and skilful officer. He harassed Sherman's flank during the march to Atlanta, and in August, 1864, led a successful raid in Sherman's rear as far north as the Kentucky line. In February, 1865, he was commissioned lieutenant-general, and continued in command of the cavalry in Johnston's army until its surrender. He served as a major-general in the Spanish-American War. He died in Brooklyn, January 25, 1906.

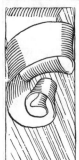

course that he should be the commander of the troops who flocked to his standard. From the very outset he evinced his extraordinary capacity for war, and in his long career of great achievement no defeat or failure was ever charged to him. . . .

When Forrest, with about twelve hundred men, set out in pursuit of Streight, he was more than a day behind him. Streight had several hundred more men in the saddle than Forrest, and being far in advance could replace a broken-down horse by a fresh one from the farms through which his route lay, while Forrest, when he lost a horse, lost a soldier, too; for no good horses were left for him. After a hot pursuit of five days and nights, during which he had lost two-thirds of his forces from broken-down horses, he overhauled his enemy and brought him to a parley. This conference took place in sight of a cut-off in the mountain road, Captain Morton and his horse artillery, which had been so long with Forrest, passing in sight along the road till they came to the cut-off, into which they would turn, reentering the road out of view, so that it seemed that a continuous stream of artillery was passing by. Forrest had so arranged that he stood with his back to the guns while Streight was facing them.

Forrest, in his characteristic way, described the scene to me. He said, " I seen him all the time he was talking, looking over my shoulder and counting the guns. Presently he said: ' Name of God! How many guns have you got? There's fifteen I've counted already!' Turning my head that way, I said, ' I reckon that's all that has kept up.' Then he said, ' I won't surrender till you tell me how many men you've got.' I said, ' I've got enough to whip you out of your boots.' To which he said, ' I won't surrender.' I turned to my bugler and said, ' Sound to mount!' Then he cried out ' I'll surrender!' I told him, ' Stack your arms right along there, Colonel, and march your men away down that hollow.'

"When this was done," continued Forrest, " I ordered my men to come forward and take possession of the arms.

MAJOR–GENERAL JAMES HARRISON WILSON AND STAFF

This brilliant cavalryman's demonstration of 1865 against Selma and Tuscaloosa, Alabama, in aid of General Canby s operations against Mobile and the center of the State, was one of the greatest cavalry raids in the West.   General Wilson was born in 1837, near Shawneetown, Illinois, and graduated at West Point in 1860. He was aide-de-camp to General McClellan on the Peninsula, and served in the engineering corps in the West until after Vicksburg and Chattanooga, when he was made brigadier-general of volunteers in October, 1863. In February, 1864, he was put in charge of the cavalry bureau at Washington, and later commanded the Third Division of Sheridan's reorganized cavalry.   October 5, 1864, he was brevetted major-general of volunteers for "gallant and meritorious services" during the war, and on the 24th of that month he was put in command of the cavalry corps of the Military Division of the Mississippi.   He took part in the battles of Franklin and Nashville, and in March, 1865, made his famous Selma raid.   In twenty-eight days Wilson had captured 288 guns and 6280 prisoners, including Jefferson Davis.   Five large iron works, three factories, numerous mills and immense quantities of supplies had been destroyed.   As a reward for these services, he was made major-general of volunteers on April 20, 1865.   General Wilson later served with distinction in the Spanish American War, and was also in command of the British and American troops in the siege at Pekin, China.

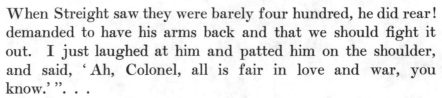

When Streight saw they were barely four hundred, he did rear! demanded to have his arms back and that we should fight it out. I just laughed at him and patted him on the shoulder, and said, 'Ah, Colonel, all is fair in love and war, you know.'". . .

Forrest knew nothing about tactics—could not drill a company. When first ordered to have his brigade ready for review, he was quite ignorant, but Armstrong told him what commands to give, and what to do with himself. . . .

Forrest will always stand as the great exponent of the power of the mounted riflemen to fight with the revolver when mounted and with the rifle on foot. His troops were not dragoons "who fought indifferently on foot or horseback," nor were they cavalry who fought only mounted and with sabers. Few of his command ever bore sabers, save some of his officers, who wore them as a badge of rank. None of Forrest's men could use the saber. He himself had no knowledge of its use, but he would encounter half a dozen expert *sabreurs* with his revolver.

GENERAL CUSTER *

It was here (Hanover, Pennsylvania, June, 1863) that the brigade first saw Custer. As the men of the Sixth, armed with their Spencer rifles, were deploying forward across the railroad into a wheat-field beyond, I heard a voice new to me, directly in rear of the portion of the line where I was, giving directions for the movement, in clear, resonant tones, and in a calm, confident manner, at once resolute and reassuring. Looking back to see whence it came, my eyes were instantly riveted upon a figure only a few feet distant, whose appearance amazed, if it did not for the moment amuse me. It was he who was giving the orders. At first, I thought he might be a staff-officer, conveying the commands of his chief. But it was at once apparent

* Personal Recollections of a Cavalryman. By J. H. Kidd, formerly Colonel, Sixth Michigan Cavalry. (Ionia, Mich.) Sentinel Printing Co.

BRIGADIER–GENERAL JOHN R. CHAMBLISS, C.S.A.

General John R. Chambliss was a Confederate cavalry leader who distinguished himself at Gettysburg. At Brandy Station, June 9, 1863, W. H. F. Lee had been wounded, and Colonel Chambliss had taken command of his brigade. On the night of June 24th Stuart left Robertson's and Jones' brigades to guard the passes of the Blue Ridge and started to move round the Army of the Potomac with the forces of Hampton, Fitzhugh Lee, and Chambliss, intending to pass between it and Centerville into Maryland and so rejoin Lee. The movements of the army forced him out of his way, so on the morning of the 30th he moved across country to Hanover, Chambliss in front and Hampton in the rear with Fitzhugh Lee well out on the flank. Chambliss attacked Kilpatrick at Hanover about 10 A.M., but was driven out before Hampton or Lee could come to his support.

MAJOR HENRY GILMOR, C.S.A.

Major Gilmor was born in Baltimore County, Maryland, in 1838. He entered the Confederate army at the outbreak of the Civil War, and was commissioned captain in 1862. In 1862–63 he was imprisoned for five months in Fort McHenry, at Baltimore, and in the latter year he raised a cavalry battalion, of which he was made major. Subsequently he commanded the First Confederate Regiment of Maryland, and in 1864 headed the advance of the forces of General Jubal A. Early into that State, and, being familiar with the country, made a successful raid north of Baltimore. He captured Frederick, Md., and created great alarm by his daring exploit so far north of the customary battlefields. In 1874 he became police commissioner of his native city. He died in 1883.

that he was *giving* orders, not transmitting them, and that he was in command of the line.

Looking at him closely, this is what I saw: An officer, superbly mounted, who sat his charger as if to the manner born. Tall, lithe, active, muscular, straight as an Indian and as quick in his movements, he had the fair complexion of a school-girl. He was clad in a suit of black velvet, elaborately trimmed with gold lace, which ran down the outer seams of his trousers, and almost covered the sleeves of his cavalry jacket. The wide collar of a navy-blue shirt was turned down over the collar of his velvet jacket, and a necktie of brilliant crimson was tied in a graceful knot at the throat, the long ends falling carelessly in front. The double rows of buttons on his breast were arranged in groups of twos, indicating the rank of brigadier-general. A soft black hat with wide brim adorned with a gilt cord, and rosette encircling a silver star, was worn turned down on one side, giving him a rakish air. His golden hair fell in graceful luxuriance nearly or quite to his shoulder, and his upper lip was garnished with a blonde mustache. A sword and belt, gilt spurs and top-boots completed his unique outfit.

A keen eye would have been slow to detect in that rider with the flowing locks and gaudy tie, in his dress of velvet and of gold, the master-spirit that he proved to be. That garb, fantastic as at first sight it appeared to be, was to be the distinguishing mark which, during all the remaining years of the war, like the white plume of Henry of Navarre, was to show us where, in the thickest of the fight, we were to seek our leader —for, where danger was, where swords were to cross, where Greek met Greek, there he was, always. Brave, but not reckless; self-confident, yet modest; ambitious, but regulating his conduct at all times by a high sense of honor and duty; eager for laurels, but scorning to wear them unworthily; ready and willing to act, but regardful of human life; quick in emergencies, cool and self-possessed, his courage was of the highest moral type, his perceptions were intuitions.

[284]

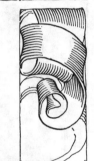

MAJOR–GENERAL HUGH JUDSON KILPATRICK

This daring cavalry leader was born in 1836 near Deckertown, New Jersey, and graduated at West Point in 1861. He entered the Federal service as captain in the Fifth New York Volunteers, generally known as Duryea's Zouaves. He was wounded at Big Bethel, June 10, 1861, and on September 25th he became lieutenant-colonel of the Second New York Cavalry. In the second battle of Bull Run, and on the left at Gettysburg, he served with conspicuous gallantry. In December, 1862, he was promoted to be colonel, and in June, 1863, to be brigadier-general of volunteers while he received the brevet of major and lieutenant-colonel in the Regular Army for repeated gallantry. In March, 1864, he made his celebrated Richmond raid and in April accompanied Sherman in his invasion of Georgia. He was wounded at Resasca, and at the close of the war he was brevetted brigadier-general in the Regular Army for "gallant and meritorious services in the capture of Fayetteville, North Carolina," and major-general for his services during the campaign under Sherman in the Carolinas. In June, 1865, he obtained the regular rank of major-general of volunteers. He died at Santiago in December, 1881.

GENERAL FITZHUGH LEE[*]

Major-General Fitzhugh Lee, or "Our Fitz" as he was affectionately called by his old comrades, won high distinction as a cavalryman in the Army of Northern Virginia, and since the war won higher distinction as a citizen.

After serving for a year at Carlisle Barracks as cavalry instructor of raw recruits, he reported to his regiment on the frontier of Texas, and was greatly distinguished in several fights for gallantry. In a fight with the Comanches, May 13, 1859, he was so severely wounded, being pierced through the lungs by an arrow, that the surgeons despaired of his life (especially as he had to be borne two hundred miles across the prairie in a horse litter), but he recovered and rejoined his command, and led a part of his company in January, 1860, in a very notable and successful fight with the Indians, in which he greatly distinguished himself in a single combat with a powerful Indian chief. . . .

In the campaign against Pope, and the Maryland Campaign (1862) his cavalry rendered most important service, of which General R. E. Lee said in his official report: "Its vigilance, activity, and courage were conspicuous; and to its assistance is due in a great measure some of the most important and delicate operations of the campaign." . . .

When Hampton was sent south, Lee was put in command of the entire cavalry corps of the Army of Northern Virginia, and only the break-up at Richmond prevented him from receiving his merited commission as lieutenant-general, which had been decided on by the Confederate President. . . .

When the war with Spain broke out he was made major-general of volunteers, and put in command of troops destined to capture Havana. After the close of the war he was kept

[*] Thirty-sixth Annual Reunion of the Association of the Graduates of the United States Military Academy, at West Point, New York, June 13, 1905.

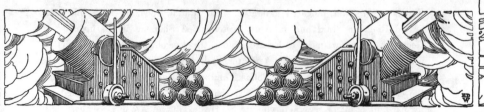

MAJOR–GENERAL LOVELL HARRISON ROUSSEAU

General Rousseau was born in Stanford, Lincoln County, Ky., in 1818. He fought in the Mexican War, distinguished himself at Buena Vista, and later settled in Louisville. In 1860 he raised the Fifth Kentucky regiment, of which he was made colonel, and in 1861 he was made brigadier-general. He served with great credit at Shiloh, and was made major-general of volunteers for gallant conduct at Perryville. He commanded the Fifth Division of the Army of the Cumberland at Stone River and at Chickamauga, and in 1864 made a cavalry raid into Alabama. In the Nashville campaign he had command of Fort Rosecrans under General Thomas, and did his share in achieving the notable results of that battle. At the time of his death in 1869 he was commander of the Department of the Gulf.

MAJOR–GENERAL GEORGE STONEMAN

General Stoneman was born at Busti, Chautauqua County, N. Y., in 1822, and graduated at West Point in 1846. Following some service in West Virginia in the early part of the war, he was appointed chief of cavalry in the Army of the Potomac. After the evacuation of Yorktown, he overtook the Confederate troops and brought on the battle of Williamsburgh in May, 1862. On November 15, 1862, he was made commander of the Third Army Corps, which he led at Fredericksburg on December 13, 1862. During Hooker's Chancellorsville campaign he led a cavalry raid toward Richmond. In April, 1864, he was made commander of a cavalry corps in the Army of the Ohio, and in the Atlanta campaign undertook a raid against Macon and Andersonville. For three months he was a prisoner.

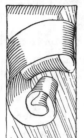

for a time in Cuba as Commander of the District of Havana, and was made brigadier-general in the regular army, where he served with distinction until he was retired.

GENERAL WHEELER

One of the most versatile soldiers of the Civil War was Joseph Wheeler, Lieutenant-General, C. S. A., Brigadier-General, U. S. A., and in the opinion of General R. E. Lee one of "the two ablest cavalry officers which the war developed."

President Davis said that General Wheeler displayed "a dash and activity, vigilance and consummate skill, which justly entitled him to a prominent place on the roll of great cavalry leaders. By his indomitable energy he was able to keep the Government and commanders of our troops advised of the enemy's movements and by preventing foraging parties from leaving the main body, he saved from spoliation all but a narrow tract of country, and from the torch millions worth of property which would otherwise have certainly been consumed."

One of his biographers (Rev. E. S. Buford) states that: "General Wheeler has commanded in more than a hundred battles, many of which, considering the numbers engaged, were the most severe recorded in the history of cavalry. Always in the front of battle, he was wounded three times, sixteen horses were shot under him, eight of his staff-officers were killed and thirty-two wounded."

At the outbreak of the war with Spain, Wheeler was appointed a major-general, U. S. V., and during the short but sharp campaign in Cuba, displayed the same energy and ability which had distinguished him in a greater conflict. In 1899 he was ordered to the Philippines, serving there until June, 1900, when he was commissioned brigadier-general, U. S. A., and in September of the same year was retired from active service. His old opponent, General Sherman, paid this tribute to his worth: "In the event of war with a foreign country, 'Joe' Wheeler is the man to command the cavalry of our army."

CHAPTER
ELEVEN

———

FAMOUS CHARGERS

———

GRANT'S FAVORITE WAR-HORSE "CINCINNATI"

THREE CHARGERS THAT BORE A NATION'S DESTINY

These three horses can fairly be said to have borne a nation's destiny upon their backs. They are the mounts used by General Grant in his final gigantic campaign that resulted in the outwearing of the Confederacy. When photographed in June, 1864, they were "in the field" with the General-in-Chief, after the ghastly battle of Cold Harbor, and before the crossing of the James River that sealed the fate of Lee's army. On the left is "Egypt," presented to Grant by admirers in Illinois, and named for the district in

IN THE FIELD WITH GENERAL GRANT

which he was bred.   The horse in the center, fully caparisoned, is "Cincinnati," also a present from a gentleman in St. Louis, who on his death-bed sent for Grant and presented him with "the finest horse in the
world."   The little black pony to the right is "Jeff Davis," captured in a cavalry raid on the plantation of
Joe Davis, brother of the Confederate President, near Vicksburg.   "Jeff Davis" looks indifferent, but
"Cincinnati" and "Egypt" have pricked up their ears.   Perhaps they were looking at General Grant.

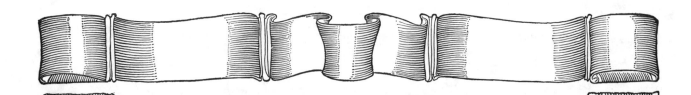

WAR–HORSES

By Theo. F. Rodenbough
Brigadier-General, United States Army (Retired)

THE battle chargers of the general officers of the Confederate and Federal armies during the American Civil War, wrote their names upon the scrolls of history by their high grade of sagacity and faithfulness. They carried their masters upon the tedious march and over the bullet-swept battlefields, and seemed to realize their importance in the conflict. The horse of the commanding officer was as well known to the rank and file as the general himself, and the soldiers were as affectionately attached to the animal as was the master.

GENERAL GRANT'S HORSES

When the Civil War broke out, my father,* General Grant, was appointed colonel of the Twenty-first Illinois Volunteer Infantry and on joining the regiment purchased a horse in Galena, Illinois. This horse, though a strong animal, proved to be unfitted for the service and, when my father was taking his regiment from Springfield, Illinois, to Missouri, he encamped on the Illinois River for several days. During the time they were there a farmer brought in a horse called "Jack." This animal was a cream-colored horse, with black eyes, mane and tail of silver white, his hair gradually becoming darker toward his feet. He was a noble animal, high spirited, very intelligent and an excellent horse in every way. He was a stallion and of considerable value. My father used him until after the battle of Chattanooga (November, 1863), as an extra horse

* This account was furnished at the author's request by General Frederick Dent Grant, U. S. A.—T. F. R.

"STONEWALL" JACKSON'S WAR–HORSE SHORTLY AFTER HIS MASTER'S DEATH

The negative of this picture, made in 1863, not long after the terrible tragedy of General Jackson's death, was destroyed in the great Richmond fire of 1865. The print is believed to be unique, and here reproduced for the first time. All day long on May 2d of 1863, "Old Sorrel," as the soldiers called him, had borne his master on the most successful flanking march of the war, which ended in the Confederate victory at Chancellorsville. There have not been many movements in military history so brilliant and decisive in their effect. At nightfall Jackson mounted "Fancy" for the last time, and rode out to reconnoiter. Galloping back to avoid the Federal bullets, he and his staff were mistaken for foes and fired upon by their own men. Jackson reeled from the saddle into the arms of Captain Milburn, severely wounded. The horse bolted toward the Union lines, but was recovered and placed in the stable of Governor John Letcher at Richmond.

and for parades and ceremonial occasions. At the time of the Sanitary Fair in Chicago (1863 or '64), General Grant gave him to the fair, where he was raffled off, bringing $4,000 to the Sanitary Commission.

Soon after my father was made a brigadier-general, (August 8, 1861), he purchased a pony for me and also another horse for field service for himself. At the battle of Belmont (November 7, 1861), his horse was killed under him and he took my pony. The pony was quite small and my father, feeling that the commanding general on the field should have a larger mount, turned the pony over to one of his aides-de-camp (Captain Hyllier) and mounted the captain's horse. The pony was lost in the battle.

The next horse that my father purchased for field service was a roan called "Fox," a very powerful and spirited animal and of great endurance. This horse he rode during the siege and battles around Fort Donelson and also at Shiloh.

At the battle of Shiloh the Confederates left on the field a rawboned horse, very ugly and apparently good for nothing. As a joke, the officer who found this animal on the field, sent it with his compliments, to Colonel Lagow, one of my father's aides-de-camp, who always kept a very excellent mount and was a man of means. The other officers of the staff "jollied" the colonel about this gift. When my father saw him, he told the colonel that the animal was a thoroughbred and a valuable mount and that if he, Lagow, did not wish to keep the horse he would be glad to have him. Because of his appearance he was named "Kangaroo," and after a short period of rest and feeding and care he turned out to be a magnificent animal and was used by my father during the Vicksburg campaign.

In this campaign, General Grant had two other horses, both of them very handsome, one of which he gave away and the other he used until late in the war. During the campaign and siege of Vicksburg, a cavalry raid or scouting party arrived at Joe Davis' plantation (the brother of Jefferson Davis,

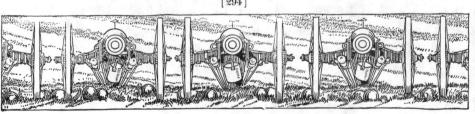

MEADE'S BATTLE–SCARRED MOUNT THREE MONTHS AFTER GETTYSBURG

"Baldy" was the horse that carried General George G. Meade from September, 1861, to the end of the war, except when "absent on sick leave." His war record is remarkable for the number of wounds from which he recovered, reporting for duty each time he was convalescent. He was wounded twice at the first battle of Bull Run, before he came into General Meade's possession. Left on the field for dead at Antietam, he was later discovered quietly grazing, with a deep wound in his neck. Again, at Gettysburg, a bullet lodged between his ribs and rendered him unable to carry his owner again until after Appomattox. "Baldy" was a bright bay horse, with white face and feet. This bullet-scarred veteran followed General Meade's hearse to his last resting-place in 1872, and survived him by a decade. The photograph was taken in October, 1863.

President of the Confederacy) and there captured a black pony which was brought to the rear of the city and presented to me. The animal was worn out when it reached headquarters but was a very easy riding horse and I used him once or twice. With care he began to pick up and soon carried himself in fine shape.

At that time my father was suffering with a carbuncle and his horse being restless caused him a great deal of pain. It was necessary for General Grant to visit the lines frequently and one day he took this pony for that purpose. The gait of the pony was so delightful that he directed that he be turned over to the quartermaster as a captured horse and a board of officers be convened to appraise the animal. This was done and my father purchased the animal and kept him until he died, which was long after the Civil War. This pony was known as " Jeff Davis."

After the battle of Chattanooga, General Grant went to St. Louis, where I was at the time, critically ill from dysentery contracted during the siege of Vicksburg. During the time of his visit to the city he received a letter from a gentleman who signed his name "S. S. Grant," the initials being the same as those of a brother of my father's, who had died in the summer of 1861. S. S. Grant wrote to the effect that he was very desirous of seeing General Grant but that he was ill and confined to his room at the Lindell Hotel and begged him to call, as he had something important to say which my father might be gratified to hear.

The name excited my father's curiosity and he called at the hotel to meet the gentleman who told him that he had, he thought, the finest horse in the world, and knowing General Grant's great liking for horses he had concluded, inasmuch as he would never be able to ride again, that he would like to give his horse to him; that he desired that the horse should have a good home and tender care and that the only condition that he would make in parting with him would be that the person receiving him would see that he was never ill-treated, and

GENERAL SHERIDAN'S "WINCHESTER"

"Winchester" wore no such gaudy trappings when he sprang "up from the South, at break of day" on that famous ride of October 19, 1864, which has been immortalized in Thomas Buchanan Read's poem. The silver-mounted saddle was presented later by admiring friends of his owner. The sleek neck then was dark with sweat, and the quivering nostrils were flecked with foam at the end of the twenty-mile dash that brought hope and courage to an army and turned defeat into the overwhelming victory of Cedar Creek. Sheridan himself was as careful of his appearance as Custer was irregular in his field dress. He was always careful of his horse. but in the field decked him in nothing more elaborate than a plain McClellan saddle and army blanket.

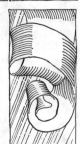

should never fall into the hands of a person that would ill-treat him. This promise was given and General Grant accepted the horse and called him "Cincinnati." This was his battle charger until the end of the war and was kept by him until the horse died at Admiral Ammen's farm in Maryland, in 1878.*

About this time (January, 1864) some people in Illinois found a horse in the southern part of that State, which they thought was remarkably beautiful. They purchased him and sent him as a present to my father. This horse was known as "Egypt" as he was raised, or at least came from southern Illinois, a district known in the State as Egypt, as the northern part was known as Canaan.

GENERAL LEE'S "TRAVELLER"

The most famous of the horses in the stables of General Lee, the Confederate commander, was "Traveller," an iron gray horse. He was raised in Greenbrier County, near Blue Sulphur Springs, and, as a colt, won first prize at a fair in Lewisburg, Virginia. When hostilities commenced between the North and the South, the horse, then known as "Jeff Davis," was owned by Major Thomas L. Broun, who had paid $175 (in gold) for him. Lee first saw the gray in the mountains of West Virginia. He instantly became attached to him, and always called him "my colt."

In the spring of 1862, this horse finally became the

* "Cincinnati" was the son of "Lexington," the fastest four-mile thoroughbred in the United States, time 7:19¾ minutes. "Cincinnati" nearly equaled the speed of his half-brother, "Kentucky," and Grant was offered $10,000 in gold or its equivalent for him, but refused. He was seventeen hands high, and in the estimation of Grant was the finest horse that he had ever seen. Grant rarely permitted anyone to mount the horse —two exceptions were Admiral Daniel Ammen and Lincoln. Ammen saved Grant's life from drowning while a school-boy. Grant says: "Lincoln spent the latter days of his life with me. He came to City Point in the last month of the war and was with me all the time. He was a fine horseman and rode my horse 'Cincinnati' every day."—T. F. R.

GENERAL ALFRED PLEASONTON AND HIS HORSE

This is the horse which General Pleasonton brought with him from Utah in 1861. This charger carried him through the Peninsular campaign when he was a major in the Second Cavalry, commanding the regiment and covering the march of the Federal army to Yorktown, August 18 and 19, 1862. It bore him at Antietam, Fredericksburg, and Chancellorsville, where Pleasonton distinguished himself by checking the flank attack of the Confederates on the Federal right, and perhaps it stepped forth a little more proudly when its owner was given command of the entire cavalry corps of the Army of the Potomac on June 7, 1863. This photograph was taken at Falmouth, Va., in the latter year. General Pleasonton is riding the same charger in the photograph of himself and Custer used to illustrate the battle of Gettysburg on page 237.

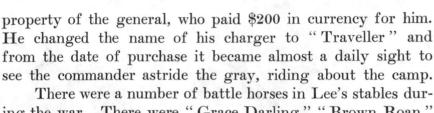

property of the general, who paid $200 in currency for him. He changed the name of his charger to "Traveller" and from the date of purchase it became almost a daily sight to see the commander astride the gray, riding about the camp.

There were a number of battle horses in Lee's stables during the war. There were "Grace Darling," "Brown Roan," "Lucy Long," "Ajax," and "Richmond," but of them all "Traveller" became the especial companion of the general. The fine proportions of this horse immediately attracted attention. He was gray in color, with black points, a long mane and long flowing tail. He stood sixteen hands high, and was five years old in the spring of 1862. His figure was muscular, with a deep chest and short back, strong haunches, flat legs, small head, quick eyes, broad forehead, and small feet. His rapid, springy step and bold carriage made him conspicuous in the camps of the Confederates. On a long and tedious march with the Army of Northern Virginia he easily carried Lee's weight at five or six miles an hour, without faltering, and at the end of the day's hard travel seemed to be as fresh as at the beginning.

The other horses broke under the strain and hardships; "Lucy Long," purchased by General "Jeb" Stuart from Stephen Dandridge and presented to Lee, served for two years in alternation with "Traveller," but in the fall of 1864 became unserviceable and was sent into the country to recuperate.* "Richmond," "Ajax," and "Brown Roan" each in turn proved unequal to the rigors of war.

* "Lucy Long," second to "Traveller" in Lee's affections, was recalled from the country just before the evacuation of Richmond; but during the confusion she was placed with the public horses and sent to Danville, and Lee lost all trace of his war-horse. A thorough search was made, and finally, in 1866, she was discovered and brought to Lexington to pass her days in leisure with General Lee and "Traveller." After a number of years the mare became feeble and seemed to lose interest in life, and when "Lucy Long" reached about thirty-three years of age a son of General Lee mercifully chloroformed the veteran war-horse of the Army of Northern Virginia.

GENERAL RUFUS INGALLS' CHARGER

Like General Grant's "Cincinnati," this horse was present at Lee's surrender at Appomattox. Major-General Rufus Ingalls was chief quartermaster of the Army of the Potomac. After the surrender he asked permission to visit the Confederate lines and renew his acquaintance with some old friends, class-mates and companions in arms. He returned with Cadmus M. Wilcox, who had been Grant's groomsman when he was married; James Longstreet, who had also been at his wedding; Heth, Gordon, Pickett, and a number of others. The American eagle is plainly visible on the major-general's saddle-cloth, which the charger is wearing. The whole outfit is spick and span, though the double bridle is not according to army regulations, and General Ingalls even enjoyed the luxury of a dog at the time this photograph was taken.

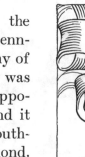

But "Traveller" sturdily accepted and withstood the hardships of the campaigns in Virginia, Maryland, and Pennsylvania. When in April, 1865, the last battle of the Army of Northern Virginia had been fought, the veteran war-horse was still on duty. When Lee rode to the McLean house at Appomattox Court House, he was astride of "Traveller," and it was this faithful four-footed companion who carried the Southern leader back to his waiting army, and then to Richmond.

When Lee became a private citizen and retired to Washington and Lee University, as its president, the veteran war-horse was still with him, and as the years passed and both master and servant neared life's ending they became more closely attached.* As the funeral cortège accompanied Lee to his last resting place, "Traveller" marched behind the hearse, his step slow and his head bowed, as if he understood the import of the occasion.

GENERAL McCLELLAN'S HORSES

While General McClellan was in command of the Army of the Potomac, in 1862, he had a number of war-horses. The favorite of them all was "Daniel Webster," soon called by the members of the general's staff "that devil Dan," because of his speed with which the staff officers had great difficulty in keeping pace. During the battle of the Antietam the great horse carried the commander safely through the day.

"Daniel Webster" was a dark bay about seventeen hands high, pure bred, with good action, never showing signs of fatigue, no matter how hard the test. He was extremely hand-

* During the life of "Traveller" after the war, he was the pet of the countryside about Lexington, Va. Many marks of affection were showered upon him. Admiring friends in England sent two sets of equipment for the veteran war-horse. Ladies in Baltimore, Md., bestowed another highly decorated set, and another came from friends at the Confederate capital, Richmond. But the set that seemed to most please "Traveller" was the one sent from St. Louis, in Missouri.

GENERAL RAWLINS' MOUNT

It is a proud little darkey boy who is exercising the horse of a general—John Aaron Rawlins, the Federal brigadier-general of volunteers, who was later promoted to the rank of major-general, U. S. A., for gallant and meritorious services during the campaign terminating with the surrender of the army under General Lee. The noble horse himself is looking around with a mildly inquiring air at the strange new instrument which the photographer is leveling at him.

some, with more than ordinary horse-sense. He was a fast walker, an important requisite in a commander's charger, but a disagreeable quality for the staff officers whose horses were kept at a slow trot. After McClellan retired to private life, "Dan" became the family horse at Orange, N. J., where he died at the age of twenty-three. McClellan said: "No soldier ever had a better horse than I had in 'Daniel Webster.'"

McClellan also had a charger named "Burns," a fiery black, named after an army friend who gave the horse to Mc-Clellan. His one failing was that at dinner time he would bolt for his oats regardless of how much depended on McClellan's presence on the battlefield at the critical moment, as in the battle of the Antietam. Running at dinner time became so much an obsession with "Burns" that McClellan was always careful not to be mounted on him at that hour of the day.*

GENERAL SHERMAN'S HORSES

General Sherman's best war-horse was killed early in the Civil War, at the battle of Shiloh, where he led the right wing of the Federal army against General A. S. Johnston's Confederate legions. Two of his other chargers were killed while being held by an orderly. Of the many horses that carried Sherman through the remaining years of the struggle, two had

* The Editor has vivid recollection of "Little Mac" in April, 1862 (then at the height of his popularity), during a ride from Fort Monroe to Big Bethel, being the first day's march of the Army of the Potomac toward Yorktown, Va. The writer commanded the escort (a squadron, Second U. S. Cavalry), and during the ten or twelve miles of the route covered at a gallop, between double lines of infantry, halted for the moment to permit the commanding general to pass, the air was literally "rent" with the cheers of the troops, filled with high hopes of an early entrance to the Confederate capital. As the brilliant staff, headed by the young chieftain of magnetic presence, with bared head, mounted on "Black Burns," swept along amid clatter of hoof, jingle of equipment, and loud hurrahs, the thought came to the writer that thus the "Little Corporal" was wont to inspire his devoted legions to loud acclaim of *Vive l'Empereur*. (T. F. R.)

GENERAL BUTTERFIELD, A WELL–MOUNTED INFANTRY GENERAL

This is a photograph of the well-mounted chief-of-staff and corps commander of the Army of the Potomac. It was the custom of generals who had been infantry officers to set their own pace, regardless of their cavalry escort. A cavalryman detailed to escort him tells the following story: "We started out with General Butterfield one day upon the Potomac to meet Confederate officers in relation to the exchange of prisoners. My regiment was ordered out to escort him. The infantry officers, accustomed to riding alone, made their way regardless of their escorts, and inside of half an hour my column was distributed over two miles of road; General Butterfield did not adapt his riding to the pace of the escort and made it very difficult for the cavalry to follow him."

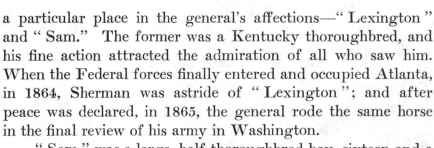

a particular place in the general's affections—"Lexington" and "Sam." The former was a Kentucky thoroughbred, and his fine action attracted the admiration of all who saw him. When the Federal forces finally entered and occupied Atlanta, in 1864, Sherman was astride of "Lexington"; and after peace was declared, in 1865, the general rode the same horse in the final review of his army in Washington.

"Sam" was a large, half-thoroughbred bay, sixteen and a half hands high. He possessed great speed, strength, and endurance. The horse made one of the longest and most difficult marches ever recorded in history, from Vicksburg to Washington, through the cities of Atlanta, Savannah, Columbia, and Richmond. He had a rapid gait, and could march five miles an hour at a walk. While under fire "Sam" was as calm and steady as his brave master. He was wounded several times, while mounted, and the fault was usually due to Sherman's disregard of the horse's anxiety to seek cover. In 1865, Sherman retired "Sam" to a well-earned rest, on an Illinois farm, where he received every mark of affection. The gallant war-horse died of extreme old age, in 1884.

GENERAL JACKSON'S HORSES

General Thomas J. ("Stonewall") Jackson, the great Southern leader, had his favorite battle charger, which at the beginning of the war was thought to be about eleven years old. On May 9, 1861, while Jackson was in command of the garrison at Harper's Ferry, a train load of supplies and horses, on the way to the Federal camps, was captured. Among the horses was one that attracted Jackson's attention. He purchased the animal from his quartermaster's department for his own personal use. The horse, named "Old Sorrel," carried Jackson over many of the bullet-swept battlefields and was with Jackson when that officer fell before the volley of his own men at the battle of Chancellorsville. During the swift campaign through the Shenandoah, in 1862, when Jackson

AN "AIDE" OF GENERAL GRANT

A photograph of little "Jeff Davis," a pony that won General Grant's approval at the siege of Vicksburg by his easy gait. General Grant was suffering with a carbuncle and needed a horse with easy paces. A cavalry detachment had captured a suitable mount on the plantation of Joe Davis, brother of the President of the Confederacy, and that is how the little black pony came by his name. The great Union general was more apt to call him "Little Jeff." The general used him throughout the siege, but he felt that the commanding general on the battlefield should have a larger mount, and "Jeff Davis" in this photograph is apparently saddled for an orderly or aide. The little horse remained with General Grant until he died.

marched his "foot cavalry" towards the citadel at Washington, the horse was his constant companion.

In 1884, a state fair was held at Hagerstown, in Maryland, and one of the most interesting sights was that of the veteran war horse, "Old Sorrel," tethered in a corral and quietly munching choice bits of vegetables and hay. Before the fair was ended nearly all the mane and hair of his tail had disappeared, having been plucked by scores of relic hunters. For many years after the cessation of hostilities, Jackson's gallant old war-horse was held in tender esteem at the South.

When the veteran battle charger died, admirers of Jackson sent the carcass to a taxidermist and the gallant steed now rests in the Soldier's Home in Richmond, Virginia.*

GENERAL SHERIDAN'S "RIENZI"

General Sheridan's charger was foaled at or near Grand Rapids, Michigan, of the Black Hawk stock, and was brought into the Federal army by an officer of the Second Michigan Cavalry. He was presented to Sheridan, then colonel of the regiment, by the officers, in the spring of 1862, while the regiment was stationed at Rienzi, Mississippi; the horse was nearly three years old. He was over seventeen hands in height, powerfully built, with a deep chest, strong shoulders, a broad forehead, a clear eye and of great intelligence. In his prime he was one of the strongest horses Sheridan ever knew, very active, and one of the fastest walkers in the Federal army. "Rienzi" always held his head high, and by the quickness of his movements created the impression that he was exceedingly impetuous, but Sheridan was always able to control him by a firm hand and a few words. He was as cool and quiet under fire as any veteran trooper in the Cavalry Corps.

At the battle of Cedar Creek, October 19, 1864, the name of the horse was changed from "Rienzi" to "Winchester," a name derived from the town made famous by Sheridan's ride

* From the Confederate Veteran.

[308]

MOUNTS FOR ALL THE CAVALRYMEN

Behind this mixed command grouped in front of the camp stand a great number of horses. There is at least one for every cavalryman in the picture, a state of affairs that did not last long; the photograph was evidently taken before the Union armies were using up five hundred horses a day. The picture illustrates one of the few quiet hours that the Federal cavalrymen enjoyed. Infantry boys are evidently fraternizing with their comrades of the cavalry at an advanced post. The horn that shows on the cap of the second man at the left of the photograph is the insignia, adopted from European light infantry, of the infantry of the Army of the Potomac. The drummer boy also belongs to the infantry arm, and the leather scabbard of the officer kneeling near the center of the picture likewise indicates the infantry. Such photographs as these are rare. Both horses and men were resting for once.

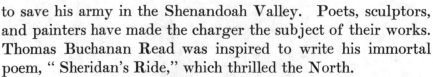

to save his army in the Shenandoah Valley. Poets, sculptors, and painters have made the charger the subject of their works. Thomas Buchanan Read was inspired to write his immortal poem, " Sheridan's Ride," which thrilled the North.

From an account of this affair in " Scribner's Magazine," by General G. W. Forsyth, who accompanied Sheridan as aide-de-camp, the following is quoted:

The distance from Winchester to Cedar Creek, on the north bank of which the Army of the Shenandoah lay encamped, is a little less than nineteen miles. As we debouched into the fields . . . the general would wave his hat to the men and point to the front, never lessening his speed as he pressed forward. It was enough. One glance at the eager face and familiar black horse and they knew him and, starting to their feet, they swung their caps around their heads and broke into cheers as he passed beyond them; and then gathering up their belongings started after him for the front, shouting to their comrades farther out in the fields, " Sheridan! Sheridan!" waving their hats and pointing after him as he dashed onward. . . . So rapid had been our gait that nearly all of the escort save the commanding officer and a few of his best mounted men had been distanced, for they were more heavily weighted and ordinary troop horses could not live at such a pace.

In one of the closing scenes of the war—Five Forks—Sheridan was personally directing a movement against the Confederates who were protected by temporary entrenchments about two feet high. The Federal forces, both cavalry and infantry, were suffering from a sharp fire, which caused them to hesitate. "Where is my battle-flag?" cried Sheridan. Seizing it by the staff, he dashed ahead, followed by his command. The gallant steed leaped the low works and landed the Federal general fairly amid the astonished Southerners. Close behind him came Merritt's cavalrymen in a resistless charge which swept the Confederates backward in confusion. The horse passed a comfortable old age in his master's stable and died in Chicago, in 1878; the lifelike remains are now in the Museum at Governor's Island, N. Y., as a gift from his owner.

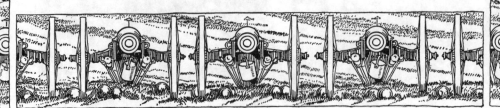

TWO FINE HORSES—THE PROVOST-MARSHAL'S MOUNTS

A couple of examples of the care given to horses at Giesboro. These two serviceable chargers belonged to Colonel George Henry Sharpe, Provost-Marshal of the Army of the Potomac. The provost-marshal of a great army must be well mounted. It is the duty of the provost-guard to arrest all criminals, take charge of deserters, follow the army and restore strag-glers to their regiments. This was no easy matter with an army of 120,000 men. Pris-oners of war were also turned over to its care to be sent back to the institutions in the North. It is no wonder that the chief provided himself with powerful mounts. This pho-tograph was taken at Brandy Station just before the strenuous campaign of the Wilderness.

GENERAL STUART'S "HIGHFLY"

The battle horse, "Highfly," carried General "Jeb" Stuart through many campaigns and had become his favored companion. The intelligence and faithfulness of the steed had many times borne the dashing cavalier through desperate perils. In the summer of 1862, at Verdiersville on the plank road between Fredericksburg and Orange, in Virginia, Stuart was stretched out upon a bench on the porch of the tavern, awaiting the arrival of General Fitzhugh Lee with whom he desired to confer on the next movement of the cavalry. "Highfly" was unbridled and grazing in the yard near the road. The clatter of horses aroused the Confederate general, and he walked to the roadway, leaving behind on the bench his hat, in which was a black plume, the pride of Stuart's heart. Suddenly, horsemen dashed around the bend in the road and Stuart was within gunshot of Federal cavalry. He was nonplussed; he had expected to see Fitzhugh Lee. Mounting his faithful and speedy bay he soon left the chagrined cavalry far behind, but the foe carried away the hat with its black plume.

GENERAL MEADE'S "BALDY"

In the first great battle of the Civil War, at Bull Run, there was a bright bay horse, with white face and feet. His rider was seriously wounded. The horse was turned back to the quartermaster to recover from his wounds received that day. Later, in September, General Meade bought the horse and named him "Baldy." Though Meade became deeply attached to the horse, his staff officers soon began to complain of the peculiar pace of "Baldy," which was hard to follow. He had a racking gait that was faster than a walk and slow for a trot and compelled the staff, alternately, to trot and then to drop into a walk, causing great discomfort.

"Baldy's" war record was remarkable. He was wounded twice at the first battle of Bull Run; he was at the battle of Drainesville; he took part in two of the seven days' fighting

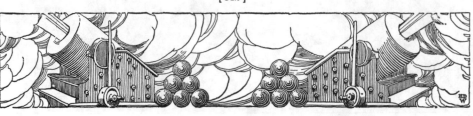

THE HALT

On this and the opposite page are shown types of the horses for which the Northern States were ransacked to furnish mounts for the staff and regimental officers of the Union armies. Small wonder that this magnificent, well-groomed animal has excited the admiration of his own master who is critically looking him over. The officer is Captain Harry Page, quartermaster of the Headquarters of the Army of the Potomac, subsequently colonel and chief quartermaster of the cavalry corps under Sheridan. This was one of the most arduous posts of duty in the entire service, and one whose necessities during the severe campaigns up the Shenandoah Valley, and around Richmond, kept the young colonel always upon his mettle. He has cultivated the ability to rest and relax when the opportunity arrives. He is evidently awaiting the arrival of his wagon-train, when he will again become active at the pitching of the tents and the parking of the wagons.

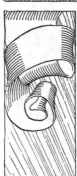

around Richmond in the summer of 1862; at Groveton, August 29th, at the second battle of Bull Run; at South Mountain and at Antietam. In the last battle the gallant horse was left on the field as dead, but in the next Federal advance "Baldy" was discovered quietly grazing on the battle-ground, with a deep wound in his neck. He was tenderly cared for and soon was again fit for duty. He bore the general at the battles of Fredericksburg and Chancellorsville. For two days "Baldy" was present at Gettysburg, where he received his most grievous wound from a bullet entering his body between the ribs, and lodging there. Meade would not part with the gallant horse, and kept him with the army until the following spring.

In the preparations of the Army of the Potomac for their last campaign, "Baldy" was sent to pasture at Downingtown, in Pennsylvania. After the surrender of Lee's army at Appomattox, Meade hurried to Philadelphia where he again met his faithful charger, fully recovered. For many years the horse and the general were inseparable companions, and when Meade died in 1872, the bullet-scarred war-horse followed the hearse. Ten years later "Baldy" died, and his head and two fore hoofs were mounted and are now cherished relics of the George G. Meade Post, Grand Army of the Republic, in Philadelphia.

GENERAL THOMAS' "BILLY"

The "Rock of Chickamauga," General George H. Thomas, possessed two intelligent war-horses, both powerful and large, and able to carry the general, who weighed nearly two hundred pounds. Both horses were bays; one named "Billy" (after Thomas' friend, General Sherman) was the darker of the two, about sixteen hands high, and stout in build. He was, like his owner, sedate in all his movements and was not easily disturbed from his habitual calm by bursting shells or the turmoil of battle. Even in retreat, the horse did not hurry his footsteps unduly, and provoked the staff by his deliberate pace.

"Billy" bore General Thomas through the campaigns in

[314]

AN OFFICER'S MOUNT

Captain Webster, whose horse this is, showed a just pride in his steed. Observe how the reins are hitched over the saddle to exhibit the arched neck to the best advantage. The equipment is regulation except for the unhooded stirrups. It has the preferable single line, curb bit, no breast strap and no martingale. The saddle is the McClellan, so-called because adopted through recommendations made by General George B. McClellan after his official European tour in 1860, although it was in reality a modification of the Mexican or Texas tree. It was an excellent saddle, and in an improved pattern remained after fifty years of trial still the standard saddle of the United States regular cavalry. In its original form it was covered with rawhide instead of leather, and when this covering split the seat became very uncomfortable to the rider. Captain Webster used a saddle cloth instead of the usual folded blanket. His horse's shiny coat shows recent thorough grooming.

middle Tennessee and northern Georgia. He was on the fields of Chickamauga and Chattanooga, and marched with the Federal host in the advance upon Atlanta. From Atlanta, he next moved to Nashville where his master engineered the crushing defeat to the Confederate arms in the winter of 1864, the last battle in which Thomas and "Billy" participated.

GENERAL HOOKER'S "LOOKOUT"

General Hooker first became acquainted with his famous charger, "Lookout," while the animal was stabled in New York, and when Louis Napoleon, the French emperor, and an English gentleman of wealth were bidding for its purchase. Napoleon repeatedly offered the owner a thousand dollars for the horse. Hooker finally obtained him and rode him in the campaigns in which he later participated.

"Lookout" was raised in Kentucky, and he was a three-quarters bred, out of a half bred mare by Mambrino. He was of a rich chestnut color, stood nearly seventeen hands high, and had long slender legs. Despite his great height, the horse was known to trot a mile in two minutes and forty-five seconds. When the battle of Chattanooga occurred, the horse was seven years old. It was here that the animal received its name of "Lookout." The grandeur of "Lookout's" stride and his height dwarfed many gallant war-horses and he has been termed the finest charger in the army.

GENERAL KEARNY'S HORSES

General Philip Kearny was a veteran of the Mexican War, with the rank of captain. It had been decided to equip Kearny's troop (First United States Dragoons) with horses all of the same color, and he went to Illinois to purchase them. He was assisted in the work by Abraham Lincoln and finally found himself in possession of one hundred gray horses. While engaged in battle before the City of Mexico, mounted upon one of the newly purchased grays, "Monmouth," Kearny was

[316]

WHEN SLEEK HORSES WERE PLENTIFUL—YORKTOWN, 1862

Confederate winter quarters near Yorktown, Virginia, which had passed into Federal hands. When McClellan moved to the Peninsula in the spring of 1862 he had but few cavalry, but every officer was provided with a handsome charger on which he pranced gaily up and down the lines. "Little Mac" himself rode preferably at full speed. His appearance was the signal for an outburst of cheering. It was to be a picnic parade of the well-equipped army to the Confederate capital. It is presumable that the portly officer in the center of the picture had lost some weight, and the chargers some sleekness before they were through with Lee and Jackson. To such an extent had overwork and disease reduced the number of cavalry horses during McClellan's retreat from the Peninsula that when General Stuart made his raid into Pennsylvania, October 11th of the same year, only eight hundred Federal cavalry could be mounted to follow him. Under date of October 21st, McClellan wrote to General Halleck: "Exclusive of the cavalry force now engaged in picketing the river, I have not at present over one thousand horses for service. Without more cavalry horses our communications from the moment we march would be at the mercy of the large cavalry force of the enemy."

wounded in an arm, which was finally amputated. During the Civil War, Kearny had many excellent animals at his command, but his most celebrated steed was "Moscow," a high-spirited white horse. On the battlefield, "Moscow" was conspicuous because of his white coat, but Kearny was heedless of the protests of his staff against his needless exposure.

Another war-horse belonging to General Kearny was "Decatur," a light bay, which was shot through the neck in the battle of Fair Oaks or Seven Pines. "Bayard," a brown horse, was ridden by Kearny at this battle, and his fame will ever stand in history through the poem by Stedman, "Kearny at Seven Pines." At the battle of Chantilly, Kearny and "Bayard" were advancing alone near the close of the struggle, when they met with a regiment of Confederate infantry. "Bayard" instantly wheeled and dashed from danger, with Kearny laying flat upon the horse's neck. A shower of bullets fell about the general and his charger. They seemed about to escape when a fatal bullet struck the general.

The leader of the Southern legions in the West, General Albert Sidney Johnston, rode a magnificent thoroughbred bay, named "Fire-eater," on the battlefield. The steed stood patiently like a veteran when the bullets and shells hurtled about him and his master, but when the command came to charge, he was all fire and vim, like that Sunday in April, 1862, the first day of the bloody battle of Shiloh.

Among the hundreds of generals' mounts which became famous by their conspicuous bravery and sagacity on the battlefields, were General Fitzhugh Lee's little mare, "Nellie Gray," which was killed at the battle of Opequon Creek; Major-General Patrick R. Cleburne's "Dixie," killed at the battle of Perryville; General Adam R. Johnson's "Joe Smith," which was noted for its speed and endurance; and General Benjamin F. Butler's war-horse, "Almond Eye," a name derived from the peculiar formation of the eyes of the horse.

CHAPTER
TWELVE

———

MOUNTING THE CAVALRY
OF THE UNION ARMY

———

AN ORDERLY WITH AN OFFICER'S MOUNT

A THOUSAND FEDERAL CAVALRY HORSES

Lovers of horses will appreciate, in this photograph of 1864, the characteristic friendly fashion in which the cavalry "mounts" are gathering in deep communion. The numerous groups of horses in the corrals of the great depot at Giesboro, D. C., are apparently holding a series of conferences on their prospects in the coming battles. Presently all those who are in condition will resolve themselves into a committee of the whole and go off to war, whence they will return here only for hospital treatment. The corrals at Giesboro could easily contain a thousand horses, and they were never overcrowded. It was not until the true value of

"TALKING IT OVER"

cavalry was discovered, from the experience of the first two years of warfare, that this great depot was established, but it was most efficiently handled. Giesboro was a great teacher in regard to the care of horses. Cavalrymen learned what to guard against. The knowledge was acquired partly from field service, but in a great measure from the opportunity for leisurely observation, an opportunity somewhat analogous to that of a physician in a great metropolitan hospital where every kind of a physical problem has to be solved.

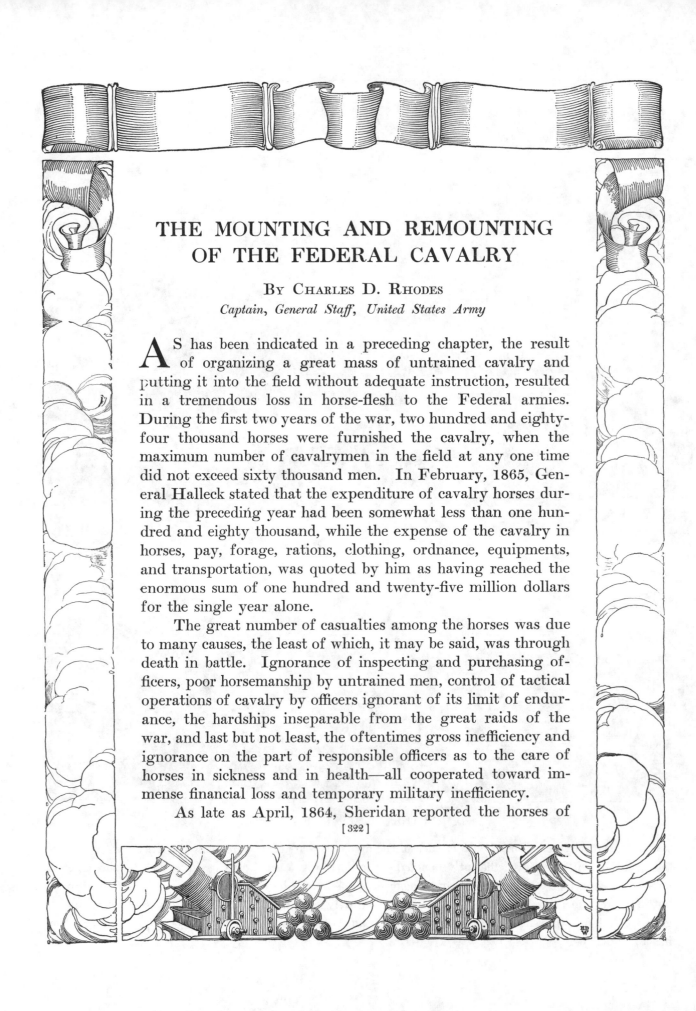

THE MOUNTING AND REMOUNTING
OF THE FEDERAL CAVALRY

By Charles D. Rhodes
Captain, General Staff, United States Army

AS has been indicated in a preceding chapter, the result of organizing a great mass of untrained cavalry and putting it into the field without adequate instruction, resulted in a tremendous loss in horse-flesh to the Federal armies. During the first two years of the war, two hundred and eighty-four thousand horses were furnished the cavalry, when the maximum number of cavalrymen in the field at any one time did not exceed sixty thousand men. In February, 1865, General Halleck stated that the expenditure of cavalry horses during the preceding year had been somewhat less than one hundred and eighty thousand, while the expense of the cavalry in horses, pay, forage, rations, clothing, ordnance, equipments, and transportation, was quoted by him as having reached the enormous sum of one hundred and twenty-five million dollars for the single year alone.

The great number of casualties among the horses was due to many causes, the least of which, it may be said, was through death in battle. Ignorance of inspecting and purchasing officers, poor horsemanship by untrained men, control of tactical operations of cavalry by officers ignorant of its limit of endurance, the hardships inseparable from the great raids of the war, and last but not least, the oftentimes gross inefficiency and ignorance on the part of responsible officers as to the care of horses in sickness and in health—all cooperated toward immense financial loss and temporary military inefficiency.

As late as April, 1864, Sheridan reported the horses of

CAVALRY STABLES AT ARLINGTON—THE GREAT CORRAL IN THE DISTANCE, 3½ MILES

INTERIOR VIEW OF CAVALRY STABLES AT ARLINGTON

The streets of Washington re-echoed throughout the war with the clatter of horses' hoofs. Mounted aides, couriers, the general staff, the officers of the various regiments stationed in and about the Capital all had their chargers, and Giesboro was too far away to stable them. In the left-hand corner of the upper picture, the Giesboro corral shown on the following pages can be seen in the distance. A glance at the photograph will show that the corral was too far away to be convenient for horses in use in Washington. It is three and a half miles as the crow flies from Arlington to the corral. The photographer has written on the face of the lower photograph the date, "June 29, 1864." At this moment Grant was swinging his cavalry toward Petersburg.

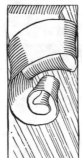

his command worn out by the mistaken use of mounted men to protect trains—a duty which could be as well and much more economically performed by infantry; and by the unnecessary picket-duty, encircling the great infantry and cavalry camps of the Army of the Potomac on an irregular curve of nearly sixty miles.

In October, 1862, when service in the Peninsula campaign and in that of the Army of Virginia, had brought the number of mounted cavalrymen down to less than a good-sized regiment, McClellan wrote Halleck:

It is absolutely necessary that some energetic measures be taken to supply the cavalry of this army with remount horses. The present rate of supply is 1,050 per week for the entire army here and in front of Washington. From this number the artillery draw for their batteries.

The demand for horses was so great that in many cases they were sent on active service before recovering sufficiently from the fatigue incident to a long railway journey. In one case reported, horses were left on railroad cars fifty hours without food or water, and were then taken out, issued, and used for immediate service in the field.

To such an extent had overwork and disease reduced the number of cavalry horses in the Army of the Potomac, that when the Confederate general, Stuart, made his daring raid into Pennsylvania, in October, 1862, only eight hundred Federal cavalrymen could be mounted to follow him.

Of course the original mounting of the cavalry, field-artillery, and field- and staff-officers caused a great demand for suitable chargers throughout the North. The draft animals required for transportation purposes increased the scarcity of suitable horses. Furthermore, with the unexpected losses during the first years of the war came such a dearth of animals suitable for the cavalry service, that in course of time almost any remount which conformed to the general specifications of a horse, was thankfully accepted by the Government.

[324]

SHELTER FOR SIX THOUSAND HORSES AT GIESBORO

Thirty-two immense stables, besides hospitals and other buildings, provided shelter for six thousand horses at the big cavalry depot, District of Columbia, but most of the stock was kept in open sheds or in corrals. The stockyards alone covered forty-five acres. The stables were large, well-lighted buildings with thousands of scrupulously clean stalls. The horses were divided into serviceable and unserviceable classes. About sixty per cent. of the horses received from the field for recuperation were returned to active service. Five thousand men were employed in August, 1863, to rush this cavalry depot to completion. Its maintenance was one of the costly items which aggregated an expenditure by the Union Government of $1,000,-000 a day during the entire period of the war—an expenditure running even as high as $4,000,000 a day.

THE BARRACKS AT GIESBORO

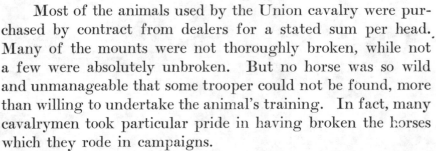

Most of the animals used by the Union cavalry were purchased by contract from dealers for a stated sum per head. Many of the mounts were not thoroughly broken, while not a few were absolutely unbroken. But no horse was so wild and unmanageable that some trooper could not be found, more than willing to undertake the animal's training. In fact, many cavalrymen took particular pride in having broken the horses which they rode in campaigns.

At the beginning of the war, when horses were being received from the West in car-load lots and shipped to the new regiments, some effort was made to organize troops of the same color—blacks, grays, bays, and sorrels—and to maintain this harmonious coloring from the remounts received from time to time. But after the regiments were fairly initiated into real campaigning and the losses in horseflesh became serious, all thought of coloring troops and regiments was abandoned, and the one idea was to secure serviceable mounts and remounts of any color, size, or description.

It is related of one cavalry colonel, whose regiment had been in several engagements and who had lost more than half his horses, that he appealed most eloquently to the quartermaster, for a supply of remounts. "Colonel," said the quartermaster in reply, "I'll tell you frankly that we haven't five pounds of horse for each man to be mounted." "That won't help much," retorted the colonel, testily; "we were thinking of riding the brutes, not of eating them."

The continual complaints as to the quality of the horses furnished, the tardiness with which remounts were supplied, and the inadequacy of conveniences for recuperating broken-down horses in the field, led to the establishment, in the year 1863, of the Cavalry Bureau, with General George Stoneman as its first chief, followed soon after by General Kenner Garrard. But it was under General James Harrison Wilson that the Cavalry Bureau reached its greatest efficiency.

This war bureau was charged with the organization and

IN BARRACKS

A COMFORTABLE SPOT

FOR THE CAVALRY TROOPER

These cavalrymen of '64 look comfortable enough in their barracks at Giesboro. When the cavalry depot was established there in '63, it was the custom to have the troopers return to the dismounted camp near Washington to be remounted and refitted. Some "coffee-coolers" purposely lost their equipments and neglected their horses in the field in order to be sent back for a time to the comfortable station. The order was finally given by General Meade to forward all horses, arms, and equipments to the soldiers in the field. While the men in this photograph are very much at ease and their lolling attitudes would seem to denote peace rather than war, they are probably none of them self-indulgent troopers who prefer this luxurious resting-place but are part of the garrison of the post charged with defending the valuable depot. There are many Civil War photographs of cattle on the hoof, but this picture contains the only representation of a sheep that has come to light.

equipment of the cavalry forces of the army, and with the providing of mounts and remounts. The inspection of horses for
the latter purpose was ordered to be made by experienced cavalry officers, while the purchasing was under the direction of
officers of the Quartermaster's Department of the army.

Under the general charge of the Cavalry Bureau, six
principal depots were established at Giesboro, District of Columbia; St. Louis, Missouri; Greenville, Louisiana; Nashville,
Tennessee; Harrisburg, Pennsylvania, and Wilmington, Delaware, for the reception, organization, and discipline of cavalry
recruits, and for the collection, care, and training of horses.

The principal depot was at Giesboro, District of Columbia,
on the north bank of the Potomac, below Washington, and
consisted of a site of about six hundred and twenty-five acres
for which the Government paid a rental of six thousand dollars
per annum. Stables, stock-yards, forage-houses, storehouses,
mess-houses, quarters, a grist-mill, a chapel, and wharves, were
soon constructed, and within three months after taking possession (August 12, 1863) provision had been made for fifteen
thousand animals; and within three months more, arrangement
had been made for the care of thirty thousand animals, although
twenty-one thousand was the largest number on hand at any
one time. The wharves afforded facilities for three steamers of
the largest class to load simultaneously; the hospitals had accommodation for two thousand six hundred and fifty horses;
five thousand men were employed during the construction
period, afterward reduced to fifteen hundred; while thirty-
two stables, besides hospitals and other buildings, gave shelter
to six thousand horses. Most of the stock was kept in open
sheds or in corrals, these stock-yards alone covering forty-five
acres, each yard being furnished with hay-racks and water-
troughs, and having free access to the river. The estimated
cost of the Giesboro Depot was $1,225,000.

The remount depot at St. Louis covered about four hundred acres, and had a force of nearly eleven hundred employees

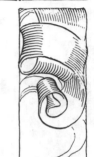

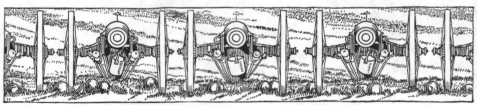

CAVALRY TO GUARD THE DISTRICT OF COLUMBIA.

Between June and December, 1863, just at the time that the Giesboro remount depot was established, four companies of the First District of Columbia Cavalry (A, B, C, and D) were organized. These commands were assigned to special service in the District of Columbia, subject only to the orders of the War Department. The thousands of mounts at Giesboro were not many miles from the track of the Confederate raiders, and presented a tempting prize to them. But early in 1864 the "District" cavalry were ordered away to southeastern Virginia, where they served with Kautz's cavalry division in the Army of the James, during the Petersburg and Appomattox campaigns. Colonel Lafayette C. Baker, in command of this cavalry, reported an encounter with Mosby, to whose depredations their organization was chiefly due, on October 22, 1863: "Sir: This morning about ten o'clock a detachment of my battalion, under command of Major E. J. Conger, and a detachment of the California battalion, under command of Captain Eigenbrodt, encountered a squad of Mosby's men some three miles this side of Fairfax Court House and near the Little River turnpike. One of Mosby's men (named Charles Mason) was shot and instantly killed. The celebrated guerrillas, Jack Barns, Ed. Stratton, and Bill Harover, were captured and forwarded to the Old Capitol Prison. These men state that they were looking for Government horses and sutlers' wagons. None of our force were injured." Colonel Baker was in the Federal Secret Service, and used these cavalrymen as his police. Eight additional companies were subsequently organized for the First District of Columbia Cavalry at Augusta, Maine, January to March, 1864, but after some service with Kautz's cavalry, these were consolidated into two companies and merged into the First Maine Cavalry.

—blacksmiths, carpenters, wagon-makers, wheelwrights, far-riers, teamsters, and laborers in many departments.

The stables were long, well-lighted buildings with thou-sands of scrupulously clean stalls. From five to ten thousand horses were usually present at the depot, nearly evenly divided between serviceable and unserviceable classes—the latter class being again divided into convalescents and condemned animals. The condemned horses were those declared unfit for further military service, and unless afflicted with some incurable dis-ability, were sold at public auction.

About fifty per cent. of the horses received from the field for recuperation were returned to active service, " fit for duty." More than half of the remainder were recuperated sufficiently to be sold as condemned animals, while less than one-fourth of the unserviceable animals received, died at the depot or were killed to prevent further suffering.

The bane of the cavalry service of the Federal armies in the field was diseases of the feet. " Hoof-rot," " grease-heel," or the " scratches " followed in the wake of days and nights spent in mud, rain, snow, and exposure to cold, and caused thousands of otherwise serviceable horses to become useless for the time being.

Sore backs became common with the hardships of cam-paigning, and one of the first lessons taught the inexperienced trooper was to take better care of his horse than he did of him-self. The remedy against recurrence of sore backs on horses was invariably to order the trooper to walk and lead the dis-abled animal. With a few such lessons, cavalry soldiers of but short service became most scrupulous in smoothing out wrinkles in saddle-blankets, in dismounting to walk steep hills, in giving frequent rests to their jaded animals, and when op-portunity offered, in unsaddling and cooling the backs of their mounts after hours in the saddle. Poor forage, sudden changes of forage, and overfeeding produced almost as much sickness and physical disability as no forage at all.

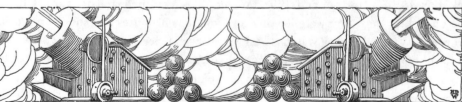

A RIDING COB

IN WASHINGTON, 1865

NOT THE SORT

FOR CAVALRY

This skittish little cob with the civilian saddle, photographed at the headquarters of the defense of Washington south of the Potomac, in 1865, was doubtless an excellent mount upon which to ride back to the Capital and pay calls. But experience soon taught that high-strung hunters and nervous cobs were of little or no use for either fighting or campaigning. When the battle was on and the shells began to scream a small proportion of these pedigreed animals was sufficient to stampede an entire squadron. They took fright and bolted in all directions. On the other hand, they were far too sensitive for the arduous night marches, and lost in nerves what they gained in speed. A few of them were sufficient to keep a whole column of horses who would otherwise be patiently plodding, heads down, actually stumbling along in their sleep, wide awake and restive by their nervous starts and terrors. The short-barreled, wiry Virginia horses, almost as tireless as army mules, proved to be far their superiors for active service.

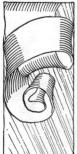

In its cantonment at Brandy Station, during the winter of 1864, the cavalry of the Army of the Potomac was nearly ruined by increasing the ration of grain to make up a deficiency in hay. During the famous Stoneman raid (March and April, 1863) an entire cavalry division was without hay for twenty-one days, in a country where but little grazing was possible. During Sheridan's last raid, in 1865, nearly three-fourths of the lameness of his horses was due to an involuntary change of forage from oats to corn.

But much of the breaking-down of cavalry horses was merely inseparable from the hardships and privations which every great war carries in its train, and which the most experienced leaders cannot foresee or prevent.

In General Sheridan's march from Winchester to Petersburg, February 27th to March 27, 1865, each trooper carried on his horse, in addition to his regular equipment, five days' rations in haversacks, seventy-five rounds of ammunition, and thirty pounds of forage. On General James H. Wilson's Selma expedition, each trooper carried, besides his ordinary kit, five days' rations, twenty-four pounds of grain, one hundred rounds of ammunition, and two extra horseshoes.

A remarkable case, illustrating the conditions surrounding the war service of cavalry regiments, was that of the Seventh Pennsylvania Cavalry. In April, 1864, this regiment started on a march from Nashville, Tennessee, to Blake's Mill, Georgia. It had nine hundred and nineteen horses fresh from the Nashville remount depot, and among its enlisted men were three hundred recruits, some of whom had never been on a horse before.

In a little over four months, the regiment marched nine hundred and two miles, not including fatiguing picket duty and troop scouting. During this period, the horses were without regular supplies of forage for twenty-six days, on scanty forage for twenty-seven days, and for seven consecutive days were without food of any kind. In one period of seventy-two

WHERE THE FEDERAL CAVALRY WAS TRAINED

Giesboro, D. C., where the cavalry of the Army of the Potomac was remounted after August, 1863, was also their drill and training camp.

A BIG RESPONSIBILITY—FORT CARROLL, GIESBORO, D. C.

Millions of dollars worth of Government property was entrusted to the men who occupied these barracks at Fort Carroll, Giesboro, D. C. The original cost of the cavalry depot was estimated at a million and a quarter dollars, and there were immense stores of fodder, medicine, cavalry equipment, and supplies at the depot, besides the value of the horses themselves. The Union Government's appropriations for the purchase of horses for the period of the war mounted to $123,864,915. The average contract price per head was $150, so that approximately 825,766 horses were used in the Union armies. Giesboro was the largest of the Government's cavalry depot, and it must have been an anxious time for those responsible for the preservation of all this wealth when Early threatened Washington.

hours, the horses remained saddled for sixty hours. During the expedition, two hundred and thirty horses were abandoned or died, and one hundred and seventy-one were killed or captured by the Confederates—a total loss of four hundred and one animals, or nearly fifty per cent. of those starting on the march. With such hardships, it is little wonder that it became necessary to send thousands of horses back to the depots for rest and recuperation.

But, of course, one of the main purposes of the great horse-depots of the Civil War period, was not to recuperate horses already in the military service, but to receive, condition, and issue thousands of animals purchased throughout the country for army use.

During the fiscal year ending June 30, 1864, the Federal Government purchased 188,718 horses in addition to 20,308 captured from the Confederates and reported; while during the first eight months of the year 1864, the cavalry of the Army of the Potomac, alone, was supplied with two complete remounts or nearly forty thousand horses.

The price paid to contractors by Federal purchasing agents averaged about $150 per head, and occasionally really high-class horses found their way into the lots received at the depots. More often, however, the reverse was the case, and the inspectors of horses were usually at their wits' ends detecting the many frauds and tricks of the horse trade, which dealers attempted to perpetrate on the Government. Men otherwise known to be of the staunchest integrity seem to lose all sense of the equity of things when it comes to selling or swapping horses; and this is particularly the case when the other party to the transaction is the Government, a corporate body incapable of physical suffering and devoid of sentiment.

The Giesboro depot received between January 1, 1864, and June 30, 1866—a period of two and one-half years—an aggregate of 170,654 cavalry horses. Of this number, 96,006 were issued to troops in the field, 1574 were issued to officers,

AN ARTILLERY OFFICER'S MOUNT   A QUARTERMASTER'S MOUNT

Mounts were required by staff and regimental officers, as well as for the cavalry and mounted artillery. So great was the demand that during the second year of the war any quadruped that answered to the general specifications of a horse was seized upon. These fine animals look as if they had been obtained early in the war. The second and third show a "U. S." brand on the shoulder.

48,721 were sold, and 24,321 died. In addition to this number, over 12,000 artillery horses were handled at the depot.

While the capacity of the St. Louis depot was thirty thousand animals, it was never completely filled—the serviceable remounts being promptly forwarded to regiments in the field, and the recuperating animals being held only long enough to render them serviceable or to determine whether they would not respond to further rest or veterinary treatment. The hospitals for the accommodation and treatment of disabled animals were probably the most complete of their kind existing at that time; but after it had been demonstrated that an animal could not be nursed back to the military service, it was a matter of economy to dispose of him to some enterprising bidder for the average price of thirty dollars per head.

The depot system or caring for Government stock, receiving those newly purchased and recuperating those returning sick or disabled from the field, proved a measure of the greatest economy to the Federal Government, in addition to its marked effect on the military efficiency of the mounted service. The value of the animals returned to duty with regiments from the St. Louis depot alone, in excess of what the same animals would have been worth at public auction as condemned articles of sale, was in a single year nearly two hundred thousand dollars more than the entire operating expenses of the plant.

When it is remembered that there were six large depots, all engaged in handling the mounts and remounts of the great Federal armies, and that the depots at Giesboro and St. Louis comprised but a part of this complex system of administration and supply, the tremendous responsibilities imposed upon the Cavalry Bureau of the Federal War Department may be appreciated and understood.

AN HONOR MAN OF THE REGULARS

First-Sergeant Conrad Schmidt of the Second United States Cavalry—a fine type of the "regular" trooper. He was decorated for galloping to the assistance of his captain, whose horse had been killed in a charge, mounting the officer behind him under fire and riding off to safety, although his own horse had been wounded in five places. This was at the Opequon, September 19, 1864.

The Photographic History
of The Civil War

———

The Decisive Battles

1864—A SHOT THAT STARTLED WASHINGTON

After the shell whirled from the Confederate General Early's gun through the little house outside of Washington City, shortly before this photograph was taken in July, 1864, consternation spread throughout the North, and surprise the world over. A most audacious swoop down the Valley of Virginia, over the Potomac and across Maryland, had carried eight thousand seasoned veterans in gray to the very gates of Washington. A shot struck near President Lincoln himself at Fort Stevens. The capital was without sufficient trained defenders. Half a million Union soldiers were scattered south of the Potomac to the Gulf, but few remained north of the river when Early appeared after forced marches that tested the heroism of his devoted troops. Hastening on the afternoon of July 11th, two army corps arrived from Grant's army. Washington was saved; reluctantly the daring Confederates retreated, and abandoned their last invasion of the North.

The Photographic History of The Civil War
The Decisive Battles

INTRODUCTION BY

FREDERICK DENT GRANT
Major-General United States Army

TEXT BY

HENRY W. ELSON
Professor of History, Ohio University

PHOTOGRAPH DESCRIPTIONS BY

JAMES BARNES
Author of "Naval Actions of 1812" and "David G. Farragut"

CONTENTS

	PAGE
FRONTISPIECE—*A Shot that Startled Washington*	4
FOREWORD	9
PREFACE	11
INTRODUCTION	
Frederick Dent Grant	13

Part I

GRANT VERSUS LEE
Henry W. Elson

THE BATTLE IN THE WILDERNESS	21
SPOTSYLVANIA AND THE BLOODY ANGLE	51
ATTACK AND REPULSE AT COLD HARBOR	79

Part II

THE SIMULTANEOUS MOVEMENTS
Henry W. Elson

DREWRY'S BLUFF IMPREGNABLE	93
TO ATLANTA—SHERMAN VERSUS JOHNSTON	99
THE LAST CONFLICTS IN THE SHENANDOAH	139

Part III

CLOSING IN
Henry W. Elson

CHARLESTON, THE UNCONQUERED PORT	169
THE INVESTMENT OF PETERSBURG	175
SHERMAN'S FINAL CAMPAIGNS	209

Contents

Part IV

PAGE

FROM WAR TO PEACE
  Henry W. Elson

  NASHVILLE—THE END IN TENNESSEE 249

  THE SIEGE AND FALL OF PETERSBURG 271

  APPOMATTOX 295

Part V

ENGAGEMENTS OF THE CIVIL WAR FROM MAY, 1864, TO MAY, 1865 . 317
  George L. Kilmer

PHOTOGRAPHIC DESCRIPTIONS THROUGHOUT THIS BOOK
  James Barnes

FOREWORD

ON April 14, 1861, Fort Sumter underwent a thirty-four-hour bombardment by the Confederate Army. As the fighting drew to a close, Union officer Major Robert Anderson lowered the flag and turned the fort over to the Confederacy. The American Civil War had begun. It would be four long, hard-fought years before the guns would finally be silenced.

The Photographic History of the Civil War: The Decisive Battles captures the images of both intense drama and horror created by this internal national conflict. This unique collection of black-and-white photographs takes the reader into the campsites and onto the battlefields where victories were won and lives were lost. The superb text and photograph descriptions present an authoritative yet sensitive portrayal of the War Between the States.

This volume focuses on the last stages of the Civil War, the decisive battles that led up to General Robert E. Lee's surrender of the Confederate Army at the court house at Appomattox. In this last year of the war, General Ulysses S. Grant organized the Union Armies for a cohesive effort against the Confederacy. In his introduction, Frederick Dent Grant writes, "Everything being prepared, orders were given for the start, and all the armies were on the move by the 6th of May, with what results the chapters that follow will tell the reader in detail."

Some of the more important battles that led to the war's end discussed here include General William Sherman's campaign through Atlanta, the Union Armies' attack and defeat at Cold Harbor, the battle of St. Petersburg and the fall of Richmond. Soon after the fall of the Confederate capital and the surrender of General Lee's army, followed the surrender of all the remaining Southern forces. The war that had divided the country had come to an end.

By the 1860s the camera was on its way to becoming an important medium for communication. The method used during this period was known as daguereotype, named after its inventor Frenchman Louis Jacques Mandé Daguerre. Using this wet-plate process, however, the Civil War photographer was unable to capture action shots. Yet this disadvantage did not prevent him from capturing on film the human and material wreckage created by the war—the wistful face of the dying young soldier or the sabotaged railroad. The Battle of Bull Run marked the beginning of American military photography.

The Civil War photographers risked constant danger of battle and worked under the most difficult conditions—the bitter cold during the winters of 1862 and 1863 and the blistering heat in the summer. Important Civil War photographers—including Mathew B. Brady, Timothy O'Sullivan and Alexander Gardner as well as other combat photographers—provided the American people with an inside look at this war through their work. These poignant photographs stirred the hearts of Americans on both sides of the Mason-Dixon line then and will continue to do so today.

K.M.B.

PREFACE

THE introduction that follows from General Frederick Dent Grant is a simple statement of the large movements during the last year of the war in mass. In it the reader will find a concise summation of what follows in detail throughout the chapters of this volume.

It is amazing to the non-military reader to find how simple was the direct cause for the tremendous results in the last year of the Civil War. It was the unification of the Federal army under Ulysses S. Grant. His son, in the pages that follow, repeats the businesslike agreement with President Lincoln which made possible the wielding of all the Union armies as one mighty weapon.

The structure of this book reflects the Civil War situation thus changed in May, 1864. No longer were battles to be fought here and there unrelated; but a definite movement was made by "GRANT VERSUS LEE" on the 4th of May, accompanied by "THE SIMULTANEOUS MOVEMENTS" of Butler, Sherman, and Sigel—all under the absolute control of the man who kept his headquarters near those of Meade, Commander of the Army of the Potomac.

Against such concentrated strokes the enfeebled Confederacy could not stand. Only the utter courage of leaders and soldiers innately brave, who were fighting for a cause they felt meant home no less than principle, prolonged the struggle during the tragic year ending with May, 1865.

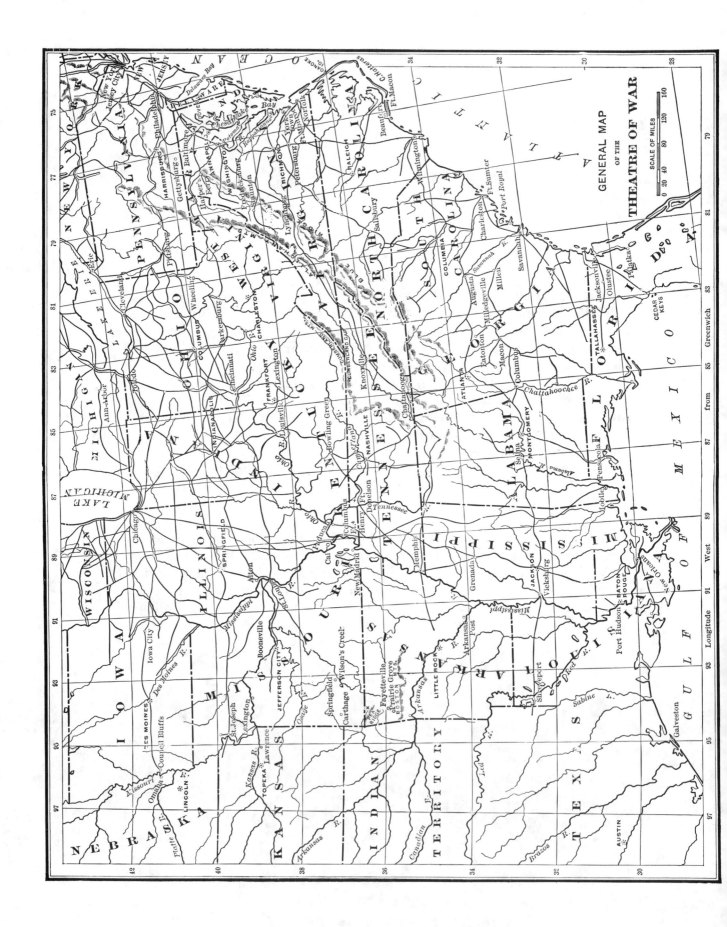

GENERAL MAP
OF THE
THEATRE OF WAR

SCALE OF MILES

0 20 40 80 120 160

INTRODUCTION

By FREDERICK DENT GRANT
Major-General, U. S. A.

GENERAL ULYSSES S. GRANT AT CITY POINT IN 1864, WITH HIS
WIFE AND SON JESSE

INTRODUCTION

By Frederick Dent Grant

Major-General, United States Army

UPON being appointed lieutenant-general, and having assumed command of all the armies in the field, in March, 1864, General Grant had an interview with President Lincoln, during which interview Mr. Lincoln stated that procrastination on the part of commanders, and the pressure from the people of the North and from Congress, had forced him into issuing his series of military orders, some of which he *knew* were wrong, and all of which *may have been* wrong; that all he, the President, wanted, or had ever wanted, was some one who would take the responsibility of action, and would call upon him, as the Executive of the Government, for such supplies as were needed; the President pledging himself to use the full powers of the Government in rendering all assistance possible. General Grant assured the President that he would do the best he could with the means at hand, and would, as far as possible, avoid annoying the administration with unnecessary demands.

His first work was to inaugurate a plan of campaign for all the armies. During the first three years of the war, the various armies had acted independently—a condition which had enabled their enemies to reenforce each point of attack by drawing troops from points of inactivity.

Having this in view, General Grant planned to move all the armies at once. He looked upon the Army of the James as the left wing, the Army of the Potomac as the center, and the troops operating under General Sherman as the right wing; all other troops being considered as cooperative

[14]

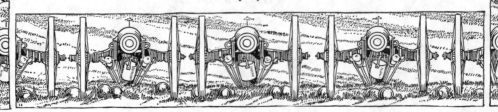

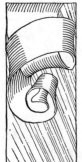

columns. He believed that by moving the whole line at the same time the greatest number of troops practicable would be brought against the armed forces of his enemy, and would prevent them from using the same force to resist the efforts of the Union army, first at one point and then at another, and that, by continuously hammering against their armies, he would destroy both them and their sources of supply.

To carry out this idea, orders were given to the various commanders—on the 2d of April to Butler; on the 4th, to Sherman, and on the 9th, to Meade. In all these orders the same general ideas were expressed. To Butler he wrote:

"You will collect all the forces from your command that can be spared from garrison duty . . . to operate on the south side of James River, Richmond being your objective point."

To Sherman he wrote:

"It is my design, if the enemy keep quiet and allow me to take the initiative in the spring campaign, to work all the parts of the army together, and somewhat toward a common center. . . . You, I propose to move against Johnston's army, to break it up, and to get into the interior of the enemy's country as far as you can, inflicting all the damage you can against their war resources."

To Meade he wrote:

"Lee's army will be your objective point. Wherever Lee goes, there you will go also."

Thus it will be seen that General Grant's plan with reference to the movements of the Army of the Potomac was similar to that of Napoleon in the Russian campaign, while his plan in reference to the whole army much resembles the plan adopted by the Allies in their campaign against France in 1813–14.

When these movements began, the situation was about as follows: In the possession of the Union was all the territory north of a line beginning at Fortress Monroe, following the Chesapeake Bay to the Potomac River, up that river to near

[15]

Washington, the northern border of Virginia as far as Harper's Ferry, covered by the Army of the Potomac; across the mountains into West Virginia, to the headwaters of the Holston River in Tennessee, down that river and the Tennessee to Chattanooga, and thence along the Memphis and Charleston Railroad to the Mississippi, which was also in Union hands. All south of that line was in the hands of the Confederates, except a few stations along the sea coast, the possession of which assisted in the blockade.

Most of the opposing troops which were east of the Mississippi had been concentrated into the armies commanded by Lee and Johnston; that commanded by Lee facing the Army of the Potomac and guarding Richmond, while that of Johnston was at Dalton, in the northern part of Georgia, facing Sherman and defending Atlanta, a great railroad center and a point of concentration of supplies for the Confederate troops, wherever they were stationed, east of the Mississippi River. Richmond and the armies under Lee and Johnston were the main objectives of the campaign.

General Grant, as commander of the Union armies, placed himself with the Army of the Potomac, where the greatest opposition was to be expected, and where he considered his personal presence would be of the greatest value, and whence he exercised general supervision over the movements of all the armies.

The main movements being against Lee and Johnston, all other troops were directed to cooperate with the main armies. The movements of detached bodies would compel the Confederates either to detach largely for the protection of his supplies and lines of communication, or else to lose them altogether.

Everything being prepared, orders were given for the start, and all the armies were on the move by the 6th of May, with what results the chapters that follow will tell the reader in detail.

Early on the morning of the 4th of May, 1864, the Army of the Potomac moved out of its camp near Culpeper Court House and, heading toward Richmond, crossed the Rapidan at Germanna and Ely's fords and entered the Wilderness. At the same time the Army of the James moved from Fortress Monroe up the James River, landing on the south side of the James near City Point, threatening Petersburg. The army in the Shenandoah valley had already started, and Sherman was about to move.

As the Army of the Potomac was marching through the Wilderness it was attacked by Lee, who had moved from his fortifications at Mine Run. The head of Lee's column met the Army of the Potomac near the Wilderness Tavern, and the struggle for military supremacy in the field began. This battle, locally known as "The Wilderness," had by the 7th of May spread along the entire line of the Federal armies, and was raging from the Atlantic Ocean to the Mississippi valley. Columns of men were engaged in battle on the James River, in the Wilderness, in the Shenandoah valley, and in northern Georgia. In a few days the question was to be determined whether the North or the South possessed the military mastery of the continent. The decision of this struggle is told in detail by the chapters which follow.

From now on the tactics of Lee and Johnston were defensive, and they awaited the assaults of the Union armies behind fortifications. The Union center attacked and maneuvered, always by the left flank, while the right wing maneuvered generally by the right flank. One flank movement after another forced the Confederates out of position after position, until their main armies were thrown back to near the James River, to Staunton, Virginia, and to the Etowah River, Georgia. In the East, the great battle of Cold Harbor was fought, and a sudden flank movement to the left was made, the crossing of the James effected, and the carrying of the outer lines of Petersburg, which city, with Richmond, was immediately laid

[17]

under siege. The junction of the armies of the James and of the Potomac now took place, and from this time on they together formed the left wing of the Union armies. The column in the Shenandoah valley had penetrated to near Staunton and Lynchburg, in Virginia; but their ammunition becoming almost exhausted, especially that for artillery, the army had to move over the mountains toward the Kanawha valley, thus leaving the Shenandoah valley open for General Early to pass through in making raids on the North; while the right wing of the Union army pushed its way on through northern Georgia to the Chattahoochee River, which it crossed, and moved toward Atlanta. The first phase of the great campaign was thus ended, and the second phase now opens before us.

As already described, the Shenandoah valley was left open to raids by Southern troops into the North, and so able a man as General Lee did not miss such an opportunity. A portion of the Confederates within the strong entrenchments of Petersburg and Richmond were detached under General Early, who marched down the Shenandoah, crossed the Potomac, and entered Maryland, penetrating as far as Washington, for the defense of which city two corps were detached from the right wing. They succeeded in saving the national capital and in driving Early's forces to the north and west, and took up the line of the Monocacy. Sheridan was given the command of the Federal defense. He soon placed himself in the valley of the Shenandoah, where his army now became the center of the Union line.

The second phase was the adoption of the policy to keep the Confederate armies within the besieged cities, Richmond, Petersburg, and Atlanta, and actively to engage the outside troops, to drive all the smaller bands to the south, to devastate the country from which supplies were drawn, and, as far as possible, to destroy the troops that gathered these supplies. In these movements the most active and most effective column was the Army of the Shenandoah, which soon sent the oppos-

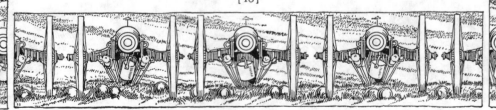

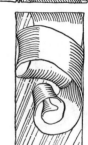

ing force, as Sheridan expressed it, "whirling through Winchester," annihilated two armies gathered to protect the Valley, and destroyed all the war supplies it contained.

In the meantime, the Confederate Government, finding that it was losing so much ground by its defensive policy, relieved Johnston, an officer of great ability, who was commanding at Atlanta. Hood was placed in charge of that wing of the army. He immediately assumed the offensive and attacked the Army of the Tennessee on the 22d of July, but was defeated and thrown back, with great losses, into his works at Atlanta.

Sherman soon followed Hood's lead by making another flank movement, which caused the fall of the city, the Confederates evacuating the place and moving to the west and north, threatening Sherman's line of supplies. Sherman followed Hood for a while, but it was soon decided to detach part of the troops under him, to concentrate them at Nashville, in Tennessee, so as to prevent an invasion of the North by Hood's army, and to abandon the lines of supplies to the rear; and then for Sherman to push on to the sea, cutting through Georgia, living off the country, and destroying as far as possible the store houses from which the army in Richmond gathered its food.

Hood followed one of the detachments from Sherman's army, and penetrated as far north as Nashville, where, in December, the decisive battle of Nashville was fought. This relieved the country in the rear of the line from menace, and one might say that the Confederacy was limited to the segment of a circle the circumference of which would pass through Richmond, Petersburg, Savannah, Atlanta, and Nashville. The policy maintained was continually to reduce the size of this circle until the Confederacy was crushed.

Sherman turned north, marching through the Carolinas. Part of the troops that had fought at Nashville under Thomas

[19]

were sent to Wilmington, under Schofield, after the fall of Fort Fisher. Sheridan's troopers were pressed forward up the Shenandoah Valley, to cross over to the headwaters of the James River, and down that stream to join the armies of the Potomac and of the James in front of Richmond and Petersburg. Stoneman moved from east Tennessee into the Virginias. The circle was contracted and the Confederacy was pressed on every side. This constituted the second phase of the great campaign, and the grand finale was about to be enacted.

As soon as Sheridan reached the Army of the Potomac, his troops were placed on the left of that army, to attack the remaining lines of communication between Richmond and the South. This forced the Confederates to detach large numbers of troops from their works, and, while thus weakened, the Army of the Potomac assaulted and carried the lines in front of Petersburg on the 2d of April, 1865. The fall of the fortifications around Petersburg opened to the Union armies all the lines of communication which the Confederates had to the south from Richmond, and forced the evacuation of that city. A race was begun by the Confederates to get beyond the Army of the Potomac and Sheridan's troopers, to join Johnston, and so possibly to overpower Sherman's army. Sheridan succeeded in heading Lee off and in forcing him from the railroad, where his supplies were, while parts of the armies of the Potomac and the James followed and pressed Lee's army in the rear, until the 9th of April, when he was nearly surrounded at Appomattox Court House and his position was such that he was forced to surrender.

With the fall of Richmond and Petersburg and the surrender of Lee, the main prop of the Confederacy was broken, and all that was now necessary was to gather in the other Southern armies. As further resistance was useless, these armies asked for terms, which were granted, and thus ended the third and last phase of the great campaign.

PART I
GRANT VERSUS LEE

———

THE BATTLES IN
THE WILDERNESS

———

WRECKAGE OF TREES AND MEN, AS THEY FELL IN THE DENSE FOREST—VICTIMS OF THE MONTH'S
ADVANCE THAT COST 40,000 UNION DEAD AND WOUNDED

ULYSSES S. GRANT

GENERAL–IN–CHIEF OF THE FEDERAL ARMY IN 1865.
BORN 1822; WEST POINT 1843; DIED 1885.

ROBERT E. LEE

GENERAL-IN-CHIEF OF THE CONFEDERATE ARMY IN 1865.
BORN 1807; WEST POINT 1829; DIED 1870.

GRANT'S FIRST MOVE AGAINST LEE

ADVANCE OF THE ARMY OF THE POTOMAC, MAY 5, 1864

The gleaming bayonets that lead the winding wagons mark the first lunge of one champion against another—the Federal military arm stretching forth to begin the "continuous hammering" which Grant had declared was to be his policy. By heavy and repeated blows he had vanquished Pemberton, Bragg, and every Southern general that had opposed him. Soon he was to be face to face with Lee's magnificent veterans, and here above all other places he had chosen to be in person. Profiting by the experience of Halleck, he avoided Washington. Sherman pleaded in vain with him to "come out West." Grant had recognized the most difficult and important task to be the destruction of Lee's army, and therefore had determined "to fight it out on this line." The Army of the Potomac was but one body of the 533,447 Federal

[24]

PONTOONS AT GERMANNA FORD ON THE RAPIDAN

BEGINNING THE "SIMULTANEOUS MOVEMENT" TO END THE WAR

troops set in motion by the supreme word of Grant at the beginning of May, 1864. East and West, the concentrated forces were to participate as much as possible in one simultaneous advance to strike the vitals of the Confederacy. The movements of Sherman, Banks, Sigel, and Butler were intended to be direct factors in the efficiency of his own mighty battering on the brave front of Lee's army. All along the line from the Mississippi to the Atlantic there was to be coöperation so that the widely separated armies of the South would have their hands full of fighting and could spare no reenforcements to each other. But it took only a few weeks to convince Grant that in Robert E. Lee, he had met more than his match in strategy. Sigel and Butler failed him at New Market and Drewry's Bluff. The simultaneous movement crumbled.

LEE'S MEN

The faces of the veterans in this photograph of 1864 reflect more forcibly than volumes of historical essays, the privations and the courage of the ragged veterans in gray who faced Grant, with Lee as their leader. They did not know that their struggle had already become unavailing; that no amount of perseverance and devotion could make headway against the resources, determination, and discipline of the Northern armies, now that they had become concentrated and wielded by a master of men like Grant. But Grant was as yet little more than a name to the armies of the East. His successes had been won on Western fields—Donelson, Vicksburg, Chattanooga. It was not yet known that the Army of the Potomac under the new general-in-chief was to prove irresistible. So these faces reflect perfect confidence.

CONFEDERATE SOLDIERS IN VIRGINIA, 1864

Though prisoners when this picture was taken—a remnant of Grant's heavy captures during May and June, when he sent some ten thousand Confederates to Coxey's Landing, Virginia, as a result of his first stroke against Lee—though their arms have been taken from them, though their uniforms are anything but "uniform," their hats partly the regulation felt of the Army of Northern Virginia, partly captured Federal caps, and partly nondescript—yet these ragged veterans stand and sit with the dignity of accomplishment. To them, "Marse Robert" is still the general unconquerable, under whom inferior numbers again and again have held their own, and more; the brilliant leader under whom every man gladly rushes to any assault, however impossible it seems, knowing that every order will be made to count.

THE BATTLE IN THE WILDERNESS

The volunteers who composed the armies of the Potomac and Northern Virginia were real soldiers now, inured to war, and desperate in their determination to do its work without faltering or failure. This fact—this change in the temper and *morale* of the men on either side—had greatly simplified the tasks set for Grant and Lee to solve. They knew their men. They knew that those men would stand against anything, endure slaughter without flinching, hardship without complaining, and make desperate endeavor without shrinking. The two armies had become what they had not been earlier in the contest, *perfect instruments of war*, that could be relied upon as confidently as the machinist relies upon his engine scheduled to make so many revolutions per minute at a given rate of horse-power, and with the precision of science itself.—*George Cary Eggleston, in "The History of the Confederate War."*

AFTER the battle of Gettysburg, Lee started for the Potomac, which he crossed with some difficulty, but with little interruption from the Federals, above Harper's Ferry, on July 14, 1863. The thwarted invader of Pennsylvania wished to get to the plains of Virginia as quickly as possible, but the Shenandoah was found to be impassable. Meade, in the mean time, had crossed the Potomac east of the Blue Ridge and seized the principal outlets from the lower part of the Valley. Lee, therefore, was compelled to continue his retreat up the Shenandoah until Longstreet, sent in advance with part of his command, had so blocked the Federal pursuit that most of the Confederate army was able to emerge through Chester Gap and move to Culpeper Court House. Ewell marched through Thornton's Gap and by the 4th of August practically the whole Army of Northern Virginia was south of the Rapidan, prepared to dispute the crossing of that river. But Meade, continuing his flank pursuit, halted at

[28]

THE COMING OF THE STRANGER GRANT

Hither, to Meade's headquarters at Brandy Station, came Grant on March 10, 1864. The day before, in Washington, President Lincoln handed him his commission, appointing him Lieutenant-General in command of all the Federal forces. His visit to Washington convinced him of the wisdom of remaining in the East to direct affairs, and his first interview with Meade decided him to retain that efficient general in command of the Army of the Potomac. The two men had known each other but slightly from casual meetings during the Mexican War. "I was a stranger to most of the Army of the Potomac," said Grant, "but Meade's modesty and willingness to serve in any capacity impressed me even more than had his victory at Gettysburg." The only prominent officers Grant brought on from the West were Sheridan and Rawlins.

Culpeper Court House, deeming it imprudent to attempt the Rapidan in the face of the strongly entrenched Confederates. In the entire movement there had been no fighting except a few cavalry skirmishes and no serious loss on either side.

On the 9th of September, Lee sent Longstreet and his corps to assist Bragg in the great conflict that was seen to be inevitable around Chattanooga. In spite of reduced strength, Lee proceeded to assume a threatening attitude toward Meade, and in October and early November there were several small but severe engagements as the Confederate leader attempted to turn Meade's flank and force him back to the old line of Bull Run. On the 7th of November, Sedgwick made a brilliant capture of the redoubts on the Rappahannock, and Lee returned once more to his old position on the south side of the Rapidan. This lay between Barnett's Ford, near Orange Court House (Lee's headquarters), and Morton's Ford, twenty miles below. Its right was also protected by entrenchments along the course of Mine Run. Against these, in the last days of November, Meade sent French, Sedgwick, and Warren. It was found impossible to carry the Confederate position, and on December 1st the Federal troops were ordered to re-cross the Rapidan. In this short campaign the Union lost sixteen hundred men and the Confederacy half that number. With the exception of an unsuccessful cavalry raid against Richmond, in February, nothing disturbed the existence of the two armies until the coming of Grant.

In the early months of 1864, the Army of the Potomac lay between the Rapidan and the Rappahannock, most of it in the vicinity of Culpeper Court House, although some of the troops were guarding the railroad to Washington as far as Bristoe Station, close to Manassas Junction. On the south side of the Rapidan, the Army of Northern Virginia was, as has been seen, securely entrenched. The Confederates' ranks were thin and their supplies were scarce; but the valiant spirit which had characterized the Southern hosts in former battles

ON THE WAY TO THE FRONT

The Streets of Culpeper, Virginia, in March, 1864. After Grant's arrival, the Army of the Potomac awoke to the activity of the spring campaign. One of the first essentials was to get the vast transport trains in readiness to cross the Rapidan. Wagons were massed by thousands at Culpeper, near where Meade's troops had spent the winter. The work of the teamsters was most arduous; wearied by long night marches—nodding, reins in hand, for lack of sleep—they might at any moment be suddenly attacked in a bold attempt to capture or destroy their precious freight. When the arrangements were completed, each wagon bore the corps badge, division color, and number of the brigade it was to serve. Its contents were also designated, together with the branch of the service for which it was intended. While loaded, the wagons must keep pace with the army movements whenever possible in order to be parked at night near the brigades to which they belonged.

still burned fiercely within their breasts, presaging many desperate battles before the heel of the invader should tread upon their cherished capital, Richmond, and their loved cause, the Confederacy.

Within the camp religious services had been held for weeks in succession, resulting in the conversion of large numbers of the soldiers. General Lee was a religious man. The influence of the awakening among the men in the army during this revival was manifest after the war was over, when the soldiers had gone back to civil life, under conditions most trying and severe. To this spiritual frame of mind may be credited, perhaps, some of the remarkable feats accomplished in subsequent battles by the Confederate army.

On February 29, 1864, the United States Congress passed a law reviving the grade of lieutenant-general, the title being intended for Grant, who was made general-in-chief of the armies of the United States. Grant had come from his victorious battle-grounds in the West, and all eyes turned to him as the chieftain who should lead the Union army to success. On the 9th of March he received his commission. He now planned the final great double movement of the war. Taking control of the whole campaign against Lee, but leaving the Army of the Potomac under Meade's direct command, he chose the strongest of his corps commanders, **W. T.** Sherman, for the head of affairs in the West. Grant's immediate objects were to defeat Lee's army and to capture Richmond, the latter to be accomplished by General Butler and the Army of the James; Sherman's object was to crush Johnston, to seize that important railroad center, Atlanta, Georgia, and, with Banks' assistance, to open a way between the Atlantic coast and Mobile, on the Gulf, thus dividing the Confederacy north and south, as the conquest of the Mississippi had parted it east and west. It was believed that if either or both of these campaigns were successful, the downfall of the Confederacy would be assured.

BELLE PLAIN, WHERE THE WAGON–TRAINS STARTED

In Grant's advance through the desolate tract guarded by Lee's veterans, extending for ten miles along the south bank of the Rapidan and for fifteen miles to the southward, he was unable to gather a particle of forage. His train of wagons in single file would have stretched from the Rapidan to Richmond. Never was a quartermaster's corps better organized than that of the Army of the Potomac in 1864. General Rufus Ingalls, Chief Quartermaster, managed his department with the precision of clockwork. The wagons, as fast as emptied, were returned to the base to be reloaded. Nevertheless within a week the losses of this well-equipped Army of the Potomac in the Wilderness campaign made dreadful reading. But with grim determination Grant wrote on May 11, 1864: "I am now sending back to Belle Plain all my wagons for a fresh supply of provisions and ammunition, and I propose to fight it out on this line if it takes all summer."

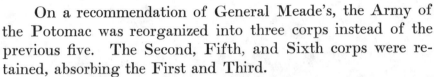

On a recommendation of General Meade's, the Army of the Potomac was reorganized into three corps instead of the previous five. The Second, Fifth, and Sixth corps were retained, absorbing the First and Third.

Hancock was in command of the Second; Warren, the Fifth; and Sedgwick, the Sixth. Sheridan was at the head of the cavalry. The Ninth Corps acted as a separate army under Burnside, and was now protecting the Orange and Alexandria Railroad. As soon as Meade had crossed the Rapidan, Burnside was ordered to move promptly, and he reached the battlefield of the Wilderness on the morning of May 6th. On May 24th his corps was assigned to the Army of the Potomac. The Union forces, including the Ninth Corps, numbered about one hundred and eighteen thousand men.

The Army of Northern Virginia consisted of three corps of infantry, the First under Longstreet, the Second under Ewell, and the Third under A. P. Hill, and a cavalry corps commanded by Stuart. A notable fact in the organization of the Confederate army was the few changes made in commanders. The total forces under Lee were about sixty-two thousand.

After assuming command, Grant established his headquarters at Culpeper Court House, whence he visited Washington once a week to consult with President Lincoln and the Secretary of War. He was given full authority, however, as to men and movements, and worked out a plan of campaign which resulted in a series of battles in Virginia unparalleled in history. The first of these was precipitated in a dense forest, a wilderness, from which the battle takes its name.

Grant decided on a general advance of the Army of the Potomac upon Lee, and early on the morning of May 4th the movement began by crossing the Rapidan at several fords below Lee's entrenched position, and moving by his right flank. The crossing was effected successfully, the line of march taking part of the Federal troops over a scene of defeat in the

CAMP IS BROKEN—THE ARMY ADVANCES

To secure for Grant the fullest possible information about Lee's movements was the task of General Sharp, Chief of the Secret Service of the Army, whose deserted headquarters at Brandy Station, Va., in April, 1864, are shown in this photograph. Here are the stalls built for the horses and the stockade for prisoners. The brick fireplace that had lent its cheer to the general's canvas house is evidence of the comforts of an army settled down for the respite of winter. Regretfully do soldiers exchange all this for forced marches and hard fighting; and to the scouts, who precede an army, active service holds a double hazard. Visitors to Federal camps often wondered at soldiers in Confederate gray chatting or playing cards with the men in blue and being allowed to pass freely. These were Federal spies, always in danger of being captured and summarily shot, not only by the Confederates, but in returning and attempting to regain their own lines.

previous spring. One year before, the magnificent Army of the Potomac, just from a long winter's rest in the encampment at Falmouth on the north bank of the Rappahannock, had met the legions of the South in deadly combat on the battlefield of Chancellorsville. And now Grant was leading the same army, whose ranks had been freshened by new recruits from the North, through the same field of war.

By eight o'clock on the morning of the 4th the various rumors as to the Federal army's crossing the Rapidan received by Lee were fully confirmed, and at once he prepared to set his own army in motion for the Wilderness, and to throw himself across the path of his foe. Two days before he had gathered his corps and division commanders around him at the signal station on Clark's Mountain, a considerable eminence south of the Rapidan, near Robertson's Ford. Here he expressed the opinion that Grant would cross at the lower fords, as he did, but nevertheless Longstreet was kept at Gordonsville in case the Federals should move by the Confederate left.

The day was oppressively hot, and the troops suffered greatly from thirst as they plodded along the forest aisles through the jungle-like region. The Wilderness was a maze of trees, underbrush, and ragged foliage. Low-limbed pines, scrub-oaks, hazels, and chinkapins interlaced their branches on the sides of rough country roads that lead through this labyrinth of desolation. The weary troops looked upon the heavy tangles of fallen timber and dense undergrowth with a sense of isolation. Only the sounds of the birds in the trees, the rustling of the leaves, and the passing of the army relieved the heavy pall of solitude that bore upon the senses of the Federal host.

The forces of the Northern army advanced into the vast no-man's land by the roads leading from the fords. In the afternoon, Hancock was resting at Chancellorsville, while Warren posted his corps near the Wilderness Tavern, in which General Grant established his headquarters. Sedgwick's corps

THE "GRAND CAMPAIGN" UNDER WAY—THE DAY BEFORE THE BATTLE

Pontoon-Bridges at Germanna Ford, on the Rapidan. Here the Sixth Corps under Sedgwick and Warren's Fifth Corps began crossing on the morning of May 4, 1864. The Second Corps, under Hancock, crossed at Ely's Ford, farther to the east. The cavalry, under Sheridan, was in advance. By night the army, with the exception of Burnside's Ninth Corps, was south of the Rapidan, advancing into the Wilderness. The Ninth Corps (a reserve of twenty thousand men) remained temporarily north of the Rappahannock, guarding railway communications. On the wooden pontoon-bridge the rear-guard is crossing while the pontonniers are taking up the canvas bridge beyond. The movement was magnificently managed; Grant believed it to be a complete surprise, as Lee had offered no opposition. That was yet to come. In the baffling fighting of the Wilderness and Spotsylvania Court House, Grant was to lose a third of his superior number, arriving a month later on the James with a dispirited army that had left behind 54,926 comrades in a month.

had followed in the track of Warren's veterans, but was ordered to halt near the river crossing, or a little south of it. The cavalry, as much as was not covering the rear wagon trains, was stationed near Chancellorsville and the Wilderness Tavern. That night the men from the North lay in bivouac with little fear of being attacked in this wilderness of waste, where military maneuvers would be very difficult.

Two roads—the old Orange turnpike and the Orange plank road—enter the Wilderness from the southwest. Along these the Confederates moved from their entrenched position to oppose the advancing hosts of the North. Ewell took the old turnpike and Hill the plank road. Longstreet was hastening from Gordonsville. The troops of Longstreet, on the one side, and of Burnside, on the other, arrived on the field after exhausting forced marches.

The locality in which the Federal army found itself on the 5th of May was not one that any commander would choose for a battle-ground. Lee was more familiar with its terrible features than was his opponent, but this gave him little or no advantage. Grant, having decided to move by the Confederate right flank, could only hope to pass through the desolate region and reach more open country before the inevitable clash would come. But this was not to be. General Humphreys, who was Meade's chief of staff, says in his "Virginia Campaign of 1864 and 1865": "So far as I know, no great battle ever took place before on such ground. But little of the combatants could be seen, and its progress was known to the senses chiefly by the rising and falling sounds of a vast musketry fire that continually swept along the lines of battle, many miles in length, sounds which at times approached to the sublime."

As Ewell, moving along the old turnpike on the morning of May 5th, came near the Germanna Ford road, Warren's corps was marching down the latter on its way to Parker's store, the destination assigned it by the orders of the day. This meeting precipitated the battle of the Wilderness.

THE TANGLED BATTLEFIELD

The Edge of the Wilderness, May 5, 1864.   Stretching away to the westward between Grant's army and Lee's lay no-man's-land—the Wilderness.   Covered with a second-growth of thicket, thorny underbrush, and twisted vines, it was an almost impassable labyrinth, with here and there small clearings in which stood deserted barns and houses, reached only by unused and overgrown farm roads.   The Federal advance into this region was not a surprise to Lee, as Grant supposed.   The Confederate commander had caused the region to be carefully surveyed, hoping for the precise opportunity that Grant was about to give him.   At the very outset of the campaign he could strike the Federals in a position where superior numbers counted little.   If he could drive Grant beyond the Rappahannock—as he had forced Pope, Burnside and Hooker before him—says George Cary Eggleston (in the "History of the Confederate War"), "loud and almost irresistible would have been the cry for an armistice, supported (as it would have been) by Wall Street and all Europe."

Meade learned the position of Ewell's advance division and ordered an attack. The Confederates were driven back a mile or two, but, re-forming and reenforced, the tide of battle was turned the other way. Sedgwick's marching orders were sending him to the Wilderness Tavern on the turnpike. He was on his way when the battle began, and he now turned to the right from the Germanna Ford road and formed several of his divisions on Warren's right. The presence of Hill on the plank road became known to Meade and Grant, about eight in the morning. Hancock, at Chancellorsville, was too far away to check him, so Getty's division of Sedgwick's corps, on its way to the right, was sent over the Brock road to its junction with the plank road for the purpose of driving Hill back, if possible, beyond Parker's store.

Warren and Sedgwick began to entrench themselves when they realized that Ewell had effectively blocked their progress. Getty, at the junction of the Brock and the Orange plank roads, was likewise throwing up breastworks as fast as he could. Hancock, coming down the Brock road from Chancellorsville, reached him at two in the afternoon and found two of A. P. Hill's divisions in front. After waiting to finish his breastworks, Getty, a little after four o'clock, started, with Hancock supporting him, to carry out his orders to drive Hill back. Hancock says: "The fighting became very fierce at once. The lines of battle were exceedingly close, the musketry continuous and deadly along the entire line. . . . The battle raged with great severity and obstinacy until about 8 P.M. without decided advantage to either party." Here, on the Federal left, and in this desperate engagement, General Alexander Hays, one of Hancock's brigade commanders, was shot through the head and killed.

The afternoon had worn away with heavy skirmishing on the right. About five o'clock Meade made another attempt on Ewell's forces. Both lines were well entrenched, but the Confederate artillery enfiladed the Federal positions. It was after

[40]

WHERE EWELL'S CHARGE SURPRISED GRANT

A photograph of Confederate breastworks raised by Ewell's men a few months before, while they fought in the Wilderness, May 5, 1864. In the picture we see some of the customary breastworks which both contending armies threw up to strengthen their positions. These were in a field near the turnpike in front of Ewell's main line. The impracticable nature of the ground tore the lines on both sides into fragments; as they swept back and forth, squads and companies strove fiercely with one another, hand-to-hand. Grant had confidently expressed the belief to one of his staff officers that there was no more advance left in Lee's army. He was surprised to learn on the 5th that Ewell's Corps was marching rapidly down the Orange turnpike to strike at Sedgwick and Warren, while A. P. Hill, with Longstreet close behind, was pushing forward on the Orange plank-road against Hancock.

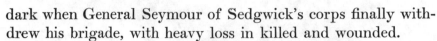

dark when General Seymour of Sedgwick's corps finally with-drew his brigade, with heavy loss in killed and wounded.

When the battle roar had ceased, the rank and file of the Confederate soldiers learned with sorrow of the death of one of the most dashing brigade leaders in Ewell's corps, General John M. Jones. This fighting was the preliminary strug-gle for position in the formation of the battle-lines of the two armies, to secure the final hold for the death grapple. The contestants were without advantage on either side when the sanguinary day's work was finished.

Both armies had constructed breastworks and were en-trenched very close to each other, front to front, gathered and poised for a deadly spring. Early on the morning of May 6th Hancock was reenforced by Burnside, and Hill by Longstreet.

Grant issued orders, through Meade, for a general attack by Sedgwick, Warren, and Hancock along the entire line, at five o'clock on the morning of the 6th. Fifteen minutes before five the Confederates opened fire on Sedgwick's right, and soon the battle was raging along the whole five-mile front. It became a hand-to-hand contest. The Federals advanced with great difficulty. The combatants came upon each other but a few paces apart. Soldiers on one side became hopelessly mixed with those of the other.

Artillery played but little part in the battle of the Wil-derness. The cavalry of the two armies had one indecisive engagement on the 5th. The next day both Custer and Gregg repulsed Hampton and Fitzhugh Lee in two separate en-counters, but Sheridan was unable to follow up the advantage. He had been entrusted with the care of the wagon trains and dared not take his cavalry too far from them. The battle was chiefly one of musketry. Volley upon volley was poured out unceasingly; screaming bullets mingled with terrific yells in the dense woods. The noise became deafening, and the wounded and dying lying on the ground among the trees made a scene of indescribable horror. Living men rushed in to take

LEE GIVES BLOW FOR BLOW

Another view of Ewell's advanced entrenchments — the bark still fresh where the Confederates had worked with the logs. In the Wilderness, Lee, ever bold and aggressive, executed one of the most brilliant maneuvers of his career. His advance was a sudden surprise for Grant, and the manner in which he gave battle was another. Grant harbored the notion that his adversary would act on the defensive, and that there would be opportunity to attack the Army of Northern Virginia only behind strong entrenchments. But in the Wilderness, Lee's veterans, the backbone of the South's fighting strength, showed again their unquenchable spirit of aggressiveness. They came forth to meet Grant's men on equal terms in the thorny thickets. About noon, May 5th, the stillness was broken by the rattle of musketry and the roar of artillery, which told that Warren had met with resistance on the turnpike and that the battle had begun. Nearly a mile were Ewell's men driven back, and then they came magnificently on again, fighting furiously in the smoke-filled thickets with Warren's now retreating troops. Sedgwick, coming to the support of Warren, renewed the conflict. To the southward on the plank road, Getty's division, of the Sixth Corps, hard pressed by the forces of A. P. Hill, was succored by Hancock with the Second Corps, and together these commanders achieved what seemed success. It was brief; Longstreet was close at hand to save the day for the Confederates.

the places of those who had fallen. The missiles cut branches from the trees, and saplings were mowed down as grass in a meadow is cut by a scythe. Bloody remnants of uniforms, blue and gray, hung as weird and uncanny decorations from remaining branches.

The story of the Federal right during the morning is easily told. Persistently and often as he tried, Warren could make no impression on the strongly entrenched Ewell—nor could Sedgwick, who was trying equally hard with Wright's division of his corps. But with Hancock on the left, in his entrenchments on the Brock road, it was different. The gallant and heroic charges here have elicited praise and admiration from friend and foe alike. At first, Hill was forced back in disorder, and driven in confusion a mile and a half from his line. The Confederates seemed on the verge of panic and rout. From the rear of the troops in gray came the beloved leader of the Southern host, General Lee. He was astride his favorite battle-horse, and his face was set in lines of determination. Though the crisis of the battle for the Confederates had arrived, Lee's voice was calm and soft as he commanded, "Follow me," and then urged his charger toward the bristling front of the Federal lines. The Confederate ranks were electrified by the brave example of their commander. A ragged veteran who had followed Lee through many campaigns, leaped forward and caught the bridle-rein of the horse. "We won't go on until you go back," cried the devoted warrior. Instantly the Confederate ranks resounded with the cry, "Lee to the rear! Lee to the rear!" and the great general went back to safety while his soldiers again took up the gage of battle and plunged into the smoke and death-laden storm. But Lee, by his personal presence, and the arrival of Longstreet, had restored order and courage in the ranks, and their original position was soon regained.

The pursuit of the Confederates through the dense forest had caused confusion and disorganization in Hancock's corps.

[44]

TREES IN THE TRACK OF THE IRON STORM

The Wilderness to the north of the Orange turnpike. Over ground like this, where men had seldom trod before, ebbed and flowed the tide of trampling thousands on May 5 and 6, 1864. Artillery, of which Grant had a superabundance, was well-nigh useless, wreaking its impotent fury upon the defenseless trees. Even the efficacy of musketry fire was hampered. Men tripping and falling in the tangled underbrush arose bleeding from the briars to struggle with an adversary whose every movement was impeded also. The cold steel of the bayonet finished the work which rifles had begun. In the terrible turmoil of death the hopes of both Grant and Lee were doomed to disappointment. The result was a victory for neither. Lee, disregarding his own safety, endeavored to rally the disordered ranks of A. P. Hill, and could only be persuaded to retire by the pledge of Longstreet that his advancing force would win the coveted victory. Falling upon Hancock's flank, the fresh troops seemed about to crush the Second Corps, as Jackson's men had crushed the Eleventh the previous year at Chancellorsville. But now, as Jackson, at the critical moment, had fallen by the fire of his own men, so Longstreet and his staff, galloping along the plank road, were mistaken by their own soldiers for Federals and fired upon. A minie-ball struck Longstreet in the shoulder, and he was carried from the field, feebly waving his hat that his men might know that he was not killed. With him departed from the field the life of the attack.

That cohesion and strength in a battle-line of soldiers, where the men can " feel the touch," shoulder to shoulder, was wanting, and the usual form and regular alignment was broken. It was two hours before the lines were re-formed. That short time had been well utilized by the Confederates. Gregg's eight hundred Texans made a desperate charge through the thicket of the pine against Webb's brigade of Hancock's corps, cutting through the growth, and wildly shouting amid the crash and roar of the battle. Half of their number were left on the field, but the blow had effectually checked the Federal advance.

While the battle was raging Grant's general demeanor was imperturbable. He remained with Meade nearly the whole day at headquarters at the Lacy house. He sat upon a stump most of the time, or at the foot of a tree, leaning against its trunk, whittling sticks with his pocket-knife and smoking big black cigars—twenty during the day. He received reports of the progress of the battle and gave orders without the least evidence of excitement or emotion. " His orders," said one of his staff, " were given with a spur," implying instant action. On one occasion, when an officer, in great excitement, brought him the report of Hancock's misfortune and expressed apprehension as to Lee's purpose, Grant exclaimed with some warmth: " Oh, I am heartily tired of hearing what Lee is going to do. Go back to your command and try to think what we are going to do ourselves."

Several brigades of Longstreet's troops, though weary from their forced march, were sent on a flanking movement against Hancock's left, which demoralized Mott's division and caused it to fall back three-quarters of a mile. Longstreet now advanced with the rest of his corps. The dashing leader, while riding with Generals Kershaw and Jenkins at the head of Jenkins' brigade on the right of the Southern battle array, was screened by the tangled thickets from the view of his own troops, flushed with the success of brilliant flank movement.

THE GRAVEYARD OF THREE CAMPAIGNS

As this photograph was taken, May 12, 1864, the dead again were being brought to unhappy Fredericksburg, where slept thousands that had fought under Burnside and Hooker. Now, once more, the sad cavalcade is arriving, freighted still more heavily. The half-ruined homes, to which some of the dwellers had returned, for the third time become temporary hospitals. It was weeks before the wounded left. The Wilderness brought death's woe to 2,246 Northern homes, and Spotsylvania added its 2,725 more. At the South, mourning for lost ones was not less widespread. As a battle, the fighting at close quarters in the Wilderness was indecisive; as a slaughter, it proved that the deadly determination on both sides was equal. Grant, as he turned his face in anguish away from the passing trains of dead and wounded, had learned a bitter lesson—not only as to the fighting blood of his new command but also of that of the foe he had come to crush.

Suddenly the passing column was seen indistinctly through an opening and a volley burst forth and struck the officers. When the smoke lifted Longstreet and Jenkins were down— the former seriously wounded, and the latter killed outright. As at Chancellorsville a year before and on the same battle-ground, a great captain of the Confederacy was shot down by his own men, and by accident, at the crisis of a battle. Jackson lingered several days after Chancellorsville, while Longstreet recovered and lived to fight for the Confederacy till the surrender at Appomattox. General Wadsworth, of Hancock's corps, was mortally wounded during the day, while making a daring assault on the Confederate works, at the head of his men.

During the afternoon, the Confederate attack upon Hancock's and Burnside's forces, which constituted nearly half the entire army, was so severe that the Federal lines began to give way. The combatants swayed back and forth; the Confederates seized the Federal breastworks repeatedly, only to be repulsed again and again. Once, the Southern colors were placed on the Union battlements. A fire in the forest, which had been burning for hours, and in which, it is estimated, about two hundred of the Federal wounded perished, was communicated to the timber entrenchments, the heat and smoke driving into the faces of the men on the Union side, and compelling them in some places to abandon the works. Hancock made a gallant and heroic effort to re-form his lines and push the attack, and, as he rode along the lines, his inspiring presence elicited cheer upon cheer from the men, but the troops had exhausted their ammunition, the wagons were in the rear, and as night was approaching, further attack was abandoned. The contest ended on the lines where it began.

Later in the evening consternation swept the Federal camp when heavy firing was heard in the direction of Sedgwick's corps, on the right. The report was current that the entire Sixth Corps had been attacked and broken. What had happened was a surprise attack by the Confederates,

[48]

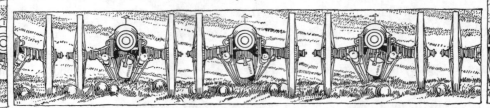

A LOSS IN "EFFECTIVE STRENGTH"—WOUNDED AT FREDERICKSBURG

Federal wounded in the Wilderness campaign, at Fredericksburg. Grant lost 17.3 per cent. of his numbers engaged in the two days' battles of the Wilderness alone. Lee's loss was 18.1 per cent. More than 24,000 of the Army of the Potomac and of the Army of Northern Virginia lay suffering in those uninhabited thickets. There many of them died alone, and some perished in the horror of a forest fire on the night of May 5th. The Federals lost many gallant officers, among them the veteran Wadsworth. The Confederates lost Generals Jenkins and Jones, killed, and suffered a staggering blow in the disabling of Longstreet. The series of battles of the Wilderness and Spotsylvania campaigns were more costly to the Federals than Antietam and Gettysburg combined.

commanded by General John B. Gordon, on Sedgwick's right flank, Generals Seymour and Shaler with six hundred men being captured. When a message was received from Sedgwick that the Sixth Corps was safe in an entirely new line, there was great rejoicing in the Union camp.

Thus ended the two days' fighting of the battle of the Wilderness, one of the greatest struggles in history. It was Grant's first experience in the East, and his trial measure of arms with his great antagonist, General Lee. The latter returned to his entrenchments and the Federals remained in their position. The first clash had been undecisive. While Grant had been defeated in his plan to pass around Lee, yet he had made a new record for the Army of the Potomac, and he was not turned from his purpose of putting himself between the Army of Northern Virginia and the capital of the Confederacy. During the two days' engagement, there were ten hours of actual fighting, with a loss in killed and wounded of about seventeen thousand Union and nearly twelve thousand Confederates, nearly three thousand men sacrificed each hour. It is the belief of some military writers that Lee deliberately chose the Wilderness as a battle-ground, as it would effectually conceal great inferiority of force, but if this be so he seems to have come to share the unanimous opinions of the generals of both sides that its difficulties were unsurmountable, and within his entrenchments he awaited further attack. It did not come.

The next night, May 7th, Grant's march by the Confederate right flank was resumed, but only to be blocked again by the dogged determination of the tenacious antagonist, a few miles beyond, at Spotsylvania. Lee again anticipated Grant's move. It is not strange that the minds of these two men moved along the same lines in military strategy, when we remember they were both military experts of the highest order, and were now working out the same problem. The results obtained by each are told in the story of the battle of Spotsylvania.

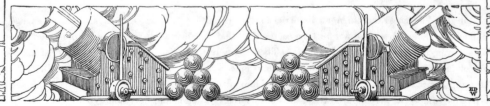

PART I
GRANT VERSUS LEE

SPOTSYLVANIA AND THE BLOODY ANGLE

QUARLES' MILL, NORTH ANNA RIVER—THE GOAL AFTER SPOTSYLVANIA

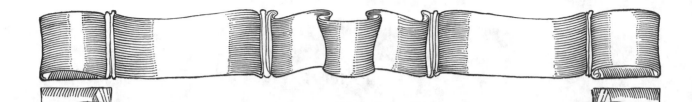

THE BATTLE OF SPOTSYLVANIA
COURT HOUSE

But to Spotsylvania history will accord the palm, I am sure, for having furnished an unexampled muzzle-to-muzzle fire; the longest roll of incessant, unbroken musketry; the most splendid exhibition of individual heroism and personal daring by large numbers, who, standing in the freshly spilt blood of their fellows, faced for so long a period and at so short a range the flaming rifles as they heralded the decrees of death. This heroism was confined to neither side. It was exhibited by both armies, and in that hand-to-hand struggle for the possession of the breastworks it seemed almost universal. It would be commonplace truism to say that such examples will not be lost to the Republic.—*General John B. Gordon, C.S.A., in "Reminiscences of the Civil War."*

IMMEDIATELY after the cessation of hostilities on the 6th of May in the Wilderness, Grant determined to move his army to Spotsylvania Court House, and to start the wagon trains on the afternoon of the 7th. Grant's object was, by a flank move, to get between Lee and Richmond. Lee foresaw Grant's purpose and also moved his cavalry, under Stuart, across the opponent's path. As an illustration of the exact science of war we see the two great military leaders racing for position at Spotsylvania Court House. It was revealed later that Lee had already made preparations on this field a year before, in anticipation of its being a possible battleground.

Apprised of the movement of the Federal trains, Lee, with his usual sagacious foresight, surmised their destination. He therefore ordered General R. H. Anderson, now in command of Longstreet's corps, to march to Spotsylvania Court House at three o'clock on the morning of the 8th. But the smoke and flames from the burning forests that surrounded

SPOTSYLVANIA COURT HOUSE

WHERE GRANT WANTED TO "FIGHT IT OUT"

For miles around this quaint old village-pump surged the lines of two vast contending armies, May 8–12, 1864.   In this picture of only a few months later, the inhabitants have returned to their accustomed quiet, although the reverberations of battle have hardly died away.   But on May 7th Generals Grant and Meade, with their staffs, had started toward the little courthouse.   As they passed along the Brock Road in the rear of Hancock's lines, the men broke into loud hurrahs. They saw that the movement was still to be southward.   But chance had caused Lee to choose the same objective.   Misinterpreting Grant's movement as a retreat upon Fredericksburg, he sent Longstreet's corps, now commanded by Anderson, to Spotsylvania.   Chance again, in the form of a forest fire, drove Anderson to make, on the night of May 7th, the march from the Wilderness that he had been ordered to commence on the morning of the 8th.   On that day, while Warren was contending with the forces of Anderson, Lee's whole army was entrenching on a ridge around Spotsylvania Court House.   "Accident," says Grant, "often decides the fate of battle."   But this "accident" was one of Lee's master moves.

Anderson's camp in the Wilderness made the position untenable, and the march was begun at eleven o'clock on the night of the 7th. This early start proved of inestimable value to the Confederates. Anderson's right, in the Wilderness, rested opposite Hancock's left, and the Confederates secured a more direct line of march to Spotsylvania, several miles shorter than that of the Federals. The same night General Ewell at the extreme Confederate left was ordered to follow Anderson at daylight, if he found no large force in his front. This order was followed out, there being no opposing troops, and the corps took the longest route of any of Lee's troops. General Ewell found the march exhausting and distressing on account of the intense heat and dust and smoke from the burning forests.

The Federal move toward Spotsylvania Court House was begun after dark on the 7th. Warren's corps, in the lead, took the Brock road behind Hancock's position and was followed by Sedgwick, who marched by way of Chancellorsville. Burnside came next, but he was halted to guard the trains. Hancock, covering the move, did not start the head of his command until some time after daylight. When Warren reached Todd's Tavern he found the Union cavalry under Merritt in conflict with Fitzhugh Lee's division of Stuart's cavalry. Warren sent Robinson's division ahead; it drove Fitzhugh Lee back, and, advancing rapidly, met the head of Anderson's troops. The leading brigades came to the assistance of the cavalry; Warren was finally repulsed and began entrenching. The Confederates gained Spotsylvania Court House.

Throughout the day there was continual skirmishing between the troops, as the Northerners attempted to break the line of the Confederates. But the men in gray stood firm. Every advance of the blue was repulsed. Lee again blocked the way of Grant's move. The Federal loss during the day had been about thirteen hundred, while the Confederates lost fewer men than their opponents.

[54]

MEADE AND SEDGWICK—BEFORE THE ADVANCE THAT BROUGHT SEDGWICK'S
DEATH AT SPOTSYLVANIA

To the right of General Meade, his chief and friend, stands Major-General John Sedgwick, commanding
the Sixth Army Corps. He wears his familiar round hat and is smiling. He was a great tease; evidently
the performances of the civilian who had brought his new-fangled photographic apparatus into camp suggested a joke. A couple of months later, on the 9th of May, Sedgwick again was jesting—before Spotsylvania Court House. McMahon of his staff had begged him to avoid passing some artillery exposed to
the Confederate fire, to which Sedgwick had playfully replied, "McMahon, I would like to know who
commands this corps, you or I?" Then he ordered some infantry before him to shift toward the right.
Their movement drew the fire of the Confederates. The lines were close together; the situation tense. A
sharpshooter's bullet whistled—Sedgwick fell. He was taken to Meade's headquarters. The Army of
the Potomac had lost another corps commander, and the Union a brilliant and courageous soldier.

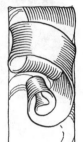

The work of both was now the construction of entrenchments, which consisted of earthworks sloping to either side, with logs as a parapet, and between these works and the opposing army were constructed what are known as abatis, felled trees, with the branches cut off, the sharp ends projecting toward the approaching forces.

Lee's entrenchments were of such character as to increase the efficiency of his force. They were formed in the shape of a huge V with the apex flattened, forming a salient angle against the center of the Federal line. The Confederate lines were facing north, northwest, and northeast, the corps commanded by Anderson on the left, Ewell in the center, and Early on the right, the latter temporarily replacing A. P. Hill, who was ill. The Federals confronting them were Burnside on the left, Sedgwick and Warren in the center, and Hancock on the right.

The day of the 9th was spent in placing the lines of troops, with no fighting except skirmishing and some sharpshooting. While placing some field-pieces, General Sedgwick was hit by a sharpshooter's bullet and instantly killed. He was a man of high character, a most competent commander, of fearless courage, loved and lamented by the army. General Horatio G. Wright succeeded to the command of the Sixth Corps.

Early on the morning of the 10th, the Confederates discovered that Hancock had crossed the Po River in front of his position of the day before and was threatening their rear. Grant had suspected that Lee was about to move north toward Fredericksburg, and Hancock had been ordered to make a reconnaissance with a view to attacking and turning the Confederate left. But difficulties stood in the way of Hancock's performance, and before he had accomplished much, Meade directed him to send two of his divisions to assist Warren in making an attack on the Southern lines. The Second Corps started to recross the Po. Before all were over Early made

THE APEX OF THE BATTLEFIELD

McCool's house, within the "Bloody Angle." The photographs were taken in 1864, shortly after the struggle of Spotsylvania Court House, and show the old dwelling as it was on May 12th, when the fighting was at flood tide all round it; and below, the Confederate entrenchments near that blood-drenched spot. At a point in these Confederate lines in advance of the McCool house, the entrenchments had been thrown forward like the salient of a fort, and the wedge-shaped space within them was destined to become renowned as the "Bloody Angle." The position was defended by the famous "Stonewall Division" of the Confederates under command of General Edward Johnson. It was near the scene of Upton's gallant charge on the 10th. Here at daybreak on May 12th the divisions of the intrepid Barlow and Birney, sent forward by Hancock, stole a march upon the unsuspecting Confederates. Leaping over the breastworks the Federals were upon them and the first of the terrific hand-to-hand conflicts that marked the day began. It ended in victory for Hancock's men, into whose hands fell 20 cannon, 30 standards and 4,000 prisoners, "the best division in the Confederate army."

CONFEDERATE ENTRENCHMENTS NEAR "BLOODY ANGLE"

Flushed with success, the Federals pressed on to Lee's second line of works, where Wilcox's division of the Confederates held them until reënforcements sent by Lee from Hill and Anderson drove them back. On the Federal side the Sixth Corps, with Upton's brigade in the advance, was hurried forward to hold the advantage gained. But Lee himself was on the scene, and the men of the gallant Gordon's division, pausing long enough to seize and turn his horse, with shouts of "General Lee in the rear," hurtled forward into the conflict. In five separate charges by the Confederates the fighting came to close quarters. With bayonets, clubbed muskets, swords and pistols, men fought within two feet of one another on either side of the entrenchments at "Bloody Angle" till night at last left it in possession of the Federals. None of the fighting near Spotsylvania Court House was inglorious. On the 10th, after a day of strengthening positions on both sides, young Colonel Emory Upton of the 121st New York, led a storming party of twelve regiments into the strongest of the Confederate entrenchments. For his bravery Grant made him a brigadier-general on the field.

a vigorous assault on the rear division, which did not escape without heavy loss. In this engagement the corps lost the first gun in its most honorable career, a misfortune deeply lamented by every man in the corps, since up to this moment it had long been the only one in the entire army which could make the proud claim of never having lost a gun or a color.

But the great event of the 10th was the direct assault upon the Confederate front. Meade had arranged for Hancock to take charge of this, and the appointed hour was five in the afternoon. But Warren reported earlier that the opportunity was most favorable, and he was ordered to start at once. Wearing his full uniform, the leader of the Fifth Corps advanced at a quarter to four with the greater portion of his troops. The progress of the valiant Northerners was one of the greatest difficulty, owing to the dense wood of low cedar-trees through which they had to make their way. Longstreet's corps behind their entrenchments acknowledged the advance with very heavy artillery and musket fire. But Warren's troops did not falter or pause until some had reached the abatis and others the very crest of the parapet. A few, indeed, were actually killed inside the works. All, however, who survived the terrible ordeal were finally driven back with heavy loss. General James C. Rice was mortally wounded.

To the left of Warren, General Wright had observed what he believed to be a vulnerable spot in the Confederate entrenchments. Behind this particular place was stationed Doles' brigade of Georgia regiments, and Colonel Emory Upton was ordered to charge Doles with a column of twelve regiments in four lines. The ceasing of the Federal artillery at six o'clock was the signal for the charge, and twenty minutes later, as Upton tells us, "at command, the lines rose, moved noiselessly to the edge of the wood, and then, with a wild cheer and faces averted, rushed for the works. Through a terrible front and flank fire the column advanced quickly, gaining the parapet. Here occurred a deadly hand-to-hand

UNION ARTILLERY MASSING
FOR THE ADVANCE THAT
EWELL'S ATTACK DELAYED
THAT SAME AFTERNOON

BEVERLY HOUSE, MAY 18, 1864

The artillery massing in the meadow gives to this view the interest of an impending tragedy. In the foreground the officers, servants, and orderlies of the headquarters mess camp are waiting for the command to strike their tents, pack the wagons, and move on. But at the very time this photograph was taken they should have been miles away. Grant had issued orders the day before that should have set these troops in motion. However, the Confederate General Ewell had chosen the 18th to make an attack on the right flank. It not only delayed the departure but forced a change in the intended positions of the division as they had been contemplated by the commander-in-chief. Beverly House is where General Warren pitched his headquarters after Spotsylvania, and the spectator is looking toward the battlefield that lies beyond the distant woods. After Ewell's attack, Warren again found himself on the right flank, and at this very moment the main body of the Federal army is passing in the rear of him. The costly check at Spotsylvania, with its wonderful display of fighting on both sides, had in its apparently fruitless results called for the display of all Grant's gifts as a military leader. It takes but little imagination to supply color to this photograph; it is full of it—full of the movement and detail of war also. It is springtime; blossoms have just left the trees and the whole country is green and smiling, but the earth is scarred by thousands of trampling feet and hoof-prints. Ugly ditches cross the landscape; the débris of an army marks its onsweep from one battlefield to another.

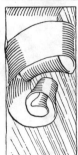

conflict. The enemy, sitting in their pits with pieces upright, loaded, and with bayonets fixed ready to impale the first who should leap over, absolutely refused to yield the ground. The first of our men who tried to surmount the works fell, pierced through the head by musket-balls. Others, seeing the fate of their comrades, held their pieces at arm's length and fired downward, while others, poising their pieces vertically, hurled them down upon their enemy, pinning them to the ground. . . . The struggle lasted but a few seconds. Numbers prevailed, and like a resistless wave, the column poured over the works, quickly putting *hors de combat* those who resisted and sending to the rear those who surrendered. Pressing forward and expanding to the right and left, the second line of entrenchments, its line of battle, and a battery fell into our hands. The column of assault had accomplished its task."

The Confederate line had been shattered and an opening made for expected support. This, however, failed to arrive. General Mott, on the left, did not bring his division forward as had been planned and as General Wright had ordered. The Confederates were reenforced, and Upton could do no more than hold the captured entrenchments until ordered to retire. He brought twelve hundred prisoners and several stands of colors back to the Union lines; but over a thousand of his own men were killed or wounded. For gallantry displayed in this charge, Colonel Upton was made brigadier-general.

The losses to the Union army in this engagement at Spotsylvania were over four thousand. The loss to the Confederates was probably two thousand.

During the 11th there was a pause. The two giant antagonists took a breathing spell. It was on the morning of this date that Grant penned the sentence, "I propose to fight it out on this line if it takes all summer," to his chief of staff, General Halleck.

During this time Sheridan, who had brought the cavalry

THE ONES WHO NEVER CAME BACK

These are some of the men for whom waiting women wept—the ones who never came back. They belonged to Ewell's Corps, who attacked the Federal lines so gallantly on May 18th. There may be some who will turn from this picture with a shudder of horror, but it is no morbid curiosity that will cause them to study it closely. If pictures such as this were familiar everywhere there would soon be an end of war. We can realize money by seeing it expressed in figures; we can realize distances by miles, but some things in their true meaning can only be grasped and impressions formed with the seeing eye. Visualizing only this small item of the awful cost—the cost beside which money cuts no figure—an idea can be gained of what war is. Here is a sermon in the cause of universal peace. The handsome lad lying with outstretched arms and clinched fingers is a mute plea. Death has not disfigured him—he lies in an attitude of relaxation and composure. Perhaps in some Southern home this same face is pictured in the old family album, alert and full of life and hope, and here is the end. Does there not come to the mind the insistent question, "Why?" The Federal soldiers standing in the picture are not thinking of all this, it may be true, but had they meditated in the way that some may, as they gaze at this record of death, it would be worth their while. One of the men is apparently holding a sprig of blossoms in his hand. It is a strange note here.

up to a state of great efficiency, was making an expedition to the vicinity of Richmond. He had said that if he were permitted to operate independently of the army he would draw Stuart after him. Grant at once gave the order, and Sheridan made a detour around Lee's army, engaging and defeating the Confederate cavalry, which he greatly outnumbered, on the 11th of May, at Yellow Tavern, where General Stuart, the brilliant commander of the Confederate cavalry, was mortally wounded.

Grant carefully went over the ground and decided upon another attack on the 12th. About four hundred yards of clear ground lay in front of the sharp angle, or salient, of Lee's lines. After the battle this point was known as the " Bloody Angle," and also as " Hell's Hole." Here Hancock was ordered to make an attack at daybreak on the 12th. Lee had been expecting a move on the part of Grant. On the evening of the 10th he sent to Ewell this message: " It will be necessary for you to reestablish your whole line to-night. . . . Perhaps Grant will make a night attack, as it was a favorite amusement of his at Vicksburg."

Through rain and mud Hancock's force was gotten into position within a few hundred yards of the Confederate breastworks. He was now between Burnside and Wright. At the first approach of dawn the four divisions of the Second Corps, under Birney, Mott, Barlow, and Gibbon (in reserve) moved noiselessly to the designated point of attack. Without a shot being fired they reached the Confederate entrenchments, and struck with fury and impetuosity a mortal blow at the point where least expected, on the salient, held by General Edward Johnson of Ewell's corps. The movement of the Federals was so swift and the surprise so complete, that the Confederates could make practically no resistance, and were forced to surrender.

The artillery had been withdrawn from the earthworks occupied by Johnson's troops on the previous night, but

DIGGING A LONELY GRAVE—AFTER SPOTSYLVANIA

If we should take out the grim reminder of war's horrors, the dead man on the litter with the stiff upturned arms, we should have a charming picture of a little Virginia farm, a cozy little house with its blossoming peach trees in the garden and the big Chinaberry tree shading the front yard. But within a stone's throw lie scores of huddled heaps distressing to gaze upon. Only a few hours before they had been living, breathing, fighting men; for here occurred Ewell's fierce attack on the 18th of May. The little farm belonged to a widow by the name of Allsop, and the garden and the ground back of the barns and outbuildings became a Confederate cemetery. Soldiers grow callous to the work of putting friends and foemen to rest for the last long sleep. Evidently this little squad of the burying detail have discovered that this man is an officer, and instead of putting him in the long trench where his comrades rest with elbows touching in soldierly alignment, they are giving him a grave by himself. Down at a fence corner on the Allsop farm they found the dead Confederate of the smaller photograph. He was of the never-surrender type, this man in the ragged gray uniform, one of the do or die kind that the bullets find most often. Twice wounded before his dauntless spirit left him was this gallant fellow; with a shattered leg that he had tied about hastily with a cotton shirt, he still fought on, firing from where he lay until he could see no longer, and he fell back and slowly bled to death from the ghastly wound in the shoulder. There was no mark on him to tell his name; he was just one of Ewell's men, and became merely a number on the tally sheet that showed the score of the game of war.

JUST "ONE OF EWELL'S MEN"

developments had led to an order to have it returned early in the morning. It was approaching as the attack was made. Before the artillerymen could escape or turn the guns upon the Federals, every cannon had been captured. General Johnson with almost his whole division, numbering about three thousand, and General Steuart, were captured, between twenty and thirty colors, and several thousand stands of arms were taken. Hancock had already distinguished himself as a leader of his soldiers, and from his magnificent appearance, noble bearing, and courage had been called "Hancock the Superb," but this was the most brilliant of his military achievements.

Pressing onward across the first defensive line of the Confederates, Hancock's men advanced against the second series of trenches, nearly half a mile beyond. As the Federals pushed through the muddy fields they lost all formation. They reached close to the Confederate line. The Southerners were prepared for the attack. A volley poured into the throng of blue, and General Gordon with his reserve division rushed forward, fighting desperately to drive the Northerners back. As they did so General Lee rode up, evidently intending to go forward with Gordon. His horse was seized by one of the soldiers, and for the second time in the campaign the cry arose from the ranks, "Lee to the rear!" The beloved commander was led back from the range of fire, while the men, under the inspiration of his example, rushed forward in a charge that drove the Federals back until they had reached the outer line of works. Here they fought stubbornly at deadly range. Neither side was able to force the other back. But Gordon was not able to cope with the entire attack. Wright and Warren both sent some of their divisions to reenforce Hancock, and Lee sent all the assistance possible to the troops struggling so desperately to restore his line at the salient.

Many vivid and picturesque descriptions of this fighting at the angle have been written, some by eye-witnesses, others by able historians, but no printed page, no cold type can

IN ONE LONG BURIAL TRENCH

It fell to the duty of the First Massachusetts Heavy Artillery of General Tyler's division to put under ground the men they slew in the sharp battle of May 18th, and here they are near Mrs. Allsop's barn digging the trench to hide the dreadful work of bullet and shot and shell. No feeling of bitterness exists in moments such as these. What soldier in the party knows but what it may be his turn next to lie beside other lumps of clay and join his earth-mother in this same fashion in his turn. But men become used to work of any kind, and these men digging up the warm spring soil, when their labor is concluded, are neither oppressed nor nerve-shattered by what they have seen and done. They have lost the power of experiencing sensation. Senses become numbed in a measure; the value of life itself from close and constant association with death is minimized almost to the vanishing point. In half an hour these very men may be singing and laughing as if war and death were only things to be expected, not reasoned over in the least.

ONE OF THE FEARLESS CONFEDERATES

convey to the mind the realities of that terrible conflict.   The
results were appalling.   The whole engagement was practically a hand-to-hand contest.   The dead lay beneath the feet
of the living, three and four layers deep.   This hitherto quiet
spot of earth was devastated and covered with the slain, wel-
tering in their own blood, mangled and shattered into scarcely
a semblance of human form.   Dying men were crushed by
horses and many, buried beneath the mire and mud, still lived.
Some artillery was posted on high ground not far from the
apex of the salient, and an incessant fire was poured into the
Confederate works over the Union lines, while other guns kept
up an enfilade of canister along the west of the salient.

The contest from the right of the Sixth to the left of the
Second Corps was kept up throughout the day along the
whole line.   Repeatedly the trenches had to be cleared of the
dead.   An oak tree twenty-two inches in diameter was cut
down by musket-balls.   Men leaped upon the breastworks,
firing until shot down.

The battle of the " angle " is said to have been the most
awful in duration and intensity in modern times.   Battle-line
after battle-line, bravely obeying orders, was annihilated.   The
entrenchments were shivered and shattered, trunks of trees
carved into split brooms.   Sometimes the contestants came so
close together that their muskets met, muzzle to muzzle, and
their flags almost intertwined with each other as they waved
in the breeze.   As they fought with the desperation of madmen,
the living would stand on the bodies of the dead to reach over
the breastworks with their weapons of slaughter.   Lee hurled
his army with unparalleled vigor against his opponent five
times during the day, but each time was repulsed.   Until three
o'clock the next morning the slaughter continued, when the
Confederates sank back into their second line of entrenchments,
leaving their opponents where they had stood in the morning.

All the fighting on the 12th was not done at the " Bloody
Angle."   Burnside on the left of Hancock engaged Early's

BETHEL CHURCH—WAITING FOR ORDERS

The couriers lounging around the church door will soon be galloping away with orders; for it is the 23d of May, and, the afternoon before, Burnside, with his Ninth Corps, arrived and took up his headquarters here, within ten miles of the North Anna. In the "sidling" movement, as the Confederate soldiers called it, begun by Grant on May 19th, the corps of Hancock and Warren were pressing forward to Guiney's Station through a strange country, over roads unknown to them, while the corps of Burnside and Wright were still demonstrating against the Confederates at Spotsylvania. Here was an opportunity for Lee to take the initiative, and with his whole force either attack Wright and Burnside, or, pushing forward by the Telegraph Road, strike Hancock alone, or at most Hancock and Warren. But Lee, fearing perhaps to risk a general contest, remained strictly on the defensive, moving his troops out along the Telegraph Road to make sure of keeping between his adversary and Richmond. Meanwhile, Burnside, followed by Wright, marched on the evening of the 21st, and next day came up with Grant's headquarters at Guiney's Station. Here he found Grant sitting on the porch, reading the despatch that told of Sherman's capture of Kingston, Georgia, and his crossing of the Etowah River. Burnside was ordered forward to Bethel Church and thence to Ox Ford, on the North Anna, there on the 24th to be held in check by Lee's faultless formation.

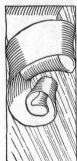

troops and was defeated, while on the other side of the salient Wright succeeded in driving Anderson back.

The question has naturally arisen why that "salient" was regarded of such vital importance as to induce the two chief commanders to force their armies into such a hand-to-hand contest that must inevitably result in unparalleled and wholesale slaughter. It was manifest, however, that Grant had shown generalship in finding the weak point in Lee's line for attack. It was imperative that he hold the gain made by his troops. Lee could ill afford the loss resistance would entail, but he could not withdraw his army during the day without disaster.

The men on both sides seemed to comprehend the gravity of the situation, that it was a battle to the death for that little point of entrenchment. Without urging by officers, and sometimes without officers, they fell into line and fought and bled and died in myriads as though inspired by some unseen power. Here men rushed to their doom with shouts of courage and eagerness.

The pity of it all was manifested by the shocking scene on that battlefield the next day. Piles of dead lay around the "Bloody Angle," a veritable "Hell's Hole" on both sides of the entrenchments, four layers deep in places, shattered and torn by bullets and hoofs and clubbed muskets, while beneath the layers of dead, it is said, there could be seen quivering limbs of those who still lived.

General Grant was deeply moved at the terrible loss of life. When he expressed his regret for the heavy sacrifice of men to General Meade, the latter replied, "General, we can't do these little tricks without heavy losses." The total loss to the Union army in killed, wounded, and missing at Spotsylvania was nearly eighteen thousand. The Confederate losses have never been positively known, but from the best available sources of information the number has been placed at not less than nine thousand men. Lee's loss in high officers was very

THE REDOUBT THAT LEE LET GO

This redoubt covered Taylor's Bridge, but its flanks were swept by artillery and an enfilading fire from rifle-pits across the river.   Late in the evening of the 23d, Hancock's corps, arriving before the redoubt, had assaulted it with two brigades and easily carried it.   During the night the Confederates from the other side made two attacks upon the bridge and finally succeeded in setting it afire.   The flames were extinguished by the Federals, and on the 24th Hancock's troops crossed over without opposition.   The easy crossing of the Federals here was but another example of Lee's favorite rule to let his antagonist attack him on the further side of a stream.   Taylor's Bridge could easily have been held by Lee for a much longer time, but its ready abandonment was part of the tactics by which Grant was being led into a military dilemma.   In the picture the Federal soldiers confidently hold the captured redoubt, convinced that the possession of it meant that they had driven Lee to his last corner.

severe, the killed including General Daniel and General Perrin, while Generals Walker, Ramseur, R. D. Johnston, and McGowan were severely wounded. In addition to the loss of these important commanders, Lee was further crippled in efficient commanders by the capture of Generals Edward Johnson and Steuart. The Union loss in high officers was light, excepting General Sedgwick on the 9th. General Webb was wounded, and Colonel Coon, of the Second Corps, was killed.

Lee's forces had been handled with such consummate skill as to make them count one almost for two, and there was the spirit of devotion for Lee among his soldiers which was indeed practically hero-worship. All in all, he had an army, though shattered and worn, that was almost unconquerable. Grant found that ordinary methods of war, even such as he had experienced in the West, were not applicable to the Army of Northern Virginia. The only hope for the Union army was a long-drawn-out process, and with larger numbers, better kept, and more often relieved, Grant's army would ultimately make that of Lee's succumb, from sheer exhaustion and disintegration.

The battle was not terminated on the 12th. During the next five days there was a continuous movement of the Union corps to the east which was met by a corresponding readjustment of the Confederate lines. After various maneuvers, Hancock was ordered to the point where the battle was fought on the 12th, and on the 18th and 19th, the last effort was made to break the lines of the Confederates. Ewell, however, drove the Federals back and the next day he had a severe engagement with the Union left wing, while endeavoring to find out something of Grant's plans.

Twelve days of active effort were thus spent in skirmishing, fighting, and countermarching. In the last two engagements the Union losses were nearly two thousand, which are included in those before stated. It was decided to abandon the attempt to dislodge Lee from his entrenchments, and to move

"WALK YOUR HORSES"

ONE OF THE GRIM JOKES OF WAR

AS PLAYED AT

CHESTERFIELD BRIDGE, NORTH ANNA

The sign posted by the local authorities at Taylor's bridge, where the Telegraph Road crosses the North Anna, was "Walk your horses." The wooden structure was referred to by the military as Chesterfield bridge. Here Hancock's Corps arrived toward evening of May 23d, and the Confederate entrenchments, showing in the foreground, were seized by the old "Berry Brigade." In the heat of the charge the Ninety-third New York carried their colors to the middle of the bridge, driving off the Confederates before they could destroy it. When the Federals began crossing next day they had to run the gantlet of musketry and artillery fire from the opposite bank. Several regiments of New York heavy artillery poured across the structure at the double-quick with the hostile shells bursting about their heads. When Captain Sleeper's Eighteenth Massachusetts battery began crossing, the Confederate cannoneers redoubled their efforts to blow up the ammunition by well-aimed shots. Sleeper passed over only one piece at a time in order to diminish the target and enforce the observance of the local law by walking his horses! The Second Corps got no further than the ridge beyond, where Lee's strong V formation held it from further advance.

to the North Anna River. On the 20th of May the march
was resumed. The men had suffered great hardships from
hunger, exposure, and incessant action, and many would fall
asleep on the line of march.

On the day after the start, Hancock crossed the Mattapony River at one point and Warren at another. Hancock
was ordered to take position on the right bank and, if practicable, to attack the Confederates wherever found. By the
22d, Wright and Burnside came up and the march proceeded.
But the vigilant Lee had again detected the plans of his
adversary.

Meade's army had barely started in its purpose to turn
the Confederates' flank when the Southern forces were on the
way to block the army of the North. As on the march from
the Wilderness to Spotsylvania, Lee's troops took the shorter
route, along main roads, and reached the North Anna ahead
of the Federals. Warren's corps was the first of Meade's
army to arrive at the north bank of the river, which it did on
the afternoon of May 23d. Lee was already on the south
bank, but Warren crossed without opposition. No sooner
had he gotten over, however, than he was attacked by the Confederates and a severe but undecisive engagement followed.
The next morning (the 24th) Hancock and Wright put their
troops across at places some miles apart, and before these two
wings of the army could be joined, Lee made a brilliant stroke
by marching in between them, forming a wedge whose point
rested on the bank, opposite the Union center, under Burnside,
which had not yet crossed the river.

The Army of the Potomac was now in three badly separated parts. Burnside could not get over in sufficient strength
to reenforce the wings, and all attempts by the latter to aid
him in so doing met with considerable disaster. The loss in
these engagements approximated two thousand on each side.

On the 25th, Sheridan and his cavalry rejoined the army.
They had been gone since the 9th and their raid was most

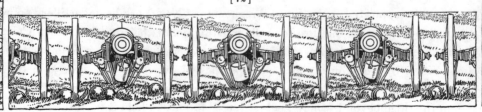

WHERE GRANT FOUND OUT HIS MISTAKE

At those white tents above Quarles' Mill dam sits Grant, at his "General Headquarters" on the 24th of May, and he has found out too late that Lee has led him into a trap. The Army of Northern Virginia had beaten him in the race for the North Anna, and it was found strongly entrenched on the south side of the stream. The corps of Warren and Wright had crossed at Jericho Mills a mile above Quarles' Mill, and Hancock's crossing had been effected so easily at the wooden bridge just below Quarles' Mill. Grant had reenforced both wings of his army before he discovered that it was divided. Lee's lines stretched southward in the form of a V, with the apex resting close to the river. The great strategist had folded back his flanks to let in Grant's forces on either side. This and the following pictures form a unique series of illustrations in panorama of the futile crossing of the North Anna by the Federals.

THE UNDISPUTED CROSSING
AT NORTH ANNA

These pictures show the pontoon-bridge laid for the crossing of the corps of Warren and Wright at Jericho Ford, about four miles farther upstream than the Chesterfield or Taylor's bridge. The Federals met with no opposition at this crossing, their sharpshooters being able to keep off the Confederates, while the pontonniers were at work. In the two upper pictures the old Jericho Mill stands on the north bank. On the eminence above it is the Gentry house and other dwellings, past which the ammunition-train is winding down the road to the crossing. Warren's Fifth Corps was soon to need its ammunition. The infantry were all across by 4:30 in the afternoon of May 23d and, advancing over the ground seen in the lower picture, formed their lines on the edge of a wood half a mile beyond the south bank. The artillery was posted on the ridge. Before Warren could get into position Lee sent the whole of Hill's Corps against him. A brigade of Cutler's division was forced back, but after some sharp fighting the Confederates were driven back into their trenches, leaving many killed and wounded, and five hundred prisoners.

THE REAR-GUARD

Thus the Federals held the approaches to their pontoon-bridge at Jericho Mill during the sultry days of May (24–26) while Grant was making up his mind that Lee's position could not be successfully attacked. The corps of Warren and Wright have all crossed the bridge, followed by the wagon-trains. Guards have been posted on either bank. The felled timber on the north bank was cut so as to allow the Federal reserve artillery to command the bridge. At either end sit two sentinels ready to challenge perfunctorily any straggler who may pass. The rest of the men have stacked arms and given themselves up to idleness, stretching their improvised shelters to shield them from the broiling sun. One man by the old mill is bathing his feet, weary with the long march.

THE CAPTURED REDAN
AND THE BRIDGE

Across this insecure foot-bridge Hancock's troop had to pass in the attack on the Confederate works which commanded Taylor's bridge on the North Anna. A tongue of land formed by the junction of Long Creek with the larger stream was the position chosen for the redan which is seen topping the ridge in the upper picture. Birney's division advanced across the bare and barren plain of the little peninsula, and pressing across the shaky little foot-bridge at the double-quick, swept up the sharp height seen in the picture above, while three sections of Tidball's battery covered the assault of Pierce and Egan As their line approached, the Confederates abandoned the redan and fled. The Federals, digging footholds in the parapet with their bayonets, clambered up and planted their colors. In taking the lower picture the camera was placed within the Confederate works looking toward the ground over which the Federals approached. The fresh earthworks in the foreground were hastily thrown up to strengthen the redan, which was originally built during the Chancellorsville campaign.

WHERE THE BATTLE–LINE WENT OVER

On the pontoon-bridge in the lower picture crossed Smyth's division of the Second Corps on the morning of May 24th. Forming in line of battle on the south bank, they advanced and carried the Confederate works that commanded Taylor's or the Chesterfield bridge above. The Confederates at once brought up reënforcements and attacked Smyth, who, also reenforced, held his position during a furious rain-storm until dark. Until the pontoons were laid, Grant could not get his army across the North Anna in sufficient force to make the attack he contemplated. The lower picture shows one of the two pontoon-bridges laid below Taylor's bridge so that its defenders could be driven off and the Federal troops enabled to use it. The railroad bridge below Taylor's had been destroyed, but still farther downstream was an old foot-bridge. A short distance above here the pontoons were laid. They can be seen in the upper picture beyond the pontonniers in the foreground, who are at work strengthening the foot-bridge so that it, too, can be used for the passage of the troops that were to retreat from the embarrassing predicament into which Lee had lured them.

successful. Besides the decisive victory over the Confederate cavalry at Yellow Tavern, they had destroyed several depots of supplies, four trains of cars, and many miles of railroad track. Nearly four hundred Federal prisoners on their way to Richmond had been rescued from their captors. The dashing cavalrymen had even carried the first line of work around Richmond, and had made a detour down the James to communicate with General Butler. Grant was highly satisfied with Sheridan's performance. It had been of the greatest assistance to him, as it had drawn off the whole of the Confederate cavalry, and made the guarding of the wagon trains an easy matter.

But here, on the banks of the North Anna, Grant had been completely checkmated by Lee. He realized this and decided on a new move, although he still clung to his idea of turning the Confederate right. The Federal wings were withdrawn to the north side of the river during the night of May 26th and the whole set in motion for the Pamunkey River at Hanovertown. Two divisions of Sheridan's cavalry and Warren's corps were in advance. Lee lost no time in pursuing his great antagonist, but for the first time the latter was able to hold his lead. Along the Totopotomoy, on the afternoon of May 28th, infantry and cavalry of both armies met in a severe engagement in which the strong position of Lee's troops again foiled Grant's purpose. The Union would have to try at some other point, and on the 31st Sheridan's cavalry took possession of Cold Harbor. This was to be the next battleground.

PART I
GRANT VERSUS LEE

———

COLD HARBOR

———

WAITING THE WORD FOR THE COLD HARBOR FLANKING MARCH
—UNION TROOPS REPULSED AT THE NORTH ANNA

TEN MINUTES WITH GENERAL GRANT, JUNE 2, 1864—THE FIRST SCENE

As the General-in-Chief of all the Federal armies sits smoking with his back to the smaller tree, two extraordinary things are happening: Grant is arriving at the tremendous decision to "fight it out" that cost him ten thousand men the next morning; and the enterprising photographer with the Union army has climbed upstairs in the little roadside meeting house (Bethesda Church, on the way to Cold Harbor), and is photographing the scene again and again. The result is a veritable "moving picture" series of Grant in the field—an opportunity without a parallel to witness the acting of history itself. The informal consultation which the pictures reveal was as near a council of war as Grant ever came.

TEN MINUTES WITH GENERAL GRANT—THE SECOND AND THIRD SCENES

It is due to the courtesy of General Horace Porter, himself an actor in these three scenes as a member of Grant's staff, that so many participants in the historic episode can here be identified. In the first picture (on the facing page) General Porter himself sits reading a newspaper on Grant's right, and on his left is General Rawlins, his chief of staff, next to Colonel Ely S. Parker. General Grant impassively listens to the report that Colonel Bowers, his adjutant-general, is reading as he stands inside the circle to the right of the picture. In the second picture (immediately above) the General-in-Chief has arisen and walked to the left, where he leans over General Meade's shoulder and consults his map. In front of them a newly arrived officer bends forward, receiving orders or reporting. Colonel Parker has passed his newspaper to another officer. The rest of the group center their looks upon Grant. Soldiers from the Third Division of the Fifth Army Corps, whose wagons are passing, stop and gaze at the men in whose hands their lives are held. At last, in the third picture, the General-in-Chief has made up his mind. He is back in his original seat and is writing out his orders. The problem has been a painful one; on the one side his conviction that his "hammering policy" is the right one; on the other the heated protest of Northern press and public against what seemed so extravagant a waste of human life. The question was, as General Porter later wrote: "Whether to attempt to crush Lee's army on the north side of the James, with the prospect, in case of success, of driving him into Richmond, capturing the city, perhaps without a siege, and putting the Confederate Government to flight; or to move the Union army south of the James without giving battle and transfer the field of operations to the vicinity of Petersburg. It was a nice question of judgment." Grant's judgment was to fight; the result, Cold Harbor.

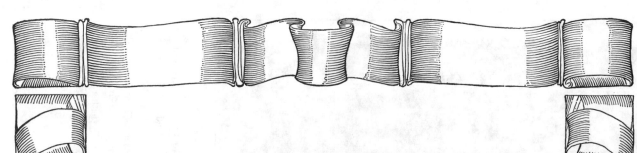

COLD HARBOR

Cold Harbor is, I think, the only battle I ever fought that I would not fight over again under the circumstances. I have always regretted that the last assault at Cold Harbor was ever made.—*General U. S. Grant in his " Memoirs."*

ACCORDING to Grant's well-made plans of march, the various corps of the Army of the Potomac set out from the banks of the North Anna on the night of May 26, 1864, at the times and by the routes assigned to them. Early on the morning of May 27th Lee set his force in motion by the Telegraph road and such others as were available, across the Little and South Anna rivers toward Ashland and Atlee's Station on the Virginia Central Railroad.

Thus the armies were stretched like two live wires along the swampy bottom-lands of eastern Virginia, and as they came in contact, here and there along the line, there were the inevitable sputterings of flame and considerable destruction wrought. The advance Federal infantry crossed the Pamunkey, after the cavalry, at Hanoverstown, early on May 28th. The Second Corps was close behind the Sixth; the Fifth was over by noon, while the Ninth, now an integral portion of the Army of the Potomac, passed the river by midnight.

On the 31st General Sheridan reached Cold Harbor, which Meade had ordered him to hold at all hazards. This place, probably named after the old home of some English settler, was not a town but the meeting-place of several roads of great strategic importance to the Federal army. They led not only toward Richmond by the way of the upper Chickahominy bridges, but in the direction of White House Landing, on the Pamunkey River.

Both Lee and Meade had received reenforcements—the

READY FOR THE ADVANCE THAT LEE DROVE BACK

Between these luxuriant banks stretch the pontoons and bridges to facilitate the rapid crossing of the North Anna by Hancock's Corps on May 24th. Thus was completed the passage to the south of the stream of the two wings of the Army of the Potomac. But when the center under Burnside was driven back and severely handled at Ox Ford, Grant immediately detached a brigade each from Hancock and Warren to attack the apex of Lee's wedge on the south bank of the river, but the position was too strong to justify the attempt. Then it dawned upon the Federal general-in-chief that Lee had cleaved the Army of the Potomac into two separated bodies. To reënforce either wing would require two crossings of the river, while Lee could quickly march troops from one side to the other within his impregnable wedge. As Grant put it in his report, " To make a direct attack from either wing would cause a slaughter of our men that even success would not justify."

former by Breckinridge, and the scattered forces in western Virginia, and by Pickett and Hoke from North Carolina. From Bermuda Hundred where General Butler was "bottled up"—to use a phrase which Grant employed and afterward regretted—General W. F. Smith was ordered to bring the Eighteenth Corps of the Army of the James to the assistance of Meade, since Butler could defend his position perfectly well with a small force, and could make no headway against Beauregard with a large one. Grant had now nearly one hundred and fourteen thousand troops and Lee about eighty thousand.

Sheridan's appearance at Cold Harbor was resented in vain by Fitzhugh Lee, and the next morning, June 1st, the Sixth Corps arrived, followed by General Smith and ten thousand men of the Eighteenth, who had hastened from the landing-place at White House. These took position on the right of the Sixth, and the Federal line was promptly faced by Longstreet's corps, a part of A. P. Hill's, and the divisions of Hoke and Breckinridge. At six o'clock in the afternoon Wright and Smith advanced to the attack, which Hoke and Kershaw received with courage and determination. The Confederate line was broken in several places, but before night checked the struggle the Southerners had in some degree regained their position. The short contest was a severe one for the Federal side. Wright lost about twelve hundred men and Smith one thousand.

The following day the final dispositions were made for the mighty struggle that would decide Grant's last chance to interpose between Lee and Richmond. Hancock and the Second Corps arrived at Cold Harbor and took position on the left of General Wright. Burnside, with the Ninth Corps, was placed near Bethesda Church on the road to Mechanicsville, while Warren, with the Fifth, came to his left and connected with Smith's right. Sheridan was sent to hold the lower Chickahominy bridges and to cover the road to White House,

IMPROVISED BREASTWORKS

The End of the Gray Line at Cold Harbor. Here at the extreme left of the Confederate lines at Cold Harbor is an example of the crude protection resorted to by the soldiers on both sides in advance or retreat. A momentary lull in the battle was invariably employed in strengthening each position. Trees were felled under fire, and fence rails gathered quickly were piled up to make possible another stand. The space between the lines at Cold Harbor was so narrow at many points as to resemble a road, encumbered with the dead and wounded. This extraordinary proximity induced a nervous alertness which made the troops peculiarly sensitive to night alarms; even small parties searching quietly for wounded comrades might begin a panic. A few scattering shots were often enough to start a heavy and continuous musketry fire and a roar of artillery along the entire line. It was a favorite ruse of the Federal soldiers to aim their muskets carefully to clear the top of the Confederate breastworks and then set up a great shout. The Confederates, deceived into the belief that an attack was coming, would spring up and expose themselves to the well-directed volley which thinned their ranks.

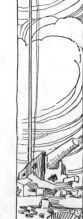

which was now the base of supplies. On the Southern side Ewell's corps, now commanded by General Early, faced Burnside's and Warren's. Longstreet's corps, still under Anderson, was opposite Wright and Smith, while A. P. Hill, on the extreme right, confronted Hancock. There was sharp fighting during the entire day, but Early did not succeed in getting upon the Federal right flank, as he attempted to do.

Both armies lay very close to each other and were well entrenched. Lee was naturally strong on his right, and his left was difficult of access, since it must be approached through wooded swamps. Well-placed batteries made artillery fire from front and both flanks possible, but Grant decided to attack the whole Confederate front, and word was sent to the corps commanders to assault at half-past four the following morning.

The hot sultry weather of the preceding days had brought much suffering. The movement of troops and wagons raised clouds of dust which settled down upon the sweltering men and beasts. But five o'clock on the afternoon of June 2d brought the grateful rain, and this continued during the night, giving great relief to the exhausted troops.

At the hour designated the Federal lines moved promptly from their shallow rifle-pits toward the Confederate works. The main assault was made by the Second, Sixth, and Eighteenth corps. With determined and firm step they started to cross the space between the opposing entrenchments. The silence of the dawning summer morning was broken by the screams of musket-ball and canister and shell. That move of the Federal battle-line opened the fiery furnace across the intervening space, which was, in the next instant, a Vesuvius, pouring tons and tons of steel and lead into the moving human mass. From front, from right and left, artillery crashed and swept the field, musketry and grape hewed and mangled and mowed down the line of blue as it moved on its approach.

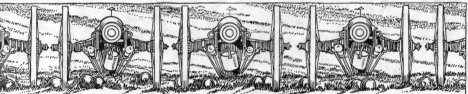

COLD HARBOR

The battle of Cold Harbor on June 3d was the third tremendous engagement of Grant's campaign against Richmond within a month. It was also his costliest onset on Lee's veteran army. Grant had risked much in his change of base to the James in order to bring him nearer to Richmond and to the friendly hand which Butler with the Army of the James was in a position to reach out to him. Lee had again confronted him, entrenching himself but six miles from the outworks of Richmond, while the Chickahominy cut off any further flanking movement. There was nothing to do but fight it out, and Grant ordered an attack all along the line. On June 3d he hurled the Army of the Potomac against the inferior numbers of Lee, and in a brave assault upon the Confederate entrenchments, lost ten thousand men in twenty minutes.

Grant's assault at Cold Harbor was marked by the gallantry of General Hancock's division and of the brigades of Gibbon and Barlow, who

WHERE TEN THOUSAND FELL

FEDERAL CAMP AT COLD HARBOR AFTER THE BATTLE

on the left of the Federal line charged up the ascent in their front upon the concentrated artillery of the Confederates; they took the position and held it for a moment under a galling fire, which finally drove them back, but not until they had captured a flag and three hundred prisoners. The battle was substantially over by half-past seven in the morning, but sullen fighting continued throughout the day. About noontime General Grant, who had visited all the corps commanders to see for himself the positions gained and what could be done, concluded that the Confederates were too strongly entrenched to be dislodged and ordered that further offensive action should cease. All the next day the dead and wounded lay on the field uncared for while both armies warily watched each other. The lower picture was taken during this weary wait. Not till the 7th was a satisfactory truce arranged, and then all but two of the wounded Federals had died. No wonder that Grant wrote, "I have always regretted that the last assault at Cold Harbor was ever made."

The three corps of the Federal army had gotten in some places as near as thirty yards to the main Confederate entrenchments, but to carry them was found impossible. The whole line was ordered to lie down, and shelter from the deadly fire was sought wherever it could be found. The advance had occupied less than ten minutes, and before an hour had passed the greater part of the fighting was over. Meade, at headquarters, was quickly made aware that each corps commander had a serious grievance against his neighbor, and, strange to say, the complaints were all phrased alike. General McMahon in "Battles and Leaders of the Civil War" explains this curious state of affairs:

"Each corps commander reported and complained to General Meade that the other corps commanders, right or left, as the case might be, failed to protect him from enfilading fire by silencing batteries in their respective fronts; Smith, that he could go no farther until Wright advanced upon his left; Hancock, that it was useless for him to attempt a further advance until Wright advanced upon his right; Wright, that it was impossible for him to move until Smith and Hancock advanced to his support on his right and left to shield him from the enemy's enfilade. These despatches necessarily caused mystification at headquarters. . . . The explanation was simple enough, although it was not known until reconnaissance had been made. The three corps had moved upon diverging lines, each directly facing the enemy in its immediate front, and the farther each had advanced the more its flank had become exposed."

Not yet understanding the real state of affairs Meade continued to issue orders to advance. To do so was now beyond human possibility. The men could only renew the fire from the positions they had gained. General Smith received a verbal order from Meade to make another assault, and he flatly refused to obey. It was long past noon, and after Grant was cognizant of the full situation, that

THE FORCES AT LAST JOIN HANDS

Charles City Court House on the James River, June 14, 1864.   It was with infinite relief that Grant saw the advance of the Army of the Potomac reach this point on June 14th.   His last flanking movement was an extremely hazardous one.   More than fifty miles intervened between him and Butler by the roads he would have to travel, and he had to cross both the Chickahominy and the James, which were unbridged.   The paramount difficulty was to get the Army of the Potomac out of its position before Lee, who confronted it at Cold Harbor.   Lee had the shorter line and better roads to move over and meet Grant at the Chickahominy, or he might, if he chose, descend rapidly on Butler and crush him before Grant could unite with him.   "But," says Grant, "the move had to be made, and I relied upon Lee's not seeing my danger as I saw it."   Near the old Charles City Court House the crossing of the James was successfully accomplished, and on the 14th Grant took steamer and ran up the river to Bermuda Hundred to see General Butler and direct the movement against Petersburg, that began the final investment of that city.

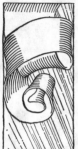

Meade issued orders for the suspension of all further offensive operations.

A word remains to be said as to fortunes of Burnside's and Warren's forces, which were on the Federal right. Generals Potter and Willcox of the Ninth Corps made a quick capture of Early's advanced rifle-pits and were waiting for the order to advance on his main entrenchments, when the order of suspension arrived. Early fell upon him later in the day but was repulsed. Warren, on the left of Burnside, drove Rodes' division back and repulsed Gordon's brigade, which had attacked him. The commander of the Fifth Corps reported that his line was too extended for further operations and Birney's division was sent from the Second Corps to his left. But by the time this got into position the battle of Cold Harbor was practically over.

After the day's conflict the field presented a scene that was indescribable. It showed war in all its horror. It is even painful to attempt a record of the actual facts, so appalling was the loss and the suffering. The groans and the moaning of the wounded during the night were heart-breaking. For three days many unfortunate beings were left lying, uncared for, where they fell. It was almost certain death to venture outside of the entrenchments. Where the heaviest assaults occurred the ground was literally covered with the dead and dying, and nearly all of them were Federal soldiers. Volunteers who offered to go to their relief were in peril of being shot, yet many went bravely out in the face of the deadly fire, to bring in their wounded comrades.

On the 5th, the Second Corps was extended to the Chickahominy, and the Fifth Corps was ordered to the rear of Cold Harbor. The Eighteenth Corps was placed along the Matadequin. Lee threatened attack on the 6th and 7th, but he soon desisted and retired to his entrenchments.

The losses to the Federal army in this battle and the engagements which preceded it were over seventeen thousand,

BACK TO THE OLD BASE

White House Landing, on the Pamunkey River, bustles with life in June, 1864. Once more, just before the battle of Cold Harbor, McClellan's old headquarters at the outset of the Peninsula Campaign of '62 springs into great activity. River steamers and barges discharge their cargoes for the army that is again endeavoring to drive Lee across the Chickahominy and back upon Richmond. Grant's main reliance was upon the inexhaustible supplies which lay at the command of the North. He knew well that the decimated and impoverished South could not long hold out against the "hammering" which the greater abundance of Federal money and men made it possible for him to keep up. Hence, without haste but without rest, he attacked Lee upon every occasion and under all conditions, aware that his own losses, even if the greater, could be made up, while those of his antagonist could not. He believed that this was the surest and speediest way to end the war, and that all told it would involve the least sacrifice of blood and treasure.

while the Confederate loss did not exceed one-fifth of that number. Grant had failed in his plan to destroy Lee north of the James River, and saw that he must now cross it.

Thirty days had passed in the campaign since the Wilderness and the grand total in losses to Grant's army in killed, wounded, and missing was 54,926. The losses in Lee's army were never accurately given, but they were very much less in proportion to the numerical strength of the two armies. If Grant had inflicted punishment upon his foe equal to that suffered by the Federal forces, Lee's army would have been practically annihilated. But, as matters stood, after the battle of Cold Harbor, with reenforcements to the Confederate arms and the comparatively small losses they had sustained, Lee's army stood on the field of this last engagement almost as large as it was at the beginning of the campaign.

For nearly twelve days the two armies lay within their entrenchments on this field, while the Federal cavalry was sent to destroy the railroad communications between Richmond and the Shenandoah valley and Lynchburg. One writer says that during this time sharpshooting was incessant, and "no man upon all that line could stand erect and live an instant." Soldiers whose terms of service had expired and were ordered home, had to crawl on their hands and knees through the trenches to the rear. No advance was attempted during this time by the Confederates, but every night at nine o'clock the whole Confederate line opened fire with musket and cannon. This was done by Lee in apprehension of the possible withdrawal by night of Grant's army.

The Federal general-in-chief had decided to secure Petersburg and confront Lee once more. General Gillmore was sent by Butler, with cavalry and infantry, on June 10th to make the capture, but was unsuccessful. Thereupon General Smith and the Eighteenth Corps were despatched to White House Landing to go forward by water and reach Petersburg before Lee had time to reenforce it.

PART II

THE SIMULTANEOUS MOVEMENTS

DREWRY'S BLUFF
IMPREGNABLE

IN BATTERY DANTZLER—CONFEDERATE GUN COMMANDING
THE RIVER AFTER BUTLER'S REPULSE ON LAND

PORT DARLING

Charles Francis Adams, who, as a cavalry officer, served in Butler's campaign, compares Grant's maneuvers of 1864 to Napoleon's of 1815. While Napoleon advanced upon Wellington it was essential that Grouchy should detain Blucher. So Butler was to eliminate Beauregard while Grant struck at Lee. With forty thousand men, he was ordered to land at Bermuda Hundred, seize and hold City Point as a future army base, and advance upon Richmond by way of Petersburg, while Grant meanwhile engaged Lee farther north. Arriving at Broadway Landing, seen in the lower picture, Butler put his army over the Appomattox on pontoons, occupied City Point, May 4th, and advanced within three miles of Petersburg, May 9th. The city might have been easily taken by a vigorous move, but Butler delayed until Beauregard arrived with a hastily gathered army and decisively defeated the Federals at Drewry's Bluff, May 10th. Like Grouchy, Butler failed.

THE MASKED BATTERY

WHERE BUTLER'S TROOPS CROSSED—BROADWAY LANDING ON THE APPOMATTOX

BUTLER "BOTTLED UP"

Butler, after his disastrous repulse at Drewry's Bluff, threw up strong entrenchments across the neck of the bottle-shaped territory which he occupied between the Appomattox and the James. That was exactly what Beauregard wanted, and the Confederate general immediately constructed field works all along Butler's front, effectually closing the neck of this "bottle." Here Butler remained in inactivity till the close of the war. He built the elaborate signal tower seen in the picture so that he could observe all the operations of the Confederates, although he could make no move against any of them. Generals Gilmore and "Baldy" Smith both urged upon Butler the laying of pontoons across the Appomattox in order to advance on Petersburg, the key to Richmond. But Butler curtly replied that he would build no bridges for West Pointers to retreat over.

BUTLER'S SIGNAL TOWER

THE LOOKOUT

THIRTEENTH NEW YORK HEAVY ARTILLERY IDLING IN WINTER QUARTERS AT BERMUDA HUNDRED

THE IMPASSABLE JAMES RIVER

The gun is in Confederate Battery Brooke—another of the defenses on the James constructed after Butler was bottled up. Here in 1865 the gunners were still at their posts guarding the water approach to Richmond. The Federals had not been able to get up the river since their first unsuccessful effort in 1862, when the hastily constructed Fort Darling at Drewry's Bluff baffled the *Monitor* and the *Galena*. Battery Brooke was situated above Dutch Gap, the narrow neck of Farrar's Island, where Butler's was busily digging his famous canal to enable the Federal gunboats to get by the obstructions he himself had caused to be sunk in the river. Even the canal proved a failure, for when the elaborate ditch was finished under fire from the Confederate batteries above, the dam was unskilfully blown up and remained an effective barrier against the passage of vessels.

AN ADVANCE DEFENSE OF RICHMOND

This Confederate gun at Battery Dantzler swept the James at a point where the river flows due south around Farrar's Island. "But-ler's Campaign" consisted merely of an advance by land up the James to Drewry's Bluff and inglorious retreat back again. Far from threatening Richmond, it enabled the Confederates to construct strong river defenses below Fort Darling on the James to hold in check the Federal fleet and assist in keeping the neck of Butler's "bottle" tightly closed. The guns at Battery Dantzler controlled the river at Trent's Reach. In a straight line from Drewry's Bluff to City Point it was but nine miles, but the James flows in a suc-cession of curves and bends at all angles of the compass, around steep bluffs, past swamp and meadow-land, making the route by water a journey of thirty miles. If the Federal gunboats could have passed their own obstructions and the Confederate torpedoes, they would still have been subjected to the fire of Battery Dantzler from their rear in attempting to reach Richmond.

ABOVE DUTCH GAP—A GUN THAT MOCKED THE FEDERALS

This huge Confederate cannon in one of the batteries above Dutch Gap bore on the canal that was being dug by the Federals. Away to the south stretches the flat and swampy country, a complete protection against hostile military operations. The Confederate cannoneers amused themselves by dropping shot and shell upon the Federal colored regiments toiling on Butler's canal. Aside from the activity of the diggers, the Army of the James had nothing to do.

PART II
THE SIMULTANEOUS MOVEMENTS

TO ATLANTA

SHERMAN'S MEN IN THE ATLANTA TRENCHES

THE MAN WHO DEFINED WAR

William Tecumseh Sherman and his staff. Leaning carelessly on the breach of the gun stands General William Tecumseh Sherman at the close of one of the war's most brilliant and successful campaigns which his military genius had made possible. The old slouch hat does not indicate that the general is holding a triumphant review of his army, but the uniform is as near full dress as Sherman ever came. "He hated fine clothes," says General Rodenbough, "and endured hardships with as much fortitude as any of his men."

In the upper picture rises the precipitous height of Rocky Face as Sherman saw it on May 7, 1864. His troops under Thomas had moved forward along the line of the railroad, opening the great Atlanta campaign on schedule time. Looking down into the gorge called Buzzard's Roost, through which the railroad passes, Sherman could see swarms of Confederate troops, the road filled with obstructions, and hostile batteries crowning the cliffs on either side. He knew that his antagonist, Joe Johnston, here confronted him in force. But it was to be a campaign of brilliant flanking movements, and Sherman sat quietly down to wait till the trusty McPherson should execute the first one.

BUZZARD'S ROOST, GEORGIA, MAY 7, 1864

In the lower picture, drawn up on dress parade, stands one of the finest fighting organizations in the Atlanta campaign. This regiment won its spurs in the first Union victory in the West at Mill Springs, Kentucky, January 19, 1862. There, according to the muster-out roll, "William Blake, musician, threw away his drum and took a gun." The spirit of this drummer boy of Company F was the spirit of all the troops from Minnesota. A Georgian noticed an unusually fine body of men marching by, and when told that they were a Minnesota regiment, said, "I didn't know they had any troops up there." But the world was to learn the superlative fighting qualities of the men from the Northwest. Sherman was glad to have all he could get of them in this great army of one hundred thousand veterans.

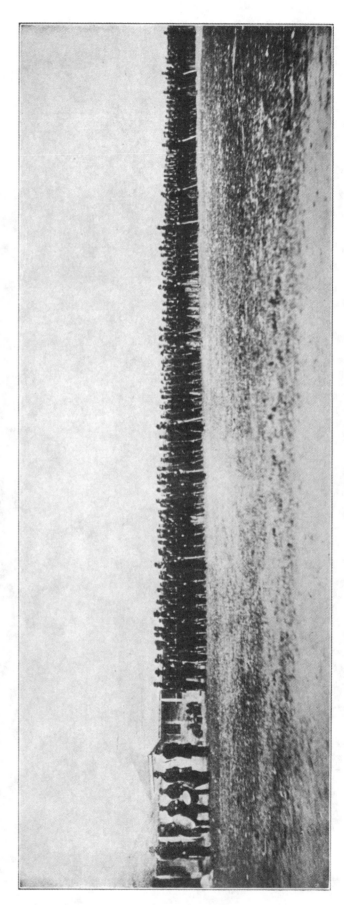

THE SECOND MINNESOTA INFANTRY—ENGAGED AT ROCKY FACE RIDGE, MAY 8–11, 1864

A REGIMENT THAT CHARGED UP KENESAW—THE ONE HUNDRED AND TWENTY-FIFTH OHIO

These are some of the men who charged upon the slopes of Kenesaw Mountain, Sherman's stumbling-block in his Atlanta campaign. They belonged to Company M of the One Hundred and Twenty-fifth Ohio, in the brigade led by the daring General Harker, Newton's division, Fourth Corps. Johnston had drawn up his forces on the Kenesaw Mountains along a line stronger, both naturally and by fortification, than the Union position at Gettysburg. But for the same reason that Lee attacked Little Round Top, Sherman, on June 27, 1864, ordered an assault on the southern slope of Little Kenesaw. The Federal forces did not pause, in spite of a terrific fire from the breastworks, till they gained the edge of the felled trees. There formations were lost; men struggled over trunks and through interlaced boughs. Before the concentrated fire of artillery and musketry they could only seek shelter behind logs and boulders. General Harker, already famous for his gallantry, cheered on his men, but as he was rushing forward he fell mortally wounded.

KENESAW MOUNTAIN IN 1864

Sherman's Stumbling Block. Thus the rugged height of Kenesaw Mountain rose in the distance to the sight of Sherman's advancing army in the middle of June, 1864. The men knew the ground, for most of them had marched over it the year before in the Chickamauga campaign. Now to its difficulties were added the strong entrenchments of Johnston's army and the batteries posted on the heights, which must be surmounted before Atlanta, the coveted goal, could be reached. But the Federals also knew that under "Old Tecumseh's" watchful eye they had flanked Johnston's army out of one strong position after another, and in little over a month had advanced nearly a hundred miles through "as difficult country as was ever fought over by civilized armies." But there was no flinching when the assaulting columns fought their way to the summit on June 27th.

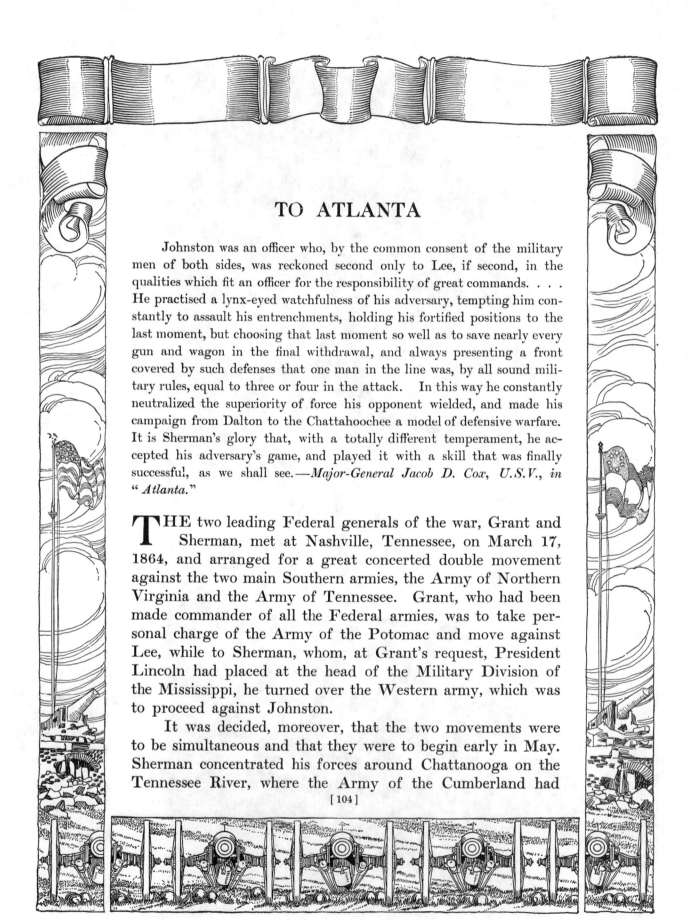

TO ATLANTA

Johnston was an officer who, by the common consent of the military men of both sides, was reckoned second only to Lee, if second, in the qualities which fit an officer for the responsibility of great commands. . . . He practised a lynx-eyed watchfulness of his adversary, tempting him constantly to assault his entrenchments, holding his fortified positions to the last moment, but choosing that last moment so well as to save nearly every gun and wagon in the final withdrawal, and always presenting a front covered by such defenses that one man in the line was, by all sound military rules, equal to three or four in the attack. In this way he constantly neutralized the superiority of force his opponent wielded, and made his campaign from Dalton to the Chattahoochee a model of defensive warfare. It is Sherman's glory that, with a totally different temperament, he accepted his adversary's game, and played it with a skill that was finally successful, as we shall see.—*Major-General Jacob D. Cox, U.S.V., in " Atlanta."*

THE two leading Federal generals of the war, Grant and Sherman, met at Nashville, Tennessee, on March 17, 1864, and arranged for a great concerted double movement against the two main Southern armies, the Army of Northern Virginia and the Army of Tennessee. Grant, who had been made commander of all the Federal armies, was to take personal charge of the Army of the Potomac and move against Lee, while to Sherman, whom, at Grant's request, President Lincoln had placed at the head of the Military Division of the Mississippi, he turned over the Western army, which was to proceed against Johnston.

It was decided, moreover, that the two movements were to be simultaneous and that they were to begin early in May. Sherman concentrated his forces around Chattanooga on the Tennessee River, where the Army of the Cumberland had

IN THE FOREFRONT—GENERAL RICHARD W. JOHNSON AT GRAYSVILLE

On the balcony of this little cottage at Graysville, Georgia, stands General Richard W. Johnson, ready to advance with his cavalry division in the vanguard of the direct movement upon the Confederates strongly posted at Dalton. Sherman's cavalry forces under Stoneman and Garrard were not yet fully equipped and joined the army after the campaign had opened. General Richard W. Johnson's division of Thomas' command, with General Palmer's division, was given the honor of heading the line of march when the Federals got in motion on May 5th. The same troops (Palmer's division) had made the same march in February, sent by Grant to engage Johnston at Dalton during Sherman's Meridian campaign. Johnson was a West Pointer; he had gained his cavalry training in the Mexican War, and had fought the Indians on the Texas border. He distinguished himself at Corinth, and rapidly rose to the command of a division in Buell's army. Fresh from a Confederate prison, he joined the Army of the Cumberland in the summer of 1862 to win new laurels at Stone's River, Chickamauga, and Missionary Ridge. His sabers were conspicuously active in the Atlanta campaign; and at the battle of New Hope Church on May 28th Johnson himself was wounded, but recovered in time to join Schofield after the fall of Atlanta and to assist him in driving Hood and Forrest out of Tennessee. For his bravery at the battle of Nashville he was brevetted brigadier-general, U. S. A., December 16, 1864, and after the war he was retired with the brevet of major-general.

spent the winter, and where a decisive battle had been fought some months before, in the autumn of 1863. His army was composed of three parts, or, more properly, of three armies operating in concert. These were the Army of the Tennessee, led by General James B. McPherson; the Army of Ohio, under General John M. Schofield, and the Army of the Cumberland, commanded by General George H. Thomas. The last named was much larger than the other two combined. The triple army aggregated the grand total of ninety-nine thousand men, six thousand of whom were cavalrymen, while four thousand four hundred and sixty belonged to the artillery. There were two hundred and fifty-four heavy guns.

Soon to be pitted against Sherman's army was that of General Joseph E. Johnston, which had spent the winter at Dalton, in the State of Georgia, some thirty miles southeast of Chattanooga. It was by chance that Dalton became the winter quarters of the Confederate army. In the preceding autumn, when General Bragg had been defeated on Missionary Ridge and driven from the vicinity of Chattanooga, he retreated to Dalton and stopped for a night's rest. Discovering the next morning that he was not pursued, he there remained. Some time later he was superseded by General Johnston.

By telegraph, General Sherman was apprised of the time when Grant was to move upon Lee on the banks of the Rapidan, in Virginia, and he prepared to move his own army at the same time. But he was two days behind Grant, who began his Virginia campaign on May 4th. Sherman broke camp on the 6th and led his legions across hill and valley, forest and stream, toward the Confederate stronghold. Nature was all abloom with the opening of a Southern spring and the soldiers, who had long chafed under their enforced idleness, now rejoiced at the exhilarating journey before them, though their mission was to be one of strife and bloodshed.

Johnston's army numbered about fifty-three thousand,

BEGINNING THE FIRST FLANK MOVEMENT

In the upper picture, presented through the kindness of General G. P. Thruston, are the headquarters of General Thomas at Ringgold, Georgia, May 5, 1864. On that day, appointed by Grant for the beginning of the "simultaneous movements" he had planned to carry out in 1864, General Sherman rode out the eighteen miles from Chattanooga to Ringgold with his staff, about half a dozen wagons, and a single company of Ohio sharpshooters. A small company of irregular Alabama cavalry acted as couriers. Sherman's mess establishment was less bulky than that of any of his brigade commanders. "I wanted to set the example," he says, "and gradually to convert all parts of that army into a mobile machine willing and able to start at a minute's notice and to subsist on the scantiest food." On May 7th, General Thomas moved in force to Tunnel Hill to begin the turning of Johnston's flank.

TUNNEL HILL, GA., BEYOND WHICH JOHNSTON OCCUPIED A STRONG POSITION IN BUZZARD'S ROOST GAP

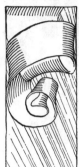

and was divided into two corps, under the respective commands of Generals John B. Hood and William J. Hardee. But General Polk was on his way to join them, and in a few days Johnston had in the neighborhood of seventy thousand men. His position at Dalton was too strong to be carried by a front attack, and Sherman was too wise to attempt it. Leaving Thomas and Schofield to make a feint at Johnston's front, Sherman sent McPherson on a flanking movement by the right to occupy Snake Creek Gap, a mountain pass near Resaca, which is about eighteen miles below Dalton.

Sherman, with the main part of the army, soon occupied Tunnel Hill, which faces Rocky Face Ridge, an eastern range of the Cumberland Mountains, north of Dalton, on which a large part of Johnston's army was posted. The Federal leader had little or no hope of dislodging his great antagonist from this impregnable position, fortified by rocks and cliffs which no army could scale while under fire. But he ordered that demonstrations be made at several places, especially at a pass known as Rocky Face Gap. This was done with great spirit and bravery, the men clambering over rocks and across ravines in the face of showers of bullets and even of masses of stone hurled down from the heights above them. On the whole they won but little advantage.

During the 8th and 9th of May, these operations were continued, the Federals making but little impression on the Confederate stronghold. Meanwhile, on the Dalton road there was a sharp cavalry fight, the Federal commander, General E. M. McCook, having encountered General Wheeler. Mc-Cook's advance brigade under Colonel La Grange was defeated and La Grange was made prisoner.

Sherman's chief object in these demonstrations, it will be seen, was so to engage Johnston as to prevent his intercepting McPherson in the latter's movement upon Resaca. In this Sherman was successful, and by the 11th he was giving his whole energy to moving the remainder of his forces by the

RESACA—FIELD OF THE FIRST HEAVY FIGHTING

The chips are still bright and the earth fresh turned, in the foreground where are the Confederate earthworks such as General Joseph E. Johnston had caused to be thrown up by the Negro laborers all along his line of possible retreat. McPherson, sent by Sherman to strike the railroad in Johnston's rear, got his head of column through Snake Creek Gap on May 9th, and drove off a Confederate cavalry brigade which retreated toward Dalton, bringing to Johnston the first news that a heavy force of Federals was already in his rear. McPherson, within a mile and a half of Resaca, could have walked into the town with his twenty-three thousand men, but concluded that the Confederate entrenchments were too strongly held to assault. When Sherman arrived he found that Johnston, having the shorter route, was there ahead of him with his entire army strongly posted. On May 15th, "without attempting to assault the fortified works," says Sherman, "we pressed at all points, and the sound of cannon and musketry rose all day to the dignity of a battle." Its havoc is seen in the shattered trees and torn ground in the lower picture.

THE WORK OF THE FIRING AT RESACA

right flank, as McPherson had done, to Resaca, leaving a detachment of General O. O. Howard's Fourth Corps to occupy Dalton when evacuated. When Johnston discovered this, he was quick to see that he must abandon his entrenchments and intercept Sherman. Moving by the only two good roads, Johnston beat Sherman in the race to Resaca. The town had been fortified, owing to Johnston's foresight, and McPherson had failed to dislodge the garrison and capture it. The Confederate army was now settled behind its entrenchments, occupying a semicircle of low wooded hills, both flanks of the army resting on the banks of the Oostenaula River.

On the morning of May 14th, the Confederate works were invested by the greater part of Sherman's army and it was evident that a battle was imminent. The attack was begun about noon, chiefly by the Fourteenth Army Corps under Palmer, of Thomas' army, and Judah's division of Schofield's. General Hindman's division of Hood's corps bore the brunt of this attack and there was heavy loss on both sides. Later in the day, a portion of Hood's corps was massed in a heavy column and hurled against the Federal left, driving it back. But at this point the Twentieth Army Corps under Hooker, of Thomas' army, dashed against the advancing Confederates and pushed them back to their former lines.

The forenoon of the next day was spent in heavy skirmishing, which grew to the dignity of a battle. During the day's operations a hard fight for a Confederate lunette on the top of a low hill occurred. At length, General Butterfield, in the face of a galling fire, succeeded in capturing the position. But so deadly was the fire from Hardee's corps that Butterfield was unable to hold it or to remove the four guns the lunette contained.

With the coming of night, General Johnston determined to withdraw his army from Resaca. The battle had cost each army nearly three thousand men. While it was in progress, McPherson, sent by Sherman, had deftly marched around

ANOTHER RETROGRADE MOVEMENT OVER THE ETOWAH BRIDGE

The strong works in the pictures, commanding the railroad bridge over the Etowah River, were the fourth fortified position to be abandoned by Johnston within a month. Pursued by Thomas from Resaca, he had made a brief stand at Kingston and then fallen back steadily and in superb order into Cassville. There he issued an address to his army announcing his purpose to retreat no more but to accept battle. His troops were all drawn up in preparation for a struggle, but that night at supper with Generals Hood and Polk he was convinced by them that the ground occupied by their troops was untenable, being enfiladed by the Federal artillery. Johnston, therefore, gave up his purpose of battle, and on the night of May 20th put the Etowah River between himself and Sherman and retreated to Allatoona Pass, shown in the lower picture.

ALLATOONA PASS IN THE DISTANCE

In taking this the camera was planted inside the breastworks seen on the eminence in the upper picture. Sherman's army now rested after its rapid advance and waited a few days for the railroad to be repaired in their rear so that supplies could be brought up. Meanwhile Johnston was being severely criticized at the South for his continual falling back without risking a battle. His friends stoutly maintained that it was all strategic, while some of the Southern newspapers quoted the Federal General Scott's remark, "Beware of Lee advancing, and watch Johnston at a stand; for the devil himself would be defeated in the attempt to whip him retreating." But General Jeff C. Davis, sent by Sherman, took Rome on May 17th and destroyed valuable mills and foundries. Thus began the accomplishment of one of the main objects of Sherman's march.

Johnston's left with the view of cutting off his retreat south by seizing the bridges across the Oostenaula, and at the same time the Federal cavalry was threatening the railroad to Atlanta which ran beyond the river. It was the knowledge of these facts that determined the Confederate commander to abandon Resaca. Withdrawing during the night, he led his army southward to the banks of the Etowah River. Sherman followed but a few miles behind him. At the same time Sherman sent a division of the Army of the Cumberland, under General Jeff. C. Davis, to Rome, at the junction of the Etowah and the Oostenaula, where there were important machine-shops and factories. Davis captured the town and several heavy guns, destroyed the factories, and left a garrison to hold it.

Sherman was eager for a battle in the open with Johnston and on the 17th, near the town of Adairsville, it seemed as if the latter would gratify him. Johnston chose a good position, posted his cavalry, deployed his infantry, and awaited combat. The Union army was at hand. The skirmishing for some hours almost amounted to a battle. But suddenly Johnston decided to defer a conclusive contest to another time.

Again at Cassville, a few days later, Johnston drew up the Confederate legions in battle array, evidently having decided on a general engagement at this point. He issued a spirited address to the army: "By your courage and skill you have repulsed every assault of the enemy. . . . You will now turn and march to meet his advancing columns. . . . I lead you to battle." But, when his right flank had been turned by a Federal attack, and when two of his corps commanders, Hood and Polk, advised against a general battle, Johnston again decided on postponement. He retreated in the night across the Etowah, destroyed the bridges, and took a strong position among the rugged hills about Allatoona Pass, extending south to Kenesaw Mountain.

Johnston's decision to fight and then not to fight was a

ENTRENCHMENTS HELD BY THE CONFEDERATES AGAINST HOOKER ON MAY 25TH

These views of the battlefield of New Hope Church, in Georgia, show the evidences of the sharp struggle at this point that was brought on by Sherman's next attempt to flank Johnston out of his position at Allatoona Pass. The middle picture gives mute witness to the leaden storm that raged among the trees during that engagement. In the upper and lower pictures are seen the

THE CANNONADED FOREST

entrenchments which the Confederates had hastily thrown up and which resisted Hooker's assaults on May 25th. For two days each side strengthened its position; then on the 28th the Confederates made a brave attack upon General McPherson's forces as they were closing up to this new position. The Confederates were repulsed with a loss of two thousand.

ANOTHER POSITION OF THE CONFEDERATES AT NEW HOPE CHURCH

cause for grumbling both on the part of his army and of the inhabitants of the region through which he was passing. His men were eager to defend their country, and they could not understand this Fabian policy. They would have preferred defeat to these repeated retreats with no opportunity to show what they could do.

Johnston, however, was wiser than his critics. The Union army was larger by far and better equipped than his own, and Sherman was a master-strategist. His hopes rested on two or three contingencies—that he might catch a portion of Sherman's army separated from the rest; that Sherman would be so weakened by the necessity of guarding the long line of railroad to his base of supplies at Chattanooga, Nashville, and even far-away Louisville, as to make it possible to defeat him in open battle, or, finally, that Sherman might fall into the trap of making a direct attack while Johnston was in an impregnable position, and in such a situation he now was.

Not yet, however, was Sherman inclined to fall into such a trap, and when Johnston took his strong position at and beyond Allatoona Pass, the Northern commander decided, after resting his army for a few days, to move toward Atlanta by way of Dallas, southwest of the pass. Rations for a twenty days' absence from direct railroad communication were issued to the Federal army. In fact, Sherman's railroad connection with the North was the one delicate problem of the whole movement. The Confederates had destroyed the iron way as they moved southward; but the Federal engineers, following the army, repaired the line and rebuilt the bridges almost as fast as the army could march.

Sherman's movement toward Dallas drew Johnston from the slopes of the Allatoona Hills. From Kingston, the Federal leader wrote on May 23d, " I am already within fifty miles of Atlanta." But he was not to enter that city for many weeks, not before he had measured swords again and again with his great antagonist. On the 25th of May, the two great

PINE MOUNTAIN, WHERE POLK, THE FIGHTING BISHOP OF THE CONFEDERACY, WAS KILLED

The blasted pine rears its gaunt height above the mountain slope, covered with trees slashed down to hold the Federals at bay; and here, on June 14, 1864, the Confederacy lost a commander, a bishop, and a hero. Lieut.-General Leonidas Polk, commanding one of Johnston's army corps, with Johnston himself and Hardee, another corps commander, was studying Sherman's position at a tense moment of the latter's advance around Pine Mountain. The three Confederates stood upon the rolling height, where the center of Johnston's army awaited the Federal attack. They could see the columns in blue pushing east of them; the smoke and rattle of musketry as the pickets were driven in; and the bustle with which the Federal advance guard felled trees and constructed trenches at their very feet. On the lonely height the three figures stood conspicuous. A Federal order was given the artillery to open upon any men in gray who looked like officers reconnoitering the new position. So, while Hardee was pointing to his comrade and his chief the danger of one of his divisions which the Federal advance was cutting off, the bishop-general was struck in the chest by a cannon shot. Thus the Confederacy lost a leader of unusual influence. Although

LIEUT.–GEN. LEONIDAS POLK, C.S.A.

a bishop of the Episcopal Church, Polk was educated at West Point. When he threw in his lot with the Confederacy, thousands of his fellow-Louisianians followed him. A few days before the battle of Pine Mountain, as he and General Hood were riding together, the bishop was told by his companion that he had never been received into the communion of a church and was begged that the rite might be performed. Immediately Polk arranged the ceremony. At Hood's headquarters, by the light of a tallow candle, with a tin basin on the mess table for a baptismal font, and with Hood's staff present as witnesses, all was ready. Hood, "with a face like that of an old crusader," stood before the bishop. Crippled by wounds at Gaines' Mill, Gettysburg, and Chickamauga, he could not kneel, but bent forward on his crutches. The bishop, in full uniform of the Confederate army, administered the rite. A few days later, by a strange coincidence, he was approached by General Johnston on the same errand, and the man whom Hood was soon to succeed was baptized in the same simple manner. Polk, as Bishop, had administered his last baptism, and as soldier had fought his last battle; for Pine Mountain was near.

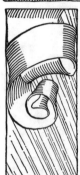
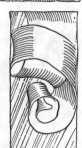

armies were facing each other near New Hope Church, about four miles north of Dallas. Here, for three or four days, there was almost incessant fighting, though there was not what might be called a pitched battle.

Late in the afternoon of the first day, Hooker made a vicious attack on Stewart's division of Hood's corps. For two hours the battle raged without a moment's cessation, Hooker being pressed back with heavy loss. During those two hours he had held his ground against sixteen field-pieces and five thousand infantry at close range. The name "Hell Hole" was applied to this spot by the Union soldiers.

On the next day there was considerable skirmishing in different places along the line that divided the two armies. But the chief labor of the day was throwing up entrenchments, preparatory to a general engagement. The country, however, was ill fitted for such a contest. The continuous succession of hills, covered with primeval forests, presented little opportunity for two great armies, stretched out almost from Dallas to Marietta, a distance of about ten miles, to come together simultaneously at all points.

A severe contest occurred on the 27th, near the center of the battle-lines, between General O. O. Howard on the Federal side and General Patrick Cleburne on the part of the South. Dense and almost impenetrable was the undergrowth through which Howard led his troops to make the attack. The fight was at close range and was fierce and bloody, the Confederates gaining the greater advantage.

The next day Johnston made a terrific attack on the Union right, under McPherson, near Dallas. But McPherson was well entrenched and the Confederates were repulsed with a serious loss. In the three or four days' fighting the Federal loss was probably twenty-four hundred men and the Confederate somewhat greater.

In the early days of June, Sherman took possession of the town of Allatoona and made it a second base of supplies,

IN THE HARDEST FIGHT OF THE CAMPAIGN—THE ONE–HUNDRED–AND–TWENTY–FIFTH OHIO

During the dark days before Kenesaw it rained continually, and Sherman speaks of the peculiarly depressing effect that the weather had upon his troops in the wooded country. Nevertheless he must either assault Johnston's strong position on the mountain or begin again his flanking tactics. He decided upon the former, and on June 27th, after three days' preparation, the assault was made. At nine in the morning along the Federal lines the furious fire of musketry and artillery was begun, but at all points the Confederates met it with determined courage and in great force. McPherson's attacking column, under General Blair, fought its way up the face of little Kenesaw but could not reach the summit. Then the courageous troops of Thomas charged up the face of the mountain and planted their colors on the very parapet of the Confederate works. Here General Harker, commanding the brigade in which fought the 125th Ohio, fell mortally wounded, as did Brigadier-General Daniel McCook, and also General Wagner.

FEDERAL ENTRENCHMENTS AT THE FOOT OF KENESAW MOUNTAIN

after repairing the railroad bridge across the Etowah River. Johnston swung his left around to Lost Mountain and his right extended beyond the railroad—a line ten miles in length and much too long for its numbers. Johnston's army, however, had been reenforced, and it now numbered about seventy-five thousand men. Sherman, on June 1st, had nearly one hundred and thirteen thousand men and on the 8th he received the addition of a cavalry brigade and two divisions of the Seventeenth Corps, under General Frank P. Blair, which had marched from Alabama.

So multifarious were the movements of the two great armies among the hills and forests of that part of Georgia that it is impossible for us to follow them all. On the 14th of June, Generals Johnston, Hardee, and Polk rode up the slope of Pine Mountain to reconnoiter. As they were standing, making observations, a Federal battery in the distance opened on them and General Polk was struck in the chest with a Parrot shell. He was killed instantly.

General Polk was greatly beloved, and his death caused a shock to the whole Confederate army. He was a graduate of West Point; but after being graduated he took orders in the church and for twenty years before the war was Episcopal Bishop of Louisiana. At the outbreak of the war he entered the field and served with distinction to the moment of his death.

During the next two weeks there was almost incessant fighting, heavy skirmishing, sparring for position. It was a wonderful game of military strategy, played among the hills and mountains and forests by two masters in the art of war. On June 23d, Sherman wrote, "The whole country is one vast fort, and Johnston must have full fifty miles of connected trenches. . . . Our lines are now in close contact, and the fighting incessant. . . . As fast as we gain one position, the enemy has another all ready."

Sherman, conscious of superior strength, was now anxious for a real battle, a fight to the finish with his antagonist.

THOMAS' HEADQUARTERS NEAR MARIETTA DURING THE FIGHTING OF
THE FOURTH OF JULY

This is a photograph of Independence Day, 1864. As the sentries and staff officers stand outside the sheltered tents, General Thomas, commanding the Army of the Cumberland, is busy; for the fighting is fierce
to-day. Johnston has been outflanked from Kenesaw and has fallen back eastward until he is actually
farther from Atlanta than Sherman's right flank. Who will reach the Chattahoochee first? There, if anywhere, Johnston must make his stand; he must hold the fords and ferries, and the fortifications that, with
the wisdom of a far-seeing commander, he has for a long time been preparing. The rustic work in the photograph, which embowers the tents of the commanding general and his staff, is the sort of thing that Civil
War soldiers had learned to throw up within an hour after pitching camp.

But Johnston was too wily to be thus caught. He made no false move on the great chessboard of war. At length, the impatient Sherman decided to make a general front attack, even though Johnston, at that moment, was impregnably entrenched on the slopes of Kenesaw Mountain. This was precisely what the Confederate commander was hoping for.

The desperate battle of Kenesaw Mountain occurred on the 27th of June. In the early morning hours, the boom of Federal cannon announced the opening of a bloody day's struggle. It was soon answered by the Confederate batteries in the entrenchments along the mountain side, and the deafening roar of the giant conflict reverberated from the surrounding hills. About nine o'clock the Union infantry advance began. On the left was McPherson, who sent the Fifteenth Army Corps, led by General John A. Logan, directly against the mountain. The artillery from the Confederate trenches in front of Logan cut down his men by hundreds. The Federals charged courageously and captured the lower works, but failed to take the higher ridges.

The chief assault of the day was by the Army of the Cumberland, under Thomas. Most conspicuous in the attack were the divisions of Newton and Davis, advancing against General Loring, successor of the lamented Polk. Far up on a ridge at one point, General Cleburne held a line of breastworks, supported by the flanking fire of artillery. Against this a vain and costly assault was made.

When the word was given to charge, the Federals sprang forward and, in the face of a deadly hail of musket-balls and shells, they dashed up the slope, firing as they went. Stunned and bleeding, they were checked again and again by the withering fire from the mountain slope; but they re-formed and pressed on with dauntless valor. Some of them reached the parapets and were instantly shot down, their bodies rolling into the Confederate trenches among the men who had slain them, or back down the hill whence they had come. General

THE CHATTAHOOCHEE BRIDGE

"One of the strongest pieces of field fortification I ever saw"—this was Sherman's characterization of the entrenchments that guarded the railroad bridge over the Chattahoochee on July 5th. A glimpse of the bridge and the freshly-turned earth in 1864 is given by the upper picture. At this river Johnston made his final effort to hold back Sherman from a direct attack upon Atlanta. If Sherman could get successfully across that river, the Confederates would be compelled to fall back behind the defenses of the city, which was the objective of the campaign. Sherman perceived at once the futility of trying to carry by assault this strongly garrisoned position. Instead, he made a feint at crossing the river lower down, and simultaneously went to work in earnest eight miles north of the bridge. The lower picture shows the canvas pontoon boats as perfected by Union engineers in 1864. A number of these were stealthily set up and launched by Sherman's Twenty-third Corps near the mouth of Soap Creek, behind a ridge. Byrd's brigade took the defenders of the southern bank completely by surprise. It was short work for the Federals to throw pontoon bridges across and to occupy the coveted spot in force.

INFANTRY AND ARTILLERY CROSSING ON BOATS MADE OF PONTOONS

Harker, leading a charge against Cleburne, was mortally wounded. His men were swept back by a galling fire, though many fell with their brave leader.

This assault on Kenesaw Mountain cost Sherman three thousand men and won him nothing. Johnston's loss probably exceeded five hundred. The battle continued but two and a half hours. It was one of the most recklessly daring assaults during the whole war period, but did not greatly affect the final result of the campaign.

Under a flag of truce, on the day after the battle, the men of the North and of the South met on the gory field to bury their dead and to minister to the wounded. They met as friends for the moment, and not as foes. It was said that there were instances of father and son, one in blue and the other in gray, and brothers on opposite sides, meeting one another on the bloody slopes of Kenesaw. Tennessee and Kentucky had sent thousands of men to each side in the fratricidal struggle and not infrequently families had been divided.

Three weeks of almost incessant rain fell upon the struggling armies during this time, rendering their operations disagreeable and unsatisfactory. The camp equipage, the men's uniforms and accouterments were thoroughly saturated with rain and mud. Still the warriors of the North and of the South lived and fought on the slopes of the mountain range, intent on destroying each other.

Sherman was convinced by his drastic repulse at Kenesaw Mountain that success lay not in attacking his great antagonist in a strong position, and he resumed his old tactics. He would flank Johnston from Kenesaw as he had flanked him out of Dalton and Allatoona Pass. He thereupon turned upon Johnston's line of communication with Atlanta, whence the latter received his supplies. The movement was successful, and in a few days Kenesaw Mountain was deserted.

Johnston moved to the banks of the Chattahoochee,

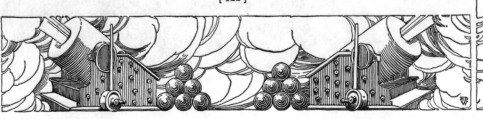

Johnston's parrying of Sherman's mighty strokes was "a model of defensive warfare," declares one of Sherman's own division commanders, Jacob D. Cox. There was not a man in the Federal army from Sherman down that did not rejoice to hear that Johnston had been superseded by Hood on July 18th. Johnston, whose mother was a niece of Patrick Henry, was fifty-seven years old, cold in manner, measured and accurate in speech. His dark firm face, surmounted by a splendidly intellectual forehead, betokened the experienced and cautious soldier. His dismissal was one of the political mistakes which too often hampered capable leaders on both sides. His Fabian policy in Georgia was precisely the same as that which was winning fame against heavy odds for Lee in Virginia.

GENERAL JOSEPH EGGLESTON
JOHNSTON, C. S. A.
BORN 1809; WEST POINT 1829; DIED 1891

LIEUTENANT–GENERAL
JOHN B. HOOD, C. S. A.
BORN 1831; WEST POINT 1853; DIED 1879

The countenance of Hood, on the other hand, indicates an eager, restless energy, an impetuosity that lacked the poise of Sherman, whose every gesture showed the alertness of mind and soundness of judgment that in him were so exactly balanced. Both Schofield and McPherson were classmates of Hood at West Point, and characterized him to Sherman as "bold even to rashness and courageous in the extreme." He struck the first offensive blow at Sherman advancing on Atlanta, and wisely adhered to the plan of the battle as it had been worked out by Johnston just before his removal. But the policy of attacking was certain to be finally disastrous to the Confederates.

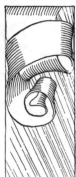

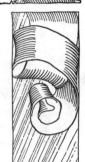

Sherman following in the hope of catching him while crossing the river. But the wary Confederate had again, as at Resaca, prepared entrenchments in advance, and these were on the north bank of the river. He hastened to them, then turned on the approaching Federals and defiantly awaited attack. But Sherman remembered Kenesaw and there was no battle.

The feints, the sparring, the flanking movements among the hills and forests continued day after day. The immediate aim in the early days of July was to cross the Chattahoochee. On the 8th, Sherman sent Schofield and McPherson across, ten miles or more above the Confederate position. Johnston crossed the next day. Thomas followed later.

Sherman's position was by no means reassuring. It is true he had, in the space of two months, pressed his antagonist back inch by inch for more than a hundred miles and was now almost within sight of the goal of the campaign—the city of Atlanta. But the single line of railroad that connected him with the North and brought supplies from Louisville, five hundred miles away, for a hundred thousand men and twenty-three thousand animals, might at any moment be destroyed by Confederate raiders.

The necessity of guarding the Western and Atlantic Railroad was an ever-present concern with Sherman. Forrest and his cavalry force were in northern Mississippi waiting for him to get far enough on the way to Atlanta for them to pounce upon the iron way and tear it to ruins. To prevent this General Samuel D. Sturgis, with eight thousand troops, was sent from Memphis against Forrest. He met him on the 10th of June near Guntown, Mississippi, but was sadly beaten and driven back to Memphis, one hundred miles away. The affair, nevertheless, delayed Forrest in his operations against the railroad, and meanwhile General Smith's troops returned to Memphis from the Red River expedition, somewhat late according to the schedule but eager to join Sherman in the advance on Atlanta. Smith, however, was directed to

PEACH–TREE CREEK, WHERE HOOD HIT HARD

Counting these closely clustered Federal graves gives one an idea of the overwhelming onset with Hood become the aggressor on July 20th. Beyond the graves are some of the trenches from which the Federals were at first irresistibly driven. In the background flows Peach-Tree Creek, the little stream that gives its name to the battlefield. Hood, impatient to signalize his new responsibility by a stroke that would at once dispel the gloom at Richmond, had posted his troops behind strongly fortified works on a ridge commanding the valley of Peach-Tree Creek about five miles to the north of Atlanta. Here he awaited the approach of Sherman. As the Federals were disposing their lines and entrenching before this position, Hood's eager eyes detected a gap in their formation and at four o'clock in the afternoon hurled a heavy force against it. Thus he proved his reputation for courage, but the outcome showed the mistake. For a brief interval Sherman's forces were in great peril. But the Federals under Newton and Geary rallied and held their ground, till Ward's division in a brave counter-charge drove the Confederates back. This first effort cost Hood dear. He abandoned his entrenchments that night, leaving on the field five hundred dead, one thousand wounded, and many prisoners. Sherman estimated the total Confederate loss at no less than five thousand. That of the Federals was fifteen hundred.

PALISADES AND *CHEVAUX-DE-FRISE* GUARDING ATLANTA

At last Sherman is before Atlanta. The photograph shows one of the keypoints in the Confederate defense, the fort at the head of Marietta Street, toward which the Federal lines were advancing from the northwest. The old Potter house in the background, once a quiet, handsome country seat, is now surrounded by bristling fortifications, palisades, and double lines of *chevaux-de-frise*. Atlanta was engaged in the final grapple with the force that was to overcome her. Sherman has fought his way past Kenesaw and across the Chattahoochee, through a country which he describes as "one vast fort," saying that "Johnston must have at least fifty miles of connected trenches with abatis and finished batteries." Anticipating that Sherman might drive him back upon Atlanta, Johnston had constructed, during the winter, heavily fortified positions all the way from Dalton. During his two months in retreat the fortifications at Atlanta had been strengthened to the utmost. What he might have done behind them was never to be known.

AFTER THE SHARPSHOOTING IN POTTER'S HOUSE

One gets a closer look at Potter's house in the background opposite. It was occupied by sharpshooters in the skirmishing and engagements by which the investing lines were advanced. So the Federals made it a special target for their artillery. After Atlanta fell, nearly a ton of shot and shell was found in the house. The fort on Marietta Street, to the northwest of the city, was the first of the inner defenses to be encountered as Sherman advanced quickly on July 21st, after finding that Hood had abandoned his outer line at Peach-Tree Creek. The vicinity of the Potter house was the scene of many vigorous assaults and much brave resistance throughout the siege. Many another dwelling in Atlanta suffered as badly as this one in the clash of arms. During Sherman's final bombardment the city was almost laid in ruins. Even this was not the end, for after the occupation Captain Poe and his engineers found it necessary, in laying out the new fortifications, to destroy many more buildings throughout the devastated town.

take the offensive against Forrest, and with fourteen thousand troops, and in a three days' fight, demoralized him badly at Tupelo, Mississippi, July 14th–17th. Smith returned to Memphis and made another start for Sherman, when he was suddenly turned back and sent to Missouri, where the Confederate General Price was extremely active, to help Rosecrans.

To avoid final defeat and to win the ground he had gained had taxed Sherman's powers to the last degree and was made possible only through his superior numbers. Even this degree of success could not be expected to continue if the railroad to the North should be destroyed. But Sherman must do more than he had done; he must capture Atlanta, this Richmond of the far South, with its cannon foundries and its great machine-shops, its military factories, and extensive army supplies. He must divide the Confederacy north and south as Grant's capture of Vicksburg had split it east and west.

Sherman must have Atlanta, for political reasons as well as for military purposes. The country was in the midst of a presidential campaign. The opposition to Lincoln's re-election was strong, and for many weeks it was believed on all sides that his defeat was inevitable. At least, the success of the Union arms in the field was deemed essential to Lincoln's success at the polls. Grant had made little progress in Virginia and his terrible repulse at Cold Harbor, in June, had cast a gloom over every Northern State. Farragut was operating in Mobile Bay; but his success was still in the future.

The eyes of the supporters of the great war-president turned longingly, expectantly, toward General Sherman and his hundred thousand men before Atlanta. "Do something—something spectacular—save the party and save the country thereby from permanent disruption!" This was the cry of the millions, and Sherman understood it. But withal, the capture of the Georgia city may have been doubtful but for the fact that at the critical moment the Confederate President made a decision that resulted, unconsciously, in a decided

THE ARMY'S FINGER–TIPS—PICKETS BEFORE ATLANTA

A Federal picket post on the lines before Atlanta. This picture was taken shortly before the battle of July 22d. The soldiers are idling about unconcerned at exposing themselves; this is on the "reserve post." Somewhat in advance of this lay the outer line of pickets, and it would be time enough to seek cover if they were driven in. Thus armies feel for each other, stretching out first their sensitive fingers—the pickets. If these recoil, the skirmishers are sent forward while the strong arm, the line of battle, gathers itself to meet the foe. As this was an inner line, it was more strongly fortified than was customary with the pickets. But the men of both sides had become very expert in improvising field-works at this stage of the war. Hard campaigning had taught the veterans the importance to themselves of providing such protection, and no orders had to be given for their construction. As soon as a regiment gained a position desirable to hold, the soldiers would throw up a strong parapet of dirt and logs in a single night. In order to spare the men as much as possible, Sherman ordered his division commanders to organize pioneer detachments out of the Negroes that escaped to the Federals. These could work at night.

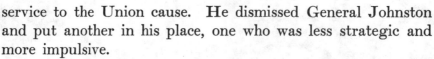
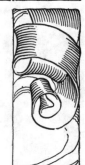

service to the Union cause. He dismissed General Johnston and put another in his place, one who was less strategic and more impulsive.

Jefferson Davis did not agree with General Johnston's military judgment, and he seized on the fact that Johnston had so steadily retreated before the Northern army as an excuse for his removal. On the 18th of July, Davis turned the Confederate Army of Tennessee over to General John B. Hood. A graduate of West Point of the class of 1853, a classmate of McPherson, Schofield, and Sheridan, Hood had faithfully served the cause of the South since the opening of the war. He was known as a fighter, and it was believed that he would change the policy of Johnston to one of open battle with Sherman's army. And so it proved.

Johnston had lost, since the opening of the campaign at Dalton, about fifteen thousand men, and the army that he now delivered to Hood consisted of about sixty thousand in all.

While Hood was no match for Sherman as a strategist, he was not a weakling. His policy of aggression, however, was not suited to the circumstances—to the nature of the country—in view of the fact that Sherman's army was far stronger than his own.

Two days after Hood took command of the Confederate army he offered battle. Sherman's forces had crossed Peach Tree Creek, a small stream flowing into the Chattahoochee, but a few miles from Atlanta, and were approaching the city. They had thrown up slight breastworks, as was their custom, but were not expecting an attack. Suddenly, however, about four o'clock in the afternoon of July 20th, an imposing column of Confederates burst from the woods near the position of the Union right center, under Thomas. The Federals were soon at their guns. The battle was short, fierce, and bloody. The Confederates made a gallant assault, but were pressed back to their entrenchments, leaving the ground covered with dead and wounded. The Federal loss in the battle

THE SCENE OF McPHERSON'S DEATH

Near the tree seen in the upper picture the brave and wise McPherson, one of Sherman's best generals, was killed, July 22d. On the morning of that day, McPherson, in excellent spirits, rode up with his staff to Sherman's headquarters at the Howard House. The night before his troops had gained a position on Leggett's Hill, from which they could look over the Confederate parapets into Atlanta. McPherson explained to Sherman that he was planting batteries to knock down a large foundry which the position commanded. Sitting down on the steps of the porch, the two generals discussed the chances of battle and agreed that they ought to be unusually cautious. McPherson said that his old classmate Hood, though not deemed much of a scholar at West Point, was none the less brave and determined. Walking down the road the two comrades in arms sat down at the foot of a tree and examined the Federal positions on a map. Suddenly the sound of battle broke upon their ears and rose to the volume of a general engagement. McPherson, anxious about his newly gained position, called for his horse and rode off. Reaching the battlefield he sent one orderly after another to bring up troops, and then riding alone through the woods to gain another part of the field, ran directly into a Confederate skirmish line. Upon his refusal to surrender a volley brought him lifeless to the ground. The battle of Atlanta, on July 22d, was Hood's second attempt to repel Sherman's army that was rapidly throwing its cordon around the city to the north and threatening to cut his rail communication with Augusta to the eastward. To prevent this, it was imperative that the hill gained by McPherson should be retaken, and Hood thought he saw his opportunity in the thinly extended Federal line near this position. His abandoned entrenchments near Peach-Tree Creek were but a ruse to lure Sherman on into advancing incautiously. Sherman and McPherson had so decided when Hood began to strike. McPherson's prompt dispositions saved the day at the cost of his life. A skilful soldier, tall and handsome, universally liked and respected by his comrades, he was cut off in his prime at the age of thirty-six.

DÉBRIS FROM THE BATTLE OF ATLANTA

of Peach Tree Creek was placed at over seventeen hundred, the Confederate loss being much greater. This battle had been planned by Johnston before his removal, but he had been waiting for the strategic moment to fight it.

Two days later, July 22d, occurred the greatest engagement of the entire campaign—the battle of Atlanta. The Federal army was closing in on the entrenchments of Atlanta, and was now within two or three miles of the city. On the night of the 21st, General Blair, of McPherson's army, had gained possession of a high hill on the left, which commanded a view of the heart of the city. Hood thereupon planned to recapture this hill, and make a general attack on the morning of the 22d. He sent General Hardee on a long night march around the extreme flank of McPherson's army, the attack to be made at daybreak. Meantime, General Cheatham, who had succeeded to the command of Hood's former corps, and General A. P. Stewart, who now had Polk's corps, were to engage Thomas and Schofield in front and thus prevent them from sending aid to McPherson.

Hardee was delayed in his fifteen-mile night march, and it was noon before he attacked. At about that hour Generals Sherman and McPherson sat talking near the Howard house, which was the Federal headquarters, when the sudden boom of artillery from beyond the hill that Blair had captured announced the opening of the coming battle. McPherson quickly leaped upon his horse and galloped away toward the sound of the guns. Meeting Logan and Blair near the railroad, he conferred with them for a moment, when they separated, and each hastened to his place in the battle-line. McPherson sent aides and orderlies in various directions with despatches, until but two were still with him. He then rode into a forest and was suddenly confronted by a portion of the Confederate army under General Cheatham. "Surrender," was the call that rang out. But he wheeled his horse as if to flee, when he was instantly shot dead, and the horse galloped back riderless.

THE FINAL BLOW TO THE CONFEDERACY'S SOUTHERN STRONGHOLD

It was Sherman's experienced railroad wreckers that finally drove Hood out of Atlanta. In the picture the rails heating red-hot amid the flaming bonfires of the ties, and the piles of twisted débris show vividly what Sherman meant when he said their "work was done with a will." Sherman saw that in order to take Atlanta without terrific loss he must cut off all its rail communications. This he did by "taking the field with our main force and using it against the communications of Atlanta instead of against its intrench-ments." On the night of August 25th he moved with practically his entire army and wagon-trains loaded with fifteen days' rations. By the morning of the 27th the whole front of the city was deserted. The Confederates concluded that Sherman was in retreat. Next day they found out their mistake, for the Federal army lay across the West Point Railroad while the soldiers began wrecking it. Next day they were in motion toward the railroad to Macon, and General Hood began to understand that a colossal raid was in progress. After the occupation, when this picture was taken, Sherman's men completed the work of destruction.

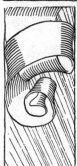

The death of the brilliant, dashing young leader, James B McPherson, was a great blow to the Union army. But thirty-six years of age, one of the most promising men in the country, and already the commander of a military department, McPherson was the only man in all the Western armies whom Grant, on going to the East, placed in the same military class with Sherman.

Logan succeeded the fallen commander, and the battle raged on. The Confederates were gaining headway. They captured several guns. Cheatham was pressing on, pouring volley after volley into the ranks of the Army of the Tennessee, which seemed about to be cut in twain. A gap was opening. The Confederates were pouring through. General Sherman was present and saw the danger. Calling for Schofield to send several batteries, he placed them and poured a concentrated artillery fire through the gap and mowed down the advancing men in swaths. At the same time, Logan pressed forward and Schofield's infantry was called up. The Confederates were hurled back with great loss. The shadows of night fell—and the battle of Atlanta was over. Hood's losses exceeded eight thousand of his brave men, whom he could ill spare. Sherman lost about thirty-seven hundred.

The Confederate army recuperated within the defenses of Atlanta—behind an almost impregnable barricade. Sherman had no hope of carrying the city by assault, while to surround and invest it was impossible with his numbers. He determined, therefore, to strike Hood's lines of supplies. On July 28th, Hood again sent Hardee out from his entrenchments to attack the Army of the Tennessee, now under the command of General Howard. A fierce battle at Ezra Church on the west side of the city ensued, and again the Confederates were defeated with heavy loss.

A month passed and Sherman had made little progress toward capturing Atlanta. Two cavalry raids which he organized resulted in defeat, but the two railroads from the

THE RUIN OF HOOD'S RETREAT—DEMOLISHED CARS AND ROLLING-MILL

On the night of August 31st, in his headquarters near Jonesboro, Sherman could not sleep. That day he had defeated the force sent against him at Jonesboro and cut them off from returning to Atlanta. This was Hood's last effort to save his communications. About midnight sounds of exploding shells and what seemed like volleys of musketry arose in the direction of Atlanta. The day had been exciting in that city. Supplies and ammunition that Hood could carry with him were being removed; large quantities of provisions were being distributed among the citizens, and as the troops marched out they were allowed to take what they could from the public stores. All that remained was destroyed. The noise that Sherman heard that night was the blowing up of the rolling-mill and of about a hundred cars and six engines loaded with Hood's abandoned ammunition. The picture shows the Georgia Central Railroad east of the town.

SHERMAN'S MEN IN THE ABANDONED DEFENSES

At last Sherman's soldiers are within the Confederate fortifications which held them at bay for a month and a half. This is Confederate Fort D, to the southwest of the city, and was incorporated in the new line of defenses which Sherman had laid out preparatory to holding Atlanta as a military post. In the left background rises the new Federal fort, No. 7. The General himself felt no such security as these soldiers at ease seem to feel. His line of communications was long, and the Confederates were threatening it aggressively.

IN POSSESSION OF THE GOAL

This Confederate fort was to the west of Peach-Tree Street, and between it and the Chatta-nooga Railroad. Here, four hundred miles from his base, Sherman, having accomplished in four months what he set out to do, rested his army. Had Johnston's skill been opposed to him till the end, the feat would hardly have been so quickly performed. Hood's impetuous bravery had made it difficult and costly enough, but Sherman's splendid army, in the hands of its aggressive leader, had faced the intrepid assaults and won.

south into Atlanta were considerably damaged. But, late in August, the Northern commander made a daring move that proved successful. Leaving his base of supplies, as Grant had done before Vicksburg, and marching toward Jonesboro, Sherman destroyed the Macon and Western Railroad, the only remaining line of supplies to the Confederate army.

Hood attempted to block the march on Jonesboro, and Hardee was sent with his and S. D. Lee's Corps to attack the Federals, while he himself sought an opportunity to move upon Sherman's right flank. Hardee's attack failed, and this necessitated the evacuation of Atlanta. After blowing up his magazines and destroying the supplies which his men could not carry with them, Hood abandoned the city, and the next day, September 2d, General Slocum, having succeeded Hooker, led the Twentieth Corps of the Federal army within its earthen walls. Hood had made his escape, saving his army from capture. His chief desire would have been to march directly north on Marietta and destroy the depots of Federal supplies, but a matter of more importance prevented. Thirty-four thousand Union prisoners were confined at Andersonville, and a small body of cavalry could have released them. So Hood placed himself between Andersonville and Sherman.

In the early days of September the Federal hosts occupied the city toward which they had toiled all the summer long. At East Point, Atlanta, and Decatur, the three armies settled for a brief rest, while the cavalry, stretched for many miles along the Chattahoochee, protected their flanks and rear. Since May their ranks had been depleted by some twenty-eight thousand killed and wounded, while nearly four thousand had fallen prisoners, into the Confederates' hands.

It was a great price, but whatever else the capture of Atlanta did, it ensured the reelection of Abraham Lincoln to the presidency of the United States. The total Confederate losses were in the neighborhood of thirty-five thousand, of which thirteen thousand were prisoners.

THE LAST CONFLICTS
IN THE SHENANDOAH

THE CAPITOL IN WAR TIME

WAR'S WRECKAGE IN THE SHENANDOAH VALLEY

Ruins of the Virginia Military Institute at Lexington, after Hunter's raid in 1864. The picture shows the blackened walls of the leading Virginia military institution after General Hunter's raid through the valley in the early summer of 1864. The "V. M. I." meant much to the people of Virginia. It was in this well-known school that "Stonewall" Jackson had served for ten years as a professor before the outbreak of the war. The cadets of the "V. M. I." had fought like veterans in a body under Breckinridge in the battle with Sigel at New Market. Possibly it was because of the school's contributions to the Confederate cause that General Hunter ordered it to be burned. At any rate, he seems to have acted solely on his own responsibility in the matter. General Grant never approved of the unnecessary destruction of schools, churches, and private property. Retaliatory movements had an important part in the operations of General Early during the remainder of the summer. Such scenes undoubtedly spurred his footsore soldiers in their march.

A CONFEDERATE REPRISAL ON PENNSYLVANIA SOIL

Chambersburg as McCausland left it. As a reprisal for Hunter's raid in the Shenandoah Valley, the Confederate General McCausland burned the town of Chambersburg, in the Cumberland Valley of Pennsylvania. One high-minded and courageous officer in McCausland's command—Colonel William E. Peters, of Virginia—refused to obey the order to apply the torch. A year before, on the march to Gettysburg, General Lee had issued in the very town of Chambersburg his famous "General Order No. 73," in which he exhorted his troops to abstain from "any unnecessary or wanton injury to private property," and General Gordon is authority for the statement that the burning of Chambersburg by his subordinate was a great shock to General Lee's sensibilities. It seems inevitable that war should leave in its train such tottering walls and roofless homes.

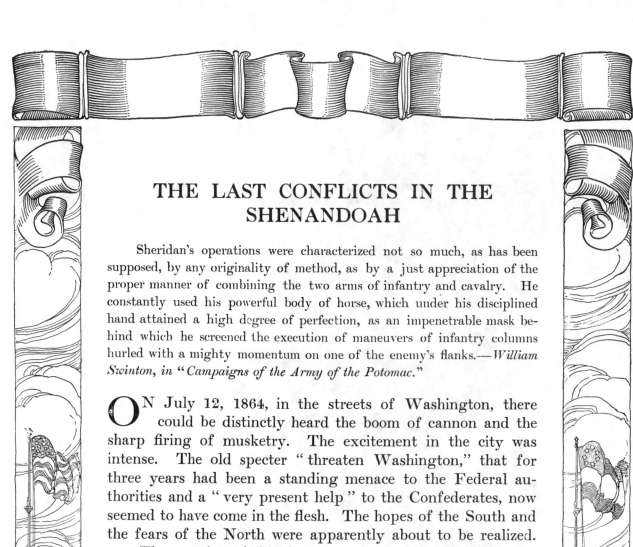

THE LAST CONFLICTS IN THE SHENANDOAH

Sheridan's operations were characterized not so much, as has been supposed, by any originality of method, as by a just appreciation of the proper manner of combining the two arms of infantry and cavalry. He constantly used his powerful body of horse, which under his disciplined hand attained a high degree of perfection, as an impenetrable mask behind which he screened the execution of maneuvers of infantry columns hurled with a mighty momentum on one of the enemy's flanks.—*William Swinton, in "Campaigns of the Army of the Potomac."*

ON July 12, 1864, in the streets of Washington, there could be distinctly heard the boom of cannon and the sharp firing of musketry. The excitement in the city was intense. The old specter "threaten Washington," that for three years had been a standing menace to the Federal authorities and a "very present help" to the Confederates, now seemed to have come in the flesh. The hopes of the South and the fears of the North were apparently about to be realized.

The occasion of this demonstration before the very gates of the city was the result of General Lee's project to relieve the pressure on his own army, by an invasion of the border States and a threatening attitude toward the Union capital. The plan had worked well before, and Lee believed it again would be effective. Grant was pushing him hard in front of Petersburg. Accordingly, Lee despatched the daring soldier, General Jubal A. Early, to carry the war again to the northward. He was to go by the beautiful and fertile Shenandoah valley, that highway of the Confederates along which the legions of the South had marched and countermarched until it had become almost a beaten track.

With that celerity of movement characteristic of Confed-

THE CAPITOL AT WASHINGTON IN 1863

When the Capitol at Washington was threatened by the Confederate armies, it was still an unfinished structure, betraying its incompleteness to every beholder. This picture shows the derrick on the dome. It is a view of the east front of the building and was taken on July 11, 1863. Washington society had not been wholly free from occasional "war scares" since the withdrawal of most of the troops whose duty it had been to guard the city. Early's approach in July, 1864, found the Nation's capital entirely unprotected. Naturally there was a flutter throughout the peaceable groups of non-combatants that made up the population of Washington at that time, as well as in official circles. There were less than seventy thousand people living in the city in 1864, a large proportion of whom were in some way connected with the Government.

erate marches, General Early prepared to sweep from the valley the fragmentary bodies of Union troops there collected. Less than a week after receiving his commission, he encountered the forces of General Hunter at Lynchburg, Virginia. There was some skirmishing, but Hunter, who did not have enough ammunition to sustain a real battle, returned westward. For three days Early's barefoot, half-clad soldiers followed the retreating columns of Hunter until the latter had safely filed his men through the passes of the Blue Ridge Mountains and into the Kanawha valley.

The Shenandoah valley was now uncovered, but not as Lee had expected. Believing that if Hunter were defeated he would retreat down the Valley, Early had been instructed to follow him into Maryland. But the Federal general had gone in the other direction, and southwestern Virginia had thereby been placed in great danger. The question was, how to draw Hunter from his new position. To pursue him further would have been a difficult task for Early. So it was decided to carry out the plans for a march into Maryland, in the hope of luring Hunter from his lair. So Early turned to the north with his seventeen thousand troops, and marching under the steady glare of a July sun, two weeks later, his approach was the signal for the Union troops at Martinsburg, under Sigel, to fall back across the Potomac to Maryland Heights. The road to Washington was thus blocked at Harper's Ferry, where Early intended to cross. He therefore was compelled to get over at Shepherdstown, while Breckenridge engaged Sigel at Harper's Ferry. Once across the river, Early's scouting parties quickly destroyed miles of the Baltimore and Ohio Railroad, cut the embankments and locks of the Chesapeake and Ohio Canal, levied contributions upon the citizens of Hagerstown and Frederick, and pushed their tattered ranks of gray in the direction of the Federal capital. On the 9th of July, the advance lines of the Confederate force came to the banks of the Monocacy, where they

PROTECTING LOCOMOTIVES FROM THE CONFEDERATE RAIDER

The United States railroad photographer, Captain A. J. Russell, labeled this picture of 1864: "Engines stored in Washington to prevent their falling into Rebel hands in case of a raid on Alexandria." Here they are, almost under the shadow of the Capitol dome (which had just been completed). This was one of the precautions taken by the authorities at Washington, of which the general public knew little or nothing at the time. These photographs are only now revealing official secrets recorded fifty years ago.

ONE OF WASHINGTON'S DEFENDERS

Heavy artillery like this was of comparatively little use in repulsing such an attack as Early might be expected to make. Not only were these guns hard to move to points of danger, but in the summer of '64 there were no trained artillerists to man them. Big as they were, they gave Early no occasion for alarm.

found General Lew Wallace posted, with eight thousand men, half of Early's numbers, on the eastern side of that stream, to contest the approach of the Southern troops.

The battle was brief but bloody; the Confederates, crossing the stream and climbing its slippery banks, hurled their lines of gray against the compact ranks of blue. The attack was impetuous; the repulse was stubborn. A wail of musketry rent the air and the Northern soldiers fell back to their second position. Between the opposing forces was a narrow ravine through which flowed a small brook. Across this stream the tide of battle rose and fell. Its limpid current was soon crimsoned by the blood of the dead and wounded. Wallace's columns, as did those of Early, bled, but they stood. The result of the battle for a time hung in the balance. Then the Federal lines began to crumble. The retreat began, some of the troops in order but the greater portion in confusion, and the victorious Confederates found again an open way to Washington.

Now within half a dozen miles of the city, with the dome of the Capitol in full view, the Southern general pushed his lines so close to Fort Stevens that he was ready to train his forty pieces of artillery upon its walls.

General Augur, in command of the capital's defenses, hastily collected what strength in men and guns he could. Heavy artillery, militia, sailors from the navy yard, convalescents, Government employees of all kinds were rushed to the forts around the city. General Wright, with two divisions of the Sixth Corps, arrived from the camp at Petersburg, and Emory's division of the Nineteenth Corps came just in time from New Orleans. This was on July 11th, the very day on which Early appeared in front of Fort Stevens. The Confederate had determined to make an assault, but the knowledge of the arrival of Wright and Emory caused him to change his mind. He realized that, if unsuccessful, his whole force would be lost, and he concluded to return. Nevertheless, he spent the 12th of July in threatening the city. In the middle of

ENTRANCE TO WASHINGTON FROM THE SOUTH—THE FAMOUS "CHAIN BRIDGE"

The sentry and vedette guarding the approach to Washington suggest one reason why Early did not make his approach to the capital from the Virginia side of the Potomac. A chain of more than twenty forts protected the roads to Long Bridge (shown below), and there was no way of marching troops into the city from the south, excepting over such exposed passages. Most of the troops left for the defense of the city were on the Virginia side. Therefore Early wisely picked out the northern outposts as the more vulnerable. Long Bridge was closely guarded at all times, like Chain Bridge and the other approaches, and at night the planks of its floor were removed.

LONG BRIDGE AND THE CAPITOL ACROSS THE BROAD POTOMAC

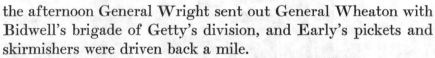

the afternoon General Wright sent out General Wheaton with Bidwell's brigade of Getty's division, and Early's pickets and skirmishers were driven back a mile.

This small engagement had many distinguished spectators. Pond in "The Shenandoah Valley" thus describes the scene: "On the parapet of Fort Stevens stood the tall form of Abraham Lincoln by the side of General Wright, who in vain warned the eager President that his position was swept by the bullets of sharpshooters, until an officer was shot down within three feet of him, when he reluctantly stepped below. Sheltered from the line of fire, Cabinet officers and a group of citizens and ladies, breathless with excitement, watched the fortunes of the fight."

Under cover of night the Confederates began to retrace their steps and made their way to the Shenandoah, with General Wright in pursuit. As the Confederate army was crossing that stream, at Snicker's Ferry, on the 18th, the pursuing Federals came upon them. Early turned, repulsed them, and continued on his way to Winchester, where General Averell, from Hunter's forces, now at Harper's Ferry, attacked them with his cavalry and took several hundred prisoners, two days later. The Union troops under Wright returned to the defenses of Washington.

The Confederate army now became a shuttlecock in the game of war, marching and countermarching up and down, in and across, the valley of the Shenandoah, in military maneuvers, with scarcely a day of rest. This fruitful valley was to be the granary for its supplies. From it, as a base of operations, Early would make his frequent forays—a constant menace to the peace of the authorities at Washington.

General Crook was sent up the Valley after him, but at Kernstown, near Winchester, on July 24th, he met a disastrous defeat and made his way to the north side of the Potomac. Early, now in undisputed possession of the Valley, followed him to Martinsburg and sent his cavalry across the

GENERAL JUBAL A. EARLY, THE CONFED-ERATE RAIDER WHO THREATENED WASHINGTON

"My bad old man," as General Lee playfully called him, was forty-eight years of age when he made the brilliant Valley campaign of the summer of 1864, which was halted only by the superior forces of Sheridan. A West Point graduate and a veteran of the Mexican War, Early became, after the death of Jackson, one of Lee's most efficient subordinates. He was alert, aggressive, resourceful. His very eccentricities, perhaps, made him all the more successful as a commander of troops in the field. "Old Jube's" caustic wit and austere ways made him a terror to stragglers, and who shall say that his fluent, forcible profanity did not endear him to men who were accustomed to like roughness of speech?

border river. With a bold movement General McCausland swept into Chambersburg and demanded a ransom of war. Compliance was out of the question and the torch was applied to the town, which in a short time was reduced to ashes. General Averell dashed in pursuit of McCausland and forced him to recross the Potomac.

The Federal authorities were looking for a " man of the hour "—one whom they might pit against the able and strategic Early. Such a one was found in General Philip Henry Sheridan, whom some have called the " Marshal Ney of America." He was selected by General Grant, and his instructions were to drive the Confederates out of the Valley and to make it untenable for any future military operations.

It was a magnificent setting for military genius. The men, the armies, and the beautiful valley combined to make it one of the great strategic campaigns of the war. The Union forces comprising the Army of the Shenandoah, as it was afterward called, amounted to about twenty-seven thousand men; the Confederates, to about twenty thousand. There was over a month of preliminary skirmishing and fighting. Cavalry raiders from both armies were darting hither and thither. Sheridan pushed up the Valley and fell back again toward the Potomac. Early followed him, only to retreat in turn toward Winchester, Sheridan now being pursuer. Both generals were watching an opportunity to strike. Both seemed anxious for battle, but both were sparring for the time and place to deliver an effective blow.

The middle of September found the Confederate forces centered about Winchester, and the Union army was ten miles distant, with the Opequon between them. At two o'clock on the morning of September 19th, the Union camp was in motion, preparing for marching orders. At three o'clock the forward movement was begun, and by daylight the Federal advance had driven in the Confederate pickets. Emptying into the Opequon from the west are two converging streams,

A HOUSE NEAR WASHINGTON STRUCK BY ONE OF EARLY'S SHELLS

The arrival of Grant's trained veterans in July, 1864, restored security to the capital city after a week of fright. The fact that shells had been thrown into the outskirts of the city gave the inhabitants for the first time a realizing sense of immediate danger. This scene is the neighborhood of Fort Stevens, on the Seventh Street road, not far from the Soldiers' Home, where President Lincoln was spending the summer. The campaign for his reëlection had begun and the outlook for his success and that of his party seemed at this moment as dubious as that for the conclusion of the war. Grant had weakened his lines about Richmond in order to protect Washington, while Lee had been able to detach Early's Corps for the brilliant Valley Campaign, which saved his Shenandoah supplies.

forming a triangle with the Winchester and Martinsburg pike as a base.

The town of Winchester is situated on this road, and was therefore at the bottom of the triangle. Before the town, the Confederate army stretched its lines between the two streams. The Union army would have to advance from the apex of the triangle, through a narrow ravine, shut in by thickly wooded hills and gradually emerging into an undulating valley. At the end of the gorge was a Confederate outwork, guarding the approach to Winchester. Both generals had the same plan of battle in mind. Sheridan would strike the Confederate center and right. Early was willing he should do this, for he planned to strike the Union right, double it back, get between Sheridan's army and the gorge, and thus cut off its retreat.

It took time for the Union troops to pass through the ravine, and it was late in the forenoon before the line of battle was formed. The attack and defense were alike obstinate. Upon the Sixth Corps and Grover's division of the Nineteenth Corps fell the brunt of the battle, since they were to hold the center while the Army of West Virginia, under General Crook, would sweep around them and turn the position of the opposing forces. The Confederate General Ramseur, with his troops, drove back the Federal center, held his ground for two hours, while the opposing lines were swept by musketry and artillery from the front, and enfiladed by artillery. Many Federal prisoners were taken.

By this time, Russell's division of the Sixth Corps emerged from the ravine. Forming in two lines, it marched quickly to the front. About the same time the Confederates were also being reenforced. General Rodes plunged into the fight, making a gallant attack and losing his life. General Gordon, with his columns of gray, swept across the summit of the hills and through the murky clouds of smoke saw the steady advance of the lines of blue. One of Russell's brigades struck the Confederate flank, and the Federal line was reestablished. As the

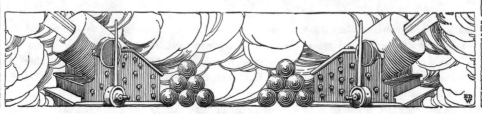

THE FIRST CONNECTICUT HEAVY ARTILLERY, ASSIGNED TO THE DEFENSE OF WASHINGTON

When Early approached Washington from the north, in 1864, the crack artillery companies, like that represented in the photograph (the First Connecticut Heavy), had all left the city to its fate. In the spring of 1862, as this picture was taken, just before the beginning of McClellan's Peninsula Campaign, Colonel Tyler was in the act of examining a despatch at the sally-port of Fort Richardson, Arlington Heights, Virginia. During the first two years of the war the Government devoted a great part of its energies to the development of a strong line of fortifications around the capital city, on both sides of the Potomac. Washington's nearness to the Confederate lines made such precautions necessary. The political significance of a possible capture of the national capital by the Confederates was fully appreciated. The retaining of large bodies of troops for the protection of Washington was a fixed policy during 1861 and 1862, as the first commander of the Army of the Potomac knew to his sorrow. As the war wore on, the increasing need of troops for the investment of Richmond, coupled with the apparent security of the capital, led to a reversal of that policy. Washington was practically abandoned, in a military sense, save for the retention of a few regiments of infantry, including a very small proportion of men who had seen actual fighting, and the forts were garrisoned chiefly by raw recruits.

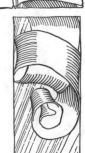

division moved forward to do this General Russell fell, pierced through the heart by a piece of shell.

The Fifth Maine battery, galloping into the field, unlimbered and with an enfilading storm of canister aided in turning the tide. Piece by piece the shattered Union line was picked up and reunited. Early sent the last of his reserves into the conflict to turn the Union right. Now ensued the fiercest fighting of the day. Regiment after regiment advanced to the wood only to be hurled back again. Here it was that the One hundred and fourteenth New York left its dreadful toll of men. Its position after the battle could be told by the long, straight line of one hundred and eighty-five of its dead and wounded.

It was three o'clock in the afternoon; the hour of Early's repulse had struck. To the right of the Union lines could be heard a mighty yell. The Confederates seemed to redouble their fire. The shivering lightning bolts shot through the air and the volleys of musketry increased in intensity. Then, across the shell-plowed field, came the reserves under General Crook. Breasting the Confederate torrent of lead, which cut down nine hundred of the reserves while crossing the open space, they rushed toward the embattled lines of the South.

At the same moment, coming out of the woods in the rear of the Federals, were seen the men of the Nineteenth Corps under General Emory, who had for three hours been lying in the grass awaiting their opportunity. The Confederate bullets had been falling thick in their midst with fatal certainty. They were eager for action. Rushing into the contest like madmen, they stopped at nothing. From two sides of the wood the men of Emory and Crook charged simultaneously. The Union line overlapped the Confederate at every point and doubled around the unprotected flanks. The day for the Southerners was irretrievably lost. They fell back toward Winchester in confusion. As they did so, a great uproar was heard on the pike road. It was the Federal cavalry under

WHERE LINCOLN WAS UNDER FIRE

This is Fort Stevens (originally known as Fort Massachusetts), north of Washington, near the Soldiers' Home, where President Lincoln had his summer residence. It was to this outpost that Early's troops advanced on July 12, 1864. In the fighting of that day Lincoln himself stood on the ramparts, and a surgeon who stood by his side was wounded. These works were feebly garrisoned, and General Gordon declared in his memoirs that when the Confederate troops reached Fort Stevens they found it untenanted. This photograph was taken after the occupation of the fort by Company F of the Third Massachusetts Artillery.

General Torbert sweeping up the road, driving the Confederate troopers before them. The surprised mass was pressed into its own lines. The infantry was charged and many prisoners and battle-flags captured.

The sun was now sinking upon the horizon, and on the ascending slopes in the direction of the town could be seen the long, dark lines of men following at the heels of the routed army. Along the crest of the embattled summit galloped a force of cavalrymen, which, falling upon the disorganized regiments of Early, aided, in the language of Sheridan, "to send them whirling through Winchester." The Union pursuit continued until the twilight had come and the shadows of night screened the scattered forces of Early from the pursuing cavalrymen. The battle of Winchester, or the Opequon, had been a bloody one—a loss of five thousand on the Federal side, and about four thousand on the Confederate.

By daylight of the following morning the victorious army was again in pursuit. On the afternoon of that day, it caught up with the Confederates, who now turned at bay at Fisher's Hill to resist the further approach of their pursuers. The position selected by General Early was a strong one, and his antagonist at once recognized it as such. The valley of the Shenandoah at this point is about four miles wide, lying between Fisher's Hill and Little North Mountain. General Early's line extended across the entire valley, and he had greatly increased his already naturally strong position. His army seemed safe from attack. From the summit of Three Top Mountain, his signal corps informed him of every movement of the Union army in the valley below. General Sheridan's actions indicated a purpose to assault the center of the Confederate line. For two days he continued massing his regiments in that direction, at times even skirmishing for position. General Wright pushed his men to within seven hundred yards of the Southern battle-line. While this was going on in full view of the Confederate general and his army, another movement was being executed

WAR DEPARTMENT OFFICIALS AND CLERKS IN WAR–TIME

Non-combatants of this type formed the main reliance of the authorities against Early's veterans in July, 1864. The forces available, prior to the arrival of the Sixth and Nineteenth Corps from Grant's army, are summarized by General Barnard thus: "The effective forces were 1,819 infantry, 1,834 artillery, and 63 cavalry north of the Potomac, and 4,064 infantry, 1,772 artillery, and 51 cavalry south thereof. There were besides, in Washington and Alexandria, about 3,900 effectives and about 4,400 (six regiments) of Veteran Reserves. The foregoing constitute a total of about 20,400 men. Of that number, however, but 9,600, mostly perfectly raw troops, constituted the garrison of the defenses. Of the other troops, a considerable portion were unavailable, and the whole would form but an inefficient force for service on the lines."

which even the vigilant signal officers on Three Top Mountain had not observed.

On the night of September 20th, the troops of General Crook were moved into the timber on the north bank of Cedar Creek. All during the next day, they lay concealed. That night they crossed the stream and the next morning were again hidden by the woods and ravines. At five o'clock on the morning of the 22d, Crook's men were nearly opposite the Confederate center. Marching his men in perfect silence, by one o'clock he had arrived at the left and front of the unsuspecting Early. By four o'clock he had reached the east face of Little North Mountain, to the left and rear of the Confederates. While the movement was being made, the main body of the Federal army was engaging the attention of the Confederates in front. Just before sundown, Crook's men plunged down the mountain side, from out of the timbered cover. The Confederates were quick to see that they had been trapped. They had been caught in a pocket and there was nothing for them to do except to retreat or surrender. They preferred the former, which was, according to General Gordon, "first stubborn and slow, then rapid, then—a rout."

After the battle of Fisher's Hill the pursuit still continued. The Confederate regiments re-formed, and at times would stop and contest the approach of the advancing cavalrymen. By the time the Union infantry would reach the place, the retreating army would have vanished. Torbert had been sent down Luray Valley in pursuit of the Confederate cavalry, with the hope of scattering it and seizing New Market in time to cut off the Confederate retreat from Fisher's Hill. But at Milford, in a narrow gorge, General Wickham held Torbert and prevented the fulfilment of his plan; and General Early's whole force was able to escape. Day after day this continued until Early had taken refuge in the Blue Ridge in front of Brown's Gap. Here he received reenforcements. Sheridan in the mean time had gone into camp at Harrisonburg, and for

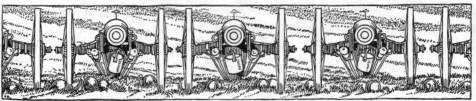

A MARYLAND VILLAGE ON THE LINE OF EARLY'S RETREAT

This is a winter scene in Poolesville, a typical village in this part of Maryland, overrun for the last time by Confederate armies in the summer of 1864. Early passed through the place on his second day's march from Washington, closely pursued by General Wright's force of Federals. After Early had made good his escape and threatened to levy heavy toll on the defenseless communities of Maryland and Pennsylvania if he were not vigorously opposed, Grant selected Sheridan for the task of clearing the Valley of Confederates and finally destroying its value as a source of supplies for Lee's army. Sheridan waited until Early had been seriously weakened before he assaulted him; but when he struck, the blows were delivered with tremendous energy. The battles of the Opequon, Fisher's Hill, and Cedar Creek (the latter made memorable by Read's famous poem, "Sheridan's Ride"), drove Early back to New Market and wholly broke the Confederate power in that part of Virginia. This photograph (loaned by **Mr. George A. Brackett**, of Annapolis), was taken when the Eighth Minnesota held it, in the winter of 1862.

some time the two armies lay watching each other. The Federals were having difficulty in holding their lines of supply.

With the Valley practically given up by Early, Sheridan was anxious to stop here. He wrote to Grant, " I think the best policy will be to let the burning of the crops in the Valley be the end of the campaign, and let some of this army go somewhere else." He had the Petersburg line in mind. Grant's consent to this plan reached him on October 5th, and the following day he started on his return march down the Shenandoah. His cavalry extended across the entire valley. With the unsparing severity of war, his men began to make a barren waste of the region. The October sky was overcast with clouds of smoke and sheets of flame from the burning barns and mills.

As the army of Sheridan proceeded down the Valley, the undaunted cavaliers of Early came in pursuit. His horsemen kept close to the rear of the Union columns. On the morning of October 9th, the cavalry leader, Rosser, who had succeeded Wickham, found himself confronted by General Custer's division, at Tom's Brook. At the same time the Federal general, Wesley Merritt, fell upon the cavalry of Lomax and Johnson on an adjacent road. The two Union forces were soon united and a mounted battle ensued. The fight continued for two hours. There were charges and countercharges. The ground being level, the maneuvering of the squadrons was easy. The clink of the sabers rang out in the morning air. Both sides fought with tenacity. The Confederate center held together, but its flanks gave way. The Federals charged along the whole front, with a momentum that forced the Southern cavalrymen to flee from the field. They left in the hands of the Federal troopers over three hundred prisoners, all their artillery, except one piece, and nearly every wagon the Confederate cavalry had with them.

The Northern army continued its retrograde movement, and on the 10th crossed to the north side of Cedar Creek. Early's army in the mean time had taken a position at the

ONE OF CHAMBERSBURG'S QUIET STREETS

The invasion of Pennsylvania had only a minor part in the plan of Early's campaign, which in a month's time had accomplished two important results: It had restored to Lee free access to the rich supplies which the Shenandoah Valley could furnish, and it had caused Grant to withdraw from his operations at Petersburg a strong force for the protection of Washington. The cavalry raid in Pennsylvania was planned as retaliation for Hunter's operations in the Shenandoah. Early succeeded in holding the "Valley of Virginia" (Shenandoah) until the concentration of Sheridan's forces compelled his retirement. Then the "Valley" finally became eliminated as an avenue of danger to Washington.

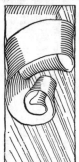

wooded base of Fisher's Hill, four miles away. The Sixth Corps started for Washington, but the news of Early at Fisher's Hill led to its recall. The Union forces occupied ground that was considered practically unassailable, especially on the left, where the deep gorge of the Shenandoah, along whose front rose the bold Massanutten Mountain, gave it natural protection.

The movements of the Confederate army were screened by the wooded ravines in front of Fisher's Hill, while, from the summit of the neighboring Three Top Mountain, its officers could view, as in a panorama, the entire Union camp. Seemingly secure, the corps of Crook on the left of the Union line was not well protected. The keen-eyed Gordon saw the weak point in the Union position. Ingenious plans to break it down were quickly made.

Meanwhile, Sheridan was summoned to Washington to consult with Secretary Stanton. He did not believe that Early proposed an immediate attack, and started on the 15th, escorted by the cavalry, and leaving General Wright in command. At Front Royal the next day word came from Wright enclosing a message taken for the Confederate signal-flag on Three Top Mountain. It was from Longstreet, advising Early that he would join him and crush Sheridan. The latter sent the cavalry back to Wright, and continued on to Washington, whence he returned at once by special train, reaching Winchester on the evening of the 18th.

Just after dark on October 18th, a part of Early's army under the command of General John B. Gordon, with noiseless steps, moved out from their camp, through the misty, autumn night. The men had been stripped of their canteens, in fear that the striking of them against some object might reveal their movements. Orders were given in low whispers. Their path followed along the base of the mountain—a dim and narrow trail, upon which but one man might pass at a time. For seven miles this sinuous line made its way through the dark

CHAMBERSBURG—A LANDMARK IN EARLY'S INVASION OF THE NORTH

After withdrawing from Washington, in July, 1864, Early sent a cavalry expedition under General McCausland to invade Pennsylvania. Chambersburg, in the Cumberland Valley, which was burned by McCausland's orders, marked the limit of the northward advance in this remarkable campaign. Early's force of ten thousand men had been detached from Lee's army of defense around Richmond on June 12th, had driven Hunter out of the Shen- andoah, and (after marching the length of that valley) had crossed the Potomac, forced back Lew Wallace with his six thousand Federals at the Monocacy, and camped within sight of the capitol's dome at Washington. Much of this marching had been at the rate of twenty miles a day, and at one time half of the command had been shoeless. The dash and endurance of the troops shone as bright as the leadership displayed by Early.

gorge, crossing the Shenandoah, and at times passing within four hundred yards of the Union pickets.

It arrived at the appointed place, opposite Crook's camp on the Federal right, an hour before the attack was to be made. In the shivering air of the early morning, the men crouched on the river bank, waiting for the coming of the order to move forward. At last, at five o'clock, it came. They plunged into the frosty water of the river, emerged on the other side, marched in "double quick," and were soon sounding a reveille to the sleeping troops of Sheridan. The minie balls whizzed and sang through the tents. In the gray mists of the dawn the legions of the South looked like phantom warriors, as they poured through the unmanned gaps. The Northerners sprang to arms. There was a bloody struggle in the trenches. Their eyes saw the flames from the Southern muskets; the men felt the breath of the hot muzzles in their faces, while the Confederate bayonets were at their breasts. There was a brief struggle, then panic and disorganization. Only a quarter of an hour of this yelling and struggling, and two-thirds of the Union army broke like a mill-dam and poured across the fields, leaving their accouterments of war and the stiffening bodies of their comrades. Rosser, with the cavalry, attacked Custer and assisted Gordon.

Meanwhile, during these same early morning hours, General Early had himself advanced to Cedar Creek by a more direct route. At half-past three o'clock his men had come in sight of the Union camp-fires. They waited under cover for the approach of day. At the first blush of dawn and before the charge of Gordon, Early hurled his men across the stream, swept over the breastworks, captured the batteries and turned them upon the unsuspecting Northerners. The Federal generals tried to stem the impending disaster. From the east of the battlefield the solid lines of Gordon were now driving the fugitives of Crook's corps by the mere force of momentum. Aides were darting hither and thither, trying to reassemble the

GENERAL PHILIP H. SHERIDAN IN THE SHENANDOAH CAMPAIGN

Two generations of schoolboys in the Northern States have learned the lines beginning, "Up from the south at break of day." This picture represents Sheridan in 1864, wearing the same hat that he waved to rally his soldiers on that famous ride from "Winchester, twenty miles away." As he reined up his panting horse on the turnpike at Cedar Creek, he received salutes from two future Presidents of the United States. The position on the left of the road was held by Colonel Rutherford B. Hayes, who had succeeded, after the rout of the Eighth Corps in the darkness of the early morning, in rallying some fighting groups of his own brigade; while on the right stood Major William McKinley, gallantly commanding the remnant of his fighting regiment—the Twenty-third Ohio.

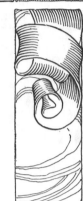

crumbling lines. The Nineteenth Corps, under Emory, tried to hold its ground; for a time it fought alone, but after a desperate effort to hold its own, it, too, melted away under the scorching fire. The fields to the rear of the army were covered with wagons, ambulances, stragglers, and fleeing soldiers.

The Sixth Corps now came to the rescue. As it slowly fell to the rear it would, at times, turn to fight. At last it found a place where it again stood at bay. The men hastily gathered rails and constructed rude field-works. At the same time the Confederates paused in their advance. The rattle of musketry ceased. There was scarcely any firing except for the occasional roar of a long-range artillery gun. The Southerners seemed willing to rest on their well-earned laurels of the morning. In the language of the successful commander, it was "glory enough for one day."

But the brilliant morning victory was about to be changed to a singular afternoon defeat. During the morning's fight, when the Union troops were being rapidly overwhelmed with panic, Rienzi, the beautiful jet-black war-charger, was bearing his master, the commander of the Federal army, to the field of disaster. Along the broad valley highway that leads from Winchester, General Sheridan had galloped to where his embattled lines had been reduced to a flying mob. While riding leisurely away from Winchester about nine o'clock he had heard unmistakable thunder-peals of artillery. Realizing that a battle was on in the front, he hastened forward, soon to be met, as he crossed Mill Creek, by the trains and men of his routed army, coming to the rear with appalling rapidity.

News from the field told him of the crushing defeat of his hitherto invincible regiments. The road was blocked by the retreating crowds as they pressed toward the rear. The commander was forced to take to the fields, and as his steed, flecked with foam, bore him onward, the disheartened refugees greeted him with cheers. Taking off his hat as he rode, he cried, "We will go back and recover our camps." The words

SHERIDAN'S CAVALRY
IN THE SHENANDOAH
GENERAL TORBERT AND HIS STAFF

Sheridan appointed General Alfred T. A. Torbert Chief of Cavalry of the Army of the Shenandoah in August, 1864. General Torbert had been a regular army officer and was now a major-general of volunteers. This photograph was taken in 1864, on the vine-covered veranda of a Virginia mansion occupied as headquarters. In all the operations in the Valley during September and October, Sheridan made such good use of the cavalry that this branch of the service leaped into prominence, and won a goodly share of the praise for eliminating the Valley of Virginia from

MAJOR–GENERAL
WILLIAM WELLS

the field of war. The portrait below is that of Major-General William Wells, of Vermont, the last commander of the Corps. During the fighting in the Valley, his rank was only that of colonel; but he commanded the second brigade in Custer's division with a daring and skill notable even in that magnificent body. Gallantry displayed previously, during Farnsworth's charge at Gettysburg, had earned him the Congressional medal of honor. With such soldiers, and with equipment and discipline steadily bettering, Sheridan's cavalry corps became a mighty arm. It swept from front to flank of his infantry, concealing the latter's movements. Its stubborn charges changed the fate of many a doubtful field.

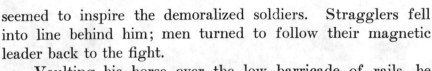

seemed to inspire the demoralized soldiers. Stragglers fell into line behind him; men turned to follow their magnetic leader back to the fight.

Vaulting his horse over the low barricade of rails, he dashed to the crest of the field. There was a flutter along the battle-line. The men from behind their protecting wall broke into thunderous cheers. From the rear of the soldiers there suddenly arose, as from the earth, a line of the regimental flags, which waved recognition to their leader. Color-bearers reassembled. The straggling lines re-formed. Early made another assault after one o'clock, but was easily repulsed.

It was nearly four o'clock when the order for the Federal advance was given. General Sheridan, hat in hand, rode in front of his infantry line that his men might see him. The Confederate forces now occupied a series of wooded crests. From out of the shadow of one of these timbered coverts, a column of gray was emerging. The Union lines stood waiting for the impending crash. It came in a devouring succession of volleys that reverberated into a deep and sullen roar. The Union infantry rose as one man and passed in among the trees. Not a shot was heard. Then, suddenly, there came a screaming, humming rush of shell, a roar of musketry mingling with the yells of a successful charge. Again the firing ceased, except for occasional outbursts. The Confederates had taken a new position and reopened with a galling fire. General Sheridan dashed along the front of his lines in personal charge of the attack. Again his men moved toward the lines of Early's fast thinning ranks. It was the final charge. The Union cavalry swept in behind the fleeing troops of Early and sent, again, his veteran army " whirling up the Valley."

The battle of Cedar Creek was ended; the tumult died away. The Federal loss had been about fifty-seven hundred; the Confederate over three thousand. Fourteen hundred Union prisoners were sent to Richmond. Never again would the gaunt specter of war hover over Washington.

PART III
CLOSING IN

CHARLESTON, THE UNCAPTURED PORT

CONFEDERATE GARRISON COOKING DINNER
IN RUINED SUMTER—1864

MAKING SAND–BAGS INSIDE FORT SUMTER IN 1864

The story of how these photographs in unconquered Sumter were secured is a romance in itself. No one, North or South, can escape a thrill at the knowledge that several of them were actually taken in the beleaguered port by George S. Cook, the Confederate photographer. This adventurous spirit was one of the enterprising and daring artists who are now and then found ready when and where great events impend. He had risked his life in 1863, taking photographs of the Federal fleet as it was bombarding Sumter. The next year, while the magnificent organization of the Northern armies was closing in day by day; while the stores and homes and public buildings of Charleston were crumbling into pitiful ruins under the bombardment; while shoes and clothing and food were soaring to unheard-of prices in the depreciated Confederate currency, Cook still ingeniously secured his precious chemicals from the New York firm of Anthony & Co., which, curiously enough, was the same that supplied Brady. Cook's method was to smuggle his chemicals through as quinine! It is only the most fortunate of chances that preserved these photographs of the Confederates defending Charleston through the nearly half century which elapsed between their taking and the publication of the PHOTOGRAPH HISTORY. Editors of the work

traveled thousands of miles and wrote thousands of letters in the search for such photographs. Of the priceless examples and specimens, several are here reproduced. How rare such pictures are may be judged by the fact that some of the men prominent and active in the circles of Confederate veterans, together with families of former Confederate generals and leaders, were unable to lay their hands on any such picture . The natural disappointment in the South at the end of the war was such that photographers were forced to destroy all negatives, just as owners destroyed all the objects that might serve as souvenirs or relics of the terrible struggle, thinking, for the moment at least, that they could not bear longer the strain of brooding over the tragedy. Constant ferreting, following up clues, digging in dusty garrets amid relics buried generations ago, interviews with organizations like the Daughters of the Confederacy (to the Charleston chapter of which acknowledgment must be made for the picture of the Charleston Zouaves)—only after such exertions did it become possible to show on these pages the countenances and bearing and drill of the men who held Charleston against the ever-increasing momentum of the Northern power.

THE TOTTERING WALLS OF THE FORT SHORED UP

THE CONFEDERATE CAMP WASHINGTON. LOCKED IN ON THE SANDY BEACH NEAR SULLIVAN INLET
WHERE THE SOUTH CAROLINA WARRIORS MAINTAINED THEIR MILITARY POST FOR FOUR YEARS

CHARLESTON'S FAMOUS ZOUAVE CADETS DRILLING AT CASTLE PINCKNEY

REMAINS OF THE CIRCULAR CHURCH AND "SECESSION HALL," WHERE SOUTH CAROLINA DECIDED TO LEAVE THE UNION

"Prodigies of talent, audacity, intrepidity, and perseverance were exhibited in the attack, as in the defense of the city, which will assign to the siege of Charleston an exceptional place in military annals." Thus spoke the expert of the French *Journal of Military Science* in 1865, only a few months after this attack and defense had passed into history. Charleston was never captured. It was evacuated only after Sherman's advance through the heart of South Carolina had done what over five hundred and fifty-seven days of continuous attack and siege by the Federal army and navy could not do—make it untenable. When, on the night of February 17, 1865, Captain H. Huguenin, lantern in hand, made his last silent rounds of the deserted fort and took the little boat for shore, there ended the four years' defense of Fort Sumter, a feat of war unsurpassed in ancient or modern times—eclipsing (says an English military critic) "such famous passages as Sale's defense of Jellalabad against the Afghans and Havelock's obdurate tenure of the residency at Lucknow." Charleston with its defenses—Forts Sumter, Moultrie, Wagner, and Castle Pinckney from the sea and the many batteries on the land side—was the heart of the Confederacy,

and some of the most vigorous efforts of the Federal forces were made to capture it. Though "closed in" upon more than once, it never surrendered. But beleaguered it certainly was, in the sternest sense of the word. It is a marvel how the photographer, Cook, managed to get his supplies past the Federal army on one side and the Federal blockading fleet on the other. Yet there he remained at his post, catching with his lens the ruins of the uncaptured fort and the untaken city in 1864. How well he made these pictures may be seen on the pages preceding and the lower picture opposite. They furnish a glimpse into American history that most people—least of all the Confederate veterans themselves—never expected to enjoy. Those who actually knew what it was to be besieged in Petersburg, invaded in Georgia, starved in Tennessee, or locked up by a blockading fleet—such veterans have been astonished to find these authenticated photographs of the garrison beleaguered in the most important of Southern ports.

ON "THE BATTERY," CHARLESTON'S SPACIOUS PROMENADE

INSIDE FORT MOULTRIE—LOOKING EASTWARD

OUTSIDE FORT JOHNSON—SUMTER IN THE DISTANCE

GRIM-VISAGED WAR ALONG THE PALMETTO SHORE-LINE OF CHARLESTON HARBOR

THE DESOLATE INTERIOR OF SUMTER IN SEPTEMBER, 1863, AFTER THE GUNS OF THE FEDERAL FLEET
HAD BEEN POUNDING IT FOR MANY WEEKS

IN CHARLESTON AFTER THE BOMBARDMENT

So long as the Confederate flag flew over the ramparts of Sumter, Charleston remained the one stronghold of the South that was firmly held. That flag was never struck. It was lowered for an evacuation, not a surrender. The story of Charleston's determined resistance did not end in triumph for the South, but it did leave behind it a sunset glory, in which the valor and dash of the Federal attack is paralleled by the heroism and self-sacrifice of the Confederate defense, in spite of wreck and ruin.

PART III
CLOSING IN

THE INVESTMENT
OF PETERSBURG

ON GRANT'S CITY POINT RAILROAD—A NEW KIND
OF SIEGE GUN

WHERE THE PHOTOGRAPHER "DREW FIRE"

June 21, 1864, is the exact date of the photograph that made this picture and those on the three following pages. A story goes with them, told by one of the very men pictured here. As he looked at it forty-six years later, how vividly the whole scene came back to him! This is Battery B, First Pennsylvania Light Artillery, known as Cooper's Battery of the Fifth Corps, under General G. K. Warren. On the forenoon of this bright June day, Brady, the photographer, drove his light wagon out to the entrenchments. The Confederates lay along the sky-line near where rose the ruined chimney of a house belonging to a planter named Taylor. Approaching Captain Cooper, Brady politely asked if he could take a picture of the battery, when just about to fire. At the command, from force of habit, the men jumped to their positions. Hardly a face was turned toward the camera. They might be oblivious of its existence. The cannoneer rams home a charge. The gunner "thumbs the vent"—but "our friend the enemy" just over the hill observes the movement,

THE MAN WHO REMEMBERED

and, thinking it means business, opens up. Away goes Brady's horse, scattering chemicals and plates. The gun in the foreground is ready to send a shell across the open ground, but Captain Cooper reserves his fire. Brady, seeing his camera is uninjured, recalls his assistant and takes the other photographs, moving his instrument a little to the rear. And the man who saw it then, sees it all again to-day just as it was. He is even able to pick out many of the men by name. Their faces come back to him. Turning the page, may be seen Captain James H. Cooper, leaning on his sword, and Lieutenant Alcorn, on the extreme right. In the photograph above is Lieutenant Miller, back of the gun. Lieutenant James A. Gardner was the man who saw all this, and in the picture on the preceding page he appears seated on the trail of the gun to the left in the act of sighting the gun. The other officers shown in this picture were no longer living when, in 1911, he described the actors in the drama that the glass plate had preserved forty-six years.

JUST AS THE CAMERA CAUGHT THEM

General Warren's Corps had arrived in front of Petersburg on the 17th of June, 1864, and Battery B of the First Pennsylvania Light Artillery was put into position near the Avery house. Before them the Confederates were entrenched, with Beauregard in command. On the 17th, under cover of darkness, the Confederates fell back to their third line, just visible beyond the woods to the left in the first picture. Early the next morning Battery B was advanced to the line of entrenchments shown above, and a sharp interchange of artillery fire took place in the afternoon. So busy were both sides throwing up entrenchments and building forts and lunettes that there had been very little interchange of compliments in the way of shells or bullets at this point until Photographer Brady's presence and the gathering of men of Battery B at their posts called forth the well-pointed salute. Men soon became accustomed to artillery

COOPER'S BATTERY BEFORE PETERSBURG

and shell-fire. It was not long before Battery B was advanced from the position shown above to that held by the Confederates on the 21st of June, and there Fort Morton was erected, and beyond the line of woods the historic Fort Stedman, the scene of some of the bloodiest fighting before Petersburg. On page 23 of volume I, another view of this scene appears; the short man in civilian's clothes, on a mound toward the left of the right-hand section, has been identified as Mr. Brady himself. There are fifteen people in this picture whom Lieutenant Gardner, of this battery, recognized after a lapse of forty-six years and can recall by name. There may be more gallant Pennsylvanians who, on studying this photograph, will see themselves and their comrades, surviving and dead, as once they fought on the firing-line.

"WHERE IS GRANT?"

This heavy Federal battery looks straight across the low-lying country to Petersburg. Its spires show in the distance. The smiling country is now to be a field of blood and suffering. For Grant's army, unperceived, has swung around from Cold Harbor, and "the Confederate cause was lost when Grant crossed the James," declared the Southern General Ewell. It was a mighty and a masterful move, practicable only because of the tremendous advantages the Federals held in the undisputed possession of the waterways, the tremendous fleet of steamers, barges, and river craft that made a change of base and transportation easy. Petersburg became the objective of the great army under Grant. His movements to get there had not been heralded; they worked like well-oiled machinery. "Where is Grant?" frantically asked Beauregard of Lee. The latter, by his despatches, shows that he could not answer with any certainty. In fact, up to the evening of the 13th of June, when the Second Corps, the advance of the Army of the Potomac, reached

HEAVY ARTILLERY JUST ARRIVED BEFORE PETERSBURG—1864

the north bank of the James, Lee could not learn the truth. By midnight of the 15th, bridges were constructed, and following the Second Corps, the Ninth began to cross. But already the Fifth and Sixth Corps and part of the Army of the James were on their way by water from White House to City Point. The Petersburg campaign had begun. Lee's army drew its life from the great fields and stock regions south and southwest of Richmond. With the siege of Petersburg, the railroad center of the state, this source of supply was more and more cut off, until six men were made to live on the allowance first given to each separate Southern soldier. Outnumbered three to one in efficient men, with the cold of winter coming on and its attendant hardships in prospect, no wonder the indomitable Southern bravery was tried to the utmost. Sherman was advancing. The beginning of the end was near.

THE BUSIEST PLACE IN DIXIE

City Point, just after its capture by Butler. From June, 1864, until April, 1865, City Point, at the juncture of the Appomattox and the James, was a point of entry and departure for more vessels than any city of the South including even New Orleans in times of peace. Here landed supplies that kept an army numbering, with fighting force and supernumeraries, nearly one hundred and twenty thousand well-supplied, well-fed, well-contented, and well-munitioned men in the field. This was the marvelous base —safe from attack, secure from molestation. It was meals and money that won at Petersburg, the bravery of full stomachs and warm-clothed bodies against the desperation of starved and shivering out-numbered men. A glance at this picture tells the story. There is no need of rehearsing charges, counter-charges, mines, and counter-mines. Here lies the reason—Petersburg had to fall. As we look back with a retrospective eye on this scene of plenty and abundance, well may the American heart be proud that only a few miles away were men of their own blood enduring the hardships that the defenders of Petersburg suffered in the last campaign of starvation against numbers and plenty.

THE TEEMING WHARVES

No signs of warfare, no marching men or bodies lying on the blood-soaked sward, are needed to mark this as a war-time photograph. No laboring boss would have fallen into the position of the man on the top of the embankment. Four years in uniform has marked this fellow; he has caught the eye of the camera and drawn up at "Attention," shoulders back, heels together, and arms hanging at his side. There is no effect of posing, no affectation here; he stands as he has been taught to stand. He is a soldier. No frowning cannon could suggest the military note more clearly. Just beyond the point to the left, above the anchorage and the busy wharves, are General Grant's headquarters at City Point. From here it was but a few minutes' ride on the rough military rail-

SUPPLIES FOR AN ARMY—BELOW, AN ENGINE OF THE U. S. MILITARY RAILROAD

way to where the one hundred and ten thousand fighting men lay entrenched with the sixty-six thousand veterans in gray opposed to them. A warship lying where these vessels lie could drop a 12-inch shell into Petersburg in modern days. From here President Lincoln set out to see a grand review and witnessed a desperate battle. Here General Sherman, fresh from his victorious march from Atlanta to the sea, came up in the little gunboat *Bat* to visit Grant. During the last days, when to the waiting world peace dawned in sight, City Point, to all intents and purposes, was the National Capital, for from here President Lincoln held communication with his Cabinet officers, and replied to Stanton's careful injunctions "to take care of himself" with the smiling assurance that he was in the hands of Grant and the army.

A MOVABLE MENACE

The 17,000-pound mortar, "Dictator," was run on a flat-car from point to point on a curve of the railroad track along the bank of
the Appomattox. It was manned and served before Petersburg, July 9–31, 1864, by Company G, First Connecticut Artillery, during
its stay. When its charge of fourteen pounds of powder was first fired, the car broke under the shock; but a second car was prepared

THE RAILROAD MORTAR

by the engineers, strengthened by additional beams, tied strongly by iron rods and covered with iron-plating. This enabled the "Dictator" to be used at various points, and during the siege it fired in all forty-five rounds—nineteen of which were fired during the battle of the Crater. It was given at last a permanent emplacement near Battery No. 4—shown on the following pages.

THE DICTATORS OF THE "DICTATOR"

Here are the men who did the thinking for the great mortar that rests so stolidly in the midst of the group. They are its cabinet ministers, artillerymen every one, versed in the art of range-finding and danger-angles, of projectory arcs and the timing of shell-fuses. In the front line the two figures from left to right are Colonel H. L. Abbott, First Connecticut Heavy Artillery, and General H. J. Hunt, Chief of Artillery. In the second, or rear line, also from left to right, the first is Captain F. A. Pratt; second (just behind Colonel Abbott), Captain E. C. Dow; fourth (just behind and to General Hunt's left), Major T. S. Trumbull.

A PERMANENT POSITION

THE RAILROAD GUN'S EXECUTIVE COMMITTEE

These nine men are the executive committee that controlled the actions of the great mortar, and a glance at them shows that they were picked men for the job—men in the prime of life, brawny and strong—they were the slaves of their pet monster. Some shots from this gun went much farther than they were ever intended, carrying their fiery trails over the Confederate entrenchments and exploding within the limits of the town itself, over two and a quarter miles. The roar of the explosion carried consternation to all within hearing. In the lower picture is the great mortar resting in the position it occupied longest, near Battery No. 4.

POINTED TOWARD PETERSBURG

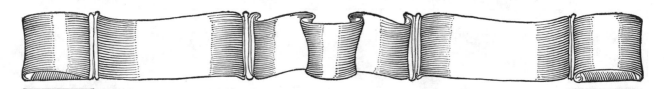

THE INVESTMENT OF PETERSBURG

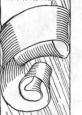

The cause was lost, but the end was not yet. The noble Army of Northern Virginia, once, twice conqueror of empire, must bite the dust before its formidable adversary.—Lieutenant-General James Longstreet, C.S.A., in "From Manassas to Appomattox."

THE disastrous failure of the Union army on the sanguinary battlefield of Cold Harbor, in June, 1864, destroyed Grant's last chance to turn the Confederate right flank north of Richmond. He could still try to turn Lee's left and invest Richmond from the north, but this would not have interfered with the lines of supply over the James River and the railroads from the South and West. The city could have resisted for an indefinite time. If Richmond were to fall, it must be besieged from the south.

The movement from Cold Harbor began after dark on June 12th, and Meade's whole army was safely over the James River at Wilcox's Landing by midnight on the 16th of June. The little city of Petersburg is situated twenty-one miles south of Richmond on the southern bank of the Appomattox, a small stream threading its way through the Virginia tidewater belt, almost parallel with the James, into which it flows. In itself the town was of little value to either army. But it was the doorway to Richmond from the south. Three railroads from Southern points converged here. To reach the Confederate capital, Petersburg must first be battered down. At this time the town ought not to have been difficult to capture, for its defenses were but weak entrenchments, and they were not formidably manned. General Smith, who reached Bermuda Hundred by water, with his corps, on the night of the 14th, was ordered by Butler, under instructions from Grant, to move on Petersburg at daylight.

THE DIGGERS AT PETERSBURG—1864

There was not a day during the whole of the nine months' siege of Petersburg that pick and shovel were idle. At first every man had to turn to and become for the nonce a laborer in the ditches. But in an army of one hundred and ten thousand men, in the maintenance of camp discipline, there were always soldier delinquents who for some infringement of military rules or some neglected duty were sentenced to extra work under the watchful eye of an officer and an armed sentry. Generally, these small punishments meant six to eight hours' digging, and here we see a group of Federal soldiers thus employed. They are well within the outer chain of forts, near where the military road joins the Weldon & Petersburg Railroad. The presence of the camera man has given them a moment's relaxation.

The Confederate forces at Petersburg were now commanded by General Beauregard. He had conjectured what Grant's plans might be, and in order to prevent the capture of the town and enable him to hold Butler at Bermuda Hundred, he called on Lee for immediate reenforcement. But the latter, not yet convinced that Grant was not moving on Richmond, sent only Hoke's division. On the day after Meade began to move his army toward the James, Lee left the entrenchments at Cold Harbor. Keeping to the right and rear of the Union lines of march, by the morning of the 16th, he had thrown a part of his force to the south side of the James, and, by the evening of the 18th, the last of the regiments had united with those of Beauregard, and the two great opposing armies were once more confronting each other—this time for a final settlement of the issue at arms. The Union army outnumbered that of the Confederates, approximately, two to one.

The contest for Petersburg had already begun. For two days the rapidly gathering armies had been combating with each other. On June 15th, General Smith pushed his way toward the weakly entrenched lines of the city. General Beauregard moved his men to an advanced line of rifle-pits. Here the initial skirmish occurred. The Confederates were driven to the entrenched works of Petersburg, and not until evening was a determined attack made upon them. At this time Hancock, "The Superb," came on the field. Night was falling but a bright moon was shining, and the Confederate redoubts, manned by a little over two thousand men, might have been carried by the Federals. But Hancock, waiving rank, yielded to Smith in command. No further attacks were made and a golden opportunity for the Federals was lost.

By the next morning the Confederate trenches were beginning to fill with Hoke's troops. The Federal attack was not made until afternoon, when the fighting was severe for three hours, and some brigades of the Ninth Corps assisted the Second and Eighteenth. The Confederates were driven back

MAHONE, "THE HERO OF THE CRATER"

General William Mahone, C. S. A. It was through the promptness and valor of General Mahone that the Southerners, on July 30, 1864, were enabled to turn back upon the Federals the disaster threatened by the hidden mine. On the morning of the explosion there were but eighteen thousand Confederates left to hold the ten miles of lines about Petersburg. Everything seemed to favor Grant's plans for the crushing of this force. Immediately after the mine was sprung, a terrific cannonade was opened from one hundred and fifty guns and mortars to drive back the Confederates from the breach, while fifty thousand Federals stood ready to charge upon the panic-stricken foe. But the foe was not panic-stricken long. Colonel McMaster, of the Seventeenth South Carolina, gathered the remnants of General Elliott's brigade and held back the Federals massing at the Crater until General Mahone arrived at the head of three brigades. At once he prepared to attack the Federals, who at that moment were advancing to the left of the Crater. Mahone ordered a counter-charge. In his inspiring presence it swept with such vigor that the Federals were driven back and dared not risk another assault. At the Crater, Lee had what Grant lacked—a man able to direct the entire engagement.

some distance and made several unsuccessful attempts during the night to recover their lost ground. Before the next noon, June 17th, the battle was begun once more. Soon there were charges and countercharges along the whole battle-front. Neither side yielded. The gray and blue lines surged back and forth through all the afternoon. The dusk of the evening was coming on and there was no prospect of a cessation of the conflict. The Union troops were pressing strongly against the Confederates. There was a terrible onslaught, which neither powder nor lead could resist. A courier, dashing across the field, announced to Beauregard the rout of his army. Soon the panic-stricken Confederate soldiers were swarming in retreat. The day seemed to be irreparably lost. Then, suddenly in the dim twilight, a dark column was seen emerging from the wooded ravines to the rear, and General Gracie, with his brigade of twelve hundred gallant Alabamians, plunged through the smoke, leapt into the works, and drove out the Federals. Now the battle broke out afresh, and with unabated fury continued until after midnight.

Early on the morning of the 18th, a general assault was ordered upon the whole Confederate front. The skirmishers moved forward but found the works, where, on the preceding day, such desperate fighting had occurred, deserted. During the night, Beauregard had successfully made a retrograde movement. He had found the old line too long for the number of his men and had selected a shorter one, from five hundred to one thousand yards to the rear, that was to remain the Confederate wall of the city during the siege. But there were no entrenchments here and the weary battle-worn soldiers at once set to work to dig them, for the probable renewal of the contest. In the darkness and through the early morning hours, the men did with whatever they could find as tools—some with their bayonets, or split canteens, while others used their hands. This was the beginning of those massive works that defied the army of Grant before Petersburg for nearly a year. By noon

WHAT EIGHT THOUSAND POUNDS OF POWDER DID

The Crater, torn by the mine within Elliott's Salient. At dawn of July 30, 1864, the fifty thousand Federal troops waiting to make a charge saw a great mass of earth hurled skyward like a water-spout. As it spread out into an immense cloud, scattering guns, carriages, timbers, and what were once human beings, the front ranks broke in panic; it looked as if the mass were descending upon their own heads. The men were quickly rallied; across the narrow plain they charged, through the awful breach, and up the heights beyond to gain Cemetery Ridge. But there were brave fighters on the other side still left, and delay among the Federals enabled the Confederates to rally and re-form in time to drive the Federals back down the steep sides of the Crater. There, as they struggled amidst the horrible débris, one disaster after another fell upon them. Huddled together, the mass of men was cut to pieces by the canister poured upon them from well-planted Confederate batteries. At last, as a forlorn hope, the colored troops were sent forward; and they, too, were hurled back into the Crater and piled upon their white comrades.

of that day they had assumed quite a defensive character. Again the Federals attempted to break the Confederate line. All during the afternoon, regiments were hurled against the newly made works. Artillery bombarded here and there with but little effect. At times the attacking force would come within thirty yards of the entrenchments, only to recoil. Night came, and in front of the trenches the ranks of the Union dead lay thickly strewn.

During these four days, divisions and batteries were being added to both armies, and when the Union assault was successfully repulsed in the twilight hours of June 18, 1864, those two grim adversaries, Grant and Lee, stood in full battle array—this time for the final combat. The siege of Petersburg began the next day.

It was a beautiful June Sabbath. There was only the occasional boom of some great gun as it thundered along the Appomattox, or the fretful fire of picket musketry, to break the stillness. But it was not a day of rest. With might and main the two armies busily plied with pick and spade and axe.

In an incredibly short time, as if by magic, impregnable bastioned works began to loom about Petersburg. More than thirty miles of frowning redoubts, connected with extended breastworks, strengthened by mortar batteries and field-works of every description, lined the fields near the Appomattox. In front were abatis—bushy entanglements and timber slashings. Bomb-proofs and parapets completed these cordons of offense and defense—the one constructed to keep the Federals out; the other to keep the Confederates in. So formidable were the works, that only twice during the siege was there any serious attempt made by either army upon the entrenchments of the other, and both assaults were failures.

It was Grant's purpose to extend his lines to the south and west, until they would finally envelop Lee's right flank, and then strike at the railroads, upon which the Confederate army and Richmond depended for supplies. On June 21st, two corps,

COLORED TROOPS AFTER THE DISASTER OF THE MINE

On July 30, 1864, at the exploding of the hidden mine under Elliott's salient, the strong Confederate fortification opposite. The plan of the mine was conceived by Colonel Henry Pleasants and approved by Burnside, whose Ninth Corps, in the assaults of June 17th and 18th, had pushed their advance position to within 130 yards of the Confederate works. Pleasants had been a mining engineer and his regiment, the Forty-eighth Pennsylvania, was composed mainly of miners from the coal regions. The work was begun on June 25th and prosecuted under the greatest difficulties. In less than a month Pleasants had the main gallery, 510.8 feet long, the left lateral gallery, 37 feet long, and the right lateral gallery, 38 feet long, all completed. While

FORT MORTON, BEFORE PETERSBURG

finishing the last gallery, the right one, the men could hear the Confederates working in the fortification above them, trying to locate the mine, of which they had got wind. It was General Burnside's plan that General Edward Ferrero's division of colored troops should head the charge when the mine should be sprung. The black men were kept constantly on drill and it was thought, as they had not seen any very active service, that they were in better condition to lead the attack than any of the white troops. In the upper picture are some of the colored troops drilling and idling in camp after the battle of the Crater, in which about three hundred of their comrades were lost. The lower picture shows the entrenchments at Fort Morton, whence they sallied forth.

the Second and Sixth, moved out of their entrenchments to capture the Weldon Railroad, and to extend the line of investment. The region to be traversed was one characteristic of the tidewater belt—dense forests and swampy lowlands, cut by many small creeks. The morning of June 22d found the two army corps in the midst of tangled wilderness. There was some delay in bringing these divisions together—thus leaving a wide gap. While the troops were waiting here, two divisions of A. P. Hill's corps were advancing against them. Hill led Mahone's division through a ravine close by. Screened by the intervening ridge, the Confederates quickly formed in line of battle, dashed through the pine forest, with a fierce, wild yell, and swiftly and suddenly burst through the gap between the two Federal corps, attacking the flank and rear of Barlow's division. A withering volley of musketry, before which the Northerners could not stand, plowed through their ranks. The Federal line was doubled upon itself. The terrific onslaught was continued by the Confederates and resulted in forging to the entrenchments and capturing seventeen hundred prisoners, four guns, and several colors. At dusk Hill returned to his entrenchments. The Second and Sixth corps were joined in a new position.

At the same time the cavalry, under General James H. Wilson, including Kautz's division, started out to destroy the railroads. The Confederate cavalry leader, General W. H. F. Lee, followed closely, and there were several sharp engagements. The Union cavalry leader succeeded, however, in destroying a considerable length of track on both the Weldon and South Side railroads between June 22d and 27th. Then he turned for the works at Petersburg, but found it a difficult task. The woods were alive with Confederates. Infantry swarmed on every hand. Cavalry hung on the Federals' flanks and rear at every step. Artillery and wagon trains were being captured constantly. During the entire night of June 28th, the Union troopers were constantly

AN OASIS IN THE DESERT OF WAR

Throughout all the severe fighting south of Petersburg the Aiken house and its inhabitants remained un-
harmed, their safety respected by the combatants on both sides. The little farmhouse near the Weldon
Railroad between the lines of the two hostile armies was remembered for years by many veterans on both
sides. When Grant, after the battle of the Crater, began to force his lines closer to the west of Petersburg
the Weldon Railroad became an objective and General Warren's command pushed forward on August 18,
1864, and after a sharp fight with the Confederates, established themselves in an advance position near
Ream's Station. Three gallant assaults by the Confederates on the three succeeding days failed to dislodge the Federals. In these engagements the tide of battle ebbed and flowed through the woods and
through thickets of vine and underbrush more impenetrable even than the "Wilderness."

harassed on every hand. They fell back in every direction. The two divisions became separated and, driven at full speed in front of the Confederate squadrons, became irreparably broken, and when they finally reached the Union lines—the last of them on July 2d—it was in straggling parties in wretched plight.

On June 25th, Sheridan returned from his raid on the Virginia Central Railroad. He had encountered Hampton and Fitzhugh Lee at Trevilian Station on June 11th, and turned back after doing great damage to the Railroad. His supply of ammunition did not warrant another engagement.

Now ensued about five weeks of quiet during which time both generals were strengthening their fortifications. However, the Federals were covertly engaged in an undertaking that was destined to result in a conspicuous failure. While the Northern soldiers were enduring the rays of a blistering July sun behind the entrenchments, one regiment was delving underneath in the cool, moist earth. It was the Forty-eighth Pennsylvania regiment of the Ninth Corps, made up mostly of miners from the upper Schuylkill coal-district of Pennsylvania. From June 25th until July 23d, these men were boring a tunnel from the rear of the Union works to a point underneath the Confederate fortifications. Working under the greatest difficulties, with inadequate tools for digging, and hand-barrows made out of cracker boxes, in which to carry away the earth, there was excavated in this time a passage-way five hundred and ten feet in length, terminating in left and right lateral galleries, thirty-seven and thirty-eight feet respectively. Into these lateral galleries eight thousand pounds of gunpowder were packed and tamped, and a fuse attached. On July 28th, everything was ready for the match to be applied and for the gigantic upheaval, sure to follow.

Grant, in order to get a part of Lee's army away, had sent Hancock's corps and two divisions of cavalry north of the James, as if he might attack Richmond. The ruse was successful. Preparations were then completed to fire the mine,

THE SAFE END OF THE MOVING BATTERY

The Federals were not the first to use a gun mounted on railway trucks. In the defense of Richmond during the Seven Days' and at the attack on Savage's Station the Confederates had mounted a field-piece on a flat-car and it did severe damage to the Federal camps. But they possessed no such formidable armored truck as this. Propelled by man-power, no puffing locomotive betrayed its whereabouts; and as it rolled along the tracks, firing a shot from time to time, it must have puzzled the Confederate outposts. This was no clumsy experimental toy, but a land gunboat on wheels, armored with iron-plating, backed by massive beams.

At the Globe Tavern General Warren made his headquarters after the successful advance of

THE GLOBE TAVERN, WELDON RAILROAD

August 18th, and from here he directed the maneuvers by which the Federal lines to the westward of Petersburg were drawn closer and closer to cut off the last of Confederate communications. The country hereabout was the theater of constant activities on both sides during the autumn, and skirmishing between the hostile forces was kept up far into November. The old tavern was the very center of war's alarms. Yet the junior officers of the staff were not wholly deprived of amenities, since the Aiken house near by domiciled no less than seven young ladies, a fact that guaranteed full protection to the family during the siege. A strong safeguard was encamped within the garden railing to protect the house from intrusion by stragglers.

tear a gap in the Confederate works, and rush the Union troops into the opening. A division of colored soldiers, under General Ferrero, was selected and thoroughly drilled to lead the charge. Everything was in readiness for a successful attack, but at the last moment the colored division was replaced by the First Division of the Ninth Corps, under General Ledlie. The explosion was to take place at half-past three on the morning of July 30th. The appointed time had come. Everything required was in its place, ready to perform its part. Less than four hundred feet in front were the Confederate works, and directly beneath them were four tons of powder waiting to perform their deadly work.

Then the Federals applied the match. The fuse sputtered as the consuming flame ate its way to the magazines within the tunnel. The men waited in breathless suspense. In another moment the earth would be rent by the subterranean upheaval. Minute after minute passed. The delay was unbearable. Something must have gone wrong. A gallant sergeant of the Forty-eighth Pennsylvania, Henry Rees by name, volunteered to enter the gallery and find out why the fuse had failed. It had parted within fifty feet of the powder. Rees returned for materials to resplice the fuse, and on the way out met Lieutenant Jacob Douty. The two men made the necessary repairs; the fire was again applied, and then—at twenty minutes to five —the ground underneath trembled as if by an earthquake, a solid mass of earth shot two hundred feet into the air, and a flame of fire burst from the vent as from a new-born volcano. Smoke rose after the ascending column. There in mid-air, earth, cannon, timbers, sand-bags, human beings, smoke, and fire, hung suspended an instant, and bursting asunder, fell back into and around the smoking crater where three hundred Confederates had met their end.

When the cloud of smoke had cleared away, the waiting troops of Ledlie charged, Colonel Marshall at the head of the Second Brigade, leading the way. They came to an immense

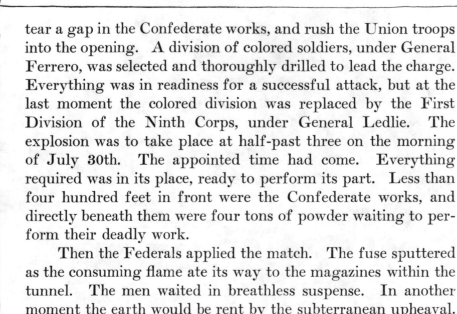

FEDERAL FIGHTERS AT REAMS' STATION

These men of Barlow's First division of the Second Corps, under command of Brigadier-General Nelson A. Miles, gallantly repulsed the second and third attacks by the Confederates upon Reams' Station, where Hancock's men were engaged in destroying the Weldon Railroad on August 24, 1864. In the upper picture is seen Company D of the famous "Clinton Guard," as the Sixty-first New York Infantry called itself. The picture was taken at Falmouth in April, 1863, and the trim appearance of the troops on dress parade indicates nothing of the heavy losses they sustained when at Fredericksburg, led by Colonel Miles, they fought with distinguished bravery against Jackson's men. Not only the regiment but its officers attained renown, for the regiment had the honor to be commanded by able soldiers. First, Francis C. Barlow was its colonel, then Nelson A. Miles, then Oscar A. Broady, and lastly George W. Scott.

opening, one hundred and seventy feet long, sixty feet wide, and thirty feet deep. They climbed the rim, looked down into the pit at the indescribable horrors, and then plunged into the crater. Here, they huddled in inextricable confusion. The two brigades poured in until the yawning pit was crowded with the disorganized mass. All semblance of organization vanished. In the confusion, officers lost power to recognize, much less to control, their own troops. A regiment climbed the slope, but finding that no one was following, went back to the crater.

The stunned and paralyzed Confederates were not long in grasping the situation. Batteries were soon planted where they could sweep the approach to the crater. This cut off the possibility of retreat. Then into the pit itself poured a stream of wasting fire, until it had become a veritable slaughter-house. Into this death-trap, the sun was sending down its shafts until it became as a furnace. Attempts were made to pass around the crater and occupy Cemetery Hill, which had been the objective of the Federals. But the withering fire prevented. The colored troops, who had been originally trained to lead in the charge, now tried to save the day. They passed by the side of the crater and started for the crest of the hill. They had not gone far when the Confederates delivered a countercharge that broke their ranks.

The Confederates were being rapidly reenforced. At eight o'clock Mahone's division of Georgians and Virginians swept onto the field, to the scene of the conflict. They had been hidden from view until they were almost ready for the charge. The Federals, seeing the intended attack, made ready to resist it. Lieutenant-Colonel Bross of the Twenty-ninth Colored regiment sprang upon the edge of the crater with the Union flag in his hand and was quickly struck down. The men began to scramble out after him, but before a line could be formed the Confederates were on them, and the Federals were driven back into the pit, already overflowing with the living and the dead. Huge missiles from Confederate mortars

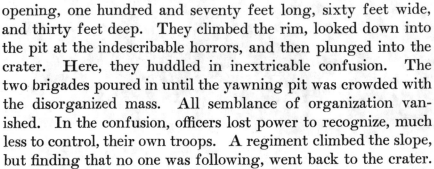

FORT MAHONE—"FORT DAMNATION"

RIVES' SALIENT

TRAVERSES AGAINST CROSS–FIRE

GRACIE'S SALIENT, AND OTHER FORTS ALONG THE TEN MILES OF DEFENSES

Dotted with formidable fortifications such as these, Confederate works stretched for ten miles around Petersburg. Fort Mahone was situated opposite the Federal Fort Sedgwick at the point where the hostile lines converged most closely after the battle of the Crater. Owing to the constant cannonade which it kept up, the Federals named it Fort Damnation, while Fort Sedgwick, which was no less active in reply, was known to the Confederates as Fort Hell. Gracie's salient, further north on the Confederate line, is notable as the point in front of which General John B. Gordon's gallant troops moved to the attack on Fort Stedman, the last desperate effort of the Confederates to break through the Federal cordon. The views of Gracie's salient show the French form of *chevaux-de-frise*, a favorite protection against attack much employed by the Confederates.

rained into the awful chasm. The muskets left by the retreating Federals were thrown like pitchforks among the huddled troops. The shouts, the explosions, the screams, and groans added to the horror of the carnage. The clay in the pit was drenched with the blood of the dead and dying. The Southerners pushed in from both sides of the crater, forming a cordon of bayonets about it. The third and final charge was made, about two in the afternoon, and the bloody fight at the crater was ended as the brigade commanders followed Burnside's order to withdraw to the Federal lines. Both of Ledlie's brigade commanders were captured in the crater. The total Federal loss in this disastrous affair was over thirty-nine hundred, of whom all but one hundred were in the Ninth Corps. The Confederates lost about one thousand.

Now came a season of comparative quiet about Petersburg, except for the strategic maneuverings of the Federals who were trying to find weak places in the Confederate walls. On August 18th, however, Grant sent General Warren to capture the Weldon Railroad. Desperate fighting was to be expected, for this was one of the important routes along which supplies came to the Confederate capital. The Federal forces moved out quietly from their camp, but the alert Beauregard was ready for them. By the time Warren had reached the railroad, near the Globe Tavern, four miles from Petersburg, he was met by a force under Heth which at once drove him back. Rallying his troops, Warren entrenched on the railroad.

The fight was renewed on the next day, when, strongly reenforced by Lee, the Confederates burst suddenly upon the Federals. Mahone thrust his gallant division through the Federal skirmish line and then turned and fought from the rear, while another division struck the right wing. The Union force was soon in confusion; more than two thousand were taken prisoners, including General Joseph Hayes, and but for the arrival of the Ninth Corps, the field would have been lost. Two days later, Lee again attacked the position by massing

THE DEFENDERS' COUNTER-MINE

The sinister burrow opens within the Confederate Fort Mahone, seen more fully at the top of the preceding page. Fort Sedgwick, directly opposite Fort Mahone, had been originally captured from the Confederates and its defenses greatly strengthened. So galling did its fire become, and so important was its position to the Confederates, that early in the siege they planned to lay a mine in order to regain it and perhaps break through the Federal lines and raise the siege. The distance across the intervening plain was but fifteen hundred feet. The Confederates ran their main gallery somewhat more than a third of this distance before finally abandoning it, the difficulties of the undertaking having proved too great. This fort was named after General William Mahone, who was conspicuously engaged in the defense of Petersburg, and whose gallant conduct at the explosion of the Federal mine under Elliott's salient saved the day to the Confederates. Weak as were the defenses of Petersburg in comparison with the strong investing works of the Federals, they withstood all assaults during nine months except when Elliott's salient was captured during the battle of the Crater.

WHERE GORDON'S MEN ATTACKED, FORT STEDMAN

At Fort Stedman was directed the gallant onslaught of Gordon's men that resulted so disastrously for the Confederates on the 25th of March. For no troops could stand the heavy artillery and musketry fire directed on them from both flanks and from the rear at daylight. What was left of this brave division, shattered and broken, drifted back to their own line. It was the forlorn hope of Lee's beleaguered army. Fort McGilvery was less than one-half a mile from the Appomattox River, just north of the City

THE POWDER MAGAZINE AT FORT McGILVERY

Point Railroad, at the extreme right of the Federal line. It was one of the earliest forts completed, being built in July, 1864. Fort Morton, named after Major St. Clair Morton, killed by a sharpshooter's bullet in July, 1864, was renowned as the place from which the mine was dug and from which the disastrous attempt to break through the Confederate lines was made on July 30th. Fort Morton lay almost in the center of the most active portion of the lines, and was about a mile south of Fort Stedman.

FORT MORTON, OPPOSITE THE CRATER

A POSITION OF COMPLETE DEFENSE, FORT MEIKLE

Almost every one of the forts in the long Federal line was named after some gallant officer who had lost his life in action. They might have been termed the memorial forts. The almost circular entrenchment, strengthened by logs and sandbags and defended by the formidable abatis of tree trunks, was named after Lieutenant-Colonel George W. Meikle, of the Twentieth Indiana Volunteers. From the position shown we are looking directly into Petersburg. Military observers have conceded that the fortifications surrounding

THE SWEEPING LINES OF FORT SEDGWICK

Petersburg were the most remarkable of any in the world. Before the end of October, 1864, the Army of the Potomac occupied a formidable cordon of defenses that stretched for more than thirty-two miles, and comprised thirty-six forts and fifty batteries. For years succeeding the war excursions were run from New York and from all parts of the country to this historic ground. It took three days to complete the tour. Then most of the forts were in the condition in which we see them pictured here.

FORT RICE, AS THE CONFEDERATES SAW IT

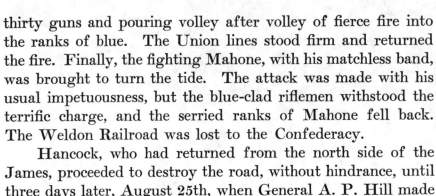

thirty guns and pouring volley after volley of fierce fire into the ranks of blue. The Union lines stood firm and returned the fire. Finally, the fighting Mahone, with his matchless band, was brought to turn the tide. The attack was made with his usual impetuousness, but the blue-clad riflemen withstood the terrific charge, and the serried ranks of Mahone fell back. The Weldon Railroad was lost to the Confederacy.

Hancock, who had returned from the north side of the James, proceeded to destroy the road, without hindrance, until three days later, August 25th, when General A. P. Hill made his appearance and Hancock retreated to some hastily built breastworks at Ream's Station. The Confederate attack was swift and terrific. The batteries broke the Union lines. The men were panic-stricken and were put to flight. Hancock tried in vain to rally his troops, but for once this splendid soldier, who had often seen his men fall but not fail, was filled with agony at the rout of his soldiers. Their rifle-pits had been lost, their guns captured and turned upon them. Finally, General Nelson A. Miles succeeded in rallying a few men, formed a new line and, with the help of some dismounted cavalry, partly regained their former position. The night came on and, under cover of darkness, Hancock withdrew his shattered columns.

The two great opposing armies had now come to a deadlock. For weeks they lay in their entrenchments, each waiting for the other to move. Each knew that it was an almost hopeless task to assail the other's position. At the end of September, General Ord, with the Eighteenth Corps, and General Birney, with the Tenth, captured Fort Harrison north of the James, securing a vantage-point for threatening Richmond. The Union line had been extended to within three miles of the South Side Railroad, and on October 27th, practically the whole Army of the Potomac was put in motion to secure this other avenue of transportation to Richmond. After severe fighting for one day the attempt was given up, and the Union troops returned to the entrenchments in front of Petersburg.

SHERMAN'S FINAL CAMPAIGNS

WAITING FOR THE MARCH TO THE SEA

After the capture of Atlanta, says Sherman, "all the army, officers and men, seemed to relax more or less and sink into a condition of idleness." All but the engineers! For it was their task to construct the new lines of fortifications surveyed by General Poe so that the city could be held by a small force while troops were detached in pursuit of Hood. The railroad lines and bridges along the route by which the army had come had to be repaired so that the sick and wounded and prisoners could be sent back to Chattanooga and the army left free of encumbrances before undertaking the march to the sea. In the picture, their work practically done, the men of the First Michigan Engineers are idling about the old salient of the Confederate lines southeast of Atlanta near which their camp

CAMP OF THE FIRST MICHIGAN ENGINEERS AT ATLANTA, AUTUMN, 1864

was pitched. The organization was the best known and one of the most efficient of the Michigan regiments. It was composed almost entirely of mechanics and trained engineers and mustered eighteen hundred strong. The work of these men dotted the whole theater of war in the West. The bridges and trestles of their making, if combined, would have to be measured by the mile, and many of them were among the most wonderful feats of military engineering. The First Michigan Engineers could fight, too, for a detachment of them under Colonel Innes at Stone's River successfully defended the army trains from an attack by Wheeler's cavalry. The march to the sea could not have been made without these men.

THE LAST TRAIN WAITING

This series of three photographs, taken a few minutes apart, tells the story of Sherman's order evicting the inhabitants of Atlanta, September, 1864. A train of cars stands empty beside the railroad station. But in the second picture piles of household effects appear on some of the cars. This disordered embarkation takes little time; the wagon train advancing in the first picture has not yet passed the camera. By the time the shutter clicked for the bottom photograph, every car was heaped with household effects—bedding and pitiful packages of a dozen kinds. Unfortunate owners dangle their feet from the cars; others, white-bonnetted women in the group, cluster around their chairs and other belongings not yet shipped. The last train of refugees was ready to leave Atlanta. Sherman outlined very clearly his reasons for ordering the evacuation of the city by its inhabitants. He wrote on September 17, 1864: "I take the ground that Atlanta is a conquered place, and I propose to use it purely for our own military purposes, which are inconsistent with its habitation by the families of a brave people. I am shipping them *all*, and by next Wednesday the town will be a real military town, with no women boring me every order I give."

CHATTELS APPEAR ON TOP OF THE CARS

THE CARS PILED HIGH WITH HOUSEHOLD GOODS—THE LAST TRAIN OF INHABITANTS READY
TO LEAVE ATLANTA

THE END OF THE RAILROAD DEPOT

The crumpled wreck is hardly recognizable as the same spacious train-shed that sheltered such human activities as those pictured opposite, yet this is the Atlanta depot. But such destruction was far from the wanton outrage that it naturally seemed to those whose careers it rudely upset. As early as September, Sherman, with Atlanta on his hands, had deemed it essential for the prosecutions of his movements and the end of the war that the city should be turned into a military post. So he determined "to remove the entire civil population, and to deny to all civilians from the rear the expected profits of civil trade. This was to avoid the necessity of a heavy garrison to hold the position, and prevent the crippling of the armies in the fields as heretofore by 'detachments' to guard and protect the interests of a hostile population." The railroad station, as the heart of the modern artery of business, was second in importance only to the buildings and institutions of the Confederate government itself, as a subject for elimination.

SHERMAN'S FINAL CAMPAIGNS

I only regarded the march from Atlanta to Savannah as a "shift of base," as the transfer of a strong army, which had no opponent, and had finished its then work, from the interior to a point on the sea coast, from which it could achieve other important results. I considered this march as a means to an end, and not as an essential act of war. Still, then as now, the march to the sea was generally regarded as something extraordinary, something anomalous, something out of the usual order of events; whereas, in fact, I simply moved from Atlanta to Savannah, as one step in the direction of Richmond, a movement that had to be met and defeated, or the war was necessarily at an end.—General W. T. Sherman, in his "Memoirs."

THE march to the sea, in which General William T. Sherman won undying fame in the Civil War, is one of the greatest pageants in the world's warfare—as fearful in its destruction as it is historic in its import. But this was not Sherman's chief achievement; it was an easy task compared with the great campaign between Chattanooga and Atlanta through which he had just passed. "As a military accomplishment it was little more than a grand picnic," declared one of his division commanders, in speaking of the march through Georgia and the Carolinas.

Almost immediately after the capture of Atlanta, Sherman, deciding to remain there for some time and to make it a Federal military center, ordered all the inhabitants to be removed. General Hood pronounced the act one of ingenious cruelty, transcending any that had ever before come to his notice in the dark history of the war. Sherman insisted that his act was one of kindness, and that Johnston and Hood themselves had done the same—removed families from their homes—in other places. The decision was fully carried out.

THE ATLANTA BANK BEFORE THE MARCH TO THE SEA

As this photograph was taken, the wagons stood in the street of Atlanta ready to accompany the Federals in their impending march to the sea. The most interesting thing is the bank building on the corner, completely destroyed, although around it stand the stores of merchants entirely untouched. Evidently there had been here faithful execution of Sherman's orders to his engineers—to destroy all buildings and property of a public nature, such as factories, foundries, railroad stations, and the like; but to protect as far as possible strictly private dwellings and enterprises. Those of a later generation who witnessed the growth of Atlanta within less than half a century after this photograph was taken, and saw tall office-buildings and streets humming with industry around the location in this photograph, will find in it an added fascination.

Many of the people of Atlanta chose to go southward, others to the north, the latter being transported free, by Sherman's order, as far as Chattanooga.

Shortly after the middle of September, Hood moved his army from Lovejoy's Station, just south of Atlanta, to the vicinity of Macon. Here Jefferson Davis visited the encampment, and on the 22d he made a speech to the homesick Army of Tennessee, which, reported in the Southern newspapers, disclosed to Sherman the new plans of the Confederate leaders. These involved nothing less than a fresh invasion of Tennessee, which, in the opinion of President Davis, would put Sherman in a predicament worse than that in which Napoleon found himself at Moscow. But, forewarned, the Federal leader prepared to thwart his antagonists. The line of the Western and Atlantic Railroad was more closely guarded. Divisions were sent to Rome and to Chattanooga. Thomas was ordered to Nashville, and Schofield to Knoxville. Recruits were hastened from the North to these points, in order that Sherman himself might not be weakened by the return of too many troops to these places.

Hood, in the hope of leading Sherman away from Atlanta, crossed the Chattahoochee on the 1st of October, destroyed the railroad above Marietta and sent General French against Allatoona. It was the brave defense of this place by General John M. Corse that brought forth Sherman's famous message, "Hold out; relief is coming," sent by his signal officers from the heights of Kenesaw Mountain, and which thrilled the North and inspired its poets to eulogize Corse's bravery in verse. Corse had been ordered from Rome to Allatoona by signals from mountain to mountain, over the heads of the Confederate troops, who occupied the valley between. Reaching the mountain pass soon after midnight, on October 5th, Corse added his thousand men to the nine hundred already there, and soon after daylight the battle began. General French, in command of the Confederates, first

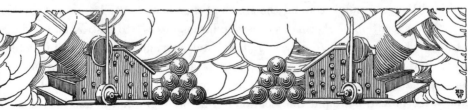

"TUNING UP"—A DAILY DRILL IN THE CAPTURED FORT

Here Sherman's men are seen at daily drill in Atlanta. This photograph has an interest beyond most war pictures, for it gives a clear idea of the soldierly bearing of the men that were to march to the sea. There was an easy carelessness in their appearance copied from their great commander, but they were never allowed to become slouchy. Sherman was the antithesis of a martinet, but he had, in the Atlanta campaign, molded his army into the "mobile machine" that he desired it to be, and he was anxious to keep the men up to this high pitch of efficiency for the performance of still greater deeds. No better disciplined army existed in the world at the time Sherman's "bummers" set out for the sea.

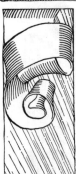

summoned Corse to surrender, and, receiving a defiant answer, opened with his guns. Nearly all the day the fire was terrific from besieged and besiegers, and the losses on both sides were very heavy.

During the battle Sherman was on Kenesaw Mountain, eighteen miles away, from which he could see the cloud of smoke and hear the faint reverberation of the cannons' boom. When he learned by signal that Corse was there and in command, he said, "If Corse is there, he will hold out; I know the man." And he did hold out, and saved the stores at Allatoona, at a loss of seven hundred of his men, he himself being among the wounded, while French lost about eight hundred.

General Hood continued to move northward to Resaca and Dalton, passing over the same ground on which the two great armies had fought during the spring and summer. He destroyed the railroads, burned the ties, and twisted the rails, leaving greater havoc, if possible, in a country that was already a wilderness of desolation. For some weeks Sherman followed Hood in the hope that a general engagement would result. But Hood had no intention to fight. He went on to the banks of the Tennessee opposite Florence, Alabama. His army was lightly equipped, and Sherman, with his heavily burdened troops, was unable to catch him. Sherman halted at Gaylesville and ordered Schofield, with the Twenty-third Corps, and Stanley, with the Fourth Corps, to Thomas at Nashville.

Sherman thereupon determined to return to Atlanta, leaving General Thomas to meet Hood's appearance in Tennessee. It was about this time that Sherman fully decided to march to the sea. Some time before this he had telegraphed to Grant: "Hood . . . can constantly break my roads. I would infinitely prefer to make a wreck of the road . . . send back all my wounded and worthless, and, with my effective army, move through Georgia, smashing things to the sea." Grant thought it best for Sherman to destroy Hood's army

CUTTING LOOSE FROM THE BASE, NOVEMBER 12TH

"On the 12th of November the railroad and telegraph communications with the rear were broken and the army stood detached from all friends, dependent on its own resources and supplies," writes Sherman. Meanwhile all detachments were marching rapidly to Atlanta with orders to break up the railroad en route and "generally to so damage the country as to make it untenable to the enemy." This was a necessary war measure. Sherman, in a home letter written from Grand Gulf, Mississippi, May 6, 1863, stated clearly his views regarding the destruction of property. Speaking of the wanton havoc wrought on a fine plantation in the path of the army, he added: "It is done, of course, by the accursed stragglers who won't fight but hang behind and disgrace our cause and country. Dr. Bowie had fled, leaving everything on the approach of our troops. Of course, devastation marked the whole path of the army, and I know all the principal officers detest the infamous practice as much as I do. Of course, I expect and do take corn, bacon, ham, mules, and everything to support an army, and don't object much to the using of fences for firewood, but this universal burning and wanton destruction of private property is not justified in war."

first, but Sherman insisted that his plan would put him on the offensive rather than the defensive. He also believed that Hood would be forced to follow him. Grant was finally won to the view that if Hood moved on Tennessee, Thomas would be able to check him. He had, on the 11th of October, given permission for the march. Now, on the 2d of November, he telegraphed Sherman at Rome: "I do not really see that you can withdraw from where you are to follow Hood without giving up all we have gained in territory. I say, then, go on as you propose." It was Sherman, and not Grant or Lincoln, that conceived the great march, and while the march itself was not seriously opposed or difficult to carry out, the conception and purpose were masterly.

Sherman moved his army by slow and easy stages back to Atlanta. He sent the vast army stores that had collected at Atlanta, which he could not take with him, as well as his sick and wounded, to Chattanooga, destroyed the railroad to that place, also the machine-shops at Rome and other places, and on November 12th, after receiving a final despatch from Thomas and answering simply, "Despatch received—all right," the last telegraph line was severed, and Sherman had deliberately cut himself off from all communication with the Northern States. There is no incident like it in the annals of war. A strange event it was, as Sherman observes in his memoirs. "Two hostile armies marching in opposite directions, each in the full belief that it was achieving a final and conclusive result in a great war."

For the next two days all was astir in Atlanta. The great depot, round-house, and machine-shops were destroyed. Walls were battered down; chimneys pulled over; machinery smashed to pieces, and boilers punched full of holes. Heaps of rubbish covered the spots where these fine buildings had stood, and on the night of November 15th the vast débris was set on fire. The torch was also applied to many places in the business part of the city, in defiance of the strict orders of

THE BUSTLE OF DEPARTURE FROM ATLANTA

Sherman's men worked like beavers during their last few days in Atlanta. There was no time to be lost; the army was gotten under way with that precision which marked all Sherman's movements. In the upper picture, finishing touches are being put to the railroad, and in the lower is seen the short work that was made of such public buildings as might be of the slightest use in case the Confederates should recapture the town. As far back as Chattanooga, while plans for the Atlanta campaign were being formed, Sherman had been revolving a subsequent march to the sea in case he was successful. He had not then made up his mind whether it should be in the direction of Mobile or Savannah, but his Meridian campaign, in Mississippi, had convinced him that the march was entirely feasible, and gradually he worked out in his mind its masterly details. At seven in the morning on November 16th, Sherman rode out along the Decatur road, passed his marching troops, and near the spot where his beloved McPherson had fallen, paused for a last look at the city. "Behind us," he says, "lay Atlanta, smouldering and in

RUINS IN ATLANTA

ruins, the black smoke rising high in air and hanging like a pall over the ruined city." All about could be seen the glistening gun-barrels and white-topped wagons, "and the men marching steadily and rapidly with a cheery look and swinging pace." Some regimental band struck up "John Brown," and the thousands of voices of the vast army joined with a mighty chorus in song. A feeling of exhilaration pervaded the troops. This marching into the unknown held for them the allurement of adventure, as none but Sherman knew their destination. But as he worked his way past them on the road, many a group called out, "Uncle Billy, I guess Grant is waiting for us at Richmond." The devil-may-care spirit of the troops brought to Sherman's mind grave thoughts of his own responsibility. He knew that success would be regarded as a matter of course, but should he fail the march would be set down as "the wild adventure of a crazy fool." He had no intention of marching directly to Richmond, but from the first his objective was the seacoast, at Savannah or Port Royal, or even Pensacola, Florida.

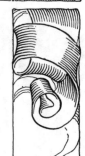

Captain Poe, who had the work of destruction in charge. The court-house and a large part of the dwellings escaped the flames.

Preparations for the great march were made with extreme care. Defective wagons and horses were discarded; the number of heavy guns to be carried along was sixty-five, the remainder having been sent to Chattanooga. The marching army numbered about sixty thousand, five thousand of whom belonged to the cavalry and eighteen hundred to the artillery. The army was divided into two immense wings, the Right, the Army of the Tennessee, commanded by General O. O. Howard, and consisting of the Fifteenth and Seventeenth corps, and the Left, the Army of Georgia, by General Henry W. Slocum, composed the Fourteenth and Twentieth corps. Sherman himself was in supreme command. There were twenty-five hundred wagons, each drawn by six mules; six hundred ambulances, with two horses each, while the heavy guns, caissons, and forges were each drawn by eight horses. A twenty days' supply of bread, forty of coffee, sugar, and salt was carried with the army, and a large herd of cattle was driven on foot.

In Sherman's general instructions it was provided that the army should march by four roads as nearly parallel as possible, except the cavalry, which remained under the direct control of the general commanding. The army was directed "to forage liberally on the country," but, except along the roadside, this was to be done by organized foraging parties appointed by the brigade commanders. Orders were issued forbidding soldiers to enter private dwellings or to commit any trespass. The corps commanders were given the option of destroying mills, cotton-gins, and the like, and where the army was molested in its march by the burning of bridges, obstructing the roads, and so forth, the devastation should be made "more or less relentless, according to the measure of such hostility." The cavalry and artillery and the foraging

THE GUNS THAT SHERMAN TOOK ALONG

In Hood's hasty evacuation of Atlanta many of his guns were left behind. These 12-pounder Napoleon bronze field-pieces have been gathered by the Federals from the abandoned fortifications, which had been equipped entirely with field artillery, such as these. It was an extremely useful capture for Sherman's army, whose supply of artillery had been somewhat limited during the siege, and still further reduced by the necessity to fortify Atlanta. On the march to the sea Sherman took with him only sixty-five field-pieces. The Negro refugees in the lower picture recall an embarrassment of the march to the sea. "Negroes of all sizes" flocked in the army's path and stayed there, a picturesque procession, holding tightly to the skirts of the army which they believed had come for the sole purpose of setting them free. The cavalcade of Negroes soon became so numerous that Sherman became anxious for his army's sustenance, and finding an old gray-haired black at Covington, Sherman explained to him carefully that if the Negroes continued to swarm after the army it would fail in its purpose and they would not get their freedom. Sherman believed that the old man spread this news to the slaves along the line of march, and in part saved the army from being overwhelmed by the contrabands.

NEGROES FLOCKING IN THE ARMY'S PATH

parties were permitted to take horses, mules, and wagons from the inhabitants without limit, except that they were to discriminate in favor of the poor. It was a remarkable military undertaking, in which it was intended to remove restrictions only to a sufficient extent to meet the requirements of the march. The cavalry was commanded by General Judson Kilpatrick, who, after receiving a severe wound at Resaca, in May, had gone to his home on the banks of the Hudson, in New York, to recuperate, and, against the advice of his physician, had joined the army again at Atlanta.

On November 15th, most of the great army was started on its march, Sherman himself riding out from the city next morning. As he rode near the spot where General McPherson had fallen, he paused and looked back at the receding city with its smoking ruins, its blackened walls, and its lonely, tenantless houses. The vision of the desperate battles, of the hope and fear of the past few months, rose before him, as he tells us, " like the memory of a dream." The day was as perfect as Nature ever gives. The men were hilarious. They sang and shouted and waved their banners in the autumn breeze. Most of them supposed they were going directly toward Richmond, nearly a thousand miles away. As Sherman rode past them they would call out, " Uncle Billy, I guess Grant is waiting for us at Richmond." Only the commanders of the wings and Kilpatrick were entrusted with the secret of Sherman's intentions. But even Sherman was not fully decided as to his objective—Savannah, Georgia, or Port Royal, South Carolina—until well on the march.

There was one certainty, however—he was fully decided to keep the Confederates in suspense as to his intentions. To do this the more effectually he divided his army at the start, Howard leading his wing to Gordon by way of McDonough as if to threaten Macon, while Slocum proceeded to Covington and Madison, with Milledgeville as his goal. Both were secretly instructed to halt, seven days after starting, at Gor-

The task of General Hardee in defending Savannah was one of peculiar difficulty. He had only eighteen thousand men, and he was uncertain where Sherman would strike. Some supposed that Sherman would move at once upon Charleston, but Hardee argued that the Union army would have to establish a new base of supplies on the seacoast before attempting to cross the numerous deep rivers and swamps of South Carolina. Hardee's task therefore was to hold Savannah just as long as possible, and then to withdraw northward to unite with the troops which General Bragg was assembling, and with the detachments scattered at this time over the Carolinas. In protecting his position around Savannah, Fort McAllister was of prime importance, since it commanded the Great Ogeechee River in such a way as to prevent the approach of the Federal fleet,

THE DEFENDER OF SAVANNAH

Sherman's dependence for supplies. It was accordingly manned by a force of two hundred under command of Major G. W. Anderson, provided with fifty days' rations for use in case the work became isolated. This contingency did not arrive. About noon of December 13th, Major Anderson's men saw troops in blue moving about in the woods. The number increased. The artillery on the land side of the fort was turned upon them as they advanced from one position to another, and sharpshooters picked off some of their officers. At half-past four o'clock, however, the long-expected charge was made from three different directions, so that the defenders, too few in number to hold the whole line, were soon overpowered. Hardee now had to consider more narrowly the best time for withdrawing from the lines at Savannah.

FORT McALLISTER—THE LAST BARRIER TO THE SEA

FROM SAVANNAH'S ROOF–TOPS—1865

No detailed maps, no written description, could show better than these clear and beautiful photographs the almost impregnable position of the city. For miles the higher ground on which it was possible to build lay on the south bank of the river. From only one direction, the westward, could Savannah be approached without difficult feats of engineering, and here the city was guarded along the lines of the Georgia Central Railroad by strong entrenchments, held by General Hardee's men. Sherman perceived that a frontal attack would not only be costly but effort thrown away, and determined that after he had taken Fort McAllister he would make a combination with the naval forces and invest the city from all sides. The march to the sea would not be completed until such a combination had been effected. On the evening of the 12th Sherman held consultation with General Howard and with General Hazen

OVER THE IMPASSABLE MARSHES

of the Fifteenth Corps. The latter received orders from Sherman in person to march down the right bank of the Ogeechee and to assault and carry Fort McAllister by storm. He was well informed as to the latter's defenses and knew that its heavier batteries pointed seaward, but that it was weak if attacked from the rear. General Hardee's brave little force of 18,000 were soon to hear the disheartening news that they were outflanked, that McAllister had fallen, and that Sherman and Admiral Dahlgren, in command of the fleet in Ossabaw Sound, were in communication. This was on the 13th of December, 1864, but it was not until nine days later that Sherman was able to send his historic despatch to President Lincoln that began with: "I beg to present you, as a Christmas gift, the City of Savannah."

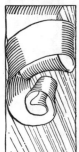

don and Milledgeville, the latter the capital of Georgia, about a hundred miles to the southeast. These two towns were about fifteen miles apart.

General Hood and General Beauregard, who had come from the East to assist him, were in Tennessee, and it was some days after Sherman had left Atlanta that they heard of his movements. They realized that to follow him would now be futile. He was nearly three hundred miles away, and not only were the railroads destroyed, but a large part of the intervening country was utterly laid waste and incapable of supporting an army. The Confederates thereupon turned their attention to Thomas, who was also in Tennessee, and was the barrier between Hood and the Northern States.

General Sherman accompanied first one corps of his army and then another. The first few days he spent with Davis' corps of Slocum's wing. When they reached Covington, the negroes met the troops in great numbers, shouting and thanking the Lord that "deliverance" had come at last. As Sherman rode along the streets they would gather around his horse and exhibit every evidence of adoration.

The foraging parties consisted of companies of fifty men. Their route for the day in which they obtained supplies was usually parallel to that of the army, five or six miles from it. They would start out before daylight in the morning, many of them on foot; but when they rejoined the column in the evening they were no longer afoot. They were astride mules, horses, in family carriages, farm wagons, and mule carts, which they packed with hams, bacon, vegetables, chickens, ducks, and every imaginable product of a Southern farm that could be useful to an army.

In the general orders, Sherman had forbidden the soldiers to enter private houses; but the order was not strictly adhered to, as many Southern people have since testified. Sherman declares in his memoirs that these acts of pillage and violence were exceptional and incidental. On one occasion Sherman

WATERFRONT AT SAVANNAH, 1865

Savannah was better protected by nature from attack by land or water than any other city near the Atlantic seaboard. Stretching to the north, east, and southward lay swamps and morasses through which ran the river-approach of twelve miles to the town. Innumerable small creeks separated the marshes into islands over which it was out of the question for an army to march without first building roads and bridging miles of waterways. The Federal fleet had for months been on the blockade off the mouth of the river, and Savannah had been closed to blockade runners since the fall of Fort Pulaski in April, 1862. But obstructions and powerful batteries held the river, and Fort McAllister, ten miles to the south, on the Ogeechee, still held the city safe in its guardianship.

FORT McALLISTER, THAT HELD THE FLEET AT BAY

saw a man with a ham on his musket, a jug of molasses under his arm, and a big piece of honey in his hand. As the man saw that he was observed by the commander, he quoted audibly to a comrade, from the general order, "forage liberally on the country." But the general reproved him and explained that foraging must be carried on only by regularly designated parties.

It is a part of military history that Sherman's sole purpose was to weaken the Confederacy by recognized means of honorable warfare; but it cannot be denied that there were a great many instances, unknown to him, undoubtedly, of cowardly hold-ups of the helpless inhabitants, or ransacking of private boxes and drawers in search of jewelry and other family treasure. This is one of the misfortunes of war—one of war's injustices. Such practices always exist even under the most rigid discipline in great armies, and the jubilation of this march was such that human nature asserted itself in the license of warfare more than on most other occasions. General Washington met with similar situations in the American Revolution. The practice is never confined to either army in warfare.

Opposed to Sherman were Wheeler's cavalry, and a large portion of the Georgia State troops which were turned over by General G. W. Smith to General Howell Cobb. Kilpatrick and his horsemen, proceeding toward Macon, were confronted by Wheeler and Cobb, but the Federal troopers drove them back into the town. However, they issued forth again, and on November 21st there was a sharp engagement with Kilpatrick at Griswoldville. The following day the Confederates were definitely checked and retreated.

The night of November 22d, Sherman spent in the home of General Cobb, who had been a member of the United States Congress and of Buchanan's Cabinet. Thousands of soldiers encamped that night on Cobb's plantation, using his fences for camp-fire fuel. By Sherman's order, everything on the

THE FIFTEEN MINUTES' FIGHT

Across these ditches at Fort McAllister, through entangling abatis, over palisading, the Federals had to fight every inch of their way against the Confederate garrison up to the very doors of their bomb-proofs, before the defenders yielded on December 13th. Sherman had at once perceived that the position could be carried only by a land assault. The fort was strongly protected by ditches, palisades, and plentiful abatis; marshes and streams covered its flanks, but Sherman's troops knew that shoes and clothing and abundant rations were waiting for them just beyond it, and had any of them been asked if they could take the fort their reply would have been in the words of the poem: "Ain't we simply got to take it?" Sherman selected for the honor of the assault General Hazen's second division of the Fifteenth Corps, the same which he himself had commanded at Shiloh and Vicksburg. Gaily the troops crossed the bridge on the morning of the 13th. Sherman was watching anxiously through his glass late in the afternoon when a Federal steamer came up the river and signaled the query: "Is Fort McAllister taken?" To which Sherman sent reply: "Not yet, but it will be in a minute." At that instant Sherman saw Hazen's troops emerge from the woods before the fort, "the lines dressed as on parade, with colors flying." Immediately dense clouds of smoke belching from the fort enveloped the Federals. There was a pause; the smoke cleared away, and, says Sherman, "the parapets were blue with our men." Fort McAllister was taken.

plantation movable or destructible was carried away next day, or destroyed. Such is the price of war.

By the next night both corps of the Left Wing were at Milledgeville, and on the 24th started for Sandersville. Howard's wing was at Gordon, and it left there on the day that Slocum moved from Milledgeville for Irwin's Cross-roads. A hundred miles below Milledgeville was a place called Millen, and here were many Federal prisoners which Sherman greatly desired to release. With this in view he sent Kilpatrick toward Augusta to give the impression that the army was marching thither, lest the Confederates should remove the prisoners from Millen. Kilpatrick had reached Waynesboro when he learned that the prisoners had been taken away. Here he again encountered the Confederate cavalry under General Wheeler. A sharp fight ensued and Kilpatrick drove Wheeler through the town toward Augusta. As there was no further need of making a feint on Augusta, Kilpatrick turned back toward the Left Wing. Wheeler quickly followed and at Thomas' Station nearly surrounded him, but Kilpatrick cut his way out. Wheeler still pressed on and Kilpatrick chose a good position at Buck Head Creek, dismounted, and threw up breastworks. Wheeler attacked desperately, but was repulsed, and Kilpatrick, after being reenforced by a brigade from Davis' corps, joined the Left Wing at Louisville.

On the whole, the great march was but little disturbed by the Confederates. The Georgia militia, probably ten thousand in all, did what they could to defend their homes and their firesides; but their endeavors were futile against the vast hosts that were sweeping through the country. In the skirmishes that took place between Atlanta and the sea the militia was soon brushed aside. Even their destroying of bridges and supplies in front of the invading army checked its progress but for a moment, as it was prepared for every such emergency. Wheeler, with his cavalry, caused more trouble. and engaged Kilpatrick's attention a large part of the time. But even he

A BIG GUN AT FORT McALLISTER

Fort McAllister is at last in complete possession of the Federals, and a group of the men who had charged over these ramparts has arranged itself before the camera as if in the very act of firing the great gun that points seaward across the marshes, toward Ossabaw Sound   There is one very peculiar thing proved by this photograph—the gun itself is almost in a fixed position as regards range and sweep of fire.   Instead of the elevating screw to raise or depress the muzzle, there has been substituted a block of wood wedged with a heavy spike, and the narrow pit in which the gun carriage is sunk admits of it being turned but a foot or so to right or left.   It evidently controlled one critical point in the river, but could not have been used in lending any aid to the repelling of General Hazen's attack.   The officer pointing with outstretched arm is indicating the very spot at which a shell fired from his gun would fall.   The men in the trench are artillerymen of General Hazen's division of the Fifteenth Corps; their appearance in their fine uniforms, polished breastplates and buttons, proves that Sherman's men could not have presented the ragged appearance that they are often pictured as doing in the war-time sketches.   That Army and Navy have come together is proved also by the figure of a marine from the fleet, who is standing at "Attention" just above the breach of the gun.   Next, leaning on his saber, is a cavalryman, in short jacket and chin-strap.

did not seriously retard the irresistible progress of the legions of the North.

The great army kept on its way by various routes, covering about fifteen miles a day, and leaving a swath of destruction, from forty to sixty miles wide, in its wake. Among the details attendant upon the march to the sea was that of scientifically destroying the railroads that traversed the region. Battalions of engineers had received special instruction in the art, together with the necessary implements to facilitate rapid work. But the infantry soon entered this service, too, and it was a common sight to see a thousand soldiers in blue standing beside a stretch of railway, and, when commanded, bend as one man and grasp the rail, and at a second command to raise in unison, which brought a thousand railroad ties up on end. Then the men fell upon them, ripping rail and tie apart, the rails to be heated to a white heat and bent in fantastic shapes about some convenient tree or other upright column, the ties being used as the fuel with which to make the fires. All public buildings that might have a military use were burned, together with a great number of private dwellings and barns, some by accident, others wantonly. This fertile and prosperous region, after the army had passed, was a scene of ruin and desolation.

As the army progressed, throngs of escaped slaves followed in its trail, "from the baby in arms to the old negro hobbling painfully along," says General Howard, "negroes of all sizes, in all sorts of patched costumes, with carts and broken-down horses and mules to match." Many of the old negroes found it impossible to keep pace with the army for many days, and having abandoned their homes and masters who could have cared for them, they were left to die of hunger and exposure in that naked land.

After the Ogeechee River was crossed, the character of the country was greatly changed from that of central Georgia. No longer were there fertile farms, laden with their Southern

THE SPOILS OF VICTORY

Here are the men that marched to the sea doing their turn as day-laborers, gleefully trundling their wheelbarrows, gathering up everything of value in Fort McAllister to swell the size of Sherman's "Christmas present." Brigadier-General W B. Hazen, after his men had successfully stormed the stubbornly defended fort, reported the capture of twenty-four pieces of ordnance, with their equipment, forty tons of ammunition, a month's supply of food for the garrison, and the small arms of the command. In the upper picture the army engineers are busily at work removing a great 48-pounder 8-inch Columbiad that had so long repelled the Federal fleet. There is always work enough and to spare for the engineers both before and after the capture of a fortified position. In the wheelbarrows is a harvest of shells and torpedoes. These deadly instruments of destruction had been relied upon by the Confederates to protect the land approach to Fort McAllister, which was

much less strongly defensible on that side than at the waterfront. While Sherman's army was approaching Savannah one of his officers had his leg blown off by a torpedo buried in the road and stepped on by his horse. After that Sherman set a line of Confederate pr soners across the road to march ahead of the army, and no more torpedoes were found. After the capture of Fort McAllister the troops set to work gingerly scraping about wherever the ground seemed to have been disturbed, trying to find and remove the dangerous hidden menaces to life. At last the ground was rendered safe and the troops settled down to the occupation of Fort McAllister where the bravely fighting little Confederate garrison had held the key to Savannah. The city was the first to fall of the Confederacy's Atlantic seaports, now almost locked from the outside world by the blockade. By the capture of Fort McAllister, which crowned the march to the sea, Sherman had numbered the days of the war. The fall of the remaining ports was to follow in quick succession, and by Washington's Birthday, 1865, the entire coast-line was to be in possession of the Federals.

SHERMAN'S TROOPS DISMANTLING FORT McALLISTER

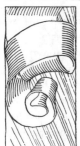

harvests of corn and vegetables, but rather rice plantations and great pine forests, the solemn stillness of which was broken by the tread of thousands of troops, the rumbling of wagon-trains, and by the shouts and music of the marching men and of the motley crowd of negroes that followed.

Day by day Sherman issued orders for the progress of the wings, but on December 2d they contained the decisive words, "Savannah." What a tempting prize was this fine Southern city, and how the Northern commander would add to his laurels could he effect its capture! The memories cling-ing about the historic old town, with its beautiful parks and its magnolia-lined streets, are part of the inheritance of not only the South, but of all America. Here Oglethorpe had bartered with the wild men of the forest, and here, in the days of the Revolution, Count Pulaski and Sergeant Jasper had given up their lives in the cause of liberty.

Sherman had partially invested the city before the middle of December; but it was well fortified and he refrained from assault. General Hardee, sent by Hood from Tennessee, had command of the defenses, with about eighteen thousand men. And there was Fort McAllister on the Ogeechee, protecting the city on the south. But this obstruction to the Federals was soon removed. General Hazen's division of the Fifteenth Corps was sent to capture the fort. At five o'clock in the afternoon of the 13th Hazen's men rushed through a shower of grape, over abatis and hidden torpedoes, scaled the parapet and captured the garrison. That night Sherman boarded the *Dandelion*, a Union vessel, in the river, and sent a message to the outside world, the first since he had left Atlanta.

Henceforth there was communication between the army and the Federal squadron, under the command of Admiral Dahlgren. Among the vessels that came up the river there was one that was received with great enthusiasm by the sol-diers. It brought mail, tons of it, for Sherman's army, the accumulation of two months. One can imagine the eagerness

With much foresight, General Hardee had not waited for Sherman's approach, but before the Federal forces could prevent, had marched out with his force with the intention of joining Johnston. There were in the neighborhood of some twenty thousand inhabitants in the city of Savannah when Sherman took possession, and the man who had made a Christmas present of their city to Lincoln had no easy task before him to preserve order and to meet the many claims made upon his time by the responsibilities of city government. But Sherman regarded the war as practically over and concluded that he would make it optional with the citizens and their families to remain in the city under a combination of military and civil government, or rejoin their friends in Augusta or the still unsurrendered but beleaguered town of Charleston. After consulting with Dr. Arnold, the Mayor, the City Council was assembled and authorized to take charge generally of the interests of those who remained. About two hundred of the families of men still fighting in the Confederate army were sent by steamer under a flag of truce to Charleston, but the great majority preferred to remain

DESTRUCTION THAT FOLLOWED WAR

RUINS AT SAVANNAH, 1865

in Savannah. During the night before the Federal occupation, fires had broken out and a scene of chaos had resulted. There is no doubt that Sherman had destroyed vast amounts of Confederate stores, that he had torn up railway tracks and burned stations, and that his army had subsisted on what supplies it could gather from the country through which it had passed, but in the bitter feelings of the times, rumors scattered by word of mouth and repeated by newspapers as deliberate accusations had gone to the extreme in stating the behavior of his army. Yet, nevertheless, many Confederate officers still in the field confided their families to Sherman's keeping and left them in their city homes. Cotton was contraband and although the Confederates sought to destroy it, as was just and proper, at Savannah thirty-one thousand bales became a prize to the army. The newspapers were not suppressed entirely and two were allowed to be published, although under the closest censorship. But as we look at the ruins of fine houses and desolated homes we begin to appreciate more fully Sherman's own solemn declaration that "War is Hell."

with which these war-stained veterans opened the longed-for letters and sought the answer to the ever-recurring question, " How are things at home? "

Sherman had set his heart on capturing Savannah; but, on December 15th, he received a letter from Grant which greatly disturbed him. Grant ordered him to leave his artillery and cavalry, with infantry enough to support them, and with the remainder of his army to come by sea to Virginia and join the forces before Richmond. Sherman prepared to obey, but hoped that he would be able to capture the city before the transports would be ready to carry him northward.

He first called on Hardee to surrender the city, with a threat of bombardment. Hardee refused. Sherman hesitated to open with his guns because of the bloodshed it would occasion, and on December 21st he was greatly relieved to discover that Hardee had decided not to defend the city, that he had escaped with his army the night before, by the one road that was still open to him, which led across the Savannah River into the Carolinas. The stream had been spanned by an improvised pontoon bridge, consisting of river-boats, with planks from city wharves for flooring and with old car-wheels for anchors. Sherman immediately took possession of the city, and on December 22d he sent to President Lincoln this message: " I beg to present to you, as a Christmas gift, the city of Savannah, with one hundred and fifty heavy guns and plenty of ammunition, and also about twenty-five thousand bales of cotton." As a matter of fact, over two hundred and fifty guns were captured, and thirty-one thousand bales of cotton. General Hardee retreated to Charleston.

Events in the West now changed Grant's views as to Sherman's joining him immediately in Virginia. On the 16th of December, General Thomas accomplished the defeat and utter rout of Hood's army at Nashville. In addition, it was found that, owing to lack of transports, it would take at least two months to transfer Sherman's whole army by sea. There-

HOMEWARD BOUND

Wagon-trains leaving Savannah. Here the wagon-trains of the victorious army are ready just outside of Savannah for the march northward. The troops, in high glee and splendid condition, again abundantly supplied with food and clothes, are impatient to be off. But a difficult country confronts them—a land of swollen streams and nearly tropical swamps like that in the lower photograph, picturesque enough, but "bad going" for teams. Near this the Fifteenth Corps passed on its way to Columbia. It is typical of the spongy ground over which the army must pass, building causeways and corduroying roads. Sherman himself rated this homeward march as a greater achievement than his much-sung "Atlanta to the Sea."

THE CAPTURED CAPITAL OF SOUTH CAROLINA

This striking photograph of Columbia will stir the memory of many a veteran. One recalls marching through the two small gates in the fence with his comrades. He points out the broken wagon wheels and old iron pipe in the foreground, and explains that they are the remains of dummy cannon which the Confederates had constructed and mounted there as Sherman's army approached. There were some real cannon in the town, however, and in a window of one of the houses one of these had been mounted and opened on the Federals, who had to bring up one of their own small guns before they could dislodge the men bravely defending Columbia.

RUINS OF THE UNFINISHED STATEHOUSE AT COLUMBIA

On the 16th of February Sherman was opposite Columbia. A few shells had been thrown into the city, but it was never under bombardment. But on the morning of the 17th the mayor had come out to surrender the city, and before the troops had entered a high wind was carrying about flakes of cotton that had in some manner become ignited. With the aid of an old fire-engine the soldiers endeavored to put out the conflagration, but much property was destroyed. In the afternoon the wind moderated and the fire was controlled.

THE CONGAREE RIVER BRIDGE

THE EMPTY PRISON

THE PRESBYTERIAN LECTURE-ROOM

HUNT'S HOUSE

FREIGHT DEPOT, SOUTH CAROLINA RAILROAD

THE CATHOLIC CONVENT

AS COLUMBIA LOOKED AFTER SHERMAN'S ARMY PASSED, IN 1865

HOME OF STATE SURGEON-GENERAL GIBBS

THE LUTHERAN CHURCH

EVANS AND COGGSWELL'S PRINTING SHOP

DESERTED MAIN STREET

THE METHODIST EPISCOPAL CHURCH, WASHINGTON STREET

THE SOUTH CAROLINA RAILROAD OFFICES

WHAT WAR BROUGHT TO THE CAPITAL OF SOUTH CAROLINA

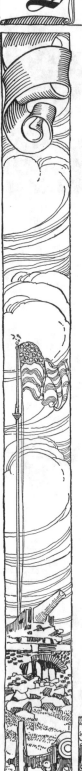

fore, it was decided that Sherman should march through the Carolinas, destroying the railroads in both States as he went. A little more than a month Sherman remained in Savannah. Then he began another great march, compared with which, as Sherman himself declared, the march to the sea was as child's play. The size of his army on leaving Savannah was practically the same as when he left Atlanta—sixty thousand. It was divided into two wings, under the same commanders, Howard and Slocum, and was to be governed by the same rules. Kilpatrick still commanded the cavalry. The march from Savannah averaged ten miles a day, which, in view of the conditions, was a very high average. The weather in the early part of the journey was exceedingly wet and the roads were well-nigh impassable. Where they were not actually under water the mud rendered them impassable until corduroyed. Moreover, the troops had to wade streams, to drag themselves through swamps and quagmires, and to remove great trees that had been felled across their pathway.

The city of Savannah was left under the control of General J. G. Foster, and the Left Wing of Sherman's army under Slocum moved up the Savannah River, accompanied by Kilpatrick, and crossed it at Sister's Ferry. The river was overflowing its banks and the crossing, by means of a pontoon bridge, was effected with the greatest difficulty. The Right Wing, under Howard, embarked for Beaufort, South Carolina, and moved thence to Pocotaligo, near the Broad River, whither Sherman had preceded it, and the great march northward was fairly begun by February 1, 1865.

Sherman had given out the word that he expected to go to Charleston or Augusta, his purpose being to deceive the Confederates, since he had made up his mind to march straight to Columbia, the capital of South Carolina.

The two wings of the army were soon united and they continued their great march from one end of the State of South Carolina to the other. The men felt less restraint in devas-

THE MEN WHO LIVED OFF THE COUNTRY — HEADQUARTERS GUARD ON THE MARCH THROUGH
NORTH CAROLINA

These men have not been picked out by the photographer on account of their healthy and well-fed appearance; they are just average samples of what the units of Sherman's army looked like as they pressed on toward Fayetteville and the last battle in the Carolinas, Bentonville, where General Johnston made a brave stand before falling back upon Raleigh. The men of the march to the sea were champions in covering ground. The condition of the roads did not seem to stop them, nor the fact that they had to fight as they pressed on. During the forced march to Bentonville the right wing, under General Howard, marched twenty miles, almost without a halt, skirmishing most of the way.

tating the country and despoiling the people than they had felt in Georgia. The reason for this, given by Sherman and others, was that there was a feeling of bitterness against South Carolina as against no other State. It was this State that had led the procession of seceding States and that had fired on Fort Sumter and brought on the great war. No doubt this feeling, which pervaded the army, will account in part for the reckless dealing with the inhabitants by the Federal soldiery. The superior officers, however, made a sincere effort to restrain lawlessness.

On February 17th, Sherman entered Columbia, the mayor having come out and surrendered the city. The Fifteenth Corps marched through the city and out on the Camden road, the remainder of the army not having come within two miles of the city. On that night Columbia was in flames. The conflagration spread and ere the coming of the morning the best part of the city had been laid in ashes.

Before Sherman left Columbia he destroyed the machine-shops and everything else which might aid the Confederacy. He left with the mayor one hundred stand of arms with which to keep order, and five hundred head of cattle for the destitute.

As Columbia was approached by the Federals, the occupation of Charleston by the Confederates became more and more untenable. In vain had the governor of South Carolina pleaded with President Davis to reenforce General Hardee, who occupied the city. Hardee thereupon evacuated the historic old city—much of which was burned, whether by design or accident is not known—and its defenses, including Fort Sumter, the bombardment of which, nearly four years before, had precipitated the mighty conflict, were occupied by Colonel Bennett, who came over from Morris Island.

On March 11th, Sherman reached Fayetteville, North Carolina, where he destroyed a fine arsenal. Hitherto, Sherman's march, except for the annoyance of Wheeler's cavalry, had been but slightly impeded by the Confederates. But

COLOR–GUARD OF THE EIGHTH MINNESOTA—WITH SHERMAN WHEN JOHNSTON SURRENDERED

The Eighth Minnesota Regiment, which had joined Sherman on his second march, was with him when Johnston's surrender wrote "Finis" to the last chapter of the war, April 26, 1865. In Bennett's little farmhouse, near Durham's Station, N. C., were begun the negotiations between Johnston and Sherman which finally led to that event. The two generals met there on April 17th; it was a highly dramatic moment, for Sherman had in his pocket the cipher message just received telling of the assassination of Lincoln.

THE END OF THE MARCH—BENNETT'S FARMHOUSE

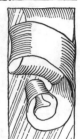

henceforth this was changed. General Joseph E. Johnston, his old foe of Resaca and Kenesaw Mountain, had been recalled and was now in command of the troops in the Carolinas. No longer would the streams and the swamps furnish the only resistance to the progress of the Union army.

The first engagement came at Averysboro on March 16th. General Hardee, having taken a strong position, made a determined stand; but a division of Slocum's wing, aided by Kilpatrick, soon put him to flight, with the loss of several guns and over two hundred prisoners.

The battle of Bentonville, which took place three days after that of Averysboro, was more serious. Johnston had placed his whole army, probably thirty-five thousand men, in the form of a V, the sides embracing the village of Bentonville. Slocum engaged the Confederates while Howard was hurried to the scene. On two days, the 19th and 20th of March, Sherman's army fought its last battle in the Civil War. But Johnston, after making several attacks, resulting in considerable losses on both sides, withdrew his army during the night, and the Union army moved to Goldsboro. The losses at Bentonville were: Federal, 1,527; Confederate, 2,606.

At Goldsboro the Union army was reenforced by its junction with Schofield, who had come out of the West with over twenty-two thousand men from the army of Thomas in Tennessee. But there was little need of reenforcement. Sherman's third great march was practically over. As to the relative importance of the second and third, Sherman declares in his memoirs, he would place that from Atlanta to the sea at one, and that from Savannah through the Carolinas at ten.

Leaving his army in charge of Schofield, Sherman went to City Point, in Virginia, where he had a conference with General Grant and President Lincoln, and plans for the final campaign were definitely arranged. He returned to Goldsboro late in March, and, pursuing Johnston, received, finally, on April 26th the surrender of his army.

[248]

PART III
CLOSING IN

NASHVILLE—THE END
IN TENNESSEE

GUARDING THE CUMBERLAND—WHERE THOMAS WATCHED
FOR HOOD AT THE NASHVILLE BRIDGE

FORT NEGLEY,

THE IMPOSING DEFENSE

OF NASHVILLE

Perched on a hill overlooking Nashville stood Fort Negley—a large, complex citadel ready for action at any time. Though it was little called upon, its very aspect would have caused an enemy much reflection ere deciding to attack. Within the work were two casemates (one of which is shown in the fine photograph above) covered with railroad iron and made bomb-proof with earth. Fort Negley was designed and built on the German polygonal system early in 1862 and was regarded as satisfying the most exacting of the Old World standards as an up-to-date fortification. By the middle of November, 1864, with Sherman well on his march to the sea, the struggle in middle Tennessee had reached a crisis. Hood had invaded the State and Thomas had confided to Schofield the task of checking the Southern army. Thomas himself sent out his couriers and drew in all the available Federal forces to Nashville. There he meant to give battle to Hood when the Confederate leader, racing Schofield, should reach the State capital. The dramatic running fight between Hood and Schofield from Columbia to Nashville is graphically described in the accompanying text.

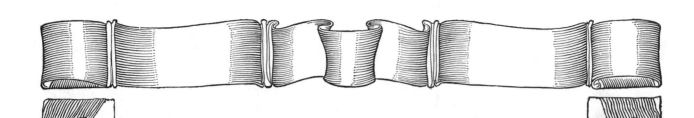

THE BATTLES OF FRANKLIN AND NASHVILLE

The Army of Tennessee under General Hood, pursuing its march northward late in November and early in December, came upon the Federal forces under General Schofield at Franklin, and General Thomas at Nashville, Tennessee, where desperate battles were fought, until Hood's army was reduced to skeleton commands and forced to retreat.—*Lieutenant-General James Longstreet, C.S.A., in " From Manassas to Appomattox."*

WHILE Hood was turning back from Atlanta in the great northward movement, which, in the hopes of the Confederacy, would bring the Army of Tennessee to the banks of the Ohio, there was gathering at and around Nashville a force to dispute the progress of Hood. General Thomas was sent by Sherman " to take care of Tennessee," and he was preparing to weld many fragmentary bodies of troops into a fighting army.

After a month of bold maneuvering, the advance of Hood's army appeared, on the 26th of October, at Decatur, on the south side of the Tennessee. It had been a time of perplexity to the Federal authorities and of intense alarm throughout the North. Hood had twice thrown his army between Sherman and the latter's base; had captured four garrisons, and destroyed thirty miles of railroad. His movements had been bold and brilliantly executed.

At Decatur, Hood found himself too far east to join with Forrest, whose cooperation was absolutely necessary to him. So he moved westward to Florence where the first division of his army, with but little opposition from Croxton's cavalry, crossed the Tennessee on the 31st. Forrest had gone down the river to intercept the Federal line of supplies. At John-

CHATTANOOGA FORTIFIED IN 1864

When Hood made his audacious movement upon Sherman's communications, by invading Tennessee — without however tempting the Northern commander from his grim course—Chattanooga was the only point in Thomas' Department, south of Nashville, which was heavily garrisoned. This town became the supply center for all the Federal posts maintained in eastern Tennessee. Therefore it had been well fortified, so strongly in fact that Thomas, who had just begun his great concentration movement, was able by December 1st to draw Steedman away to the Elk River and thence to Nashville. It was from a point on the hill a little to the right of the scene shown in the lower photograph on this page that the picture of Chattanooga fortified was taken.

CHATTANOOGA AND THE MILITARY BRIDGE

sonville he disabled the gunboats to such an extent that they were burned to prevent their falling into his hands. The fire spread to the Federal stores on the levee and $1,500,-000 of Government property thereby was destroyed. The garrison held firm. Forrest withdrew his troops and crossed the river above the town. He had received orders to join Hood as quickly as possible and reached Florence on November 14th. General Hood was now free to invade Tennessee. Sherman had sent the Fourth Corps, under Stanley, and the Twenty-third, under Schofield, the latter in command of both, back to Thomas, and this force was now at Pulaski to oppose Hood.

On the morning of November 19th, the army of Hood was put in motion. The day was disagreeable. It snowed and rained, and there was sleet and ice for the men to face. Over the slippery roads the army trudged, led by the cavalry of the daring Forrest. The wary Hood did not choose to be " checked at Pulaski," but passed adroitly by on the other side, urging his ranks forward toward Columbia on the Duck River.

At midnight of the 23d, General Schofield learned of the movements of Hood. He knew that if the latter reached Columbia he could easily capture the garrison at that place and then be free to cross the river and cut him off from Thomas. The sleeping troops were quickly aroused and in an hour were making their way through the night to Columbia, twenty-one miles distant. Another column, led by General Cox, starting somewhat later, was pushing rapidly over another road to the same point. It was a race between the armies of Hood and Schofield for the crossing at Columbia. The weary, footsore Federals barely won. Cox, by taking a cross-road, came to the rescue only a few miles south of Columbia, as Forrest was driving the Federal cavalry back, and the little army was saved.

The Union army entrenched itself for battle. Works were thrown up while the wagon trains were retreating beyond the river. But it was found impracticable to hold the position. All during the night of the 27th, there was a steady stream of

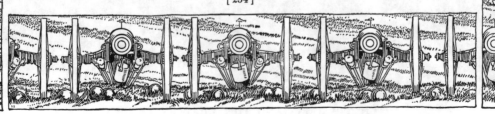

THE "BUSINESS OF WAR" AT AN ALABAMA RAILROAD STATION—FEDERALS CON–
CENTRATING AT STEVENSON BEFORE THE NASHVILLE BATTLE

Early in the winter of 1864, this station in the little Alabama town fairly hummed with the movement of men and horses and supplies. Schofield's division of Thomas' army was being concentrated there for the campaign which culminated, in the middle of December, at the bloody battle of Nashville. A business-like crowd is shown in this picture, of soldiers and citizens, with more than one commanding figure in the foreground. The railroad played a part most important and most vulnerable in the Western campaigns.

men, wagons, and artillery, passing over to the north side of Duck River. Not until daylight did the rear guard burn the railroad bridge and scuttle the pontoon boats, behind them.

The 28th of November was a suspiciously quiet day in front of Columbia. Not so, along other parts of the river bank. About noon, at various points, squads of Confederate cavalry appeared, indicating their purpose to cross, which was finally accomplished.

At daybreak the next morning, with Hood himself in the lead, the Confederate army, headed by one of its most courageous divisions, was quickly marching again to intercept the retreat of Schofield. Spring Hill, fifteen miles north of Columbia, was the objective of Hood. This was a brilliant piece of strategy, and the Confederate general hurried his columns along that he might reach the point first. Succeeding in this he could easily turn the Union flank, and nothing could save that army. It all depended on who should win the race.

The Confederates marched lightly. It was a beautiful, crisp morning and the men were in high hopes. There was every prospect of their winning, since the Union army was heavy and it moved sluggishly. To save the Federal wagon train, and its contents of food, clothing, and ammunition, which was slowly moving along the roads to the north, with only the little force of warriors in blue interposing between them and the eager Confederate legions, General Stanley was ordered forward, to make a dash to the rescue. As he neared the town he saw on his right the Confederate columns abreast of him on a parallel road. A little further on, he was informed that Forrest's cavalry was approaching rapidly from the east.

No time was now to be lost. Although his men were weary from their hurried march, they were pushed forward at the double-quick into town. The opposing forces met on the edge of the village; a light skirmish followed, in which the Federals secured the main approaches to the town.

Schofield's army was in a splendid position to invite attack.

RUSHING A FEDERAL BATTERY OUT OF JOHNSONVILLE

When Thomas began to draw together his forces to meet Hood at Nashville, he ordered the garrison at Johnsonville, on the Tennessee, eighty miles due west of Nashville, to leave that place and hasten north. It was the garrison at this same Johnsonville that, a month earlier, had been frightened into panic and flight when the bold Confederate raider, Forrest, appeared on the west bank of the river and began a noisy cannonade. New troops had been sent to the post. They appear well coated and equipped. The day after the photograph was taken (November 23d) the encampment in the picture was broken.

The forces were widely scattered, and the situation was indeed critical. The afternoon of November 29th records a series of lost opportunities to the Confederates. From noon until seven o'clock in the evening the little force of Stanley was completely isolated from the main army. Hood had sufficient troops literally to crush him, to cut off the retreat of Schofield, and thereby to defeat that wing of the Federal army. During the afternoon and evening there were various attempts made on the Union lines, which were stoutly resisted. The vigor of the repulse, the lack of concentration in the attack and, perhaps, the coming of evening saved the day for the Federals.

The Confederates bivouacked for the night near the pike. Brightly their camp-fires gleamed, as the Federal wagon trains and the columns of Northern soldiers trudged along through a moonless night, within a few rods of the resting Confederates. The Southern troops were plainly visible to the Federals, as they were seen moving about the camp. There was constant apprehension lest the Southern army should fall upon the passing army, but the officer who was ordered to block the Federal march made but a feeble and partial attack. Hood realized that he had lost the best opportunity for crushing Schofield that the campaign had offered, and deplored the failure most bitterly.

Schofield reached Spring Hill about seven in the evening. At the same hour the last company of his troops was leaving Columbia, about eleven miles away. All through the night the procession continued. The intrepid Stanley stood guard at a narrow bridge, as the long train wended its way in the darkness over the hills in the direction of Nashville. At daybreak, as the rear wagons safely passed, and the skirmishers were called in, the advance columns, under Cox, were reaching the outskirts of Franklin.

This village, situated on a bend of the Harpeth River, was admirably located for a great battle. On the north and west, it was protected by the river. Beyond the stream, to the

FORT NEGLEY, LOOKING TOWARD THE CONFEDERATE CENTER AND LEFT, AS HOOD'S VETERANS THREATENED THE CITY

It was Hood's hope that, when he had advanced his line to the left of the position shown in this photograph, he might catch a weak spot in Thomas' forces. But Thomas had no weak spots. From the casemate, armored with railroad iron, shown here, the hills might be easily seen on which the Confederate center and left were posted at the opening of the great battle of Nashville.

THE PRIZE OF THE NASHVILLE CAMPAIGN—THE STATE CAPITOL

north, were three prominent hills, giving excellent elevations for batteries, and commanding a broad plain that lay in front of the town. These were utilized by the Federals. To the south were low ridges on which an attacking party might entrench.

Schofield had not expected to give battle at Franklin. He was hurrying his men to reach the protecting entrenchments of Nashville. But he would not be taken unawares. Though his men had marched and fought by turns for a week, by day and night, until they were on the point of exhaustion, yet the tired and hungry troops, before they had prepared their morning meal, laid down the musket and took up the spade. Soon entrenchments stretched along on two sides of the town. Batteries of artillery were placed at the front and in the rear, guarding the lines of probable attack. To this protecting haven, the weary regiments, one by one, filed, until, by noon, the last one had safely found its way to the entrenched walls of Franklin. The wagon trains passed over the Harpeth and the troops would soon follow after. But this was not to be. Even then, the Confederate vanguard was close at hand.

It was a glorious Indian summer afternoon. For two hours the Federal troops had been looking through the hazy atmosphere to the eastward hills. The day was already beginning to wane, when from the wooded ridge there emerged the stately columns of the army of Hood. On a rise in front of the Union lines stood Wagner's two brigades, in uniforms of blue. They were stationed, unsupported, directly in front of the Confederate approach. It was evident that "some one had blundered." But there they stood, waiting for the impact of the line in gray. A concentrated roar of musketry burst forth and they were engulfed in the on-sweeping torrent.

The Confederate ranks plunged on, carrying the helpless brigades along. With tremendous momentum they rushed toward the works. The guns along the Federal line were silent. They dare not fire on their own routed men. The weight of the oncoming mass of humanity broke through the first line of

A STATE HOUSE STOCKADED

Shortly after the occupation of Nashville by the Union forces in February, 1862, General Morton, of the U. S. Corps of Engineers, began work on its fortifications. Around the capitol were built earth parapets and stockades, and enough room was provided to mount fifteen guns. The strong, massive structure, plentifully supplied with water, could easily accommodate a regiment of infantry—enough in

THE STOCKADE AND THE PARAPET

such a citadel to hold an entire army at bay. This, however, was but a part of the entire line of defenses he planned. He was intending to fortify Morton and Houston Hills, and a third on which Fort Negley was actually constructed. The pictures show the city which the works were built to defend, but which Morton was prepared to leave to the enemy if forced to retreat within his lines.

THE NASHVILLE CAPITOL FORTIFIED

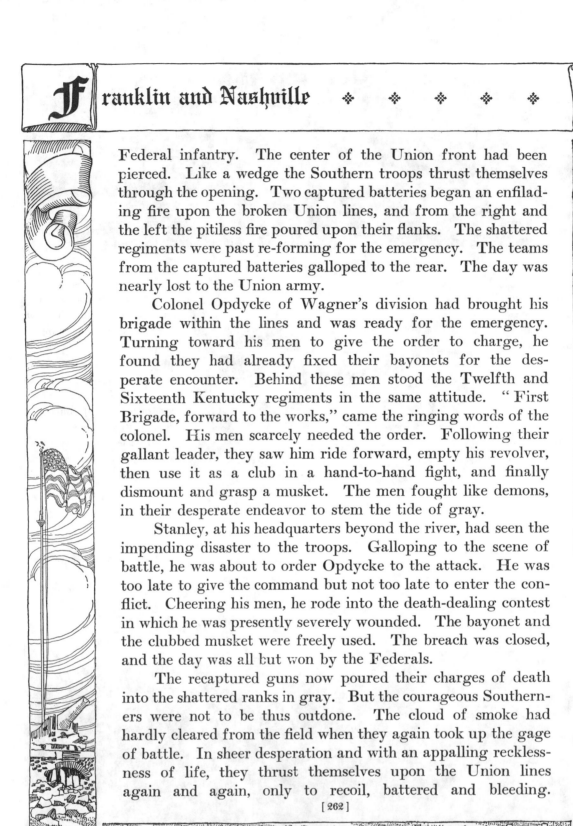

Federal infantry. The center of the Union front had been pierced. Like a wedge the Southern troops thrust themselves through the opening. Two captured batteries began an enfilading fire upon the broken Union lines, and from the right and the left the pitiless fire poured upon their flanks. The shattered regiments were past re-forming for the emergency. The teams from the captured batteries galloped to the rear. The day was nearly lost to the Union army.

Colonel Opdycke of Wagner's division had brought his brigade within the lines and was ready for the emergency. Turning toward his men to give the order to charge, he found they had already fixed their bayonets for the desperate encounter. Behind these men stood the Twelfth and Sixteenth Kentucky regiments in the same attitude. "First Brigade, forward to the works," came the ringing words of the colonel. His men scarcely needed the order. Following their gallant leader, they saw him ride forward, empty his revolver, then use it as a club in a hand-to-hand fight, and finally dismount and grasp a musket. The men fought like demons, in their desperate endeavor to stem the tide of gray.

Stanley, at his headquarters beyond the river, had seen the impending disaster to the troops. Galloping to the scene of battle, he was about to order Opdycke to the attack. He was too late to give the command but not too late to enter the conflict. Cheering his men, he rode into the death-dealing contest in which he was presently severely wounded. The bayonet and the clubbed musket were freely used. The breach was closed, and the day was all but won by the Federals.

The recaptured guns now poured their charges of death into the shattered ranks in gray. But the courageous Southerners were not to be thus outdone. The cloud of smoke had hardly cleared from the field when they again took up the gage of battle. In sheer desperation and with an appalling recklessness of life, they thrust themselves upon the Union lines again and again, only to recoil, battered and bleeding.

THOMAS—THE "ROCK OF CHICKAMAUGA" WHO BECAME THE "SLEDGE OF NASHVILLE"

Major-General George Henry Thomas, Virginia-born soldier loyal to the Union; commended for gallantry in the Seminole War, and for service in Mexico; won the battle of Mill Spring, January 19, 1862; commanded the right wing of the Army of the Tennessee against Corinth and at Perryville, and the center at Stone's River. Only his stability averted overwhelming defeat for the Federals at Chickamauga. At Lookout Mountain and Missionary Ridge he was a host in himself. After Sherman had taken Atlanta he sent Thomas back to Tennessee to grapple with Hood. How he crushed Hood by his sledge-hammer blows is told in the accompanying text. Thomas, sitting down in Nashville, bearing the brunt of Grant's impatience, and ignoring completely the proddings from Washington to advance before he was ready, while he waited grimly for the psychological moment to strike the oncoming Confederate host under Hood, is one of the really big dramatic figures of the entire war. It has been well said of Thomas that every promotion he received was a reward of merit: and that during his long and varied career as a soldier no crisis ever arose too great for his ability.

Evening fell upon the battling hosts, and long into the night there was heard the sharp volleys of musketry. Thus closed one of the fiercest of the minor struggles of the Civil War. At midnight, Schofield withdrew from the trenches of Franklin and fell back to Thomas at Nashville.

Many gallant Southern leaders fell on the battlefield of Franklin, whose loss to the Confederacy was irreparable. Five generals and a long list of field-officers were among the killed. General Patrick Cleburne, a native of Ireland and a veteran of the British army, and General John Adams, both fell in the desperate charges at the breach in the Federal lines when Wagner's brigades were swept headlong from the front of the battle-line.

Hood appeared before the army of Thomas, on December 2d. Preparations at once began in both camps for the decisive contest. Hood was furnishing his army with supplies and with shoes, and throwing up entrenchments parallel to those of the Union army. Thomas was remounting his cavalry and increasing the strength of his works. The city was well fortified. On the surrounding hills the forts bristled with cannon. But the Federal commander was not ready for battle.

Thomas was not a born military strategist. But he was a remarkable tactician. No battle of the war was better planned and none was so nearly carried out to the letter of the plan as the battle of Nashville. It has been said that this plan of Thomas is the only one of the entire war that is now studied as a model in European military schools.

But Thomas was not acting quickly enough to satisfy Grant and the Washington authorities. Day after day, telegrams and messages poured in on him, giving advice and urging immediate action. Thomas stood firm. Finally an order for his removal was issued but never delivered. In a telegram to Halleck, Thomas stated that if it was desirable to relieve him of his command he would submit without a murmur.

Finally, preparations were completed. But, just then a

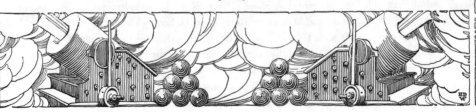

THIRTY-TWO OHIO REGIMENTS FOUGHT AT NASHVILLE—A TYPICAL GROUP OF VETERANS, FROM THE
ONE–HUNDRED–AND–TWENTY–FIFTH—"OPDYCKE'S TIGERS"

Ohio's part in 1861–65 was a large one, promptly and bravely played.   Thirty-two regiments, besides cavalry companies and artillery
batteries from that State, were in service in the operations around Nashville.   Colonel Emerson Opdycke, afterwards brevetted major-
general, commanded the One-Hundred-and-Twenty-fifth Ohio as part of the rear-guard at Spring Hill.   Some of these troops are
shown above   The lads in the lower picture made up the band of the One-Hundred-and-Twenty-fifth.

THE "TIGER BAND" OF THE ONE–HUNDRED–AND–TWENTY–FIFTH OHIO BEFORE NASHVILLE

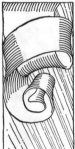

severe storm of freezing rain poured down upon the waiting armies and held the country in its frigid grasp. The ground was covered with a glare of ice. Horses and men slid and sprawled on the slippery surface. It was impossible to move an army under such conditions. Still the bombardment of messages from the East continued.

On December 14th, the ice began to melt. That night Thomas called a council of his corps commanders and laid before them his well-matured plans for the morrow's battle. Then he telegraphed to Grant that the ice had melted and the attack would be made in the morning. Had the storm continued, the attack must have been postponed and Thomas probably would not have been the hero of Nashville. Even as it was, Logan was hurrying from the East toward that city to take command of the army. When he reached Louisville, in Kentucky, on the 17th, he heard that the battle was over and he came no farther.

At four on the morning of December 15th, reveille sounded through the Union camp of fifty-five thousand soldiers. Two hours later, the men were standing in array of battle. The air was soft and even balmy. A heavy river-fog hung over the lowlands and across the city. In the dense pall, regiments of soldiers, like phantom warriors, moved across the country.

By nine o'clock the sun had pierced the mist and to the observers on the hilltops it was a brilliant spectacle. The battle-lines were rapidly forming. With the precision of a well-oiled machine, the battalions were moving to their places. Squadrons of cavalry were passing along the lowlands to take their position in the battle-line. Great guns glinted through embrasures ready to vomit forth their missiles of destruction.

The plan of the battle of Nashville as formed by Thomas was simple—a feint attack on the opposing army's right, the striking of a sudden and irresistible blow on his left, followed by successive attacks until the Southern army was battered into

THOMAS ADVANCING HIS OUTER LINE AT NASHVILLE, DECEMBER 16TH

Camp-fires were still smouldering along the side of the abatis where the lens caught the field of Nashville, while Thomas' concentric forward movement was in progress. Note the abatis to the right of the picture, the wagons moving and ready to move in the background, and the artillery on the left. White tents gleam from the distant hills. A few straggling soldiers remain. The Federals are closing with Hood's army a couple of miles to the right of the scene in the picture.

GUARDING THE LINE DURING THE ADVANCE

disorganization and routed. About forty-five thousand Federals were actually engaged at Nashville. Against them Hood mustered some thirty-eight thousand Confederates.

At eight o'clock, Steedman sent Colonels Morgan and Grosvenor to demonstrate on the Confederate right. This was gallantly done, in the face of a severe fire, and so closely did it resemble a genuine attack that Hood was completely deceived. At once, he drew troops from his center to strengthen the endangered flank. Then on the Union right, infantry and dismounted cavalry moved out against the weakened Confederate left.

The cooperation of these two arms of the service was almost perfect. Soon, the battle was raging along the entire front. The Federal forces were gradually converging. The Confederate lines were being crowded from their first position. Montgomery Hill, the salient point of the Confederate defense, was a strong position commanding a view of the surrounding country. It was here that one of the most daring assaults of the day was made. At one o'clock, Colonel Post's brigade dashed up the hill, direct at the works on the summit. The color-bearers forged rapidly ahead. At the top, without a moment's hesitation, the troops plunged across the works, capturing guns and men.

Still, the flail of war kept pounding at the Confederate center. Hour after hour, the Union lines, compact and unyielding, battered the ranks of the Southern troops. As the sun set on the evening of that day, the army of Hood found itself more than two miles from the place it occupied in the morning.

The new day found the Confederate general still undaunted. During the night he had formed a new line of battle. It was shorter, stronger, and more compact than that of the preceding day. Works had been thrown up in front, while behind rose a range of hills. These were strongly fortified. The second position was stronger than the first.

NASHVILLE WATCHING THE FIGHT TO A FINISH BETWEEN HOOD AND THOMAS

When Hood attacked Nashville, early in December, 1864, the Union army, under Thomas, was entrenched in a semi-circle on the wooded hills about the city, both flanks resting on the Cumberland River. Hundreds of spectators watched the fighting from the other hills. The picture at the top of this page was taken on the heights to the east, on December 15th. The view at the bottom was looking northwest. The spectators caught by the alert photographer might not have realized the tremendous significance of the struggle going on before them, but they could all witness the mathematical precision of Thomas' tactics. The checking of Hood at Nashville made Sherman's position secure in the heart of the Confederacy.

THE BATTLEFIELD FROM THE MILITARY COLLEGE

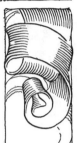

It was past noon before Thomas was ready to repeat the tactics of the preceding day. On the Confederate right was Overton's Hill, a strongly fortified position. Colonel Post was designated to lead the Federal attack. Supported by a brigade of negro troops, the assaulting columns moved up the steep ascent. With precision the lines marched toward the crest of the hill. All was well until the final dash was to be made, when a withering fire drove them back to the foot of the hill.

The extreme Confederate left also rested upon a hill. To Colonel McMillen was given the task of wresting it from the possession of the Southern troops. Forming his regiments,— the One hundred and fourteenth Illinois, the Ninety-third Indiana, the Tenth Minnesota, the Seventy-second Ohio and the Ninety-fifth Ohio—into two lines, he rapidly moved forward. The approaching lines of attack were received with a hail of musketry, and grape and canister from the Confederate artillery. But unwaveringly the cheering ranks carried the position.

The success of this charge on the right inspired the left, and again the attempt to carry Overton's Hill was made, this time successfully. These successes of the Union lines became contagious. A general forward movement was made along the entire front. It was irresistible. No troops could withstand such an impact. Hood's splendid and courageous army was routed. From thirty-eight thousand men who entered the fight it was reduced to a remnant. Flinging aside muskets and everything that would impede progress, the army that was to revivify the hopes of the failing Confederacy was fleeing in utter confusion along the Franklin pike through Brentwood Pass. This Confederate Army of Tennessee had had a glorious history. It had fought with honor from Donelson and Shiloh to Atlanta and Nashville. It had been at Murfreesboro, Chickamauga, Lookout Mountain, and Missionary Ridge. Now, shattered and demoralized, it was relentlessly pursued beyond the Tennessee River, never again to emerge as a fighting army in the Southwest.

PART IV

FROM WAR TO PEACE

———

THE SIEGE AND FALL
OF PETERSBURG

———

UNION PICKET NEAR FORT MAHONE,
THE CONFEDERATE STRONGHOLD

THE FINISHED PRODUCT

It is winter-time before Petersburg. Grant's army, after the assault of October 27th, has settled down to the waiting game that can have but one result. Look at the veterans in this picture of '64—not a haggard or hungry face in all this group of a hundred or more. Warmly clad, well-fed, in the prime of manly vigor, smiling in confidence that the end is almost now in sight, these are the men who hold the thirty-odd miles of Federal trenches that hem in Lee's ragged army. Outdoor life and constant "roughing it" affects men variously. There was many a young clerk from the city, slender of limb, lacking in muscle, a man only in the embryo, who finished his three or five years' term of service with a constitution of iron and sinews like whip-cords. Strange to say, it was the regiments from up-country and the backwoods, lumbermen and farmers, who after a short time in camp began to show most the effect of hardship

UNION VETERANS OF TRENCH AND FIELD BEFORE PETERSBURG—1864

and sickness. They had been used to regular hours, meals at certain times, and always the same kind of food—their habits had been formed, their sleep had not been interfered with; their stomachs, by which they could tell the time of day, rebelled at being obliged to go empty, their systems had to learn new tricks. But the city recruit, if possessed of no physical ailment or chronic trouble, seemed to thrive and expand in the open air—he was a healthy exotic that, when transplanted, adapted itself to the new soil with surprising vigor—being cheated of his sleep, and forced to put up with the irregularities of camp life was not such a shock for him as for the "to bed with the chickens and up with the lark" countryman. This is no assuming of facts—it is the result of experience and record. But here are men of city, farm, and backwoods who have become case-hardened to the rugged life.

PETERSBURG THE BESIEGED CITY

Thus we see Petersburg as, with a powerful glass, it might have been seen from the north bank of the Appomattox, looking south over the ruined town in April, 1865. As the railroad center south of Richmond, it was, at the outbreak of the war, one of the largest cities of Virginia. It was Grant who first utilized its importance in leading up to the capture of the capital. Although all missiles apparently evince a

THE RUINED MILL

selective intelligence, at times in any bombardment there are naturally objects which give range to the gunners and become targets for their aim. Chimneys and smokestacks, and, alas! in some cases, steeples, were picked out between the sights before the lanyard was pulled. In Petersburg the churches suffered least, but buildings such as the mill and the gas-house, with its 80-foot stack, were crumbled into ruins.

WHERE THE LIGHT FAILED—GAS WORKS AT PETERSBURG

BOLINGBROKE STREET—HISTORIC HOUSES BOMBARDED

In the houses down this quiet street, liable at any moment to be pierced by shot, as some of these have been, the women of Peters-burg, with all the courage the daughters of the South invariably have shown, went bravely about their self-imposed tasks, denying themselves all luxuries and frequently almost the necessities of life, to help feed and take care of the men in the trenches that faced the Federal lines. During the siege, from June, 1864, to April, 1865, led by the wives of some of the officers high in com-mand, the Petersburg citizens, and the women especially, exhibited high heroism in nursing the wounded and aiding the army. This street was named after a distinguished Revolutionary family, whose mansion during the Revolution had been seized and made the headquarters of Benedict Arnold. Arnold, after his defection from the Continental cause, had been sent into Virginia to destroy the property of prominent Revolutionists.

A BATTERED RELIC OF COLONIAL DAYS IN PETERSBURG

This beautiful old mansion on Bolingbroke Street could look back to the days of buckles and small clothes; it wears an aggrieved and surprised look, as if wondering why it should have received such buffetings as its pierced walls, its shattered windows and doorway show. Yet it was more fortunate than some of its near-by neighbors, which were never again after the visitation of the falling shells fit habitations for mankind. Many of these handsome residences were utterly destroyed, their fixtures shattered beyond repair; their wainscoting, built when the Commonwealth of Virginia was ruled over by the representative of King George, was torn from the walls and, bursting into flames, made a funeral pyre of past comforts and magnificence. The havoc wrought upon the dwellings of the town was heavy; certain localities suffered more than others, and those residents who seemed to dwell in the safest zones had been ever ready to open their houses to the sick and wounded of Lee's army. As Grant's troops marched in, many pale faces gazed out at them from the windows, and at the doorsteps stood men whose wounds exempted them from ever bearing arms again.

THE SHATTERED DOORWAY

THE DEMOLISHED DINING–ROOM

OF A

HANDSOME MANSION

HAVOC OF BOMBARDMENT

IN A

PETERSBURG HOME

In this room, nearly a hundred years before, the red-coated officers of His Britannic Majesty's troops had gathered at the long mahogany table, which, with the glittering sideboards and the old portraits, had furnished the apartment. They were unbidden guests and were invaders. It was with enforced courtesy that the lady of the house, whose husband and two sons were wearing the blue and buff of the Continental Army, received them. And now, in 1865, this lady's descendents, the heirs to the old mansion, have been forced to move by another invasion that brought home to them the stern decrees of war. The two maiden ladies of proud lineage had been forced in the early stages of the siege to move their belongings to a safer place. The house had been stripped of furnishings; against the noble old walls the Federal guns had knocked for admittance, presenting no billet of lodgment with a sweeping bow, but rudely bursting in. After the war was over, its occupants came back; but still, if you should visit them, they could point out to you the traces of the siege.

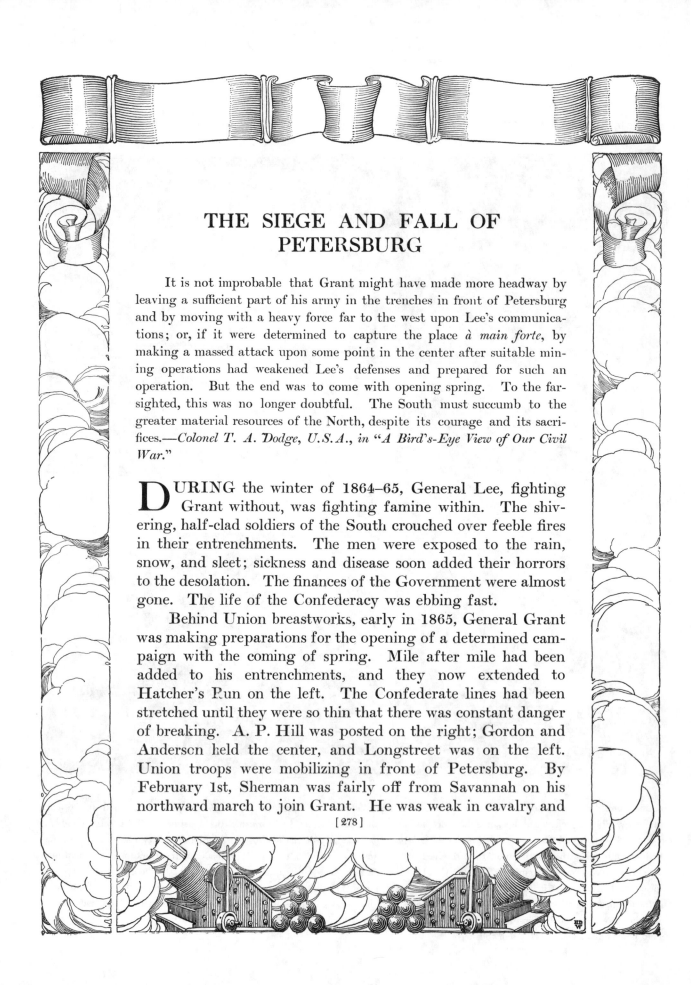

THE SIEGE AND FALL OF PETERSBURG

It is not improbable that Grant might have made more headway by leaving a sufficient part of his army in the trenches in front of Petersburg and by moving with a heavy force far to the west upon Lee's communications; or, if it were determined to capture the place *à main forte*, by making a massed attack upon some point in the center after suitable mining operations had weakened Lee's defenses and prepared for such an operation. But the end was to come with opening spring. To the far-sighted, this was no longer doubtful. The South must succumb to the greater material resources of the North, despite its courage and its sacrifices.—*Colonel T. A. Dodge, U.S.A., in "A Bird's-Eye View of Our Civil War."*

DURING the winter of 1864–65, General Lee, fighting Grant without, was fighting famine within. The shivering, half-clad soldiers of the South crouched over feeble fires in their entrenchments. The men were exposed to the rain, snow, and sleet; sickness and disease soon added their horrors to the desolation. The finances of the Government were almost gone. The life of the Confederacy was ebbing fast.

Behind Union breastworks, early in 1865, General Grant was making preparations for the opening of a determined campaign with the coming of spring. Mile after mile had been added to his entrenchments, and they now extended to Hatcher's Run on the left. The Confederate lines had been stretched until they were so thin that there was constant danger of breaking. A. P. Hill was posted on the right; Gordon and Anderson held the center, and Longstreet was on the left. Union troops were mobilizing in front of Petersburg. By February 1st, Sherman was fairly off from Savannah on his northward march to join Grant. He was weak in cavalry and

APPROACHING THE POST OF DANGER—PETERSBURG, 1865

A FEW STEPS NEARER THE PICKET LINE

IN BEHIND THE SHELTER

For nine months of '64–'65 the musket-balls sang past these Federal picket posts, in advance of Federal Fort Sedgwick, called by the Confederates "Fort Hell." Directly opposite was the Confederate Fort Mahone, which the Federals, returning the compliment, had dubbed "Fort Damnation." Between the two lines, separated by only fifty yards, sallies and counter-sallies were continual occurrences after dark. In stealthy sorties one side or the other frequently captured the opposing pickets before alarm could be given. No night was without its special hazard. During the day the pastime here was sharp-shooting with muskets and rifled cannon.

Grant determined to bring Sheridan from the Shenandoah, whence the bulk of Early's forces had been withdrawn, and send him to assist Sherman. Sheridan left Winchester February 27th, wreaking much destruction as he advanced, but circumstances compelled him to seek a new base at White House. On March 27th he formed a junction with the armies of the Potomac and the James. Such were the happenings that prompted Lee to prepare for the evacuation of Petersburg. And he might be able, in his rapid marches, to outdistance Grant, join his forces with those of Johnston, fall on Sherman, destroy one wing of the Union army and arouse the hopes of his soldiers, and prolong the life of his Government.

General Grant knew the condition of Lee's army and, with the unerring instinct of a military leader, surmised what the plan of the Southern general must be. He decided to move on the left, destroy both the Danville and South Side railroads, and put his army in better condition to pursue. The move was ordered for March 29th.

General Lee, in order to get Grant to look another way for a while, decided to attack Grant's line on the right, and gain some of the works. This would compel Grant to draw some of his force from his left and secure a way of escape to the west. This bold plan was left for execution to the gallant Georgian, General John B. Gordon, who had successfully led the reverse attack at Cedar Creek, in the Shenandoah, in October, 1864. Near the crater stood Fort Stedman. Between it and the Confederate front, a distance of about one hundred and fifty yards, was a strip of firm earth, in full view of both picket lines. Across this space some deserters had passed to the Union entrenchments. General Gordon took advantage of this fact and accordingly selected his men, who, at the sound of the signal gun, should disarm the Federal pickets, while fifty more men were to cross the open space quickly with axes and cut away the abatis, and three hundred others were to rush through the opening, and capture the fort and guns.

SECURITY FROM SURPRISE

THE MOLE–HILL RAMPARTS, NEAR THE CRATER

These well-made protections of sharpened spikes, as formidable as the pointed spears of a Roman legion, are *chevaux-de-frise* of the Confederates before their main works at Petersburg. They were built after European models, the same as employed in the Napoleonic wars, and were used by both besiegers and besieged along the lines south of the Appomattox. Those shown in this picture were in front of the entrenchments near Elliott's salient and show how effectually it was protected from any attempt to storm the works by rushing tactics on the part of the Federal infantry. Not far from here lies the excavation of the Crater.

At four o'clock on the morning of March 25, 1865, Gordon had everything in readiness. His chosen band wore white strips of cloth across the breast, that they might distinguish each other in the hand-to-hand fight that would doubtless ensue. Behind these men half of Lee's army was massed to support the attack. In the silence of the early morning, a gunshot rang out from the Confederate works. Not a Federal picket-shot was heard. The axemen rushed across the open and soon the thuds of their axes told of the cutting away of the abatis. The three hundred surged through the entrance, overpowered the gunners, captured batteries to the right and to the left, and were in control of the situation. Gordon's corps of about five thousand was on hand to sustain the attack but the remaining reserves, through failure of the guides, did not come, and the general found himself cut off with a rapidly increasing army surrounding him.

Fort Haskell, on the left, began to throw its shells. Under its cover, heavy columns of Federals sent by General Parke, now commanding the Ninth Corps, pressed forward. The Confederates resisted the charge, and from the captured Fort Stedman and the adjoining batteries poured volley after volley on Willcox's advancing lines of blue. The Northerners fell back, only to re-form and renew the attack. This time they secured a footing, and for twenty minutes the fighting was terrific. Again they were repulsed. Then across the brow of the hill swept the command of Hartranft. The blue masses literally poured onto the field. The furious musketry, and artillery directed by General Tidball, shrivelled up the ranks of Gordon until they fled from the fort and its neighboring batteries in the midst of withering fire, and those who did not were captured. This was the last aggressive effort of the expiring Confederacy in front of Petersburg, and it cost three thousand men. The Federal loss was not half that number.

The affair at Fort Stedman did not turn Grant from his plans against the Confederate right. With the railroads here

PRAYERS FOR RELIEF AND PRAYERS FOR VICTORY

This church at Petersburg stood near the tobacco warehouses shown in the lower picture, and here the Federal prisoners confined in the old brick building were praying for victory as they listened to the boom of cannon and the rattle of musketry through the terrible winter of '64 and '65. But every Sunday, in this church, prayers to the God of Battles for relief from the invader were raised in fervent zeal of spirit. In all the camps, and in all the cities of the North and South, throughout the war, each side, believing firmly in the justice of its cause, had regularly and earnestly thus appealed to the Almighty for the triumph of its arms.

In the Southern army in particular, religious fervor was high. During the previous winter, while Lee's troops were encamped on the Rapidan, revivals had swept nearly every soldier into the church. General Gordon says that "not only on the Sabbath day, but during the week, night after night, for long periods these services continued, increasing in attendance and interest until they brought under religious influence the

WHERE PRAYER ROSE FOR THE WANING CAUSE

WHERE PRISONERS PRAYED FOR LIBERTY

great body of the army. Along the mountainsides and in the forest, where the Southern camps were pitched, the rocks and woods rang with appeals for holiness and consecration, with praises for past mercies and earnest prayers for future protection and deliverance. Thousands of these brave followers of Southern banners became consistent and devoted soldiers of the Cross." And the same officer recalls that during the siege of Petersburg, especially after the attack on Fort Stedman, religious devotion was uncooled. "From the commander-in-chief to the privates in the ranks, there was a deep and sincere religious feeling in Lee's army. Whenever it was convenient or practicable, these hungry but unyielding men were holding prayer-meetings. Their supplications were fervent and often inspiring."

On the memorable 2d of April, in the Richmond church in which he had been baptized and confirmed scarcely three years before, President Jefferson Davis received the ominous tidings sent by Lee to the capital of the Confederacy that both Petersburg and Richmond would have to be evacuated before the morning of April 4th. There followed a night of terror.

destroyed, Richmond would be completely cut off. On the morning of the 29th, as previously arranged, the movement began. Sheridan swept to the south with his cavalry, as if he were to fall upon the railroads. General Warren, with fifteen thousand men, was working his way through the tangled woods and low swamps in the direction of Lee's right. At the same time, Lee stripped his entrenchments at Petersburg as much as he dared and hurried General Anderson, with infantry, and Fitzhugh Lee, with cavalry, forward to hold the roads over which he hoped to escape. On Friday morning, March 31st, the opposing forces, the Confederates much reenforced, found themselves at Dinwiddie Court House. The woods and swamps prevented the formation of a regular line of battle. Lee made his accustomed flank movement, with heavy loss to the Federals as they tried to move in the swampy forests. The Northerners finally were ready to advance when it was found that Lee had fallen back. During the day and night, reenforcements were coming in from all sides. The Confederates had taken their position at Five Forks.

Early the next afternoon, the 1st of April, Sheridan, reenforced by Warren, was arranging his troops for battle. The day was nearly spent when all was in readiness. The sun was not more than two hours high when the Northern army moved toward that of the South, defended by a breastwork behind a dense undergrowth of pines. Through this mass of timber the Federals crept with bayonets fixed. They charged upon the Confederates, but, at the same time, a galling fire poured into them from the left, spreading dismay and destruction in their midst. The intrepid Sheridan urged his black battle-charger, the famous Rienzi, now known as Winchester, up and down the lines, cheering his men on in the fight. He seemed to be everywhere at once. The Confederate left was streaming down the White Oak Road. But General Crawford had reached a cross-road, by taking a circuitous route, and the Southern army was thus shut off from retreat. The Federal

 [Concluded on page 294]

To this gallant young Georgia officer, just turned thirty-three at the time, Lee entrusted the last desperate effort to break through the tightening Federal lines, March 25, 1865. Lee was confronted by the dilemma of either being starved out of Petersburg and Richmond, or of getting out himself and uniting his army to that of Johnston in North Carolina, to crush Sherman before Grant could reach him. Gordon was to begin this latter, almost impossible, task by an attack on Fort Stedman, which the Confederates believed to be the weakest point in the Federal fortifications. The position had been captured from them in the beginning, and they knew that the nature of the ground and its nearness to their own lines had made it difficult to strengthen it very much. It was planned to surprise the fort before daylight. Below are seen the rabbit-like burrows of Gracie's Salient, past which Gordon led his famished men. When the order came to go forward, they did not flinch, but hurled them-

GENERAL JOHN B. GORDON,
C. S. A.

Stedman. They were to be followed by a division. Through the gap which the storming parties were expected to open in the Federal lines, Gordon's columns would rush in both directions and a cavalry force was to sweep on and destroy the pontoon bridges across the Appomattox and to raid City Point, breaking up the Federal base. It was no light task, for although Fort Stedman itself was weak, it was flanked by Battery No. 10 on the right and by Battery No. 11 on the left. An attacking party on the right would be exposed to an enfilading fire in crossing the plain; while on the left the approach was difficult because of ravines, one of which the Confederate engineers had turned into a pond by damming a creek. All night long General Gordon's wife, with the brave women of Petersburg, sat up tearing strips of white cloth, to be tied on the arms of the men in the storming parties so that they could tell friend from foe in the darkness and confusion of the assault. Before the sleep-dazed

selves bravely against fortifications far stronger than their own. Three columns of a hundred picked men each moved down the slope shown on the left and advanced in the darkness against Federals could offer effective resistance, Gordon's men had possession of the fort and the batteries. Only after one of the severest engagements of the siege were the Confederates driven back.

GRACIE'S SALIENT—AFTER GORDON'S FORLORN HOPE HAD CHARGED

PRISONERS TO PHIL SHERIDAN

This group of the five thousand Confederate prisoners captured March 31st is eloquent of the tragedy in progress. Dire was the extremity of the Confederate cause in March, 1865. The words of the gallant leader in the last desperate and forlorn hope that charged Fort Stedman, General Gordon, give a pen-picture of the condition of the Southern fighting men: "Starvation, literal starvation, was doing its deadly work. So depleted and poisoned was the blood of many of Lee's men from insufficient and unsound food that a slight wound, which would probably not have been reported at the beginning of the war, would often cause blood-poison, gangrene and death, yet the spirits of these brave men seemed to rise as their condition grew more desperate." But not only was it physical ailments and consequent inability to fight their best which brought about the downfall, it was numbers, the overwhelming numbers that were opposed against them. In an interview with General Gordon, Lee laid before him his reports, which showed how completely he understood the situation. Of his own fifty thousand men but thirty-five thousand were fit for duty. Lee's estimate

FULL RATIONS AT LAST

of the forces of Grant was between one hundred and forty thousand and one hundred and fifty thousand. Coming up from Knoxville was Schofield with an estimated force of thirty thousand superb troops. From the valley Grant was bringing up nearly twenty thousand more, against whom, as Lee expressed it, he "could oppose scarcely a vidette." Sherman was approaching from North Carolina, and his force when united with Scofield's would reach eighty thousand. It was impossible, and yet it was after this, that Gordon made his charge. South of Hatcher's Run, at the very westernmost part of the Confederate entrenchments, Sheridan fell upon the Confederate flank. It was a complete victory. With General Merritt and General Griffin sweeping in, the cavalry charged the works and five thousand Confederates were taken prisoners, besides those killed and wounded. The Federal loss was less than seven hundred. This was the last day of March. Lined up here we see some of these captured thousands about to receive their first square meal in many months,

APRIL SECOND—WHERE LEE WATCHED

From this mound General Lee watched the final Federal attack begin near Hatcher's Run on the morning of April 2, 1865. It was a serious party of officers that gathered in this battery on the inner line of Confederate fortifications before Petersburg. On the preceding days at Hatcher's Run, and again at Five Forks, Lee had attempted to break through the besiegers, but the efforts were futile, and no sooner had they ceased than the Federal army began to gather itself for the last grapple. All night of April 1st, till four in the morning, the Federal artillery had kept up a terrific bombardment along the whole line, and at daybreak Lee saw the Sixth Corps advancing to the assault. As they broke through the Confederate lines and wheeled to attack Fort Gregg, Lee called his staff about him, telling them to witness a most gallant defense. A moment later they saw the Stars and Stripes unfurled over the parapet. The depleted and worn-out Confederates had spent themselves to the last gasp. Not even Lee's veterans could fight starvation and overwhelming numbers at once. "This is a sad business!" were Lee's words as he turned to his staff. Couriers were bringing in reports of disasters all along his lines, and he gave the orders necessary for the holding of such of the interior defenses as would enable the Army of Northern Virginia to abandon Petersburg and Richmond.

APRIL SECOND—"THIS IS A SAD BUSINESS"

As his general watched, this boy fought to stem the Federal rush—but fell, his breast pierced by a bayonet, in the trenches of Fort Mahone. It is heart-rending to look at a picture such as this; it is sad to think of it and to write about it. Here is a boy of only fourteen years, his face innocent of a razor, his feet unshod and stockingless in the bitter April weather. It is to be hoped that the man who slew him has forgotten it, for this face would haunt him surely. Many who fought in the blue ranks were young, but in the South there were whole companies made up of such boys as this. At the battle of Newmarket the scholars of the Virginia Military Institute, the eldest seventeen and the youngest twelve, marched from the classrooms under arms, joined the forces of General Breckinridge, and aided by their historic charge to gain a brilliant victory over the Federal General Sigel. The never-give-in spirit was implanted in the youth of the Confederacy, as well as in the hearts of the grizzled veterans. Lee had inspired them, but in addition to this inspiration, as General Gordon writes, "every man of them was supported by their extraordinary consecration, resulting from the conviction that he was fighting in the defense of home and the rights of his State. Hence their unfaltering faith in the justice of the cause, their fortitude in the extremest privations, their readiness to stand shoeless and shivering in the trenches at night and to face any danger at their leader's call."

AT FORT MAHONE—THE FIRST TO MEET THE ONSLAUGHT

The tall young Southerner stretched here was outside the walls of Fort Mahone, and with scores of comrades met the first shock when the onsweep of the massed lines in blue came roaring down like a torrent upon the outer works. His musket, with the ramrod out, lies beside him, showing that he has even stayed to load; the ground is strewn with cartridges frantically torn open; his hands are grasped tightly over the gaping wound through his body; he will be laid away to rest on the very spot he has so splendidly defended.

"YOU WILL SEE
A BRAVE
DEFENSE"

THREE SOLDIERS
WHO BORE OUT
LEE'S PROPHECY

bayonet and clubbed musket did bloody work here; men rolled and grappled with each other in the half darkness of the early dawn, rising to their knees to fight again. It was relentless, terrible, and from the romantic point of view magnificent. Yet as we look at these poor heaps of clay, the magnificence has vanished; horror and sorrow are the sensations that are aroused. Dead "Reb" or fallen "Yank," these men who fell, though their voices are stilled, cry from their gory beds that such things may come to pass no more—their faces and forms, twisted as they fell, speak more eloquently than any words could, for peace.

When Lee, looking toward Fort Gregg as the Federals attacked on April 2d, said, "You will see a brave defense," he spoke from intimate knowledge of his men. But even if they had been twice the number, they could not have done more than they did. If they had had three lives apiece they might have laid them down no more bravely nor uselessly. God was on the side of the bigger army. But in the outflanking trenches filled with mud, in the corners of the abatis, in the angles of the walls, and in the very last ditch, groups of men in gray fought with the desperation almost of wild animals with retreat cut off. The

FRESH AMMUNITION IN THE PATH OF THE CHARGE

A veritable battle-photograph, in the fresh path of the charge within the Confederate works that had so long held the Federals back. This picture was taken very shortly after the rattle of their muskets had rung the knell of Petersburg. Beyond the parapet are the Federal lines and the intervening plain over which the men came at the double-quick that morning. Some regiment has halted here to replenish its ammunition. Boxes of cartridges have been hurried up and impatiently broken open. There was no time for the eager men to fill pouches and belts. Grabbing handfuls of the cartridges, they have thrust them into their pockets or the breasts of their jackets. Then, leaving many of the boxes but half emptied, they pressed on, loading as they ran. The picture is an eloquent bit of still life; even the belts and cartridge-pouches cast away in impatience tell of the hurry and heat of battle.

It was the grand old Sixth Corps that crowned its splendid record on April 2d in the last great charge of the war upon an entrenched position. Silently the troops had been brought out on the night of the 1st and placed in position just in the rear of their own picket line. The darkness hid the intended movement even from the watchful eyes of the Confederate pickets. Orders for the strictest silence had been imposed upon each man. But suddenly the pickets broke out firing, and it was only with great exertions that the officers quieted the Federal outposts. The men in the columns had maintained their positions without a sound—not a shot fired, not a word uttered. At half-past four in the early morning a signal gun from Fort Fisher boomed and flashed through the early light. Rushing forward, breaking the Confederate line of outposts, down streamed the blue masses upon the main line of the defenses. Into their faces the men in gray poured deadly volleys from behind the earthworks and lines of spiked abatis. The latter were rolled aside, carried by main force and tossed into the ditches. General Wright, in command of this

ABATIS AND DEFENDER IN THE DITCH

AFTER THE LAST GREAT CHARGE

body of men, knew from the shouts even before he saw the flag upon the breastworks that the wedge had been driven home. Leaving behind their own dead and wounded lying mingled with the bodies of the brave defenders, without waiting for orders, men from each division of the Sixth Corps pressed ahead, broke up the South Side Railroad and cut the telegraph wires. When the officers had at length calmed the ardor of their troops and re-formed the lines, a large part of the corps wheeled to the left and dashed along the Confederate entrenchments, soon overcame all resistance and swept victoriously forward as far as Hatcher's Run, capturing artillery and a large number of prisoners. There they were again re-formed, marched back to the original point of attack, and thence pushed forward in conjunction with the Twenty-fourth Corps to complete the investment of Petersburg. In this advance some Confederate batteries, very dashingly handled, inflicted considerable loss until they were driven behind the inner lines of entrenchment, when the Union troops were halted with their left resting on the Appomattox. Petersburg had fallen. The end was only a week away.

cavalry had dismounted and was doing its full share of work. The Confederates soon found themselves trapped, and the part of their army in action that day was nearly annihilated. About five thousand prisoners were taken.

With night came the news of the crushing blow to Lee. General Grant was seated by his camp-fire surrounded by his staff, when a courier dashed into his presence with the message of victory. Soon from every great gun along the Union line belched forth the sheets of flame. The earth shook with the awful cannonade. Mortar shells made huge parabolas through the air. The Union batteries crept closer and closer to the Confederate lines and the balls crashed into the streets of the doomed city. The bombardment of Petersburg was on.

At dawn of the 2nd of April the grand assault began. The Federal troops sprang forward with a rush. Despite the storms of grape and canister, the Sixth Corps plunged through the battery smoke, and across the walls, pushing the brave defenders to the inner works. The whole corps penetrated the lines and swept everything before it toward Hatcher's Run. Some of the troops even reached the South Side Railroad, where the brave General A. P. Hill fell mortally wounded.

Everywhere, the blue masses poured into the works. General Ord, on the right of the Sixth Corps, helped to shut the Confederate right into the city. General Parke, with the Ninth Corps, carried the main line. The thin gray line could no longer stem the tide that was engulfing it. The Confederate troops south of Hatcher's Run fled to the west, and fought General Miles until General Sheridan and a division from Meade appeared on the scene. By noon the Federals held the line of the outer works from Fort Gregg to the Appomattox. The last stronghold carried was Fort Gregg, at which the men of Gibbon's corps had one of the most desperate struggles of the war. The Confederates now fell back to the inner fortifications and the siege of Petersburg came to an end.

PART IV
FROM WAR TO PEACE

———

APPOMATTOX

———

IN THE WAKE OF LEE'S RETREAT

THE RUINS OF RAILROAD

BRIDGE AT PETERSBURG

APRIL, 1865

The scene that met the eyes of the Union cavalry on April 3d. The ashes of a bridge, locomotive, train and all, as they had fallen the day before on the gravelly shore of the Appotomax. When the lines southeast and west of the city were captured on April 2d, Lee had seen that retreat was the only resource left. His haggard but undaunted veterans began this final movement at eight o'clock in the evening, passing to the north side of the Appomattox by the pontoon, Pocahontas and "railroad" bridges. These were given to the flames immediately after crossing, in order to hinder the pursuit. Though there were in the fields of Mississippi and Alabama supplies enough to feed Lee's army for a whole year, the means of transportation was so poor that all through the winter they had suffered from hunger. Now the only avenue of supply that had remained in their control was seized by the Union armies. The possibility of joining with Johnston's forces, or of making a last stand where the pursuer should put himself at a disadvantage, was the hope which sustained the famished heroes in gray as they left behind them the burning bridge.

THE CAPITAL OF THE CONFEDERACY FALLEN

The ruins of the armory in the foreground, the pillars of the Petersburg and Richmond Railroad bridge across the James, a few houses in Manchester beyond the stream—this picture of desolation revives the scenes of wild commotion in Richmond on the 2d and 3d of April, 1865. On the 2d, a quiet Sunday, Jefferson Davis, at morning service in St. Paul's Church, received a despatch from General Lee, announcing the imminent fall of Petersburg and the necessity of retreating that night. Mr. Davis left his seat calmly; but by half-past eleven a strange agitation began to appear in the streets, and by noon the worst was known. A hubbub of excitement, the rumbling of trains and rattling of wagons filled the afternoon. By sunset bands of ruffians made their appearance on the prin-

THE DESERT AND THE WASTE PLACES IN RICHMOND, APRIL, 1865

cipal streets.   That night was full of the pandemonium of flight.   Orders for the burning of the arsenals and all public buildings were issued before the officers of government left the city.   To prevent drunkenness the alcoholic liquor was emptied into the gutters.   The explosion of the magazines threw high into the air burning fragments which fell upon the adjacent buildings in Richmond and even across the river in Manchester.   The hundreds of blazing piles lighted up the river with the brightness of day as it rushed sparkling beneath the high-arched bridges past the flaming cities.   At early dawn, amid the roar of the explosions and of the falling buildings, the clatter of Union cavalry was heard in the streets.   The capital of the Confederacy had fallen.

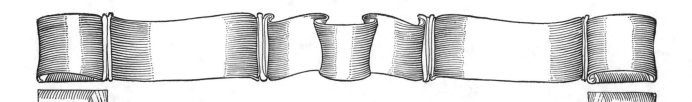

APPOMATTOX

I now come to what I have always regarded—shall ever regard—as the most creditable episode in all American history—an episode without a blemish, imposing, dignified, simple, heroic. I refer to Appomattox. Two men met that day, representative of American civilization, the whole world looking on. The two were Grant and Lee—types each. Both rose, and rose unconsciously, to the full height of the occasion—and than that occasion there has been none greater. About it, and them, there was no theatrical display, no self-consciousness, no effort at effect. A great crisis was to be met; and they met that crisis as great countrymen should. Consider the possibilities; think for a moment of what that day might have been; you will then see cause to thank God for much.—*General Charles Francis Adams, U.S.V., in Phi Beta Kappa Address delivered at the University of Chicago, June 17, 1902.*

WE are now to witness the closing scene of one of the greatest tragedies ever enacted on the world's stage. Many and varied had been the scenes during the war; the actors and their parts had been real. The wounds of the South were bleeding; the North was awaiting the decisive blow. Thousands of homes were ruined. Fortunes, great and small, had melted away by the hundreds of millions. In Richmond, the citadel of the waning Confederacy, the people were starving. The Southern army, half clad and without food, was but a shadow of its once proud self. Bravely and long the men in gray had followed their adored leader. Now the limit of endurance had been reached.

It was the second day of April, 1865. Lee realized that after Petersburg his beloved Richmond must fall. The order was given for the movement to begin at eight o'clock that night. The darkness of the early morning of the 3d was suddenly transformed into a lurid light overcasting the heavens

TWELVE HOURS AFTER, AT THE PETERSBURG COURTHOUSE

The night of April 2d was a tense one for the Federal troops in the trenches. The brigade of Colonel Ralph Ely was to charge at four o'clock in the morning, but at half-past two he learned that only the Confederate picket-lines remained. His command was formed for attack and advanced quickly across the opposing works. It then re-formed and pushed into the town, arriving at the courthouse shortly after four o'clock. At 4.28 A.M. the flag of the First Michigan Sharpshooters was floating from the staff. Major Lounsberry, in command of the detachment, was met in front of the courthouse by three citizens with a flag of truce, who surrendered the town in the name of the mayor and common council. The committee were assured of the safety of private property, and, according to the report of the mayor, so long as the brigade was in the city "the conduct of both officers and men was such as to reflect [honor] on our cause and cast a luster of glory over the profession of arms." This is one of the series of photographs taken April 3d by the enterprising artist with the Federal army; and the clock-face in the courthouse tower shows that the picture was made at ten minutes of four that afternoon.

for miles around the famous city whose name had become a household word over the civilized world. Richmond was in flames! The capital of the Confederacy, the pride of the South, toward which the Army of the Potomac had fought its way, leaving a trail of blood for four weary years, had at last succumbed to the overwhelming power of Grant's indomitable armies.

President Davis had received a despatch while attending services at St. Paul's church, Sunday morning, the 2d, advising him that the city must be evacuated that night, and, leaving the church at once, he hastened the preparations for flight with his personal papers and the archives of the Confederate Government. During that Sabbath day and night Richmond was in a state of riot. There had been an unwarranted feeling of security in the city, and the unwelcome news, spreading like an electric flash, was paralyzing and disastrous in its effect. Prisoners were released from their toils, a lawless mob overran the thoroughfares, and civic government was nullified. One explosion after another, on the morning of the 3d, rent the air with deafening roar, as the magazines took fire. The scene was one of terror and grandeur.

The flames spread to the city from the ships, bridges, and arsenal, which had been set on fire, and hundreds of buildings, including the best residential section of the capital of the Confederacy, were destroyed.

When the Union army entered the city in the morning, thousands of the inhabitants, men, women, and children, were gathered at street corners and in the parks. in wildest confusion. The commissary depot had been broken open by the starving mob, and rifled of its contents, until the place was reached by the spreading flames. The Federal soldiers stacked arms, and heroically battled with the fire, drafting into the work all able-bodied men found in the city. The invaders extinguished the flames, and soon restored the city to a state of order and safety. The invalid wife of General Lee, who was

IN PETERSBURG—AFTER NINE MONTHS OF BATTERING

This fine mansion on Bolingbroke Street, the residential section of Petersburg, has now, on the 3d of April, fallen into the hands of straggling Union soldiers. Its windows have long since been shattered by shells from distant Federal mortars; one has even burst through the wall. But it was not till the night of April 2d, when the retreat of the Confederate forces started, that the citizens began to leave their homes. At 9 o'clock in the morning General Grant, surrounded by his staff, rode quietly into the city. The streets were deserted. At length they arrived at a comfortable home standing back in a yard. There he dismounted and sat for a while on the piazza. Soon a group of curious citizens gathered on the sidewalk to gaze at the commander of the Yankee armies. But the Union troops did not remain long in the deserted homes. Sheridan was already in pursuit south of the Appomattox, and Grant, after a short conference with Lincoln, rode to the west in the rear of the hastily marching troops. Bolingbroke Street and Petersburg soon returned to the ordinary occupations of peace in an effort to repair the ravages of the historic nine months' siege.

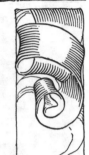

exposed to danger, was furnished with an ambulance and corporal's guard until the danger was past.

President Lincoln, who had visited Grant at Petersburg, entered Richmond on the 4th of April. He visited President Davis' house, and Libby Prison, then deserted, and held a conference with prominent citizens and army officers of the Confederacy. The President seemed deeply concerned and weighted down with the realization of the great responsibilities that would fall upon him after the war. Only ten days later the nation was shaken from ocean to ocean by the tragic news of his assassination.

General Lee had started on his last march by eight o'clock on the night of the 2d. By midnight the evacuation of both Petersburg and Richmond was completed. For nine months the invincible forces of Lee had kept a foe of more than twice their numerical strength from invading their stronghold, and only after a long and harassing siege were they forced to retreat. They saw the burning city as their line of march was illuminated by the conflagration, and emotions too deep for words overcame them. The woods and fields, in their fresh, bright colors of spring, were in sharp contrast to the travel-worn, weather-beaten, ragged veterans passing over the verdant plain. Lee hastened the march of his troops to Amelia Court House, where he had ordered supplies, but by mistake the train of supplies had been sent on to Richmond. This was a crushing blow to the hungry men, who had been stimulated on their tiresome march by the anticipation of much-needed food. The fatality of war was now hovering over them like a huge black specter.

General Grant did not proceed to Richmond, but leaving General Weitzel to invest the city, he hastened in pursuit of Lee to intercept the retreating army. This pursuit was started early on the 3d. On the evening of that date there was some firing between the pursuing army and Lee's rear guard. It was Lee's design to concentrate his force at Amelia Court

SUPPORTING THE PURSUIT OF LEE'S ARMY

A Federal wagon-train moves out of Petersburg to feed the troops pursuing Lee, in those early April days of '65. The Army of Northern Virginia has taken no supply trains on its hurried departure from Petersburg and Richmond. It depends on forage. Within the next week Grant's troops are to be brought almost to a like pass. If the surrender had not come when it did, the pursuit would have been brought to a stop for the time being by lack of subsistence. The South Side Railroad, which crossed Indian Town Creek on the trestle shown in the smaller picture, was the only railroad line in the possession of the Confederates at the end of the siege of Petersburg. It was their only avenue of supplies, but Sheridan's victory at Five Forks made it possible to cut the line. Lee was thus compelled to evacuate both Richmond and Petersburg. The bridge is to the west of Petersburg on the main line of the railroad.

THE LAST RAILROAD INTO PETERSBURG

House, but this was not to be accomplished by the night of the 4th. Not until the 5th was the whole army up, and then it was discovered that no adequate supplies were within less than fifty miles. Subsistence could be obtained only by foraging parties. No word of complaint from the suffering men reached their commander, and on the evening of that disappointing day they patiently and silently began the sad march anew. Their course was through unfavorable territory and necessarily slow. The Federals were gaining upon their retreating columns. Sheridan's cavalry had reached their flank, and on the 6th there was heavy skirmishing. In the afternoon the Federals had arrived in force sufficient to bring on an engagement with Ewell's corps in the rear, at Sailor's Creek, a tributary of the Appomattox River. Ewell was surrounded by the Federals and the entire corps captured. General Anderson, commanding the divisions of Pickett and Johnson, was attacked and fought bravely, losing many men. In all about six thousand Confederate soldiers were left in the hands of the pursuing army.

On the night of the 6th, the remainder of the Confederate army continued the retreat and arrived at Farmville, where the men received two days' rations, the first food except raw or parched corn that had been given them for two days. Again the tedious journey was resumed, in the hope of breaking through the rapidly-enmeshing net and forming a junction with Johnston at Danville, or of gaining the protected region of the mountains near Lynchburg. But the progress of the weak and weary marchers was slow and the Federal cavalry had swept around to Lee's front, and a halt was necessary to check the pursuing Federals. On the evening of the 8th, Lee reached Appomattox Court House. Here ended the last march of the Army of Northern Virginia.

General Lee and his officers held a council of war on the night of the 8th and it was decided to make an effort to cut their way through the Union lines on the morning of the next day. On the 7th while at Farmville, on the south side of the

WAITING TO PRESS THE ADVANTAGE

This is a scene near the railroad station on April 3, 1865. Muskets of the Federal troops are stacked in the foreground. Evidences of the long bombardment appear in the picture. The foot-bridge shown in the smaller picture is at the point where the old river road crossed the run west of Old Town Creek. In the distance can be seen the trestle of the South Side Railroad. This bridge shook under the hurrying feet of Meade's heavy advancing column, as the pursuit of Lee was pressed.

ON THE LINE OF PURSUIT

Appomattox River, Grant sent to Lee a courteous request for the surrender of the Army of Northern Virginia, based on the hopelessness of further resistance on the part of that army. In reply, Lee expressed sympathy with Grant's desire to avoid useless effusion of blood and asked the terms of surrender.

The next morning General Grant replied to Lee, urging that a meeting be designated by Lee, and specifying the terms of surrender, to which Lee replied promptly, rejecting those terms, which were, that the Confederates lay down their arms, and the men and officers be disqualified for taking up arms against the Government of the United States until properly exchanged. When Grant read Lee's letter he shook his head in disappointment and said, " It looks as if Lee still means to fight; I will reply in the morning."

On the 9th Grant addressed another communication to Lee, repeating the terms of surrender, and closed by saying, " The terms upon which peace can be had are well understood. By the South laying down their arms they will hasten that most desirable event, save thousands of human lives, and hundreds of millions of property not yet destroyed. Sincerely hoping that all our difficulties may be settled without the loss of another life, I subscribe myself, etc."

There remained for Lee the bare possibility, by desperate fighting, of breaking through the Federal lines in his rear. To Gordon's corps was assigned the task of advancing on Sheridan's strongly supported front. Since Pickett's charge at Gettysburg there had been no more hopeless movement in the annals of the war. It was not merely that Gordon was overwhelmingly outnumbered by the opposing forces, but his hunger-enfeebled soldiers, even if successful in the first onslaught, could count on no effective support, for Longstreet's corps was in even worse condition than his own. Nevertheless, on the morning of Sunday, the 9th, the attempt was made. Gordon was fighting his corps, as he said, " to a frazzle," when Lee came at last to a realizing sense of the futility of it all and

THE FRESHET THAT DELAYED GRANT'S PURSUIT

The roads leading west from Petersburg crossed and recrossed the Appomattox and its tributaries. The spring floods impeded, though they did not actually check, Grant's impetuous pursuit of Lee. By the time Lee had reached Amelia Court House (April 5th), Grant's van was at Jetersville. Lee halted to bring up provisions; as he said in his official report, the ensuing delay proved fatal to his plans. The provisions that he expected to find at Amelia Court House were captured by the Federals.

THE FLOODED APPOMATTOX

ordered a truce. A meeting with Grant was soon arranged on the basis of the letters already exchanged. The conference of the two world-famous commanders took place at Appomattox, a small settlement with only one street, but to be made historic by this meeting. Lee was awaiting Grant's arrival at the house of Wilmer McLean. It was here, surrounded by staff-officers, that the terms were written by Grant for the final surrender of the Army of Northern Virginia. The terms, and their acceptance, were embodied in the following letters, written and signed in the famous " brick house " on that memorable Sunday:

APPOMATTOX COURT HOUSE, VIRGINIA,
APRIL 9, 1865.

GENERAL: In accordance with the substance of my letter to you of the 8th instant, I propose to receive the surrender of the Army of Northern Virginia on the following terms, to wit: Rolls of all the officers and men to be made in duplicate, one copy to be given to an officer to be designated by me, the other to be retained by such officer or officers as you may designate. The officers to give their individual paroles not to take up arms against the Government of the United States until properly exchanged; and each company or regimental commander to sign a like parole for the men of their commands. The arms, artillery, and public property to be parked and stacked, and turned over to the officers appointed by me to receive them. This will not embrace the side-arms of the officers, nor their private horses or baggage. This done, each officer and man will be allowed to return to his home, not to be disturbed by the United States authority so long as they observe their paroles and the laws in force where they may reside.

U. S. GRANT, *Lieutenant-General.*

General R. E. Lee.

HEADQUARTERS ARMY OF NORTHERN VIRGINIA,
APRIL 9, 1865.

GENERAL: I have received your letter of this date containing the terms of the surrender of the Army of Northern Virginia as proposed by you. As they are substantially the same as those expressed in your

THE LANDMARK OF THE CONFEDERATES' LAST STAND

The Union army, after the fall of Petersburg, followed the streaming Confederates, retreating westward, and came upon a part of Gordon's troops near High Bridge over the Appomattox, where the South Side Railroad crosses the river on piers 60 feet high. Hancock's (Second) Corps arrived on the south bank just after the Confederates had blown up the redoubt that formed the bridge head, and set fire to the bridge itself. The bridge was saved with the loss of four spans at the north end, by Colonel Livermore, whose party put out the fire while Confederate skirmishers were fighting under their feet. A wagon bridge beside it was saved by the men of Barlow's division. Mahone's division of the Confederate army was drawn up on a hill, north of the river behind redoubts, but when Union troops appeared in force the Confederates again retreated westward along the river.

HIGH BRIDGE

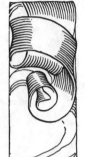

letter of the 8th instant, they are accepted. I will proceed to designate the proper officers to carry the stipulation into effect.

R. E. LEE, *General.*

Lieutenant-General U. S. Grant.

When Federal officers were seen galloping toward the Union lines from Appomattox Court House it was quickly surmised that Lee had surrendered. Cheer after cheer was sent up by the long lines throughout their entire length; caps and tattered colors were waved in the air. Officers and men alike joined in the enthusiastic outburst. It was glad tidings, indeed, to these men, who had fought and hoped and suffered through the long bloody years.

When Grant returned to his headquarters and heard salutes being fired he ordered it stopped at once, saying, " The war is over; the rebels are our countrymen again; and the best sign of rejoicing after the victory will be to abstain from all demonstration in the field."

Details of the surrender were arranged on the next day by staff-officers of the respective armies. The parole officers were instructed by General Grant to permit the Confederate soldiers to retain their own horses—a concession that was most welcome to many of the men, who had with them animals brought from the home farm early in the war.

There were only twenty-eight thousand men to be paroled, and of these fewer than one-third were actually bearing arms on the day of the surrender. The Confederate losses of the last ten days of fighting probably exceeded ten thousand.

The Confederate supplies had been captured by Sheridan, and Lee's army was almost at the point of starvation. An order from Grant caused the rations of the Federal soldiers to be shared with the " Johnnies," and the victorious " Yanks " were only too glad to tender such hospitality as was within their power. These acts of kindness were slight in themselves, but they helped immeasurably to restore good feeling and to

APPOMATTOX STATION—LEE'S LAST ATTEMPT TO PROVISION HIS RETREATING ARMY

At this railroad point, three miles from the Court House, a Confederate provision train arrived on the morning of April 8th. The supplies were being loaded into wagons and ambulances by a detail of about four thousand men, many of them unarmed, when suddenly a body of Federal cavalry charged upon them, having reached the spot by a by-road leading from the Red House. After a few shots the Confederates fled in confusion. The cavalry drove them on in the direction of Appomattox Court House, capturing many prisoners, twenty-five pieces of artillery, a hospital train, and a large park of wagons. This was Lee's last effort to obtain food for his army.

FEDERAL SOLDIERS WHO PERFORMED ONE OF THE LAST DUTIES AT APPOMATTOX

A detail of the Twenty-sixth Michigan handed out paroles to the surrendered Confederates.

McLEAN'S RESIDENCE AT THE BEGINNING OF THE WAR—BEAUREGARD'S HEADQUARTERS AT BULL RUN

THE HOMES

OF

WILMER McLEAN

By an extraordinary coincidence the two historic houses on this and the facing page belonged to the same man. In 1861, Wilmer McLean lived near Manassas Station, and his house was chosen by General Beauregard as headquarters. In the engagement of July 18th, preceding the great battle, a Federal cannon-ball landed in the fireplace and spoiled the general's dinner. During the famous battle of the following Sunday the household was subject to the constant alarms of a long-fought field. To avoid the scene of active military operations McLean removed to the village of Appomattox and spent nearly four years tranquilly enough. But he found himself once more the center of warlike activity. Only half a mile west of the town Grant's messenger had found Lee resting under an apple-tree. After read-

ing Grant's letter, he started with his military secretary for Appomattox Court House. In the village they met Wilmer Mc-Lean, who, after stopping for a moment at the first house they came to, conducted the party to his own home. It was Sunday, three years and nine months since that Sunday of Bull Run. At half-past one, April 9th, the negotiations took place to the left of the central doorway; during them General Lee sat by a small oval table near the window, half hidden by the pillar at the top of the step. For the table General Sheridan paid Mr. McLean twenty dollars in gold. The rest of the furniture used on that historic occasion was largely seized by others of those present. The house itself remained no longer in obscurity, but became one of the most famous land-marks in American history.

associate for all time with Appomattox the memory of reunion rather than of strife. The things that were done there can never be the cause of shame to any American. The noble and dignified bearing of the commanders was an example to their armies and to the world that quickly had its effect in the genuine reconciliation that followed.

The scene between Lee and his devoted army was profoundly touching. General Long in his "Memoirs of Lee" says: "It is impossible to describe the anguish of the troops when it was known that the surrender of the army was inevitable. Of all their trials, this was the greatest and hardest to endure." As Lee rode along the lines of the tried and faithful men who had been with him at the Wilderness, at Spotsylvania, and at Cold Harbor, it was not strange that those ragged, weather-beaten heroes were moved by deep emotion and that tears streamed down their bronzed and scarred faces. Their general in broken accents admonished them to go to their homes and be as brave citizens as they had been soldiers.

Thus ended the greatest civil war in history, for soon after the fall of the Confederate capital and the surrender of Lee's army, there followed in quick succession the surrender of all the remaining Southern forces.

While these stirring events were taking place in Virginia, Sherman, who had swept up through the Carolinas with the same dramatic brilliancy that marked his march to the sea, accomplishing most effective work against Johnston, was at Goldsboro. When Johnston learned of the fall of Richmond and Lee's surrender he knew the end had come and he soon arranged for the surrender of his army on the terms agreed upon at Appomattox. In the first week of May General "Dick" Taylor surrendered his command near Mobile, and on the 10th of the same month, President Jefferson Davis, who had been for nearly six weeks a fugitive, was overtaken and made a prisoner near Irwinsville, Georgia. The Southern Confederacy was a thing of the past.

PART V

ENGAGEMENTS OF
THE CIVIL WAR

MAY 1864—MAY 1865

THE END

RUINS OF THE RICHMOND ARSENAL,
APRIL 1865

ENGAGEMENTS OF THE CIVIL WAR

WITH LOSSES ON BOTH SIDES

MAY, 1864—JUNE, 1865

CHRONOLOGICAL summary and record of historical events, and of important engagements between the Union and the Confederate armies, in the Civil War in the United States, showing troops participating, losses and casualties, collated and compiled by George L. Kilmer from the official records of the Union and Confederate armies filed in the United States War Department. Minor engagements are omitted; also some concerning which statistics, especially Confederate, are not available.

MAY, 1864.

1 to 8.—Hudnot's Plantation, and near Alexandria, La. *Union,* Lee's Cav. Division of Gen. Banks' army; *Confed.,* Troops of Gen. Richard Taylor's command. Losses: *Union, 33* killed, 87 wounded; *Confed.,* 25 killed, 100 wounded.

4 to 21.—Yazoo City expedition, including Benton and Vaughan, Miss. *Union,* 11th, 72d, and 76th Ill., 5th Ill. Cav., 3d U. S. Colored Cav., 7th Ohio Battery; *Confed.,* Troops of Gen. Jos. E. Johnston's command. Losses: *Union, 5* killed, 20 wounded.

5 to 17.—Kautz's Cavalry Raid from Suffolk to City Point, Va. *Union,* 5th and 11th Pa. Cav., 3d N. Y. Cav., 1st D. C. Cav., 1 section 4th Wis. Battery; *Confed.,* Holcombe Legion, detachment 59th Va. and Home Guards. Losses: *Union,* 14 killed, 60 wounded, 27 missing; *Confed.,* 180 (about) wounded and captured.

5.—Roanoke River, N. C. *Union,* gunboats, *Ceres, Commodore Hull, Mattabesett, Sassacus, Seymour, Wyalusing, Miama,* and *Whitehead; Confed.,* iron-clad ram *Albemarle.* Losses: *Union, 5* killed, 26 wounded; *Confed.,* 57 captured.

—Dunn's Bayou, Red River, La. *Union,* 56th Ohio, gunboats *Signal, Covington,* and transport *Warner; Confed.,* Gen. Richard Taylor's command on shore.

Losses: *Union, 35* killed, 65 wounded, 150 missing; *Confed.**

5 to 7.—Wilderness, Va. *Union,* Forces commanded by Gen. U. S. Grant; Army of the Potomac, Maj.-Gen. George G. Meade; Second Corps, Maj.-Gen. Hancock; Fifth Corps, Maj.-Gen. Warren; Sixth Corps, Maj.-Gen. Sedgwick; Cavalry Corps, Maj.-Gen. Sheridan; and Ninth Corps, Maj.-Gen. Burnside. *Confed.,* Army of Northern Virginia, Gen. R. E. Lee; First Corps, Lieut.-Gen. Longstreet; Second Corps, Lieut.-Gen. Ewell; Third Corps, Lieut.-Gen. A. P. Hill; Cavalry Corps, Maj.-Gen. Stuart. Losses: *Union,* 2246 killed, 12,137 wounded, 3383 missing; *Confed.* (estimate) 2000 killed, 6000 wounded, 3400 missing; *Union,* Brig.-Gens. Wadsworth and Hays killed; *Confed.* Gens. Jones and Jenkins killed, and Stafford, Longstreet, and Pegram wounded.

5 to 9.—Rocky Face Ridge, Ga., including Tunnel Hill, Mill Creek Gap, and Buzzard's Roost. *Union,* Military Division of the Mississippi, commanded by Gen. W. T. Sherman: Army of the Cumberland, Maj.-Gen. Thomas; Army of the Tennessee, Maj.-Gen. McPherson; Army of the Ohio, Maj.-Gen. John M. Schofield, Elliott's and Stoneman's Cavalry; *Confed.,* Army of Tennessee, Gen. J. E. Johnston, commanding; Hardee's Corps, Hood's Corps, Wheeler's Cavalry.

* No record found.

[318]

FORT MORGAN FALLEN AFTER A STUBBORN DEFENSE

Among the decisive events of 1864 was the Union victory of Mobile Bay, August 23d. These smoke-blackened walls of the citadel, Fort Morgan, its shattered face, are silent witnesses to the stubborn nature of the defense, and the folds of the American flag in the distance proclaim the success of Farragut's attack. Gradually the Confederacy was being hemmed in and its resources exhausted. The bay fight itself took place on the morning of August 5th. The success of Admiral Farragut at New Orleans in the previous year had made him eager to close the remaining great gulf port to the blockade runners. After several months of effort he secured the necessary coöperation of a land force, and of four monitors to deal with the powerful Confederate ram *Tennessee*. The naval operations were entirely successful, but Fort Morgan had received hardly a scratch, and the commander sturdily refused to surrender. A constant bombardment of two weeks was necessary to reduce it, during which the woodwork caught fire and threatened to set off the great powder magazines. It was only when defense was obviously futile that General Page raised the white flag of surrender.

Engagements of the Civil War

Losses: *Union,* 200 killed, 637 wounded; *Confed.,* 600 killed and wounded.

6.—James River, near City Point, Va. *Union,* gunboat *Commodore Jones; Confed.,* Torpedo operators on shore. Losses: *Union,* 23 killed, 48 wounded and gunboat destroyed.

6 and 7.—Richmond and Petersburg Railroad, near Chester Station, Va. *Union,* Portion of Tenth and Eighteenth Corps; *Confed.,* Hagood's Brigade. Losses: *Union,* 48 killed, 256 wounded; *Confed.,* 50 killed, 200 wounded.

7.—Bayou La Mourie, La. *Union,* Portion of Sixteenth Corps; *Confed.,* Gen. Taylor's command. Losses: *Union,* 10 killed, 31 wounded.

8.—Todd's Tavern, Va. *Union,* Sheridan's Cav.; *Confed.,* Stuart's Cav. Losses: *Union,* 40 killed, 150 wounded; *Confed.,* 30 killed, 150 wounded.

8 to 18.—Spotsylvania, Fredericksburg Road, Laurel Hill, and Ny. River, Va. *Union,* Army of the Potomac, Maj.-Gen. Meade; *Confed.,* Army of Northern Virginia, Gen. R. E. Lee. Losses: *Union,* 2725 killed, 13,416 wounded, 2258 missing; *Confed.,* 1000 killed, 5000 wounded, 3000 missing; *Union,* Maj.-Gen. Sedgwick and Brig.-Gens. Rice and Stevenson killed; *Confed.* Gens. Daniel and Perrin killed; Maj.-Gen. Ed. Johnson and Brig.-Gen. Steuart captured.

9.—Varnell's Station, Ga. *Union,* First Div. McCook's Cav.; *Confed.,* Wheeler's Cav. Losses: *Union,* 4 killed, 25 wounded, 100 captured.

9 and 10.—Swift Creek or Arrowfield Church, Va. *Union,* Tenth and Eighteenth Corps, Army of the James; *Confed.,* Gen. Beauregard's command. Losses: *Union,* 90 killed, 400 wounded; *Confed.,* 500 killed, wounded, and missing.
—Cloyd's Mountain and New River Bridge, Va. *Union,* 12th, 23d, 34th, and 36th Ohio, 9th, 11th, 14th, and 15th W. Va., 3d and 4th Pa. Reserves; *Confed.,* Gen. A. G. Jenkins' command. Losses: Union, 108 killed, 508 wounded; *Confed.,* 600 killed and wounded, 300 missing.

9 to 25.—Sheridan's Cavalry Raid in Virginia, including engagements at Beaver Dam Station, South Anna Bridge, Ashland, and Yellow Tavern. *Union,* Sheridan's Cav.; *Confed.,* Stuart's Cav.

Losses: *Union,* 50 killed, 174 wounded, 200 missing; *Confed.,* killed and wounded not recorded, 100 captured; *Confed.,* Maj.-Gen. J. E. B. Stuart and Brig.-Gen. Jas. B. Gordon killed.

12 to 16.—Fort Darling, Drewry's Bluff, Va. *Union,* Army of the James, Gen. B. F. Butler, commanding; Tenth Corps; Eighteenth Corps; *Confed.,* Gen. Beauregard's command. Losses: *Union,* 390 killed, 2380 wounded, 1390 missing; *Confed.,* 400 killed, 2000 wounded, 100 missing.

12 to 17.—Kautz's Raid on Petersburg and Lynchburg Railroad, Va. *Union,* 6 killed, 28 wounded.

13 to 16.—Resaca, Ga. *Union,* Fourth, Fourteenth, Twentieth, and Cavalry Corps, Army of the Cumberland, Maj.-Gen. Thomas; Fifteenth and Sixteenth Corps, Army of the Tennessee, Maj.-Gen. McPherson, and Twenty-third Corps, Army of the Ohio, Maj.-Gen. Schofield; *Confed.,* Army of Tennessee, Gen. J. E. Johnston, commanding; Army of Mississippi, Lieut.-Gen. Leonidas Polk. Losses: *Union,* 600 killed, 2147 wounded; *Confed.,* 300 killed, 1500 wounded, 1000 missing.

15.—New Market, Va. *Union,* Maj.-Gen. Sigel's command; *Confed.,* Gen. J. C. Breckinridge's command. Losses: *Union,* 93 killed, 482 wounded, 256 missing; *Confed.,* 42 killed, 522 wounded.

18.—Rome and Kingston, Ga. *Union,* Second Division of Fourteenth Corps and Cavalry, Army of the Cumberland. *Confed.,* Gen. Johnston's command. Losses: *Union,* 16 killed, 59 wounded.
—Bayou De Glaize or Calhoun Station, La. *Union,* Portions of Sixteenth, Seventeenth Corps, and Cavalry of Nineteenth Corps; *Confed.,* Gen. Taylor's command. Losses: *Union,* 60 killed, 300 wounded; *Confed.,* 500 killed and wounded.

19 to 22.—Cassville, Ga. *Union,* Twentieth Corps, Maj.-Gen. Hooker; *Confed.,* Gen. Johnston's command. Losses: *Union,* 10 killed, 46 wounded.

20.—Bermuda Hundred, Va. *Union,* Tenth and Eighteenth Corps, Army of the James; *Confed.,* Gen. Beauregard's command. Losses: *Union,* 702 killed and wounded. *Confed.,* (estimate) 700 killed, wounded, and missing.

While the navy was perfecting the blockade along the coast, General Grant at Petersburg was trying to get across Lee's entrenchments. In the fall a partially successful attempt was made on the lines between Petersburg and Richmond. On the night of September 28th–29th, the Tenth Army Corps under General D. B. Birney, and the Eighteenth Army Corps under General Ord, crossed the James near this place, drove back the Confederate skirmishers, and by half-past seven in the morning advanced three miles north through the dense woods to Fort Harrison. Stannard's division then came upon open ground before a strong line of earthworks mounting

WHERE ORD CROSSED THE JAMES

heavy guns, and protected by a battery on the crest of a hill. The troops charged fourteen hundred yards across a deeply plowed field in the face of a galling fire of artillery and musketry. After a pause at the foot of a hill, the head of the column carried the parapet of the fort and planted the flag on one of its massive traverses. In an attempt to drive the Confederates entirely from the position General Ord was severely wounded. On September 30th the Confederate General R. H. Anderson, commanding Longstreet's Corps, attacked the captured fort, making three separate charges, but was repulsed with a loss of some two thousand men.

PALISADES AND PARAPET AT FORT HARRISON

Engagements of the Civil War

23 to 28.—North Anna River, Jericho Ford or Taylor's Bridge, and Totopotomoy Creek, Va. *Union,* Second, Fifth, and Ninth Corps, Army of the Potomac, Maj.-Gen. Meade; *Confed.,* Army of Northern Virginia, Gen. R. E. Lee. Losses: *Union,* 186 killed, 942 wounded, 165 missing; *Confed.,* 2000 killed and wounded.

24.—Wilson's Wharf, Va. *Union,* 10th U. S. Colored, 1st D. C. Cav., Battery B U. S. Colored Artil.; *Confed.,* Fitzhugh Lee's Cav. Losses: *Union,* 2 killed, 24 wounded; *Confed.,* 20 killed, 100 wounded.

25 to June 4.—Dallas, Ga., also called New Hope Church and Allatoona Hills. *Union,* Fourth, Fourteenth, Twentieth, and Cavalry Corps, Army of the Cumberland, Maj.-Gen. Thomas; Twenty-third Corps, Maj.-Gen. Schofield; Fifteenth, Sixteenth, and Seventeenth Corps, Army of the Tennessee, Maj.-Gen. McPherson—Division of the Mississippi, Maj.-Gen. Sherman; *Confed.,* Army of Tennessee, Gen. J. E. Johnston, commanding. Losses: *Union,* 2400 killed, wounded, and missing; *Confed.,* 369 killed, 1921 wounded.

26 to 29.—Decatur and Moulton, Ala. *Union,* 1st, 3d, and 4th Ohio Cav., Second Cavalry Division; *Confed.,* Roddey's Cav. Losses: *Union,* 48 killed and wounded; *Confed.,* 60 killed and wounded.

27 and 28.—Hanovertown, Hawes' Shop, and Salem Church, Va. First and Second Divisions, Cavalry Corps, Maj.-Gen. Sheridan; *Confed.,* detachments of Lee's Army. Losses: *Union,* 25 killed, 119 wounded, 200 missing; *Confed.,* 475 killed, wounded, and missing.

30.—Hanover and Ashland, Va. *Union,* Wilson's Cavalry; *Confed.,* Young's Cav. Losses: *Union,* 26 killed, 130 wounded. —Old Church, Va. *Union,* Torbert's Cavalry; *Confed.,* Cavalry of the Army of Northern Virginia. Losses: *Union,* 16 killed, 74 wounded.

JUNE, 1864.

1 to 12.—Cold Harbor, Va., including Gaines' Mill, Salem Church, and Hawes' Shop. *Union,* Second, Fifth, Sixth, Ninth, and Eighteenth Corps and Sheri-dan's Cavalry; *Confed.,* Army of Northern Virginia, reinforced by the fresh divisions of Breckinridge, Pickett, and Hoke. Losses: *Union,* 1844 killed, 9077 wounded, 1816 missing; *Confed.,* 1200 killed and wounded, 500 missing.

2.—Bermuda Hundred, Va. *Union,* Tenth Corps; *Confed.,* Gen. Beauregard's command. Losses: *Union,* 25 killed, 100 wounded; *Confed.,* 100 killed and wounded.

4.—Panther Gap, W. Va. *Union,* Hayes's Brigade of Second Division, Army of West Virginia; *Confed.,* Gen. Breckinridge's command. Losses: *Union,* 25 killed and wounded; *Confed.,* 25 killed and wounded.

5.—Piedmont, W. Va. *Union,* portion of Army of West Virginia, commanded by Maj.-Gen. Hunter; *Confed.,* Gen. Vaughn's Cav. Losses: *Union,* 130 killed, 650 wounded; *Confed.,* 460 killed, 1450 wounded, 1060 missing. *Confed.* Gen. W. E. Jones killed.

6.—Old River Lake or Lake Chicot, Ark. *Union,* Sixteenth Corps; *Confed.,* Marmaduke's Cav. Losses: *Union,* 40 killed, 70 wounded; *Confed.,* 100 killed and wounded.

9.—Mt. Sterling, Ky. *Union,* Burbridge's Cav; *Confed.,* Morgan's Cav. Losses: *Union,* 35 killed, 150 wounded; *Confed.,* 50 killed, 200 wounded, 250 captured.

9 to 30.—Kenesaw Mountain, Marietta or Big Shanty, Ga., including general assault on the 27th, Pine Mt., Golgotha, Culp's House, and Powder Springs. *Union,* Fourth, Fourteenth, and Twentieth Corps, Army of the Cumberland, Maj.-Gen. Thomas; Fifteenth, Sixteenth, and Seventeenth Corps, Army of the Tennessee, Maj. Gen. McPherson; Twenty-third Corps, Maj.-Gen. Schofield. Division of the Mississippi, Maj.-Gen. W. T. Sherman; *Confed.,* Army of Tennessee—Gen. J. E. Johnston, commanding. Losses: *Union,* 1370 killed, 6500 wounded, 800 missing; *Confed.,* 468 killed, 3480 wounded, missing not recorded. *Union,* Brig.-Gen. Harker killed and Col. D. McCook mortally wounded; *Confed.,* Lieut.-Gen. Polk killed.

10.—Petersburg, Va. *Union,* portion of Tenth Corps and Kautz's Cav.; *Confed.,* Gen. R. E. Colston's command. Losses: *Union,* 20 killed, 67 wounded.

THE OPPOSING

LINES

NEAR RICHMOND

This picture represents the main bomb-proof at Fort Brady. After the capture of Fort Harrison the Union authorities strengthened that position by constructing a line of fortifications southward to the James. Fort Brady was at the southern end, commanding the river. The bomb-proof was built of heavy cross timbers, covered with fifteen feet of solid earth, and its entrances were at such an angle as to be safe from any cross-fire. The lower

picture shows similar precautions of the Confederates. Though Fort Harrison was lost, Fort Gilmer, a little farther north, was held, and a line of entrenchments was strengthened from the rear of Harrison to the James. This particular picture shows a ditch twenty-seven feet deep dug to prevent the running of mines from the adjacent Federal lines. The man in shirt-sleeves standing in the ditch is General Peter S. Michie, acting Chief Engineer for the Union armies about Petersburg. He had directed the construction of Fort Brady, and is now, in April, 1865, investigating the Confederate engineering operations.

A WELL–PROTECTED MAGAZINE, FORT BRADY

THE 27–FOOT DITCH AT FORT GILMER, GUARD AGAINST FEDERAL MINES

Engagements of the Civil War

—Brice's Cross Roads, near Guntown, Miss. *Union*, 81st, 95th, 108th, 113th, 114th, and 120th Ill., 72d and 95th Ohio, 9th Minn., 93d Ind., 55th and 59th U. S. Colored, Brig.-Gen. Grierson's Cavalry, the 4th Mo., 2d N. J., 19th Pa., 7th and 9th Ill., 7th Ind., 3d and 4th Iowa, and 10th Kan. Cav., 1st Ill. and 6th Ind. Batteries, Battery F 2d U. S. Colored Artil; *Confed.*, Forrest's Cav. Losses: *Union*, 223 killed, 394 wounded, 1623 missing; *Confed.*, 96 killed, 396 wounded.

—Cynthiana and Kellar's Bridge, Ky. *Union*, 168th and 171st Ohio; *Confed.*, Morgan's Cav. Losses: *Union*, 21 killed, 71 wounded, 980 captured; *Confed.**

10 and 11.—Lexington, W. Va. *Union*, Second Division Army of West Virginia; *Confed.*, McCausland's Cav. Losses: *Union*, 6 killed, 18 wounded.

11 and 12.—Cynthiana, Ky. *Union*, Burbridge's Cav.; *Confed.*, Morgan's Cav. Losses: *Union*, 150 killed and wounded; *Confed.*, 300 killed and wounded, 400 captured.

—Trevilian Station, Va. *Union*, Sheridan's Cav.; *Confed.*, Gen. Wade Hampton's Cav. Losses: *Union*, 102 killed, 470 wounded, 435 missing; *Confed.* (incomplete) 59 killed, 258 wounded, 295 missing.

13.—White Oak Swamp Bridge, Va. *Union*, Wilson's and Crawford's Cav.; *Confed.*, detachments of the Army of Northern Virginia. Losses: *Union*, 50 killed, 250 wounded.

14.—Lexington, Mo. *Union*, Detachment 1st Mo. Cav. Losses: *Union*, 8 killed, 1 wounded.

15.—Samaria Church, Malvern Hill, Va. *Union*, Wilson's Cav.; *Confed.*, Hampton's Cav. Losses: *Union*, 25 killed, 3 wounded; *Confed.*, 100 killed and wounded.

15 to 19.—Petersburg, Va., commencement of the siege that continued to its fall (April 2, 1865). *Union*, Tenth and Eighteenth Corps, Army of the James, Maj.-Gen. B. F. Butler; Second, Fifth, Sixth, and Ninth Corps, Army of the Potomac, Maj.-Gen. Geo. G. Meade; *Confed.*, Gen. Beauregard's command, reenforced by two divisions of Lee's army on June 18th. Losses: *Union*, 1688 killed, 8513 wounded, 1185 missing; *Confed.* (estimate), 5000 killed, wounded, and missing.

16.—Otter Creek, near Liberty, Va. *Union*, Hunter's command in advance of the Army of West Virginia; *Confed.*, McCausland's Cav. Losses: *Union*, 3 killed, 15 wounded.

17 and 18.—Lynchburg, Va. *Union*, Sullivan's and Crook's divisions and Averell's and Duffié's Cav., Army of West Virginia; *Confed.*, Gen. Jubal Early's command. Losses: *Union*, 100 killed, 500 wounded, 100 missing; *Confed.*, 200 killed and wounded.

19.—Destruction of the *Confed.* cruiser *Alabama*, off Cherbourg, France, by U. S. cruiser *Kearsarge*. Losses: *Union*, 3 wounded; *Confed.*, 9 killed, 21 wounded, 10 drowned, and 70 captured.

21.—Salem, Va. *Union*, Averell's Cav.; *Confed.*, Gen. McCausland's Cav. Losses: *Union*, 6 killed, 10 wounded; *Confed.*, 10 killed and wounded.

22 and 23.—Weldon Railroad, Williams' Farm or Jerusalem Plank Road, Va. *Union*, Second and Sixth Corps and First Division of Fifth Corps, Army of the Potomac; *Confed.*, Gen. A. P. Hill's Corps. Losses: *Union*, 142 killed, 654 wounded, 2166 missing; *Confed.**

22 to 30.—In front of Petersburg, Va. *Union*, Fifth, Ninth, Tenth, and Eighteenth Corps; *Confed.*, Army of Northern Virginia. Losses: *Union*, 112 killed, 506 wounded, 800 missing.

—Wilson's Raid on the Weldon Railroad, Va. *Union*, Kautz's and Wilson's Cav.; *Confed.*, Gen. W. H. F. Lee's Cav. Losses: *Union*, 71 killed, 262 wounded, 1119 missing; *Confed.*, 365 killed and wounded.

23 and 24.—Jones's Bridge and Samaria Church, Va. *Union*, Torbert's and Gregg's Cavalry Divisions; *Confed.*, Hampton's Cav. Losses: *Union*, 54 killed, 235 wounded, 300 missing; *Confed.*, 250 killed and wounded.

25 to 29.—Clarendon, St. Charles River, Ark. *Union*, 126th Ill. and 11th Mo., 9th Iowa and 3d Mich. Cav., Battery D 2d Mo. Artil.; *Confed.*, Gen. Price's command. Losses: *Union*, 1 killed, 16 wounded; *Confed.*, 30 killed and wounded.

* No record found.

THE LAST PORT CLOSED

Fort Fisher, captured January 15, 1865. With the capture of Fort Fisher, Wilmington, the great importing depot of the South, on which General Lee said the subsistence of his army depended, was finally closed to all blockade runners. The Federal navy concentrated against the fortifications of this port the most powerful naval force ever assembled up to that time—fifty-five ships of war, including five ironclads, altogether carrying six hundred guns. The upper picture shows the nature of the palisade, nine feet high, over which some two thousand marines attempted to pass; the lower shows interior of the works after the destructive bombardment.

INSIDE FORT FISHER—WORK OF THE UNION FLEET

Engagements of the Civil War

1 to 31.—In front of Petersburg, including Deep Bottom, New Market, and Malvern Hill, on the 27th, and Federal mine explosion on the 30th under a Confederate fort. *Union*, Second, Fifth, Ninth, Tenth, and Eighteenth Corps; *Confed.*, Army of Northern Virginia. Losses: *Union*, 853 killed, 3468 wounded, 1558 missing; *Confed.**

2 to 5.—Nickajack Creek or Smyrna, Ga. *Union*, troops under command of Maj.-Gen. Sherman; *Confed.*, Gen. Johnston's command. Losses: *Union*, 60 killed, 310 wounded; *Confed.*, 100 killed and wounded.

2 to 10.—Expedition from Vicksburg to Jackson, Miss. *Union*, First Division, Seventeenth Corps; *Confed.*, Gen. Wirt Adam's command. Losses: *Union*, 220 killed, wounded, and missing; *Confed.**

3.—Fort Johnson, James Island, S. C. *Union*, Troops of Department of the South; *Confed.*, Gen. W. B. Taliaferro's command. Losses: *Union*, 19 killed, 97 wounded, 135 missing; *Confed.**

4 to 7.—Bolivar and Maryland Heights, Va. *Union*, Maj.-Gen. Sigel's Reserve Division; *Confed.*, Gen. Jubal Early's command. Losses: *Union*, 20 killed, 80 wounded.

5 to 7.—John's Island, S. C. *Union*, Maj.-Gen. Foster's troops; *Confed.*, Gen. W. B. Taliaferro's command. Losses: *Union*, 16 killed, 82 wounded; *Confed.*, 33 killed, 92 wounded.

5 to 18.—Smith's Expedition, La Grange, Tenn., to Tupelo, Miss. *Union*, First and Third Divisions Sixteenth Corps, one brigade U. S. Colored Troops and Grierson's Cav.; *Confed.*, Forrest's Cav. Losses: *Union*, 85 killed, 567 wounded; *Confed.*, 210 killed, 1049 wounded, 149 missing.

6 to 10.—Chattahoochee River, Ga. *Union*, Army of the Ohio, Maj.-Gen. Schofield; Army of the Tennessee, Maj.-Gen. McPherson; Army of the Cumberland, Maj.-Gen. Thomas—Division of the Mississippi, Maj.-Gen. W. T. Sherman; *Confed.*, Gen. J. E. Johnston's command. Losses: *Union*, 80 killed, 450 wounded, 200 missing.

7.—Solomon's Gap and Middletown, Md. *Union*, 8th Ill. Cav., Potomac Home Brigade, and Alexander's Baltimore Battery; *Confed.*, Gen. Early's command. Losses: *Union*, 5 killed, 20 wounded.

9.—Monocacy, Md. *Union*, First and Second Brigades of Third Division, Sixth Corps, and detachment of Eighth Corps; *Confed.*, Gordon's, Breckinridge's and Rodes' divisions under Gen. Jubal Early. Losses: *Union*, 98 killed, 594 wounded, 1188 missing; *Confed.**

11 to 22.—Rousseau's raid in Alabama and Georgia, including Ten Islands and Stone's Ferry, Ala., and Auburn and Chewa Station, Ga. *Union*, 8th Ind., 5th Iowa, 9th Ohio, 2d Ky., and 4th Tenn. Cav., Battery E 1st Mich. Artil.; *Confed.*, Troops of Gen. J. E. Johnston's command. Losses: *Union*, 3 killed, 30 wounded; *Confed.*, 95 killed and wounded.

12.—Fort Stevens, Washington, D. C. *Union*, Part of Nineteenth Corps, First and Second Divisions Sixth Corps, Marines, Home Guards, citizens, and convalescents; *Confed.*, Gen. Early's command. Losses: *Union*, 280 killed and 319 wounded; *Confed.**

17 and 18.—Snicker's Gap and Island Ford, Va. *Union*, Army of West Virginia, Maj.-Gen. Crook and portion of Sixth Corps; *Confed.*, Gen. Early's command. Losses: *Union*, 30 killed, 181 wounded, 100 missing.

18.—Ashby's Gap, Va. *Union*, Duffié's Cav.; *Confed.** Losses: *Union*, 124 killed and wounded.

19 and 20.—Darksville, Stevenson's Depot, and Winchester, Va. *Union*, Averell's Cav.; *Confed.*, Cavalry of Gen. Early's command. Losses: *Union*, 38 killed, 175 wounded, 300 captured; *Confed.*, 300 killed and wounded, 300 captured.

20.—Peach Tree Creek, Ga. *Union*, Fourth, Fourteenth, and Twentieth Corps, Maj.-Gen. Geo. H. Thomas; *Confed.*, Gen. J. B. Hood's army. Losses (estimates): Union, 300 killed, 1410 wounded; *Confed.*, 1113 killed, 2500 wounded, 1183 missing.

22.—Atlanta, Ga. (Hood's first sortie.) *Union*, Fifteenth, Sixteenth, and Seventeenth Corps, Maj.-Gen. McPherson;

* No record found.

THE REFUGE OF THE DEFENDERS

When the wounded leaders (Lamb and Whiting) in command of Fort Fisher saw it was impossible to hold out much longer, they were removed on stretchers along the sea-coast to Battery Buchanan, pictured at the bottom of the page. The spent musket-balls from the stubborn battle still raging in the fort fell like hailstones around the party. The garrison itself soon retreated to Buchanan, where two miles of level sand separated them from the Federal troops, now in full possession of the fort. But they were defenseless, for the guns in Buchanan had been spiked, and no means of escape was at hand. Consequently, when the Federal General J. C. Abbot arrived in the night with two regiments, Colonel Lamb surrendered to him and his superior, General A. H. Terry, the works, with the force of a thousand men and some sixty officers. Though the Federal army captured Fort Fisher, the coöperation of the fleet was necessary to success. During the two days of almost ceaseless bombardment a thousand tons of shot and shell were poured upon the defenses, wrecking nearly every gun and wounding or killing those of the garrison who dared to man the pieces.

Confed., Gen. J. B. Hood's command. Losses: *Union,* 500 killed, 2141 wounded, 1000 missing; *Confed.,* 2482 killed, 4000 wounded, 2017 missing. *Union,* Gen. McPherson killed.

23 and 24.—Kernstown and Winchester, Va. *Union,* Portion of Army of West Virginia; *Confed.,* Gen. Early's command. Losses: *Union,* 1200 killed and wounded; *Confed.,* 600 killed and wounded.

26.—Wallace's Ferry, Ark. *Union,* 15th Ill. Cav., 60th and 56th U. S. Colored Troops, Co. E 2d U. S. Colored Artil.; *Confed.,* Gen. Price's command. Losses: *Union,* 16 killed, 32 wounded; *Confed.,* 150 wounded.

26 to 31.—Stoneman's raid to Macon, Ga. *Union,* Stoneman's and Garrard's Cav.; *Confed.,* Cavalry of Gen. Hood's army, local garrisons and Home Guards. Losses: *Union,* 100 killed and wounded, 900 missing; *Confed.**

—McCook's raid to Lovejoy's Station, Ga. *Union,* 1st Wis., 5th and 8th Iowa, 2d and 8th Ind., 1st and 4th Tenn., and 4th Ky. Cav.; *Confed.,* detachments of Gen. Hood's command. Losses: *Union,* 100 killed and wounded, 500 missing.

27.—Mazzard Prairie, Fort Smith, Ark. *Union,* 6th Kan. Cav.; *Confed.,* Gen. Price's command. Losses: *Union,* 12 killed, 17 wounded, 152 captured; *Confed.,* 12 killed, 20 wounded.

28.—Atlanta, Ga. (Second sortie; at Ezra Church.) *Union,* Fifteenth, Sixteenth, and Seventeenth Corps, Maj.-Gen. Howard; *Confed.,* Gen. Hood's command. Losses: *Union,* 100 killed, 600 wounded; *Confed.,* 642 killed, 3000 wounded, 1000 missing.

28 to Sept. 2.—Siege of Atlanta, Ga. *Union,* Army of the Military Division of the Mississippi, Maj.-Gen. W. T. Sherman; *Confed.,* Army of Tennessee, Gen. J. B. Hood, commanding. Losses: Careful estimates place the casualties at between 30,000 and 35,000 on each side.

AUGUST, 1864.

1 to 31.—In front of Petersburg, Va. *Union,* Second, Fifth, Ninth, and Eighteenth Corps; *Confed.,* Army of Northern Virginia. Losses: *Union,* 158 killed, 623 wounded, 296 missing; *Confed.**

2.—Green Springs, W. Va. *Union,* 153d Ohio; *Confed.,* troops of Gen. J. H. Morgan's command. Losses: *Union,* 1 killed, 5 wounded, 90 missing; *Confed.,* 5 killed, 22 wounded.

5 to 23.—Forts Gaines and Morgan, Mobile Bay, Ala. *Union,* Thirteenth Corps and Admiral Farragut's fleet of war vessels; *Confed.,* fleet commanded by Admiral Buchanan and land forces under Gen. D. H. Maury. Losses: *Union,* 145 killed, 170 wounded; *Confed.,* 12 killed, 20 wounded, 280 captured.

7.—Moorefield, Va. *Union,* 14th Penna., 8th Ohio, 1st and 3d W. Va., and 1st N. Y. Cav.; *Confed.,* McCausland's and Bradley T. Johnson's Cav. Losses: *Union,* 9 killed, 22 wounded; *Confed.,* 100 killed and wounded, 400 missing.

9.—Explosion of ammunition at City Point, Va. Losses: *Union,* 70 killed, 130 wounded.

10 and 11.—Berryville Pike, Sulphur Springs Bridge and White Post, Va. *Union,* Torbert's Cav.; *Confed.,* Gen. Early's command. Losses: *Union,* 30 killed, 70 wounded, 200 missing.

13.—Near Snicker's Gap, Va. *Union,* 144th and 149th Ohio; *Confed.,* Gen. R. H. Anderson's command. Losses: *Union,* 4 killed, 10 wounded, 200 missing; *Confed.,* 2 killed, 3 wounded.

14 to 18.—Strawberry Plains, Va. *Union,* Second and Tenth Corps and Gregg's Cav.; *Confed.,* detachments from Gen. Lee's army at Petersburg. Losses: *Union,* 327 killed, 1855 wounded, 1400 missing; *Confed.* (estimate), 1000 killed, wounded, and missing.

15.—Fisher's Hill, near Strasburg, Va. *Union,* Sixth and Eighth Corps and 1st Cav. Division Army of the Potomac; *Confed.,* Gen. Early's command. Losses: *Union,* 30 wounded.

16.—Crooked Run, Front Royal, Va. *Union,* Merritt's Cav.; *Confed.,* Kershaw's division and Fitzhugh Lee's Cav. Losses: *Union,* 13 killed, 58 wounded; *Confed.,* 30 killed, 150 wounded, 300 captured.

17.—Gainesville, Fla. *Union,* 75th Ohio Mounted Inf. Losses: *Union,* 16 killed, 30 wounded, 102 missing.

* No record found.

RUINS OF CHARLESTON—EVACUATED FEBRUARY 18, 1865

A center of Southern civilization lies in ashes. The Circular Church has been reduced to bare blackened walls and topless tower. The famous Mills House, to the right, has been swept by the flames. The private mansions in the foreground are completely destroyed, nothing but the steps remaining of the one in front. But the photograph, taken only two months later, shows also a mighty power of recuperation. The scaffolding is already up for the repair of the steeple of the church. The evacuation of Charleston had not been the result of any Federal attack, but of Sherman's advance through the heart of South Carolina. On February 17th the city was reluctantly evacuated.

—Winchester, Va. *Union,* New Jersey Brigade of Sixth Corps and Wilson's Cav.; *Confed.,* Gen. Early's command. Losses: *Union,* 50 wounded, 250 missing.

18, 19, and 20.—Six-mile House, Weldon Railroad, Va. *Union,* Fifth and Ninth Corps and Kautz's and Gregg's Cav.; *Confed.,* Gen. A. P. Hill's corps, Bushrod Johnson's division, Dearing's brigade and Hampton's Cav. Losses: *Union,* 251 killed, 1155 wounded, 2879 missing; *Confed.**

18 to 22.—Raid on the Atlanta and West Point Railroad. *Union,* Kilpatrick's Cav.; *Confed.,* W. H. Johnson's Cav. Losses: *Union,* 400 wounded.

21.—Summit Point, Berryville, and Flowing Springs, Va. *Union,* Sixth Corps, and Merritt's and Wilson's Cav.; *Confed.,* Rodes' and Ramseur's divisions. Losses: *Union,* 600 killed and wounded; *Confed.,* 400 killed and wounded.

—Memphis, Tenn. *Union,* detachments of 8th Iowa and 113th Ill., 39th, 40th, and 41st Wis., 61st U. S. Colored, 3d and 4th Iowa Cav., Battery G 1st Mo. Lt. Artil.; *Confed.,* Forrest's Cav. Losses: *Union,* 30 killed, 100 wounded; *Confed.,* 100 killed and wounded.

21 and 22.—Oxford, Miss. *Union,* 4th Iowa, 11th and 21st Mo., 3d Iowa Cav., 12th Mo. Cav.; *Confed.,* Forrest's Cav. Losses: *Confed.**

23.—Abbeville, Miss. *Union,* 10th Mo., 14th Iowa, 5th and 7th Minn., 8th Wis.; *Confed.,* Forrest's Cavalry. Losses: *Union,* 20 wounded; *Confed.,* 34 killed, wounded, and missing.

24.—Jones' Hay Station and Ashley Station, Ark. *Union,* 9th Iowa and 8th and 11th Mo. Cav.; *Confed.,* Troops of Gen. Price's command. Losses: *Union,* 5 killed, 41 wounded; *Confed.,* 60 wounded.

24 and 25.—Bermuda Hundred, Va. *Union,* Tenth Corps; *Confed.,* troops of Gen. Lee's command. Losses: *Union,* 31 wounded; *Confed.,* 61 missing.

24 to 27.—Halltown, Va. *Union,* portion of Eighth Corps; *Confed.,* Gen. Early's command. Losses: *Union,* 30 killed, 141 wounded; *Confed.,* 130 killed and wounded.

25.—Smithfield and Shepherdstown or Kearneysville, Va. *Union,* Merritt's and Wilson's Cav.; *Confed.,* Gen. Early's command. Losses: *Union,* 10 killed, 90 wounded, 100 missing; *Confed.,* 300 killed and wounded.

—Ream's Station, Va. *Union,* Second Corps and Gregg's Cav.; *Confed.,* Gen. A. P. Hill's command. Losses: *Union,* 140 killed, 529 wounded, 2073 missing; *Confed.,* 720 killed and wounded.

29.—Smithfield, Va. *Union,* Third Division Sixth Corps and Torbert's Cav.; *Confed.,* Gen. Early's command. Losses: *Union,* 10 killed, 90 wounded; *Confed.,* 200 killed and wounded.

31 and Sept. 1.—Jonesboro, Ga. *Union,* Fourteenth, Fifteenth, Sixteenth, Seventeenth Corps and Cavalry Corps; *Confed.,* Gen Hardee's Corps, Gen. S. D. Lee's Corps, Army of Tennessee, Gen. J. B. Hood, commanding. Losses: *Union,* 1149 killed and wounded; *Confed.,* 1400 killed, wounded, and missing.

SEPTEMBER, 1864.

1 to 8.—Rousseau's pursuit of Wheeler in Tenn. *Union,* Rousseau's Cav., 1st and 4th Tenn., 2d Mich., 1st Wis., 8th Iowa, 2d and 8th Ind., and 6th Ky.; *Confed.,* Wheeler's Cav. Losses: *Union,* 10 killed, 30 wounded; *Confed.,* 300 killed, wounded, and captured.

1 to Oct. 30.—In front of Petersburg. *Union,* Army of the Potomac; *Confed.,* Army of Northern Virginia. Losses: *Union,* 170 killed, 822 wounded, 812 missing; *Confed.**

2.—Federal occupation of Atlanta, Ga. (Evacuation by Hood's rear-guard during the night of the 1st.) *Union,* Twentieth Corps. Losses: *Confed.,* 200 captured.

3 and 4.—Berryville, Va. *Union,* Eighth and Nineteenth Corps and Torbert's Cav.; *Confed.,* Anderson's command. Losses: *Union,* 30 killed, 182 wounded, 100 missing; *Confed.,* 25 killed, 100 wounded, 70 missing.

4.—Greenville, Tenn. *Union,* 9th and 13th Tenn., and 10th Mich. Cav.; *Confed.,* Morgan's Cav. Losses: *Union,* 6 wounded; *Confed.,* 10 killed, 60 wounded, 75 missing; *Confed.,* Gen. John H. Morgan killed.

* No record found.

THE UNION PHOTOGRAPHER IN SUMTER AT LAST

The shapeless ruins of Sumter, demolished by eighteen months of almost constant fire from Federal batteries, appear in the top picture, of April 14, 1865, the anniversary of Major Anderson's evacuation in 1861. Next comes the Federal fleet dressed with flags for the celebration; and below, a group at the foot of the pole listening to Henry Ward Beecher. In the foreground stand the soldiers and sailors who had taken part in the ceremonies of raising on the shining white staff the very flag that had been lowered exactly four years earlier.

RAISING THE FLAG, APRIL 14TH

On the night of this gala occasion President Lincoln was shot in Washington. Sumter had in a sense become a symbol of the Confederacy. Repeated efforts had been made to conquer its garrisons. But with a tenacity of purpose typical of the South, its shattered walls were transformed into an earthwork impregnable to assault and lending the aid of its six heavy guns to the defenses of Charleston Harbor. It was evacuated only on the night of February 17th, when South Carolina needed every man that could possibly be summoned to oppose Sherman.

Engagements of the Civil War

10.—Capture of Fort Hell, Va. *Union,* 99th Pa., 20th Ind., 2d U. S. Sharpshooters. Losses: *Union,* 20 wounded; *Confed.,* 90 prisoners.

13.—Lock's Ford, Va. *Union,* Torbert's Cav.; *Confed.,* Gen. Early's command. Losses: *Union,* 2 killed, 18 wounded; *Confed.,* 181 captured.

16.—Sycamore Church, Va. *Union,* 1st D. C. and 13th Pa. Cav. Losses: *Union,* 400 killed, wounded, and captured; *Confed.,* 50 killed and wounded.

16 and 18.—Fort Gibson, Ind. Ter. *Union,* 79th U. S. Colored and 2d Kan. Cav. Losses: *Union,* 38 killed, 48 missing.

19 to 22.—Winchester and Fisher's Hill, Va. *Union,* Sixth, Eighth, and 1st and 2d Divisions of the Nineteenth Corps, Averell's and Torbert's Cav., Maj.-Gen. Phil. Sheridan; *Confed.,* Gen. Jubal Early's command. Losses: *Union,* 749 killed, 4440 wounded, 357 missing; *Confed.,* 250 killed, 1777 wounded, 2813 captured; *Union,* Brig.-Gens. Russell and Mulligan killed; *Confed.,* Maj.-Gen. Rodes and Brig.-Gen. Godwin killed.

23.—Athens, Ala. *Union,* 106th, 110th, and 114th U. S. Colored, 3d Tenn. Cav., re-enforced by 18th Mich. and 102d Ohio; *Confed.,* Forrest's Cav. Losses: *Union,* 950 missing; *Confed.,* 5 killed, 25 wounded.

26 and 27.—Pilot Knob or Ironton, Mo. *Union,* 47th and 50th Mo., 14th Iowa, 2d and 3d Mo. Cav., Battery H 2d Mo. Lt. Artil.; *Confed.,* Gen. Sterling Price's command. Losses: *Union,* 28 killed, 56 wounded, 100 missing; *Confed.,* 1500 killed and wounded.

27.—Centralia, Mo. *Union,* three cos. 39th Mo.; *Confed.,* Price's forces. Losses: *Union,* 122 killed, 2 wounded.

—Marianna, Fla. *Union,* 7th Vt., 82d U. S. Colored and 2d Maine Cav.; *Confed.,* Troops of Col. A. B. Montgomery's command, including Anderson's militia. Losses: *Union,* 32 wounded; *Confed.,* 81 missing.

28 and 30.—New Market Heights or Laurel Hill, Va. *Union,* Tenth and Eighteenth Corps and Kautz's Cav.; *Confed.,* Gen. R. S. Ewell's command, supported by Longstreet's Corps under R. H. Anderson. Losses: *Union,* 400 killed, 2029 wounded; *Confed.,* 2000 killed and wounded.

30 and Oct. 1.—Poplar Springs Church, Va. *Union,* First Division Fifth Corps and Second Division Ninth Corps; *Confed.,* Gen. A. P. Hill's Corps. Losses: *Union,* 187 killed, 900 wounded, 1802 missing; *Confed.* (estimate), 800 killed and wounded, 100 missing.

—Arthur's Swamp, Va. *Union,* Gregg's Cav.; *Confed.,* Hampton's Cav. Losses: *Union,* 60 wounded, 100 missing; *Confed.**

OCTOBER, 1864.

2.—Waynesboro, Va. *Union,* portion of Custer's and Merritt's Cav.; *Confed.,* Gen. Early's command. Losses: *Union,* 50 killed and wounded.

—Saltville, Va. *Union,* 11th and 13th Ky. Cav., 12th Ohio, 11th Mich., 5th and 6th U. S. Colored Cav., 26th, 30th, 35th, 37th, 39th, 40th, and 45th Ky. Mounted Inf.; *Confed.,* Gen. Breckinridge's Infantry, Col. Giltner's Cav., 13th Va. Reserves (Home Guards). Losses: *Union,* 54 killed, 190 wounded, 104 missing; *Confed.,* 18 killed, 71 wounded, 21 missing.

5.—Allatoona Pass, Ga. *Union,* 7th, 12th, 50th, 57th, and 93d Ill., 39th Iowa, 4th Minn., 18th Wis., and 12th Wis. Battery; *Confed.,* Gen. French's command. Losses: *Union,* 142 killed, 352 wounded, 212 missing; *Confed.,* 122 killed, 443 wounded, 234 missing.

7 and 13.—Darbytown Road Va. *Union,* Tenth Corps and Kautz's Cav.; *Confed.,* troops of Gen. R. E. Lee's command. Losses: *Union,* 105 killed, 502 wounded, 206 missing; *Confed.**

9.—Tom's Brook, Fisher's Hill or Strasburg, Va. *Union,* Merritt's, Custer's and Torbert's Cav.; *Confed.,* Rosser's and Lomax's Cav. Losses: *Union,* 9 killed, 67 wounded; *Confed.,* 100 killed and wounded, 180 missing.

13.—Reconnaissance to Strasburg, Va. *Union,* Maj.-Gens. Emory's and Crook's troops; *Confed.,* Gen. Early's command. Losses: *Union,* 30 killed, 144 wounded, 40 missing.

—Dalton, Ga. *Union,* troops under Col. Johnson, 44th U. S. Colored; *Confed.,*

* No record found.

The calm sunlight of April, 1865, is falling on the northern face of the fort which had withstood a severer bombardment than any other fortification attacked during the Civil War. This wall was across the fort from the one upon which the heavy Union batteries on Morris Island concentrated their fire. But many a shot passing over the southern wall struck this rampart from the inside, making breaches that had to be patched with gabions. Patched in this way it continued to the end of the war, frowning across the waters of the bay upon the blockading fleet and the Union batteries. Thus it looked when, on February 18, 1865, Colonel Bennet, in command of the United States forces at Charleston, was rowed across from Cummins Point toward Fort Moultrie. Forty yards east of Sumter he met a boat filled with musicians who had been left behind by the Confederates. He directed one of his subordinates to proceed to Sumter and raise the American flag above the ramparts—for the first time in four years.

SUMTER ONCE MORE IN PEACE

THE DESERTED DEFENSES

Sumter, inside the face of which the outside is shown above. The skill with which gabions were employed to strengthen the ramparts is apparent. A description of the relinquishment of the position follows in the words of Major John Johnson: "On the night of the 17th of February, 1865, the commander, Captain Thomas A. Huguenin, silently and without interruption effected the complete evacuation. He has often told me of the particulars, and I have involuntarily accompanied him in thought and feeling as, for the last time, he went the rounds of the deserted fort. The ordered casements with their massive guns were there, but in the stillness of that hour his own footfall alone gave an echo from the arches overhead. The labyrinthine galleries, as he traversed them, were lighted for a moment by his lantern; he passed out from the shadows to step aboard the little boat awaiting him at the wharf, and the four years' defense of Fort Sumter was at an end."

WITHIN THE DEADLY ZONE AT PETERSBURG

The officers' quarters of Fort Sedgwick, a bomb-proof structure, was a post of honor in the Federal line, as it invariably drew the hottest fire. It stands immediately behind the salient at which the guns were served. On the right is the "Blessed Well" of Fort Damnation. The commands garrisoning this fort were changed more frequently than any other. Regiments were continually moved from one part of the line to the camps near City Point to recuperate, while fresh troops were brought up from that base to take their places. General John Grubb Park commanded the Ninth Corps, and it was this body of Federal troops that advanced from behind Fort Sedgwick and, supported by its guns, seized the Confederate entrenchments opposite in an assault made on April 2, 1865.

A WINTER DUG-OUT

CAVE DWELLERS

A CONFEDERATE MILL IN '65—WHERE THE SOUND OF THE GRINDING WAS LOW

The wonder is that Lee's starving army was able to hold out as long as it did. This well-built flour-mill was one of many which in times of peace carried on an important industry in the town. But long before the siege closed, all the mills were empty of grain and grist. Could Lee have kept the flour-mills of Petersburg and Richmond running during the last winter of the war, disaster would not have come to his famished forces so early in 1865. At the beginning of the year but one railroad, a canal, and a turnpike remained by which supplies could be gotten into Petersburg from Wilmington, N. C., and Charleston, S. C. These were the last two ports that the blockade-runners still dared venture into with supplies for the Confederacy. Not only was food scarce, but the deserters from Lee's army, averaging about a hundred daily, revealed plainly the fact that the Confederate troops with their threadbare, insufficient clothing, were in a most pitiable condition. Not only was food lacking, but ammunition was running low. During 1864 the supply of percussion-caps for the Confederate army had been kept up only by melting the copper stills throughout the South. Now even these were exhausted, and there were no more supplies of copper in sight. Hundreds of heartrending letters were intercepted and sent to Lee's headquarters. "Mothers, wives, and sisters wrote of their inability to respond to the appeals of hungry children for bread or to provide proper care and remedies for the sick, and in the name of all that was dear appealed to the men to come home.

THE FINAL CAPTURE—FORT MAHONE

It is April 3, 1865. On the parapet in the middle of the line of officers stands Lieutenant J. B. Krepps, of the Second Pennsylvania Heavy Artillery. The regiment was attached to the Ninth Corps, of which Potter's division had captured the fort on the previous afternoon. "Fort Damnation," as it was called by the Federal soldiers, was the last to fall in the general assault. Potter's men gained possession of it only after the most desperate fighting from traverse to traverse. Even then, after a breathing space, the Confederates, in a brave assault, recaptured a portion of the works and held on until driven back by a brilliant charge of Griffin's men.

CHEERING THE VICTORS OF PETERSBURG, APRIL 3D

Here, on the gabioned parapet of "Fort Hell" (Sedgwick), the garrison left behind, with shouts and waving of hats and firing of muskets, are signalling their enthusiasm at the success of their comrades, who now hold the works of the old antagonist, "Fort Damnation," across the way. Such scenes were enacted all along the lines on the 3d, when the victory became assured. The long siege of nearly a year was over and the men knew that its consequences were momentous. If there were to be more fighting it would be against a retreating army, without any of the weary waiting in cramped fortifications. The army was soon to be on the move; Lee was already evacuating Petersburg.

Gen. Hood's advance troops. Losses: *Union*, 400 missing.

15.—Glasgow, Mo. *Union*, 43d Mo., and detachments of 17th Ill., 9th Mo. Militia, 13th Mo. Cav., 62d U. S. Colored; *Confed.*, Gen. Sterling Price's command. Losses: *Union*, 400 wounded and missing; *Confed.*, 50 killed and wounded.

19.—Cedar Creek, Va. (Sheridan's Ride.) *Union*, Sixth Corps, Eighth Corps, and First and Second Divisions Nineteenth Corps, Merritt's, Custer's, and Torbert's Cav.; *Confed.*, Gen. Jubal Early's army. Losses: *Union*, 644 killed, 3430 wounded, 1591 captured or missing; *Confed.*, 320 killed, 1540 wounded, 1050 missing; *Union*, Brig.-Gen. Bidwell and Col. Thoburn killed; *Confed.*, Maj.-Gen. Ramseur killed.

26 to 29.—Decatur, Ala. *Union*, 18th Mich., 102d Ohio, 68th Ind., and 14th U. S. Colored; *Confed.*, Gen. J. B. Hood's army. Losses: *Union*, 10 killed, 45 wounded, 100 missing; *Confed.*, 100 killed, 300 wounded.

27.—Hatcher's Run, Va. *Union*, Gregg's Cav., Second and Third Divisions Second Corps, Fifth and Ninth Corps; *Confed.*, Gen. Hill's Corps, Fitzhugh Lee's and M. C. Butler's Cav. Losses: *Union*, 166 killed, 1047 wounded, 699 missing; *Confed.*, 200 killed, 600 wounded, 200 missing (Federal estimate).

—Destruction at Plymouth, N. C., of the *Confed.* ram *Albemarle*, by Lieut. W. B. Cushing, U. S. N., and 14 officers and men. Losses: *Union*, 2 drowned, 11 captured. *Confed.**

—Morristown, Tenn. *Union*, Gen. Gillem's Cav.; *Confed.*, Forrest's Cav. Losses: *Union*, 8 killed, 42 wounded; *Confed.*, 240 missing.

27 and 28.—Fair Oaks, Va. *Union*, Tenth and Eighteenth Corps and Kautz's Cav.; *Confed.*, Gen. Longstreet's command. Losses: *Union*, 120 killed, 783 wounded, 400 missing; *Confed.*, 60 killed, 311 wounded, 80 missing.

28 and 30.—Newtonia, Mo. *Union*, Col. Blunt's Cav.; *Confed.*, Gen. Price's command. Losses: *Confed.*, 250 killed and wounded.

29.—Beverly, W. Va. *Union*, 8th Ohio Cav.; *Confed.*, troops of Gen. Breckinridge's command. Losses: *Union*, 8 killed, 25 wounded, 13 missing; *Confed.*, 17 killed, 27 wounded, 92 missing.

NOVEMBER, 1864.

5.—Fort Sedgwick or Fort Hell, Va. *Union*, Second Corps; *Confed.*, troops of Gen. Lee's Army of Northern Virginia. Losses: *Union*, 5 killed, 10 wounded; *Confed.*, 15 killed, 35 wounded.

12.—Newtown and Cedar Springs, Va. *Union*, Merritt's, Custer's, and Powell's Cav.; *Confed.*, troops of Gen. Early's command. Losses: *Union*, 84 wounded, 100 missing; *Confed.*, 150 killed, wounded, and missing.

13.—Bull's Gap., Tenn. *Union*, 8th, 9th, and 13th Tenn. Cav.; *Confed.*, advance of Gen. Hood's army. Losses: *Union*, 5 killed, 36 wounded, 200 missing; *Confed.**

17.—Bermuda Hundred, Va. *Union*, 209th Pa.; *Confed.*, troops of Gen. Lee's army. Losses: *Union*, 10 wounded, 120 missing; *Confed.*, 10 wounded.

21.—Griswoldville, Ga. *Union*, Walcutt's Brigade First Division, Fifteenth Corps, and First Brigade Third Division Cav.; *Confed.*, Gen. Gustavus W. Smith's Georgia Militia. Losses: *Union*, 13 killed, 69 wounded; *Confed.*, 5 killed, 472 wounded, 2 missing.

22.—Rood's Hill, Va. *Union*, Torbert's Cav.; *Confed.*, Gen. Early's command. Losses: *Union*, 18 killed, 52 wounded; *Confed.**

24.—Lawrenceburg, Campbellville, and Lynnville, Tenn. *Union*, Hatch's Cav.; *Confed.*, Cavalry of Hood's army. Losses: *Union*, 75 killed and wounded; *Confed.*, 50 killed and wounded.

26.—Sandersville, Ga. *Union*, Third Brigade First Division, Twentieth Corps; *Confed.*, Wheeler's Cav. Losses: *Union*, 100 missing; *Confed.*, 100 missing.

26 to 29.—Sylvan Grove, Waynesboro', Browne's Cross Roads, Ga. *Union*, Kilpatrick's Cav.; *Confed.*, Wheeler's Cav. Losses: *Union*, 46 wounded; *Confed.**

29 and 30.—Spring Hill and Franklin, Tenn. *Union*, Fourth and Twenty-third Corps and Cav.; *Confed.*, Gen. J. B. Hood's army. Losses: *Union*, 189 killed, 1033 wounded, 1104 missing; *Confed.*, 1750 killed, 3800 wounded, 702 missing.

* No record found.

HAVOC UNCONFINED—THE RICHMOND ARSENAL

As the camera clicks in April, 1865, the long-defended citadel of the Confederacy is at last deserted; its munitions of war no longer ready for service against an enemy; its armies at a distance, retreating as rapidly as their exhausted condition permits. These fire-blasted and crumbling walls are a fit symbol of the condition of the South at the close of the war. The scene at this arsenal on the night of April 2d was one of the most brilliant and splendid of the whole conflict. The arsenal was near the Richmond & Petersburg Railroad at the James River. The high-arched bridges ablaze across the stream, the deafening reports of exploding magazines, the columns of white smoke rising high into the sky lurid from thousands of shells bursting in the arsenal, the falling of the broken fragments among the already panic stricken fugitives—all these features created a scene such as the world has seldom witnessed. Early in the morning of April 3d the clatter of Federal cavalry was heard in the streets. The Stars and Stripes waved. Richmond was the capital of the Confederacy no longer.

Union, Maj.-Gens. Stanley and Bradley wounded; *Confed.,* Maj.-Gen. Cleburne, Brig.-Gens. Adams, Strahl, Gist, and Granbury killed, Maj.-Gen. Brown and Brig.-Gens. Carter, Manigault, Quarles, Cockrell, and Scott wounded.

30.—Honey Hill or Grahamsville, S. C. *Union,* 25th Ohio, 56th and 155th N. Y., 26th, 32d, 35th, and 102d U. S. Colored, 54th and 55th Mass. Colored; *Confed.,* Georgia Militia under Gen. G. W. Smith, S. C. Battery. Losses: *Union,* 91 killed, 631 wounded; *Confed.,* 8 killed, 42 wounded.

DECEMBER, 1864.

1.—Stony Creek Station, Weldon Railroad, Va. *Union,* Gregg's Cav.; *Confed.,* Capt. Waldhauer's command and Gen. Fitzhugh Lee's Cav. Losses: *Union,* 40 wounded; *Confed.,* 175 captured.

1 to 14.—In front of Nashville, Tenn. *Union,* Fourth, Twenty-third Corps; First and Third divisions of Sixteenth Corps; Wilson's Cav.; *Confed.,* Gen. Hood's army. Losses: *Union,* 16 killed, 100 wounded; *Confed.**

1 to 31.—In front of Petersburg. *Union,* Army of the Potomac; *Confed.,* troops of Lee's army. Losses: *Union,* 40 killed, 329 wounded; *Confed.**

4.—Block-house No. 7, Tenn. *Union,* Gen. Milroy's troops; *Confed.,* Gen. Bate's division of Hood's army. Losses: *Union,* 100 killed, wounded, and missing; *Confed.,* 87 killed, wounded and missing.

5 to 8.—Murfreesboro', Tenn. *Union,* Gen. Rousseau's troops; *Confed.,* Gen. Bate's command. Losses: *Union,* 30 killed, 175 wounded; *Confed.,* 197 missing.

6 to 9.—Deveaux's Neck, S. C. *Union,* 56th, 127th, 144th, 155th, and 157th N. Y., 25th Ohio, 26th, 32d, 33d, 34th, and 102d U. S. Colored, 54th and 55th Mass. Colored, 3d R. I. Artil., Naval brigade Bat. F, 3d N. Y. Lt. Art., and gunboats; *Confed.,* troops of Gen. Samuel Jones' command. Losses: *Union,* 39 killed, 390 wounded, 200 missing; *Confed.,* 400 killed and wounded.

7 to 11.—Weldon Railroad Expedition. *Union,* Fifth Corps, Third Division of

Second Corps, and Second Division Cavalry Corps, Army of the Potomac; *Confed.,* Gen. A. P. Hill's command. Losses: *Union,* 100 killed and wounded; *Confed.**

8 and 9.—Hatcher's Run, Va. *Union,* First Division, Second Corps, 3d and 13th Pa. Cav., 6th Ohio Cav.; *Confed.,* Gen. Hill's command. Losses: *Union,* 125 killed and wounded; *Confed.**

8 to 28.—Raid to Gordonsville, Va. *Union,* Merritt's and Custer's Cav.; *Confed.,* Cavalry of Gen. Early's army. Losses: *Union,* 43 killed and wounded. *Confed.**

10 to 21.—Siege of Savannah, Ga. *Union,* Fourteenth, Fifteenth, Seventeenth, and Twentieth Corps of Sherman's army; *Confed.,* Gen. W. J. Hardee's command. Losses: *Union,* 200 killed and wounded; *Confed.* (estimate), 800 killed, wounded, and missing.

12 to 21.—Federal raid from Bean's Station, Tenn., to Saltville, Va., including Abingdon, Glade Springs, and Marion. *Union,* Stoneman's Cav.; *Confed.,* Gen. J. C. Breckinridge's command. Losses: *Union,* 20 killed, 123 wounded; *Confed.,* 126 wounded, 500 missing.

13.—Fort McAllister, Ga. *Union,* Second Division of Fifteenth Corps; *Confed.,* Garrison commanded by Maj. W. G. Anderson. Losses: *Union,* 24 killed, 110 wounded; *Confed.,* 48 killed and wounded, 200 missing.

15 and 16.—Nashville, Tenn. *Union,* Fourth Corps; First and Third Divisions Thirteenth Corps; Twenty-third Corps; Wilson's Cav., and detachments colored troops, convalescents; *Confed.,* Gen. J. B. Hood's army. Losses: *Union,* 387 killed, 2558 wounded; *Confed.,* 4462 killed, wounded, and missing.

17.—Franklin, Tenn. *Union,* Wilson's Cav.; *Confed.,* Forrest's Cav. Losses: *Confed.,* 1800 wounded and sick captured. (Incident of Hood's retreat from Nashville.)

25.—Fort Fisher, N. C. *Union,* Tenth Corps and North Atlantic Squadron, commanded by Rear-Admiral D. D. Porter; Flag-Ship, *Malvern;* Iron-Clads: *Canonicus, Mahopac, Monadnock, New Ironsides, Saugus;* Screw-Frigates: *Colorado, Minnesota, Wabash;* Side-Wheel Steamers (first class): *Powhatan, Susque-*

* No record found.

EMPTY VAULTS—THE EXCHANGE BANK, RICHMOND, 1865

The sad significance of these photographs is all too apparent. Not only the bank buildings were in ruins, but the financial system of the entire South. All available capital had been consumed by the demands of the war, and a system of paper currency had destroyed credit completely. Worse still was the demoralization of all industry. Through large areas of the South all mills and factories were reduced to ashes, and everywhere the industrial system was turned topsy-turvy. Truly the problem that confronted the South was stupendous.

WRECK OF THE GALLEGO FLOUR MILLS

Engagements of the Civil War

hanna; Screw Sloops: *Brooklyn, Juniata, Mohican, Shenandoah, Ticonderoga, Tuscarora;* Screw Gun-Vessels: *Kansas, Maumee, Nyack, Pequot, Yantic;* Screw Gun-Boats: *Chippewa, Huron, Seneca, Unadilla;* Double-Enders: *Iosco, Mackinaw, Maratanza, Osceola, Pawtuxet, Pontoosuc, Sassacus, Tacony;* Miscellaneous Vessels: *Fort Jackson, Monticello, Nereus, Quaker City, Rhode Island, Santiago de Cuba, Vanderbilt;* Powder Vessel: *Louisiana;* Reserve: *A. D. Vance, Alabama, Britannia, Cherokee, Emma, Gettysburg, Governor Buckingham, Howquah, Keystone State, Lilian, Little Ada, Moccasin, Nansemond, Tristram Shandy, Wilderness; Confed.,* North Carolina troops in garrison, commanded by Col. William Lamb, Gen. Hoke's Division outside. Losses: *Union,* 8 killed, 38 wounded; *Confed.,* 3 killed, 55 wounded, 280 prisoners.

28.—Egypt Station, Miss. *Union,* 4th and 11th Ill. Cav., 7th Ind., 4th and 10th Mo., 2d Wis., 2d N. J., 1st Miss. and 3d U. S. Colored Cav.; *Confed.,* troops of Gen. Gardner's army under Gen. Gholson. Losses: *Union,* 23 killed, 88 wounded; *Confed.,* 500 captured; *Confed.,* Brig.-Gen. Gholson killed.

JANUARY, 1865.

11.—Beverly, W. Va. *Union,* 34th Ohio and 8th Ohio Cav.; *Confed.,* Gen. Breckinridge's command. Losses: *Union,* 5 killed, 20 wounded, 583 missing; *Confed.**

12 to 15.—Fort Fisher, N. C. *Union,* Portions of Twenty-fourth and Twenty-fifth Corps and Admiral Porter's fleet; Same ships as Dec. 25th above, with the exception that the *Nyack, Keystone State,* and *Quaker City* were not present and the *Montgomery, Cuyler, Aries, Eolus, Fort Donelson,* and *Republic* had been added to the fleet; *Confed.,* Same as Dec. 25th above. Losses: *Union,* 184 killed, 749 wounded; *Confed.,* 400 killed and wounded, 2083 captured.

25 to Feb. 9.—Combahee River and River's Bridge, Salkahatchie, S. C. *Union,* Fifteenth and Seventeenth Corps; *Confed.,* Wade Hampton's Cav. Losses: *Union,* 138 killed and wounded; *Confed.**

FEBRUARY, 1865.

5 to 7.—Dabney's Mills, Hatcher's Run, Va. *Union,* Fifth Corps and First Division Sixth Corps and Gregg's Cav.; *Confed.,* troops of Gen. A. P. Hill's and Gen. J. B. Gordon's Corps. Losses: *Union,* 171 killed, 1181 wounded, 186 missing; *Confed.,* 1200 killed and wounded; *Confed.,* Gen. Pegram killed.

8 to 14.—Williston, Blackville, and Aiken, S. C. *Union,* Kilpatrick's Cav.; *Confed.,* Wheeler's Cav. Losses: *Union *; Confed.,* 240 killed and wounded, 100 missing.

10.—James Island, S. C. *Union,* Maj.-Gen. Gillmore's command; *Confed.,* troops of Gen. Hardee's command. Losses: *Union,* 20 killed, 76 wounded; *Confed.,* 20 killed, and 70 wounded.

11.—Sugar Loaf Battery, Federal Point, N. C. *Union,* Portions of Twenty-fourth and Twenty-fifth Corps; *Confed.,* Gen. Hoke's command. Losses: *Union,* 14 killed, 114 wounded. *Confed.**

16 and 17.—Columbia, S. C. *Union,* Fifteenth Corps, Army of the Tennessee, commanded by Major-General John A. Logan; *Confed.,* troops of Gen. Beauregard's command. Losses: *Union,* 20 killed and wounded; *Confed.**

18 to 22.—Fort Anderson, Town Creek, and Wilmington, N. C. *Union,* Twenty-third and Twenty-fourth Corps, and Porter's gunboats; *C o n f e d.,* Gen. Hoke's command. Losses: *Union,* 40 killed, 204 wounded; *Confed.,* 70 killed, 400 wounded, 375 missing.

22.—Douglas Landing, Pine Bluff, Ark. *Union,* 13th Ill. Cav.; *Confed.,* troops of Gen. Kirby Smith's command. Losses: *Union,* 40 killed and wounded; *Confed.,* 26 killed and wounded.

27 to March 25.—Cavalry raid in Virginia. *Union,* First and Third divisions of Sheridan's Cav.; *Confed.,* Gen. Jubal Early's command. Losses: *Union,* 35 killed and wounded; *Confed.,* 1667 prisoners.

MARCH, 1865.

2.—Waynesboro, Va. *Union,* Sheridan's Cavalry Corps. *Confed.,* Maj.-Gen. Jubal Early's command, Rosser's Cav.

* No record found.

[342]

SIGNS OF PEACE—CONFEDERATE ARTILLERY CAPTURED AT RICHMOND AND WAITING SHIPMENT

Never again to be used by brother against brother, these Confederate guns captured in the defenses about Richmond are parked near the wharves on the James River ready for shipment to the national arsenal at Washington, once more the capital of a united country. The reflection of these instruments of destruction on the peaceful surface of the canal is not more clear than was the purpose of the South to accept the issues of the war and to restore as far as in them lay the bases for an enduring prosperity. The same devotion which manned these guns so bravely and prolonged the contest as long as it was possible for human powers to endure, was now directed to the new problems which the cessation of hostilities had provided. The restored Union came with the years to possess for the South a significance to be measured only by the thankfulness that the outcome had been what it was and by the pride in the common traditions and common blood of the whole American people. These captured guns are a memory therefore, not of regret, but of recognition, gratitude, that the highest earthly tribunal settled all strife in 1865.

COEHORNS, MORTARS, LIGHT AND HEAVY GUNS

Engagements of the Civil War

Losses: *Union* *; *Confed.*, killed and wounded not recorded, 1603 captured

8 to 10.—Wilcox's Bridge, N. C. *Union*, Palmer's, Carter's, and Ruger's Divisions, of Gen. Schofield's command; *Confed.*, forces under Gen. Bragg from Hood's Army of Tennessee, and Hoke's North Carolina division. Losses: *Union*, 65 killed, 379 wounded, 953 missing; *Confed.*, 1500 killed, wounded, and missing.

16.—Averysboro', N. C. *Union*, Twentieth Corps and Kilpatrick's Cav.; *Confed.*, Gen. Hardee's command. Losses: *Union*, 93 killed, 531 wounded; *Confed.*, 108 killed, 540 wounded, 217 missing.

19 to 21.—Bentonville, N. C. *Union*, Fourteenth, Fifteenth, Seventeenth, and Twentieth Corps, and Kilpatrick's Cav.; *Confed.*, Gen. J. E. Johnston's army and Wade Hampton's Cav. Losses: *Union*, 194 killed, 1112 wounded, 221 missing; *Confed.*, 239 killed, 1694 wounded, 673 missing.

20 to April 6.—Stoneman's raid into Southwestern Va. and North Carolina. *Union*, Palmer's, Brown's, and Miller's Cavalry Brigades; *Confed.**. Losses.*

22 to April 24.—Wilson's Raid, Chickasaw, Ala., to Macon, Ga. *Union*, Gen. James H. Wilson's Cav.; *Confed.*, Forrest's Cav., local garrison and State Militia. Losses: *Union*, 63 killed, 345 wounded, 63 missing; *Confed.*, 22 killed, 38 wounded, 6766 prisoners.

25.—Fort Stedman, in front of Petersburg, Va. *Union*, First and Third Divisions Ninth Corps; *Confed.*, Gen. John B. Gordon's Corps, supported by Lee's artillery in the forts. Losses: *Union*, 70 killed, 424 wounded, 523 captured; *Confed.*, about 3000 killed, wounded and missing (Federal estimate).
—Petersburg Trenches. Second and Sixth Corps; *Confed.*, Gen. R. E. Lee's command. Losses: *Union*, 103 killed, 864 wounded, 209 missing; *Confed.*, killed and wounded not recorded, 834 captured.

26 to April 9.—Siege of Mobile, Ala., including Spanish Fort and Fort Blakely. *Union*, Thirteenth and Sixteenth Corps and Acting Rear-Admiral Thatcher's fleet; *Confed.*, Gen. D. H. Maury's land forces, five gunboats under Commodore Farrand. Losses: *Union*, 213 killed, 1211 wounded; *Confed.*, 500 killed and wounded, 3000 to 4000 captured.

29.—Quaker Road, Va. *Union*, Warren's Fifth Corps and Griffin's First Division, Army of the Potomac; *Confed.*, Part of Gen. R. E. Lee's Army. Losses: *Union*, 55 killed, 306 wounded; *Confed.*, 135 killed, 400 wounded, 100 missing.

31.—Boydton and White Oak Roads, Va. *Union*, Second and Fifth Corps; *Confed.*, part of Gen. R. E. Lee's command. Losses: *Union*, 177 killed, 1134 wounded, 556 missing; *Confed.*, 1000 killed, 235 missing.
—Dinwiddie C. H., Va. *Union*, First, Second, and Third Divisions Cavalry of the Army of the Potomac; *Confed.*, Cav. under Gen. Fitzhugh Lee and Gen. W. H. F. Lee. Losses: *Union*, 67 killed, 354 wounded; *Confed.*, 400 killed and wounded.

APRIL, 1865.

1.—Five Forks, Va. *Union*, First, Second, and Third Cav. Divisions and Fifth Corps; *Confed.*, Gen. Geo. E. Pickett's command, Gen. Fitzhugh Lee's Cav., including Rosser's and Munford's Divisions. Losses: *Union*, 124 killed, 706 wounded; *Confed.**

2.—Selma, Ala. *Union*, Second Division Cav., Military Division of the Mississippi; Forrest's Cav. Losses: *Union*, 42 killed, 270 wounded, 7 missing; *Confed.*, killed and wounded,* 2700 captured.
—Fall of Petersburg, Va. *Union*, Second, Sixth, Ninth, and Twenty-fourth Corps; *Confed.*, Part of Gen. A. P. Hill's and Gen. J. B. Gordon's Corps. Losses: *Union*, 296 killed, 2565 wounded, 500 missing; *Confed.*, killed and wounded not recorded, 3000 prisoners (estimate).

3.—Fall of Richmond, Va. *Union*, Gen. Weitzel's command; *Confed.*, Local Brigade and other forces under command of Gen. R. S. Ewell. Losses: *Confed.*, 6000 prisoners, of whom 500 were sick and wounded.

5.—Amelia Springs, Va. *Union*, Crook's Cav.; *Confed.*, Gary's Cav. Losses: *Union*, 20 killed, 96 wounded; *Confed.**

* No record found.

One of the proudest days of the nation— May 24, 1865—here lives again. The true greatness of the American people was not displayed till the close of the war. The citizen from the walks of humble life had during the contest become a veteran soldier, equal in courage and fighting capacity to the best drilled infantry of Marlborough, Frederick the Great, or Napoleon. But it remained to be seen whether he would return peacefully to the occupations of peace. European nations made dark predictions. "Would nearly a million men," they asked, "one of the mightiest military organizations ever trained in war, quietly lay aside this resistless power and disappear into the unnoted walks of civil life?" Europe with its standing armies thought not. Europe was mistaken. The disbanded veterans lent the effectiveness of military order and discipline to the industrial and commercial development of the land they had come to love with an increased devotion. The pictures are of Sherman's troops marching

THE RETURN OF THE SOLDIERS—THE GRAND REVIEW

THE SAME SCENE, A FEW SECONDS LATER

down Pennsylvania Avenue. The horsemen in the lead are General Francis P. Blair and his staff, and the infantry in flashing new uniforms are part of the Seventeenth Corps in the Army of Tennessee. Little over a year before, they had started with Sherman on his series of battles and flanking marches in the struggle for Atlanta. They had taken a conspicuous and important part in the battle of July 22d east of Atlanta, receiving and finally repulsing attacks in both front and rear. They had marched with Sherman to the sea and participated in the capture of Savannah. They had joined in the campaign through the Carolinas, part of the time leading the advance and tearing up many miles of railway track, and operating on the extreme right after the battle of Bentonville. After the negotiations for Johnston's surrender were completed in April, they set out on the march for the last time with flying colors and martial music, to enter the memorable review at Washington in May, here preserved.

Engagements of the Civil War

6.—Sailor's Creek, Va. *Union,* Second and Sixth Corps and Sheridan's Cav.; *Confed.,* Gen. R. S. Ewell's command, and part of Gen. R. H. Anderson's. Losses: *Union,* 166 killed, 1014 wounded; *Confed.,* 6000 killed, wounded, and captured. (Federal estimate.)

7.—High Bridge and Farmville, Appomattox River, Va. *Union,* Second Corps and portion of Twenty-fourth Corps; *Confed.,* rearguard of Gordon's and Longstreet's Corps and Fitzhugh Lee's Cav. Losses: *Union,* 571 killed, 71 wounded, and missing; *Confed.**

8 and 9.—Appomattox C. H., Va. *Union,* Twenty-fourth Corps, one division of the Twenty-fifth Corps and Sheridan's Cav.; *Confed.,* Gen. Fitzhugh Lee's Cav. Losses: *Union,* 200 killed and wounded; *Confed.,* 500 killed and wounded.

9.—Gen. R. E. Lee surrendered the Army of Northern Virginia to the Army of the Potomac and the Army of the James; Lieut.-Gen. U. S. Grant. *Confed.,* surrendered and paroled, 27,805.

12 and 13.—Montgomery, Ala. *Union,* Second Brigade, First Division Cav.; *Confed.,* Gen. D. W. Adams' command. Losses: not recorded.

16.—West Point, Ga. *Union,* 2d and 4th Ind. Cav., 18th Indpt. Bat. Ind. Light Artil.; *Confed.,* Brig.-Gen. R. C. Tyler with 300 men. Losses: *Union,* 7 killed, 29 wounded; *Confed.,* 19 killed, 28 wounded, 218 missing. Brig.-Gen. R. C. Tyler killed. Last organized Confederate resistance East of the Mississippi.
—Columbus, Ga. *Union,* Fourth Division Cav.; *Confed.,* Gen. D. W. Adams' command. Losses: *Union,* 6 killed, 24 missing; *Confed.,* killed and wounded not recorded, 1200 captured.

26.—Gen. Jos. E. Johnston surrendered the Army of Tennessee and other commands to the Army of the Tennessee, the Army of Georgia and the Army of Ohio; Maj.-Gen. W. T. Sherman. *Confed.,* surrendered and paroled, 31,243.

MAY, 1865.

4.—Gen. Richard Taylor surrendered with Army of the Department of Alabama to Maj.-Gen. E. R. S. Canby. *Confed.,* surrendered, 42,293.

10.—Capture of Jefferson Davis, President of the Confederate States of America, at Irwinsville, Ga., by the 1st Wis. and 4th Mich. Cav. Losses: *Union,* 2 killed, 4 wounded, caused by the pursuing parties firing into each other.
—Tallahassee, Fla. Surrender of Gen. Samuel Jones' command to detachment of Wilson's U. S. Cav. under Maj.-Gen. McCook. *Confed.,* surrendered, 8000.

11.—Chalk Bluff, Ark. Surrender of Gen. Jeff. Thompson's command to forces under Gen. M. Grenville Dodge; *Confed.,* surrendered, 7454.

12 and 13.— Palmetto Ranch, near Brownsville, Tex. *Union,* 34th Ind., 62d U. S. Colored and 2d Tex. Cav. under command Col. F. H. Barrett; *Confed.,* troops commanded by Brig.-Gen. Jas. H. Slaughter. Losses: *Union,* 115 killed and wounded; *Confed.**

23 and 24.—Grand Review of the Federal armies on Pennsylvania Avenue, Washington. Lieut.-Gen. U. S. Grant, Maj.-Gen. George G. Meade and Maj.-Gen. W. T. Sherman occupied the reviewing stand.

26.—Surrender of Gen. E. Kirby Smith (Army of the Trans-Mississippi Department) to Maj.-Gen. E. R. S. Canby. *Confed.,* surrendered, 17,686.
—In addition to the surrenders noted above, there were paroled at Cumberland, Maryland, and other stations, 9337; in the Department of Washington, 3390; in Virginia, Tennessee, Alabama, Louisiana, and Texas, 13,922; at Nashville and Chattanooga, Tenn., 5029. Miscellaneous paroles in the Department of Virginia amounted to 9072. Total number paroled, according to the statistics of the War Department, was 174,223.

* No record found.

Review of Twentieth Army Corps, May 24, 1865. To the strains of popular airs the Grand Army of the Republic marched from the shadow of the Capitol to the front of the Executive Mansion. But amid the bayonets flashing in the sunlight each soldier was saddened by the thought of companions in arms who were not by his side and who would never return to waiting mother or sweetheart. In the Union armies alone three hundred and fifty-nine thousand men had lain down their lives in the Civil War, and the losses in the Southern armies raised the total to over seven hundred thousand. Most of these were young fellows, their years of vigorous activity yet unlived. If by a sudden catastrophe Cleveland or Pittsburgh were utterly destroyed, the loss to the nation would not be so great. Behind the glamor of military achievement lies the cruel cost to be compensated for only by the necessity for deciding the questions that had threatened the foundations of the American nation.

"WHEN THIS CRUEL WAR IS OVER"

READY TO TILL THE FIELDS OF PEACE

The record of the Twentieth Corps was distinguished. It was engaged in the constant battling and skirmishing of the Atlanta Campaign. In the final operations these troops were the first to enter the city on the morning of September 2, 1864, and it was to General Slocum, their commander, that the mayor surrendered. For two months they held Atlanta and its approaches from the North while the rest of Sherman's army was engaged in attacking Hood's retreating columns. In the march to the sea the corps was commanded by General A. S. Williams. At Savannah the troops again had the honor of being the first to enter an evacuated city, the second division marching in on the morning of December 21, 1864. In the march through the Carolinas the corps was in the thick of the fight at Bentonville, repulsing successive attacks with the aid of its artillery. Another change in the commanding officer was made on April 2d, when General J. A. Mower succeeded General A. S. Williams.

A NATION'S JOY AND GRIEF—"WELCOME BRAVE SOLDIERS" BELOW CRAPE AND THE FLAG AT HALF-MAST FOR LINCOLN

THE MARCH OF THE GRAND ARMY

This vivid photograph has been identified, by one who witnessed the procession, as a view on F Street, Washington. The jaunty bearing of the men in front is as striking to the reader now as it was to that eye-witness nearly half a century ago. The view on the page facing shows the signs of joy and grief mingled on the same day. The flag at half mast, the windows draped in crape, express silently the grief that filled the heart of both North and South at the news of Lincoln's assassination. The vision of his majestic figure now rose calmly and grandly above the animosities of the stormy conflict as one to whom every section of the land he saved could point with pride, and say, "Here is an American." All sections could join, too, in applauding the banner, "Welcome Brave Soldiers." For in the war all were Americans, and all can join in pride over the courage of the American soldier from North and South. The soldiers who led in the battle line, Blue and Gray alike, led also in reëchoing the words of Webster: "Union now and forever, one and inseparable."

THE FINAL ACT OF THE DRAMA

This is the finale, the last tableau of the Great Drama of the Civil War—a drama that for four years had held the stage of half a continent with all civilization for an audience. In late April of '65 a photographer visited Point Lookout Prison, Maryland, and was present when the last Confederate prisoners took the oath of allegiance to the flag under whose shadow they stand as their hands touch simultaneously the Bibles—one held by each group of four. At the desk, administering the oath, sits the Commander of the Department of St. Mary's, General James Barnes, who since recovering from his wounds at Gettysburg had been in charge of more captured Confederates than there were in Lee's last army. It is a moving

THE LAST CONFEDERATE PRISONERS TAKE THE OATH AT POINT LOOKOUT

sight; it stirs the emotions, to look at the faces of these men, now returning from exile to their war-ridden country and desolated homes. Theirs is the hardest task in all the world—to conquer defeat and begin anew, under changed surroundings and conditions, the struggle for existence. Bravely the Southerners faced it, as bravely as they had faced the line of blue-clad men who are their enemies no longer. Long before fifty years had passed, when again the war cloud had risen and the country called for men, during the Spanish War, in the great camps at Chickamauga—"the sons of those sires, at the same camp-fires, cheered one flag where their fathers fought."

1865

THE WILDERNESS OF WAR BEFORE PETERSBURG—HOMES GONE, TREES BLASTED, THE EARTH ITSELF RIVEN,
SPLIT AND SCARRED—YET BY THE EVEN MORE GLORIOUS VICTORIES OF PEACE, SUCH
WASTES IN A FEW YEARS WERE MADE TO BLOSSOM AGAIN.

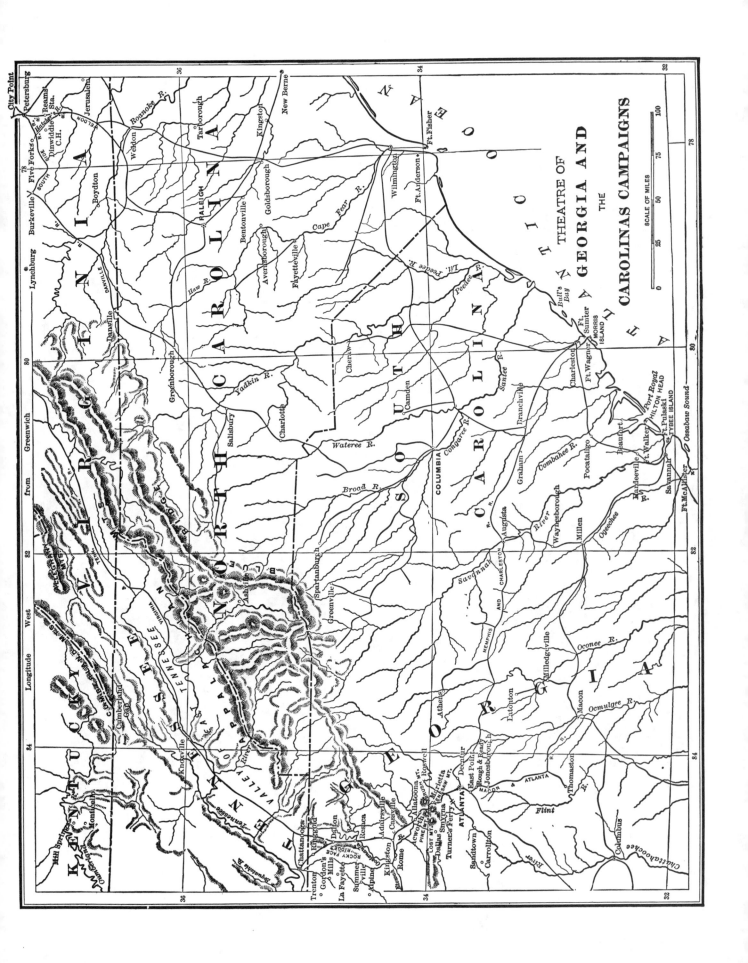

THEATRE OF
GEORGIA AND
THE
CAROLINAS CAMPAIGNS

SCALE OF MILES

0   25   50   75   100